ExamSim

Experience realistic, simulated exams on your own computer with Osborne's interactive ExamSim software. This computer-based test engine offers both standard and adaptive test modes, knowledge-based and product simulation questions like those found on the real exams, and review tools that help you study more efficiently. Intuitive controls allow you to move easily through the program: mark difficult or unanswered questions for further review and skip ahead, then assess your performance at the end.

Knowledge-based questions present challenging material in a multiple-choice format. Answer treatments not only explain why the correct options are right, they also tell you why the incorrect answers were wrong.

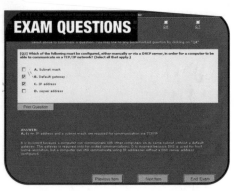

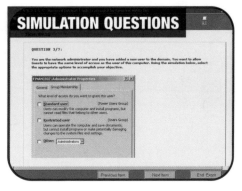

Realistic Windows 2000 product **simulation questions** test the skills you need to pass the exam—these questions look and feel like the simulation questions on the actual exam!

Additional CD-ROM Features

- Complete hyperlinked e-book for easy information access and self-paced study

- **DriveTime** audio tracks offer concise review of key exam topics for in the car or on the go!

System Requirements:

A PC running Internet Explorer version 5 or higher

Detailed **Score Reports** provide score analysis and history to chart your progress and focus your study time.

MCSE Windows® 2000
Directory Services
Administration Study Guide

(Exam 70-217)

MCSE Windows® 2000
Directory Services
Administration Study Guide

(Exam 70-217)

Syngress Media, Inc.

Osborne/McGraw-Hill

New York   Chicago   San Francisco   Lisbon   London   Madrid
Mexico City   Milan   New Delhi   San Juan   Seoul   Singapore   Sydney   Toronto

Osborne/**McGraw-Hill**
2600 Tenth Street
Berkeley, California 94710
U.S.A.

For information on translations or book distributors outside the U.S.A., or to arrange bulk purchase discounts for sales promotions, premiums, or fund-raisers, please contact Osborne/**McGraw-Hill** at the above address.

**MCSE Windows 2000 Directory Services Administration Study Guide
(Exam 70-217)**

4567890 DOC DOC 01987654321

Book P/N 0-07-212378-8   and   CD P/N 0-07-212379-6
parts of
ISBN 0-07-212380-X

Publisher Brandon A. Nordin	**Acquisitions Coordinator** Tara Davis	**Proofreaders** Pat Mannion Linda Medoff Paul Medoff
Vice President and Associate Publisher Scott Rogers	**Series Editors** Dr. Thomas W. Shinder Debra Littlejohn Shinder	**Indexer** Jack Lewis
Editorial Director Gareth Hancock	**VP, Worldwide Business Development Global Knowledge** Richard Kristof	**Computer Designers** Gary Corrigan Roberta Steele
Associate Acquisitions Editor Timothy Green	**Technical Editor** Neil Ruston	**Illustrator** Michael Mueller
Editorial Management Syngress Media, Inc.	**Technical Reviewer** Brian Collins	**Series Design** Roberta Steele
Project Editors Patty Mon Maribeth A. Corona	**Copy Editor** Darlene Bordwell	**Cover Design** Will Voss

This book was composed with Corel VENTURA™ Publisher.

FOREWORD

From Global Knowledge

At Global Knowledge we strive to support the multiplicity of learning styles required by our students to achieve success as technical professionals. In this series of books, it is our intention to offer the reader a valuable tool for successful completion of the MCSE Windows 2000 Certification exams.

As the world's largest IT training company, Global Knowledge is uniquely positioned to offer these books. The expertise gained each year from providing instructor-led training to hundreds of thousands of students worldwide has been captured in book form to enhance your learning experience. We hope that the quality of these books demonstrates our commitment to your lifelong learning success. Whether you choose to learn through the written word, computer-based training, Web delivery, or instructor-led training, Global Knowledge is committed to providing you the very best in each of those categories. For those of you who know Global Knowledge, or those of you who have just found us for the first time, our goal is to be your lifelong competency partner.

Thank you for the opportunity to serve you. We look forward to serving your needs again in the future.

Warmest regards,

Duncan Anderson
President and Chief Executive Officer, Global Knowledge

The Global Knowledge Advantage

Global Knowledge has a global delivery system for its products and services. The company has 28 subsidiaries, and offers its programs through a total of 60+ locations. No other vendor can provide consistent services across a geographic area this large. Global Knowledge is the largest independent information technology education provider, offering programs on a variety of platforms. This enables our multi-platform and multi-national customers to obtain all of their programs from a single vendor. The company has developed the unique Competus™ Framework software tool and methodology which can quickly reconfigure courseware to the proficiency level of a student on an interactive basis. Combined with self-paced and on-line programs, this technology can reduce the time required for training by prescribing content in only the deficient skills areas. The company has fully automated every aspect of the education process, from registration and follow-up, to "just-in-time" production of courseware. Global Knowledge Network through its Enterprise Services Consultancy, can customize programs and products to suit the needs of an individual customer.

Global Knowledge Classroom Education Programs

The backbone of our delivery options is classroom-based education. Our modern, well-equipped facilities staffed with the finest instructors offer programs in a wide variety of information technology topics, many of which lead to professional certifications.

Custom Learning Solutions

This delivery option has been created for companies and governments that value customized learning solutions. For them, our consultancy-based approach of developing targeted education solutions is most effective at helping them meet specific objectives.

Self-Paced and Multimedia Products

This delivery option offers self-paced program titles in interactive CD-ROM, videotape and audio tape programs. In addition, we offer custom development of interactive multimedia courseware to customers and partners. Call us at 1-888-427-4228.

Electronic Delivery of Training

Our network-based training service delivers efficient competency-based, interactive training via the World Wide Web and organizational intranets. This leading-edge delivery option provides a custom learning path and "just-in-time" training for maximum convenience to students.

ARG

American Research Group (ARG), a wholly-owned subsidiary of Global Knowledge, one of the largest worldwide training partners of Cisco Systems, offers a wide range of internetworking, LAN/WAN, Bay Networks, FORE Systems, IBM, and UNIX courses. ARG offers hands on network training in both instructor-led classes and self-paced PC-based training.

Global Knowledge Courses Available

Network Fundamentals

- Understanding Computer Networks
- Telecommunications Fundamentals I
- Telecommunications Fundamentals II
- Understanding Networking Fundamentals
- Implementing Computer Telephony Integration
- Introduction to Voice Over IP
- Introduction to Wide Area Networking
- Cabling Voice and Data Networks
- Introduction to LAN/WAN protocols
- Virtual Private Networks
- ATM Essentials

Network Security & Management

- Troubleshooting TCP/IP Networks
- Network Management
- Network Troubleshooting
- IP Address Management
- Network Security Administration
- Web Security
- Implementing UNIX Security
- Managing Cisco Network Security
- Windows NT 4.0 Security

IT Professional Skills

- Project Management for IT Professionals
- Advanced Project Management for IT Professionals
- Survival Skills for the New IT Manager
- Making IT Teams Work

LAN/WAN Internetworking

- Frame Relay Internetworking
- Implementing T1/T3 Services
- Understanding Digital Subscriber Line (xDSL)
- Internetworking with Routers and Switches
- Advanced Routing and Switching
- Multi-Layer Switching and Wire-Speed Routing
- Internetworking with TCP/IP
- ATM Internetworking
- OSPF Design and Configuration
- Border Gateway Protocol (BGP) Configuration

Authorized Vendor Training

Cisco Systems

- Introduction to Cisco Router Configuration
- Advanced Cisco Router Configuration
- Installation and Maintenance of Cisco Routers
- Cisco Internetwork Troubleshooting
- Cisco Internetwork Design
- Cisco Routers and LAN Switches
- Catalyst 5000 Series Configuration
- Cisco LAN Switch Configuration
- Managing Cisco Switched Internetworks
- Configuring, Monitoring, and Troubleshooting Dial-Up Services
- Cisco AS5200 Installation and Configuration
- Cisco Campus ATM Solutions

Bay Networks

- Bay Networks Accelerated Router Configuration
- Bay Networks Advanced IP Routing
- Bay Networks Hub Connectivity
- Bay Networks Accelar 1xxx Installation and Basic Configuration
- Bay Networks Centillion Switching

FORE Systems

- FORE ATM Enterprise Core Products
- FORE ATM Enterprise Edge Products
- FORE ATM Theory
- FORE LAN Certification

Operating Systems & Programming

Microsoft

- Introduction to Windows NT
- Microsoft Networking Essentials
- Windows NT 4.0 Workstation
- Windows NT 4.0 Server
- Advanced Windows NT 4.0 Server
- Windows NT Networking with TCP/IP
- Introduction to Microsoft Web Tools
- Windows NT Troubleshooting
- Windows Registry Configuration

UNIX

- UNIX Level I
- UNIX Level II
- Essentials of UNIX and NT Integration

Programming

- Introduction to JavaScript
- Java Programming
- PERL Programming
- Advanced PERL with CGI for the Web

Web Site Management & Development

- Building a Web Site
- Web Site Management and Performance
- Web Development Fundamentals

High Speed Networking

- Essentials of Wide Area Networking
- Integrating ISDN
- Fiber Optic Network Design
- Fiber Optic Network Installation
- Migrating to High Performance Ethernet

DIGITAL UNIX

- UNIX Utilities and Commands
- DIGITAL UNIX v4.0 System Administration
- DIGITAL UNIX v4.0 (TCP/IP) Network Management
- AdvFS, LSM, and RAID Configuration and Management
- DIGITAL UNIX TruCluster Software Configuration and Management
- UNIX Shell Programming Featuring Kornshell
- DIGITAL UNIX v4.0 Security Management
- DIGITAL UNIX v4.0 Performance Management
- DIGITAL UNIX v4.0 Intervals Overview

DIGITAL OpenVMS

- OpenVMS Skills for Users
- OpenVMS System and Network Node Management I
- OpenVMS System and Network Node Management II
- OpenVMS System and Network Node Management III
- OpenVMS System and Network Node Operations
- OpenVMS for Programmers
- OpenVMS System Troubleshooting for Systems Managers
- Configuring and Managing Complex VMScluster Systems
- Utilizing OpenVMS Features from C
- OpenVMS Performance Management
- Managing DEC TCP/IP Services for OpenVMS
- Programming in C

Hardware Courses

- AlphaServer 1000/1000A Installation, Configuration and Maintenance
- AlphaServer 2100 Server Maintenance
- AlphaServer 4100, Troubleshooting Techniques and Problem Solving

About Syngress Media

Syngress Media creates books and software for Information Technology professionals seeking skill enhancement and career advancement. Its products are designed to comply with vendor and industry standard course curricula, and are optimized for certification exam preparation. You can contact Syngress via the Web at www.syngress.com.

Contributors

Pawan K. Bhardwaj (MCSE, MCP+I, CCNA) is a technical trainer, consultant, and a freelance author based in Jalandhar City, India. He has spent 13 years in the IT industry in India and the US working on various systems and network support levels. He has been involved in designing and implementing LAN and WAN solutions for several small- and medium-sized companies that include a large publishing house and an e-commerce Web site.

Pawan has contributed to the following Osborne/**McGraw-Hill** books: *MCSE Windows 2000 Professional Study Guide, MCSE Windows 2000 Server Study Guide, MCSE Windows 2000 Directory Services Administration Study Guide,* and *MCSE Windows 2000 Accelerated Test Yourself Practice Exams.* He can be reached via e-mail at pawan_bhardwaj@hotmail.com.

Michael Cross (MCSE, MCPS, MCP+I, CNA) is a Microsoft Certified System Engineer, Microsoft Certified Product Specialist, Microsoft Certified Professional + Internet, and a Certified Novell Administrator. Michael is the network administrator, Internet specialist, and a programmer for the Niagara Regional Police Service in Ontario, Canada. In addition to administering the service's network, programming and providing support to a user base of more than 800 civilian and uniform users, he is webmaster of their Web site at www.nrps.com.

Michael also owns KnightWare, a company that provides consulting, programming, networking, Web page design, computer training, and various other services. He has served as an instructor for private colleges and technical schools in London and in Ontario, Canada. A freelance writer for several years, Michael has been published more than two dozen times in numerous books and anthologies. He currently resides in St. Catharines, Ontario, Canada.

Brian K. Doré (MCSE, MCT) is the Coordinator of the Microsoft Authorized Academic Training Program (AATP) at the University of Louisiana at Lafayette. In addition to managing the program, he also teaches Windows 2000 certification courses at the university. Prior to his current position, he worked nine years for the University Computing Support Services Department supporting a wide variety of computer systems. Brian also spent five years as a software developer at a privately held company. Brian and his wife, Jennifer, live in Carencro, Louisiana. He can be reached via e-mail at bkd@louisiana.edu.

Damon Merchant (CCDP, CCNP, CCNA, CCDA, MCSE, MCP, CNE, and CNA) is the President of Corbus Systems, Inc., an information technology firm in Detroit, Michigan. He has about ten years' experience in networking. Not only is he a network engineering guru, he is also a seasoned software developer. His most recent application, Touch-Tone Administrator for NT, allows network administrators to manage their Windows NT networks from a telephone. Damon also provides training and technical workshops for IT professionals. In his spare time, Damon enjoys playing basketball, ping pong, video games, weight lifting, and candlelight dinners with his wife, Lortensia.

More information about Damon Merchant and his software products can be found at his company's Web site, www.corbus-systems.com. Damon can be e-mailed at damon@corbus-systems.com.

Michael Seamans (MCSE, MCP) is a networking consultant for Long and Associates in Rochester, New York, where he is currently contracting with the Eastman Kodak Company supporting their digital camera division. He has been a Microsoft Certified System Engineer for more than three years and he has more than ten years of IT management experience with the White House, United States Army, National Reconnaissance Office, and the Eastman Kodak Company. During his career, Michael has worked on many extensive and diverse projects involving the deployment of Windows NT and Windows 2000 networks, along with projects involving other technologies such as Lotus Notes and Microsoft Systems Management Server.

Michael lives with his wife, Denelle, and their four children, Joshua, Brittany, Mikaela, and Tyler. He can be reached at mseamans@rochester.rr.com,

mseamans@kodak.com, or through his Web site at http://home.rochester.
rr.com/seamans.

Debra Littlejohn Shinder (MCSE, MCP+I, MCT) is an instructor in the
AATP program at Eastfield College, Dallas County Community College District,
where she has taught since 1992. She is webmaster for the cities of Seagoville and
Sunnyvale, Texas, as well as for the family Web site at www.shinder.net. She and her
husband, Dr. Thomas W. Shinder, provide consulting and technical support
services to Dallas area organizations. She is also the proud mom of a daughter,
Kristen, who is currently serving in the U.S. Navy in Italy, and a son, Kris, who
is a high school chess champion. Deb has been a writer for most her life and has
published numerous articles in both technical and nontechnical fields. She can be
contacted at deb@shinder.net.

Martin Wuesthoff (MCSE, MCT, CNE, A+, N+) is a Certified Technical
Trainer for New Horizons Computer Learning Center in Trumbull, Connecticut.
He currently teaches the entire Windows 2000 track as well as the NT 4.0 track and
A+ certification courses. A lifelong teacher, Martin's philosophy is that all of the
knowledge in the world is of no use in the classroom if a teacher cannot clearly
transfer it from his head to the students.

Martin and his wife, Michelle, are the proud parents of three children: Erik, 7,
their biological son; and Noel, 2, and Emilee, 6 months—two beautiful girls
adopted from Korea. He would like to dedicate his portion of this book to the girls'
birth mothers, wherever they are, for having the courage and strength to give their
daughters a better life and for blessing their family as a result.

Technical Editor

Neil Ruston (MCSE, CNE) is currently working for Perot Systems at a large
Swiss bank in London. Originally, Neil designed and implemented Netware
systems, but more recently, he has focused on Windows NT and Windows 2000
network design. Neil participated in the Microsoft-sponsored Joint Deployment
Programme (JDP), which involved the design and implementation of a large, global
Active Directory. He dedicates this book to his wife, who regularly endured his late
nights at the PC.

Technical Reviewer

Brian M. Collins (MCNE, MCSE, MCT, CTT) is a technical trainer for Network Appliance, Inc., in Sunnyvale, California. A technology-industry veteran of 20 years, his employment background includes U.S. Navy electronics, semiconductor industry robotics, software development in several languages, and system administration. Brian's hobbies include hiking, operating systems, and coding. When not traveling the world training for NetApp, Brian can be found in the Santa Cruz Mountains of California, 30 miles from the center of Silicon Valley.

Series Editors

Thomas W. Shinder, M.D. (MCSE, MCP+I, MCT), is a technology trainer and consultant in the Dallas-Ft. Worth metroplex. Dr. Shinder has consulted with major firms, including Xerox, Lucent Technologies, and FINA Oil, assisting in the development and implementation of IP-based communications strategies. Dr. Shinder attended medical school at the University of Illinois in Chicago and trained in neurology at the Oregon Health Sciences Center in Portland, Oregon. His fascination with interneuronal communication ultimately melded with his interest in internetworking and led him to focus on systems engineering. Tom works passionately with his beloved wife, Deb Shinder, to design elegant and cost-efficient solutions for small- and medium-sized businesses based on Windows NT/2000 platforms.

   Debra Littlejohn Shinder (MCSE, MCP+I, MCT) is an instructor in the AATP program at Eastfield College, Dallas County Community College District, where she has taught since 1992. She is webmaster for the cities of Seagoville and Sunnyvale, Texas, as well as for the family Web site at www.shinder.net. She and her husband, Dr. Thomas W. Shinder, provide consulting and technical support services to Dallas area organizations. She is also the proud mom of a daughter, Kristen, who is currently serving in the U.S. Navy in Italy, and a son, Kris, who is a high school chess champion. Deb has been a writer for most her life, and has published numerous articles in both technical and nontechnical fields. She can be contacted at deb@shinder.net.

ACKNOWLEDGMENTS

W e would like to thank the following people:

- Richard Kristof of Global Knowledge, for championing the series and providing access to some great people and information.

- All the incredibly hard-working folks at Osborne/McGraw-Hill: Brandon Nordin, Scott Rogers, Gareth Hancock, and Tim Green for their help in launching a great series and being solid team players. In addition, Tara Davis and Patty Mon, for their help in fine-tuning the book.

- Monica Kilwine at Microsoft Corporation, for being patient and diligent in answering all our questions.

CONTENTS AT A GLANCE

1	Introduction to Windows 2000 Directory Services Administration	1
2	Installing the Components of Active Directory	49
3	Configuring Active Directory	125
4	Troubleshooting Active Directory	175
5	Domain Name Service for Active Directory	217
6	Implementing and Troubleshooting Group Policy	277
7	Managing Software and Network Configuration Using Group Policy	339
8	Installing and Configuring the RIS Service	395
9	Using Remote Installation Service to Install the Client Machine	443
10	Managing, Monitoring, and Optimizing Active Directory Components	493
11	Managing Active Directory and Domain Name Service Replication	561
12	Active Directory Security Solutions	609
A	About the CD	665
B	About the Web Site	671
	Glossary	673
	Index	765

CONTENTS

Foreword . . . . *v*

About the Contributors . . . . *ix*

Acknowledgments . . . . *xiii*

Preface . . . . *xxix*

Introduction . . . . *xxxv*

1   Introduction to Windows 2000 Directory Services Administration **1**

What Is Windows 2000 Directory Services Administration?   2

    The Role of a Directory Service   5

    Features of a Global Directory Service   8

    Active Directory Structure 13

Overview of Exam 70-217 15

    Exam Objectives 16

What We'll Cover in This Book 31

    Knowledge 31

    Concepts 31

    Practical Skills 31

What You Should Already Know 33

    Microsoft Networking Concepts 33

    Windows 2000 Concepts 34

    Directory Services Terminology 34

    For Networking Newbies and NT Pros 37

    ✓ Two-Minute Drill 40

  Q&A Self Test 42

    Self Test Answers 45

2   Installing the Components of Active Directory **49**

Installing Active Directory 50

    Data Collation 51

Prerequisites 52

DCPROMO 54

Verifying Successful Installation 64

Exercise 2-1: Installing Active Directory 67

Creating Sites 71

What Is a Site? 71

How to Create a Site 72

Exercise 2-2: Creating New Sites in the Active

Directory 74

Creating Subnets 75

What Is a Subnet? 75

How to Create a Subnet 76

Exercise 2-3: Creating Subnets in Active Directory 78

Creating Site Links 79

What Is a Site Link? 79

How to Create a Site Link 79

Exercise 2-4: Creating Site Links in Active Directory 82

Assigning Bridgehead Servers 83

What Is a Bridgehead Server? 83

How to Create a Bridgehead Server 84

Exercise 2-5: Designating a Server as a

Bridgehead Server 87

Creating Site Link Bridges 88

What Is a Site Link Bridge? 89

How to Create a Site Link Bridge 90

Exercise 2-6: Creating Site Link Bridges

in Active Directory 95

Creating Connection Objects 96

What Are Connection Objects? 96

How to Create Connection Objects 97

Exercise 2-7: Creating Connection Objects

for Active Directory Domain Controllers 100

Creating Global Catalog Servers 101

What Is a Global Catalog Server? 102

How to Create a Global Catalog Server 102

Exercise 2-8: Defining Global Catalog Servers
in Active Directory 104

✓ Two-Minute Drill 107

Q&A Self Test 110

Lab Question 115

Self Test Answers 117

Lab Answer 122

3 Configuring Active Directory **125**

Verifying Active Directory Installation 126

Verifying the Domain Controller 126

Exercise 3-1: Verifying the Domain
from My Network Places 127

Verifying the DNS Server 128

Exercise 3-2: Verifying the Domain Controller
from Active Directory Users and Computers 129

Exercise 3-3: Verifying the DNS Server 130

Moving Server Objects Between Sites 131

Exercise 3-4: Creating a Server Object in a Site 132

When to Move Objects 133

How to Move Objects 134

Exercise 3-5: Moving Server Objects from One Site
to Another 134

Exercise 3-6: Removing a Server Object from a Site 136

Transferring Operations Master Roles 138

What Are the Operations Master Roles? 138

When to Transfer Roles, and Why 140

How to Transfer Roles 141

Exercise 3-7: Transferring the Schema Master Role 142

Exercise 3-8: Identifying the Present
Assignment of Roles 144

Exercise 3-9: Transferring Domainwide Assignment
of Operations Master Roles 146

Implementing an Organizational Unit Structure 150

OU Design Overview 150

Creating the OU Structure 152

Exercise 3-10:   Creating an Organizational Unit 153

Exercise 3-11:   Creating an Object 156

✓ Two-Minute Drill 161

Q&A Self Test 163

Lab Question 167

Self Test Answers 169

Lab Answer 172

4   Troubleshooting Active Directory **175**

Back Up and Restore Active Directory 176

Components and Files that Make Up AD 176

Backing Up Active Directory Components 181

Restoring Active Directory Components 193

Exercise 4-1:   Backing Up Active Directory 194

Performing a Restore of Active Directory 194

Recovering from a System Failure 203

✓ Two-Minute Drill 206

Q&A Self Test 208

Lab Question 211

Self Test Answers 213

Lab Answer 215

5   Domain Name Service for Active Directory **217**

Installing, Configuring, and Troubleshooting Domain Name
Service for Active Directory 218

Understanding Domain Name Service 219

Overview of Active Directory and Domain Name
Service Interoperability 220

Exercise 5-1:   Installing DNS 226

Integrating Active Directory Domain Name Service
with a Non-Active Directory Domain Name Service 234

Configure Zones for Dynamic Updates 237

Managing, Monitoring, and Troubleshooting Domain
Name Service 239
    Other Management Tasks 239
    Exercise 5-2: Viewing Resource Records
    Through DNS Console 247
    The Performance Console 248
    Domain Name Service Event Log 256
    Additional Troubleshooting Tools 256
    Managing Replication of Domain Name Service Data 258
    ✓ Two-Minute Drill 262
  Q&A Self Test 264
    Lab Question 268
    Self Test Answers 270
    Lab Answer 275

6 Implementing and Troubleshooting Group Policy **277**
Creating a Group Policy Object 278
    What Are GPOs? 279
    Deciding Where to Apply a Group Policy Object
    in the Organizational Unit Structure 281
    How to Create the Policy 281
    Exercise 6-1: Creating a Group Policy Object 284
Linking an Existing Group Policy Object 285
    An Overview of Group Policy Object Location
    in Active Directory 285
    How to Link a Group Policy Object, and Why 286
    Exercise 6-2: Linking a Group Policy Object 288
Delegating Administrative Control of Group Policy 289
    Why Delegate Control? 289
    How to Delegate Control of Group Policy Objects 289
    Exercise 6-3: Delegating Control
    of a Group Policy Object 295
Modifying Group Policy Inheritance 296
    What Is Inheritance? 296

Managing Inheritance 298

How to Change the Group Policy Object Inheritance 299

Exercise 6-4: Modifying Group Policy Inheritance 300

Filtering Group Policy Settings 301

Why Filter a Group Policy Object? 302

How to Apply a Filter to a Group Policy Object 303

Exercise 6-5: Filtering Group Policy

Using Security Groups 308

Modifying Group Policy 309

Changing the Policy 310

Exercise 6-6: Deleting a Group Policy 313

Controlling User Environments Using Administrative Templates 314

What Can the Administrator Control? 315

How to Create and Import Templates 316

Exercise 6-7: Controlling Environments

with Administrative Templates 318

Assigning Script Policies to Users and Computers 320

User vs. Computer Scripts 321

Exercise 6-8: Assigning Script Policies 323

✓ Two-Minute Drill 326

Q&A Self Test 328

Lab Question 332

Self Test Answers 333

Lab Answer 337

**7 Managing Software and Network Configuration
Using Group Policy** **339**

Deploying Software Using Group Policy 341

Windows Installer and .MSI Files 341

Exercise 7-1: Creating an .MSI Package

Using WinINSTALL LE 343

When to Use GPOs to Deploy Software, and Why 346

Applying the Package to an Organizational Unit 348

Exercise 7-2: Creating a Group Policy Object

to Deploy Software 351

Maintaining Software Using Group Policy 356

  Software Upgrades 356

  Exercise 7-3: Deploying a Software Upgrade 358

  Redeploying Software 359

  Removing Software 360

Configuring Deployment Options 361

  Filtering the Package 362

  Miscellaneous Deployment Options 363

  Exercise 7-4: Changing Categories 366

  Exercise 7-5: Categorizing Packages 367

  Using Transforms 368

Troubleshooting During Software Deployment 369

  Common Deployment Problems 369

  Event Viewer 371

  Exercise 7-6: Checking the Windows Installer Service

    in Event Viewer 372

Managing Network Configuration Using Group Policy 374

  Configuring Internet Explorer 375

  Other Configurable Options 377

  ✓ Two-Minute Drill 385

Q&A Self Test 387

  Lab Question 391

  Self Test Answers 392

  Lab Answer 394

8 Installing and Configuring the RIS Service 395

What Is Remote Installation Services? 396

  PXE and Supported Hardware 397

  Exercise 8-1: Installing RBFG.EXE and Checking

    Network Card Compatibility 398

  How RIS Works 399

  RIS Components 400

Creating a RIS Server 401

  Prerequisites 401

Installing RIS 402

Exercise 8-2: Installing RIS 403

Authorizing a RIS Server 404

Why Authorize a RIS Server? 405

The Authorization Process 405

Exercise 8-3: Authorizing a RIS Server 406

Configuring a RIS Server 407

Types of Images 407

RISetup and CD-Based Images 407

Exercise 8-4: Running RISetup 409

Computer Account Creation 413

Exercise 8-5: Associating an Answer File
with a CD-Based Image 414

Exercise 8-6: Choosing a Naming
and Placement Scheme 420

Exercise 8-7: Assigning Permissions to Users 422

Troubleshooting RIS 429

Common Errors 429

The Troubleshooter 429

Exercise 8-8: Accessing the RIS Troubleshooter 430

✓ Two-Minute Drill 433

Q&A Self Test 435

Lab Question 438

Self Test Answers 439

Lab Answer 441

**9 Using Remote Installation Service
to Install the Client Machine** **443**

Preparing for Installation 444

Supported Hardware 445

Unsupported Hardware 447

Group Policy Settings 447

Exercise 9-1: Restricting Client Installation Options ... 447

Exercise 9-2: Restricting the Operating System
Image Options 449

Installing an Image to a Client Machine 452

    Creating the RIS Boot Disk 452

    Exercise 9-3: Creating a Remote Installation Boot Disk . . . 453

    Installation Scenarios 454

    Exercise 9-4: Prestaging a Client Computer 458

    Exercise 9-5: Running the Remote Installation
    Preparation Wizard 463

    Installation Options 466

Troubleshooting 469

    Network Errors 470

    Exercise 9-6: Stopping and Restarting the BINL Service . . . 473

    Hardware Issues 475

  ✓ Two-Minute Drill 479

Q&A Self Test 481

    Lab Question 485

    Self Test Answers 487

    Lab Answer 491

**10 Managing, Monitoring, and Optimizing
Active Directory Components** **493**

Managing Active Directory Objects 494

    Moving Active Directory Objects 495

    Exercise 10-1: Moving User Accounts
    Within a Domain 497

    Exercise 10-2: Moving an Organizational Unit
    from One Domain to Another 501

    Publishing Resources in Active Directory 503

    Exercise 10-3: Publishing a Shared Folder
    in Active Directory 505

    Exercise 10-4: Publishing a Non-Windows Printer
    in Active Directory 507

    Locating Objects in Active Directory 508

    Exercise 10-5: Viewing Published Network Services
    in Active Directory 509

Exercise 10-6: Searching for a Shared Folder
in Active Directory 511
Creating and Managing Accounts Manually or by Scripting ... 513
Exercise 10-7: Creating User Accounts in a Domain 514
Controlling Access to Active Directory Objects 519
Exercise 10-8: Setting Permissions on Active
Directory Objects 521
Delegating Administrative Control of Objects
in Active Directory 525
Exercise 10-9: Delegating Control of Active
Directory Objects 527
Managing Active Directory Performance 532
Monitoring, Maintaining, and Troubleshooting Domain
Controller Performance 532
Exercise 10-10: Monitoring Active Directory
Performance 536
Monitoring, Maintaining, and Troubleshooting Active
Directory Components 539
Exercise 10-11: Adding a New Schema Attribute 544
Exercise 10-12: Adding a New Schema Class 545
✓ Two-Minute Drill 550
Q&A Self Test 552
Lab Question 556
Self Test Answers 557
Lab Answer 560

**11 Managing Active Directory and Domain
Name Service Replication** **561**
Managing and Troubleshooting Active Directory Replication 562
What Is Active Directory Replication? 563
How Domain Controllers Track Changes 567
Network and Knowledge Consistency Checker Topology 571
Overview of Sites, Subnets, Links, and Replication 574
Managing Intrasite Replication 577
Managing Intersite Replication 578

Troubleshooting Active Directory Replication 582
    Exercise 11-1: Using the Active Directory
    Replication Monitor 584
Managing and Troubleshooting Domain Name Service Replication . . . 587
    Windows 2000 DNS Features 588
    Troubleshooting Domain Name Service Replication 593
    Exercise 11-2: Creating Primary and Secondary
    DNS Zones 594
    ✓ Two-Minute Drill 597
  Q&A Self Test 599
    Lab Question 603
    Self Test Answers 604
    Lab Answer 607

12 Active Directory Security Solutions **609**
Configuring and Troubleshooting Security
in a Directory Services Infrastructure 610
    Applying Security Policies Using Group Policy 610
    Security Configuration and Analysis 613
    Exercise 12-1: Creating a New Group Policy Object 614
    Exercise 12-2: Using Group Policy Editor
    to Change Security Settings 615
    Exercise 12-3: Setting Up a Working Security Database . . . 622
    Exercise 12-4: Setting Security on System Services 625
    Implementing an Audit Policy 626
    Exercise 12-5: Setting Security on a File System 627
    Exercise 12-6: Setting Up Audit Policy
    on a Domain Controller 631
    Exercise 12-7: Setting Up Audit Policies
    on a Stand-Alone Computer 633
    Exercise 12-8: Auditing Active Directory Objects 635
    Exercise 12-9: Auditing Access to Files and Folders 638
Monitoring and Analyzing Security Events 640
    Events to Monitor 640
    Archiving Security Logs 644

Exercise 12-10: Configuring a Security Log 645

Clearing Security Logs 646

Interpreting Security Events 647

✓ Two-Minute Drill 652

Q&A Self Test 654

Lab Question 658

Self Test Answers 660

Lab Answer 663

A   About the CD **665**

Installing CertTrainer 666

System Requirements 666

CertTrainer 666

ExamSim 667

Saving Scores as Cookies 668

E-Book 668

CertCam 669

DriveTime 669

Help 670

Upgrading 670

B   About the Web Site **671**

Get *What* You Want *When* You Want It 672

Glossary **673**

Index **765**

This book's primary objective is to help you prepare for the MCSE Implementing and Administering a Microsoft Windows 2000 Directory Services Infrastructure exam under the new Windows 2000 certification track. As the Microsoft program transitions from Windows NT 4.0, it will become increasingly important that current and aspiring IT professionals have multiple resources available to assist them in increasing their knowledge and building their skills.

At the time of publication, all the exam objectives have been posted on the Microsoft Web site and the beta exam process has been completed. Microsoft has announced its commitment to measuring real-world skills. This book is designed with that premise in mind; its authors have practical experience in the field using the Windows 2000 operating systems in hands-on situations and have followed the development of the product since early beta versions.

Because the focus of the exams is on application and understanding, as opposed to memorization of facts, no book by itself can fully prepare you to obtain a passing score. It is essential that you work with the software to enhance your proficiency. Toward that end, this book includes many practical step-by-step exercises in each chapter that are designed to give you hands-on practice as well as guide you in truly learning Microsoft Windows 2000 Directory Services, not just learning *about* it.

In This Book

This book is organized in such a way as to serve as an in-depth review for the MCSE Implementing and Administering a Microsoft Windows 2000 Directory Services Infrastructure exam for both experienced Windows NT professionals and newcomers to Microsoft networking technologies. Each chapter covers a major aspect of the exam, with an emphasis on the "why" as well as the "how to" of working with and supporting Windows 2000 as a network administrator or engineer.

On the CD

The CD-ROM contains the CertTrainer software. CertTrainer comes complete with ExamSim, Skill Assessment tests, CertCam movie clips, the e-book (electronic version of the book), and Drive Time. CertTrainer is easy to install on any Windows 98/NT/2000 computer and must be installed to access these features. You may, however, browse the e-book direct from the CD without installation. For more information on the CD-ROM, please see Appendix A.

In Every Chapter

We've created a set of chapter components that call your attention to important items, reinforce important points, and provide helpful exam-taking hints. Take a look at what you'll find in every chapter:

- Every chapter begins with the **Certification Objectives**—what you need to know in order to pass the section on the exam dealing with the chapter topic. The Objective headings identify the objectives within the chapter, so you'll always know an objective when you see it!

- **Exam Watch** notes call attention to information about, and potential pitfalls in, the exam. These helpful hints are written by authors who have taken the exams and received their certification—who better to tell you what to worry about? They know what you're about to go through!

- **Practice Exercises** are interspersed throughout the chapters. These are step-by-step exercises that allow you to get the hands-on experience you need in order to pass the exams. They help you master skills that are likely to be an area of focus on the exam. Don't just read through the exercises; they are hands-on practice that you should be comfortable completing. Learning by doing is an effective way to increase your competency with a product. The practical exercises will be very helpful for any simulation exercises you may encounter on the MCSE Implementing and Administering a Microsoft Windows 2000 Directory Services Infrastructure exam.

- The **CertCam** icon that appears in many of the exercises indicates that the exercise is presented in .avi format on the accompanying CD-ROM. These .avi clips walk you step-by-step through various system configurations and are narrated by Thomas W. Shinder, M.D., MCSE.

■ **On the Job** notes describe the issues that come up most often in real-world settings. They provide a valuable perspective on certification- and product-related topics. They point out common mistakes and address questions that have arisen from on the job discussions and experience.

■ **From the Classroom** sidebars describe the issues that come up most often in the training classroom setting. These sidebars highlight some of the most common and confusing problems that students encounter when taking a live Windows 2000 training course. You can get a leg up on those difficult to understand subjects by focusing extra attention on these sidebars.

■ **Scenario & Solution** sections lay out potential problems and solutions in a quick-to-read format:

SCENARIO & SOLUTION

Is Active Directory scalable?	Yes! Unlike the Windows NT security database, which is limited to approximately 40,000 objects, Active Directory supports literally millions of objects.
Is Active Directory compatible with other LDAP directory services?	Yes! Active Directory can share information with other directory services that support LDAP versions 2 and 3, such as Novell's NDS.

■ The **Certification Summary** is a succinct review of the chapter and a restatement of salient points regarding the exam.

■ The **Two-Minute Drill** at the end of every chapter is a checklist of the main points of the chapter. It can be used for last-minute review.

■ The **Self Test** offers questions similar to those found on the certification exams. The answers to these questions, as well as explanations of the answers, can be found at the end of each chapter. By taking the Self Test after completing each chapter, you'll reinforce what you've learned from that chapter while becoming familiar with the structure of the exam questions.

■ The **Lab Question** at the end of the Self Test section offers a unique and challenging question format that requires the reader to understand multiple chapter concepts to answer correctly. These questions are more complex and more comprehensive than the other questions, as they test your ability to take all the knowledge you have gained from reading the chapter and apply it to complicated, real-world situations. These questions are aimed to be more difficult than what you will find on the exam. If you can answer these questions, you have proven that you know the subject!

The Global Knowledge Web Site

Check out the Web site. Global Knowledge invites you to become an active member of the Access Global Web site. This site is an online mall and an information repository that you'll find invaluable. You can access many types of products to assist you in your preparation for the exams, and you'll be able to participate in forums, online discussions, and threaded discussions. No other book brings you unlimited access to such a resource. You'll find more information about this site in Appendix B.

Some Pointers

Once you've finished reading this book, set aside some time to do a thorough review. You might want to return to the book several times and make use of all the methods it offers for reviewing the material:

1. *Re-read all the Two-Minute Drills,* or have someone quiz you. You also can use the drills as a way to do a quick cram before the exam. You might want to make some flash cards out of 3 × 5 index cards that have the Two-Minute Drill material on them.

2. *Re-read all the Exam Watch notes.* Remember that these notes are written by authors who have taken the exam and passed. They know what you should expect—and what you should be on the lookout for.

3. *Review all the S&S sections* for quick problem solving.

4. *Re-take the Self Tests.* Taking the tests right after you've read the chapter is a good idea, because the questions help reinforce what you've just learned. However, it's an even better idea to go back later and do all the questions in the book in one sitting. Pretend that you're taking the live exam. (When you go through the questions the first time, you should mark your answers on a

separate piece of paper. That way, you can run through the questions as many times as you need to until you feel comfortable with the material.)

5. *Complete the Exercises.* Did you do the exercises when you read through each chapter? If not, do them! These exercises are designed to cover exam topics, and there's no better way to get to know this material than by practicing. Be sure you understand why you are performing each step in each exercise. If there is something you are not clear on, re-read that section in the chapter.

MCSE Certification

This book is designed to help you pass the MCSE Implementing and Administering a Microsoft Windows 2000 Directory Services Infrastructure exam. At the time this book was written, the exam objectives for the exam were posted on the Microsoft Web site, and the beta exams had been completed. We wrote this book to give you a complete and incisive review of all the important topics that are targeted for the exam. The information contained here will provide you with the required foundation of knowledge that will not only allow you to succeed in passing the MCSE Implementing and Administering a Microsoft Windows 2000 Directory Services Infrastructure exam, but will also make you a better Microsoft Certified Systems Engineer.

The nature of the Information Technology industry is changing rapidly, and the requirements and specifications for certification can change just as quickly without notice. Microsoft expects you to regularly visit their Web site at http://www.microsoft.com/mcp/certstep/mcse.htm to get the most up-to-date information on the entire MCSE program.

Let's look at two scenarios. The first applies to the person who has already taken the Windows NT 4.0 Server (70-067), Windows NT 4.0 Workstation (70-073), and Windows NT 4.0 Server in the Enterprise (70-068) exams. The second scenario covers the situation of the person who has not completed those Windows NT 4.0 exams and would like to concentrate ONLY on Windows 2000.

In the first scenario, you have the option of taking all four Windows 2000 core exams, or you can take the Windows 2000 Accelerated Exam for MCPs if you have already passed exams 70-067, 70-068, and 70-073. (Note that you must have passed those specific exams to qualify for the Accelerated Exam; if you have fulfilled your NT 4.0 MCSE requirements by passing the Windows 95 or Windows 98 exam as your client operating system option, and did not take the NT Workstation Exam, you don't qualify.)

After completing the core requirements, either by passing the four core exams or the one Accelerated exam, you must pass a "design" exam. The design exams

Core Exams		
Candidates Who Have *Not* Already Passed Windows NT 4.0 Exams All Four of the Following Core Exams Required:	**OR**	**Candidates Who Have Passed 3 Windows NT 4.0 Exams (Exams 70-067, 70-068, and 70-073) Instead of the Four Core Exams on Left, You May Take:**
Exam 70-210: Installing, Configuring and Administering Microsoft Windows 2000 Professional		**Exam 70-240:** Microsoft Windows 2000 Accelerated Exam for MCPs Certified on Microsoft Windows NT 4.0. The accelerated exam will be available until December 31, 2001. It covers the core competencies of exams **70-210, 70-215, 70-216,** and **70-217.**
Exam 70-215: Installing, Configuring and Administering Microsoft Windows 2000 Server		
Exam 70-216: Implementing and Administering a Microsoft Windows 2000 Network Infrastructure		
Exam 70-217: Implementing and Administering a Microsoft Windows 2000 Directory Services Infrastructure		

PLUS – All Candidates – One of the Following Core Exams Required:
***Exam 70-219:** Designing a Microsoft Windows 2000 Directory Services Infrastructure
***Exam 70-220:** Designing Security for a Microsoft Windows 2000 Network
***Exam 70-221:** Designing a Microsoft Windows 2000 Network Infrastructure

PLUS – All Candidates – Two Elective Exams Required:
Any current MCSE electives when the Windows 2000 exams listed above are released in their live versions. **Electives scheduled for retirement will not be considered current.** Selected third-party certifications that focus on interoperability will be accepted as an alternative to one elective exam.
***Exam 70-219:** Designing a Microsoft Windows 2000 Directory Services Infrastructure
***Exam 70-220:** Designing Security for a Microsoft Windows 2000 Network
***Exam 70-221:** Designing a Microsoft Windows 2000 Network Infrastructure
Exam 70-222: Upgrading from Microsoft Windows NT 4.0 to Microsoft Windows 2000
*Note that some of the Windows 2000 core exams can be used as elective exams as well. An exam that is used to meet the design requirement cannot also count as an elective. Each exam can only be counted once in the Windows 2000 Certification.

include Designing a Microsoft Windows 2000 Directory Services Infrastructure (70-219), Designing Security for Microsoft Windows 2000 Network (70-220), and Designing a Microsoft Windows 2000 Network Infrastructure (70-221). One design exam is REQUIRED.

You also must pass two exams from the list of electives. However, you cannot use the design exam that you took as an elective. Each exam can only count once toward certification. This includes any of the MCSE electives that are current when the Windows 2000 exams are released. In summary, you would take a total of at least two more exams, the upgrade exam and the design exam. Any additional exams would be dependent on which electives the candidate may have already completed.

In the second scenario, if you have not completed, and do not plan to complete, the Core Windows NT 4.0 exams, you must pass the four core Windows 2000 exams, one design exam, and two elective exams. Again, no exam can be counted twice. In this case, you must pass a total of seven exams to obtain the Windows 2000 MCSE certification.

How to Take a Microsoft Certification Exam

If you have taken a Microsoft Certification exam before, we have some good news and some bad news. The good news is that the new testing formats will be a true measure of your ability and knowledge. Microsoft has "raised the bar" for its Windows 2000 certification exams. If you are an expert in the Windows 2000 operating system, and can troubleshoot and engineer efficient, cost-effective solutions using Windows 2000, you will have no difficulty with the new exams.

The bad news is that if you have used resources such as "brain-dumps," boot-camps, or exam-specific practice tests as your only method of test preparation, you will undoubtedly fail your Windows 2000 exams. The new Windows 2000 MCSE exams will test your knowledge, and your ability to apply that knowledge in more sophisticated and accurate ways than was expected for the MCSE exams for Windows NT 4.0.

In the Windows 2000 exams, Microsoft will use a variety of testing formats that include product simulations, adaptive testing, drag-and-drop matching, and possibly even "fill in the blank" questions (also called "free response" questions). The test-taking process will measure the examinee's fundamental knowledge of the Windows 2000 operating system rather than the ability to memorize a few facts and then answer a few simple multiple-choice questions.

In addition, the "pool" of questions for each exam will significantly increase. The greater number of questions combined with the adaptive testing techniques will enhance the validity and security of the certification process.

We will begin by looking at the purpose, focus, and structure of Microsoft certification tests, and examine the effect that these factors have on the kinds of questions you will face on your certification exams. We will define the structure of exam questions and investigate some common formats. Next, we will present a strategy for answering these questions. Finally, we will give some specific guidelines on what you should do on the day of your test.

Why Vendor Certification?

The Microsoft Certified Professional program, like the certification programs from Cisco, Novell, Oracle, and other software vendors, is maintained for the ultimate purpose of increasing the corporation's profits. A successful vendor certification program accomplishes this goal by helping to create a pool of experts in a company's software and by "branding" these experts so companies using the software can identify them.

We know that vendor certification has become increasingly popular in the last few years because it helps employers find qualified workers and because it helps software vendors like Microsoft sell their products. But why vendor certification rather than a more traditional approach like a college degree in computer science? A college education is a broadening and enriching experience, but a degree in computer science does not prepare students for most jobs in the IT industry.

A common truism in our business states, "If you are out of the IT industry for three years and want to return, you have to start over." The problem, of course, is *timeliness*; if a first-year student learns about a specific computer program, it probably will no longer be in wide use when he or she graduates. Although some colleges are trying to integrate Microsoft certification into their curriculum, the problem is not really a flaw in higher education, but a characteristic of the IT industry. Computer software is changing so rapidly that a four-year college just can't keep up.

A marked characteristic of the Microsoft certification program is an emphasis on performing specific job tasks rather than merely gathering knowledge. It may come as a shock, but most potential employers do not care how much you know about the theory of operating systems, networking, or database design. As one IT manager put it, "I don't really care what my employees know about the theory of our network.

We don't need someone to sit at a desk and think about it. We need people who can actually do something to make it work better."

You should not think that this attitude is some kind of anti-intellectual revolt against "book learning." Knowledge is a necessary prerequisite, but it is not enough. More than one company has hired a computer science graduate as a network administrator, only to learn that the new employee has no idea how to add users, assign permissions, or perform the other day-to-day tasks necessary to maintain a network. This brings us to the second major characteristic of Microsoft certification that affects the questions you must be prepared to answer. In addition to timeliness, Microsoft certification is also job-task oriented.

The timeliness of Microsoft's certification program is obvious and is inherent in the fact that you will be tested on current versions of software in wide use today. The job task orientation of Microsoft certification is almost as obvious, but testing real-world job skills using a computer-based test is not easy.

Computerized Testing

Considering the popularity of Microsoft certification, and the fact that certification candidates are spread around the world, the only practical way to administer tests for the certification program is through Sylvan Prometric or Vue testing centers, which operate internationally. Sylvan Prometric and Vue provide proctor testing services for Microsoft, Oracle, Novell, Lotus, and the A+ computer technician certification. Although the IT industry accounts for much of Sylvan's revenue, the company provides services for a number of other businesses and organizations, such as FAA pre-flight pilot tests. Historically, several hundred questions were developed for a new Microsoft certification exam. The Windows 2000 MCSE exam pool is expected to contain hundreds of new questions. Microsoft is aware that many new MCSE candidates have been able to access information on test questions via the Internet or other resources. The company is very concerned about maintaining the MCSE as a "premium" certification. The significant increase in the number of test questions, together with stronger enforcement of the NDA (non-disclosure agreement) will ensure that a higher standard for certification is attained.

Microsoft treats the test-building process very seriously. Test questions are first reviewed by a number of subject matter experts for technical accuracy and then are presented in a beta test. Taking the beta test may require several hours, due to the large number of questions. After a few weeks, Microsoft Certification uses the statistical feedback from Sylvan to check the performance of the beta questions. The beta test group for the Windows 2000 certification series included MCTs, MCSEs, and members of Microsoft's rapid deployment partners groups. Because the exams will be normalized based on this population, you can be sure that the passing scores will be difficult to achieve without detailed product knowledge.

Questions are discarded if most test takers get them right (too easy) or wrong (too difficult), and a number of other statistical measures are taken of each question. Although the scope of our discussion precludes a rigorous treatment of question analysis, you should be aware that Microsoft and other vendors spend a great deal of time and effort making sure their exam questions are valid.

The questions that survive statistical analysis form the pool of questions for the final certification exam.

Test Structure

The questions in a Microsoft form test will not be equally weighted. From what we can tell at the present time, different questions are given a value based on the level of difficulty. You will get more credit for getting a difficult question correct, than if you got an easy one correct. Because the questions are weighted differently, and because the exams will likely use the adapter method of testing, your score will not bear any relationship to how many questions you answered correctly.

Microsoft has implemented *adaptive* testing. When an adaptive test begins, the candidate is first given a level-three question. If it is answered correctly, a question from the next higher level is presented, and an incorrect response results in a question from the next lower level. When 15 to 20 questions have been answered in this manner, the scoring algorithm is able to predict, with a high degree of statistical certainty, whether the candidate would pass or fail if all the questions in the form were answered. When the required degree of certainty is attained, the test ends and the candidate receives a pass/fail grade.

Adaptive testing has some definite advantages for everyone involved in the certification process. Adaptive tests allow Sylvan Prometric or Vue to deliver more tests with the same resources, as certification candidates often are in and out in 30 minutes or less. For candidates, the "fatigue factor" is reduced due to the shortened testing time. For Microsoft, adaptive testing means that fewer test questions are exposed to each candidate, and this can enhance the security and, therefore, the overall validity of certification tests.

One possible problem you may have with adaptive testing is that you are not allowed to mark and revisit questions. Since the adaptive algorithm is interactive, and all questions but the first are selected on the basis of your response to the previous question, it is not possible to skip a particular question or change an answer.

Question Types

Computerized test questions can be presented in a number of ways. Some of the possible formats are used on Microsoft certification exams and some are not.

True/False

We are all familiar with True/False questions, but because of the inherent 50 percent chance of guessing the correct answer, you will not see questions of this type on Microsoft certification exams.

Multiple Choice

The majority of Microsoft certification questions are in the multiple-choice format, with either a single correct answer or multiple correct answers. One interesting variation on multiple-choice questions with multiple correct answers is whether or not the candidate is told how many answers are correct.

EXAMPLE:

Which two files can be altered to configure the MS-DOS environment? (Choose two.)

or

Which files can be altered to configure the MS-DOS environment? (Choose all that apply.)

You may see both variations on Microsoft certification exams, but the trend seems to be toward the first type, where candidates are told explicitly how many answers are correct. Questions of the "choose all that apply" variety are more difficult and can be merely confusing.

Graphical Questions

One or more graphical elements are sometimes used as exhibits to help present or clarify an exam question. These elements may take the form of a network diagram, pictures of networking components, or screen shots from the software on which you are being tested. It is often easier to present the concepts required for a complex performance-based scenario with a graphic than with words.

Test questions known as *hotspots* actually incorporate graphics as part of the answer. These questions ask the certification candidate to click a location or graphical element to answer the question. For example, you might be shown the diagram of a network and asked to click an appropriate location for a router. The answer is correct if the candidate clicks within the *hotspot* that defines the correct location.

Free Response Questions

Another kind of question you sometimes see on Microsoft certification exams requires a *free response* or type-in answer. An example of this type of question might present a TCP/IP network scenario and ask the candidate to calculate and enter the correct subnet mask in dotted decimal notation.

Simulation Questions

Simulation questions provide a method for Microsoft to test how familiar the test taker is with the actual product interface and the candidate's ability to quickly implement a task using the interface. These questions will present an actual Windows 2000 interface that you must work with to solve a problem or implement a solution. If you are familiar with the product, you will be able to answer these questions quickly, and they will be the easiest questions on the exam. However, if you are not accustomed to working with Windows 2000, these questions will be difficult for you to answer. This is why actual hands-on practice with Windows 2000 is so important!

Knowledge-Based and Performance-Based Questions

Microsoft Certification develops a blueprint for each Microsoft certification exam with input from subject matter experts. This blueprint defines the content areas and objectives for each test, and each test question is created to test a specific objective.

The basic information from the examination blueprint can be found on Microsoft's Web site in the Exam Prep Guide for each test.

Psychometricians (psychologists who specialize in designing and analyzing tests) categorize test questions as knowledge based or performance based. As the names imply, knowledge-based questions are designed to test knowledge, while performance-based questions are designed to test performance.

Some objectives demand a knowledge-based question. For example, objectives that use verbs like *list* and *identify* tend to test only what you know, not what you can do.

EXAMPLE:

Objective: Identify the MS-DOS configuration files.

Which two files can be altered to configure the MS-DOS environment? (Choose two.)

A. COMMAND.COM

B. AUTOEXEC.BAT

C. IO.SYS

D. CONFIG.SYS
   Correct answers: B, D

Other objectives use action verbs like *install, configure,* and *troubleshoot* to define job tasks. These objectives can often be tested with either a knowledge-based question or a performance-based question.

EXAMPLE:

Objective: Configure an MS-DOS installation appropriately using the PATH statement in AUTOEXEC.BAT.

Knowledge-based question:

What is the correct syntax to set a path to the D: directory in AUTOEXEC.BAT?

A. SET PATH EQUAL TO D:

B. PATH D:

C. SETPATH D:

D. D:EQUALS PATH
Correct answer: B

Performance-based question:

Your company uses several DOS accounting applications that access a group of common utility programs. What is the best strategy for configuring the computers in the accounting department so that the accounting applications will always be able to access the utility programs?

A. Store all the utilities on a single floppy disk and make a copy of the disk for each computer in the accounting department.

B. Copy all the utilities to a directory on the C: drive of each computer in the accounting department and add a PATH statement pointing to this directory in the AUTOEXEC.BAT files.

C. Copy all the utilities to all application directories on each computer in the accounting department.

D. Place all the utilities in the C: directory on each computer, because the C: directory is automatically included in the PATH statement when AUTOEXEC.BAT is executed.
Correct answer: B

Even in this simple example, the superiority of the performance-based question is obvious. Whereas the knowledge-based question asks for a single fact, the performance-based question presents a real-life situation and requires that you make a decision based on this scenario. Thus, performance-based questions give more bang (validity) for the test author's buck (individual question).

Testing Job Performance

We have said that Microsoft certification focuses on timeliness and the ability to perform job tasks. We have also introduced the concept of performance-based questions, but even performance-based multiple-choice questions do not really measure performance. Another strategy is needed to test job skills.

Given unlimited resources, it is not difficult to test job skills. In an ideal world, Microsoft would fly MCP candidates to Redmond; place them in a controlled environment with a team of experts; and ask them to plan, install, maintain, and troubleshoot a Windows network. In a few days at most, the experts could reach a valid decision as to whether each candidate should or should not be granted MCDBA or MCSE status. Needless to say, this is not likely to happen.

Closer to reality, another way to test performance is by using the actual software and creating a testing program to present tasks and automatically grade a candidate's performance when the tasks are completed. This *cooperative* approach would be practical in some testing situations, but the same test that is presented to MCP candidates in Boston must also be available in Bahrain and Botswana. The most workable solution for measuring performance in today's testing environment is a *simulation* program. When the program is launched during a test, the candidate sees a simulation of the actual software that looks, and behaves, just like the real thing. When the testing software presents a task, the simulation program is launched and the candidate performs the required task. The testing software then grades the candidate's performance on the required task and moves to the next question. Microsoft has introduced simulation questions on the certification exam for Internet Information Server 4.0. Simulation questions provide many advantages over other testing methodologies, and simulations are expected to become increasingly important in the Microsoft certification program. For example, studies have shown that there is a very high correlation between the ability to perform simulated tasks on a computer-based test and the ability to perform the actual job tasks. Thus, simulations enhance the validity of the certification process.

Another truly wonderful benefit of simulations is in the area of test security. It is just not possible to cheat on a simulation question. In fact, you will be told exactly what tasks you are expected to perform on the test. How can a certification candidate cheat? By learning to perform the tasks? What a concept!

Study Strategies

There are appropriate ways to study for the different types of questions you will see on a Microsoft certification exam.

Knowledge-Based Questions

Knowledge-based questions require that you memorize facts. There are hundreds of facts inherent in every content area of every Microsoft certification exam. There are several keys to memorizing facts:

- **Repetition**   The more times your brain is exposed to a fact, the more likely you are to remember it.

- **Association**   Connecting facts within a logical framework makes them easier to remember.

- **Motor Association**   It is often easier to remember something if you write it down or perform some other physical act, like clicking a practice test answer.

We have said that the emphasis of Microsoft certification is job performance, and that there are very few knowledge-based questions on Microsoft certification exams. Why should you waste a lot of time learning filenames, IP address formulas, and other minutiae? Read on.

Performance-Based Questions

Most of the questions you will face on a Microsoft certification exam are performance-based scenario questions. We have discussed the superiority of these questions over simple knowledge-based questions, but you should remember that the job-task orientation of Microsoft certification extends the knowledge you need to pass the exams; it does not replace this knowledge. Therefore, the first step in preparing for scenario questions is to absorb as many facts relating to the exam content areas as you can. In other words, go back to the previous section and follow the steps to prepare for an exam composed of knowledge-based questions.

The second step is to familiarize yourself with the format of the questions you are likely to see on the exam. You can do this by answering the questions in this study guide, by using Microsoft assessment tests, or by using practice tests on the included CD-ROM. The day of your test is not the time to be surprised by the construction of Microsoft exam questions.

At best, performance-based scenario questions really do test certification candidates at a higher cognitive level than knowledge-based questions. At worst, these questions can test your reading comprehension and test-taking ability rather than your ability to use Microsoft products. Be sure to get in the habit of reading the question carefully to determine what is being asked.

The third step in preparing for Microsoft scenario questions is to adopt the following attitude: multiple-choice questions aren't really performance based. It is all a cruel lie. These scenario questions are just knowledge-based questions with a story wrapped around them.

To answer a scenario question, you have to sift through the story to the underlying facts of the situation and apply your knowledge to determine the correct answer. This may sound silly at first, but the process we go through in solving real-life problems is quite similar. The key concept is that every scenario question (and every real-life problem) has a fact at its center, and if we can identify that fact, we can answer the question.

Simulations

Simulation questions really do measure your ability to perform job tasks. You must be able to perform the specified tasks. There are two ways to prepare for simulation questions:

1. Get experience with the actual software. If you have the resources, this is a great way to prepare for simulation questions.

2. Use the practice test on this book's accompanying CD-ROM, as it contains simulation questions similar to those you will find on the Microsoft exam. You can find additional practice tests at www.syngress.com and www.osborne.com.

Signing Up

Signing up to take a Microsoft certification exam is easy. Sylvan Prometric or Vue operators in each country can schedule tests at any testing center. There are, however, a few things you should know:

1. If you call Sylvan Prometric or Vue during a busy time, get a cup of coffee first, because you may be in for a long wait. The exam providers do an excellent job, but everyone in the world seems to want to sign up for a test on Monday morning.

2. You will need your social security number or some other unique identifier to sign up for a test, so have it at hand.

3. Pay for your test by credit card if at all possible. This makes things easier, and you can even schedule tests for the same day you call, if space is available at your local testing center.

4. Know the number and title of the test you want to take before you call. This is not essential, and the Sylvan operators will help you if they can. Having this information in advance, however, speeds up and improves the accuracy of the registration process.

Taking the Test

Teachers have always told you not to try to cram for exams because it does no good. If you are faced with a knowledge-based test requiring only that you regurgitate facts, cramming can mean the difference between passing and failing. This is not the case, however, with Microsoft certification exams. If you don't know it the night before, don't bother to stay up and cram.

Instead, create a schedule and stick to it. Plan your study time carefully, and do not schedule your test until you think you are ready to succeed. Follow these guidelines on the day of your exam:

1. Get a good night's sleep. The scenario questions you will face on a Microsoft certification exam require a clear head.

2. Remember to take two forms of identification—at least one with a picture. A driver's license with your picture and social security or credit card is acceptable.

3. Leave home in time to arrive at your testing center a few minutes early. It is not a good idea to feel rushed as you begin your exam.

4. Do not spend too much time on any one question. You cannot mark and revisit questions on an adaptive test, so you must do your best on each question as you go.

5. If you do not know the answer to a question, try to eliminate the obviously wrong answers and guess from the rest. If you can eliminate two out of four options, you have a 50 percent chance of guessing the correct answer.

6. For scenario questions, follow the steps we outlined earlier. Read the question carefully and try to identify the facts at the center of the story.

Finally, we would advise anyone attempting to earn Microsoft MCDBA and MCSE certification to adopt a philosophical attitude. The Windows 2000 MCSE will be the most difficult MCSE ever to be offered. The questions will be at a higher cognitive level than seen on all previous MCSE exams. Therefore, even if you are the kind of person who never fails a test, you are likely to fail at least one Windows 2000 certification test somewhere along the way. Do not get discouraged. Microsoft wants to ensure the value of your certification. Moreover, it will attempt to do so by keeping the standard as high as possible. If Microsoft certification were easy to obtain, more people would have it, and it would not be so respected and so valuable to your future in the IT industry.

1

Introduction to Windows 2000 Directory Services Administration

CERTIFICATION OBJECTIVES

1.01	What Is Windows 2000 Directory Services Administration?
1.02	Overview of Exam 70-217
1.03	What We'll Cover in This Book
1.04	What You Should Already Know
✓	Two-Minute Drill
Q&A	Self Test

Welcome to Windows 2000 and one of Microsoft's most important core topics for the Windows 2000 Microsoft Certified Systems Engineer (MCSE) certification track. The Active Directory is one of the most exciting new features in Windows 2000. This new and improved, sophisticated directory service provides administrators with a flexible, powerful tool that simplifies many day-to-day activities.

The *Active Directory (AD)* is the "heart" of the Windows 2000 Server domain controller and of Windows 2000 networking. Creating and implementing an Active Directory infrastructure present the systems administrator with both a challenge and an opportunity. Knowledge of NT networking provides a good foundation for learning many aspects of Windows 2000, but when it comes to directory services, Windows 2000 is a whole new world and presents an entirely new way of accomplishing administrative tasks, as well as the ability to accomplish many tasks that simply were not possible to accomplish in Windows NT—at least, not without third-party add-on software.

The Windows 2000 Active Directory can support a huge scope of features and capabilities in an enterprise environment. Microsoft designed Windows 2000 and Active Directory with the enterprise network in mind. The company's goal in developing the new operating system and directory service was scalability that would extend to large and complex network configurations.

This book will help prepare you to not only pass Microsoft certification exam 70-217, Implementing and Administering a Windows 2000 Directory Services Infrastructure, but it will also prepare you for the exciting experience of applying your knowledge and skills to your real-world network.

CERTIFICATION OBJECTIVE 1.01

What Is Windows 2000 Directory Services Administration?

In order to answer that question, let's break the exam topic down into its component parts. First, and most basic: what do we really mean by *implementing and administering?* The *American Heritage Dictionary* defines *implementing* as "putting into practical effect, or carrying out," and it defines *administering* as "having charge of" or simply "managing." (These definitions should appeal to the "control freak" side of your nature—and anyone who wants to manage an entire enterprise network must have at least a mild dose of that in his or her personality.)

What exactly is it, then, that we are "carrying out" and then "managing"? A *directory*, in this context, is a database that contains information about objects and their attributes. Most of us are already familiar with the basic directory concept; consider a telephone directory. The "objects" a telephone directory contains are names, and the attributes of each object include the phone number and address associated with that name. Directories utilized by network operating systems can, of course, be much more complex. The *directory service* is the component that organizes the objects into a logical and accessible structure and provides for a means of searching and locating objects within the directory. The directory service includes the entire directory *and* the method of storing it on the network.

Finally, let's look at the word *infrastructure*. Returning again to our trusty dictionary, we find that an infrastructure is defined as "an underlying base or foundation for an organization or system."

Putting it all together, we can conclude that exam 70-217 covers how to put into practice a plan that will provide a foundation for the use of a networkwide database holding information about objects on the network (such as user and computer accounts, resources, and network services) and make that information quickly and easily available to authorized users, applications, and operating system services. Furthermore, it will test you on the skills required to maintain, optimize, troubleshoot, and oversee the use of that database throughout your enterprise network.

The Active Directory includes the following specific features:

- A *data store* (another term for the directory), which stores information about Active Directory objects. Active Directory objects include shared resources such as servers, files, printers, and user and computer accounts.

- A set of rules, called the *schema*, which defines the classes of objects and attributes contained in the directory, the constraints and limits on instances of these objects, and the format of their names.

- The *global catalog (GC)* that contains information about all the objects in the directory. The GC allows users and administrators to find directory information without having to know which server or domain actually contains the data.

- A means of *querying and indexing* this information, so that objects and their properties can be published and found by network users (or by applications that need to access them).

- A *replication service*, which distributes directory data across the enterprise network. All domain controllers in a domain participate in replication and contain a complete copy of all directory information for their domain. Changes to directory data are automatically replicated to all domain controllers in the domain.

- A *security subsystem* that provides for a secure logon process to the network as well as access control on both directory data queries and data modifications.

- The ability to join domains into a *domain tree* and join trees in a *forest*, creating a trust relationship that allows for easy access by all users in the multidomain network to all resources for which their accounts have the appropriate access permissions.

- The means to exert *granular control* over entire sites, domains, or organizational units (OUs) through the use of Group Policy, making management of an enterprise-level network easier for the administrator.

SCENARIO & SOLUTION

How does the Active Directory namespace differ from the NT domain namespace?	The NT namespace is *flat*—that is, all domains are on an equal "level." The Active Directory namespace is hierarchical; domains exist in a "tree" structure in which a root domain spawns "child" domains, which can in turn have children of their own. The name of the child includes the name of the parent; thus a domain named *training.tacteam.net* is the child of a parent domain named *tacteam.net*.
How do Active Directory trust relationships between domains differ from NT trusts?	Active Directory trusts use Kerberos authentication, an industry standard, to provide for explicit *two-way transitive* trust relationships between all domains in a tree or a forest of trees. NT trusts are one way, and each must be created explicitly.
How does Active Directory achieve compatibility with other directory services?	Active Directory is compatible with the LDAP standards, which makes it compatible with other LDAP directory services such as Novell's directory services.

FROM THE CLASSROOM

Standard Industry Terms

As you begin to study and work with the Windows 2000 Active Directory, you will encounter sometimes confusing or unfamiliar terms such as *LDAP* and *X.500*. These terms refer to established standards and protocols. If you have experience with other directory services such as Novell Directory Services (NDS), you may already be familiar with them. If not, think of your introduction to Microsoft networks; you learned that organizations such as the International Organization for Standardization (ISO) and the Institute of Electrical and Electronics Engineers (IEEE) established standards adhered to by networking products vendors (for example, the 802 specifications governing physical and data link level protocols). *X.500* is a directory services standard developed by the International Telecommunication Union (ITU) and published by ISO. It is based on the *Directory Access Protocol (DAP)*. The *Lightweight Directory Access Protocol (LDAP)* is, as you might guess, a variation of DAP and is supported by many vendors. Novell's and Cisco's networking products, as well as Microsoft's Active Directory, are LDAP compatible, which allows for interoperability between different directory services.

—Debra Littlejohn Shinder, MCSE, MCP+I, MCT

The Role of a Directory Service

Directory services are good—in fact, they are *necessary* components of any complex networking system. In an object-oriented operating system such as Windows, there must be some means of keeping track of all the system's objects (users, groups, computers, printers, folders, and files and other network resources) and an easy way to locate and access them when you need to use them.

Directory Services in Windows NT

One thing that we should clarify: The directory service itself is not a new thing in Windows 2000. NT uses directory services, too. In fact, NT uses a multiplicity of directory services: DNS, with its database of host names and IP addresses; WINS, with its own database of NetBIOS names and IP addresses; the browse service, to keep up with shared network resources; and the Security Accounts Manager (SAM) database that handles information about security objects (users and groups) and permissions. NT uses NT Directory Services (NTDS) to manage users and groups. It is a flat database and is not extensible, but it does offer such features as single sign-on to access network resources across the enterprise.

The databases used by NT were not well integrated to work together, and locating particular objects could be difficult. For instance, if you needed to access a particular shared folder, you needed to know which server that folder resided on in order to access it. With the Active Directory, objects can be *published* and will appear in the directory; users can access a shared folder without ever knowing—or needing to know—on what computer's hard disk the folder is physically located.

on the
Job

Long-time network administrators who have worked with Novell's network operating systems will quickly see the parallel here: The difference between the NT Directory Services and Active Directory is like the difference between the NetWare 3x bindery, which was a flat database, and the NetWare 4x and 5x hierarchically structured NDS tree. Furthermore, just as Novell designated moving from NetWare 3x to version 4 as a "migration" as opposed to an "upgrade," the switch from NT to Windows 2000 should be viewed in the same light.

Advantage of Active Directory

Unfortunately, NT's ways of storing information had some serious limitations. For instance, the number of security objects that could be contained in the SAM database was restricted by the fact that the entire database had to fit into the domain controller's RAM. This resulted in a Microsoft-recommended maximum of about 40,000 accounts in a domain. In contrast, one of the biggest advantages of Active Directory is its *scalability;* because security accounts information, along with information about many other types of objects, is stored in the Active Directory and stored on a partition on the domain controllers' hard disks, there is no such limit on the number of accounts. One domain can contain literally millions of objects.

Interoperability of Directory Services

Along with the Active Directory, Microsoft introduced the *Active Directory Services Interface (ADSI),* a set of COM interfaces supplied as a Software Development Kit (SDK) that allows developers to enable their applications to use directory services. This structure gives users a single point of access to one or more directories, which can be based on LDAP, NDS, or NTDS.

Microsoft designed Active Directory to be a consolidation point for isolating, migrating, centrally managing, and reducing the number of directories that companies have and use in their networks. Toward that end, migration tools are provided to allow administrators to more easily migrate from other directory services, such as NTDS or NDS, to the Active Directory. Third-party programs are also available to assist in migration and/or allow for integration with multiple operating systems and services such as Banyan Vines and NDS.

Replication of Directory Information

The directory information is stored in a file named NTDS.DIT. This file must be located on an NTFS-formatted partition or volume on the Windows 2000 domain controller. The directory data can be divided into two categories: private and public. *Public data* is stored on a shared system volume. This volume is replicated to all domain controllers within the domain.

The data that is replicated includes domain data, configuration data, and schema data. *Domain data* is what we generally think of as directory information—that is, information about domain objects. Examples are user and computer account attributes, published shared folders, printers, and other resources. The *configuration data* is information about the directory structure, such as the names of domains and trees and where the domain controllers and global catalog servers are located in the domain. *Schema data* refers to the definitions of classes, object types, and attributes that you can store in the directory.

on the
job

Windows 2000 provides for the means to modify or extend the schema, but it is not a task for the timid. Microsoft refers to schema modification as "an advanced and complex operation best handled programmatically." In other words, the usual way for the schema to be modified is for developers to write applications that will modify it. Unfortunately, when an application changes the schema incorrectly, the administrator may have to perform schema modification as part of the troubleshooting process.

It is a good practice to disconnect the domain controller serving as the schema operations master from the network prior to making the changes; that way, you can test the change before the schema update is replicated to the other domain controllers. Remember, the schema master's role is forestwide, so changes to the schema impact every domain in every tree in the forest. In fact, because a change to the schema constitutes such serious business, it is recommended that they always be tested in a lab environment first, so that any unexpected effects will be isolated from your production network.

Features of a Global Directory Service

What do we mean by a *global* directory service? Microsoft uses the term to refer to a directory service that is scalable to the enterprise level, compatible with Internet and industry standards, and integrated fully with the operating system. Some features of Active Directory that have been incorporated to ensure that it meets these criteria include:

- Support for major standards such as the Dynamic Domain Name System (DDNS), Dynamic Host Configuration Protocol (DHCP), LDAP, and Kerberos

- Open programming interfaces and protocols such as Active Directory Service Interfaces (ADSI) and the Security Support Provider Interface (SSPI)

- Centralized management using a consistent management interface

- Customization and control of the user desktop and environment

- Directory-enabled applications and easier application deployment and configuration

- Integration of security services, based on standardized authentication protocols

Let's take a brief look at what each of these features means.

Support for Major Standards

Windows 2000 Server and the Active Directory support and work together with Internet and industry standards, including:

- Dynamic Domain Name System (DDNS)
- Dynamic Host Configuration Protocol (DHCP)
- Lightweight Directory Access Protocol (LDAP)
- Transmission Control Protocol/Internet Protocol (TCP/IP)

Dynamic Domain Name System   DDNS support and integration in the Active Directory allows for the creation of a global naming structure compatible with standard DNS conventions, while including the benefits of the "dynamic" aspect of this improved version of DNS. The DNS dynamic update protocol is a new specification to the DNS standard that permits hosts that store name information in DNS to dynamically register and update their records. This applies to DNS zones maintained by DNS servers that are able to accept and process dynamic update messages. Note that DDNS is supported only by Berkeley Internet Name Domain (BIND) versions 8.x and above. BIND is an implementation of DNS distributed with UNIX.

Dynamic Host Configuration Protocol   DHCP's new integration with Active Directory provides a means of authorizing DHCP servers in the directory, so that "rogue" (unauthorized) DHCP servers can be detected and prevented from allocating IP addresses on the network.

Lightweight Directory Access Protocol   LDAP compatibility translates into better interoperability between applications and directory services. Microsoft provides LDAP support in client products such as Microsoft Outlook, NetMeeting, and Internet Explorer and in server products such as Site Server and Exchange Server.

on the **job**

LDAP will also be the method used by Microsoft Exchange Server for directory migration and synchronization with Windows 2000 Server. You can also use the Active Directory Connector to replicate directory objects between a Microsoft Exchange Server directory (version 5.5 or later) and the AD directory service.

Transmission Control Protocol/Internet Protocol   TCP/IP is, of course, the standard set of protocols required for computers to communicate on the Internet. TCP/IP works on a huge diversity of operating systems and platforms and enables connectivity between dissimilar systems all over the world. The Windows 2000 implementation of TCP/IP has added several enhancements, such as support for large TCP receive windows and Selective Acknowledgements, both of which can improve the performance of this powerful, flexible, but relatively slow protocol stack.

Open Programming Interfaces and Protocols

True global status and interoperability require open interfaces and protocols that enable third parties to more easily develop applications that work in the Active Directory environment. These include:

- The Active Directory Services Interface (ADSI)
- The Security Services Provider Interface (SSPI)

Active Directory Services Interface   ADSI consists of a set of high-level, language-independent directory service programming interfaces, which support the ability to work with resources provided by Windows NT Server 4.0, Novell NetWare 3.x, and NetWare 4.x (including the Novell Directory Services). ADSI is the primary application programming interface (API) to be used for developing applications for the Windows 2000 Server Active Directory. ADSI's purpose is to provide software developers with a standardized, easy-to-use, object-oriented way to write application programs using tools such as Java, C, C++, or Visual Basic that can access information from multiple directories and synchronize data between directories.

Security Services Provider Interface   SSPI allows developers to utilize the integrated security benefits of Windows 2000, such as single sign-on and authentication. SSPI is used to access the security features of the Active Directory.

SSPI is the component of the security subsystem that reduces the amount of code needed at the application level to support multiple security protocols by providing a generic interface for the authentication mechanisms that are based on shared-secret or public key protocols.

Centralized Management and a Consistent Management Interface

The Active Directory serves as a central repository for all information about system configuration, user profiles, and applications. This repository allows administrators to manage distributed desktops, network services, and directory-enabled applications from one central location, using a consistent management interface: the Microsoft Management Console (MMC). It also provides network administrators with a consistent way to monitor and manage network devices, such as routers, through system profiles provided by the Active Directory.

The MMC is a tool that is used to create, save, and open collections of administrative tools, called *consoles*. Consoles contain snap-ins, wizards, and documentation that are used for managing hardware, software, and networking components in Windows 2000. See Figure 1-1 for an example of an MMC—in this case, the AD Sites and Services console.

All MMC snap-ins present this same common interface, with the *console tree* shown on the left and the *details pane* on the right. This Windows Explorer-like

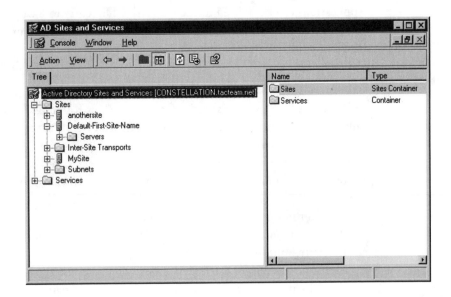

FIGURE 1-1

An example of the Microsoft Management Console with the Active Directory Sites and Services snap-in

interface makes it easier for administrators to perform management tasks, without being required to learn to navigate a different interface for each administrative tool.

Customization and Control of the User Environment

The Windows 2000 Active Directory supports customization and personalization of the user desktop and environment. Features in Windows 2000 Server and Windows 2000 Professional use information stored in Active Directory to determine where users store their documents, where their personal settings are saved, and the general configuration of their environments.

Through application of Group Policies, administrators can control the environments of users to whatever extent is desired, all the way to "locking down" the desktop. Group Policy for a site, domain, or organizational unit is implemented through the Active Directory, and the Group Policy settings define the components of the user's desktop environment that a systems administrator needs to manage.

Directory-Enabled Applications and Easier Deployment and Configuration

Applications can be written to use the Active Directory to locate services that are published to the directory and to centrally store application configuration and installation information.

Integration of Security Services

In Windows 2000, strong security features, such as Kerberos authentication and public key certificates, are directly integrated with the directory services. Let's briefly examine how this differs from the NT model.

In NT 4.0, the SAM database and the characteristics of the NTLM trust relationship combined to limit security to three levels within the domain: global groups, local groups, and individual users. With Active Directory, the database is distributed throughout the enterprise. This means security can be administered with much more granularity and flexibility. One example is the ability to delegate administrative authority at the OU level.

The Windows 2000 Distributed Security Services use the Active Directory as the central repository for account information and domain security policy. This is a big improvement over registry-based implementation in terms of both performance and scalability. It is also easier to manage because the Active Directory provides replication and availability of account information to multiple domain controllers and can be administered remotely.

Active Directory Structure

The Active Directory has both a *physical structure*, defined by sites for purposes of optimizing replication and logon authentication traffic, and a *logical structure*, defined by domains, which can be joined into trees, and trees combined to create forests. If you are not familiar with these terms, see the section on directory services terminology later in this chapter.

Active Directory Physical Structure

The physical structure of the Active Directory is based on Active Directory sites. A *site* is a group of computers in an IP subnet or group of subnets that have a high-performance connection. Sites are completely independent of domains; that is, a site can span more than one domain, and a domain can span multiple sites.

Using Sites to Optimize Logon Authentication Traffic   The Active Directory uses sites to optimize the flow of network traffic across slow wide area network (WAN) links. In other words, if you have two sites, connected by a 56Kbps link, it is more efficient for a user logon to be authenticated by a domain controller at the same site as the computer from which the user is logging on, because the traffic will not have to travel over the slow link.

Using Sites to Optimize Directory Replication Traffic   Sites are also used in optimizing directory replication. The traffic generated by the replication of directory information from one domain controller to another can have a major impact on network bandwidth if those domain controllers are separated by a slow link. Thus replication between separate sites (*intersite replication*) is handled differently from replication traffic within the same site (*intrasite replication*). For instance, you can schedule intersite replication to take place after business hours or increase the interval between instances of replication to reduce the load on the network at peak usage times.

Active Directory Logical Structure

The logical structure of the Active Directory is based on *domains*. NT administrators are already familiar with the term, but Windows 2000 Active Directory domains differ in many ways from NT domains. NT domains are all "peers" on the network, and they operate independently. Users who belong to one NT domain cannot access the resources of a different domain unless the administrator explicitly creates a *trust relationship* between the two domains. Even then, the trust is not two way; the *trusting* domain's resources are available to users in the *trusted* domain, but the opposite is not true. Another separate trust must be established for that to happen.

Trees and Forests   An important feature of the Windows 2000 domain structure is the ability to join domains in trees. A *tree* is a group of domains that share a contiguous namespace and all of which have a two-way transitive trust with one another.

Multiple trees can be joined into a *forest*. The root domains of each tree also share two-way transitive trusts with those of every other trust in the forest. All domains in a forest share a common schema, configuration, and global catalog.

The Nature of Trusts   A *transitive trust* is one in which the trust relationship is *transferred* through intermediary domains. In other words, if Domain A trusts Domain B, and Domain B trusts Domain C, then Domain also trusts Domain C in a transitive relationship. Kerberos trusts, used by Active Directory, are transitive, while NTLM trusts, used in NT-based networks, are nontransitive.

The Hierarchy of Domains   The way in which domains are arranged within a tree is *hierarchical.* A *hierarchy* is a way of organizing objects in such a way that there is a single "root" object from which others branch off and in which each object "belongs to" the object above it. The object to which it belongs is called its *parent object,* and each object directly beneath another in the hierarchy is called a *child object.* See Figure 1-2 for an illustration of a domain hierarchy.

Note that the name of each child domain also includes the full name of its parent. This is what is meant by a *contiguous namespace.*

The hierarchical structure of a domain tree

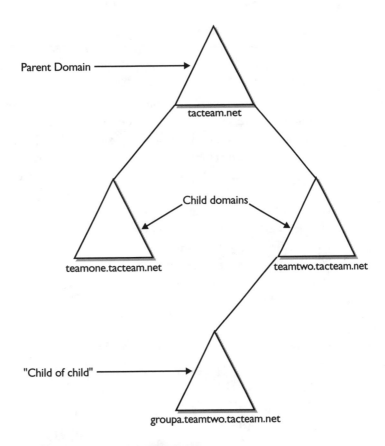

Parent Domain

tacteam.net

Child domains

teamone.tacteam.net

teamtwo.tacteam.net

"Child of child"

groupa.teamtwo.tacteam.net

CERTIFICATION OBJECTIVE 1.02

Overview of Exam 70-217

The Windows 2000 certification exams can be divided into two groups: the core implementing and administering exams and the design electives. Each category has a different focus; the design exams are concerned with planning issues, whereas the cores deal with the "nitty gritty" of everyday work with the network and the operating system and its components. It might seem logical (or *chronological*) to learn design first, since after all a directory services infrastructure (or other network infrastructure) must be designed before it can be implemented and administered. However, you will almost certainly find it easier to study and test on the core topics first. The design exam questions are more complex, requiring a higher level of cognition and the ability to dissect, analyze, evaluate, and then devise a plan based on multiple sources of information. You will find that studying for this exam, Implementing and Administering a Directory Services Infrastructure, will lay the foundation needed to prepare for 70-221, the directory services infrastructure design exam.

This exam, 70-217, covers an amazing number of complex topics. Not only must you be able to demonstrate your ability to install, configure, and troubleshoot the Windows 2000 Active Directory components as well as DNS for Active Directory; you must also be able to implement Active Directory security solutions and deploy Windows 2000 via the Remote Installation Service (RIS). Finally, you should be able to manage, monitor, and optimize the desktop environment by using Group Policy, and you must be able to use Group Policy to deploy application software.

Exam Objectives

The objectives stated by Microsoft for this exam involve many skills, most of which will be new to experienced NT administrators (although the concepts won't necessarily be). In this section we break the objectives down into broad categories and discuss a little about each.

Installing, Configuring, and Troubleshooting the Active Directory

It is recommended that you practice installing the Active Directory in various situations (for example, on a domain controller for a new domain, on a new domain controller for an existing domain, on a new domain controller that is to become the root of a new tree in an existing forest).

In order to meet this objective, you must know much more than simply how to run the Active Directory Installation Wizard (see Figure 1-3).

The Active
Directory
Installation
wizard walks
you through
the process of
promoting a
Windows 2000
server to a
domain
controller

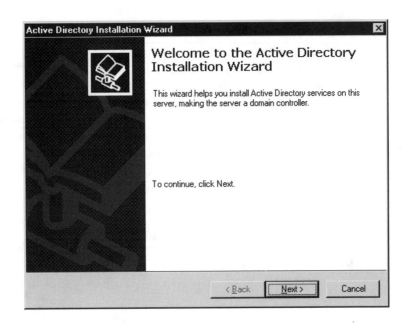

```
Active Directory Installation Wizard                              [X]

            Welcome to the Active Directory
            Installation Wizard

            This wizard helps you install Active Directory services on this
            server, making the server a domain controller.

            To continue, click Next.

                              < Back      Next >        Cancel
```

exam
Watch

To start the Active Directory installation process, type DCPROMO at the command line. Remember that installing Active Directory on a server makes that server a Windows 2000 domain controller. The DCPROMO command is also used when you want to demote a domain controller to a member or standalone server and remove Active Directory from its hard disk. Expect questions on installation issues on the exam, and be sure you also understand how to verify the installation of Active Directory once it's done.

Sites and Subnets   In addition to demonstrating your ability to install the Active Directory, the first objective requires that you be able to create active sites and subnets and then make site links, site link bridges, and connection objects to establish a replication topology between those sites. You must also know how to move server objects from one site to another.

Special Domain Controller Roles Domain controllers can take on several different, special roles in a Windows 2000 forest or domain. You must understand these specialized roles and their impact on the network. Particularly, you should know how to create and use global catalog servers and operations masters and how to transfer operations master roles from one DC to another.

■ **Global Catalog Servers** The *global catalog server* is a domain controller that contains a partial replica of every domain in Active Directory. The global catalog holds a replica of every object in Active Directory, but it includes only some of the objects' attributes—those most often used in search operations.

A domain controller can be enabled or disabled as a global catalog server via the Active Directory Sites and Services MMC, by double-clicking the server name, right-clicking NTDS Settings | Properties, and checking the Global Catalog checkbox, as shown in Figure 1-4. (Later in the book, you will go

---

A domain controller can be enabled as a global catalog server by checking the checkbox in the NTDS Settings Properties window

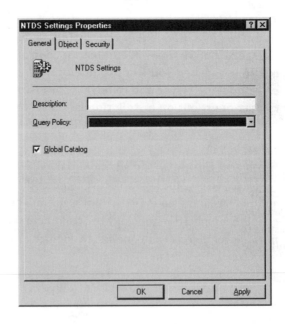

through all the steps involved in making a domain controller a global catalog server.)

A user must generally have access to a global catalog server to successfully log onto the network, because the global catalog is needed to determine to what groups the user belongs.

Network performance is increased if the domain controller at a site is also a global catalog server, so it can fulfill queries about all the objects in the entire forest. The down side is that if you make too many domain controllers global catalog servers, the replication traffic on your network could be increased.

■ **Operations Masters**   Active Directory "levels the playing field" by making domain controllers more equal—doing away with the roles of Primary Domain Controller (PDC) and Backup Domain Controller (BDC). Windows 2000 introduces *multimaster replication,* wherein a read/write copy of the directory is kept on all DCs. Nonetheless, there are still some tasks that must be performed in a *single-master* fashion. This means one domain controller must be designated as the one "in charge" of that particular operation (at least, for a period of time). These tasks are referred to as *single-master operations* and the domain controllers that take on the role of handling them are called *operations masters.*

FROM THE CLASSROOM

Flexible Single-Master Operations

You may hear the term *flexible single-master operations* or simply *FSMO* (pronounced *fiz-mo*). This was the term used to describe the operations masters in the beta versions of Windows 2000. The roles were described as

"flexible" because they could be transferred from one domain controller to another within the domain or forest. (Some operations master roles are domainwide and others are forestwide.)

—*Debra Littlejohn Shinder, MCSE, MCP+I, MCT*

The operations master roles are as follows:

- Schema master
- Domain-naming master
- Infrastructure master
- Relative ID (RID) master
- PDC emulator

SCENARIO & SOLUTION

What does the schema master do?	The DC designated as schema master controls updates and modifications to the schema. This role is forestwide because a common schema is shared by all domains in a forest. There can be only one schema master in the forest, and changes to the schema can be made only through that machine.
What does the domain-naming master do?	The domain-naming master is the domain controller that oversees the addition or removal of domains within the forest. Like the schema master, this is a forestwide role.
What does the infrastructure master do?	There is an infrastructure master for each domain, and it updates the group-to-user references when group members are changed.
What does the RID master do?	The RID master, a domainwide role, is a DC that allocates relative ID sequences to the DCs in its domain. A RID is a unique security identifier assigned each time a user, group, or computer object is created.
What does the PDC emulator do?	This domain controller emulates a Windows NT PDC if there are Windows NT BDCs in the domain, processing password changes and replicating the information to the BDCs. If the domain operates in native mode, with only Windows 2000 DCs, the PDC emulator receives preferential replication of password changes performed by other DCs, serving as a sort of clearinghouse for password authentication.
Can one domain controller serve more than one operations master role at a time?	Yes. One domain controller can perform two or more operations master roles simultaneously. This would obviously be necessary in a small network that had fewer than five domain controllers.

The Organizational Unit Structure   The next part of this first objective specifies that you be able to implement an OU structure. *Organizational units* are container objects in the Active Directory that can be created within a domain for purposes of administrative boundaries. OUs can contain users, groups, computers, printers, and even other OUs.

In Windows NT, the smallest administrative boundary was the domain. This meant that if you gave a user administrative authority, he or she had administrative privileges for the entire domain. It was difficult to delegate authority this way, and this difficulty resulted in the creation of multiple domains on a network that otherwise would have needed only one or two. Having all these separate domains was made an even greater headache because of the nature of trust relationships in NT.

Windows 2000 OUs solve this problem. Now it is simple to create an OU, place in it those resources over which you want an individual to have authority, and assign the user administrative privileges *for that OU only*. Organizational units function as both administrative and security boundaries because Group Policy can be applied to an OU as well.

Creating an effective OU structure requires that you analyze carefully the administrative functions in your organization's network and use the ability to *nest* OUs (place one inside another) to accomplish your purpose(s).

Organizational units are created and managed via the Active Directory Users and Computers management console (see Figure 1-5).

Back Up and Restore Active Directory   The last part of this exam objective deals with backing up the Active Directory information and restoring the Active Directory from backup.

- **Authoritative Restore**   You should know how to perform an *authoritative restore*. This is a type of restoration operation performed on a Windows 2000 domain controller in which the objects that are in the restored directory replace all existing copies of those objects via replication. Only replicated *system state data*—that is, Active Directory data and File Replication Service data—is authoritatively restored. The NTDSUTIL.EXE tool is used to perform an authoritative restore, which can be done only by an administrator.

- **System Failure Recovery**   You should also know how to recover from a system failure. This means being able to demonstrate your ability to back up

FIGURE 1-5

Organizational units can be created and managed via the Active Directory Users and Computers MMC

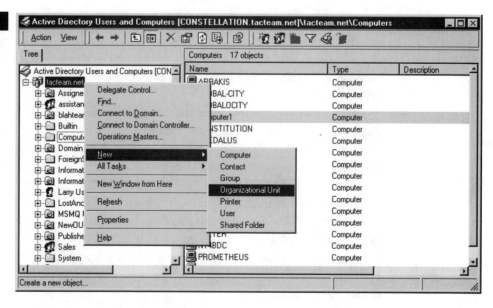

the Windows 2000 Registry and restore it to recover from a system failure. The Registry can be backed up using the Windows 2000 Backup utility to back up the system state data.

You should know how to create and use an Emergency Repair Disk (ERD) to recover from a failure when you are unable to open the Backup utility to restore the Registry. The ERD is created using the Backup utility and contains information about your current system configuration that is used to repair the system when the computer will not start and/or when system files are damaged.

Installing, Configuring, Managing, Monitoring, and Troubleshooting DNS for Active Directory

The next objectives deal with DNS and how to integrate Active Directory DNS zones with non-AD zones. The *DNS Server* service is designed to interoperate with the Active Directory in Windows 2000; by integrating DNS zones with the Active Directory, you can benefit from new features in Windows 2000 DNS—in particular, dynamic updates and record aging and scavenging features. DNS updates can be conducted via multimaster replication in the same way other directory information is replicated between domain controllers.

Directory-integrated DNS zones are stored in the Active Directory tree under the domain object container, and each zone is located in a DNS zone container labeled with the name of the zone. Integration optimizes replication planning for the network and provides for secure updates of DNS zone files.

Zone Configuration The exam objectives require that you be familiar with the process of configuring DNS zones, using both standard zone storage (which relies on a text-based file with the .DNS extension located in **the <systemroot>\System32\ Dns** folder on each DNS server) and directory-integrated zone storage using the Active Directory database.

Managing, Monitoring, and Troubleshooting DNS Furthermore, you should be able to manage, monitor, and troubleshoot Windows 2000 DNS. You should know that DNS is configured through the Computer Management console, accessible as a node in the Services and Applications section of the console tree (see Figure 1-6) or through the DNS administrative tool, which will bring up only the DNS console.

FIGURE 1-6

The Computer Management console can be used to manage Windows 2000 DNS

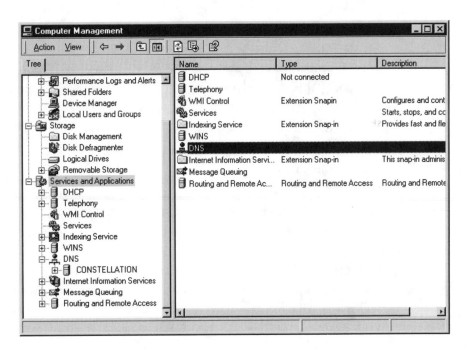

Be sure you understand the basics of Windows 2000 DNS, such as:

■ How to install and configure a Windows 2000 DNS server

■ How the DNS query process works when a client wants to resolve a fully qualified domain name (FQDN)

■ How reverse lookups work and how to add a reverse-lookup zone

■ How to use the DNS server log, viewed via Event Viewer, to monitor DNS events

■ How to trace logging to a text-based file of DNS server activity

■ How to use DNS counters in the System Monitor (accessed via Performance in the Administrative Tools menu)

■ How to use DNS Notify for notifying a select set of secondary servers for a zone when it is updated

You should know the purpose of the various DNS resource records, including:

■ **Host (A)**   For mapping a DNS domain name to an IP address used by a computer.

■ **Alias (CNAME)**   For mapping an alias DNS domain name to another primary or canonical name.

■ **Mail Exchanger (MX)**   For mapping a DNS domain name to the name of a computer that exchanges or forwards mail.

■ **Pointer (PTR)**   For mapping a reverse DNS domain name based on the IP address of a computer that points to the forward DNS domain name of that computer.

■ **Service location (SRV)**   For mapping a DNS domain name to a specified list of DNS host computers that offer a specific type of service, such as Active Directory domain controllers.

Installing, Configuring, Managing, Monitoring, Optimizing, and Troubleshooting Change and Configuration Management

This next series of exam objectives revolves around Windows 2000 Group Policy, an integral feature of Active Directory. *Group Policy* serves some of the same functions as Windows NT's system policies, but it does much more. You can think of Group Policy as "System Policy on steroids."

For exam 70-217, it is vitally important that you know all aspects of installing, configuring, managing, optimizing, monitoring, and troubleshooting Group Policy; you should expect several questions on the exam that come from this broad objective.

Group Policy is a complex topic; entire books could be written about it (and no doubt will be). You will benefit greatly from actually working with this feature until you become comfortable with its many exciting features.

Group Policy Objects A *group policy object (GPO)* is a collection of policy settings. Local GPOs are stored on all Windows 2000 computers; nonlocal GPOs are stored on domain controllers and managed via the Group Policy MMC that you create for each GPO (see Figure 1-7).

As shown in Figure 1-7, user rights, audit policies, and security policies are just a few of the many policies implemented via the Group Policy management console.

FIGURE 1-7

Group Policy is managed via the Group Policy MMC

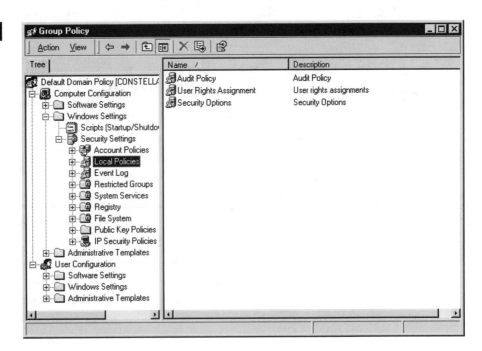

Group Policy can be applied to sites, domains, or OUs, and you can filter the policy application by associating security groups with GPOs.

exam

Watch

For this exam, you should know how to create a new GPO and how to link an existing GPO as well as how to modify Group Policy. Acquaint yourself with the default GPOs and their components, and practice working with Group Policy, both local and otherwise.

Delegation of Control   Another important area in which to practice is delegation of administrative authority, which can be done easily using the Delegation of Control wizard. There are basically three ways to define the delegation of administration responsibilities:

- You can delegate permissions to change properties on a particular container.
- You can delegate permissions to create and delete objects of a specific type under an organizational unit, such as users, groups, or printers.
- You can delegate permissions to update specific properties on objects of a specific type under an organizational unit.

on the

Job

You can delegate administration of particular resources to a specific individual or group. This technique does away with the need for multiple administrators to have authority over an entire domain or site. The user or group who has been granted the appropriate permissions can even turn around and delegate administration of a subset of his, her, or their accounts and resources to someone else. This makes for a flexible and granular means of assigning administrative responsibilities—particularly useful in large, enterprise-level organizations.

Group Policy Inheritance   Group Policy is generally inherited by child containers from their parent containers. This means that if you have assigned a specific Group Policy to a high-level parent container, that Group Policy applies to all containers beneath the parent container, including the user and computer objects in each container. On the other hand, if you explicitly specify a Group Policy setting for a child container, the child container's Group Policy setting overrides the parent container's setting.

■ **Blocking Inheritance**   You can modify the behavior of Group Policy inheritance. For example, inheritance can be blocked at the site, domain, or OU level.

■ **Enforcing Inheritance**   Another way in which you can modify default Group Policy behavior is to enforce inheritance using the No Override option. This option forces all child containers to inherit the policies of the parent container, even if Block Inheritance is in effect.

Implementing and Troubleshooting Group Policy

This objective requires that you understand the basics of using Group Policy to control various aspects of the user environment, including software deployment and management.

Using Group Policy to Manage the User Environment   For the exam, you must be able to use Group Policy to control and manage users' environments and troubleshoot problems that may arise as a result of Group Policy conflicts or misapplication.

You should be familiar with using *administrative templates,* which are ASCII files that provide a source for Group Policy to generate user interface settings. You should also be able to assign script policies to users and computers. Group Policy can be used to specify four types of scripts: logon, logoff, startup, and shutdown. Group Policy includes extensions for deployment of these script types.

Windows 2000 also includes the *Windows Scripting Host (WSH),* used to run Visual Basic Script and JavaScript without the need to embed the scripts in a HyperText Markup Language (HTML) document.

Managing Software via Group Policy   The *Software Installation* component of Group Policy is used to deploy and manage application software throughout the organization. Applications that include Windows Installer files can be assigned to a user or computer or *published* (made available for installation) to users.

Exam 70-217 requires that you be familiar with deploying application software in each of these three ways and that you understand how to maintain and deploy software upgrades and configure your deployment options. You should also be able to demonstrate your ability to troubleshoot common problems that can occur during software deployment.

Using Remote Installation Services

The Windows 2000 *Remote Installation Services (RIS)* are designed to allow administrators to set up unattended installations on multiple client machines. These services are part of the IntelliMirror Technology.

Windows 2000 provides the *Remote Installation Preparation (RIPrep)* wizard to prepare an existing installation of Windows 2000 Professional and then replicate the image to a designated remote installation server.

Installing and Configuring Remote Installation Services   For this exam, you should be familiar with RIS installation and configuration issues and know how to install the RIS, including the prerequisites for installation, such as:

- Hardware requirements for both server and client
- A DNS server on the network
- An authorized DHCP server on the network
- Active Directory installed on the network

Troubleshooting Remote Installation Services   Be familiar with common RIS-related problems and know how to use the RIS troubleshooter included in the Windows 2000 Server Help component.

RIS Security Issues   Be sure you understand the security features incorporated into RIS, including authorization of RIS servers. When a remote installation server attempts to start on the network, Active Directory is queried, and the server computer's name or IP address is compared with the list of authorized remote installation servers. If a match is found, the remote installation server is authorized and can start on the network. If a match is not found, the server is not authorized and the services will not work.

Also be aware of the required permissions for creating new computer accounts on the network and know how to set permissions for prestaged computer accounts using the Active Directory Users and Computers console.

SCENARIO & SOLUTION

Does RIS support remote installation of Windows 2000 Server CD-based or RIPrep operating system images?	No. RIS does not support installing Windows 2000 Server remotely.
When you use the RIPrep image feature in RIS, are file attributes and security settings preserved?	Yes. File attributes and security settings defined on the source computer are preserved on the destination computer.
Does the RIPrep wizard support multiple disks/partitions on a client computer?	No. RIPrep supports only one disk with one partition.
What are the hardware requirements for the RIS server?	The requirements are a Pentium or Pentium-compatible 166MHz or higher chip, 128MB RAM, 2GB disk space, a network interface card (NIC), and a CD-ROM.
What are the hardware requirements for a RIS client?	The requirements are a Pentium or Pentium-compatible 166MHz or higher chip, 32MB RAM (64MB recommended), a minimum 800MB disk, PXE DHCP–based boot ROM version .99c or greater
Can RIS be installed on the same drive as the system volume?	No.
Does RIS support the Encrypting File System (EFS) or Distributed File System (DFS)?	No.

Managing, Monitoring, and Optimizing the Components of Active Directory

At the heart of Active Directory administration are the daily tasks of managing, monitoring, and optimizing the objects and performance of the directory.

Active Directory Objects   You should be very familiar with how to create objects, such as user and computer accounts, in the directory—both manually and with scripts. You need to practice moving these objects from one container to another in the directory and understand the effects of such moves. Be able to publish resources such as shared folders and printers in the directory and how to locate those resources for access.

As an administrator, you must also be well versed in controlling access to directory objects using Active Directory object permissions and know how to use the Delegation of Control wizard to delegate administrative authority over directory objects to a user or group.

Active Directory Performance Exam 70-217 will ask you about the basics of monitoring, maintaining, and troubleshooting domain controllers. You should understand how to use the Performance counters in System Monitor to establish a baseline and measure the performance of the DCs and the Active Directory components.

Active Directory Replication Optimizing Active Directory replication, especially in a multisite network, is an important topic on the exam. To meet exam objectives, you must know the difference between *intersite* and *instrasite* replication and the configuration options available to you for each:

- **Intersite replication** You must know how to manage replication of directory information between sites, especially how to optimize network bandwidth by modifying the interval and/or scheduling of replication events.

- **Intrasite replication** This refers to replication between domain controllers that are located within the same site.

Configuring, Managing, Monitoring, and Troubleshooting Active Directory Security Solutions

Security features are tightly integrated into Active Directory. It is important that you be aware of how the new Windows 2000 security components work, how they can be configured, and how to deploy them in a way that will provide a controlled yet accessible environment for your network users. You should also know how to troubleshoot security issues, which are a common source of access problems.

Be particularly aware of the following aspects of Active Directory security:

- Creating, deploying, and modifying Group Policy security policies
- Using the Security Configuration and Analysis feature and security templates
- Establishing audit policies
- Monitoring, analyzing the impact of, and responding to security-related events

CERTIFICATION OBJECTIVE 1.03

What We'll Cover in This Book

This book covers the topics of each exam objective, along with information on additional resources, tips on common points of confusion, and details often overlooked in the directory services planning/design process and in preparing for the design exam.

Knowledge

In the beginning of each chapter, we provide you with a foundation of knowledge on which conceptual comprehension and practical design skills can be built. This includes definitions of new terms, explanations of processes, and discussion of relationships between components.

We cross-reference subjects that appear elsewhere in the book, that tie in to the topic of the chapter, and/or that will aid you in understanding the material presented in the chapter.

Concepts

In addition to basic knowledge-based information such as definitions and relationships, we provide an overview of the concepts behind the skills-based exercises. For example, managing the replication DNS data via Active Directory involves a particular skill set. An understanding of the *concepts* of both DNS and directory replication is necessary in order to perform the task correctly.

As much as possible, the authors attempt to make all abstract concepts easy to understand, using analogies and graphical illustrations.

Practical Skills

The heart of Windows 2000 exam preparation is development of practical skills: the ability not just to know about the operating system but also to use the operating system to perform common network administration tasks. The exam questions are expected to be performance based, as is obvious from the wording of the exam objectives, almost all of which use verbs such as "create, configure, manage, implement, deploy, modify," and the like. These are action verbs, indicating that you should be able to *perform* the designated tasks.

The exercises in this and other exam preparation books often involve problem solving—determining which solution is appropriate for a given situation. Other questions are more task oriented, geared toward exercises that simulate using the operating system interface. More so than with the NT exams, it is imperative that you do the practical exercises in each chapter of this book, that you experiment with various options, and that you gather hands-on experience in performing the tasks about which you read. Many of the exam questions are relatively simple for those who have worked with Windows 2000 and actually used the Active Directory for day-to-day tasks in their own networks—and almost impossible to answer for someone who hasn't gone through the processes themselves. In this book, we attempt to simulate the Windows 2000 working environment as much as possible by liberal use of graphic illustrations and detailed descriptions of every aspect of the environment in which you are working; however, there is no substitute for *doing it yourself.*

If you are new to computer networking and are not already employed in the field as you study for these exams, see the section "What You Need to Know If You're New to Networking" later in this chapter for some tips on how to get that all-important hands-on experience.

Some of the practical skills areas with which you should be sure you're familiar before taking this exam include:

- Installing the Active Directory
- Working with subnets and sites
- Working with Windows 2000 DNS
- Working with Group Policy
- Managing Active Directory objects
- Configuring Active Directory replication options
- Using the Remote Installation Services (RIS)

CERTIFICATION OBJECTIVE 1.04

What You Should Already Know

Because Microsoft's target audience for the Implementing and Administering a Windows 2000 Directory Services Infrastructure exam (and the other Windows 2000 exams) is those who have experience working with large multisite, multidomain NT networks, there is a presumption that you will have mastered the knowledge, concepts, and terminology presented in the Windows NT 4.0 certification exams.

If you do not have extensive real-world networking experience and you have not already attained the Windows NT MCSE, you should take extra time to ensure that you are familiar with Microsoft networking concepts, Windows 2000 concepts, and the terminology that is peculiar to directory services and Active Directory.

Microsoft Networking Concepts

Certainly anyone attempting to pass the Windows 2000 certification exams should have hands-on experience in deploying and using a Microsoft network. Whether you work with a multinational corporate internetwork or a small home network, the basic concepts of getting computers to communicate with one another are the same.

It is highly recommended that if you are new to the field, you take a basic networking course or work through a text on networking and operating system essentials to familiarize yourself with such basic concepts as:

- Peer-to-peer and client-server networking
- Network architectures and local area network (LAN) and WAN topologies
- Networking hardware and software, including client operating systems such as Windows for Workgroups, Windows 95 and Windows 98, Windows NT Workstation, and Windows 2000 Professional

■ The Open Systems Interconnection (OSI) and U.S. Department of Defense (DoD) networking models, the IEEE specifications, and Internet standards published as requests for comments (RFCs)

Windows 2000 Concepts

We also recommend that you study and take exams 70-210 and 70-215, which focus on the Windows 2000 Professional and Server operating systems, respectively. Be familiar with the many ways in which Windows 2000 differs from its predecessor, Windows NT 4.0, as well as the ways in which the two systems are alike.

Once again, we stress the importance of actually working with Windows 2000 on a day-to-day basis. Get to know the Active Directory "up close and personal," and it will no longer seem as mysterious, complex, or as much of a challenge to master (although it will remain challenging enough).

Be especially certain that you understand such Windows 2000 concepts as:

■ Transitive trust relationships

■ Hierarchical domain structure

■ The role of Active Directory sites

■ How OUs fit into the Active Directory structure

Also be familiar with the administrative tools that come with Windows 2000 Server and the Microsoft Management Console (MMC), including how to create custom MMCs.

Directory Services Terminology

For readers who are beginning their study of Windows 2000 with little exposure to real-life networking, one of the most important (and perhaps most tedious) tasks is to "learn the language" of computer networking. For this exam, that includes the specific terms peculiar to directory services. Otherwise, as you read through the study material, you may feel as though you're floating in a sea of acronyms and unfamiliar words.

In this book, our policy is to spell out all acronyms in full the first time they appear and to define new terms within the text, whenever possible. However, what is a well-known term to a long-time networking professional may be "new" to you, and in a book this size, trying to flip back through the pages to find the first occurrence of a word or term could be a time-consuming process.

We suggest that you make liberal use of the glossary. If you run across a word or term for which you're unsure about the meaning and it's not obvious from the context, don't just skim over it and hope it will be clarified later. Taking the time to look up the word or term may seem to slow your study, but in actuality it's one of the best ways to ensure that you remember the meaning later.

As we start, be sure you know the meanings of the following terms:

- **Active Directory Services Interface (ADSI)**   This is a set of COM interfaces that enables Windows 9x, Windows NT, and Windows 2000 applications to access Active Directory and other directory services.

- **Application Programming Interface (API)**   A set of routines used by a program to request and carry out lower-level services performed by the computer's operating system or other component, which provides the program with a way to communicate with the system.

- **Authentication**   The method used by the system to verify a user's logon credentials.

- **Child domain**   A domain located directly beneath another (parent) domain in the Active Directory domain tree, which includes the parent domain's name as part of its namespace.

- **Client Installation Wizard (CIW)**   The interface in RIS that makes installation options available to clients.

- **Delegation**   Assignment of administrative authority over a portion of the namespace to a user or group.

- **Directory**   A database containing information about objects.

- **Directory service**   The method by which directory information is stored and accessed by users and applications.

- **Distinguished Name**   A unique name that identifies an object and its location in a tree, which includes the relative distinguished name plus the names of container objects and domains in which the object resides.

- **Domain**   In Windows 2000, a collection of computers that share a common directory database, security policies, and security relationships with other domains and that represent a single security boundary of a Windows 2000 network. Domains can be joined in trees, which can in turn be joined in forests.

- **Domain tree**   A collection of Windows 2000 domains that share two-way transitive trust relationships, a contiguous namespace, and common schema, configuration, and global catalog.

- **Forest**   A group of one or more Windows 2000 domain trees that share schema, configuration, and global catalog but do not share a contiguous namespace.

- **Globally Unique Identifier (GUID)**   A 128-bit number assigned to an object when it is created, guaranteed to be unique on the network.

- **Group Policy**   The Windows 2000 feature used for controlling the behavior of user desktops, setting security, and deploying software.

- **Group Policy Object (GPO)**   A collection of Group Policy settings stored at the domain level and applied to sites, domains, or OUs.

- **Intersite replication**   Replication traffic between sites.

- **Intrasite replication**   Replication traffic within a site.

- **Kerberos version 5**   The latest version of the industry-standard security protocol used to handle authentication in Windows 2000 trust relationships.

- **Lightweight Directory Access Protocol (LDAP)**   A set of proposed standards outlined in RFC 2251, which provides for compatibility among directory services.

- **Multimaster replication**   The replication model used by Windows 2000 in which all domain controllers are capable of accepting and replicating changes in directory information to other domain controllers.

- **Native mode**   The domain condition in which all the domain controllers are running Windows 2000 (there are no "down-level" or NT domain controllers) and native mode has been explicitly enabled by an administrator, allowing the use of features not available in mixed mode.

- **Object**   An entity that is described by a set of attributes. An object could be a file, a user account, or a printer, and its attributes might include a name, location, and others, depending on the nature (class) of the object.

- **Organizational Unit (OU)**   A container object in Active Directory, which can be created within a domain for purposes of administrative boundaries. OUs can contain users, groups, computers, printers, and even other OUs.

- **Parent object**   An object inside which another object resides (for example, a folder can be a parent object that contains a file, its "child").

- **Relative Distinguished Name (RDN)**   The part of an object's distinguished name that is an attribute of the object.

- **Remote Installation Services (RIS)**   A software service by which an administrator can set up new client computers remotely (via unattended installation).

- **Replication**   The act of copying information from one computer to one or more computers to synchronize the data.

- **Schema**   A description of the object classes and attributes stored in Active Directory.

- **Site**   One or more "well-connected" IP subnets.

- **Subnet**   A part of a divided network that shares a network address with other parts of the network and is distinguished by a subnet address.

- **Trust relationship**   A relationship between domains in which a trusting domain will honor the logon authentication of a trusted domain.

- **User Principal Name (UPN)**   A user account name plus a domain name in which the account resides, with the two separated by an @ sign (for example, deb@shinder.net).

- **Zone**   A subtree of the DNS database that is administered as a single entity.

- **Zone transfer**   The method by which DNS servers synchronize data.

For Networking Newbies and NT Pros

Readers of this book who are studying for Exam 70-217 will not all be at the same level of experience and expertise. We recognize this fact, and throughout the text, we attempt to offer special tips that are geared toward people who are beginning their networking careers with the study of Windows 2000. We also provide information that targets readers who have mastered the basics of Windows NT and are already very familiar with Microsoft networking.

What You Need to Know If You're New to Networking

As mentioned, if you are new to computer networking, we recommend that you take a course or study a good book in basic networking concepts before you sit for the mandatory core exams. Even if you are following the Windows 2000 MCSE certification track, it would benefit you to study one of the NT 4.0 Networking Essentials study guides and/or take the Windows 2000 Network and Operating Systems Essentials course.

You will find that familiarizing yourself with basic networking and Active Directory concepts will benefit you in many ways. Not only will the knowledge provide a solid foundation for the material you will study in the process of obtaining Microsoft certification, but most employers will expect you, as an MCP or MCSE, to be familiar with these fundamental concepts.

The very best investment a networking neophyte can make, though, is building your own network from the ground up. Even a simple two-computer thinnet will give you a taste of the challenges faced by enterprise pros in the field. Many of the setup, maintenance, and troubleshooting scenarios associated with large production networks can be simulated on a smaller scale with a small home network. Deploy Active Directory on your test network and learn how it really works. Even on such a small scale, the experience will teach you many valuable lessons about the difference between a plan that "looks good on paper" and one that really works in the field.

New Ways of Working for Experienced NT Administrators

If you are already certified and/or experienced in NT 4.0, you may be tempted to skip some parts of this book, such as those that discuss familiar protocols or services such as DNS. But don't skip too much! Windows 2000 is built on the NT kernel, and you will find much in the new operating system that feels like "home"—but the Active Directory of Windows 2000 differs drastically from the rather feeble directory services of NT. You will also discover, as you delve deeper, that there are many fundamental changes, even to "old friends" such as DNS.

NT professionals need to guard against the possibility that their experience and mastery of the earlier operating system will be their biggest enemy on the Windows

2000 certification exams. Expect questions that try to "trick" exam takers by providing solutions that *would* have been correct if you were using NT or that measure whether you're aware of the differences between the two operating systems (just as there were traditionally questions on the NT certification exams that used experience with Windows 9x against a test taker in the same way).

We certainly don't advise NT pros to forget everything you ever knew about network operating systems, but we do encourage you not only to study Windows 2000, but to actually use it on a day-to-day basis. If possible, upgrade your primary workstation to Windows 2000 Professional so that the slightly different ways of performing routine tasks, the subtle differences in the interface, become second nature to you. Work with Windows 2000 Server or Advanced Server on the job if you can, at home or in the classroom if not. The real differences between NT and Windows 2000 show themselves in the server products. As you work with the Windows 2000 network, consider how design decisions that were made during the pre-implementation stage affect their ease of administration (or lack thereof) on a day-to-day basis.

Your NT experience can put you a step ahead of the networking newcomers—*if* you remember not to make too many assumptions (generally a good policy to follow in all areas of life).

CERTIFICATION SUMMARY

This chapter provided a brief introduction to the many Active Directory concepts and design issues that are discussed in this book. We have given you an overview of the topics you might expect to see in exam 70-217, as well as some tips on the background information you will need before you begin to study for the Implementing and Administering a Windows 2000 Active Directory Infrastructure exam.

We offered some advice for brushing up on Active Directory terminology and wrapped up with information aimed at particular types of exam candidates, such as networking newbies and NT "old pros." We also included a brief description of each exam objective provided by Microsoft.

The subsequent chapters of this book address each exam objective in detail and provide practical exercises geared toward teaching you the exam material in a hands-on, step-by-step process.

TWO-MINUTE DRILL

What Is Windows 2000 Directory Services Administration?

❏ A *directory* is a database that contains information about objects and their attributes; a *directory service* is the component that organizes the objects in a logical and accessible structure and provides a means of locating them within the directory.

❏ Active Directory offers far greater *scalability* than NT's directory service, NTDS, allowing for millions of security objects in a domain, compared with about 40,000 allowed in NT.

❏ Directory data includes domain data, configuration data, and schema data, and this data is replicated to all domain controllers in the domain so that each has an identical read/write copy of the directory database on its hard disk.

❏ Some advantages of Active Directory that make it a *global directory service* include support for Internet and industry standards such as LDAP, DNS, DHCP, and TCP/IP and its centralized management through a consistent management interface, the MMC.

Overview of Exam 70-217

❏ The Active Directory has both a *physical structure*, defined by sites, and a *logical structure*, defined by domains. Domain structure is *hierarchical*, with domains joined in a *tree;* trees themselves are joined into *forests,* in which all domains share a common schema, configuration, and global catalog.

❏ Installing the Active Directory is done by running the command DCPROMO.EXE on a Windows 2000 Server, which starts the Active Directory Installation wizard. The same command and wizard are used to demote a domain controller to member or stand-alone server status and remove the directory.

❏ Active Directory uses *multimaster replication;* however, some operations must be performed as *single-master operations.* For this purpose, five special roles, called *operations masters,* are assigned to one domain controller per forest or per domain (depending on the role) which include *schema master, domain naming master, infrastructure master, RID master,* and *PDC emulator.*

❑ *Organizational units (OUs)* are container objects that represent the smallest administrative boundary in Active Directory and can contain users, groups, computers, printers, and other OUs.

❑ DNS is thoroughly integrated in Active Directory, and DNS zone information can be replicated via either standard zone storage or directory-integrated zone storage, which optimizes replication because the information is stored in the directory.

❑ *Group Policy* is used to control user environments, deploy software, and otherwise exercise flexible, granular administrative control. *Group policy objects (GPOs)* are collections of Group Policy settings that can be applied to sites, domains, or OUs and filtered by security groups.

What We'll Cover in This Book

❑ *Remote Installation Services (RIS)* are used to install Windows 2000 Professional in unattended mode on multiple computers.

❑ Active Directory resources, such as shared folders and printers, can be *published* to the directory and easily located by network users, who don't have to be aware of the objects' physical locations to find and access them.

❑ The Windows 2000 certification core exams will focus on performance-based questions that measure skills rather than just knowledge.

What You Should Already Know

❑ Windows 2000 Active Directory uses two-way transitive trust relationships between all domains in a tree or forest.

❑ Setting up a network from scratch and using it on a day-to-day basis—even if it is only a two-computer simple home network—will help you tremendously in understanding the concepts and application of those concepts as you study Windows 2000 and the Active Directory.

❑ Prior to beginning your study of how to implement and administer a Windows 2000 directory services infrastructure, you should familiarize yourself with common Active Directory terminology, as outlined in this chapter.

SELF TEST

The following questions will help you measure your understanding of the material presented in this chapter. Read all the choices carefully because there may be more than one correct answer. Choose all correct answers for each question.

What Is Windows 2000 Directory Services Administration?

1. "An underlying base or foundation for an organization or system" is the definition of which of the following?

    A. Active Directory

    B. An infrastructure

    C. Directory services

    D. Attributes

2. Which of the following distributes directory data across the enterprise network and is participated in by all domain controllers in a Windows 2000 domain?

    A. Global catalog

    B. Security subsystem

    C. Data store

    D. Replication

3. Which of the following definitions describes the schema?

    A. A set of rules defining the classes of objects and attributes contained in the directory

    B. A means of querying and indexing information

    C. A map of the physical structure of the directory and how replication occurs between sites

    D. A collection of domains that share a contiguous namespace

4. Which of the following is true of Active Directory? Select all that apply.

    A. The Active Directory namespace is flat.

    B. The Active Directory is LDAP compatible.

    C. The Active Directory uses Kerberos authentication.

    D. The Active Directory uses explicit two-way, nontransitive trust relationships between domains, by default.

5. Which of the following is an example of directory data that is replicated? Select all that apply.

  A. Configuration data

  B. Site data

  C. Global data

  D. Domain data

6. Which of the following is the set of high-level, language-independent directory service programming interfaces that support the ability to work with resources provided by other operating systems and directory services?

  A. SSPI

  B. TCP/IP

  C. ADSI

  D. ADSL

7. In Windows 2000's Active Directory environment, which of the following is used to customize and control the user environment?

  A. System Policy

  B. Group Policy

  C. Audit Policy

  D. Windows Explorer

8. How can Active Directory sites benefit a large network with multiple geographic locations? Select all that apply.

  A. To optimize logon authentication traffic

  B. To optimize directory replication traffic

  C. To optimize broadcast traffic

  D. To optimize routing

9. Which of the following describes a hierarchical structure or arrangement?

  A. All objects are peers, on the same "level."

  B. There are numerous "roots" that spawn branches.

  C. Objects residing beneath other objects are known as *child objects*, and those above them are known as *parent objects*.

  D. The namespace is noncontiguous.

10. Which of the following commands would you use if you wanted to demote a Windows 2000 Server domain controller to member server status and remove the Active Directory?

    A. DCDEMOTE.EXE

    B. DCPROMO.EXE

    C. DCPROMOTE.EXE

    D. DCDEMO.EXE

11. Which of the following describes a domain controller that contains a partial replica of every domain in Active Directory but includes only some of the objects' attributes—those most often used in search operations?

    A. Primary domain controller

    B. Replica server

    C. Global catalog server

    D. All domain controllers

12. Which of the following operations master roles is forestwide? Select all that apply.

    A. Schema master

    B. Infrastructure master

    C. RID master

    D. Domain-naming master

13. Which of the following can be placed into OUs? Select all that apply.

    A. Other OUs

    B. Printers

    C. Schemas

    D. Sites

14. Which of the following is true of an authoritative restore? Select all that apply.

    A. It can be performed on all Windows 2000 Servers but not on Windows 2000 Professional machines.

    B. It restores only replicated system state data.

    C. It is performed using the NTDSUTIL.EXE utility.

    D. It can be done by administrators, server operators, and power users.

SELF TEST ANSWERS

What Is Windows 2000 Directory Services Administration?

1. ☑ **B.** An *infrastructure* is defined as "an underlying base or foundation for an organization or system."
    ☒ **A** is incorrect because the Active Directory is an example of a directory service. **C** is incorrect because a directory service is defined as a means of organizing directory information and providing a way to search and locate objects within the directory. **D** is incorrect because attributes are the properties of an object.

2. ☑ **D.** Replication is the process of distributing directory data across the network.
    ☒ **A** is incorrect because a global catalog is a subset of information about all the objects in the directory, used to find directory information. **B** is incorrect because the security subsystem is the means of providing secure logon and access control. **C** is incorrect because the data store is another term for directory.

3. ☑ **A.** The schema is the set of rules that defines the classes of objects and attributes contained in the directory.
    ☒ **B** is incorrect because the schema does not pertain to queries and indexing. **C** is incorrect because a map of the physical structure of the directory showing how replication occurs is the replication topology. **D** is incorrect because a collection of domains that share a contiguous namespace is a domain tree.

4. ☑ **B and C.** The Active Directory is LDAP compatible and uses Kerberos authentication, an industry standard.
    ☒ **A** is incorrect because the NT namespace is flat, whereas the Active Directory namespace is hierarchical. **D** is incorrect because the Active Directory trusts are implicit two-way transitive trust relationships.

5. ☑ **A and D.** Configuration data and domain data, along with schema data, are the three types of directory data that are replicated.
    ☒ **B and C** are incorrect because there is no such specific data type as site data or global data.

6. ☑ **C.** The Active Directory Services Interface (ADSI) is the programming interface that supports interoperability with other operating systems and directories and is used for developing applications for Windows 2000 Server.
    ☒ **A** is incorrect because SSPI is the Security Services Provider Interface. **B** is incorrect because TCP/IP, Transmission Control Protocol/Internet Protocol, is the standard protocol

stack used for communication on large networks and the Internet. **D** is incorrect because ADSL is Asymmetric Digital Subscriber Line, a high-performance telephone service.

7. ☑ **B.** Group Policy is the component used to control the user environment in Windows 2000 Active Directory networks.
   ☒ **A** is incorrect because System Policy was used in NT networks to control the user environment. **C** is incorrect because audit policy is used to track logons/logoffs, access to objects, and other activities. **D** is incorrect because the Windows Explorer is used for file management.

8. ☑ **A and B.** Establishing separate sites for areas connected by slow WAN links, you can optimize both logon authentication traffic and directory replication traffic because you can configure interval and scheduling of intersite replication, and the Active Directory client will seek a domain controller within its site to log onto.
   ☒ **C** is incorrect because sites do not affect broadcast traffic. **D** is incorrect because sites do not affect routing of packets.

9. ☑ **C.** In a hierarchical structure such as a domain tree, objects residing beneath other objects are known as *child objects,* and those above them are known as *parent objects.*
   ☒ **A** is incorrect because the objects are not all on the same level, as they would be in a flat structure. **B** is incorrect because each hierarchy has only one root. **D** is incorrect because the namespace is contiguous, with the full name of each child object containing the full name of its parent.

10. ☑ **B.** The DCPROMO.EXE command invokes the Active Directory Installation wizard, which is used to both promote a Windows 2000 server to domain controller and demote a domain controller to member or standalone server.
    ☒ **A, C,** and **D** are incorrect because there are no such commands as DCDEMOTE.EXE, DCPROMOTE.EXE, and DCDEMO.EXE.

11. ☑ **C.** The global catalog server is a domain controller that contains a partial replica of every domain in Active Directory. The global catalog holds a replica of every object in Active Directory, but it includes only some of the objects' attributes—those most often used in search operations.
    ☒ **A** is incorrect because the primary domain controller is the master domain controller on a Windows NT network. **B** is incorrect because there is no such thing as a replica server. **D** is incorrect because not all domain controllers are global catalog servers.

12. ☑ **A and D.** The schema master and domain-naming master are the two operations masters whose roles are forestwide, and there can be only one of each in a forest.

☒ **B** and **C** are incorrect because both the infrastructure and RID master roles are domainwide, so there is one for each domain.

13. ☑ **A** and **B.** Organizational units can contain other OUs (called *nesting),* printers, users, groups, shared folders, and other network resources.
☒ **C** is incorrect because a schema is a set of rules that applies to an entire forest. **D** is incorrect because sites are components of the physical directory structure.

14. ☑ **B** and **C.** An authoritative restore is performed using the NTDSUTIL.EXE utility, and only replicated and system state data such as Active Directory data and File Replication Service data are restored.
☒ **A** is incorrect because it can be performed only on Windows 2000 domain controllers, not all servers. **D** is incorrect because it can be performed only by administrators.

2

Installing the Components of Active Directory

CERTIFICATION OBJECTIVES

2.01	Installing Active Directory
2.02	Creating Sites
2.03	Creating Subnets
2.04	Creating Site Links
2.05	Assigning Bridgehead Servers
2.06	Creating Site Link Bridges
2.07	Creating Connection Objects
2.08	Creating Global Catalog Servers
✓	Two-Minute Drill
Q&A	Self Test

I n Chapter 2, you will learn about installing and configuring Active Directory (AD). Although installing AD is relatively easy (as is shown later in this chapter), tailoring AD to your specific domain needs is much more complex. You must examine and address many intricate details in your network design before starting to lay out and install your domain.

Such details as sites, site links, connection objects, and global catalogs are only a few of the details you need to think about before jumping into creating a network design. All these details, when properly planned and organized, will provide a very fast, reliable, and trouble-free environment for AD and your network overall.

If you have not realized it by now, Windows 2000 is a totally new concept, different from Windows NT 3.51 and 4.0. It requires much more planning and design than did Windows NT 3.51 and 4.0. This is primarily due to the addition of Domain Name Service (DNS) and AD to Windows 2000. Although it requires more planning and design, Windows 2000 will show the fruits of your labor by providing you with a high-performance network capable of meeting all your enterprise needs.

CERTIFICATION OBJECTIVE 2.01

Installing Active Directory

Before sitting down and building your domain, you need to have completed your homework. First, you must have thoroughly researched your network needs. This process includes not only looking at what you are currently doing on your network but also assessing what Windows 2000 can do for your network in the future.

Next, you should plan how to design your network based on the information gathered through your research. Here is where you will decide on such matters as how many domains you need in your network, how many servers you need to act as domain controllers, where to place domain controllers, and placement of global catalog servers. The last step is the fun one: installing your domain controllers and configuring AD.

Although we've presented a very high-level view of the planning stage to the implementation stage, this is a logical path you should take to the end result, which is a fully functional Windows 2000 network that is capable of handling the most stressful of situations your network can throw at it.

Data Collation

One of the most important things you can do to ensure a successful deployment of Windows 2000 is to thoroughly research your current network. You must dig deep and examine everything you are doing inside your network. Some of the things on which you should concentrate your efforts are:

- Number of domains in your enterprise. Determine whether they are still needed and whether a restructuring of your domain could be useful or required.

- Special domain-specific services such as Directory Replication for logon scripts, policies, and roaming profiles.

- Management of specific maintenance tasks such as account management, delegation of authority, and group policy management throughout your enterprise. These are only a few of the tasks that may need to be managed by individuals on a full-time basis, depending on the size of your network.

At the same time you are analyzing your current network, you need to keep in mind the new technologies that Windows 2000 brings to your network. These new technologies may have such a direct, positive impact that it might make sense to not only migrate to Windows 2000 but also to change your network infrastructure to use these new technologies to your company's benefit. Some of the new technologies that could directly impact your network are:

- **Transitive trusts**   With Windows 2000, all domains within your enterprise tree have implicit *transitive trust relationships* with each other. This means that anywhere in your domain structure, you can access another domain's resources, if you have the proper permissions to access that resource. For example, in Windows 2000, if Domain A trusts Domain B, and Domain B trusts Domain C, then Domain A trusts Domain C, and vice versa. In Windows NT models, by contrast, there are no implicit transitive trusts. For Domain A to trust Domain C, as in the Windows 2000 example, you must *explicitly* create a two-way trust relationship between Domain A and Domain C. This requirement creates an administrative nightmare when many domains enter the picture. Windows 2000 eliminates this problem.

- **Active Directory sites**   Using the concept of *sites* within AD allows administrators to define resource "boundaries" for domain clients. Clients within a site use only those resources located within the site and can use resources outside the site only in certain circumstances. This setup eliminates such problems as remote site systems authenticating over slow wide area network (WAN) links to main office systems. A good example is a client in a remote office in London being authenticated by a domain controller in the New York headquarters office over a 128K ISDN link. This authentication could be quite expensive, not to mention a huge performance hit for the client. Using sites within Windows 2000 allows administrators to control clients' use of resources.

■ **Virtual Private Networking (VPN)**   With improved VPN functionality and the addition of L2TP and IPSec to Windows 2000, companies can rethink their strategies of providing remote access services to employees. Companies that provide RAS to employees for business use usually incur the considerable costs of long distance connections. Using a VPN can eliminate this expense. Employees can dial into the Internet locally and tunnel to a VPN server provided by the company. Using L2TP to provide the tunnel, and IPSec to encrypt the data, you can use the Internet as your RAS backbone and eliminate the company's added RAS expense.

These are only a few of the technologies that could affect the way you currently do business in your company. You must make sure that you look at all angles—past, present, and future—to make the most of your upgrade or migration to Windows 2000.

Prerequisites

Once you have analyzed all your network needs and designed your network topology and Active Directory, covering special needs such as multiple domains to support remote sites, AD schema modifications to support enterprise applications, and location of global catalogs, you can start to move to the next phase of your migration, which is resource planning. You need to decide what resources you need and where to deploy them. One of the largest factors in choosing your resources is the prerequisite for Windows 2000 and Active Directory.

Although hardware requirements can vary with each network, dependent on network load, users, and resources such as storage and memory, it is safe to assume that the vast number of IT offices around the world will not implement Windows

2000 on systems that Microsoft specifies as the minimum requirements. According to Microsoft, you can install Windows 2000 Server/Advanced Server on a Pentium 166MHz system with 64MB of memory. If you want Windows 2000 to do more than just sit on your network, however, you require a system that is a little more robust than this one. Recommended minimums are more realistic, which are in the neighborhood of a Pentium II 400MHz system with at least 128MB of memory.

As for the prerequisites for Active Directory, you need two things:

- **A DNS server installed on your network** This DNS server must be at least BIND 8.1.2 compliant, which supports the requirement for service resource records (SRVs) per RFC 2052. SRVs are required to support services within Windows 2000 such as Kerberos and global catalog. Using Microsoft's implementation of DNS is *not* required (Dynamic DNS is also *not* required) but is *strongly* encouraged. As you will see later when installing Active Directory via the DCPROMO process, you can install AD without using Microsoft's DNS, but doing so becomes much more cumbersome and labor intensive (which Windows 2000 strives to eliminate).

- **One disk with at least 250MB of storage** It is preferred, as you will see later, that the AD database and logs be stored on separate disks. The AD database requires a minimum of 200MB; the AD log requires a minimum of 50MB. The AD database and log files do not require an NT File System (NTFS) partition, but it is recommended, not only for its fault tolerance but also due to its transactional logging of all disk activity. These features of NTFS make it perfect to use for A. (Note that it is recommended that you have at least 1GB of disk space to install the server—the 250MB is in addition to that.)

Once you have all your prerequisites filled and your design is finalized, the next step is to put a CD in a drive and start installing!

exam
⚲atch

Make sure you understand the requirements for the Active Directory database and log files and for installing the Shared System Folder (SYSVOL). The requirements for these two parts of AD are commonly confused with one another. Individually, the AD database and log files do not require NTFS, but AD as a concept does require NTFS, because the SYSVOL folder must have an NTFS 5.0 partition.

An excellent source for information regarding network and infrastructure design is the Windows 2000 Server Resource Kit, specifically the Distributed Systems Guide and Deployment Planning Guide supplements. These supplements contain an enormous amount of information on planning, installing, and managing AD, not to mention that they are great resources to help study for certification tests. Having a resource kit, both Server and Professional, is highly recommended. You'll find it extremely handy to have this information available at a moment's notice when questions about your network operations arise!

DCPROMO

Once you have installed and configured your first Windows 2000 server, your next step is to promote it to create your domain structure. Initially, your first Windows 2000 domain controller is your most important server, the one you will use to create your whole AD structure and root domain, and, most likely, the one that will house your DNS server, if you choose to use Microsoft's DNS.

Using DCPROMO

Starting the DCPROMO process is quite easy. To start your journey, choose Start | Run. In the text box, type **DCPROMO** and click OK. The Active Directory Installation Wizard window signals the beginning of the AD installation on your system. Before starting this process, we should probably look at the various scenarios you might run across when you use DCPROMO.

DCPROMO Scenarios

When starting the DCPROMO process to install Active Directory, you are faced with your first decision: to create a new domain or to create a domain controller in an existing domain (see Figure 2-1). First-time installations require you to select the option to install a domain controller for a new domain.

One of the shortcomings of Windows NT 4.0 was the inability to demote and promote primary domain controllers (PDCs) to backup domain controllers (BDCs) to member servers, and vice versa. With DCPROMO, you can promote and demote member servers to domain controllers with ease. The only caveat to this capability (and it is a big one) is that you must remember that if you demote your last domain controller to a member server, you will lose your Active Directory, because your last domain controller contains the last copy of your domain's Active Directory.

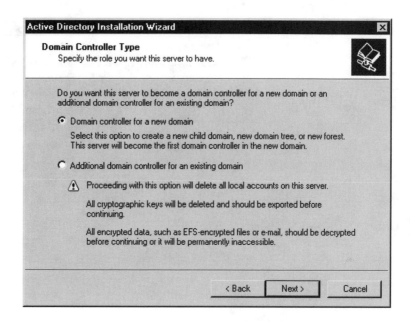

FIGURE 2-1

Installing a new
domain or adding
to an existing
domain

Selecting the option to install a new domain brings up another window in which
you have to choose to create your own domain tree or add your domain to an existing
tree (see Figure 2-2). Again, first-time domain installations must choose to create a
new domain tree. Choosing to create a new domain tree results in a third, and last,
choice, which asks whether you want to create a new forest of domain trees or connect
this tree to an existing forest (see Figure 2-3).

Creating your own forest results in establishing your own root domain from
which all other trees or child domains will attach (e.g., MICROSOFT.COM,
INTEL.COM, etc.). Selecting this option makes your domain controller the top
level of your domain tree. Once you select this option, Windows 2000 prompts you
for the fully qualified domain name (FQDN) of the domain you are installing. This
information is used to register this domain controller in DNS and start the process
of installing AD.

Selecting the second option, placing the domain tree into an existing forest,
establishes a transitive trust with the root domain to which you attach. Selecting this
option prompts you for Enterprise Administrator-equivalent credentials in order to
establish a transitive trust with the root domain of the tree to which you are attaching
(see Figure 2-4).

FIGURE 2-2

Creating a new
domain tree or
child domain

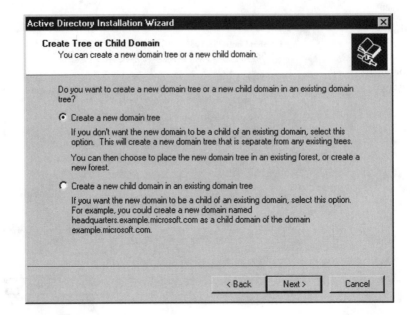

FIGURE 2-3

Creating your
own forest
or joining an
existing forest

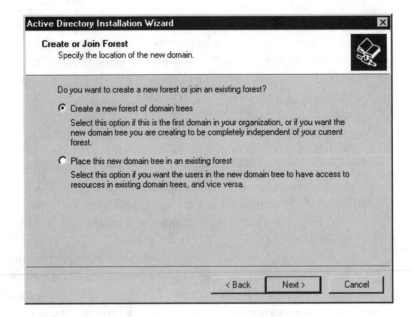

Moving On

Before you progress any further, you must have chosen how you will install your domain controller. Selecting the second option shown in Figures 2-1, 2-2, and 2-3 yields a Network Credentials window, as shown in Figure 2-4.

Keep in mind that the credentials you use to add or create a new forest or domain must have Enterprise Administrator-equivalent rights. Adding or creating a new domain controller requires either Enterprise or Domain Administrator-equivalent rights.

Once you enter your credentials or if you have chosen different options, you are presented with the New Domain Name window (see Figure 2-5). This is where you name your new Windows 2000 domain by its DNS domain name (e.g., W2K.NET).

exam
ⓦatch

You do not enter the name of a domain controller in the DNS domain name; however, you will later see that the first part of the DNS name is used as the NetBIOS name for the domain (see Figure 2-6).

FIGURE 2-4

The Network
Credentials
window

Active Directory Installation Wizard   ☒

Network Credentials
   Provide a network user name and password.

Type the user name, password, and user domain of the network account you wish to use for this operation.

User name: _____

Password: _____

Domain: _____

< Back   Next >   Cancel

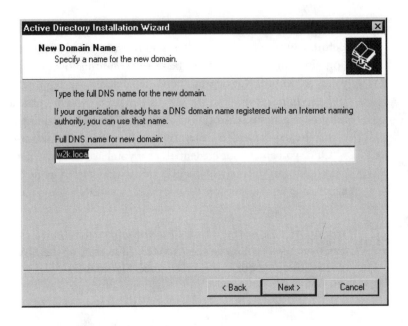

 on the job *When planning your network, keep in mind the naming of your resources. If you currently have any systems named with characters such as the period (.) or the underscore (_), you must plan to rename these resources, because Windows 2000 does not permit the use of these special characters for system names. The reason for not allowing special characters is that these characters are used by DNS to either delineate domain names (e.g., WWW.MICROSOFT.COM) or to signify service resource records in DNS (e.g., _KERBEROS, _GC). These special characters must be eliminated before starting to migrate any of these resources to Windows 2000.*

After you enter your domain's name, the next window in the Active Directory installation process is the NetBIOS Domain Name window. Here, you specify the NetBIOS domain name to be used by legacy systems such as Windows 95, Windows 98, and Windows NT 4.0. It is recommended that, as pointed out earlier in the chapter, the NetBIOS name assigned to the domain be taken from the leftmost name listed in your DNS name (e.g., W2K assigned from the domain W2K.NET). Windows 2000 uses this format to assign a default NetBIOS domain (refer back to Figure 2-6). Unless you have an urgent need to name your DNS domain and your NetBIOS domain differently, it is recommended that you use the default name assigned by Windows 2000. Using this format, you also help eliminate any possible confusion that could arise from using different naming conventions.

FIGURE 2-6

Assigning a
NetBIOS
name for
legacy systems

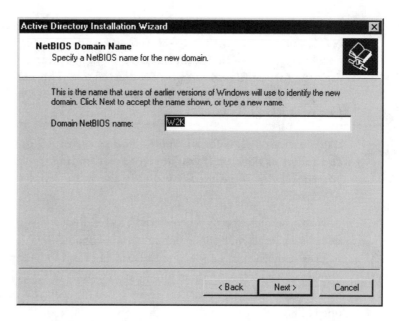

Next, you specify where your AD database and AD log files will be installed. As stated in the Database and Log Locations window, you should, for performance and recoverability reasons, install the database and log file on separate partitions (see Figure 2-7).

FIGURE 2-7

Installing your
Active Directory
database and log
files

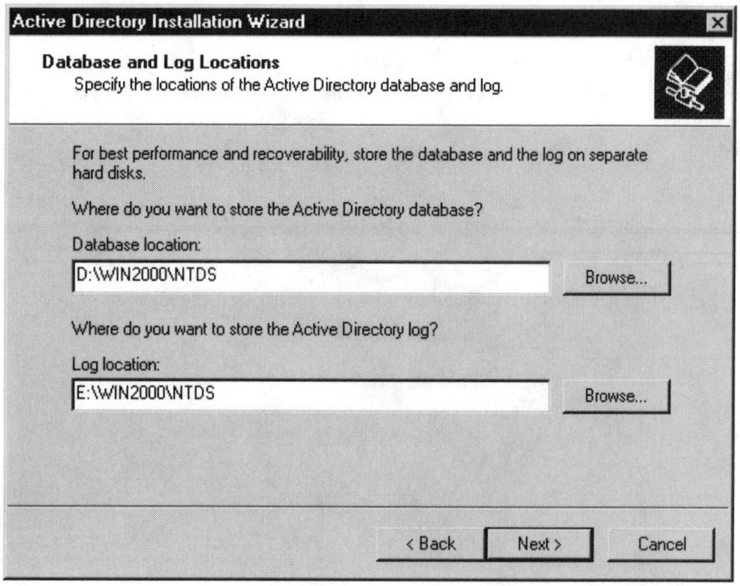

on the **job** *When installing your domain controllers, format two drives for AD using NTFS. Format one with a 4K-cluster size and use it for your Active Directory database, because the database uses 4K pages. Next, format the second drive for your AD log file and use an 8K-cluster size. The AD log file uses 8K pages. This procedure sets your AD files to optimal size and helps reduce fragmentation problems.*

on the **job** *Using dynamic disks for AD allows you to resize AD drives on your domain controllers as needed. If you have underestimated the size of your AD database, you can always dynamically increase the volume size to accommodate the AD database.*

Next, you must specify where your SYSVOL folder will be installed. The SYSVOL folder is where all your public files reside (see Figure 2-8).

Files such as logon scripts and policies that need to be replicated to all other domain controllers in the domain are placed in SYSVOL. Note that your SYSVOL folder needs to be placed on a NTFS 5.0 partition, so you need to plan for at least one NTFS 5.0 partition on your domain controller(s).

Once you have specified the location for your SYSVOL folder, Windows 2000 tries to contact DNS to determine whether it supports dynamic updates. If it cannot find a DNS server that is authoritative in the domain, a notification window appears, stating that Windows 2000 cannot find a DNS server (see Figure 2-9).

FIGURE 2-8

Specifying the location for the SYSVOL folder

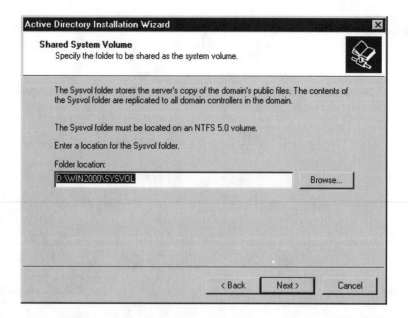

FIGURE 2-9

The window
indicating
Windows 2000
is unable to
contact a
DNS server

Once you click OK, another window appears, stating that DNS is not installed. You must select whether you want Windows 2000 to install DNS on your current system or to install DNS on another system (see Figure 2-10). This is one of your biggest decisions when installing Windows 2000, especially if you are installing your first domain controller, because once you start installing more domain controllers, it becomes increasingly hard to reverse your decision and use a different DNS solution. Make sure that you have carefully planned your DNS solution *before* installing your domain controllers!

DNS is certainly a key concept within Windows 2000 and will definitely be key in the certification exams. Make sure that you know DNS and how it works within Windows 2000. You may know DNS outside Windows 2000, but you need to know it inside Windows 2000 to understand exactly how DNS interacts with Windows 2000. Keep in mind these facts about DNS:

DNS is required for Windows 2000 to operate, although Dynamic DNS is not required.

Your DNS solution, if you choose not to use Microsoft's DNS implementation, must be at least BIND 8.1.2 compliant, because this version supports RFC 2052 SRVs. Note: Documentation on this point varies. BIND 8.1.1 does support all the requirements for AD in Windows 2000, although Microsoft TechNet article Q237675 states that there are flaws in BIND 8.1.1 that BIND version 8.1.2 fixes. Keep this in mind during examinations; Microsoft might use BIND version 8.1.1 in DNS questions because it technically supports all the requirements for AD in Windows 2000 also.

If you choose not to install DNS on your domain controller(s), Windows 2000 generates your manual DNS settings in a file called NETLOGON.DNS. These entries must be made on your DNS server(s). The number of times you install these DNS settings is dependent on the number of DNS servers you have and whether you are using Zone transfers.

FIGURE 2-10

Deciding to install
DNS or configure
DNS separately

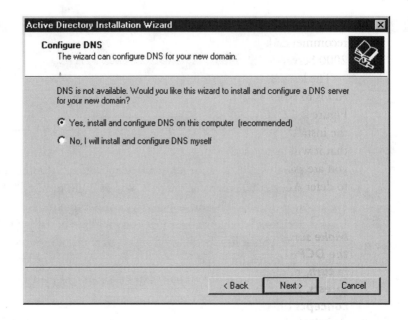

Regardless of your DNS selection, once you click Next, you are asked about
setting default permissions for User and Group objects (see Figure 2-11).

FIGURE 2-11

The default
Permissions
window

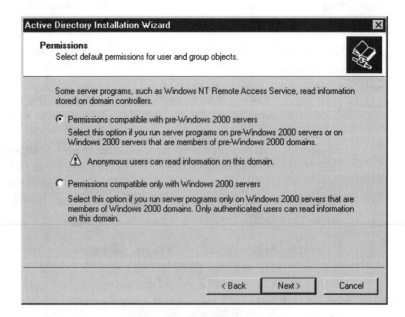

As shown in Figure 2-11, if you have any pre-Windows 2000 servers, it is recommended that you select the Permissions Compatible with Pre-Windows 2000 Servers option to avoid possible problems with these systems later.

The last step in the DCPROMO process before Windows 2000 starts configuring AD is to specify a password to be used for Directory Services Restore Mode (see Figure 2-12). Once you set this password and click Next, Active Directory begins the installation process. During the installation process, if DCPROMO determines that it will be a lengthy process to replicate all the objects currently stored in AD, you are asked whether you want to proceed with replication or whether you want to defer AD replication until the domain controller is rebooted.

exam
ⓦatch

Make sure you have a good grasp on the all the setup scenarios involved with the DCPROMO process. Having a good understanding of this process will, in turn, allow you to understand the concepts of domain structures such as forests, trees, and domains. These concepts can be confusing at times. These concepts and how domains are added to an existing domain structure will definitely be covered in the certification tests.

FIGURE 2-12

Specifying the
Directory
Services Restore
Mode password

Verifying Successful Installation

After you successfully complete the installation of AD, the Active Directory Installation Wizard reports that it has successfully installed AD (see Figure 2-13).

To further verify that AD has been installed correctly, check your DNS server to see if the correct DNS entries have been made. When you install AD on a domain controller, approximately 15 DNS entries are made for the server in question, if your DNS solution supports Dynamic DNS.

If you do not have the Active Directory Installation Wizard automatically install your domain controller in DNS, Windows 2000 generates all the DNS entries necessary for you to register your domain controller manually in DNS. Windows 2000 places these DNS entries in a file named NETLOGON.DNS under the %SystemRoot%\System32\config directory. All the entries in this file must be made on your DNS server(s) if you choose to install DNS separately or if your DNS servers do not support Dynamic DNS. Figure 2-14 shows an example of the NETLOGON.DNS file.

on the **Job**

If your DNS server(s) is configured for zone transfers, you might need to enter the required DNS entries on only one of your DNS servers.

FIGURE 2-13

Completing the
Active Directory
installation

FIGURE 2-14   Example of a NETLOGON.DNS file

```
; w2k.local. 600 IN A 192.168.1.1

; _ldap._tcp.w2k.local. 600 IN SRV 0 100 389 excalibur.w2k.local.

; _ldap._tcp.pdc._msdcs.w2k.local. 600 IN SRV 0 100 389 excalibur.w2k.local.

; _ldap._tcp.gc._msdcs.w2k.local. 600 IN SRV 0 100 3268 excalibur.w2k.local.

; _ldap._tcp.26e4eec0-bffc-4aaf-a635-9839c512c149.domains._msdcs.w2k.local.
600 IN SRV 0 100 389 excalibur.w2k.local.

; gc._msdcs.w2k.local. 600 IN A 192.168.1.1

; 72552f1f-ebc2-49ef-8811-ed04add14317._msdcs.w2k.local. 600 IN CNAME
excalibur.w2k.local.

; _kerberos._tcp.dc._msdcs.w2k.local. 600 IN SRV 0 100 88
excalibur.w2k.local.

; _ldap._tcp.dc._msdcs.w2k.local. 600 IN SRV 0 100 389 excalibur.w2k.local.

; _kerberos._tcp.w2k.local. 600 IN SRV 0 100 88 excalibur.w2k.local.

; _gc._tcp.w2k.local. 600 IN SRV 0 100 3268 excalibur.w2k.local.

; _kerberos._udp.w2k.local. 600 IN SRV 0 100 88 excalibur.w2k.local.

; _kpasswd._tcp.w2k.local. 600 IN SRV 0 100 464 excalibur.w2k.local.

; _kpasswd._udp.w2k.local. 600 IN SRV 0 100 464 excalibur.w2k.local.
```

Along with checking DNS to make sure that the appropriate DNS entries have been made (whether in DNS or the NETLOGON.DNS file), you should check several other things to make sure AD has been completed successfully:

1. Check the SYSVOL share to make sure that it contains:
   A. The SYSVOL share
   B. The NETLOGON share
   C. Policy and Script folders

2. Check the Active Directory Users and Computers snap-in to ensure that your domain controller has been placed in the Domain Controllers container for the AD domain that you specified.

3. Check the Directory Services Restore Mode boot option to make sure that not only does this option work, but it works with the password you provided. When your Directory Service has problems, it is not the time to find out that your recovery option does not work.

SCENARIO & SOLUTION

I want to use only FAT32 for easy access to my system in case of a system failure. How can I do this?	You need at least one NTFS 5.0 partition on your system for your SYSVOL and Active Directory folders and files.
My company has its own DNS solution. Can I use this DNS solution, or do I have to use Microsoft's implementation of DNS for Windows 2000?	As long as the DNS solution supports SRVs, as stated in RFC 2052, you can use this DNS solution.
I have systems with names such as MY_SERVER and DEPT_RESOURCE. How will they impact my migration strategy?	DNS does not support the use of underscore and other unicode characters, but Microsoft recommends that you not use them due to incompatibility with other non-W2K DNS servers.
I want to use my own DNS solution, but I am afraid that I will make configuration errors. How can I install my domain controllers without making errors?	Windows 2000 automatically generates a file called NETLOGON.DNS that contains all DNS entries that need to be made on your DNS server(s).
Do I have to create a forest when I install my first domain controller? What is the difference between a tree and a forest?	When you install your first domain controller, you install it with the thought that it is the first domain controller in the network. It is the root of your domain or the root for several trees, which collectively create a forest. A forest is simply a collection of connected trees.

EXERCISE 2-1

Installing Active Directory

In this exercise, we install Active Directory on a Windows 2000 server. The exercise covers two scenarios: how to install Windows 2000 using Microsoft DNS via Dynamic DNS and how to install AD using a non-Microsoft DNS solution.

For this exercise, you need a single system installed with either Windows 2000 Server or Advanced Server. Do not use any other domain controllers in this exercise. In addition, make sure you have at least one NTFS drive to allow for the installation of the SYSVOL folder.

To fully complete this exercise, it is recommended you follow the exercise from the beginning instead of starting in the middle, because the first part of the exercise sets up the environment for later sections of the exercise.

First, install AD using Microsoft DNS:

1. To start installing Active Directory, choose Start | Run. Type in **DCPROMO** and click OK.

2. The Active Directory Installation Wizard appears to start the installation of Active Directory. Click Next to start installing AD.

3. The first window to appear is the Domain Controller Type. Because you are working with a single server, make sure you select the Domain Controller for a New Domain option. This option lets Windows 2000 know that you are installing a root domain controller for a new domain. This root serves as the parent domain for all other domains added to it.

4. Next, the Create Tree or Child Domain window appears. You must select whether this domain will join an existing domain (become a child domain) or will be a standalone domain. Select the Create a New Domain Tree to make a standalone domain. We use this option because we are not connecting our domain to any existing domains. Click Next.

5. In the Create or Join Forest window, you have the choice of joining your new domain to an existing forest or creating your own forest. Although you are installing only one domain controller, you are actually installing the root for a new domain, tree, and forest with your single domain controller. Select the Create a New Forest of Domain Trees option to create your new forest. Click Next.

6. At the New Domain window, you must type in the name of the new domain. Remember, this is the DNS domain name and *not* the Windows NT NetBIOS domain name. For this exercise, use the DNS domain name **W2K.LOCAL.** When you have entered the DNS domain name, click Next.

7. In the NetBIOS domain name window, enter the NetBIOS name you want to use for this domain. This NetBIOS domain name is used by legacy systems to identify the domain. It is recommended that you use the last section of the DNS domain name as the NetBIOS name. Given our DNS name of W2K.LOCAL, we would use W2K as the NetBIOS name. Enter **W2K** as the NetBIOS name and click Next.

8. At the Database and Log Locations window, you must specify where the Active Directory database and log will be located. As covered earlier in the chapter, it is recommended, but not required, to install AD files not only on separate drives but also on NTFS drives for better performance and fault tolerance. Specify the locations for your database and log files and click Next.

9. When the Shared System Volume window appears, you must specify where your SYSVOL folder will be installed. As the window states, it must be on an NTFS 5.0 volume. Place the SYSVOL folder on your NTFS drive and click Next to continue the installation process.

10. At this point, you are presented with an information window stating that the Installation Wizard cannot contact a DNS server that handles the name W2K.LOCAL to determine whether it supports Dynamic DNS. Click OK and you will continue the installation by moving to the Configure DNS window.

11. For this exercise, select the Windows 2000 Install and Configure DNS on This Computer option. Later in this exercise, you will select the option to install and configure DNS yourself. Click Next.

12. In the Permissions window (refer back to Figure 2-11), you must select the default permissions to be applied to this domain controller. Since we are using only one Windows 2000 server, select Permissions Compatible Only with Windows 2000 Servers. Click Next.

13. The last window the Active Directory Wizard shows is the Directory Services Restore Mode Administrator Password window. Here you must specify the password to be used for the Directory Services Restore Mode boot menu option in Windows 2000. This boot option is used to help troubleshoot problems in the AD. Once you specify the password, click Next.

14. The Active Directory Wizard Summary window appears, with all your selections listed. Review this window carefully before proceeding, because once you click Next, Windows 2000 starts installing AD and there is no Back or Cancel button to allow you to change your installation settings.

15. Once AD has completed its installation, the wizard opens a notification window. Click Finish to complete the installation process. Once you click Finish, you are prompted to reboot to have your changes take place.

Now let's uninstall AD on a server:

1. To start uninstalling AD, choose Start | Run. Type **DCPROMO** and click OK.

2. The Active Directory Installation Wizard appears, ready to start the removal of AD. Click Next to start the removal process.

3. If the server you are demoting is a global catalog server, you receive an information window stating such. The window also reminds you to make sure that there are other global catalog servers available to users before removing AD from the system on which you are working.

4. Next, the Remove Active Directory window appears with a message warning about the consequences of removing AD from this system. *Before* you click Next to proceed, *carefully read* the warning messages provided! Failure to read these warnings can have a huge impact on your network operations. If this is the last domain controller in your domain, check the "This server is the last domain controller in the domain" check box before clicking Next.

5. After clicking Next, you must authenticate with Enterprise Administrator credentials. This is a security safeguard to prevent accidental or intentional removal of AD from domain controllers. Enter the appropriate credentials and click Next.

6. Because this system will be demoted to a member server, Windows 2000 prompts you to enter a local Administrator password. Enter a password for the server to use and click Next.

7. The Active Directory Wizard now has all the information it needs to remove AD. Note that the wizard has summarized all your selections and has specified all the consequences of those actions. To start removing AD from this system, click Next.

8. Windows 2000 starts the demotion process. There is no Cancel or Back button available once you reach this step, so make *absolutely sure* that you want to proceed.

9. When the process has completed, a window appears, stating that Windows 2000 has finished removing Active Directory. Click Finish and another window appears, stating that the system must be rebooted for the changes to take effect. Click Restart to finish the removal process.

Now we'll install Active Directory using non-Microsoft DNS servers:

1. Follow Steps 1–10 for installing Active Directory using Microsoft DNS.

2. In the Configure DNS window, select the No option to install and configure DNS yourself.

3. Continue to follow Steps 12–15 for installing Active Directory using Microsoft DNS.

4. Once Active Directory has finished installing, open Explorer and navigate to the `%SystemRoot%\System32\config` folder. Find and open the NETLOGON.DNS file. You will notice that Windows has made all the DNS entries you need to manually install your domain controller in DNS. This file can now be e-mailed to your DNS administrator(s) to be added to DNS.

CERTIFICATION OBJECTIVE 2.02

Creating Sites

Once you have successfully installed AD on your domain controllers, it is time to start modifying it to fit your domain. One of the first things you need to do is start defining your network's logical layout by planning your network's sites within Active Directory. Using the information gathered through researching your networks, you list your sites in AD to help define how physical boundaries should be laid out in your network. Sites, as you will see, help define how domain controllers should replicate and how workstations use resources. Sites help you cut down unnecessary WAN traffic and help make Windows 2000 and AD perform more efficiently.

Sites help partition and group your network in a way that makes logical sense. A good example is a company located in a large metropolitan area. The company has an east-side site and a west-side site. You do not want east-side systems authenticating or using services over your WAN connection to your west-side site.

What Is a Site?

By definition, a *site* is a collection of subnets and domain controllers that are well connected. The definition of *well connected* can vary from network to network, so you must use care when planning. Basically, *well connected* means a collection of subnets and domain controllers that are connected by some sort of high-speed medium such as a 10MB Ethernet network. Several of these subnets grouped together make a site.

Site boundaries are usually determined where there are slower media, such as a 56K dial-up connection or even possibly an ISDN connection. In these locations, a site usually terminates each end of the slow medium.

In general, WAN links should be considered a good dividing line for sites. Including domain controllers in a site that crosses a WAN link could be disastrous because replication traffic and service requests could easily consume all the WAN's bandwidth, resulting in very slow performance for the network overall.

When you install your first domain controller, the site object named Default First-Site-Name is created in the Sites object container, and your domain controller is placed there. As recommended throughout this chapter, you should give all your objects meaningful names; sites are no exception. It is a good idea to rename the Default First-Site-Name to a name that is meaningful within your network.

When you have all your sites created, each domain controller will exist as a certain site. If you properly set up your sites and subnets beforehand, all your domain controllers will be *automatically* placed in their correct sites when they are installed.

How to Create a Site

To create a site, you must use the Active Directory Sites and Services MMC snap-in and create a new site by right-clicking the Sites folder and selecting New | Site (see Figure 2-15).

After you elect to create a new site, a new Site window appears (see Figure 2-16) to create a new site and assign a site link to it. Note that if you want a different site link, you can either create a new site link before creating your site, or you can assign a different site link after the site is created. One of the Catch-22 situations with site links is that you cannot create one without having at least two sites created, but you cannot create a site without first assigning a site link. How do you get out of this loop? Windows 2000 provides DEFAULTIPSITELINK as the default site link. When you create a new site, your site is placed in DEFAULTIPSITELINK by default, unless you place it in another available site link. Once you have at least two sites created in DEFAULTIPSITELINK, you can create other site links using the sites within DEFAULTIPSITELINK.

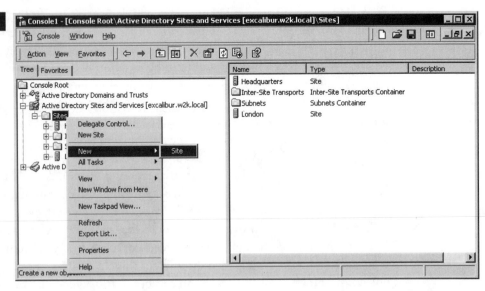

FIGURE 2-15

Creating a new site in Active Directory

FIGURE 2-16

The New
Object–Site
window

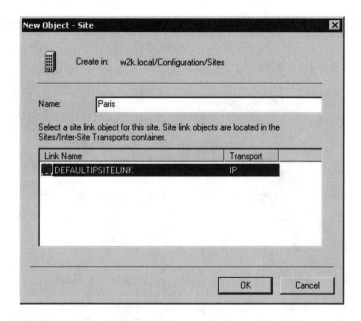

Site links, as you see later in the chapter, are a means of linking two or more sites
for replication purposes. Site links help specify preferred replication paths as well as
specifying the frequency with which sites should replicate with each other. Each site
in Active Directory has at least one associated site link.

on the
job

*For all objects that you create in Active Directory that are associated with
locations (such as London or Paris), it is a good idea to name the objects after
those locations so it is clear what each object is and where it belongs in the Active
Directory. When you use more than one location for an object, the locations
should be concatenated together (such as London–Paris). Using this type of
naming convention allows you to easily identify AD objects and their purposes.*

Once you create a new site by clicking OK, a notification window appears (see
Figure 2-17) reminding you that there might be several other housekeeping items
that you must complete before you can use the new site.

Linking the new site to other sites, as appropriate; adding necessary subnets; and
installing or moving domain controllers into this new site are among the tasks you
need to make sure are completed before your site is finished.

FIGURE 2-17

New site object
notification
window

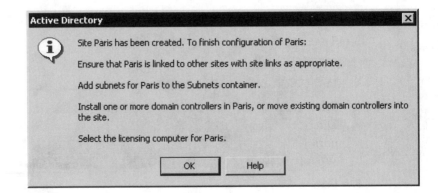

Active Directory

Creating New Sites in the Active Directory

In this exercise you learn how to create new sites and move servers from one site to another. For this exercise, you need to use Windows 2000 Server or Advanced Server and have installed Active Directory via the DCPROMO process:

1. Verify that you are logged on to your domain as Administrator.

2. To open an empty Microsoft Management Console, choose Start | Run. Type **MMC** in the text box and click OK.

3. Click the Console menu item and select the Add/Remove snap-in pop-up menu item.

4. From the Standalone tab, click Add. From the Add Standalone snap-in, click the Active Directory Sites and Services snap-in, and then click Add. After adding the snap-in, click Close, and then click OK to close the Add snap-in window.

5. Expand the Active Directory Sites and Services snap-in by double-clicking the snap-in. A Sites object appears underneath the Active Directory Sites and Services entry. If you double-click the Sites object, you see the Inter-Site Transports, Default-First-Site, and Subnets objects. You work with these objects in later exercises.

EXERCISE 2-2

6. To create a site, right-click Sites and select New Site from the pop-up context menu.

7. In the New Object–Site window, type the name of your new site.

8. Select a site link to assign to this site, and click OK. Click OK in the Active Directory information window. Practice creating sites by repeating Steps 6–8 until you understand the concept. Try creating a site that already exists. What happens?

9. Find the domain controller you are using (most likely under Default-First-Site, unless you have already moved it) in one of your sites. Select this domain controller and right-click it. Select Move from the pop-up context menu.

10. In the Move Server window, select the site you want to move the server into, and click OK. Open the destination site to find the server you moved. Repeat Steps 9 and 10 to move the server back to its original position.

11. Delete all the sites you created except two, because you will use them for future exercises. Delete sites by right-clicking the site and selecting Delete from the pop-up context menu. Try deleting the site that contains your server. What happens?

CERTIFICATION OBJECTIVE 2.03

Creating Subnets

As explained previously in this chapter, subnets play a vital role in determining where domain controllers and services, such as DNS, are located. If subnets are not defined within Active Directory, sites and services cannot be accurately reflected in your domain structure, leading to uncontrolled and inefficient directory replication and resource usage.

What Is a Subnet?

Subnets are the means by which network traffic is routed through a network. Dependent on the subnet mask, each IP address is divided into two separate sections: a network address and a host address. Think of an IP address as directions on how to reach a friend's house. Your friend gives you the address, and you break the address down, first by the name of the street (the network address of the IP address), and then, once you find the street, by the house number (the host address of the IP address).

Subnets work much the same way. First, a message is routed to a remote destination using the network ID portion of the IP address. Once the message arrives at the correct subnet, the packet is broadcast to all systems on that subnet. The system with the correct destination IP address is the one that responds. All others ignore the packet.

Consider another example. Your friend told you what street he lived on, but he forgot to tell you the house number. If you knocked on all the doors on the street that he lived on, eventually you would find his house. IP addresses work in the same fashion, but much faster.

Using subnets in Active Directory allows you to group a series of subnets together to form a site. Subnets are the building blocks of sites.

How to Create a Subnet

Subnets are easy to create within Active Directory. From the Active Directory Sites and Services snap-in, open Sites, right-click Subnets, and select New | Subnet to create a new subnet, as shown in Figure 2-18.

FIGURE 2-18

Creating a new subnet in Active Directory

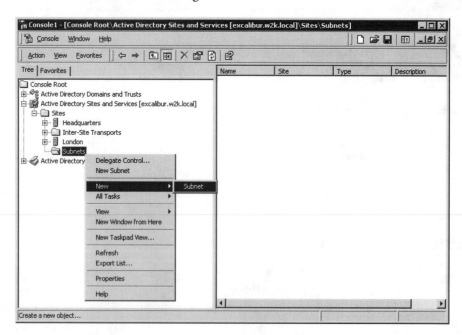

Once you elect to create a new subnet, you need to enter the information for a new subnet along with its corresponding subnet mask. After entering this information, you need to assign the subnet to a specific site. In Figure 2-19, the Default-First-Site has been renamed Headquarters, and a London site has been created. Also in Figure 2-19, you can see that subnet 192.168.1.0 will be assigned to the Headquarters site. A subnet can be assigned to only one site, so you must remember that you cannot split a subnet into two different sites.

Also note that underneath the address and mask is the subnet name, which, in this case, is 192.168.1.0/24. The */24* represents the number of subnet mask bits used for the subnet mask. It is an acceptable representation of the subnet mask, instead of using 192.168.1.0/255.255.255.0.

Finally, Windows 2000 does not allow subnet masks that do not have *contiguous* bit masks. Examples such as /20, 255.255.240.0, and /26, 255.255.255.192 are valid, but a subnet mask such as 255.255.255.193 is not because this mask cannot be represented using this type of subnet annotation.

Once you have created all your sites and subnets, you are ready to link the sites together for an efficient replication topology for AD.

FIGURE 2-19

Assigning a
subnet to a site

CertCam 2-3

EXERCISE 2-3

Creating Subnets in Active Directory

In this exercise, we create subnets and assign them to different sites in Active Directory:

1. Verify that you are logged on to your domain as Administrator.

2. Open the MMC, click the Console menu item, and select the Add/Remove snap-in pop-up menu item.

3. From the Standalone tab, click Add. From the Add Standalone snap-in, click the Active Directory Sites and Services snap-in, and click Add. After adding the snap-in, click Close, and then click OK to close the Add snap-in window.

4. Expand the Active Directory Sites and Services snap-in by double-clicking the snap-in. A Sites object appears underneath the Active Directory Sites and Services entry. Double-clicking the Sites object shows the Subnets object.

5. To create a new subnet, right-click the Subnet object and select New Subnet from the pop-up context menu.

6. In the New Object–Subnet window, enter the new subnet address and subnet mask that you want to create. Notice that as you enter each octet of the subnet mask, the subnet's actual name starts to appear underneath the subnet mask entry.

7. At the bottom, select a site to which this subnet will be assigned. Once you select your site, click OK to create the subnet object. Repeat Steps 5–7 to create several other subnets. Try different combinations of subnet addresses and subnet masks. What happens when you try to use a subnet mask of 255.192.255.0? Why?

8. Once you have created all your subnets, select a subnet. Right-click the subnet and select Properties from the pop-up context menu. A subnet Properties window appears, in which you can enter a description for the subnet and change the site to which this subnet is assigned. Change the subnet's site assignment and click OK. Does anything happen?

9. Delete all your subnet objects, with the exception of two. To delete, either highlight the subnet object and press the DELETE key, or right-click the subnet object and select Delete from the pop-up context menu.

CERTIFICATION OBJECTIVE 2.04

Creating Site Links

Once your sites and subnets have been placed in the Active Directory, the next step is to link your sites together. Site links allow you to communicate to the *Knowledge Consistency Checker (KCC)* what *cost* links are, how frequently they should replicate, and when they should replicate.

The KCC is a built-in process that runs on all domain controllers. Although the KCC can, and will, build the replication topology for the whole forest or domain, it also uses the site links you designate to replicate between sites. Creating links between domain controllers in the same site is not necessary, because the KCC assumes that there is a well-connected network between all domains and domain controllers in the site. Therefore, the KCC creates the most favorable connections to all domain controllers for replication purposes.

What Is a Site Link?

As stated earlier, site links are a method of defining how sites replicate traffic between each other. Because some WAN links (for example, an overseas ISDN connection) might be slower or more costly than others, you can set link costs appropriately so these links are used only as a last resort. Not only does this procedure cut operational costs, but it also guarantees efficient use of WAN links and the best speed of service for your network. Without site links, all WAN links would be treated the same, which could result in degraded service and higher operational costs for your network.

How to Create a Site Link

All site links are created in the Active Directory Sites and Services MMC snap-in under the Sites object. Underneath the Sites object, you will find an object called Inter-Site Transports (see Figure 2-20). This object is where you will create all site links.

FIGURE 2-20

Locating
Inter-Site
Transports
to create a
new site link

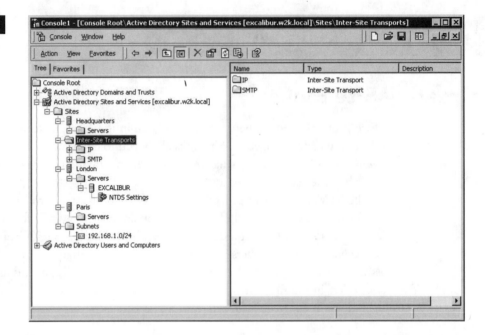

As you can tell from Figure 2-20, there are two objects beneath the Inter-Site Transports object. These are the IP and SMTP site link objects. Any link created under IP uses IP as its transport protocol; and any link created under SMTP uses SMTP as its transport protocol.

What is the difference between IP and SMTP, you ask? *Simple Mail Transfer Protocol (SMTP) site links* are used when low-speed, *asynchronous* replication is necessary between sites. SMTP site links take advantage of the fact that, because they are asynchronous, they can process several replication transactions at the same time. *Internet Protocol (IP) site links* must communicate *synchronously,* which requires each replication transaction to complete before another transaction can start. SMTP site links take into consideration the possibility that it may not be desirable to have synchronous IP site link replication over slow links.

exam
Ⓦatch

You should be aware of the terms used with site links. Although you might see IP and remote procedure call (RPC)-based communications referred to or implied as being separate, they are, in fact, one and the same. RPC is used when discussing replication within a domain or site, whereas IP is used when discussing replication between sites. In fact, the two are equal, because they are actually RPC over IP (much in the same way NetBIOS is carried over IP).

exam
ⓦatch

The certification tests are sure to have several knowledge-based questions regarding the use of SMTP and IP-based site links. Make sure that you not only understand the difference between the SMTP and IP site links, but you also understand the difference between asynchronous and synchronous communications. The basic difference between the two is that with asynchronous communications, you can have several outstanding replication transactions (without acknowledgment) without delaying communications, whereas with synchronous communications, your current transaction must be acknowledged before you can continue communications.

To create a site link, open the Active Directory Sites and Services MMC snap-in and navigate to Sites | Inter-Site Transports. From here, right-click either IP or SMTP for your site link transport and select New Site Link from the context menu. A new site link object window appears (see Figure 2-21) so that you can link the proper sites together.

Note that in Figure 2-21, the site link is named HQ-London because the site link contains the sites Headquarters and London. As stated earlier in the chapter, it is recommended that you name your objects appropriately so that they are not confusing to others who view them. Using location names for such objects as sites and site links helps describe them and their purpose.

FIGURE 2-21

Creating a new
site link object

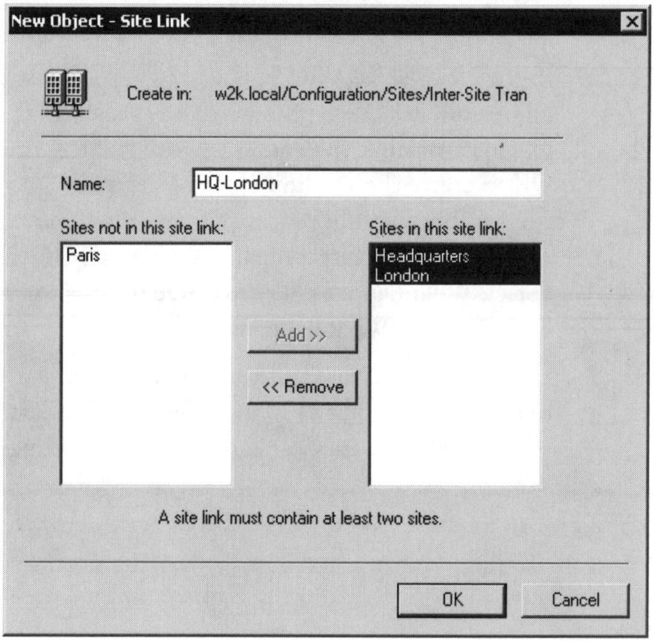

CertCam 2-4

Creating Site Links in Active Directory

In this exercise, you create site links for sites within Active Directory. You also modify existing site links by varying link costs and replication schedules:

1. Verify that you are logged on to your domain as Administrator.

2. Open the MMC, click the Console menu item, and select the Add/Remove snap-in pop-up menu item.

3. From the Standalone tab, click Add. From the Add Standalone snap-in, click the Active Directory Sites and Services snap-in, and click Add. After adding the snap-in, click Close, and then click OK to close the Add snap-in window.

4. Expand the Active Directory Sites and Services snap-in by double-clicking the snap-in. A Sites object appears underneath the Active Directory Sites and Services entry. Double-clicking the Sites object shows the Inter-Site Transports object.

5. Underneath Inter-Site Transports, you will find both the IP and SMTP objects. For this exercise, you may create Site link objects in either the IP or SMTP object, but keep in mind that when you do use either IP or SMTP, you are actually selecting the *replication protocol* that the site link will use. Select either IP or SMTP and right-click the object. Select New Site Link from the pop-up context menu to create a new site link.

6. In the New Object–Site Link window, you must enter the name of the site link before the OK button becomes available. Next, select at least two sites to which this link will connect. Once you have made your selections, click OK to create the site link object. Create several site links until you are comfortable with this process. *Do not edit any site links until you are instructed to do so.* Try to create a site link with exactly the same name under the IP object. What happens? Try to create the exact same site link under the SMTP object. What happens? Why?

7. Once you have created all your site links, select a site link and double-click it to edit. The site link's Properties window appears. Notice in the bottom-left corner that there are Cost and Replication settings along with a Change

Schedule button for this site link. Link costs can be incremented or decremented by factors of 1, while replication times can be incremented or decremented by factors of 15 minutes. If you click the Change Schedule button, a window appears that allows you to tell Windows 2000 when this link is available to pass replication traffic.

8. Work with the open site link and change its costs, replication frequency, and replication schedule to familiarize yourself with how each setting works for the site link. Try to set the replication frequency to 0. What happens? Try to modify a site link so that it only has one site. What happens?

CERTIFICATION OBJECTIVE 2.05

Assigning Bridgehead Servers

Once you have designed the layout of your network, it is time to start thinking about load balancing your network traffic, specifically your Active Directory replication. Keep in mind that not only do you have to contend with replication traffic consuming precious bandwidth, but you also need to remember that there is a server receiving all this replication traffic that needs to be processed quickly. Using bridgehead servers allows you to partially load-balance your replication traffic by assigning certain servers to receive replication traffic from other sites.

What Is a Bridgehead Server?

Bridgehead servers are much like connection objects. Bridgehead servers are inbound-only connections that specify which server(s) in a site receives replication traffic from other sites. They act as the "bridge" into the site for replication traffic; once the replication traffic is received over the bridgehead server, it then replicates all the AD changes from other sites to all the domain controllers within its own site. This designated bridgehead server acts as a shield for all other domain controllers in the site because it takes on the extra responsibility of receiving AD replication from other sites and then replicates those changes to all other domain controllers in its own site.

As you can imagine, this places an extra burden on the bridgehead server, which not only has to keep up with bridgehead replication but also has to keep up with replication within its own site. This is why you should only specify high-end servers as bridgehead servers within your sites. Assigning a low-end server as a bridgehead server, especially with several sites, will crush it.

As you will see later, the KCC handles all replication connections such as connection objects and bridgehead servers. The KCC can automatically assign bridgehead servers, but if you have very few high-end servers and many average to low-end servers, it may be beneficial to assign your own bridgehead servers instead of allowing the KCC to assign them. You can create your own bridgehead servers, but you have to use care when assigning them, because the KCC cannot automatically select an alternative bridgehead server if a preferred one is unavailable. Allowing the KCC to manage all bridgehead servers makes for more efficient management of replication connections, but it also has the potential of placing the replication burden on systems on which you do not desire to have this burden placed.

How to Create a Bridgehead Server

Creating a bridgehead is relatively simple. All you need to do is select the server to become the bridgehead server and decide what replication transport you will allow it to use. In the Active Directory Sites and Services MMC snap-in, navigate to Sites | *<Site name>* | Servers | *<Server name>* (see Figure 2-22).

Right-click the server and select Properties from the pop-up context menu. The server Properties window appears, as shown in Figure 2-23.

From here you can select the transport on which the bridgehead server will receive replication traffic from other sites. Click OK, and you have created your Bridgehead server.

FIGURE 2-22   Selecting a server to become a bridgehead server

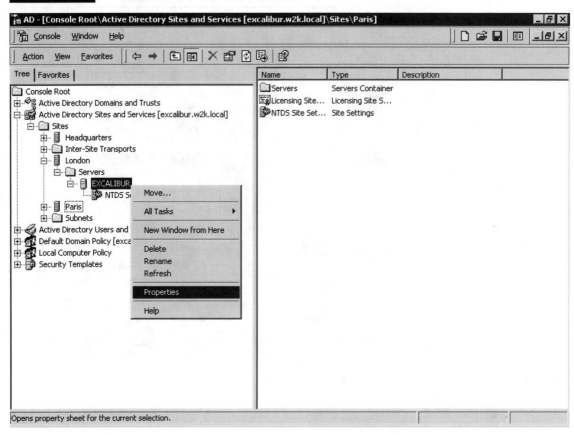

FIGURE 2-23

Designating a
server to be a
bridgehead server

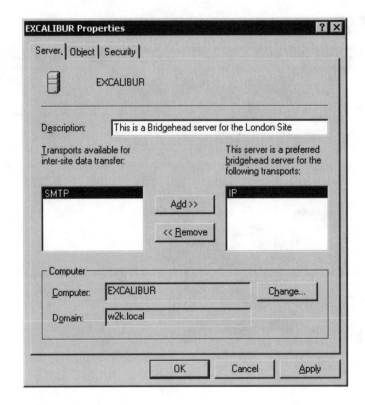

Designating a Server as a Bridgehead Server

In this exercise, you designate your Active Directory server as a bridgehead server. Your server must have AD already installed to complete this exercise:

1. Verify that you are logged on to your domain as Administrator.

2. Open the MMC, click the Console menu item, and select the Add/Remove snap-in pop-up menu item.

3. From the Standalone tab, click Add. From the Add Standalone snap-in, click the Active Directory Sites and Services snap-in, and click Add. After adding the snap-in, click Close, and then click OK to close the Add snap-in window.

4. Before navigating down the Active Directory Sites and Services snap-in, make sure you have chosen the server you want to designate as a bridgehead server.

5. Expand the Active Directory Sites and Services snap-in by double-clicking the snap-in. Navigate to Sites | *<Site name>* | Servers | *<Server name>*.

6. Right-click the server that you have chosen to be a bridgehead server, and click the Properties context menu item.

7. In the Properties window, select the transport that will accept replication traffic, and click Add to add the transport to the list of preferred bridgehead servers.

8. Click OK to save your changes.

CERTIFICATION OBJECTIVE 2.06

Creating Site Link Bridges

If your network has several sites, you can model the routing of your network by creating site link bridges, which also allow you to efficiently distribute AD replication so that backup links are used when they are needed. This technique allows companies to cut costs and ensure efficient use of resources when they are needed. In Figure 2-24, you can see how the use of site link bridges allows the employment of faster, more efficient WAN connections and how backup connections can be used only when needed.

FIGURE 2-24   Effective use of a site link bridge

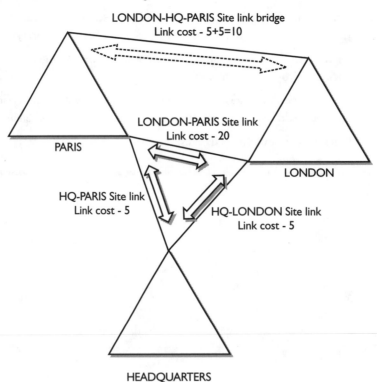

What Is a Site Link Bridge?

A *site link bridge* allows network administrators to "tell" Windows 2000 networks how to route replication traffic from one site to another. Using site link bridges allows administrators to route replication traffic to best fit their networks and build efficient routing of AD replication. Without the use of site link bridges, replication traffic might have to use slower, less efficient, and possibly more costly WAN connections. As a network administrator, you want to ensure that your company uses its resources efficiently.

Site link bridges are a way of connecting or linking sites with one another without creating massive numbers of site links. Think of a large corporation with 20 satellite offices around the country. Creating the large number of site links needed to link all these sites is not practicable and can possibly become a performance bottleneck. Creating one site link bridge that consists of the minimum number of site links needed to link all your sites guarantees that your sites replicate correctly. All links within a site link bridge are considered transitive; therefore, if Site A is linked to Site B, and Site B is linked to Site C, then Site A is connected to Site C.

Looking at Figure 2-24, you could remove the London-Paris site link and use a London-HQ-Paris site link bridge, which would allow you to:

- Route your replication traffic exclusively from London through HQ to Paris, thereby using a more efficient replication route (as specified by the low link costs for the site links HQ-London and HQ-Paris)

- Remove one unnecessary site link because the site link bridge London-HQ-Paris serves the same function as a London-Paris site link

One other point to keep in mind is that if your network is fully IP routable, Active Directory automatically links your network without any assistance, which means that you do not have to create site link bridges to link site objects. If this feature is not desired, you must disable the Bridge All Site Links option for the IP transport object. By right-clicking the IP Inter-Site transport object and selecting Properties from the context menu, you can disable the Bridge All Site Links option by unchecking the check box. Doing so allows you to create site link bridges as you desire.

How to Create a Site Link Bridge

To create a site link bridge, open the Active Directory Sites and Services MMC snap-in. Navigate to Sites | Inter-site Transports and find both the IP and SMTP objects. Right-click the object under which you want to create the site link bridge, and select New Site Link Bridge from the context menu (see Figure 2-25).

Once you select the New Site Link Bridge context menu, a New Object–Site Link Bridge window appears (see Figure 2-26). You must select at least two site links to create a new site link bridge.

Again, the general recommendation is that you create or name your site link bridges in much the same manner as your site links, which is to use the names of the sites that you are linking. Looking at Figure 2-26, you can see that two site links, HQ-London and HQ-Paris, are both selected, making the site link bridge London-HQ-Paris. Once you have created your site link bridge, you can double-click it to add comments, add or delete site links, and so on (see Figure 2-27).

FIGURE 2-25

Creating a new site link bridge

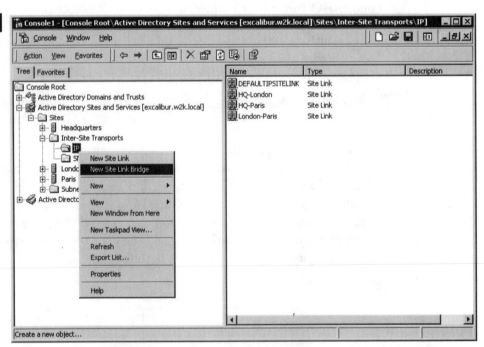

FIGURE 2-26

Creating a new
site link bridge

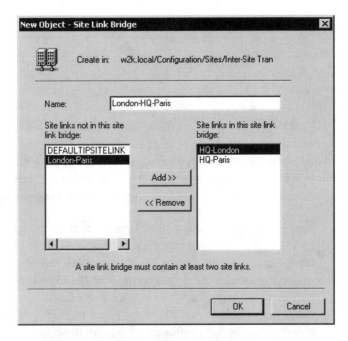

FIGURE 2-27

Editing the
site link bridge
properties

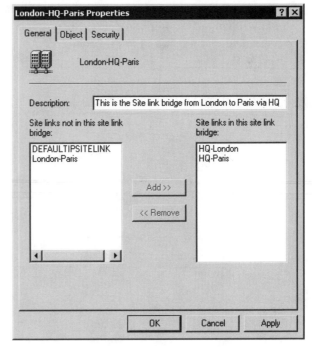

Note that when you create your site link bridge, it does not have a *link cost* assigned to it. The link cost is computed by adding the link costs of all the site links that make up the site link bridge. Care must be taken when creating site link bridges so that Active Directory properly uses them and that backup links are used when the site link bridge loses a link.

exam

Watch

Make sure you are careful about the difference between site links and site link bridges. Remember that site links contain link costs and replication times, whereas site link bridges are a set of site links grouped together to form a site link bridge. Site link bridges have no link cost, because their link cost is a dynamic cost dependent on the links included in the site link bridge.

on the

Job

Looking at Figure 2-27, you will notice that this site link bridge object has a Security tab. Remember that everything you create is an object and is therefore stored in the Active Directory. You can use this fact to your advantage by modifying an object's access control list (ACL) so that only certain persons can access it. For example, if you create a site link bridge so that your replication traffic must take a certain route, you can modify the object's ACL so that only a certain person(s) and/or group(s) can modify this site link bridge. Keep this feature in mind when modifying your Active Directory. If you have dedicated administrative duties, you can delegate certain aspects of the Active Directory to an individual or group of individuals.

FROM THE CLASSROOM

Getting a Good Grasp

After reading more than half this chapter, you should be starting to get a good idea of how Active Directory handles replication through the placement of domain controllers, subnet assignments, and the use of sites, site links, and site link bridges. This, by far, is the hardest concept to understand in using and administering Windows 2000, because there is so much complexity involved with AD replication.

AD replication is much like a set of nesting dolls. First, domain controllers within each domain replicate between each other. Second, you can have several domains (such as ABC.COM and 123.COM) that are in the same site. Not only do a domain's domain controllers replicate with each other within

their own domain, but each domain replicates Active Directory and schema data with each other because of the use of global catalogs. Third, domain controllers from different sites must replicate with one another, so site links and site link bridges provide the mechanisms to replicate between sites. Before moving on in the chapter, make sure that you really understand the concepts already covered; as in some subjects, such as mathematics, these concepts build on one another. If you do not have a good grasp of one concept, it can affect how you understand future concepts. Make sure you know all the mechanisms involved with Active Directory because the certification tests expect that you know this information by heart.

—*Michael Seamans, MCSE*

SCENARIO & SOLUTION

I want to route replication traffic through my high-speed backbone and use my backup links only when needed. How do I go about this?	Make sure you use site link bridges to route your replication traffic as desired. Using site link bridges allows you to specify which site links to use to get from Site A to Site B.
Sites are too confusing. Can't I just put all of my domain controllers into one site?	You might be able to put all of your domain controllers into a single site, but you must remember the golden rule with Sites: Domain controllers that are linked via slow connections need to be placed in separate sites and connected via site links. Failing to do so will result in poor Active Directory and network performance.
I've got domain controllers on the same subnet, but they are in different buildings. I want to put domain controllers in a site for each building. Should I keep all of them in the same site, or should I put them in their own separate sites?	If you have domain controllers on the same subnet, the assumption is that they are "well connected" by some means (such as a 10MB LAN). If this is the case, there is no need to create separate sites, unless your AD structure requires that you create sites for each building. If this is the case, you need to put the domain controllers on different subnets to accommodate the different sites.
I've got a remote site that uses a 56K connection. What type of site link should I use?	Typically, you would use an SMTP site link, because that type takes advantage of the fact that the link is slower and allows the link to use asynchronous replication. A replication then becomes more efficient because you can now have several replication transactions without having to wait for a response.
I've got a high-speed connection between my headquarters and overseas sites. Unfortunately, the connection can be unreliable at times. How should I configure my site link(s)?	First, you should use an SMTP site link due to the fact that the link can be unreliable. An SMTP site link can have outstanding replication transactions and still work, whereas an IP site link must wait for its replication transaction to complete before starting another. Also, if you have other ways to connect to your overseas site, you might want to configure your site links and site link bridges to use this link only when necessary. Setting a high link cost for this site link allows you to use this link only when necessary.

EXERCISE 2-6

Creating Site Link Bridges in Active Directory

In this exercise, you learn how to create site link bridges in Active Directory:

1. Verify that you are logged on to your domain as Administrator.

2. Open the MMC, click the Console menu item, and select the Add/Remove snap-in pop-up menu item.

3. From the Standalone tab, click Add. From the Add Standalone snap-in, click the Active Directory Sites and Services snap-in, and click Add. After adding the snap-in, click Close, and then click OK to close the Add snap-in window.

4. Expand the Active Directory Sites and Services snap-in by double-clicking the snap-in. A Sites object appears underneath the Active Directory Sites and Services entry. Double-clicking the Sites object shows the Inter-Site Transport object.

5. Double-click the Inter-Site Transport object to show the IP and SMTP objects. As in Site links, you can create site link bridges using either IP or SMTP as the transport. The only stipulation is that you must use site links from the same protocol object (in other words, an IP site link bridge may use only site links from the IP protocol object).

6. Right-click either the IP or SMTP object and select New Site Link Bridge from the pop-up context menu. The New Object–Site Link Bridge window appears. In this window, you must specify a name for the site link bridge and select at least two site links to create the site link bridge. Once you have selected these, click OK to save the object.

7. Repeat Steps 5 and 6 to create several more site link bridges until you understand the process. Try to create a new site link bridge under a protocol object that does not have at least two site links in it. What happens? Try to create a site link bridge with the same name as a current site link bridge. What happens?

CERTIFICATION OBJECTIVE 2.07

Creating Connection Objects

Connection objects are aptly named because they are exactly what their name implies. Connection objects enable inbound connections to every domain controller in your network. The KCC, as discussed earlier, automatically handles the creation and management of all connection objects as well as establishing a replication topology between all domain controllers.

What Are Connection Objects?

Connection objects are *inbound-only* connections to domain controllers. The KCC cannot create outbound connection objects. As stated, the KCC manages all connection objects and creates a replication topology automatically, without administrators needing to configure their own topologies. Some of the reasons that you might want to create manual connection objects include these:

- **Changing the replication scheduling for connection objects** When the KCC creates a connection object automatically, it sets the replication schedule for the connection object. The only way to change the replication schedule is to take ownership of the connection object. Taking ownership of the connection allows you to change the replication schedule, but it also makes the connection object a manual object instead of an automatically created object made and managed by the KCC. This becomes important when deciding to depend on the KCC for replication or making your own connection objects and planning your own replication topology.

- **Creating your own replication topology** You might need to create your own replication topology, based on your network topology.

exam
Watch

If you need to manually create connection objects, you must keep in mind that the KCC does not automatically reconfigure the replication topology when you use manual connection objects. If you have only one manual connection object from Server A to Server B and this connection object fails for whatever reason, your replication topology will fail. If the KCC manages all connection objects, it automatically rebuilds the replication topology if a server in the topology fails. When you use manual connection objects only, the KCC cannot use automatic connection objects and must rely on several backup manual connection objects to duplicate what the KCC does automatically.

You must use care when deciding on a connection strategy. In most situations, it is probably best to let the KCC automatically manage connections in your network. If you desire to create your own replication topology, you can create a manual replication topology along with the KCC-generated replication topology. This gives you the benefit of being able to create your own replication topology, at the same time leaving the KCC-generated connections in place in case a domain controller drops from the replication scheme. In this case, the KCC re-creates the replication topology automatically, without interruption of replication.

How to Create Connection Objects

To create a connection object, open the Active Directory Sites and Services MMC snap-in and navigate to the site in question. Once you reach your site, navigate to Server | *<Server name>* | NTDS settings. At the NTDS settings object, right-click to create a New Active Directory Connection (see Figure 2-28).

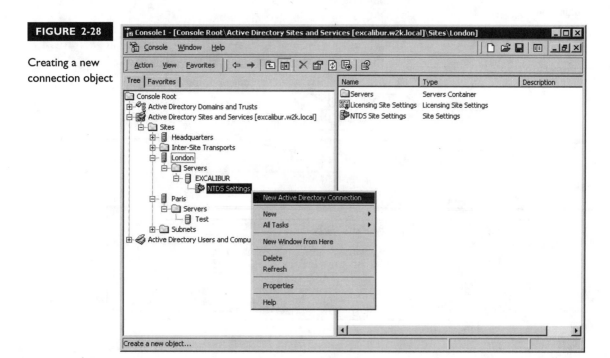

FIGURE 2-28

Creating a new connection object

When you select the New Active Directory Connection context menu option, a connection object Properties window appears for you to select the domain controller with which this connection object will be associated. Select your domain controller and click OK.

Next, you must name your connection object. As recommended in the past, name your connection object with both domain controller names. This makes it obvious what two domain controllers this connection object is connecting. Once you name your connection object, it appears as a connection object in your NTDS settings. Double-click to edit and modify the object (see Figure 2-29).

Looking at Figure 2-29, you can see that not only can you select the transport method (IP, RPC, or SMTP), you can also change the scheduling of replication by clicking Change Schedule.

FIGURE 2-29

Editing the connection object

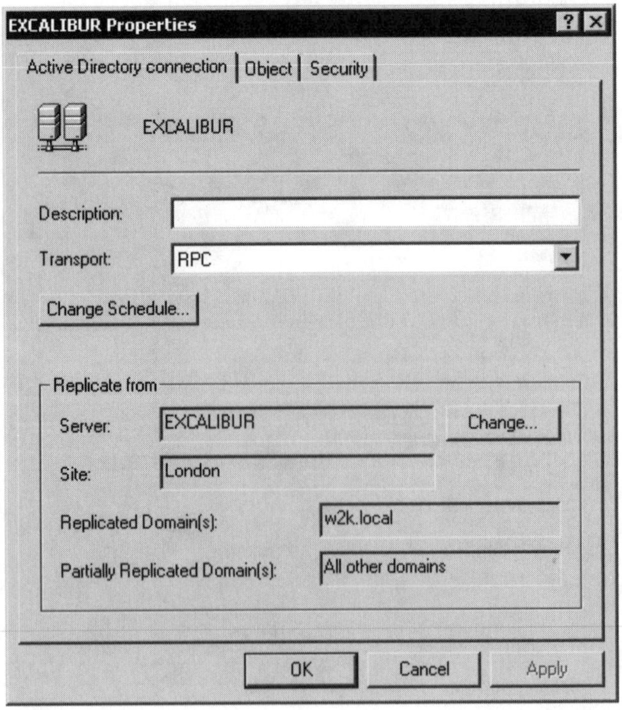

Make sure that if you make manual connection objects, you create the connection objects with the correct transport. By default, manual connection objects are assigned the RPC transport. If you need to use IP or SMTP transports, you must configure the connection object appropriately. In addition, remember that if you configure a connection object to use an IP or SMTP transport, make sure you have defined the proper site link(s) and/or site link bridge(s). Having a connection object created with an SMTP transport and no SMTP links configured results in no replication occurring on the domain controller with this connection object!

Earlier in the chapter, we clarified the difference between RPC, IP, and SMTP connections. Basically, RPC and IP connections are one and the same, although the terms are used to describe replication connections at different levels. RPC is used at the domain controller level, whereas IP is used at the Sites level of replication. Another point to keep in mind is that RPC replication (mostly used for intrasite replication) does not compress replication data, because it assumes that connections are using well-connected media, whereas IP replication (mostly used for intersite replication) does compress replication data for efficient use of bandwidth.

RPC and IP connections use synchronous communications, which require each replication transaction to be acknowledged before the next transaction can take place. SMTP connections use asynchronous communications, which allow several replication transactions to be unacknowledged while still allowing communications to continue.

When looking at these protocols, we normally associate RPC and IP connections with faster network connectivity because they are more efficient yet less tolerant of network problems than SMTP connections. SMTP connections are more tolerant of network problems, such as noisy lines, and perform well with lower-speed network connections. That is why they are sometimes favored over IP connections when administrators create site links. When you create connections that require you to choose among RPC, IP, and SMTP protocols, look at exactly where you will be applying these connections; that will help you determine what protocol to use.

Remember that you can change the replication schedule only on connection objects that you manually create. You can change the scheduling of replication on automatically generated objects, but for these changes to be permanent, you must change these objects from automatically generated connections to manual ones.

CertCam 2-7

EXERCISE 2-7

Creating Connection Objects for Active Directory Domain Controllers

In this exercise, you create manual connection objects for domain controllers in Active Directory. You also learn how to change the replication frequency for manually created connection objects:

1. Verify that you are logged on to your domain as Administrator.

2. Open the MMC, click the Console menu item, and select the Add/Remove snap-in pop-up menu item.

3. From the Standalone tab, click Add. From the Add Standalone snap-in, click the Active Directory Sites and Services snap-in, and click Add. After adding the snap-in, click Close, and then click OK to close the Add snap-in window.

4. Expand the Active Directory Sites and Services snap-in by double-clicking the snap-in. To create a new Active Directory connection, select which domain controller you would like to make the connection. Navigate to Sites | *<Site name>* | Servers | *<Server name>* | NTDS Settings. Right-click NTDS setting from the context menu, and select the New Active Directory Connection menu item.

5. Next, select a domain controller from the Find Domain Controllers window, and click OK. This is the domain controller that will replicate to the domain controller that you are using. The New Object–Connection window appears so that you can name the connection. Name the connection object, and click OK. You will find the object located under NTDS Settings for the selected server. To familiarize yourself with creating connection objects, repeat Steps 4 and 5 to create more connection objects.

6. To edit a connection object, select a connection object and double-click. A Properties window for the connection object opens, showing several settings for the object, including its transport, the domain that the connection object is replicating from, and a Change Schedule button to allow changes in replication scheduling. First, change the transport for the connection object by clicking the drop-down box for Transports. Select a different transport.

7. You can change the replicating server that uses this manual connection object by clicking Change next to the Replicate From Server entry. A Find Domain Controllers window appears. Select the domain controller to which you want to reassign this connection object, and click OK. The new domain controller selected now replicates with the domain controller with which you are currently working.

8. Finally, click Change Schedule to work with the replication schedule for this manual connection. The replication schedule shows several settings for replications per hour. You can specify replication to occur once, twice, or four times per hour. You can also specify that no replication occur during certain hours. This option is useful to limit the amount of replication during your network's peak operational hours. To change replication times, select the time frame that you want to modify, then click one of the replication frequencies to change the replication schedule. Once you have modified the replication schedule, click OK to save the changes. Try modifying the replication schedule so that there is no replication at all, and save the configuration. What happens? Do you think that Active Directory would allow this choice? Why or why not?

CERTIFICATION OBJECTIVE 2.08

Creating Global Catalog Servers

To finish the configuration of your Windows 2000 network, you need to consider the placement of *global catalog servers* within your network. Global catalog servers must be strategically placed and, as you have seen from all the other objects you created in this chapter, creating too many of any one global catalog can lead to unwanted replication and resource usage. When creating global catalog servers, keep the following in mind:

■ Each global catalog server has to bear the burden of extra replication and must have enough storage capacity to hold partial replicas of all objects from other domains in the network.

■ Global catalog servers are required for the logon process; therefore, placement of global catalog servers is crucial to performance on your network. Inefficient placement of a global catalog server can translate to poor performance for a segment of your network. As a general guideline, it is recommended that you have at least one global catalog server in each site, if possible, to provide adequate resources for your network. The drawback is, as explained previously, increased replication traffic on your network. If your network can handle the traffic, having a global catalog server in each site may be beneficial.

on the Job *The only exception to the rule that a global catalog server must be available on the network to fulfill logon requests is the Administrator account. The Administrator account is allowed to log on to the network, by default, because the Administrator, logically, needs to access the network in order to fix any problems.*

What Is a Global Catalog Server?

A *global catalog server* holds both a full copy of the local Active Directory as well as a partial replica of all objects from all other domains in the network. Many objects from other domains are not stored in the global catalog because some of this information is not critical enough to be replicated through AD. This storage scheme not only cuts down on replication, but it also relieves some processing pressure on global catalog servers to keep up with replication of non-essential AD information.

How to Create a Global Catalog Server

Creating a global catalog server is very simple (much simpler than making the decision to designate a domain controller as a global catalog). Using the Active Directory Sites and Services MMC snap-in, drill down to the server that you want to make a global catalog server by navigating to Sites | *<Site name>* | Servers | *<Server name>* | NTDS Settings. Right-click the NTDS Settings object and select Properties from the context menu. The NTDS Settings Properties window appears, as shown in Figure 2-30.

The NTDS
Settings window

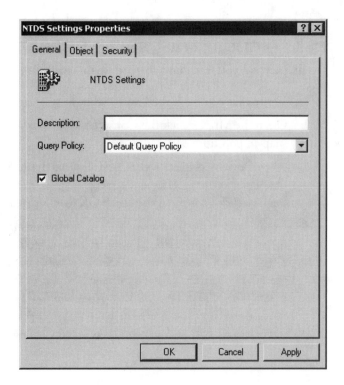

Creating a global catalog server is as easy as checking the global catalog check box, as shown in Figure 2-30. Once you check this box and click OK, the server in question becomes a global catalog server. Remember that the *first domain controller* you install automatically becomes a global catalog server because a global catalog server is necessary for logons to occur.

EXERCISE 2-8

Defining Global Catalog Servers in Active Directory

In this exercise, you learn how to set domain controllers as global catalog servers:

1. Verify that you are logged on to your domain as Administrator.

2. Open the MMC, click the Console menu item, and select the Add/Remove snap-in pop-up menu item.

3. From the Standalone tab, click Add. From the Add Standalone snap-in, click the Active Directory Sites and Services snap-in, and click Add. After adding the snap-in, click Close, and then click OK to close the Add snap-in window.

4. Expand the Active Directory Sites and Services snap-in by double-clicking the snap-in. To set a domain controller as a global catalog server, navigate to Sites | *<Site name>* | Servers | *<Server name>* | NTDS Settings. Right-click the NTDS Settings object and select Properties from the pop-up context menu. The NTDS Settings Properties window appears. On the General tab, the last item on the tab is a Global Catalog check box. To set the selected server as a global catalog, click the Global Catalog check box, and click OK.

SCENARIO & SOLUTION

I need to have my domain controllers updated as quickly as possible. Can I manually adjust their replication times?	You can manually adjust replication times by adjusting the frequency at which controllers replicate. This is done through the NTDS Settings for a server object. You can only adjust replication from once per hour to four times per hour.
I want to create my own replication topology so that I know how my domain controllers are replicating at all times and that they are replicating to the nearest domain controller. Can this be done?	The short answer is, "Yes." Keep one *very* important thing in mind, however: When you create manual connection objects, the KCC uses these over automatically generated ones. If a connection between two domain controllers has only one manually created connection object and it fails, the KCC will not compensate for that failure. You must make sure that your replication topology is solid before deciding to make an all-manual replication topology.
Do I need to have a global catalog server? I have only a single domain.	Even though you have only one domain, you still must have at least one global catalog server. Fortunately, when you install your first domain controller, it is automatically installed as a global catalog server.
Our company is very large, and our network will have a forest with several domains. What is the impact of having several domains and using global catalog servers?	Each global catalog server keeps a listing of its local domain as well as a partial listing of important objects from all other domains. Having a network with several domains places an additional replication burden on your domain controllers that serve as global catalog servers. This burden is multiplied by the number of global catalog servers you have throughout your network, again because of replication. You must carefully choose how many global catalog servers you will have and scale them appropriately.

CERTIFICATION SUMMARY

In this chapter, we covered the necessary steps to install, configure, and optimize Active Directory for any given network.

First, we covered the DCPROMO process and the various scenarios that one could face when installing a domain controller. Next, we covered the concept of sites and subnets. Subnets are groups of systems located locally on a network that, when combined with other subnets in a local geographic area, form a site. Sites are a collection of "well-connected" subnets and domain controllers. Sites form a logical partition of network systems, which, when used by clients, allows for efficient use of resources and Active Directory replication.

We then covered site links and site link bridges, which allow for connecting separate sites for Active Directory replication and resources. Site links allow sites to replicate with one another; site link bridges allow the ability to route AD replication according to your existing network topology. Site link bridges can be configured to use more favorable, and faster, network links over those that are more costly and slower.

Last, we looked at connection objects and global catalog servers. Connection objects are inbound-only connections to domain controllers that allow Active Directory replication. We discussed global catalog server placement, and it was discovered that the placement of too many global catalog servers could dramatically increase network traffic.

TWO-MINUTE DRILL

Installing Active Directory

❑ When using a non-Microsoft DNS solution, you must use a version of DNS that is BIND version 8.1.2 or higher. This version supports service resource records (SRVs), which are a requirement for Windows 2000.

❑ Active Directory requires at least one NTFS partition.

❑ The SYSVOL folder stores all your public files and contains the NETLOGON share, from which all file replication takes place. The SYSVOL folder must be installed on an NTFS 5.0 partition.

❑ When you choose to install DNS separately, Windows 2000 automatically generates all the DNS entries required for Active Directory and places them in the NETLOGON.DNS file under the %SystemRoot%\System32\config directory.

Creating Sites

❑ Sites help partition your Active Directory into logical groups based primarily on location. Sites allow clients to use local resources and replicate AD traffic efficiently.

❑ Sites, by definition, are a group of subnets and domain controllers that are well connected. The definition of *well connected* can vary from network to network, but in most cases the term is defined as a local area network-equivalent connection.

❑ Slow network connections usually create site boundaries, and they usually connect two sites.

Creating Subnets

❑ Subnets help map domain controllers to Active Directory sites. If all your subnets and sites are properly defined before installing the remaining domain controllers in your network, they will be properly placed in the correct site when they are added to the Active Directory via DCPROMO.

❑ Subnets are annotated in the form of 0.0.0.0/24. The first number is the IP subnet address; the second number is the subnet bit mask. With this type of subnet annotation, you cannot use subnet masks such as 255.255.129.0 or 255.255.255.127. The subnet bit mask assumes that the mask is a set of contiguous masking bits.

❑ When creating a subnet, you may associate the subnet with only one site. This requirement makes it impossible to split a subnet between two different sites.

Creating Site Links

❑ Site links tell AD how to connect sites within your network.

❑ Site links tell AD the links that are most favorable for AD replication.

❑ Site links control the frequency of AD replication between sites.

❑ Site links can use either IP or SMTP as their transport. IP uses synchronous communications for higher-speed and higher-quality connections; SMTP uses asynchronous communications for lower-speed and lower-quality connections.

Assigning Bridgehead Servers

❑ A bridgehead server acts as a "bridge" into a site by being a receiving point for Active Directory replication from other sites. When other sites use this bridgehead server, the bridgehead server then replicates the changes received to all other domain controllers in the site.

❑ Bridgehead servers receive a larger amount of replication traffic because they must receive replication traffic from all other sites as well as keeping up with replication traffic within their own sites.

❑ The Knowledge Consistency Checker (KCC) can, and does, create its own bridgehead server topology, but you can override this topology by designating your own bridgehead servers. Be aware that the KCC cannot automatically select alternate bridgehead servers if you have designated a bridgehead server manually. If you choose to manually assign a bridgehead server, make sure that you designate several bridgehead servers to compensate for any lost servers.

Creating Site Link Bridges

❑ Site link bridges are much like site links, but they allow you to model AD replication to your network topology. You can build site link bridges that allow you to route replication traffic over the most favorable, high-speed connections in your network.

❑ Site link bridges must consist of at least two site links.

❑ Site link bridges do not have assigned link costs; rather, they have a cost assigned to them by adding together all the costs of the site links that make up the site link bridge.

Creating Connection Objects

❑ The KCC creates and manages all connection objects between all domain controllers.

❑ The KCC can adjust the replication topology for domain controllers using automatically generated connection objects; it cannot automatically adjust manual connection objects.

❑ You can change the replication schedule for connection objects, but if they are automatically generated objects, you must take ownership of the connection object, which, in turn, makes the connection object a manual object.

Creating Global Catalog Servers

❑ Global catalog servers are required for the logon process.

❑ Global catalog servers hold a full replica of the local AD and a partial replica of all other domains.

❑ Placement of too many global catalog servers on your network can dramatically increase network traffic.

SELF TEST

The following questions will help you measure your understanding of the material presented in this chapter. Read all the choices carefully because there might be more than one correct answer. Choose all correct answers for each question.

Installing Active Directory

1. What are two DNS requirements for Active Directory? Choose two.

   A. Dynamic DNS for supporting dynamic registration of systems and resources

   B. Support for service resource records

   C. DNS must be BIND version 8.1.2 compliant

   D. Installation of at least one Microsoft DNS server to support Active Directory

2. You have started the DCPROMO process to install Active Directory. When you get to the SYSVOL installation point, you remember that you did not build this server with NTFS drives. What options must you have to be able to continue the installation?

   A. Select a path to install the SYSVOL folder, finish the installation, and then CONVERT the drive on which the SYSVOL folder is installed to NTFS.

   B. Run the CONVERT utility on a system drive to convert it from FAT16 or 32 to NTFS.

   C. Install the SYSVOL folder on a FAT16 or 32 drive; NTFS is required for the Active Directory database and log files.

   D. Select a path to install the SYSVOL folder, finish the installation, and then move the SYSVOL folder to a NTFS drive.

3. What is the minimum requirement for installing the Active Directory database and log files?

   A. An NTFS 5.0 volume with at least 250MB of free space to support the database and log files.

   B. Two partitions or drives on which to separately install the database and log files. The drives must both be NTFS 5.0 partitions.

   C. At least one drive or partition with at least 250MB of free space to support the database and log files.

   D. One NTFS 5.0 drive or partition with at least 200MB to support the Active Directory database file and one drive or partition with at least 50MB to support the Active Directory log file.

Creating Sites

4. What are the functions of sites within Active Directory? Choose two.

   A. Sites are a way to logically group subnets and domain controllers together based on well-connected networks.

   B. Sites help partition the Active Directory based on the location of domains and domain controllers.

   C. Sites are Active Directory objects on which domain controllers are placed in order to manage them.

   D. Sites are objects that Windows 2000 uses to group subnets and domain controllers together to efficiently replicate Active Directory.

5. When creating a site, what must you assign to the site?

   A. A site link; at least one site link must be assigned to the site

   B. A subnet; at least one subnet must be assigned to the site

   C. A site link bridge; the site must be attached by at least one site link bridge

   D. Nothing; a site can be created without assigning any additional objects to the site

Creating Subnets

6. Which subnet mask is invalid for subnet 224.240.16.0?

   A. 255.255.255.192

   B. 255.192.0.0

   C. 255.192.255.0

   D. 255.255.192.0

7. What is the purpose of using subnets in Active Directory?

   A. Subnets enable Active Directory to perform replication with domain controllers.

   B. Subnets define where domain controllers exist.

   C. Subnets are used by sites to define site boundaries. Domain controllers placed within sites are members of the subnets that exist within these sites.

   D. Subnets define how site links and site link bridges route replication traffic.

Creating Site Links

8. What is the main function of a site link?

    A. Site links connect two or more sites for Active Directory replication.

    B. Site links allow administrators to specify the best network route to use for replication.

    C. Site links allow you to create and control your own replication topology.

    D. Site links allow you to connect two or more connection objects to enforce the best replication topology.

9. The International Vacations Company has a main headquarters in New York and a remote office on the island of Cyprus. The company's Windows 2000 domain has two sites, a New York site and a Cyprus site. The only network link between the sites is a 56K link that has some reliability problems during bad weather. What is the best site link transport to use for this situation?

    A. Use an IP transport for the site link to guarantee that the replication data is received.

    B. Use an SMTP transport for the site link to compensate for the slow link and the unreliability of the network connection.

    C. Use a combination of IP and SMTP transports, which will create two site links for Active Directory replication. This will ensure that your Active Directory information will be replicated without data loss or corruption due to a bad network connection.

10. When creating a site link, what must be configured when the link is created?

    A. At least two sites must be added to the link.

    B. The link cost must be configured for the new link.

    C. The replication frequency must be set for the new link.

    D. At least two site link bridges must be added to the link.

Assigning Bridgehead Servers

11. What is the function of a bridgehead server?

    A. Links domain controllers within a site for replication purposes

    B. Links sites together for replication purposes

    C. Serves as a focal point for replication within a site

    D. Serves as a focal point for replication between sites

12. What is the difference between a KCC-generated bridgehead server and a manually assigned bridgehead server?

A. KCC-generated bridgehead servers are optimized for efficient replication.

B. There is no difference between KCC and manually generated bridgehead servers; they are both managed by the KCC.

C. Manually assigned bridgehead servers cannot be managed by the KCC.

D. You can create several manual bridgehead servers; the KCC creates only one bridgehead server per site.

Creating Site Link Bridges

13. Given the following scenario, what would be the best solution? Site A is connected by a LAN to Site B; Site B is connected by a T1 connection to Site C; Site C is connected by an ISDN connection to Site D; Site D is connected to Site A by a 56K dial-up connection. Site A is also connected to Site C by an ISDN connection. Link costs for each connection are shown here.

Site Link	Link Cost
AB	2
BC	4
CD	7
AC	7
AD	16

What is the best strategy to replicate traffic between Site A and Site D?

A. Create site link bridge ABCD to route replication traffic from Site A to Site D.

B. No further links need to be created; Site A and Site D are connected via site link AD.

C. Create a site link bridge ACD to route replication traffic from Site A to Site D.

D. Create a site link bridge using two Site AD links; this will double the speed at which replication occurs, which, in turn, makes the connection more efficient.

14. What is the main difference between site links and site link bridges?

A. Site links help duplicate your network configuration for efficient routing of replication traffic.

B. Site link bridges help duplicate your network configuration for efficient routing of replication traffic.

C. Site links route pass-through replication traffic through other sites to help it reach its destination.

D. Site link bridges do not use link costs.

Creating Connection Objects

15. What is the function of the Knowledge Consistency Checker (KCC)?

    A. Checks the validity and integrity of manually created connection objects

    B. Manages the creation of automatically generated connection objects and maintains the replication topology

    C. Automatically readjusts the replication topology when manual connection objects are created

    D. Creates additional connection objects as replication traffic increases; as replication traffic decreases, it removes the additional connection objects

16. What must you do to modify the replication schedule for an automatically generated connection object?

    A. You cannot change the replication schedule for automatically generated connection objects.

    B. You must make a manual connection object to link the two domain controllers that are already connected by an automatically generated connection object. Once the manual connection is created, you can modify the replication schedule.

    C. You must modify the automatically generated connection object.

    D. You must make your own replication topology with manual connection objects to be able to change replication schedules.

17. You are an administrator for a large Windows 2000 network. Your network management personnel have approached you with data that prove that one of the domains in your network is generating excessive replication traffic. The situation needs to be controlled immediately, because the replication traffic represents a total of 28 percent of all traffic for several subnets. The domain in question is not complex; three domain controllers are well connected by three subnets and are in the same site in the Active Directory. What can you do to immediately reduce the replication load on the network?

    A. Create a whole new set of manual connection objects and modify their replication schedules for off-hours replication.

    B. Create several new site links and site link bridges to redistribute the replication load over underutilized subnets.

    C. Manually create connection objects and a replication topology to route replication traffic to underutilized subnets.

    D. Modify the replication schedules for all automatically generated connections so replication occurs during off-hours.

Creating Global Catalog Servers

18. What are the effects of removing all your global catalog servers? Choose two.

A. You drastically cut Active Directory replication traffic within your network.

B. You place a greater replication load on Active Directory because it must create more connection objects to handle the increased replication traffic load created by removing all the global catalog servers.

C. You will not be able to log on to the domain.

D. You will not be able to reach or use Active Directory information in other domains.

LAB QUESTION

Your company, ABC.COM, is planning a migration from Windows NT 4.0 to Windows 2000. In the course of planning and research, the company gathered the following information:

Master domain: ALPHABET

Resource domains: NUMBERS, LETTERS

ALPHABET consists of three servers, one PDC (CROWN) and two BDCs (SIGNATURE and STAGECOACH), all on subnet 192.168.1.0.

NUMBERS consists of two servers, one PDC (STINGRAY) and one BDC (THUNDERBIRD), both on subnet 10.10.1.0.

LETTERS consists of three servers, one PDC (RANGER) and two BDCs (MILLIE and SOCKS), also on subnet 10.10.1.0.

ALPHABET is wholly located in the main business building; NUMBERS and LETTERS are both located in another building but separated from the main business building. For reliability and availability reasons, the company prefers that all systems remain in place. The concept of "upgrade in place" is in effect for all domain controllers in the network.

The building in which ALPHABET is located does not have very good WAN connectivity to other resources external to its building. The fastest WAN connection from this building is a 128K ISDN link. WAN connectivity will not be upgraded until next year because current IT resources are fully dedicated to this migration project. Since NUMBERS and LETTERS are in the same building, they are connected via high-speed networks (10MB Ethernet connectivity).

ABC.COM is also planning a divisional split; its R&D division will become its own entity, ABCFUTURES. LETTERS is planned as ABCFUTURES' domain, so you must plan your Windows 2000 domain structure accordingly. The R&D division will have its own domain name, ABCFUTURES.COM. You must make sure that ABC.COM and ABCFUTURES.COM are their own entities, but they still must be able to share resources.

ABC.COM has the following subnets free: 10.10.20.0, 192.168.2.0, and 10.220.1.0.

Your task, given the information from the research, is to plan a Windows 2000 domain for optimal performance.

SELF TEST ANSWERS

Installing Active Directory

1. ☑ **B**, Support for service resource records, and **C**, DNS must be BIND version 8.1.2 compliant. DNS must be compliant with BIND version 8.1.2 or higher in order to support the requirement for SRVs because that was the first version to support SRV records.

   ☒ **A** is incorrect because Dynamic DNS is not required for Active Directory operations. Dynamic DNS makes life easier by automatically registering systems in DNS, but it is not required for Windows 2000 or Active Directory to operate. **D** is incorrect because Microsoft DNS is not required for Active Directory. You can install Windows 2000 and Active Directory without using Microsoft DNS, as long as your DNS solution is BIND 8.1.2 compliant.

2. ☑ **B**. Run the CONVERT utility on a system drive to convert it from FAT16 or 32 to NTFS. If you can get exclusive access to a system drive to run the CONVERT utility, you can convert the drive from FAT16 or 32 to NTFS and then install the SYSVOL folder on that drive.

   ☒ **A** and **D** are both incorrect because you cannot install the SYSVOL folder on a FAT16 or 32 partition. If you attempt to do so, you will receive an error message and you will not be able to proceed. Even if it were possible to install the SYSVOL folder on a FAT16 or 32 folder, you still would not be able to move the SYSVOL folder. **C** is incorrect because you cannot install the SYSVOL folder on a FAT16 or 32 drive. It is stated in the Shared System Volume window that you must have an NTFS drive to install the SYSVOL folder.

3. ☑ **C**. At least one drive or partition with at least 250MB of free space to support the database and log files. The only requirement to install the Active Directory database and log files is to have at least 250MB of free space on any drive; 200MB is the minimum for the AD database and 50MB is the minimum for the AD log. It is recommended that you place the database file and log file on separate drives for better performance, but it is not a requirement.

   ☒ **A** is incorrect because Active Directory does not require NTFS drives to be installed. **B** is incorrect because it is not a requirement to have two separate drives for the AD database and log; also, as stated earlier, NTFS drives are not required. **D** is incorrect because, as stated earlier, it is not a requirement to install AD on separate drives.

Creating Sites

4. ☑ **A**, sites are a way to logically group subnets and domain controllers together based on well-connected networks, and **D**, sites are objects that Windows 2000 uses to group subnets and domains controllers together to efficiently replicate Active Directory. Sites are used to

logically group subnets and domain controllers together because they all use well-connected media, such as a 10MB Ethernet network. These subnets and domain controllers are grouped together in sites to efficiently replicate AD objects. AD changes that must be replicated between sites assume that the link between the sites is a slow connection and that replication will occur less frequently as replication occurs within a site.

☒   **B** is incorrect because sites have nothing to do to AD partitioning. Site creation is driven by the location of subnets, domain controllers, and usually, slow network connections such as WAN connections. **C** is incorrect because, although sites do hold domain controllers, they do not hold them for the purpose of managing them. This is a function of organizational units within Active Directory. Organizational units are containers that can hold objects such as domain controllers; Group Policy can be used to manage them.

5. ☑   **D.** Nothing; a site can be created without assigning any additional objects to the site. This makes it easy to create sites to hold future domain controllers, without having to define any additional objects for the site.

☒   **A, B,** and **C** are all incorrect because you do not need to assign any object to a site when it is created.

Creating Subnets

6. ☑   **C.** 255.192.255.0. This subnet mask is invalid because you cannot create a contiguous subnet bit mask with this subnet mask.

☒   **A, B,** and **D** are all valid subnet masks: 255.255.255.192 translates to subnet mask annotation /26, 255.192.0.0 translates to /10, and 255.255.192.0 translates to /18.

7. ☑   **C.** Subnets are used by sites to define site boundaries. Subnets define the boundaries of sites within Active Directory. Subnets, when grouped together, form a site. Subnets, when assigned to sites, allow Active Directory to understand where domain controllers are located.

☒   **A** is incorrect because subnets do not directly enable Active Directory to perform replication. Several other steps and objects are involved in enabling Active Directory replication. **B** is incorrect because subnets help define the site boundaries of sites. Site objects define where domain controllers exist. To better understand, look at the Active Directory Sites and Services snap-in and look at sites and at subnets. Notice that subnets are listed under sites. Also notice that domain controllers are listed under Sites | Servers. **D** is incorrect because subnets have no interaction with site links or site link bridges.

Creating Site Links

8. ☑ **A.** Site links connect two or more sites for Active Directory replication. Site links act as point-to-point links between sites to enable Active Directory replication.

☒ **B** is incorrect because you cannot route replication to fit your network topology with site links. This is a function of site link bridges. **C** is incorrect because you do not create replication topologies with site links. This is a function of connection objects and the KCC. **D** is incorrect because connecting connection objects is not in any way a function of site links.

9. ☑ **B.** Use an SMTP transport for the site link to compensate for the slow link and unreliability of the network connection. SMTP transports use asynchronous communications via the SMTP protocol to pass Active Directory replication. Because SMTP uses asynchronous communications, several replication transactions can be outstanding while replication continues. With synchronous communications, each transaction must finish before the next one starts. With slow and/or unreliable network connectivity, asynchronous communication is a necessity to get the job completed.

☒ **A** is incorrect because the IP transport uses synchronous communication. As stated earlier, synchronous communication does not perform well under slow and unreliable conditions. **C** is incorrect because, whereas using both transports will get the job done, it is inefficient because only one connection is required, and SMTP replication can fulfill this requirement. It is also inefficient because the use of two transports doubles the amount of replication traffic over this link, which consumes more bandwidth.

10. ☑ **A.** At least two sites must be added to the link. When a site link is created, it is naturally assumed that you are creating the site link because you have at least two sites that you want to link for replication purposes. Because of this assumption, Windows 2000 requires that you add at least two sites to the site link.

☒ **B** and **C** are incorrect because you cannot configure the link cost and replication frequency settings until the link is actually created. Once the link is created, you can edit the link and change these properties. **D** is incorrect because site links build site link bridges, not vice versa.

Assigning Bridgehead Servers

11. ☑ **D.** Serves as a focal point for replication between sites. A bridgehead server acts as a "bridge" into a site by receiving all AD replication traffic from other sites. Once received, all AD changes are replicated to all other domain controllers within the site.

☒ **A** and **B** are both incorrect because bridgehead servers do not link anything. They are inbound-only connections. **C** is incorrect because a bridgehead server functions only between sites, not within sites.

12. ☑ **C**. Manually assigned bridgehead servers cannot be managed by the KCC. When manually assigned bridgehead servers are created, the KCC cannot assign an alternative bridgehead server if the server in question fails. You must compensate by assigning more servers within your site as manual bridgehead servers.

☒ **A** is incorrect because the KCC has nothing to do with optimizing replication links. Remember that bridgehead server connections are inbound-only connections. **B** is incorrect because there is a difference between KCC-generated and manually assigned bridgehead server connections. **D** is incorrect because the KCC creates bridgehead servers as needed. The KCC does not care whether it creates 1 bridgehead server or 20.

Creating Site Link Bridges

13. ☑ **A**. Create site link bridge ABCD to route replication traffic from Site A to Site D. Using this site link bridge is the most efficient means of replicating Active Directory information from Site A to Site D.

☒ **B** is incorrect because using site link AD is less efficient than using the site link bridge ABCD. **C** is incorrect because site link bridge ACD is also less efficient than site link bridge ABCD, although site link bridge ACD is a more direct route. **D** is incorrect because you cannot add the same site link twice in a site link bridge; even if this were possible, it still would not double the speed at which the site link bridge replicates.

14. ☑ **B**. Site link bridges help duplicate your network configuration for efficient routing of replication traffic. You can use the basic layout of your network to mirror the replication routing using site link bridges to replicate to other sites as needed. Using the appropriate site links within your site link bridge, you can efficiently route replication traffic over your high-speed networks and leave the slower, more costly links as a backup for your network.

☒ **A** is incorrect because site links do not allow you to duplicate your network configuration for efficient routing of replication traffic. This is a function of site link bridges. **C** is incorrect because site links do not route pass-through replication traffic through other sites to reach its destination. This is a function of site link bridges. **D** is incorrect because, although site link bridges cannot manually set link costs, they are computed based on the site links that make up the site link bridge. This link cost is used to determine the best site link bridge to use for Active Directory replication. If a site were to drop out, all the site link bridges would have to recalculate their link costs from the remaining links available. At this point, it is determined whether the current site link bridge is still appropriate to use or whether there is now a lower-cost site link or site link bridge available for replication.

Creating Connection Objects

15. ☑ **B.** Manages the creation of automatically generated connection objects and maintains the replication topology. The KCC manages all aspects of the replication topology, from creating the automatically generated connection objects to maintaining the replication topology for all domain controllers in the forest. It manages such objects as site links to ensure that replication is being performed in accordance with all the settings for each object.

    ☒ **A** is incorrect because the KCC does not manage or interact with manually created connection objects. **C** is incorrect because the KCC does not readjust the replication topology for manually created connection objects. It is imperative to remember that if you have a single, manual connection object between two domain controllers and this connection fails for whatever reason (for example, the domain controller fails), the KCC does not adjust the replication topology unless an automatically generated connection object exists between the two domain controllers. **D** is incorrect because the KCC does not create additional connection objects based on replication traffic. The KCC only monitors the replication topology of the network, manages automatically generated connection objects, and adjusts the replication topology if a domain controller becomes unavailable.

16. ☑ **C.** Modify the automatically generated connection object. You can modify the replication schedule for automatically generated connection objects, keeping in mind that once you modify the automatically generated connection object, it becomes a manually generated connection object, which the KCC will not automatically manage.

    ☒ **A** is incorrect because the statement is totally false. You can change the replication schedule for automatically generated connection objects. **B**, although technically correct, does not modify or replace the replication schedule for the automatically generated connection object. If you create a manual connection object, both the automatic replication and the manually set replication occur. **D** is incorrect because you do not need to create your own replication topology with manual connection objects to be able to change replication schedules. The KCC generates the most favorable replication topology; therefore, it is recommended to let the KCC manage the replication between domain controllers unless there is an urgent need to modify this replication strategy in some way.

17. ☑ **D.** Modify the replication schedules for all automatically generated connections so replication occurs during off-hours. Modifying the replication schedules allows you to adjust the times that replication occurs and how frequently it occurs.

☒   **A** is incorrect because creating a set of manual connection objects, although allowing you to adjust the replication schedule, still leaves the automatically created connection objects. Modifying the automatically created connection objects correctly adjusts the replication schedules and eliminates the redundant effort of creating more connection objects. **B** is incorrect because creating new site links and site link bridges will not allow you to adjust the amount of replication traffic generated. Furthermore, the question stated that the domain in question is in one site, so site links and site link bridges would not help. **C** is incorrect because, although you can create manual connection objects and replication topology, you cannot guarantee that this new replication strategy will use underutilized subnets to pass its replication traffic.

Creating Global Catalog Servers

18.   ☑   **C**, you will not be able to log on to the domain, and **D**, you will not be able to reach or use Active Directory information in other domains. A global catalog server is required for the logon process; without a global catalog server, no one can log on to the network. The only exception to this rule is the Administrator account. In addition, without any global catalog servers, resources and objects in other domains will be unavailable.

☒   **A** is incorrect because, although you will substantially cut replication traffic by reducing global catalog servers to zero, cutting access to your network is not an acceptable result of reducing your replication traffic. **B** is incorrect because in Active Directory you do not increase replication loads by removing global catalogs; furthermore, Active Directory will not create more connection objects to handle increasing replication traffic. Connection objects for domain controllers have nothing to do with replication traffic.

LAB ANSWER

ABC.COM and ABCFUTURES.COM have their own namespace; this fact automatically assumes that two different trees are needed. Because they need to share resources, these trees need to be connected. Two or more connected trees make a forest.

Next, because Windows 2000 has better performance and replication over Windows NT 4.0, most Master Domain architectures using Resource domains can either be collapsed into the Master domain or left as a Resource domain and connected to the Master as a child domain later. In this example, for simplicity, it is better to collapse the NUMBERS domain into the ALPHABET domain, which will result in ABC.COM. Keep in mind that in Windows 2000, new objects and concepts, such as organizational units in Active Directory and sites, allow you to redefine your network so that you are not forced to create a Resource domain. You can take advantage of these features to help simplify your network's design.

See Chapter 3, Configuring Active Directory, for information regarding organizational units and their placement in the Active Directory.

Since NUMBERS will be collapsed into the ALPHABET domain, you have to create two different sites. You can name your sites anything, but for this example, let's say HQ is the site where the ALPHABET domain resides and CHANDLER is the site where the NUMBERS domain resides. LETTERS is in the same building as NUMBERS, but it must have a different site; therefore, we use the Site name CHANDLERRESEARCH.

The domain controllers are placed in each site as shown here (obviously, your names will not match):

Site HQ: CROWN, SIGNATURE, and STAGECOACH

Site CHANDLER: STINGRAY and THUNDERBIRD

Site CHANDLERRESEARCH: RANGER, MILLIE, and SOCKS

Keep in mind that once these domain controllers are migrated to Windows 2000, they are then known by their DNS domain names (STINGRAY.ABC.COM, RANGER.ABCFUTURES.COM, etc.).

You must remember that all the domain controllers in the NUMBERS and LETTERS domains are on the same subnet. They are not only in different domains; they are in separate sites, which requires that they be on different subnets. During your migration, you must assign new IP addresses to all the domain controllers in the NUMBERS domain. We use the IP subnet 192.168.2.0 since it is listed as a free IP subnet.

Once your subnets and sites are designed, you must create your site links. Because the ABC.COM domain has HQ and CHANDLER sites, you must create a HQ-CHANDLER site link for replication purposes. Although NUMBERS and LETTERS exist in the same building, they exist in different trees and domains. They also require a site link for replication. For the best replication performance, the site link between ABC.COM and ABCFUTURES.COM should be between the CHANDLER and CHANDLERRESEARCH sites rather than HQ and CHANDLERRESEARCH. Using HQ-CHANDLERRESEARCH would add replication bandwidth to an already slow WAN connection. If you handle replication using a CHANDLER-CHANDLERRESEARCH site link, the HQ-CHANDLER site link replicates the changes received by the CHANDLER-CHANDLERRESEARCH site link.

Last, we must assign global catalog servers. Since each domain requires a global catalog server, you need at least one global catalog server in the ABC.COM and ABCFUTURES.COM domains. Since the NUMBERS and LETTERS domains are in the same building, you will get optimal global catalog and Active Directory replication if you place both global catalog servers in this building. You may assign any server in either domain as a global catalog server, but for this example, we use STINGRAY in NUMBERS and SOCKS in LETTERS.

At this point, you are finished designing the new Windows 2000 domain structure that will exist for ABC.COM. Figure 2-31 shows the exact layout of the domain.

FIGURE 2-31   Domain design of ABC.COM and ABCFUTURES.COM

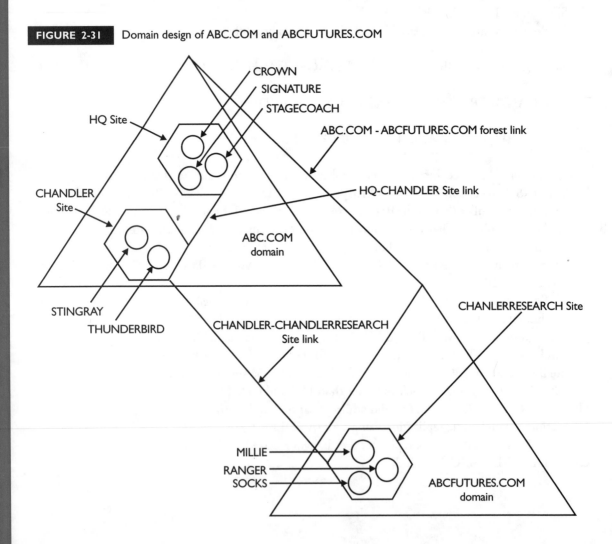

3

Configuring
Active Directory

CERTIFICATION OBJECTIVES

3.01	Verifying Active Directory Installation
3.02	Moving Server Objects Between Sites
3.03	Transferring Operations Master Roles
3.04	Implementing an Organizational Unit Structure
✓	Two-Minute Drill
Q&A	Self Test

I n the previous chapter, you learned about installation of Active Directory on a Windows 2000 Server. AD components must be configured in order to get benefits from this new feature of the Windows 2000 Server operating system. The topics that we discuss in this chapter include verification of AD installation, creating and moving server objects between sites, transferring operations master roles, and implementing an organizational unit (OU) structure.

Once the Active Directory is installed and you have verified the domain controller and the Domain Name System (DNS) server, you need to decide on the operations master roles for various domain controller computers in the network. You also need to create OUs in the Active Directory that will be the containers for AD objects. Depending on the requirements of your organization, a careful plan has to be chalked out before implementing an OU structure.

CERTIFICATION OBJECTIVE 3.01

Verifying Active Directory Installation

The first thing you should do after installation of Active Directory is to check whether it has been installed properly and is functioning in the desired way. When you start a Windows 2000 Server domain controller computer, the Configure Your Server dialog box appears by default if you have not cleared the Show This Screen At Startup check box. If you click the Active Directory option in the list on the left-hand side, you will notice that the screen that appears next tells you that Active Directory is installed. See Figure 3-1.

The addition of Active Directory management snap-ins in the Administrative tools is another indication that the installation is complete. However, this is merely an indication of the installation. This section discusses the methods of more detailed verification of Active Directory installation.

Verifying the Domain Controller

Active Directory is installed on a member server to promote it to a domain controller. You may want to check whether the domain controller that you recently upgraded from a member server is available on the network. There are several different ways to accomplish this check, but the two methods described here are the ones that give you

FIGURE 3-1

The Configure
Your Server
dialog box after
Active Directory
installation

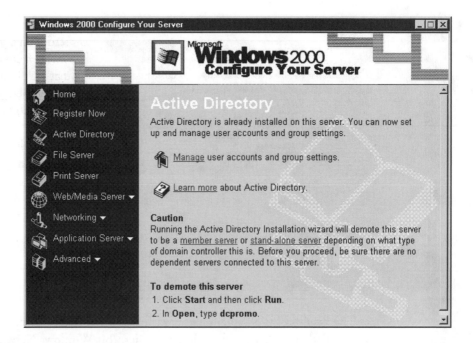

immediate verification information. Exercises 3-1 and 3-2 will help you verify
the domain controller from My Network Places and from Active Directory Users
and Computers.

CertCam 3-1

EXERCISE 3-1

Verifying the Domain from My Network Places

1. Log on to the domain controller using the domain administrator username
   and password.

2. Close the Windows 2000 Configure Your Server Wizard that appears.

3. Double-click My Network Places on the desktop or right-click and select
   Open. This step opens the My Network Places window.

4. Double-click the Entire Network icon. This opens the Microsoft Windows
   Network window. Notice that the domain icon appears.

5. Double-click the name of the domain. This displays the newly installed
   domain, as shown here:

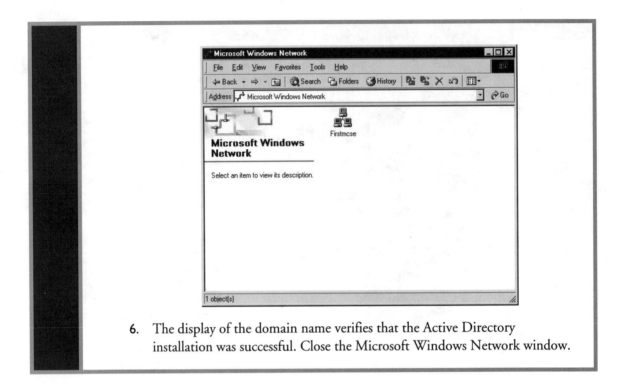

6. The display of the domain name verifies that the Active Directory installation was successful. Close the Microsoft Windows Network window.

Verifying the DNS Server

When the DNS server is installed, a DNS management tool is added to the Administration tools. In Exercise 3-3, we verify that the DNS server works correctly by performing a test from the DNS server properties.

Automatic Testing of DNS Server

The DNS configuration can also be tested automatically at specified time intervals. You might notice that the Perform Automatic Testing At The Following Interval option in the DNS Properties sheet allows you to specify time intervals in minutes. If selected, this option performs automatic testing at specified intervals. If you want to perform periodic tests, fill in the interval time and click Apply.

EXERCISE 3-2

Verifying the Domain Controller from Active Directory Users and Computers

1. Log on to the domain controller with a domain username and password.

2. Click Start | Programs | Administrative Tools, and select Active Directory Users and Computers. This step opens the Active Directory Users and Computers console.

3. Click the plus (+) sign before the name of the domain to expand it. Click the Domain Controllers icon.

4. Notice that the name of the domain controller appears on the right-hand pane, as shown here:

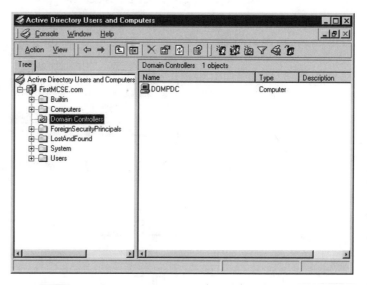

5. Close the Active Directory window. This step completes the verification of the domain controller.

Verifying the DNS Server

1. Log on to the domain controller as an administrator.

2. Click Start | Programs | Administrative Tools, and select DNS. This step opens the DNS console.

3. Right-click the name of the DNS server, and select Properties. This step opens the DNS Properties sheet.

4. Click the Monitoring tab. Look for "Select a test type." Notice there are two types of test options.

5. Select both test options: A Simple Query Against This DNS Server and A Recursive Query To Other DNS Servers:

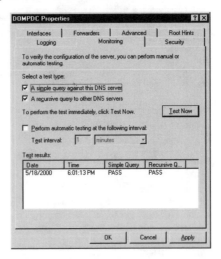

6. Click the Test Now button to start the test immediately. It takes only a moment or two for the test to complete.

7. Notice that the Test Results portion of the dialog box shows PASS for both simple and recursive query tests.

8. This completes the DNS server verification. Close the DNS properties dialog box. Close the DNS console.

SCENARIO & SOLUTION

I know I have installed Active Directory. Why is there a need for verification?	It is necessary to verify that AD was installed properly.
How do I verify that the DCPROMO has upgraded my member server to domain controller?	Browse the domain from My Network Places. If your server was upgraded, you will find it listed as one of the domain controllers.
What is the purpose of performing simple and recursive queries in the Monitoring tab of DNS server properties?	These queries ensure that the DNS is working properly and the present configuration has no problems.

CERTIFICATION OBJECTIVE 3.02

Moving Server Objects Between Sites

Several tasks are necessary to maintain Active Directory sites. These tasks include maintenance of server settings. Performing one or more of the site maintenance activities might be required on a regular basis in order to get the best benefits of the Active Directory services of Windows 2000. This section explains how to perform the following maintenance processes:

- Creating a Server object in a site
- Moving Server objects between sites
- Removing a Server object from a site

Creating a Server Object in a Site

In order to help you understand the procedure, we first create a dummy Server object in Active Directory Sites and Services. When this process is complete, you perform exercises that explain how to move and remove this Server object. This procedure holds true for creating member servers and domain controllers in the site. Exercise 3-4 shows the procedure to create a Server object.

Creating a Server Object in a Site

1. Log on to the domain controller as a domain administrator.

2. Click Start | Programs | Administrative Tools, and select Active Directory Sites and Services. This choice opens the Active Directory Sites and Services console.

3. Click the plus (+) sign before the site in which you want to create the Server object to expand it. Notice that the existing Server objects are listed in the Servers folder.

4. Right-click the Server folder and select New. Click Server, as shown here:

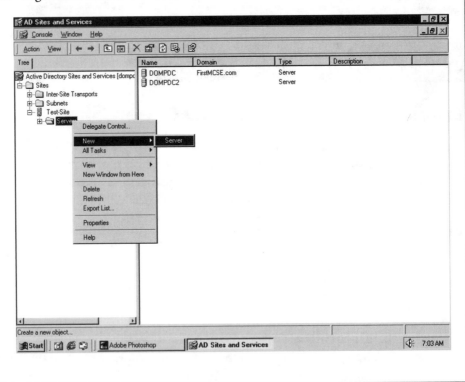

5. The New Object—Server dialog box appears, prompting you to type the name of the new Server Object. Type the name of the new Server object, as shown here:

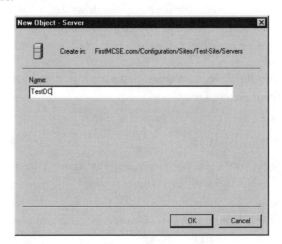

6. Click OK. Notice that the new Server object is now listed under the Servers folder.

The procedure for creating a domain controller Server object in a site is not a substitute for installing a domain controller in a site. The domain controller must first be installed using the Active Directory Installation Wizard. Once it is installed, the Domain Controller object will be moved automatically to the Domain Controllers container in the Active Directory in the Sites and Services console.

When to Move Objects

Requirements of any organization change from time to time, with a changing competitive landscape or through mergers or acquisitions, for example. The Active Directory Server objects that you designed and created at the time of deployment of Windows 2000 might no longer be suitable to fulfill the needs of your organization after some time. This situation calls for regular maintenance of Active Directory objects. Server objects are ones that you might need to move from one site to another in order to attain seamless network performance.

In today's competitive business scenario, sometimes small and medium-sized companies merge their operations to form a bigger organization. If both the constituent companies have Windows 2000-based domains, they might need to restructure the Active Directory components. Creating new site containers and moving site objects will be a part of such an Active Directory restructuring.

exam
ⓦatch

You need domain administrator rights to move or remove Server objects from Active Directory.

How to Move Objects

Server objects are moved using the Active Directory Sites and Services console. Exercise 3-5 will help you understand the process of moving Server objects between sites. The procedure is good for moving both domain controllers and member servers from one site to another. You need at least two domain controllers in order to complete this exercise.

The next most important part of this discussion is removal of Server objects from the site that are no longer in use. This procedure is detailed in Exercise 3-6.

CertCam 3-5

EXERCISE 3-5

Moving Server Objects from One Site to Another

1. Log on to the domain controller as a domain administrator.

2. Click Start | Programs | Administrative Tools, and select Active Directory Sites and Services. This choice opens the Active Directory Sites and Services console.

3. Click the + sign before the site from which you want to move the Server object in order to expand it. Select the Server object you want to move to a different site.

4. Right-click the Server object and select Move, as shown here:

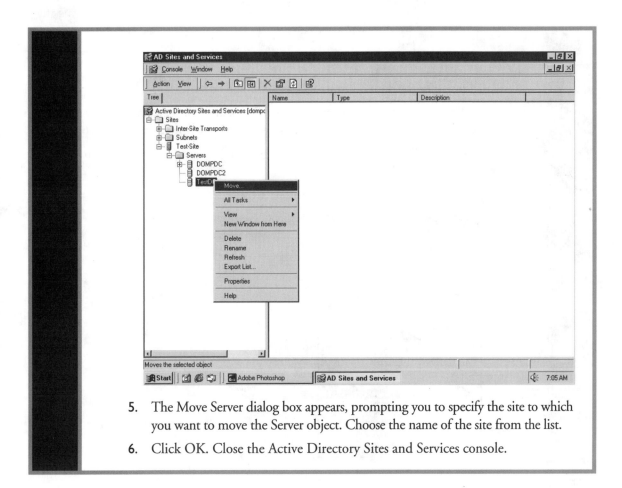

5. The Move Server dialog box appears, prompting you to specify the site to which you want to move the Server object. Choose the name of the site from the list.

6. Click OK. Close the Active Directory Sites and Services console.

on the job

Usually, you remove a Server object from a site only when it is no longer required or has been inoperative for a long time. If you want to remove the object only temporarily, remove the NTDS Settings objects for the server instead. This option allows you to reactivate the server any time you need it again. When you bring the server online later, the Active Directory creates a new NTDS Settings object for the server. To be on the safer side, even if you will not need the Server object again, it is best to first delete the NTDS Settings object for that server and remove the Server object at a later date.

EXERCISE 3-6

Removing a Server Object from a Site

1. Log on to the domain controller as a domain administrator.

2. Click Start | Settings | Administrative Tools, and select Active Directory Sites and Services. This step opens the Active Directory Sites and Services console.

3. Select the Server object that is no longer required and that you want to remove from the site.

4. Right-click the Server object and select Delete.

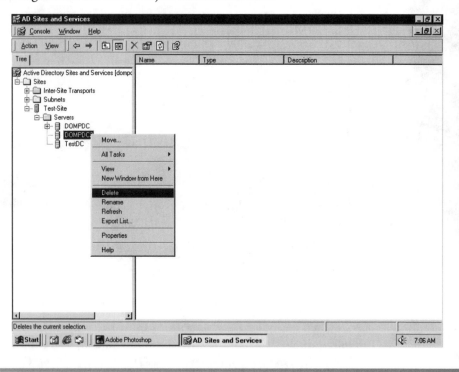

5. Notice that the following warning message appears on the screen.

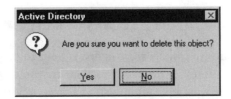

6. As a built-in safety feature against accidental removal of an object, No is the default selection in this warning dialog box. Click Yes to remove the Server object.

7. Notice that the Server object no longer appears under the tree. Close the Active Directory Sites and Services console.

SCENARIO & SOLUTION

Which of the Active Directory consoles is used to manage server objects?	Active Directory Sites and Services is used to create, remove, and move server objects between sites.
Why should there be a need to move server objects once they have been created for one site?	It is necessary to move server objects as the needs of a company change.
Can I use the New Server option from Active Directory Sites and Services to promote a member server to domain controller?	No. Member servers are promoted to domain controllers using the DCPROMO command. Creating servers in Active Directory is altogether a different operation.

CERTIFICATION OBJECTIVE 3.03

Transferring Operations Master Roles

Domain controllers are assigned various roles, depending on their location in the domain forest or domain tree. The *operations master roles* are assigned to enable single-master replication instead of multimaster replication. *Single-master replication* ensures that no two domain controllers are assigned the same operations master role in the domain. One domain controller holds the master copy of a particular component of Active Directory, and others act as its backups. In this section, we discuss various operations master roles, their significance in the domain forest or domain tree, and methods to transfer roles among domain controllers.

To start, we take a closer look at the term *operations master roles* and the purpose of these roles.

What Are the Operations Master Roles?

When you have more than one domain controller in your network, the *File Replication System* keeps the domain controllers synchronized. Each domain controller participates in the replication system to keep its database up to date. This *multimaster replication* is a built-in feature of Active Directory.

In some situations, this multimaster replication does not allow you to make changes to the domain. Making changes calls for assigning some operations to one or more domain controllers that are single master. This way you can prevent other domain controllers from performing the same operations at the same time. These specified domain controllers then perform single-master operations when assigned operations master roles. The single-master role ensures that only one domain controller keeps the specific AD data, and others remain as backups.

There are five types of operations master roles in an AD forest. These roles must be assigned to one or more domain controllers for proper functioning of the replication in the network. It is necessary to understand various operations master roles in order to maintain the domain controllers.

There are two primary types of operations master roles, each having its particular significance:

- Forestwide operations master roles
- Domainwide operations master roles

Forestwide Operations Master Roles

The *forestwide operations master roles* must be unique to a particular domain forest. There are two roles, both of which are unique—in other words, you cannot have more than one schema master role or domain-naming master role in a single domain forest. The following are the two types of forestwide operations BDCs master roles.

Schema Master Role   There can be only one *schema master* in a domain forest. The domain controller assigned this role is in charge of all changes and modifications to the forest schema.

Domain-Naming Master Role   As with the schema master, there can be only one domain controller having the *domain-naming master role*. This domain controller is in charge of any additions or deletions of domains in the forest.

exam
Ⓦatch

It is important to note that the forestwide operations master roles are unique in the forest. You cannot have more than one domain controller with the same forest-wide operations master role.

Domainwide Operations Master Roles

The *domainwide operations master roles* are relative ID (RID) master, primary domain controller (PDC) emulator, and infrastructure master. These roles are also unique to the domain.

Relative ID Master Role   The domain controller holding this role is responsible for generating a security ID for each object created in the domain. When you create a user, group, or computer object, it is assigned a security ID that consists of two parts: a domain security ID and a relative ID (RID). The *domain security ID* is the same for all objects created in the domain. The *relative ID* of the object is unique to the object. No two objects can have an identical relative ID. Whenever you want to move an object across domains, you must do it from the domain controller that has the RID master role.

Primary Domain Controller Emulator Role   As its name suggests, the domain controller assigned the PDC emulator role acts as a Windows NT primary domain controller when there are non-Windows 2000 computers in the network or when some Windows NT backup domain controllers (BDCs) still exist on the network. The domain controller acting as PDC emulator actually behaves as a PDC to all BDCs. This role is also unique to the domain and can be assigned to only one domain controller. This feature is very useful in Windows 2000 networks working in mixed mode.

Even if a Windows 2000 network is running in native mode, meaning that there are no Windows NT domain controllers, the domain controller that has the PDC emulator role gets replication information on password changes from other domain controllers.

on the Job *Users on a network keep changing their passwords for secrecy and data security. In a Windows 2000 network that has several domain controllers, a password change at one domain controller might take time to replicate to other domain controllers. However, if a user changes a password and the change has not been passed on to all domain controllers, there is no need to worry. The logon request is first sent to the domain controller acting as PDC emulator before refusing to log the user on. Hence, it is incorrect to say that the PDC emulator role is useful only in mixed-mode environments.*

Infrastructure Master Role   As with other domainwide master roles, only one domain controller can be assigned the infrastructure master role in a domain. The domain controller hosting this role is connected to the global catalog and takes care of updating information when there are changes in group memberships. When a member of a group is moved from one domain to another, that group might not reflect the member's presence in the group for a while. The domain controller that has the infrastructure master role takes care of the new location of the member.

When to Transfer Roles, and Why

If your network is very small and has only one domain controller computer, all the operations master roles are assigned to it by default. However, for reasons of providing redundancy, it is never a good decision to keep a single computer as domain controller. There should be at least two domain controllers, even if the network is very small: one that acts as an operations master domain controller and the other that acts as a standby operations master domain controller. These domain controllers must be direct replication partners for normal operation. This ensures that if for some reason one of the domain controllers fails, the other is ready to take over.

When the network is large, you must assign the domainwide operations master roles first. When this is done, the forestwide operations master roles can be assigned. Usually, when you install the first domain controller in the forest, both schema master and domain-naming master roles are assigned to the same domain controller. Usually, when you install the first domain controller, it will host all the operations master roles.

The question is, why change operations master roles? One thing is certain: The schema master and the domain-naming master roles should be assigned to the same domain controller. The only roles that are changed among domain controllers are the domainwide operations master roles. The following are some of the reasons for transferring operations master roles:

- **Load balancing**   Transfer of roles among domain controllers enables you to balance the load among various domain controllers.

- **Changes in the network**   When the network is growing at a fast pace and changes take place very frequently, you might need to transfer operations master roles from one domain controller to another for the network to run smoothly.

- **Maintenance and hardware upgrades**   Another reason for transferring operations master roles is maintenance. When a domain controller is taken offline for repairs, the role that this domain controller was performing must be transferred to another domain controller within the same domain.

Due to rapid changes in technology and the needs of organizations, server hardware needs to be upgraded occasionally. New hardware replaces old servers. So, you need to transfer to another domain controller the particular operations master role to which the obsolete server is assigned.

How to Transfer Roles

Let's look at how to transfer these roles from one domain controller to another. The exercises that follow will be helpful in explaining the procedures required to accomplish the job of transferring roles. In practice, you transfer only the domainwide operations master roles, although you can transfer any of the forestwide roles, too. The transfer operations take place only in a single domain.

Identifying and Transferring Forestwide Operations Master Roles

The forestwide schema master role can be viewed and transferred using the Active Directory Schema snap-in. The Active Directory Schema snap-in is not installed to any domain controller by default. You need to install it from the Control Panel using Add/Remove Programs and install all the Administrative tools. Once this is done, follow the steps in Exercise 3-7 to check which domain controller is responsible for this role. This procedure also explains how the schema master role can be transferred.

exam
ⓌatcH

The MCSE exams have several questions based on simulations. It is important to note that the two forestwide operations master roles are viewed and changed from two different AD snap-ins. The schema role is changed from the Active Directory Schema snap-in; the domain-naming role is changed from Active Directory Domains and Trusts.

EXERCISE 3-7

Transferring the Schema Master Role

1. Log on to the domain controller as a domain administrator.

2. Click Start | Run, and type **mmc** in the open box. Click OK. This step opens a blank MMC.

3. Click Console, and select Add/Remove Snap-in from the drop-down menu. Another dialog box appears. Select Active Directory Schema. Click Add. Notice that Active Directory Schema now appears in the left-hand side of the console.

4. Right-click Active Directory Schema, and select Change Domain Controller from the menu. This step opens the Change Domain Controller dialog box:

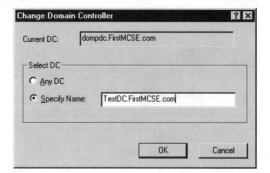

5. The Change Domain Controller dialog box gives you two options to change the schema master role, as shown above. The Any DC option lets Active Directory select a domain controller for the purpose. The Specify Name option enables you to specify the name of the domain controller yourself.

6. Type the name of the new domain controller, and click OK. This step closes the Change Domain Controller dialog box.

7. Right-click Active Directory Schema again, and select Operations Master. This choice brings up the Change Operations Master Role dialog box:

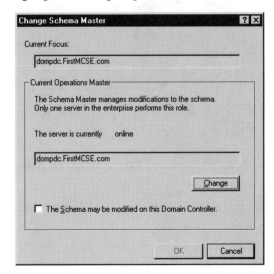

8. To transfer the schema master role, click the Change button.

The domain-naming master role is changed from the Active Directory Domains and Trusts snap-in. Making this change requires that you first connect to the domain controller that will host the new domain-naming master role. This is done from the console root. Right-click the console root, and select Change Domain Controller. Select the domain controller that will host the role. Follow these steps to view or change the assignment of this role:

9. Open the Active Directory Domains and Trusts console.

10. Right-click Active Directory Domains and Trusts, and select Operations Master.

11. The Change Operations Master dialog box appears, as shown in the following illustration. The dialog box shows the name of the domain controller that is responsible for this role.

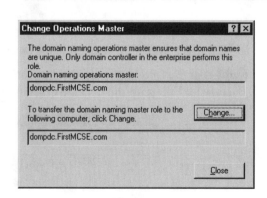

12. Click Change to transfer this role to another domain controller.

13. Click Close to close the dialog box. Close the Active Directory Domains and Trusts console.

Identifying the Current Assignment of Domainwide Operations Masters Role

In order to transfer the domainwide operations master roles in a domain from one server to another, it is necessary to know what role is currently assigned to various domain controllers. Exercise 3-8 explains how to get this information.

In order to get complete information on domain controllers that hold various operations master roles, you need to connect to them using the Connect To option from the Active Directory Users and Computers drop-down menu.

Transfer of domainwide operations master role assignments can be performed for any of the roles following the steps given in Exercise 3-9.

CertCam 3-8

Identifying the Present Assignment of Roles

1. Log on to a domain controller as an administrator.

2. Click Start | Programs | Administrative Tools, and select Active Directory Users and Computers. This step opens the Active Directory Users and Computers console.

3. Right-click the Active Directory Users and Computers node from the Console tree, and select Operations Master:

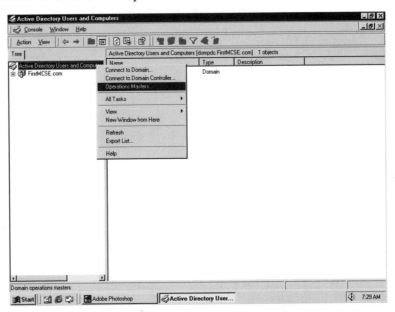

4. The Operations Master dialog box opens. Notice in the following illustration that there are three tabs: RID, PDC, and Infrastructure.

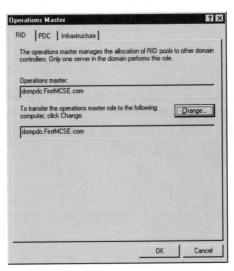

5. The RID tab is the default view that shows the name of the relative ID master in the Operations Master box.

6. Click the PDC or Infrastructure tab to view the name of the appropriate domain controller that holds the respective operations master role.

7. Click Cancel to close the Operations Master dialog box.

EXERCISE 3-9

Transferring Domainwide Assignment of Operations Master Roles

1. Log on to the domain controller as a domain administrator.

2. Click Start | Programs | Administrative Tools, and select Active Directory Users and Computers. This choice opens the Active Directory Users and Computers console.

3. Click the Console menu, and select Connect to Domain.

4. The Connect to Domain dialog box opens. Type the domain name as shown. Click OK. You could also click the Browse button to search for the domain name.

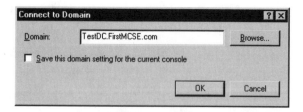

5. Right-click Active Directory Users and Computers in the console tree, and select Operations Master. This choice opens the Operations Master dialog box.

6. To change any of the roles, select the RID, PDC, or Infrastructure tab. Click Change. For example, if you need to transfer the PDC role to the new domain controller, click the PDC tab, and click Change.

7. Click OK to confirm and close the Operations Master dialog box.

Seizing an Operations Master Role

Computer hardware and networking issues can often either bring down servers or cause connectivity problems. When the server is a domain controller and assigned to one or more operations master roles, it is necessary to either transfer the role to another domain controller or, under certain circumstances, *seize* the role.

If the server will be offline for long or cannot be brought up again, you might want to seize the role and assign it to another domain controller. Seizing the role is done as a last resort step to keep the AD-based functions running properly in the network. Seizure of a role is also called *forceful transfer of an operations master role.* In any case, you must first determine the length of time the failed domain controller will remain offline. If the server that is experiencing problems will be available online again, you must wait. It is notable that domain controllers for which schema, domain-naming, or RID roles have been seized must never be brought online again. If you still want to use the same server as a domain controller, reformat its hard drive and reinstall Windows 2000 Server OS on it.

Operations master roles are seized using the NTDSUTIL command-line tool that is a part of the Windows 2000 Server Resource Kit and is included in the setup CD-ROM. This utility is used for several other administrative tasks for AD maintenance.

The following sections briefly discuss the impact of the failure of domain controllers that are assigned various operations master roles.

Seizing Schema Master   If the domain controller assigned the role of schema master is offline for very short periods, it will not make much difference. Even domain administrators are not able to notice such short durations unless they try to make some changes in the schema. You must seize the role only if the server will be permanently offline.

Seizing Domain-Naming Master   Failure of a domain controller assigned the role of domain-naming master is also not visible if the failure duration is very short. However, if the domain administrator is trying to add or remove domains in the forest, the operation will not be successful. You must seize the role only if the server will be permanently offline.

Seizing RID Operations Master   The failure for short periods of a domain controller that performs the role of RID master has no immediate effect on the network. The effect is visible only if the domain administrator tries to add or delete any objects during the period when the RID operations master domain controller is offline. This is because the RID domain controller assigns RIDs and the administrator is not able to get a RID for the new object. You must seize the role only if the server will be permanently offline.

Seizing PDC Emulator Operations Master   Failure of a domain controller holding this role affects network users. If you have even one Windows NT backup domain controller in the network or you have some clients that are not running Windows 2000, this role must be seized immediately and assigned to another domain controller. The role can be reassigned to the original domain controller when it is back online.

Seizing Infrastructure Operations Master   The failure of a domain controller assigned the infrastructure operations master role also does not make any immediate impact on the network. The domain administrator feels its absence only if he or she is trying to move or rename user or group accounts during the period when this particular domain controller is not available. The domain controller hosting the infrastructure role is connected to the global catalog, and if you want to transfer this role to another domain controller, you must ensure that it has good connection to the global catalog.

exam
ⓦatch

When the schema, domain-naming master, or RID roles have been seized from a domain controller, they must not be brought online again without you first reformatting your computer's hard drive and reinstalling Windows 2000 Server. Other roles such as PDC emulator and infrastructure can be seized and reassigned to the original domain controllers when they are back online.

Table 3-1 summarizes various operations master roles, their scopes, and the Active Directory snap-in that is used to manage each of them.

TABLE 3-1	Operations Master Role	Scope	Description	Managed from Which Snap-in?
Summary of Operations Master Roles	Schema	Forest	Controls updates and modifications to the schema	Active Directory Schema snap-in
	Domain Naming	Forest	Controls addition or deletion of domains in the forest	Active Directory Domains and Trusts snap-in
	Relative ID	Domain	Controls allocation of domain security IDs and object security IDs to objects	Active Directory Users and Computers snap-in
	PDC emulator	Domain	Processes password changes and acts as PDC for Windows NT BDCs	Active Directory Users and Computers snap-in
	Infrastructure	Domain	Controls renaming or groups and keeps track of changes in membership	Active Directory Users and Computers snap-in

SCENARIO & SOLUTION

My domain has 10 domain controllers that are working fine. Why should there be a need for transferring operations master roles?	There may be one or more reasons for transferring these roles. Hardware failures, maintenance, or upgrades are the most important reasons.
I want all domain controllers in the domain to take one or more operations master roles. How do I accomplish this?	The operations master roles can be distributed among one or more domain controllers, but one role cannot be given to more than one domain controller.
Which Active Directory console is used to transfer operations master roles within a domain?	Use Active Directory Users and Computers to manage domainwide operations master roles.
One of the domain controllers holding the PDC emulator master role has gone down. What should I do?	Seize the role immediately and assign it to another domain controller.
I seized the domain-naming role from a domain controller when it was down. Can I put it back on the network after repairs?	No. A domain controller whose domain-naming master role has been seized must not be put back in the network without first reformatting its hard drive and reinstalling Windows 2000 Server on it.

CERTIFICATION OBJECTIVE 3.04

Implementing an Organizational Unit Structure

Organizational units (OUs) are created based on the needs and functions of your organization. Your organization might be a small one with only a single domain, or it might be a large organization spread around the globe and consisting of several domains. You need to address many factors while planning and implementing the OU structure. In a large organization, all the domains might not have similar requirements, but at the same time the business goals remain the same.

The most important thing to remember in implementing an OU structure is that there must always be room for the future growth of the organization and its business needs. The discussion that follows will help you understand the various factors that you must take care of while designing and implementing an organizational structure.

OU Design Overview

OUs are containers in Active Directory that reflect the hierarchy of your organization. The OU structure must be designed to fulfill the current business needs, at the same time leaving room for growth. The structure should be designed in such a way that the administration burdens are manageable. When working for a large, globally dispersed organization, you must design the OU structure in a flexible manner so that local administrators can implement the designs in their own way.

Some of the important design considerations for the OUs are as follows:

- **Organization structure** Keep in mind the structure of the organization. This structure should be reflected in the domain. Keep different departments or different locations in separate OUs.

- **Ease of administration** When designing an OU for a multidomain, multilocation organization, you must consider delegation of administrative authorities to lower-level administrators. The top-level administrators should be made responsible for delegating administrative responsibilities.

- **Room for change and growth** Keep in mind that the business needs of a company keep changing to accommodate due to changes in the market or competition. You must design the OU structure in such a way that there is scope for change and future growth.

- ■ **Group policies**   To control the working environment for users and user groups within your domain, you must plan group policies for them. These group policies must be placed below their respective administrative areas so that the lower-level administrators are able to manage them. Objects such as users, computers, and network resources must be grouped so that they are easy to locate in Active Directory.

- ■ **Restricted access**   Create an environment for the users that gives them access to only the resources they are supposed to view and use. Other resources can be restricted from them. User accounts, computers, printers, and other Active Directory objects must have proper access set for them. Care must be taken that even after setting the most restrictive access permissions, users should have no difficulty performing their jobs.

In addition to these considerations, the Active Directory allows you to perform the following actions on the OUs:

- ■ Objects created in one OU can be moved to another OU.

- ■ OUs can be created, removed, or moved from one domain to another.

- ■ Changes in OUs do not create any significant load on current network traffic.

- ■ Organizational properties can be changed at any time.

There are three main hierarchy models from which you can choose. These are:

- ■ **Function based**   This model can be designed and implemented based on the functions of various units or departments and divisions of the organization. For example, you can have an administration unit, a marketing unit, and a research unit.

- ■ **Location based**   This model is suitable for organizations that have divisions located in different parts of the country or the globe. Each location is considered an OU. For example, the company can create three OUs based on its operations in the East Coast, the central United States, and the West

Coast. The office in New York can be in charge of operations in New York, Boston, and Washington, D.C., making one OU. The office in Dallas can be in charge of operations in Dallas and Chicago, making a second OU. The third OU can consist of offices in Seattle and Los Angeles.

- **Function and location based**   This mixed model is based on requirements with regard to both functions and locations of the organization.

With careful consideration of all factors, you can achieve a good plan for your OU structure. While planning, you must be careful to ensure that the structure you design suits the business needs of the company and allows for future growth. You should not change it time and again.

Creating the OU Structure

OUs are created using the Active Directory Users and Computers snap-in. Each OU represents an important part of the organization's hierarchy. You must plan the OUs and document your plans before starting the creation process. The OUs should fulfill the business requirements of your organization. If the organization consists of more than one domain, each domain can create its own OUs following the guidelines set by the parent domain.

Two parts of this section describe the following important processes necessary to implement the OU structure:

- Creating an organizational unit
- Creating objects in a domain.

Each of these processes is explained with the help of step-by-step exercises. Exercise 3-10 explains the steps necessary to create an OU in a domain. When you have designed and documented the complete OU structure, you can follow the same procedure to create other OUs.

exam
ⓦatch

The exam could contain simulation-based questions from the design part of an OU. Therefore, it is important to understand the important points of planning an organizational structure.

CertCam 3-10

Creating an Organizational Unit

EXERCISE 3-10

1. Log on to the domain controller as a domain administrator.

2. Click Start | Programs | Administrative Tools, and select Active Directory Users and Computers. This choice opens the Active Directory Users and Computers console.

3. Locate the domain in which you want to create the OU. If you are creating the OU under an existing OU, locate it and click the plus (+) sign to expand it. Otherwise, you need not expand the domain tree.

4. Select the container in which you want to create the OU. Right-click the container and select New, and click Organization Unit from the drop-down menu. This process is shown in the following illustration. You can also click the Action menu and select New, and click Organization Unit from there.

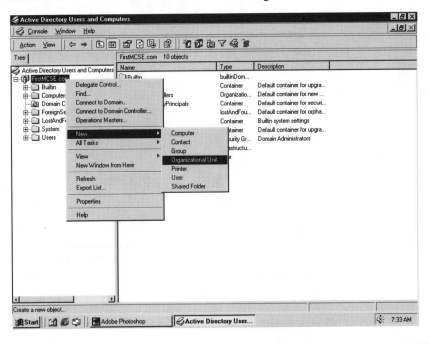

5. The New Object—Organizational Unit dialog box appears. Type the name of an organization unit. Click OK.

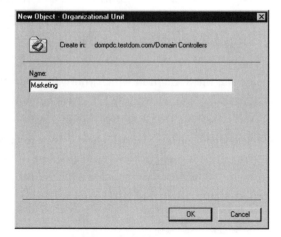

6. Notice that the newly created Organization Unit object is now displayed in Active Directory Users and Computers.

7. To create additional OUs under this new object, expand the new container and repeat Steps 4 and 5. You can create as many OUs as required.

Setting OU Properties

Once you have created an OU, you might want to set its properties. Each OU has a set of properties that are assigned to it by default when it is created. Additional properties can be set from the Properties sheet of the OU. Figure 3-2 shows the Properties sheet for the OU we created in Exercise 3-10. This illustration shows the Object and Security tabs that are visible when you enable the Advanced View by clicking View from the MMC menu and selecting Advanced features.

The tabs in the OU Properties sheet are as follows:

- **General** This tab gives the description and location details of the OU, such as its street address, city, state, ZIP or postal code, and country.

- **Managed By** Describes the name of the OU manager, location of the office, and other address details.

FIGURE 3-2

The organizational unit Properties sheet

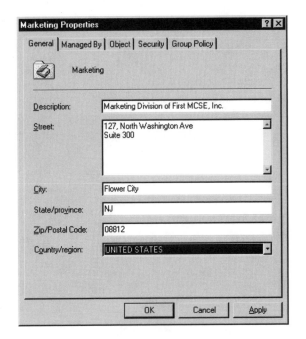

- **Object**   This tab gives details of the object.
- **Security**   This tab gives details of the security parameters currently applicable to the OU.
- **Group Policy**   This tab gives details of the group policy applied to the OU.

Any of these properties can be changed for an OU by opening the OU's Properties sheet and selecting an appropriate tab. The properties you define or set on an OU can be used as search criteria for locating an OU. In other words, if you have carefully entered the information in the Properties sheet, it could be helpful at a later date. For example, a newly appointed domain administrator can use the name of the city or the description to search for an OU or its other details.

on the **job**

In practice, you will create OUs and objects under an OU after a careful study of all the aspects of your organizational requirements. It is a good idea to document the design so that even if you leave the organization, the document remains as a reference for anyone who replaces you.

Creating an Object

Once you have created an OU, you need to create various objects under that unit, such as users, groups, or computers. The OU that you created works as a container or storage space for all the objects that you create under the unit. These objects are the ones that need your day-to-day administration.

The process for creating objects under an OU is more or less similar to creating an OU itself. For practice, let's create a user account. Exercise 3-11 explains the procedure.

EXERCISE 3-11

Creating an Object

1. Log on to the domain controller as a domain administrator.

2. Click Start | Programs | Administrative Tools, and select Active Directory Users and Computers. This choice opens the Active Directory Users and Computers console.

3. Select the OU under which you want to create the new object. Right-click the OU and click New. Select User from the drop-down menu that appears. This choice opens the New Object—User dialog box.

4. Type the first, middle initial, and last name of the user. Also type the user logon name. Notice that the Full Name and the Pre-Windows 2000 User Logon Name boxes are automatically filled.

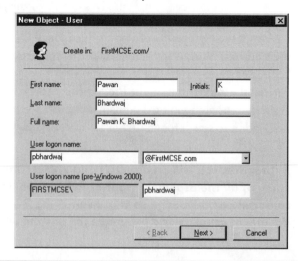

5. Click Next. The dialog box that appears prompts you to specify a password and password settings for the user. Type an initial password for the user, and check the User Must Change Password At Next Logon check box. It is a good practice to let the user choose his or her own password.

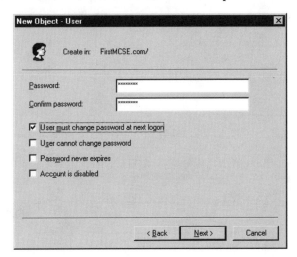

6. Click Next. A summary screen shows various settings you made for the new user.

7. Click Finish to close the dialog box. This completes the creation of a new user object in the OU.

When the new object is created, you can double-click it to see or change its properties. Figure 3-3 shows the membership properties of a user.

FIGURE 3-3

User membership
properties

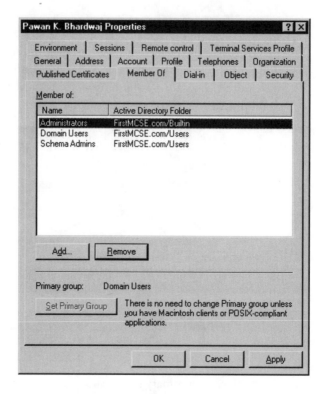

Other OU objects, such as computers, groups, and printers, can be created using the same procedure. When you create a group, you are given a choice to select the scope of the group. This scope cannot be changed later if the domain is working in mixed mode.

FROM THE CLASSROOM

Designing an OU Structure

Design of an OU is a huge responsibility; it is unlikely that you will be the only person assigned this job. If the organization you work for is small, you will probably have no problems designing an excellent working model. But if the company is large and has multiple locations, you might well be a member of a design and implementation team. A good knowledge of design factors will help you perform your job with excellence. Active Directory is new to everyone working in the Windows NT environment. AD and its benefits are one of the main features of Windows 2000 for upgrading your domain to this new platform. In most cases, organizations have predefined group policies in effect. If you are responsible for the structural design for AD, keep the following important things in mind:

1. Study the organizational structure in detail. Grab every piece of document that you can lay your hands on for details on the current setup.

2. Consult each person that is affected by the new design. Keep notes of your meetings.

3. Keep future growth of the organization in mind. Use a model that is most flexible and will not need changes very frequently.

4. Do not rush to implement things that you have designed. Prepare a test lab and conduct experiments first to get a feel for how the new design will take shape.

5. Make one change at a time. Keep a slow pace so that you can go back in case there are problems.

And finally, as I insist in all my writings, documentation must not be ignored at any cost. You might not be a member of the organization tomorrow. Documentation will help the person who replaces you in continuing to work successfully in the environment you create.

—*Pawan K. Bhardwaj, MCSE, MCP+I, CCNA*

CERTIFICATION SUMMARY

After the installation of Active Directory on a Windows 2000 Server to promote it to become a domain controller, it is necessary to verify that the AD components are working well. If the newly promoted domain controller is listed in the Active Directory Users and Computers console under the Domain Controllers container, it is verified that the installation is successful. Another way to verify the new domain controller is from My Network Places. The DNS server is verified from the Administrative tools DNS option, which again opens the Active Directory Users and Computers console. The simple and recursive queries from the Monitoring tab must show a Pass result.

Server objects are moved between sites for many purposes that include maintenance, performance, and change in needs of an organization. The Active Directory Sites and Services console can be used to move Server objects or remove an inoperative Server object. A preferred way of removing a Server object from the Active Directory is to remove the NTDS settings object for that server. This gives you the option of bringing the server online again. When the server is no longer required, it can be removed permanently.

Operations master roles are assigned to specific domain controller computers to configure single-master replication. The schema master role and the domain-naming master role are forestwide operations master roles. RID master, PDC emulator master, and infrastructure master are domainwide operations master roles. These roles can be transferred from one domain controller to another when some domain controller is unavailable on the network for maintenance purposes. It is not advisable to seize any role from any domain controller except the PDC emulator master role unless it is evident that a particular domain controller will never be online again.

Design of an organizational unit in Active Directory calls for a careful study of various requirements of the organization. In addition, organization structure, administration, future growth of the company, and group policies are some other factors that must be considered while you are designing an OU. An organizational structure is created from the Active Directory Users and Computers console. A similar procedure is adopted for creating objects under the OU container.

TWO-MINUTE DRILL

Verifying Active Directory Installation

❑ If the Active Directory tab in the Configure Your Server dialog box shows that Active Directory is installed in your computer, this is the first indication that the installation is successful. You can also browse the network to see that the domain controller is installed.

❑ Open Active Directory Users and Computers, and click Domain Controllers to verify that the domain controller is present.

❑ The DNS server is verified from the Active Directory Users and Computers console.

❑ The Monitoring tab from the DNS server Properties dialog box allows you to perform simple and recursive queries to verify that the DNS server is working well.

Moving Server Objects Between Sites

❑ The Active Directory Sites and Services console is used to create, remove, and move Server objects.

❑ Expand the Servers objects under the name of the site. Select the Server object you want to move and right-click it. Select Move. Specify the site name to which you want to move the Server object.

❑ A Server object is permanently removed from a site only when you are certain that the server will not be brought online again. Otherwise, you can remove the NTDS settings object for that server.

Transferring Operations Master Roles

❑ Schema master and domain-naming master are forestwide operations master roles. These roles are unique to the forest.

❑ Relative ID master, PDC emulator master, and infrastructure master roles are domainwide operations master roles and are unique to the domain. Only one instance of these master roles are to be defined in each domain, although a single domain controller can perform more than one of these roles.

❑ Transfer of roles is done for the reasons of load balancing, maintenance, network changes, and hardware upgrades. Except for the domain controller that is assigned the role of PDC emulator master, the domain controllers can be taken offline for short periods without having to transfer the role to another domain controller.

❑ It is not recommended to seize any role from any domain controller except the PDC emulator role, which is necessary for normal network operations. Roles are seized using the NTDSUTIL tool.

Implementing an Organizational Unit Structure

❑ The OU design must reflect the structure of an organization and should be easy to administer. There must be enough scope for growth and changes in the organizational structure.

❑ The three models that can be adapted for designing OUs are function based, location based, and function and location based.

❑ An OU is created from the Active Directory Users and Computers console after a careful design is done.

❑ When you have created the OUs, you can create objects such as users, groups, computers, and printers following the same procedure in the Active Directory Users and Computers console.

SELF TEST

The following questions will help you measure your understanding of the material presented in this chapter. Read all of the choices carefully because there may be more than one correct answer. Choose all correct answers for each question.

Verifying Active Directory Installation

1. You have just installed Active Directory on a Windows 2000 Server using the DCPROMO command. How will you verify that the server has been promoted to a domain controller?

   A. From My Network Places

   B. From Control Panel

   C. From Start menu

   D. Any of the above

2. Which of the following tabs is used to test the DNS server configuration using a recursive query?

   A. Monitoring

   B. Advanced

   C. Forwarders

   D. Interfaces

3. You want to test the DNS server configuration by performing single simple and recursive query tests at a later time. Which of the following options can you use from the Monitoring tab of DNS properties to accomplish this goal?

   A. Use the Schedule tab to set the test time.

   B. Check Perform Automatic Testing At The Following Intervals.

   C. Fill up the test interval timing and click Test Now.

   D. None of the above.

Moving Server Objects Between Sites

4. Which of the following Active Directory consoles is used to move Server objects between sites?

   A. Users and Computers

   B. Sites and Services

C. Schema

D. Domains and Trusts

5. How can you create a Server object in Active Directory?

A. By running the DCPROMO command

B. From the Active Directory Domains and Trusts console

C. Select the Servers folder in a site, click New from the Console menu, and click Server

D. None of the above

6. Which of the following constitute a reason for moving a Server object from one site to another? Choose all that apply.

A. Active Directory maintenance

B. The server is to be taken offline

C. The server is no longer needed

D. Reorganization

7. The Windows 2000-based network in your multilocation network has seven domain controllers. Four of these domain controllers are located at the company head office, where you are in charge of domain network operations. You are using Active Directory and configured it when the network was upgraded from Windows NT to Windows 2000. One of the servers at your location has been exhibiting some problems for a number of days, and you want to take it off the network so that you can fix the problems. What must you do with this server in Active Directory?

A. Delete the Server object from the site.

B. Rename the Server object temporarily.

C. Delete the NTDS Settings object of the server.

D. Export the server to a dummy site.

Transferring Operations Master Roles

8. Which of the following methods can be used to install the Active Directory Schema snap-in?

A. From the Control Panel, Add/Remove Programs.

B. From Active Directory, create a new Server object.

C. Run DCPROMO and select Schema.

D. Any of the above.

9. Which of the following operations master roles is responsible for additions and deletions of domains in the domain forest?

   A. Relative ID master

   B. Primary domain controller emulator master

   C. Schema master

   D. Domain-naming master

10. You are one of the network administrators of a large company that has three domains, and nearly 12 domain controllers are located at the office where you work. A domain controller in one of the domains is exhibiting performance problems, and you want to relieve some of its domain responsibilities. You figure out that the problems are due to the operations master roles assigned to this computer. Which of the following would be an appropriate action if you have to offload some of the roles from this domain controller?

    A. Promote the domain controller to forest level.

    B. Assign the domainwide roles to other domain controllers.

    C. Distribute the domainwide roles among two or three domain controllers.

    D. Seize all the roles from this domain controller.

11. You want to add more RAM in one of the domain controllers that is holding the relative ID master role. You are sure that this action will take only half an hour and then the domain controller will be back on the network again. What will be the impact of taking this server off the domain for half an hour?

    A. Users will not be able to work.

    B. You will not be able to create new objects in Active Directory.

    C. Users will not be able to log on to the domain.

    D. None of the above.

12. Which of the following Active Directory consoles is used to transfer the infrastructure master role from one domain controller to another?

    A. Schema

    B. Users and Computers

    C. Domains and Trusts

    D. Sites and Services

13. You are the network administrator of a medium-sized organization that has only one domain, but several domain controllers are sharing the domain responsibilities. One of the domain controllers has not been behaving properly for the previous three days and has suddenly failed due to the problematic network adapter. This domain controller is assigned the role of PDC emulator master. Changing the network adapter in this computer will take nearly two hours because you have to reconfigure all network properties. What should you do with the operations master role that this domain controller is holding?

    A. Seize the role from this domain controller.

    B. Transfer the role to another domain controller.

    C. Restore Active Directory when the domain controller is up again.

    D. Do nothing, because there will be no effect on the network.

14. One of the domain controllers on your network has been take offline due to a problem in its display adapter. You need to order a new display adapter for this controller; it will take three to four days before the domain controller can be repaired. The domain controller is responsible for the RID master role in the network. You immediately seized its role and assigned it to another working domain controller. What should you do with this domain controller when the problem is resolved?

    A. Reassign the role to this domain controller.

    B. Shift the domain controller to another network segment.

    C. Reformat the domain controller's hard disk and reinstall Windows 2000 Server.

    D. Do nothing. Simply connect it to the network.

Implementing an Organizational Unit Structure

15. Which of the following play a vital role in design of an organizational unit of a company? Choose all that apply.

    A. Company hierarchy

    B. Company directors

    C. Company requirements

    D. Future growth

    E. All of the above

16. Which of the following actions can be performed on a working organizational unit named Marketing that is meant for the sales department of a company? Consider that the OU has several functional objects. Choose all that apply.

    A. It can be deleted any time without affecting the domain.

    B. Its properties can be changed.

    C. The organizational unit can be moved to another domain.

    D. All of the above.

17. Which of the following Active Directory consoles is used to create organizational units in a domain?

    A. Users and Computers

    B. Domains and Trusts

    C. Sites and Services

    D. Schema

LAB QUESTION

Current Situation
You are the network administrator of a Windows 2000 domain in your company that has five domain controllers. The domainwide operations master roles are split among three domain controllers. One of these three servers is named PreW2kDom and is assigned the PDC operations master role. This server is showing performance problems and you intend to take it offline for maintenance. This down time could span several days. You want to assign the role to another domain controller named W2kDom01.

Required Result
Transfer the domainwide operations master role assigned to the PreW2kDom domain controller to the W2kDom01 domain controller.

Suggested Steps
These are the recommended steps to complete the required result. You are to find out any missing or incorrect steps:

1. Logon to PreW2kDom as domain administrator.

2. Click Start | Programs | Administrative Tools, and select Active Directory Domains and Trusts.

3. Select the domain controller from the left-hand pane. From the Console menu, click Operations Master.

4. You will see the Operations Master dialog box. Click the PDC tab.

5. Click Change. Click OK to close the Operations Master dialog box.

6. Close the Active Directory console.

Did you notice any missing or incorrect steps?

SELF TEST ANSWERS

Verifying Active Directory Installation

1. ☑ **D. Any of the above.** Any of the given methods can be used to verify that the server has been prompted to a domain controller. You can use My Network Places on the desktop to browse the entire network to see that the server is shown as a domain controller. Control Panel contains an applet for Administrative tools. These tools show icons for Active Directory components after the installation. Similarly, you can use the Start menu, point to Programs, and click Administrative tools, and you will see that Active Directory tools are listed in the options.

   ☒ This explanation makes **A, B,** and **C** invalid choices.

2. ☑ **A. Monitoring.** The Monitoring tab is used from the DNS server properties to test the DNS server configuration by simple and recursive queries. You can choose to test the DNS server immediately or perform automatic testing at specified intervals.

   ☒ **B** is incorrect because the Advanced tab has advanced settings for the DNS server. **C** is incorrect because the Forwarders tab has no option to test the DNS server. **D** is incorrect because the Interfaces tab also gives you no option to test the DNS server configuration.

3. ☑ **D. None of the above.** None of the given answers satisfies the requirements in the question. If you need to perform the simple and recursive query tests only once at a later time, you must do it using the Test Now tab. The tests can be performed immediately, whenever you decide to do so.

   ☒ **A** is incorrect because there is no Schedule tab in the Monitoring window of DNS properties. **B** is incorrect because the automatic testing at specified intervals will result in repeated tests, whereas you want to perform only one-time testing. **C** is incorrect because when you use the automatic testing option, you are supposed to click the Apply tab. However, this choice does not satisfy the requirement given in the question.

Moving Server Objects Between Sites

4. ☑ **B. Sites and Services.** The Server objects are moved between sites using the Active Directory Sites and Services console. Click Start | Programs | Administrative Tools, and select Active Directory Sites and Services. The Server objects are listed under the Servers container in the Sites folder.

   ☒ **A, C,** and **D** are incorrect because none of the consoles listed in these answers is appropriate to move Server objects between sites.

5. ☑   C. Select the Servers folder in a site, click New from the Console menu, and click Server. To create a Server object in Active Directory, you must open the Sites and Services console and first select the site in which you want to create the Server object. Expand the Site and click the Servers folder. From here you can either right-click and select New, then select Server, or use the Console menu and select New, and click Server.

☒   A is incorrect because the DCPROMO command is used to promote a member server to domain controller. Creating Server objects is altogether different from the DCPROMO command. B is incorrect because the Domains and Trusts console is not used to create Server objects in a site. D is an inappropriate choice because there is a correct answer.

6. ☑   A and D. Active Directory maintenance and reorganization of a company can be two potential reasons for moving a Server object from one site to another. Whenever your company restructures due to growth, you might need to move Active Directory Server objects from one site to another.

☒   B is incorrect because if the server is to be taken offline, there is no use moving it to another site. C is incorrect because if the server is no longer needed, it is better to remove it from the Active Directory site.

7. ☑   C. Delete the NTDS Settings object of the server. When you have a problem with any server that is an object in the Active Directory site, the best way to take it offline is to delete its NTDS Settings object. This enables you to bring the server online again after repairs and reactivate it.

☒   A is incorrect because the server must not be deleted from the site if it will be put back in service. B is an inappropriate choice because renaming the Server object is not a solution to the problem. D is incorrect because a Server object that will only temporarily be unavailable on the network should not be renamed.

Transferring Operations Master Roles

8. ☑   A. From the Control Panel, Add/Remove Programs. Select Install All Administrative Tools. When this is done, run MMC from the Start menu to open an empty console. Click Console, then click Add/Remove snap-in, and select Active Directory Schema from the dialog box that appears.

☒   B is incorrect because adding a new Server object in Active Directory is altogether a different function from adding Schema snap-in. C is incorrect because running DCPROMO again on the domain controller will demote it to a member server. D is incorrect because there is only one correct answer.

9. ☑   D. Domain-naming master. The domain controller holding the domain-naming master role is responsible for keeping track of any additions and deletions of domains in a forest.

☒ **A** is incorrect because the relative ID master role is at the domain level and cannot keep track of forest information such as addition and deletion of domains. **B** is incorrect because the primary domain controller master is also a domain-level role. **C** is incorrect because the schema master role is not responsible for addition and deletion of domains in the forest, although a single domain controller can have both schema and domain-naming master roles.

10. ☑ **C.** Distribute the domainwide roles among two or three domain controllers. The best way to share the load among domain controllers is to distribute the operations master roles among them. However, care must be taken that no two domain controllers are assigned the same role.

☒ **A** is incorrect because taking the domain controller to the forest level is an inappropriate action to resolve the problem. **B** is incorrect because assigning the domainwide roles to other domain controllers means that more than one domain controller will be assigned the same operations master roles, which is not possible. **D** is an inappropriate choice because seizing any role from a domain controller is the last-resort action that is taken only if the server goes down and will not be put back in service again.

11. ☑ **B.** You will not be able to create new objects in Active Directory. The relative ID master role is responsible for assigning domain IDs and object IDs to the new objects that are created in the domain. When the domain controller handling this role is taken offline, you might not be able to create new objects in the domain, such as users, computers, or printers.

☒ **A** is incorrect because there will be no effect on users' normal working methods. **C** is incorrect because the absence of a domain controller with the RID master role will not affect users who log on during this period. **D** is an invalid choice because a correct answer exists.

12. ☑ **B.** Users and Computers. The correct Active Directory console to transfer the infrastructure master role from one domain controller to another is the Users and Computers console. You first need to connect the domain controller that will hold the role, and then use this console to transfer it.

☒ **A** is incorrect because the Schema console is used to view and change the schema master role. **C** is incorrect because the Domains and Trusts console is used to change the domain-naming master role. **D** is an invalid choice because the Sites and Services console cannot be used to transfer any operations master roles.

13. ☑ **A.** Seize the role from this domain controller. The PDC emulator master role is critical for normal operation of the network. If the domain controller goes down for any reason, you must seize the role immediately and assign it to another domain controller.

☒ **B** is incorrect because the domain controller in question has already gone down and is out of the network. It is not possible to transfer the role. Moreover, the PDC emulator role is very critical and must be seized immediately. **C** is an invalid choice because the action suggested is of no use. **D** is incorrect because if you do nothing to reassign the role to another domain controller, normal operation of the network can be affected.

14. ☑ **C.** Reformat the domain controller's hard disk and reinstall Windows 2000 Server. When the RID master role is seized from any domain controller, it must not be put back on the network without formatting its hard drive and reinstalling Windows 2000 on it. This is true for other operations master roles such as schema master and domain-naming master roles, too. Other roles can be seized and given back to the same domain controllers when they are repaired and put back on the network.

☒ **A** is incorrect because reassigning the RID master role to the same domain controller is not recommended. **B** is incorrect because shifting the location of the domain controller to another network segment is also not a resolution to the problem. **D** suggests an incorrect option because the domain controller must not be connected to the network without you first reformatting its hard drive and reinstalling Windows 2000 on it.

Implementing an Organizational Unit Structure

15. ☑ **A, C, and D.** The design of an organizational unit for a company depends on several factors, including the hierarchy of the company, its requirements, and its expected future growth.

☒ **B** is incorrect because the design of an OU is independent of the directors of the company, although they might play an important role in decision making. **E** is an invalid choice because we have only three correct options.

16. ☑ **B and C.** The only two actions that can be performed on a functional organizational unit are that its properties can be changed and it can be moved to another domain.

☒ **A** is incorrect because a functional OU cannot be deleted without affecting the domain. **D** is an invalid choice because there are only two correct answers.

17. ☑ **A.** Users and Computers. The OUs are created and managed from the Users and Computers snap-in of the Active Directory console.

☒ **B, C, and D** are incorrect because none of the consoles given in these answers can be used for creating OUs in a domain.

LAB ANSWER

In the steps given, there are missing as well as incorrect steps. Step 2 suggests you open the Active Directory Domains and Trusts console. This step is incorrect because the transfer of domainwide operations master roles is done from the Active Directory Users and Computers console. Therefore, Step 2 should read:

Click Start | Programs | Administrative Tools, and select Active Directory Users and Computers.

On the other hand, the step to connect to the W2kDom01 domain controller is missing. Before you try to transfer an operations master role to another server, you must first connect from the snap-in to the server to which the role is to be transferred.

Therefore, the following steps must be completed after Step 2 and before Step 3:

- From the Console menu, click Connect to Domain Controller. This choice opens the Connect to Domain dialog box.
- Select W2kDom01 from the Domain box. Click OK.

4

Troubleshooting Active Directory

CERTIFICATION OBJECTIVES

4.01   Back Up and Restore Active
        Directory

✓   Two-Minute Drill

Q&A   Self Test

T his chapter explains the backup and restore procedures for Active Directory. This important chapter introduces you to the Backup Wizard and the Restore Wizard. You will learn about NTBACKUP options and the NTDSUTIL utility. This chapter also introduces you to the components that make up Active Directory (AD).

CERTIFICATION OBJECTIVE 4.01

Back Up and Restore Active Directory

One of the most important tasks as a Windows 2000 network administrator is performing system backups. Unfortunately, this task is underrated and sometimes overlooked by many network administrators. Priority is usually given to other, more visible activities such as upgrades to software that impacts end users. Backup solutions and backup problems are postponed until higher-priority activities are complete. This is not smart administration! Nobody cares about backups until they need a restore. So, if you value your job, perform regular backups, do a restore to save the day, and be a hero in the eyes of upper management. Otherwise, the only hero you will be is the guy flipping burgers for satisfied customers.

exam
Ⓦatch

Because exam 70-217 focuses on skills needed to prepare for and recover from system failure in the Windows 2000 Active Directory, it is imperative that you understand the fundamentals of backing up and restoring Active Directory.

Components and Files that Make Up AD

One of the most important backups you can perform in a Windows 2000 environment is a backup of Active Directory. The importance of AD stems from the abundance of network resources stored within it. These resources, or *objects,* consist of user data, groups, servers, databases, printers, services, computers, and security policies. If AD became corrupt, users might not be able to log on and gain access to printers, servers, and other network resources.

Architecture

Active Directory uses a layered architecture to provide directory services to client applications. The AD architecture consists of three primary services layers and the data store. Above the three service layers are the protocols and application programming interfaces (APIs) that allow clients to interface with directory services. Figure 4-1 shows the Active Directory architecture.

The three primary service layers are as follows:

- Directory System Agent (DSA)
- Database Layer
- Extensible Storage Engine (ESE)

The protocols and APIs for client directory services are:

- LDAP/ADSI
- Messaging API (MAPI)
- Security Accounts Manager (SAM)
- Replication (REPL)

Directory System Agent   The *DSA service layer* builds a hierarchical structure from the parent/child relationships stored in the directory. This layer provides the APIs necessary for directory access calls. Without this layer, for example, clients using LDAP would not be able to gain access to directory services.

Database Layer   The *database layer* provides an interface between client applications and the directory database. This layer prevents client applications from directly accessing the directory database. All application calls must first pass through the database layer. This system prevents bad application calls from adversely impacting the directory database.

Extensible Storage Engine (ESE)   The *Extensible Storage Engine (ESE)* sits between the database layer and the directory data store. It directly accesses individual records in the directory data store based on the relative distinguished name attribute of the object. This is the only layer that directly manipulates the directory data store. The directory data store is located in the \systemroot>\NTDS folder in a file called

NTDS.DIT. This file can be administered with the NTDSUTIL tool on the domain controller. (The NTDSUTIL tool is discussed later in this chapter.) A file named ESENT.DLL is the dynamic link library (DLL) file that controls the ESE. Each request to the DSA is treated as an individual transaction and is recorded to log files associated with the NTDS.DIT file on the domain controller. This means that whenever a user, printer, or server object is added, deleted, or modified, ESE appends an entry to a log file.

LDAP/ADSI   Clients that support LDAP use it to gain access to the DSA. Windows 2000 clients use LDAP, as do Windows 98 and Windows 95 clients with the Active Directory client installed. *LDAP*, or *Lightweight Directory Access Protocol,* is the primary directory access protocol for manipulation of Active Directory information. It defines how directory clients can access a directory server, perform directory operations, and share directory data. The LDAP protocol is used to add, modify, and delete Active Directory information. LDAP is also used to request and retrieve data from Active Directory. Versions 2 and 3 of LDAP are supported by Windows 2000 Active Directory. You can find more information about the two LDAP versions in RFC 1777 for LDAP version 2 and RFC 2251 for LDAP version 3.

ADSI, or *Active Directory Service Interface,* is an API that can be used to access information in Active Directory. The ADSI API set is accessed with programming environments such as Microsoft Visual Basic and Microsoft Visual C++. ADSI allows programmers to design applications that manipulate objects in Active Directory.

Messaging API (MAPI)   *Messaging API,* or *MAPI,* is an API set that is used by applications such as Microsoft Outlook and Microsoft Exchange to send and receive e-mail. MAPI clients connect to the DSA using the MAPI remote procedure call (RPC) address book provider interface. Similar to ADSI, the MAPI API set can be used with programming environments such as Microsoft Visual Basic and Microsoft Visual C++. This flexibility allows programmers to design applications that integrate messaging services with Active Directory objects such as users and groups, for example.

Security Accounts Manager (SAM)   The *SAM,* or *Security Accounts Manager,* is used to authenticate users during login. The SAM is used only by Windows NT 4.0 and earlier clients to gain access to the DSA. By comparison, Windows 2000 clients use LDAP to gain access to the DSA. Additionally, SAM is also used to replicate to and from Windows NT domain controllers in a mixed-mode Active Directory.

Replication (REPL)   *REPL*, or *replication*, is the process that replicates DSA data between domain controllers. When replication occurs, Active Directory DSAs connect to one another using a proprietary RPC. This RPC is the replication transport between DSAs on domain controllers.

Components

Active Directory allows company resources to be accessible from a central and logical location, regardless of physical location. The logical components that make up AD are:

- Domains
- Organizational units (OUs)
- Trees
- Forests

These components relate to each other in a hierarchical manner.

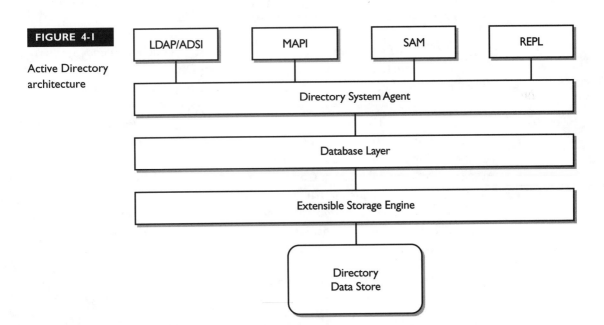

FIGURE 4-1

Active Directory architecture

Domains Administrators of previous Windows operating systems such as Windows NT 4.0 will be familiar with the concept of *domains*. In Active Directory, the domain is the core unit of logical structure. A domain can store literally millions of directory objects, including users, printers, documents, and other network resources. A domain contains only information about objects within it. A domain does not contain information about objects within other domains.

Organizational Units *Organizational units,* or *OUs,* provide a method for subdividing domains into smaller, more manageable pieces. This manageability is achieved by organizing directory objects within a domain into logical groups that are parallel to the functional or business structure of your organization.

Objects that can be contained in an OU are users, groups, printers, file shares, computers, and even other OUs from the same domain. OUs are helpful when you want to delegate administrative responsibility to specific areas of Active Directory. For example, the sales department of your organization might have its own network administrator. Let's assume that the user accounts and sales resources are located in an OU named SALES. The enterprise network administrator could assign administrative authority to the sales network administrator for the SALES OU. This means the sales network administrator would only have administrative control over directory objects for which he or she was responsible.

Trees *Trees* further organize AD by grouping Windows 2000 domains together. To better organize trees, Windows 2000 domains use DNS as the naming system to facilitate a true domain hierarchy. The logical structure of a tree is actually an upside-down tree. In other words, the root is at the top, with the leaves at the bottom. The first domain created is normally the *root,* or *parent domain,* of the tree. For example, corbus-systems.com is the parent domain of Corbus Systems, Inc. Additional domains underneath the root are considered *leaves,* or *child domains.* An example of a child domain at Corbus Systems, Inc., is detroit.corbus-systems.com. Notice that the parent domain name is appended at the end of the child domain name. However, the relative domain name of the child domain is simply detroit. All child domains append the parent domain name to their relative domain name.

All domains within a specific tree share the following:

- **Common schema** Define object types that can be stored within Active Directory.

- **Global catalog** Central repository of object information in the Active Directory tree.

Forests   *Forests* further organize AD by grouping Windows 2000 trees together. Forests can contain multiple AD trees. This is helpful when multiple parent domains need to be created or a company merger takes place. Let's say Corbus Systems, Inc., merged with ACME Corporation. Before the merger, the root of Corbus Systems, Inc., was corbus-systems.com, and the root of ACME Corporation was acme.com. Since the root, or parent, domains of the two merging companies are not contiguous, meaning they do not share a common parent domain, they cannot be added to the same tree. In this case, they both retain their individual tree structure and are added as trees to a common forest within Active Directory.

All trees within a forest share the following:

- Common schema
- Common global catalog

exam
ⓦatch   *Two trees can be merged only if they share a common schema before the merge begins.*

Backing Up Active Directory Components

As you know by now, backing up Active Directory is a very important task. The objects contained within the domains, OUs, trees, and forests are the critical components that must be backed up to ensure recovery in case of Active Directory failure. But before we can attempt a backup, the following tasks must be performed:

- Make sure all files to be backed up are closed.
- Verify that your backup device is on the Windows 2000 Hardware Compatibility List (HCL).
- The backup device should be configured and powered on.
- The proper backup media are inserted properly in the backup device.
- The Task Scheduler service should be running if scheduled backups are to be performed. Otherwise, this is not necessary for backups that will run immediately.

After the preliminary tasks are performed, you can use one of the following two methods for backup:

- Backup Wizard
- NTBACKUP

In addition to the backup tools that ship with Windows 2000, third-party backup utilities such as Veritas Backup Exec 8 can be used to back up Active Directory. More third-party backup utilities will be on the market soon. Third-party utilities are usually more robust than the tools that ship with an operating system.

on the **job**

As companies become increasingly dependent on electronic filing, the need for solid backup procedures becomes imperative. The Windows 2000 backup system is the answer to this growing need.

exam **Watch**

The NTBACKUP command invokes the same Backup Wizard dialog that appears when you choose Start | Programs | Accessories | System Tools.

The Backup Wizard

Windows 2000 improves on previous versions of Windows NT by providing a GUI-based *Backup Wizard* to simplify the backup process. This section steps you through using the Windows 2000 Backup Wizard. The next section covers the command-line backup utility NTBACKUP.

Perform the following steps when performing a backup using the Backup Wizard:

1. Log on to the appropriate domain as a user with administrative rights or in the Backup Operators group, preferably Administrator.

2. Start the Backup program by choosing Start | Programs | Accessories | System Tools | Backup.

3. At the Welcome screen, click the button that corresponds to the Backup Wizard (see Figure 4-2).

4. At the Backup Wizard Welcome screen, click Next.

5. At the What to Back Up screen (see Figure 4-3), click Only Back Up the System State Data. This backs up Active Directory if the server is a domain controller. In addition to AD, the system state data includes the following:

   - SYSVOL directory
   - Windows 2000 registry
   - System boot files
   - Certificate Services database
   - COM+ Class Registration database

FIGURE 4-2

The Backup
Wizard's main
Welcome screen

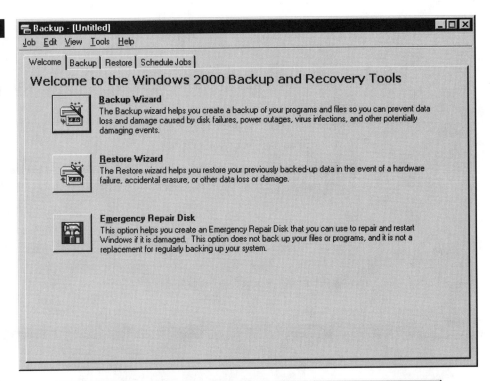

FIGURE 4-3

The What to
Back Up screen

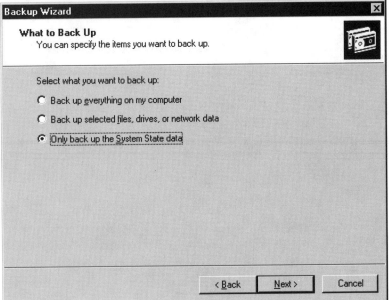

6. You also have the option of manually making your backup selections by clicking the Backup tab. Be sure to click the System State check box (see Figure 4-4).

7. At the Where to Store the Backup screen (see Figure 4-5), you must complete the following fields:

   - **Backup media type**   This is the media type of the target device. This parameter can be a tape or a file.

   - **Backup media or filename**   This is the name of the backup media or the name and path of the target backup file. Backup files can be located on the local hard disk, removable disk, or shared drive.

8. At the Completing the Backup Wizard screen (see Figure 4-6), click Finish to complete the backup job configuration with the default parameters and skip the remaining steps. If you want to change the default parameters, click Advanced and proceed to Step 9.

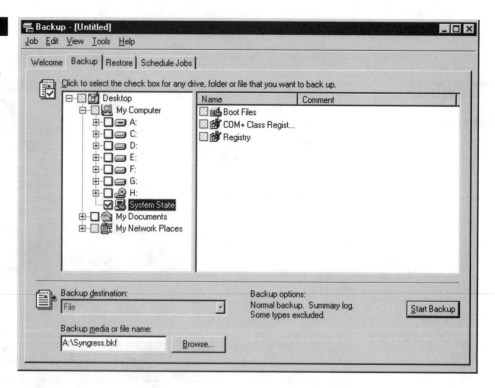

FIGURE 4-4

The manual backup selection screen

FIGURE 4-5

The Where to Store the Backup screen

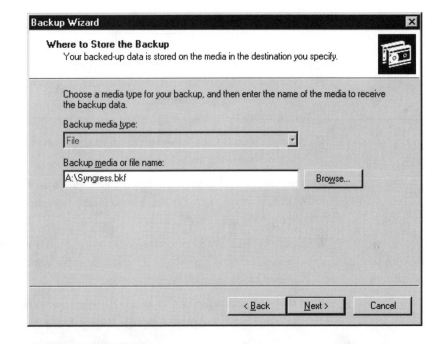

FIGURE 4-6

The Completing the Backup Wizard screen

9. At the Type of Backup screen, select the type of backup operation to be performed for the job. The following list defines the backup types available for selection:

- **Normal**   This option copies all the files that were selected for backup and then resets the archive bit. When the archive bit of a file has been set, the backup system knows that the file has just been created or modified.

- **Copy**   This option copies all the files that were selected for backup but does not reset the archive bit.

- **Incremental**   This option copies all the files that were selected for backup that have the archive bit set. This option resets the archive bit of the files that get copied.

- **Differential**   This option copies all the files that were selected for backup and that have the archive bit set. This option does *not* reset the archive bit of the files that get copied.

- **Daily**   This option copies all the files that were selected for backup and that were modified on the day the backup was performed. The archive bit is *not* reset.

10. At the Type of Backup screen (see Figure 4-7), you also have the option of backing up the contents of files that have migrated to remote storage. This option is selected by clicking the Backup Migrated Remote Storage Data check box. The Remote Storage Service allows infrequently used files to be archived to remote storage, thus saving valuable disk space.

11. Click Next and proceed to the How to Back Up screen.

12. At the How to Back Up screen, click the Verify Data After Backup check box to allow the backup system to verify the backed-up data. This option almost doubles the overall backup time. You should not select this option if you do not have a large enough backup window.

on the
Üob   *Many network administrators have lost their jobs due to corrupt backups. To prevent this from happening to you, always perform backups with the data verification option on. Furthermore, you should perform periodic restores just to be sure that your backups are working properly.*

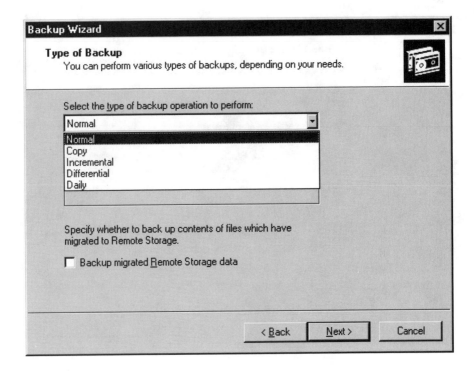

FIGURE 4-7

The Type of
Backup screen

13. At the How to Back Up screen (see Figure 4-8), you can also configure the backup system to use hardware compression, if it is available. As a rule, hardware compression performs better than software compression. This option can be selected by clicking the Use Hardware Compression check box.

14. Click Next to proceed to the Media Options screen.

15. At the Media Options screen, you can instruct the backup system to perform one of the following actions if the archive media already contains backups:

   ■ **Append this backup to the media** Allows you to have multiple backup jobs on a single tape.

   ■ **Replace the data on the media with this backup** Overwrites all previous backup jobs with the current backup job.

FIGURE 4-8

The How to
Back Up screen

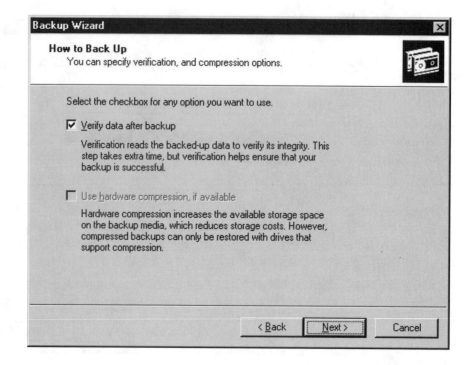

16. Also, at the Media Options screen (see Figure 4-9), you have the option of allowing only the owner and the administrator access to the backup data and any backups appended to the media. This option is selected by clicking the corresponding check box. This option is available only when the Replace option is selected. It should be selected if the backup contains a copy of the AD/system state.

17. At the Backup Label screen (see Figure 4-10), you can provide a name for the following labels:

- **Backup label**   Relate to individual backup jobs on a tape. There can be one or more backup labels per tape.

- **Media label**   Relate to a whole tape. There is only one media label per tape.

FIGURE 4-9

The Media
Options screen

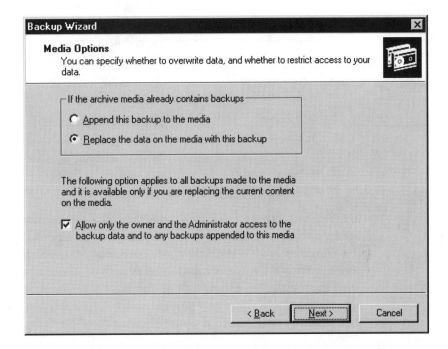

FIGURE 4-10

The Backup
Label screen

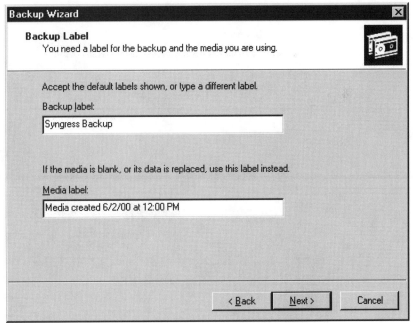

18. At the When to Back Up screen (see Figure 4-11), you are given the option to run the backup job now or schedule it to run later. To run the backup job now, select the Now option. To schedule a time for the backup job to run later, select the Later option. You are then able to configure a name and start date for the job. Click the Set Schedule button to configure the days and times for the backup job to run.

19. Finally, you are returned to the Completing the Backup Wizard screen (see Figure 4-12). If you are satisfied with the options you selected for your backup job, click Finish. If your backup job was configured to run now, it will start immediately. Otherwise, it will start when scheduled.

on the job

In many small companies, an administrative assistant with a limited IT background is responsible for performing network backups. For this reason, the Windows 2000 Backup Wizard is the tool of choice for making backup configuration easy. Unfortunately, this ease of use does not scale well for large companies with hundreds of domain controllers and thousands of clients. For these larger companies, an elaborate backup plan should be implemented and, possibly, a more robust third-party backup utility deployed.

FIGURE 4-11	

The When to Back Up screen

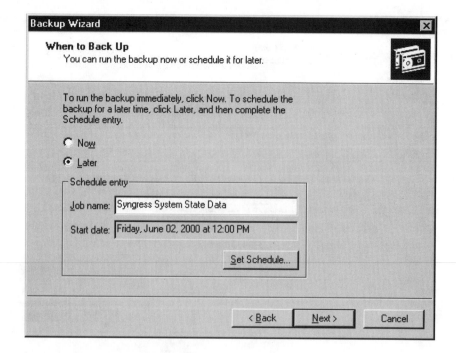

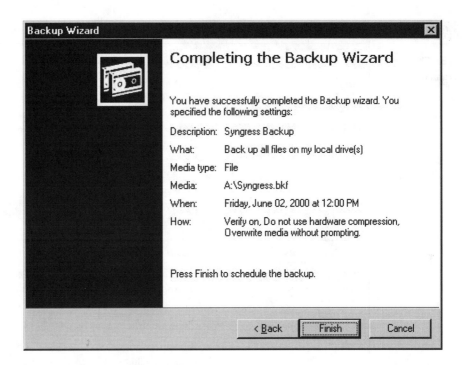

FIGURE 4-12

The final options
of the Completing
the Backup
Wizard screen

NTBACKUP

NTBACKUP is the command-line version of the backup system. It invokes the
same (GUI) Wizard dialog box that appears when you choose Start | Programs |
Accessories | System Tools. The NTBACKUP utility has many parameters of
which you should be aware. To effectively use this utility, you must review these
parameters. With a good understanding of NTBACKUP, you can make powerful
backup scripts using any text editor. NTBACKUP is strictly for backups. It cannot
perform restores of any kind. The NTBACKUP syntax follows:

```
ntbackup backup [systemstate] "bks file name" /J {"job name"}
[/P {"pool name"}] [/G {"guid name"}] [/T { "tape name"}] [/N
{"media name"}] [/F {"file name"}] [/D {"set description"}] [/DS
{"server name"}] [/IS {"server name"}] [/A] [/V:{yes|no}]
[/R:{yes|no}] [/L:{f|s|n}] [/M {backup type}] [/RS:{yes|no}]
[/HC:{on|off}]
```

Table 4-1 describes the NTBACKUP parameters.

TABLE 4-1	Parameter	Description
NTBACKUP Parameters	systemstate	Backs up the system state data.
	bks file name	Specifies the name of the selection information file.
	/J {"*job name*"}	Specifies the name of the backup job.
	/P {"*pool name*"}	Specifies the media pool from which you want to use media. The following switches cannot be used with this option: /A /G /F /T.
	/G {"*guid name*"}	Specifies the name of the tape that this job will overwrite or append to. Do not use with /P.
	/T {"*tape name*"}	Specifies the name of the tape that this job will overwrite or append to. Do not use with /P.
	/N {"*media name*"}	Specifies the new name of the tape. Do not use with /A.
	/F {"*file name*"}	Specifies the logical disk path and filename of the file to which the backup will be copied. The following switches cannot be used with this option: /P /G /T.
	/D {"*set description*"}	Specifies the label name for each backup set.
	/DS {"*server name*"}	Backs up the Directory Service file of the specified Microsoft Exchange Server.
	/IS {"*server name*"}	Backs up the Information Store file of the specified Microsoft Exchange Server.
	/A	Instructs the backup system to perform an append operation. Either /G or /T must be used with this option. Do not use /P with this option.
	/V:{yes|no}	Instructs the backup system to verify files on backup media after backup.
	/R:{yes|no}	Access to this backup is limited to the owner or members of the Administrators group.
	/L:{f|s|n}	Specifies the type of log file to be created during the backup: f: Full (logs every copied file, errors, and other backup events) s: Summary (logs errors and important backup events) n: None (no log file is created)

TABLE 4-1	Parameter	Description
NTBACKUP Parameters *(continued)*	/M {*backup type*}	Specifies the backup type as one of the following: Normal Copy Differential Incremental Daily
	/RS:{yes|no}	Instructs the backup system to back up the removable storage database.
	/HC:{on|off}	Instructs the backup system to use hardware compression.
	/UM	Finds the first available medium, formats it, and uses it for the current backup operation. The following media pools are searched: Free pool, Import pool, Unrecognized pool, and Backup pool. /P must be used with this option. Not applicable to tape loaders, only stand-alone tape devices.

Restoring Active Directory Components

Backups would be meaningless if you were not able to perform a restore from the backed-up data. It is a good practice to periodically perform a restore from backed-up data to verify that your data is being backed up properly. The Verify After Backup option does not catch everything. For example, if your backup selections do not include all the data you want to be backed up, the backup system still runs without error. Remember, it is better to be safe than sorry! So perform that periodic restore and have some peace of mind.

SCENARIO & SOLUTION

I need to create a backup job to run immediately. How do I do that?	Use the Backup Wizard.
How do I run a backup job from a script?	Use NTBACKUP.

Backing Up Active Directory

The following exercise creates a Windows 2000 backup job that backs up Active Directory. The job starts immediately and stores the backup file onto the local hard drive. This exercise should not be done on a production server.

1. Log on to the domain controller as Administrator.

2. Start the backup from the Start menu.

3. At the Welcome screen, select the Backup Wizard.

4. At the Backup Wizard Welcome screen, click Next.

5. At the What to Back Up screen, click Only Back Up the System State Data option.

6. At the Where to Store the Backup screen, select File as the backup media type and give it the filename **Exercise1** on the local hard drive.

7. At the Completing the Backup Wizard screen, click Finish, and watch your backup job in progress.

Performing a Restore of Active Directory

Windows 2000 introduces two restore methods: authoritative and non-authoritative. These two methods will be covered shortly. Before we can perform the actual restore, we must perform the following tasks:

- Log on to the Windows 2000 domain as a member of the Backup Operators or Administrator group.

- Verify that you can access all shares and file locations that require files to be restored.

- Verify that the medium containing the data you want restored is in the backup device.

- Verify that the Remote Storage Manager is running. This is necessary only if you are restoring from a media pool.

e x a m
ⓦ a t c h

Be sure you know the difference between an authoritative restore and a
non-authoritative restore.

What Is a Non-authoritative Restore?

When system state data changes on a domain controller participating in replication, it is given a higher update sequence number than the system state data of other domain controllers. Since the replicating controller's system state data has a higher update sequence number, the other domain controllers in the replication system know that it has the most up-to-date data. The system state data with the highest update sequence number in the Active Directory replication system gets replicated to the other domain controllers participating in replication.

When a non-authoritative restore is performed, the system state data that is restored maintains the same update sequence number it had when it was last backed up. In other words, the domain controller will be restored to its last backup state. So, if your backup is five days old, odds are that other domain controllers have more current system state data with higher update sequence numbers. Once entered back into the replication topology, the domain controller receives any updates made since that backup. This means that your restored data can potentially be overwritten with another domain controller's system state data. This is not an issue when there is only one domain controller, because there are no other domain controllers from which to receive replication updates.

What Is an Authoritative Restore?

What happens if Active Directory becomes corrupt? What happens if, for example, a disgruntled employee deletes an entire Active Directory tree? In such a case, the AD replication system replicates both the corrupt data and the sabotaged data. The quickest way to resolve this problem is to perform a restore. Unfortunately, a non-authoritative restore is overwritten by the unwanted system state data of other domain controllers. The solution is to perform an authoritative restore. An authoritative restore is similar to a non-authoritative restore. The main difference is that an authoritative restore modifies the update sequence number of the restored system state data to have the highest number in the Active Directory replication system. This means that the restored system state data is replicated to all the other domain controllers in the Active Directory replication system. As a result, the corruption of Active Directory is removed from domain controllers receiving the replica.

Performing a Restore

To perform an authoritative restore, you must first perform a non-authoritative restore as follows:

1. Reboot the domain controller that will have its system state data restored. System state data can be restored only on the local computer. Currently, there is no method for performing remote system state data restores.

2. At the screen that allows you to select your operating system, press the F8 key. This brings up the Windows 2000 Advanced Options Menu (see Figure 4-13).

3. Select Directory Services Restore Mode from the Windows 2000 Advanced Options menu. This choice prevents the domain controller from connecting to the network during the restore process (see Figure 4-14).

4. Select Microsoft Windows 2000 Server from the operating system selection screen.

5. Log on to the server as Administrator. Use the password specified during the promotion of the server to DC status, not the domain administrator password.

6. A pop-up box informs you that you are running in Safe mode. Click OK and continue.

7. Select Programs | Accessories | System Tools | Backup from the Windows 2000 Start menu.

FIGURE 4-13

The operating system selection screen

```
Please select the operating system to start:

    Microsoft Windows 2000 Server
Use ↑ and ↓ to move the highlight to your choice.
Press Enter to choose.




For troubleshooting and advanced startup options for Windows 2000, press F8.
```

FIGURE 4-14

The Windows 2000 Advanced Options menu

```
Windows 2000 Advanced Options Menu
Please select an option:

    Safe Mode
    Safe Mode with Networking
    Safe Mode with Command Prompt

    Enable Boot Logging
    Enable VGA Mode
    Last Known Good Configuration
    Directory Services Restore Mode (Windows 2000 domain controllers only)
    Debugging Mode

Use ↑ and ↓ to move the highlight to your choice.
Press Enter to choose.


Press ESCAPE to disable safeboot and boot normally.
```

8. Select the Restore Wizard from the Welcome to the Windows 2000 Backup and Recovery Tools screen.

9. Click Next at the Welcome to the Restore Wizard screen.

10. At the What to Restore screen (see Figure 4-15), select the media and files you want to restore, and click Next.

11. Review the settings you have selected, and click Advanced to modify advanced restore parameters (see Figure 4-16).

12. At the Where to Restore screen (see Figure 4-17), select one of the following locations for the restored data:

   ■ **Original location**   Restores files to their original location, thus replacing corrupted or lost data.

   ■ **Alternate location**   Restores files to a location other than the original. Maintains the file and folder hierarchy. This option requires that a path be specified.

   ■ **Single folder**   Restores all files to a single folder without maintaining the file and folder hierarchy. This option requires that a path be specified.

13. Click Next and proceed to the How to Restore screen.

FIGURE 4-15

The What to
Restore screen

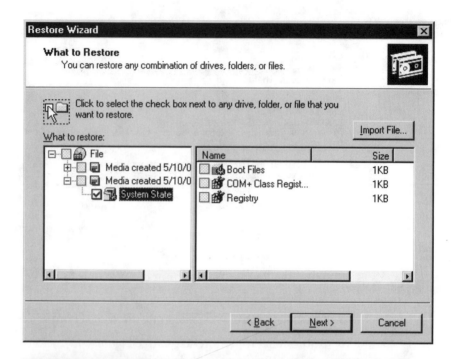

FIGURE 4-16

The Completing
the Restore
Wizard screen

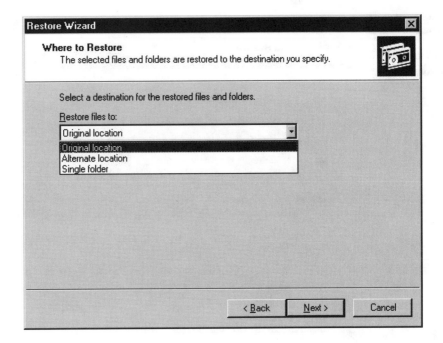

FIGURE 4-17

The Where to
Restore screen

14. At the How to Restore screen (see Figure 4-18), select one of the following options to instruct the Backup system what to do when restoring files that already exist:

- **Do not replace the file on my disk (recommended).** Restores any lost directory components, such as organizational units and leaf objects.

- **Replace the file on disk only if it is older than the backup copy.** Ensures that the most recent copy of the file exists on the computer.

- **Always replace the file on disk.** Replaces files on disk with restored files, even if the files on disk are newer.

15. Click Next and proceed to the Advanced Restore Options screen.

16. At the Advanced Restore Options screen (see Figure 4-19), select from the following restore options you want to use:

- **Restore security.** Applies the original security settings to the files being restored. This option is available only if you are restoring data originally from NTFS to an NTFS partition.

FIGURE 4-18

The How to
Restore screen

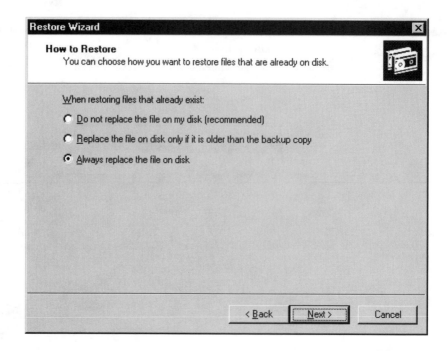

- **Restore Removable Storage Management database.** Restores the media pools and RSM database located in *systemroot*\system32\Ntmsdata.

- **Restore junction points, not the folders and file data they reference.** Restores the junction points needed if drives were mounted in the partition being restored.

17. Click Next, and proceed to the Completing the Restore Wizard screen.

18. At the Completing the Restore Wizard screen (see Figure 4-20), verify your restore settings, and click Finish to start the restore.

To this point, we have been performing a standard non-authoritative restore. The following steps extend the non-authoritative restore and perform an authoritative restore.

19. After the non-authoritative restore (Steps 1–18) completes, reboot your computer and press F8 at the operating system selection screen.

20. Select Directory Services Restore Mode from the Windows 2000 Advanced Startup Options menu.

FIGURE 4-19

The Advanced
Restore Options
screen

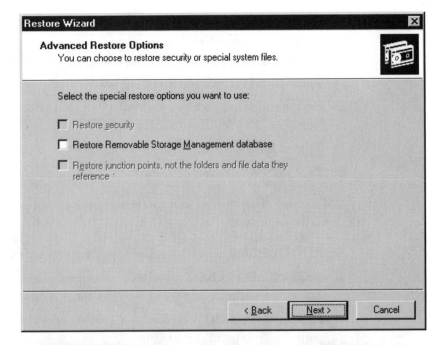

FIGURE 4-20

The final options
of the Completing
the Restore
Wizard screen

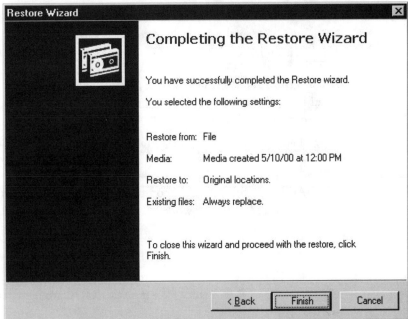

21. Select Windows 2000 Server from the operating system selection screen, and log on as Administrator. Use the password specified during the promotion of the server to DC status, not the domain administrator password.

22. Click OK on the Safe Mode pop-up box.

23. Open a command prompt by selecting Programs | Accessories | Command Prompt from the Start menu.

24. Type **ntdsutil** at the command prompt, and press ENTER.

25. Type **authoritative restore** at the ntdsutil prompt.

At this point, the following four commands are available to you for performing an authoritative restore:

- **RESTORE DATABASE.** Authoritatively restores the entire database.

- **RESTORE DATABASE VERINC** *<version increase>*. Authoritatively restores the entire directory and overrides the version increase.

- **RESTORE SUBTREE** *<subtree distinguished name>*. Restores a select portion or subtree of the directory.

- **RESTORE SUBTREE** *<subtree distinguished name>***VERINC** *<version increase>*. Authoritatively restores directory subtree and overrides the version increase.

The *VERINC option* should be used in situations that require more control over the authoritative restore process. When the VERINC option is not used, the version increase is automatically calculated.

26. Type **quit** to exit Authoritative Restore Mode.

27. Type **quit** again to exit the NTDSUTIL utility.

28. At this point, restart the computer in Normal Mode with the computer connected to the network.

29. This final step ensures the integrity of the computer's group policy. If you are performing an authoritative restore of the entire directory:

- Copy the SYSVOL directory from the alternate location over the existing SYSVOL directory *after* the SYSVOL share has been published.

If you are performing an authoritative restore of a portion of the directory:

■ Copy the policies folder corresponding to the restored objects from the alternate location *after* the SYSVOL share is published to the existing policies location.

exam
Watch *Make sure you know what NTDSUTIL is used for and how to use it. Know the commands associated with this utility.*

Recovering from a System Failure

Total system failure has a way of happening at the most inconvenient time. We could put the blame on Murphy's Law: If anything can go wrong, it will. In other words, if there is a possibility of your production Windows 2000 server crashing while you are on vacation, it will crash. Since you are the network administrator, in this scenario you would be called in from your vacation to get the production server up and running. For this reason, you should always know your options for disaster recovery and have some type of plan or policy in place to ensure that you or your backup can be successful. Some potential causes of system failure are:

■ Hard drive failure

■ Power failure

■ Systems software failure

■ Negligent use of deletion or modification commands

■ Damaging viruses

■ Sabotage

■ Natural disaster

SCENARIO & SOLUTION

How do I perform a non-authoritative restore?	Use Restore Wizard.
How can I perform an authoritative restore?	Use Restore Wizard and NTDSUTIL.

FROM THE CLASSROOM

An Introduction to NTDSUTIL

Like NTBACKUP, NTDSUTIL is a command-line utility for the Windows 2000 Active Directory. In addition to allowing authoritative restores to be performed, NTDSUTIL performs the following functions:

- Database maintenance of the Active Directory store

- Management and control of the flexible single master operations (FSMO)

- Cleaning up metadata left behind by domain controllers that were removed from the network without being properly uninstalled.

The NTDSUTIL utility supports the following menu modes:

- Authoritative restore

- Domain management

- Files

- Metadata cleanup

- Roles

- IPDeny List

- LDAP policies

- Pop-ups

- Security Account Management

- Semantic database analysis

- Help

- Quit

Each of these menu modes contains submenus and commands that facilitate the management of Active Directory. A solid foundation of the NTDSUTIL commands allows you to design powerful scripts that can manipulate the Windows 2000 environment.

—*Damon Merchant, MCSE, CNE, CCDP, CCNP*

Restoring from Backup Media

Restoring from backup media is a common method of recovering from system failure. The key to success, though, is to perform regular backups *before* system failure. In the event of system failure, perform the appropriate restore using the most recent media.

SCENARIO & SOLUTION

What do you do if an entire subtree was deleted from Active Directory from one of many domain controllers that participate in replication?	Perform an authoritative restore of the subtree that was deleted to give the system state data of the domain controller the highest update sequence number in the replication system.
What do you do when Active Directory on the only domain controller on your network becomes corrupt?	Perform a non-authoritative restore, because there will be no other domain controllers to update the restored data with system state with higher update sequence numbers.

Restoring Via a Replica

Another method of recovering from system failure is to let the other domain controllers replicate their data to the failed system. This method assumes that data on other domain controllers is current and accurate. Active Directory replication is covered in greater depth in Chapter 11.

CERTIFICATION SUMMARY

This chapter was designed to help you understand the importance of being prepared for disaster and actually recovering from disaster. Backups were explained for disaster preparation; restores were explained for disaster recovery. This chapter also identified the main components of Active Directory.

You learned about various backup options available for Windows 2000. You learned how to back up Active Directory using the Windows 2000 Backup Wizard. You were also introduced to the NTBACKUP scripting utility.

Restoring AD was also covered in this chapter. You learned how to perform a restore using the Windows 2000 Restore Wizard. You also learned about authoritative restores, which are created by performing a non-authoritative restore and then using the NTDSUTIL utility.

TWO-MINUTE DRILL

Back Up and Restore Active Directory

- ❑ DSA provides APIs for directory access calls.
- ❑ The database layer provides an interface between client applications and the directory database.
- ❑ ESE sits between the database layer and the directory data store.
- ❑ LDAP/ADSI is used to gain directory access.
- ❑ MAPI is used to send and receive e-mail.
- ❑ SAM authenticates users during login.
- ❑ REPL distributes directory trees across domain controllers in different domains within a forest.
- ❑ Logical components of Active Directory consist of domains, organizational units, trees, and forests.
- ❑ Windows 2000 Backup Wizard provides a GUI-based method for backing up Active Directory.
- ❑ System state data consists of the SYSVOL directory, Windows 2000 registry, system boot files, Certificate Services database, and COM+ Class Registration database.
- ❑ Backups can be stored to a file or a tape.
- ❑ A Normal backup copies all selected files and resets the archive bit.
- ❑ A Copy backup copies all selected files and does not reset the archive bit.
- ❑ An Incremental backup copies all selected files that have the archive bit set, and it does reset the archive bit.
- ❑ A Differential backup copies all selected files that have the archive bit set, but it does not reset the archive bit.
- ❑ A Daily backup copies all selected files that were modified on the day of the backup.

❑ The Verify Data After Backup option instructs the backup system to check the files on the media after the backup is complete.

❑ Backups can be scheduled or configured to run immediately from the When to Back Up screen.

❑ The NTBACKUP utility provides parameters that can be used for scripting backup jobs in Windows 2000.

❑ A non-authoritative restore retains the original update sequence numbers of restored data.

❑ An authoritative restore gives restored data the highest update sequence numbers in the Active Directory replication system.

❑ Data can be restored to its original location, an alternate location, or to a single folder.

❑ The NTDSUTIL utility allows you to perform an authoritative restore.

SELF TEST

The following questions will help you measure your understanding of the material presented in this chapter. Read all the choices carefully because there might be more than one correct answer. Choose all correct answers for each question.

Back Up and Restore Active Directory

1. What are the three primary service layers of the Active Directory architecture? Choose all that apply.

   A. Directory System Agent

   B. Database Layer

   C. Extensible Storage Engine

   D. Link Support Layer

2. You are designing an application that allows network administrators to manage Active Directory objects. What API set should you be using?

   A. SAM

   B. TAPI

   C. MAPI

   D. ADSI

3. You are designing an application that will allow users to send and receive e-mail. What API should you be using?

   A. SAM

   B. TAPI

   C. MAPI

   D. ADSI

4. You have Windows NT 4.0 clients that need access to Active Directory. What is used to authenticate them?

   A. SAM

   B. LDAP

   C. MAPI

   D. TAPI

5. Name the logical components that make up Active Directory. Choose all that apply.

    A. Domains

    B. Organizational units

    C. Trees

    D. Forests

6. If the parent domain is named ACME.com and the relative name of the child domain is DAFFY, what is the distinguished domain name of the child domain?

    A. ACME.com

    B. DAFFY

    C. DAFFY.ACME.com

    D. ACME.com.DAFFY

7. All domains within a specific tree share which of the following?

    A. Common schema

    B. Identical users

    C. Global catalog

    D. Identical printers

8. You are about to perform a backup. The backup will run immediately and will not be scheduled. What should you do before starting? Choose all that apply.

    A. Make sure all files to be backed up are closed.

    B. Verify that the backup device is on the Windows 2000 HCL.

    C. Make sure the backup medium is inserted properly in the backup device.

    D. Start the Task Scheduler service.

9. What two methods can be used to back up a Windows 2000 system? Choose all that apply.

    A. Backup Wizard

    B. Restore Wizard

    C. NTBACKUP

    D. NTDSUTIL

10. You have been instructed to back up the system state data. As a result, what information will be backed up? Choose all that apply.

A. SYSVOL directory

B. Windows 2000 registry

C. System boot files

D. Certificate Services database

E. COM+ Class Registration database

11. You are designing a backup strategy. You want to back up all files that were modified on the day of the backup. What option should you use?

A. Daily

B. Normal

C. Incremental

D. Differential

12. What option of NTBACKUP backs up the system state data?

A. /J "systemstate"

B. /N "systemstate"

C. /D "systemstate"

D. systemstate

13. You are performing a restore of data that needs to be updated by other domain controllers in the replication system. What type of restore should you perform?

A. Non-authoritative

B. Authoritative

C. Permissive

D. Passive

14. What key brings up the Windows 2000 Advanced Options Menu from the operating system selection screen?

A. F1

B. F2

C. F6

D. F8

E. F10

15. From the Start menu, what program would you select to run the Restore Wizard?

   A. Programs | Accessories | System Tools | Restore

   B. Programs | Accessories | System Tools | Backup

   C. Programs | Accessories | System Tools | Restore Wizard

   D. Programs | Accessories | System Tools | Backup Wizard

16. What utility allows you to perform an authoritative restore?

   A. NTBACKUP

   B. Backup Wizard

   C. NTDSUTIL

   D. Restore Wizard

17. What command authoritatively restores the entire directory database?

   A. RESTORE DATABASE

   B. DATABASE RESTORE

   C. RESTORE SUBTREE

   D. SUBTREE RESTORE

LAB QUESTION

For this lab exercise, you need access to a Windows 2000 domain controller running Active Directory services. Perform the following tasks and observe the results:

1. Log in to the domain as Administrator.

2. Access Active Directory and create a subtree under the root called LabEx1.

3. Back up the system state data using the Backup Wizard steps described earlier in this chapter.

4. Access Active Directory again and delete the subtree you just created.

5. Reboot the domain controller and press F8 at the operating system selection screen.

6. Select Directory Services Restore Mode from the Windows 2000 Advanced Options menu.

7. Select Microsoft Windows 2000 Server from the operating system selection screen.

8. Log on to Windows 2000 as Administrator.

9. Start the Backup program from the Start menu.

10. Select the Restore Wizard.

11. Step through the Restore Wizard and make sure System State data is selected for restore.

12. Make sure that the data will be restored to its original location and replace any existing files.

13. Restart the domain controller and log on as Administrator.

14. Access the Windows 2000 Active Directory.

What are your observations? How would you take this lab exercise even further and perform an authoritative restore?

SELF TEST ANSWERS

Back Up and Restore Active Directory

1. ☑ **A, B**, and **C**. Directory System Agent, Database Layer, and Extensible Storage Engine are all correct because they combine to make the Active Directory architecture.
   ☒ **D** is incorrect because the Link Support Layer is used by NetWare 3.12 clients to gain access to NetWare 3.12 servers.

2. ☑ **D**. ADSI is an API that allows programmers to write applications that manipulate Active Directory objects.
   ☒ **A** is incorrect because SAM is a security database used by Windows NT 4.0 clients to authenticate to the Active Directory. **B** is incorrect because TAPI is used for designing telephony applications. **C** is incorrect because MAPI is used by messaging applications.

3. ☑ **C**. MAPI is an API used to design messaging applications.
   ☒ **A** is incorrect because SAM is a security database used by Windows NT 4.0 clients to authenticate to Active Directory. **B** is incorrect because TAPI is used for designing telephony applications. **D** is incorrect because ADSI is an API that allows programmers to write applications that manipulate Active Directory objects.

4. ☑ **A**. SAM is used by Windows NT 4.0 clients to authenticate to the Windows 2000 Active Directory.
   ☒ **B** is incorrect because LDAP is used by Windows 2000 clients to authenticate to the Active Directory. **C** is incorrect because MAPI is an API used to design messaging applications. **D** is incorrect because TAPI is an API used to design telephony applications.

5. ☑ **A, B, C**, and **D**. Active Directory is made of domains, organizational units, trees, and forests.

6. ☑ **C**. DAFFY.ACME.com is the correct combination of relative child domain name and parent domain name.
   ☒ **A** is incorrect because ACME.com is the parent domain. **B** is incorrect because DAFFY is the relative name of the child domain. **D** is incorrect because ACME.com.DAFFY is not a valid domain name.

7. ☑ **A** and **C**. Common schema and global catalog are shared by all domains within a specific tree.
   ☒ **B** and **D** are incorrect because each domain contains only information about objects (users and printers) within it.

8. ☑ **A, B, and C.** Closing files to be backed up, verifying that the backup device is on the Windows 2000 HCL, and making sure the backup medium is inserted properly in the backup device are all tasks that should all be performed before starting a backup.
   ☒ **D** is incorrect because the Task Scheduler service is necessary only for scheduled backup jobs. This is not a scheduled backup.

9. ☑ **A and C.** Backup Wizard and NTBACKUP use the backup system to perform backups.
   ☒ **B and D** are incorrect because Restore Wizard and NTDSUTIL are used to perform restores.

10. ☑ **A, B, C, D, and E.** All the answers are correct because they are all included in the system state data.

11. ☑ **A.** The Daily option backs up all files that were modified on the day of the backup.
    ☒ **B** is incorrect because the Normal option backs up all files and resets the archive bit. **C** is incorrect because the Incremental option backs up all files that have the archive bit set and resets the archive bit. **D** is incorrect because the Differential option backs up all files that have the archive bit set, without resetting the archive bit.

12. ☑ **D.** The systemstate parameter instructs the backup system to back up the system state data.
    ☒ **A** is incorrect because /J "systemstate" names the backup job "systemstate." **B** is incorrect because /N "systemstate" names the tape "systemstate." **C** is incorrect because /D "systemstate" labels the backup set "systemstate."

13. ☑ **A.** A non-authoritative restore retains the original update sequence numbers, which allow more recent data from other domain controllers to update the restored data.
    ☒ **B** is incorrect because authoritative restores give the restored data the highest update sequence numbers in the replication system, which causes the restored data to be replicated to all the domain controllers in the replication system. **C and D** are both incorrect because there are no backups called Permissive or Passive in Windows 2000.

14. ☑ **D.** F8 brings up the Windows 2000 Advanced Options Menu.
    ☒ **A, B, C, and E** are incorrect because F1, F2, F6, and F10 have no function at the operating system selection screen.

15. ☑ **B.** Programs | Accessories | System Tools | Backup brings up the Welcome screen that allows you to select the Restore Wizard.
    ☒ **A, C, and D** are all incorrect because they do not exist in the Start menu.

16. ☑ C. NTDSUTIL is a command-line utility that allows you to perform an authoritative restore.

☒ A is incorrect because NTBACKUP is a command-line utility used to perform backups. B is incorrect because the Backup Wizard is a GUI-based interface that allows you to perform backups. D is incorrect because the Restore Wizard is a GUI-based interface that allows you to perform non-authoritative restores.

17. ☑ A. RESTORE DATABASE is an NTDSUTIL command that instructs the system to perform an authoritative restore of the entire directory database.

☒ B and D are incorrect because DATABASE RESTORE and SUBTREE RESTORE are invalid commands. C is incorrect because RESTORE SUBTREE is an NTDSUTIL command that instructs the system to perform an authoritative restore only on a subtree of the directory.

LAB ANSWER

You should see the LabEx1 subtree under the root. The restore of the system state data put the deleted subtree back into the Active Directory. If you had to perform an authoritative restore, you would additionally use the NTDSUTIL command RESTORE SUBTREE LabEx1.

5

Domain Name Service for Active Directory

CERTIFICATION OBJECTIVES

5.01   Installing, Configuring, and
        Troubleshooting Domain Name
        Service for Active Directory

5.02   Managing, Monitoring, and
        Troubleshooting Domain Name
        Service

✓   Two-Minute Drill

Q&A   Self Test

I f you're unfamiliar with the concept of the Domain Name System (DNS), don't worry. You've probably already benefited from DNS and didn't even realize it. DNS has been a vital component of the Internet for decades. As we'll see, with Windows 2000 Server, DNS is an integral part of Active Directory.

DNS is analogous to a telephone book. It maps computer names to IP addresses, and vice versa. When you want to find a person's telephone number, you look in the phone book, see the person's name, and cross-reference it to the person's phone number. Using DNS, a host computer contacts a DNS server when it wants to find a computer, and the server provides the IP address that identifies this computer on a TCP/IP network. The best example of this process is when you enter the address of a Web site into your browser. You enter the name of a site, and a DNS server provides an IP address, which your browser then uses to connect to that site. On a network, a computer uses DNS running on a Windows 2000 server to resolve the name of a computer it needs to contact.

In this chapter, we discuss the importance of DNS on a Windows 2000 network that uses Active Directory. We show you how to install DNS on Windows 2000 Server, and we see how to configure, manage, and monitor DNS and discuss what you can do to troubleshoot problems that could result.

CERTIFICATION OBJECTIVE 5.01

Installing, Configuring, and Troubleshooting Domain Name Service for Active Directory

In this section, we discuss how to install, configure, and troubleshoot DNS for Active Directory. You learn how DNS can be installed, as well as the importance and function of zones, dynamic updates, and more. We also talk about interoperability issues and show you how to integrate Active Directory DNS with non-Active Directory DNS. In doing so, we discuss the Berkeley Internet Name Domain (which is also referred to by the acronym BIND), MS-DNS, and non-MS DNS servers.

Before jumping ahead to installing DNS on your Windows 2000 server, you need to understand what DNS is and why it's important to your network. So let's review how DNS works.

Understanding Domain Name Service

To understand the importance of DNS name resolution, it's best to look at how DNS came into play on networks. The origins of DNS reside in the evolution of the Internet. In the late 1970s, when the Internet was ARPANET—a network developed by the Department of Defense's Advance Research Project Agency—it consisted of several hundred computers. ARPANET resolved computer names to IP addresses through a file called HOSTS.TXT, which was updated every week or so with new names and addresses. The file resided on a computer at the Stanford Research Institute's Network Research Center (SRI-NIC), and other computers copied the file from SRI-NIC as needed.

As the number of computers in ARPANET increased, this method of name resolution became problematic. The HOSTS.TXT file became larger and larger, taking more time to copy from SRI-NIC, and needed to be updated daily. Because all network traffic had to go through SRI-NIC, it became a bottleneck. To deal with these and other problems, the Domain Name System was created.

At this point, you might be wondering what these issues on the Internet have to do with your local area network (LAN). However, LANs experience similar issues to what occurred with ARPANET. To resolve names, a network could use a file called HOSTS. On a Windows 2000 machine, this file can be found in the folder \%Systemroot%\ System32\Drivers\Etc. HOSTS is a local text file that can be used for name resolution. Each line of the HOSTS file contains an IP address, followed by one or more machine names. When the local computer needs to find a particular server, it can look at this file to find the host's name, and cross-reference it with the IP address that identifies it on the network. However, as new servers are added to the network, you would need to either copy an updated HOSTS file to each computer or go to every computer on the network and modify this file. Should a computer not receive the updated HOSTS file, it wouldn't be able to find the new server. If there is a large or increasing number of computers on your network, this can be a daunting task—similar problems to ARPANET's, with the same solution: Domain Name System.

DNS stores the names and IP addresses of computers in a distributed database. It also uses a client/server model for name resolution. Computers on a network contact a DNS server to resolve names to IP addresses, and vice versa. Later in this chapter, we explore how DNS resolves these names and IP addresses.

Overview of Active Directory and Domain Name Service Interoperability

Active Directory and DNS are tightly integrated in Windows 2000 Server. This is due to the incorporation of namespaces into Active Directory. In DNS, a namespace is a vertical or hierarchical structure that outlines the domains, subdomains, and hosts making up the domain namespace tree.

The domain namespace is generally referred to as a *tree*, with smaller elements branching off larger ones. In other words, as shown in Figure 5-1, domain names can include hosts and other domains, which together make up their fully qualified domain names. For example, a domain called exampledns.com might include computers such as ftp.exampledns.com or subdomains such as finance.exampledns.com. Subdomains might also include host names, identifying specific host computers. For example, a computer called NTSERVER in the finance subdomain of exampledns.com appears with the structure ntserver.finance.exampledns.com.

FIGURE 5-1

Domains can contain subdomains and hosts

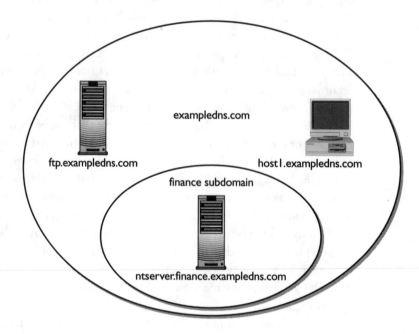

exampledns.com

ftp.exampledns.com

host1.exampledns.com

finance subdomain

ntserver.finance.exampledns.com

The main part of the domain namespace consists of top-level domains. These top-level domains are identified by the suffixes in which they end. These include

- **com**   Commercial organizations.
- **edu**   Educational institutions and universities.
- **org**   Nonprofit organizations.
- **net**   Networks (i.e., Internet backbone).
- **gov**   Government agencies that are not part of the military.
- **num**   Phone numbers.
- **arpa**   Reverse DNS (explained later in this chapter).
- *xx*   Country codes consisting of two letters. For example, a Canadian domain might end in .ca.

Branching off top-level domains are second-level domains. Second-level domains can consist of hosts and subdomains. As mentioned, subdomains are domains within a domain, whereas hosts are computers within a specific domain or subdomain.

Because Active Directory uses the Internet concept of namespaces, it requires DNS. If DNS wasn't installed and configured, Active Directory would be unable to work as expected. This is because Active Directory uses DNS as its domain naming and location service. Domain names in Windows 2000 are also DNS names, and DNS name resolution is needed on a network to locate Windows 2000 domain controllers.

In the domain name system, the namespace is a logical representation of your network and its resources. Upon installing DNS, you have the option of dividing up these namespaces into "zones." Although the namespace represents the logical structure of network resources, zones are used to provide physical storage of resources. In calling it "physical storage," we're obviously not referring to a closet or an area of an office where you keep the server. In DNS, name servers store information for resolving names in a hierarchical database. In this database, there can be subtrees called *zones*. These zones act as administrative units. Much the same way that you can manage files on a hard disk by organizing them into folders, you can manage resources in DNS using zones. Zones can consist of a domain or a domain with subdomains; and as we see later in this chapter, they are an important part of the Windows 2000 DNS Server.

Installing Domain Name Service

With Microsoft, all roads lead to Rome. In other words, Microsoft provides multiple ways for installing DNS on a Windows 2000 server. As we see in this section, you can install DNS when you install or upgrade to Windows 2000 Server. You can also install DNS separately as part of the process of installing Active Directory and promoting a server to the role of domain controller.

DNS needs to be installed on a Windows 2000 Server when it is the only server on a network and the server is acting as the domain controller. It also needs to be installed when a Windows 2000 Server computer is promoted to domain controller and should be installed if you expect to promote a server to domain controller in the future. The exception is when existing DNS servers—such as those running BIND—are used on a network. As we see later in this chapter, if existing DNS servers are running on your network, you don't necessarily need to install DNS on a domain controller.

on the
job

You can also install DNS on multiple Windows 2000 servers in your network as part of a redundancy or fault-tolerance plan. If one server goes down, the other server can still provide DNS services to the network or that particular subnet.

You can install DNS during your setup of Windows 2000 Server. From the screen in which you select the components to install with Windows 2000 Server, select the Networking Services component, and then click the button labeled Details. This displays a listing of various network-related services and protocols. In this listing, you'll see a subcomponent labeled Domain Name System (DNS). By clicking the check box beside this entry, a check mark appears in the box. This mark indicates that you've selected DNS to be installed with Windows 2000 Server. Clicking OK confirms this selection and returns you to the previous menu. Clicking the Next button continues you on your way to installing Windows 2000 Server with DNS.

Once all the files have been copied onto your system and Windows 2000 Server starts for the first time, you will be asked if you want to configure your server. The Configure Your Server dialog box, shown in Figure 5-2, offers you three choices:

- This is the only server in my network.

- One or more servers are already running on my network.

- I will configure this server later.

FIGURE 5-2

The Configure
Your Server
dialog box

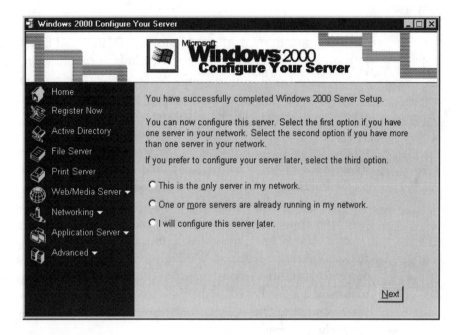

What occurs next depends on which of these items you select.

If you select "This is the only server in my network," and click Next, Windows automatically configures your server as a domain controller and sets up Active Directory, DHCP, and DNS on your network. It does this because these are core services of a Windows 2000 network.

If you select "One or more servers are already running on my network," it is assumed that you already have a server running on your network. You can select the services you want to run on this server from the menu on the left. If you select Networking, a submenu of several networking components appears. In this listing, you'll see DNS. By clicking this item, you see information on DNS and a hyperlink that launches Microsoft Management Console with the DNS snap-in. This snap-in is used to manage DNS and is a topic we discuss later in this chapter.

If you select "I will configure this server later," you can exit the configuration process and configure the server at a later time. If you select this option, you can start the configuration process later by selecting Configure Your Server from the Administrative Tools folder found under Programs on the Windows Start menu.

If you select "This is the only server in my network," and click Next, you see a screen informing you that Active Directory, DHCP, and DNS will automatically be configured on the server. Several hyperlinks are available on this screen; these hyperlinks can be clicked to display help on these aforementioned items. Clicking Next again displays a screen that requires you to enter information to set up your server as a domain controller. Here you enter the name of your domain. This might be a group name, such as Finance. You are also prompted for your registered name on the Internet. This is something like www.<*yourdomainname*>.com, where <*yourdomainname*> is the name of your domain. If you haven't registered a name on the Internet, you just type the word **local**.

Clicking Next displays a screen telling you that upon clicking the Next button, Windows invokes a wizard that installs and configures the components previously selected. After copying the necessary files and configuring these components, the Active Directory Installation Wizard runs in unattended mode and Windows 2000 Server reboots. After rebooting, the Configure Server screen appears, allowing you to manage and further configure these services. This is the same screen that appears when you select "One or more servers are already running on my network" from the server choices screen.

If you didn't install DNS when you installed your Windows 2000 Server, don't worry. DNS can be installed through Add/Remove Programs. This is an applet found in the Control Panel that can be used to install various Windows components.

When you open Add/Remove Programs, you see a dialog box with three buttons on the left-hand side. These are

- Change or Remove Programs, which is used to add or remove applications such as Microsoft Office
- Add New Programs, which displays options to install applications from a CD or floppy disk or from the Windows Update Web site
- Add/Remove Windows Components, which allows you to install or uninstall components that were offered when you initially set up Windows 2000 Server

Because DNS is a component of the Windows 2000 Server operating system, you would click the Add/Remove Windows Components option to install DNS. Upon doing so, the Windows Components Wizard, similar to that shown in Figure 5-3, would appear.

When you select the component labeled Networking Services and click the Details button, a listing of various services is displayed. In this listing of subcomponents, you will see an item labeled Domain Name System (DNS). Beside the entry is a check box. If this check box appears with a check mark in it, DNS is already installed. However, if no check mark appears, you need to click the check box to select DNS to be installed. Click OK to confirm your choice to install DNS.

This brings you back to the Windows Components Wizard. Click the Next button to continue. The screen that appears next, called Configuring Components, is where DNS—and any other components selected—is installed and configured. Once completed, a new screen appears stating that installation is complete. Click the Finish button to end the installation process.

FIGURE 5-3

The Windows
Components
Wizard

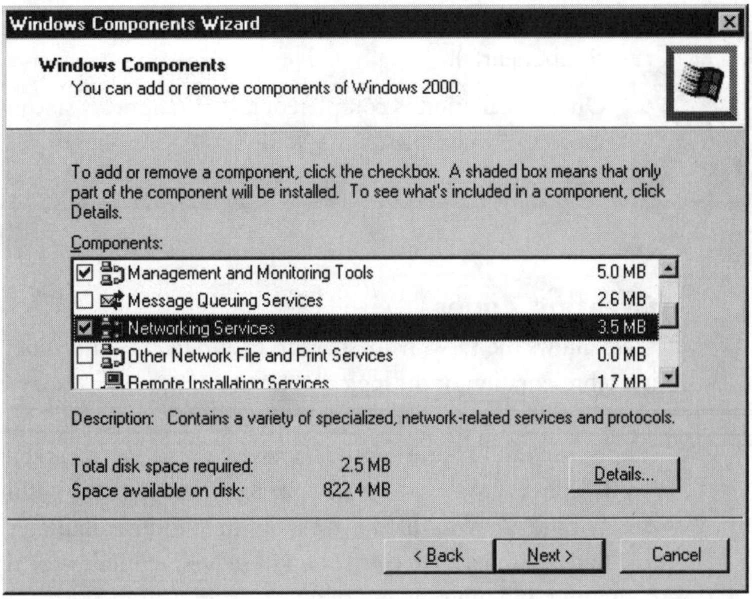

CertCam 5-1

EXERCISE 5-1

Installing DNS

1. From the Windows Start menu, select Settings, and then click Control Panel. When the Control Panel folder opens, double-click Add/Remove Programs.

2. On the left side of the dialog box that appears, click Add/Remove Windows Components.

3. When the Windows Components Wizard appears, select Networking Services from the listing of available components to install, and then click the Details button.

4. From the listing of subcomponents that appears, find the entry called Domain Name System (DNS). If a check mark appears in the check box beside this entry, click Cancel in each dialog box. The check mark indicates it is already installed. If no check mark appears, click the check box to select it, and click OK.

5. Click Next to allow the wizard to install and configure the selected component(s).

6. Once installation is completed, a screen appears stating that you have successfully completed the Windows Components Wizard. Click Finish.

Creating Zones

DNS allows the DNS namespace to be broken up into zones. The DNS namespace is a representation of the logical structure of network resources, whereas zones act as organizational units of this representation. A zone is a domain or a domain with subdomains and appears in the hierarchy of the DNS database as a subtree. In other words, zones allow you to store your resources logically within the namespace. If you think of the way your hard drive looks in Windows Explorer, a zone is analogous to a folder. Rather than containing files, DNS contains the names and addresses of computers and other necessary information. In DNS, a zone stores information about DNS domains and acts as the authoritative source of information about domains.

To find these resources, *lookup zones* can be created. There are two different types of lookup zones that can be used in DNS. They are

- Forward lookup zones, which allow you to make forward lookup queries
- Reverse lookup zones, which allow you to make reverse lookup queries

These zones are used to find resources on the network when a query is made to a DNS server and are explained in this section.

Forward lookup queries resolve a name to an IP address, and forward lookup zones are used to make these queries possible. A forward lookup query is the type of query most often performed by DNS. A computer asks the name server where a computer is located on a network by asking for its IP address. You'll remember that an IP address identifies each host computer running TCP/IP on the network. An example of an IP address is 197.200.10.1. You can break this address down into two parts:

- **Network ID, which is also called the network address.** This is used to identify a segment of the network within larger TCP/IP networks. For example, the network ID of 197.200.10.1 might be 197.200. This section of the IP address identifies that section of the network in a larger network.

- **Host ID, which is also called the host address.** This identifies a server, host computer, router, or TCP/IP device in a network. Each workstation, server, or the like must have a unique host ID or conflicts will occur on the network. For example, the host ID of 197.200.20.1 might be 20.1.

When a forward lookup query is made, an attempt is made to by the local name server to resolve the name to an IP address. If the name server can't resolve the query, it passes the query to other name servers for resolution.

To illustrate what happens, let's say a client has queried a forward lookup for ftp.thislan.net. The computer that is querying the name server is outside this zone, so this is one way in which it happens:

1. The client passes the query for the FTP server named to its local name server.

2. The name server checks its zone database but cannot find the name-to-address mapping for this computer name. Since the DNS server doesn't have authority over the zone called thislan.net, it passes the query to a DNS root server.

3. The local name server passes the query to a net name server, which responds by referring the local name server to the name servers in thislan.net.

4. The local name server sends a request to the name server at thislan.net. Since this name server has authority over the thislan.net zone, it returns the IP address for the FTP server.

5. The local name server responds to the client computer (which initially made the query) by sending the IP address for the computer called ftp.thislan.net. Now that the name has been resolved, the client can now connect to the FTP server.

A name server cannot resolve a query for a host in a zone over which it doesn't have authority. If a name server can't resolve a query, it passes the query to other name servers. The local name server then caches the results to reduce traffic, should the same name resolution be required in the future.

Just as forward lookup zones enable forward lookup queries, reverse lookup zones enable *reverse lookup queries,* which are used to resolve an IP address to a name. However, reverse lookup queries are performed somewhat differently than forward lookup queries. The DNS database is indexed by name rather than IP address, so name servers would bog down if they attempted looking through every domain name in numerous DNS servers to find to whom an IP address belonged. To deal with the need of resolving IP addresses to names, a special domain called in-addr.arpa was created for DNS. Like other domains, in-addr.arpa follows a hierarchical naming scheme, but it is based on IP addresses rather than names.

The way the in-addr.arpa domain is set up is the reverse of other domains in DNS. The subdomains do not have names but are named after numbers in an IP address, and the order of octets in the IP address is reversed. For example, if a network had the network ID of 200.100.10., it would be reversed into 10.100.200.in-addr.arpa. The reason for this reversal is that IP addresses get more specific from left to right, and domain names get less specific from left to right. By reversing the octets, the speed of a search is increased.

exam
Ⓦatch

Remember, name servers have authority over certain zones. One name server might have authority over one particular zone while other name servers would have authority over other zones. If a name server can't resolve a query, it passes the query to other name servers. The local name server then caches the results to reduce traffic, should the same name resolution be required in the future.

There are several ways to create zones for DNS on a Windows 2000 server. When a server is installed as or promoted to domain controller, the option is given to install DNS and add new zones automatically as part of the installation of Active Directory. When you elect to install and configure DNS using the Active Directory Installation Wizard, new zones are created based on the DNS name you gave during the process of installing or promoting the server to a domain controller. This isn't to say that the computer must be a domain controller to be a DNS server. You can install DNS on any Windows 2000 server, and—as we see in the paragraphs that follow—set up new zones through the DNS Console.

Once Active Directory and DNS have been installed, zones are created using DNS Console. DNS Console is the Microsoft Management Console (MMC) with the DNS snap-in. You can start MMC with the DNS snap-in in one of several ways:

- The easiest method is to click the DNS item found in Programs | Administrative Tools on the Windows Start menu. This step starts the DNS Console.

- In Configure Your Server, which is available in Programs | Administrative Tools on the Windows Start menu, select Networking from the menu on the left. This choice expands a listing of components to configure. Click DNS in this listing, and then click the hyperlink for Manage DNS.

- From the Windows Start menu, click the Run command; then type **MMC**, and press OK. This sequence starts the Microsoft Management Console. From the Console menu, click Add/Remove Snap-in to bring up a new dialog box. On the Standalone tab, click the Add button to display a list of available snap-ins. Select DNS from the listing, and then click the Add button. Click Close to exit this listing, and then click OK.

Once DNS Console (Microsoft Management Console with the DNS snap-in) has started, you are ready to begin creating new zones.

When you start this program, you see a screen similar to that shown in Figure 5-4. The name of the DNS server on your system appears in the left window. To configure your DNS server, right-click the DNS server name, and choose "Configure the server" from the context menu that appears. This choice starts the Configure DNS Server Wizard. It is important to note that if a server has been promoted and DNS is already configured, this wizard is unavailable. It is available only for unconfigured DNS servers. To set up new zones on a configured DNS server, you would use the New Zone Wizard, which is explained later in this chapter.

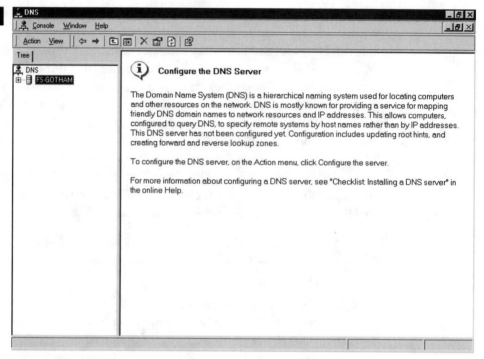

FIGURE 5-4

Microsoft
Management
Server with DNS
Snap-in

The first screen of the wizard is an introduction screen. Clicking the Next button displays a screen that asks you if you would like to create a forward lookup zone now or create one later using the New Zone Wizard (discussed later). Two options appear on this screen. The first is "Yes, create a forward lookup zone." If this is selected and you click the Next button, you continue through the configuration process. The second option is "No, do not create a forward lookup zone." If you select this option and click Next, you reach the end of the configuration wizard.

If you choose to set up a forward lookup zone, the next screen you see asks you the type of zone you want to create. There are three types of zones you can choose to configure:

■ Active Directory-integrated

■ Standard primary

■ Standard secondary

The type of zone chosen determines how Windows 2000 Server obtains and stores zone information.

When *Active Directory-integrated* is chosen as the zone type, a master copy of the new zone is created and integrated in Active Directory. Information on the zone is stored in Active Directory. We discuss this zone type in greater detail later in this chapter.

Standard primary is the second option on this screen. When selected as the zone type, a master copy of the new zone is also created. However, unlike the previous type, the data is stored in a text file. This allows you to exchange DNS data with other DNS servers that use text-based storage methods.

Standard secondary is a zone type that creates a replica of the existing zone and stores this data in a read-only, standard text file. If this option is chosen, clicking the Next button displays a screen that asks you for the name of the new zone. After entering the name and clicking Next, you must then specify the DNS server or servers from which to copy the zone. To do this, you need to enter the IP address of each server you want to copy the zone. Clicking Next brings you to the final screen of the wizard. Clicking Finish confirms your settings and creates a replica of the existing zone.

If you select standard primary as the zone type, clicking Next asks you to enter the name of the new zone. After entering the name, clicking Next gives you the option of creating a new zone file or using an existing one from another computer. The zone file is the filename of the database that contains information about this zone. Zone files have the extension .DNS. If you would like to use an existing file, you can select an option on this screen and enter the filename. To use such a file, you must first place it in the %systemroot%\system32\dns folder on the server that is running DNS. If you would like to use a file that's currently located on a BIND server—explained later in this chapter—you need to change its extension to .DNS and then copy it into the aforementioned directory on the DNS server.

Clicking Next, you see a screen that asks if you'd like to create a reverse lookup zone. As when you were asked about creating a forward lookup zone, you have two options:

- Yes, create a reverse lookup zone
- No, do not create a reverse lookup zone

If you choose not to create a reverse lookup zone, clicking Next brings you to the final screen of the wizard. Choosing to create one and clicking Next displays additional screens asking you to provide information. As we go through them, you'll see that many are the same as those seen when making forward lookup zones.

The first screen we see, after electing to create a reverse lookup zone and clicking Next, asks the type of zone to create. The zones offered as choices here are the same as those we discussed for a forward lookup zone.

Regardless of which type you choose to create, the next screen asks you to identify the reverse lookup zone by entering the network ID or name of the zone. After you provide this information, clicking Next allows you to enter the name for the zone file. The default name for this file is the network ID you entered previously, followed by in-addr.arpa.dns. You'll remember that a domain with in-addr.arpa is used for reverse lookups. On this screen, you can also use an existing file. To use such a file, you must first place it in the %systemroot%\system32\dns folder on the server that is running DNS.

Clicking Next brings you to the end of the wizard. You can click Cancel to discard the work you've done. Clicking Finish creates the new zones.

Once you've configured your DNS server, you can still add zones. In DNS Console, right-click the DNS server appearing in the left window of the console. When the context menu appears, select the item called New Zone. This choice starts the New Zone Wizard and takes you through the same process of installing new zones that was previously discussed. Should you want to create a new forward lookup zone, you can right-click the Forward Lookup Zone folder, and select New Zone. The New Zone Wizard starts, taking you through the process of creating only a forward lookup zone. Should you want to create a new reverse lookup zone, you can right-click the Reverse Lookup Zone folder, and select New Zone. This choice takes you through creating only a reverse lookup zone.

Switching to Active Directory-Integrated Zones

As mentioned earlier in this chapter, Active Directory-integrated zones can be created when you configure your DNS server or using the New Zone Wizard. When Active Directory-integrated is chosen as the zone type, a master copy of the new zone is created and integrated in Active Directory, and information on the zone is stored in Active Directory.

There are a number of differences between Active Directory-integrated zones and standard zones. Among these differences are the ways they perform updates. In an Active Directory-integrated zone, updates to DNS are performed using a multimaster update model. What this means is that any DNS server with authority over the zone is an authoritative source for the zone. A master copy of zone information is stored in Active Directory. Since Active Directory is fully replicated to every domain controller on the network, every DNS server has a duplicate of the data. Each time a zone is added, these zones are replicated to other domain controllers automatically, if they are of type Active Directory-integrated. If a DNS server goes down, any domain controller with DNS can perform updates and process requests from clients to perform updates.

In a standard zone, DNS updates are performed using a *single-master update model*. In this model, a single DNS server acts as the primary authoritative source for the zone. It maintains a master copy of the zone, and other secondary servers send requests to update their copies of the database. If the primary server experiences problems and becomes unavailable, these updates can't be processed.

Another difference between these types of zones deals with replication schedules. In an Active Directory-integrated zone, separate replication scenarios don't need to be maintained, since Active Directory and DNS data are replicated together according to the schedules and rules attributed to Active Directory replication. In standard zones, data needs to be replicated independently of Active Directory data. This means that—in non-Active Directory-integrated zones—you need to maintain two replication schedules: one for Active Directory and another for DNS data.

exam
ⓌatcH

Be aware of the differences between Active Directory-integrated zones and standard (non-Active Directory-integrated) zones. This knowledge will not only help you in the exam, it will give you a better idea of which zone type to use on your own network.

After reviewing the differences between Active Directory-integrated and standard DNS, you might decide at some point to switch from non-integrated to Active Directory-integrated. This switch is often made when considering the need for redundancy. To eliminate a single point of failure, additional DNS servers are added to a network. Rather than adding secondary standard servers to a network, you might want to convert your existing primary standard server. When a DNS server is Active Directory-integrated, changes to a zone on one server are replicated to other servers. As we see later in this chapter, this functionality eliminates the need for a zone transfer (i.e., replicating data from a primary standard server to secondary servers on the network).

To change a zone type, you use the DNS Console. In the tree pane (the left pane), select the zone you would like to convert. You then right-click the zone and select Properties from the context menu, or you can select Properties from the Action menu. On the General tab of the zone's properties, the top section indicates the status of the zone (i.e., whether it is running or paused). Below this, you see the zone type for this particular zone. This type indicates whether the zone is standard primary, standard secondary, or Active Directory-integrated. To the right of this, you see a button labeled Change.

Changing the zone type is done through the Change Zone Type dialog box, which is displayed when you click the Change button. The dialog box that appears has three options. The first allows you to change the zone type to Active Directory-integrated so that zone data is saved in Active Directory. The second option is to change the zone to standard primary, which stores the zone data in a text file. The third option is to change the zone to standard secondary, which copies an existing zone to this server. By selecting Active Directory-integrated, you convert your primary or secondary zone to Active Directory-integrated. Clicking OK confirms your selection and converts the zone.

Integrating Active Directory Domain Name Service with a Non-Active Directory Domain Name Service

With all the discussion of Active Directory DNS, you might think that the DNS that comes with Windows 2000 Server is the only DNS around. When you consider that a majority of name servers on the Internet run UNIX machines, as well as the number of large organizations running UNIX and BIND, this is clearly not the case. For this reason, there is an obvious need for Active Directory DNS to be compatible and interoperable with non-Active Directory DNS environments.

Overview of Berkeley Internet Name Domain

BIND, an acronym for the Berkeley Internet Name Domain, is an implementation of DNS that is written for UNIX machines. Windows 2000 DNS server works with BIND, but certain considerations need to be taken into account when mixing these systems.

A major issue when mixing environments deals with zone transfers. Zone transfers occur when DNS servers exchange their data so that information about the zone is synchronized. By default, zone transfers are performed using a *fast zone transfer* format. This format uses compression and allows multiple records to be sent in TCP messages. More recent versions of BIND are capable of handling this format. The problem occurs when older versions of BIND are used on a network. BIND servers running software prior to version 4.9.4 do not support the fast transfer format. Therefore, you should enable this option only if you are running a version of BIND higher than this version.

Enabling and disabling zone transfers can be done through the DNS Console. By right-clicking the DNS server and selecting Properties, you can bring up a Properties sheet for that server. Clicking the Advanced tab allows you to modify how your DNS server performs zone transfers. On this tab, you will see a server option entitled BIND Secondaries. If the check box beside this option is selected, fast zone transfer format is enabled. To disable it, click the check box so that it is deselected.

Another issue that often arises with BIND is the ability to deploy Active Directory. There are certain DNS requirements for deploying Active Directory, and if these requirements aren't met, the DNS server is unable to support Active Directory. This situation can happen if older versions of BIND are running on servers. In such cases, you can do one of two things. First, you can upgrade to a more recent version of BIND. Versions 8.1.2 and higher of BIND meet the requirements for Active Directory. Second, you could migrate current DNS zones to Windows 2000 DNS servers and stop using the DNS servers running older versions of BIND.

Microsoft Domain Name Service vs. Non-Microsoft Domain Name Service Servers

With all the advances in Windows 2000 DNS Server, a number of differences have arisen among Microsoft DNS in Windows NT Server 4.0, BIND, and other third-party DNS servers. It would take an entire chapter to list the similarities and differences between every DNS server on the market. When push comes to shove, all that really matters to someone who's implementing Windows 2000 DNS Server is how to integrate it with other DNS servers.

We discuss interoperability configurations in the next section, but here it's important to realize that the Microsoft DNS that came with Windows NT 4.0 doesn't support Active Directory, because Active Directory wasn't part of a Windows operating system until Windows 2000 Server. This is the same situation as when you have older versions of BIND running in your current environment.

As we see later in this chapter, a feature of Windows 2000 DNS is support for dynamic updates. This feature allows client computers to register and dynamically update resource records with DNS servers when changes occur. This is not a feature found in Windows NT 4.0 DNS Server or versions of BIND prior to version 4.9.7. That might make you think that Windows 2000 DNS can't be deployed in environments that are running non-dynamic DNS. That is not the case, as we see in the next section.

Configuring a Domain Name Service Server to Interoperate with Non-Microsoft and Microsoft Domain Name Service Servers

There are a number of ways to make Microsoft 2000 DNS Server interoperable with non-dynamic DNS servers. Non-dynamic DNS servers are servers running older implementations of Microsoft DNS and servers that use BIND. In this section, we discuss those options and show how you can integrate Windows 2000 DNS Server into an environment running Microsoft DNS, which was available in Windows NT Server 4.0, or BIND.

For DNS servers on Windows NT Server 4.0 machines, the first option is perhaps the most obvious. You can upgrade Windows NT 4.0 DNS servers to Windows 2000. With all name servers running Windows 2000 DNS Server, you have the best possible system in terms of support. Rather than having to remember the procedures and features of different systems, you have to remember only how to run a single DNS system. In addition, you can have each DNS server Active Directory-integrated, which requires less maintenance than other types of DNS.

The second option might not seem very different from the first, because it also means giving up other DNS servers. You can migrate zones from non-dynamic DNS servers to your Windows 2000 DNS servers. The migration is from DNS servers that are authoritative sources of other name servers. Once the zones are migrated to Windows 2000 DNS, you then stop using the other DNS servers.

You'll remember that when you set up DNS on Windows 2000 Server, you can select standard primary as the zone type. When setting up a standard primary server, you have the option of creating a new zone file or using an existing one from another computer. Using an existing zone file gives you the ability to use a file from a current DNS server, such as one running BIND or DNS running on a Windows NT 4.0 Server. The zone file specified here is the filename of the database that contains information about this zone. To use such a file, you must first place it in the %systemroot%\system32\dns folder on the server that is running DNS. However, you need to remember that the filename of this standard text database uses the file extension .DNS. The DNS server service on Windows NT Server 4.0 already uses a standard text file with the extension .DNS. However, if you want to use a file from a BIND server, you need to change its extension to .DNS and then copy it into the %systemroot%\system32\dns directory on the DNS server.

Another option is to delegate child DNS domains under the parent DNS domain on your Windows 2000 DNS Server. Active Directory domain names that don't have the same name as the root of the zone can also be set up as subdomains. To give you an example, let's say your Active Directory domain is called test.masterofmydomain.gov, and the zone containing this name is masterofmydomain.gov. You could delegate test.masterofmydomain.gov to your Windows 2000 DNS Server.

Finally, you could integrate Windows 2000 DNS into an existing domain space used on non-dynamic DNS servers. To do this, you delegate subdomains used by the domain controller locator records to a Windows 2000 server. The records referred to here are resource records, which are contained in the DNS database to identify resources in a domain. Later in this chapter, we discuss resource records in more detail.

Depending on the needs of your network, you use one of these options to integrate Windows 2000 DNS into an environment running BIND or Windows NT 4.0 DNS. This technique allows you to either replace these DNS servers or have these different DNS servers running together on the network.

Configure Zones for Dynamic Updates

As we see in the section on managing DNS, when changes are made to a domain over which a name server has authority, you need to manually make changes to the zone database file on the primary name server. However, there is a way to avoid this extra work and have DNS update itself automatically. DNS in Windows 2000 Server has the ability to perform dynamic updates. This ability is called *Dynamic DNS,* or *DDNS.*

What Are Dynamic Updates?

Dynamic updates allow client computers to register and dynamically update resource records with DNS servers when changes occur. This ability is especially useful on networks in which DHCP is used to automatically assign IP addresses to clients. When the client logs on to the network, it requests an IP address from a DHCP server. If you configure this server as a secondary name server, it passes information on this new client to the DNS primary name server, which updates the zone database.

 on the job

In setting up your DNS server this way, it's important to realize two facts. First, the DHCP server doesn't have to be a DNS server to perform this role. It is, however, a recommended method. Second, Windows 2000 DHCP servers have the ability to dynamically update records on behalf of hosts.

Configuring the Zone

Configuring a zone to use dynamic updates is done through the DNS console. To configure a zone to use DDNS, right-click on the forward or reverse lookup zone you want to configure. From the context menu that appears, select Properties to display the properties of that zone.

As shown in Figure 5-5, the General tab of the zone includes a drop-down list labeled "Allow dynamic updates?" This drop-down list has up to three values:

- Yes, which enables dynamic updates for the zone.

- No, which disables dynamic updates for the zone.

- Only Secure Updates, which allows only dynamic updates that use secure DNS. Secure updates specify that only users, groups, or computers that have been granted the right to write to the zone or record have the ability to update the record. Setting this option is done through the Security tab on the Properties sheet of the zone or record. Setting the Only Secure Updates option is a recommended method, but the option appears only if the zone type is Active Directory-integrated. This option does not appear in standard primary or standard secondary zones.

FIGURE 5-5

Setting dynamic updates through a zone's Properties sheet

SCENARIO & SOLUTION

What is the difference between a network ID and a host ID?	IP addresses are broken into two parts. The network ID is used to identify a network within a larger network. For example, the network ID identifies your LAN when it is connected to the Internet. The host ID is used to identify client computers that are members of this network.
What is the difference between a forward lookup zone and a reverse lookup zone?	Forward lookup queries resolve a name to an IP address, and forward lookup zones are used to make these queries possible. Reverse lookup zones make reverse lookup queries possible so that IP addresses can be resolved to friendly computer or domain names.
Where is zone information stored in Active Directory-integrated zones and standard primary zones?	Active Directory-integrated zone types store data on a zone by integrating the data in Active Directory. Information on the zone is stored in Active Directory. Standard primary zones have a database file that's saved to the hard drive, and information on the zone is stored in this file.

CERTIFICATION OBJECTIVE 5.02

Managing, Monitoring, and Troubleshooting Domain Name Service

Now that you've installed DNS server and created zones for your network, you're ready to begin the next steps in running Windows 2000 DNS Server on your network: managing, monitoring, and troubleshooting. In this section, we discuss a number of tools that can help you in these endeavors. We take you through using the DNS Console, which is the Microsoft Management Console with the DNS snap-in added. We also look at tools such as Performance Monitor and the DNS Event Log.

This section also looks at another important part of DNS: replication of DNS data. We show you how zone transfers and replication take place, how to configure DNS in this regard, and things to consider when dealing with Active Directory-integrated zones.

Other Management Tasks

DNS Console is the core tool for managing your DNS server. It is the Microsoft Management Console with the DNS snap-in added, and it replaces the DNS Manager program that was used in Windows NT Server 4.0. Earlier in this chapter, we saw how DNS Console can be used to configure new DNS servers, add forward and reverse lookup zones, and perform other tasks. However, DNS Console allows you to make a number of other configurations to DNS as it works on your network.

exam
ⓦatch

DNS Console is the Microsoft Management Console with the DNS snap-in added. DNS Console is designed for Windows 2000 DNS Server and can be used only to manage Windows 2000 DNS Servers.

As shown in Figure 5-6, DNS Console has a Windows Explorer–like interface, which is made up of two windows. The left window shows the DNS tree, which appears as a series of folders and subfolders. This window shows servers running DNS and the forward and reverse lookup zones contained within them. When you select a folder in this tree, the contents within appear in the window on the right-hand side. This view allows you to easily navigate the DNS tree and the subtrees that branch from it.

At the top of the console, you will see three menus: Console, Window, and Help. The Console menu contains different elements, depending on how DNS Console has been started. If you've started Microsoft Management Console and then added the DNS snap-in, this menu contains commands for adding snap-ins as well as other commands used by MMC. If you've started DNS Console by selecting DNS from

FIGURE 5-6

DNS Console

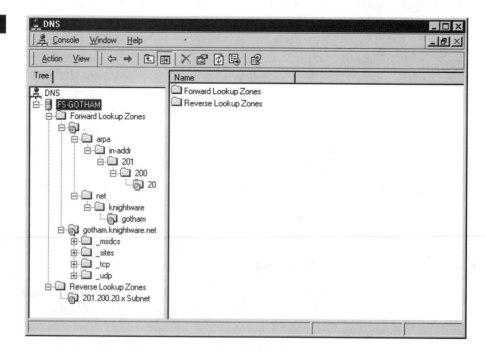

Programs | Administrative Tools in the Windows Start menu, the only command that appears under the Console menu is Exit. The Window menu contains commands to manage the way windows are organized in the console; Help contains commands to invoke help for MMC and the DNS Console.

Beneath these menus are two other menus: Action and View. The Action menu contains commands that perform various tasks related to the item that is selected in the left window of the console. As with the View menu, elements in this menu can change depending on which item is selected and are the same commands that appear when you right-click an item to invoke the context menu. We discuss the Action menu in greater detail after first looking at the View menu's contents.

The View menu allows you to determine how elements appear in the console windows. The Choose Columns command under View allows you to modify columns appearing in the right window. It brings up a dialog box that allows you to change column orders or hide and show specific columns.

Beneath Choose Columns are four commands to determine how items appear. The Large Icons option shows items as big icons with text beneath them. The Small Icons option shows items as small icons with text beside them. The List option shows a listing of items; Details shows a listing of items with detailed information beside them. Details organizes this information in a range of columns.

Beneath the previous section of commands, you will find up to three commands that allow you to toggle certain viewing preferences on and off. Advanced allows you to toggle Advanced View Mode on and off. This mode allows you to see items that are for advanced users. For example, if Advanced View Mode is on, you are able to see a folder for Cached Lookups under the DNS Server. These lookups contain DNS requests that have been fulfilled and cached for future use. If the DNS server is selected, the View menu shows a third item in this section: Message. This item is used to toggle the viewing of messages in the results pane. Finally, the Filter item in this section displays a dialog box that allows you to specify the information that is viewed in the windows. This dialog box allows you to filter information by name and limit the number of items displayed in DNS Console.

The final item on the View menu is Customize, which displays a dialog box with check boxes that allow you to determine what items are shown or hidden in the console. Items include the console tree (the left pane of the console), the standard menus (Action and View), the standard toolbar, the status bar, the description bar, navigation tabs, and snap-in menus and toolbars.

The Action menu contains a number of commands that perform actions related to the item selected. When the top of the tree (labeled DNS) is selected, the first command on this menu is Connect to Computer. This command is used to add a server to the DNS Console. When Connect to Computer is clicked, the Select Target Computer dialog box opens. Two options are available in this dialog box:

- This Computer, which is selected if you want to manage the server on which you're currently working.

- The Following Computer, which is used to specify a remote server you want to manage. If this option is selected, you need to specify the computer name or IP address.

Once you've selected one of these options, ensure that the "Connect to the specified computer now" check box is selected, and click OK.

DNS Console can be used to manage the server you're working on as well as other remote Windows 2000 DNS servers.

Beneath the Connect to Computer command are other commands that are common to the Action menu when any item is selected in the console. The New Window from Here option opens a new window, with the top level of the tree the item that was selected when this command was used. For example, if a DNS server were selected, it would be at the top of the tree. You can navigate between windows using the Windows menu of the console. The Refresh command refreshes the display of the current selection, so changes appear. The Export List command exports the current list to a file; the Help command is used to display help options on DNS.

The Update Server Data Files option on the Action menu is used to force a DNS server to write in-memory changes to the zone file. In standard primary zones, changes are written at predetermined intervals or when the server is shut down. In Active Directory-integrated zones, you don't need to worry about this command, because data is written immediately to the Active Directory-integrated database.

Aging and Scavenging

The New Zone command starts the New Zone Wizard, which we discussed earlier in this chapter. This command appears when a DNS server, the Forward Lookup Zone folder, or the Reverse Lookup Zone folder is selected. If the DNS server is selected, the next item on the Action menu is Set Aging/Scavenging for All Zones. *Aging and scavenging features* in Windows 2000 DNS are used to clean up resource records that may not have been removed. (We discuss record types later in this chapter.) When dynamic updates are used, resource records are automatically added to zones when a computer goes on the network and registers with DNS. These records have a date/time stamp on them, showing when they were created or refreshed. If the computer improperly disconnects from the network, these records could be left behind in the zone. Aging and scavenging remove these records so they don't accumulate and cause problems for the DNS zone.

When the Set Aging/Scavenging for All Zones command is selected, a dialog box used to configure settings appears. Click the check box labeled "Scavenge stale resource records" so that it appears checked. Below this option are two sections with drop-down lists. They are

- No-refresh interval, which is the interval of time from when the record was last refreshed and its date/time stamp was set to when the record next becomes eligible to have its date/time stamp refreshed

- Refresh interval, which is the interval of time from the earliest date and time when the record is eligible to have its date/time stamp refreshed to when the record becomes eligible to be scavenged and removed from the zone

Once you click OK, a confirmation box appears. To have your settings apply to your Active Directory-integrated zones, select the check box in this dialog box. Click OK to confirm your settings.

exam
ⓦatch

Any configurations you make in Set Aging/Scavenging for All Zones become default properties for the server and apply toward Active Directory-integrated zones. If standard primary zones are used, you need to set properties for each zone by selecting the zone and setting the appropriate properties.

Even though the Set Aging/Scavenging for All Zones has been configured and you've ensured that the "Scavenge stale resource records" check box has been selected, this option is enabled only for Active Directory-integrated zones. It's important to remember that standard primary zones need to have this feature manually enabled. If you don't manually enable "Scavenge stale resource records" for each standard primary zone, this feature will still be disabled for those zones.

To set the aging/scavenging properties for a zone, select a zone and then choose Properties from the Action menu. On the General tab, click the Aging button. A dialog box appears with the same elements found in Set Aging/Scavenging for All

Zones. Click the "Scavenge stale resource records" check box, and then modify the other properties as desired. When you click OK, aging/scavenging for that zone become enabled.

Once you have set aging/scavenging for zones, you can select the DNS server in the console, and click "Scavenge stale resource records" on the Action menu. This starts the scavenging of stale resource records. To have scavenging done automatically, you can select the DNS server in the console, and click Properties on the Action menu. On the Advanced tab, you will see a check box labeled "Enable automatic scavenging of stale records." Ensure that this check box has a check mark in it, and then use the "Scavenging period" drop-down list to adjust the interval in hours or days at which you want scavenging to occur.

The Cache and TTL

The Clear Cache command on the Action menu is used to clear the DNS Server Cache. As we mentioned earlier, when DNS Server processes a forward or reverse lookup query, it might not have a mapping for the computer for which you're searching. This is the case if the name server doesn't have authority over a zone of which the domain or server for which you're searching is a part. To find the domain or server, other name servers are queried. The name server then caches the query results to reduce network traffic, should you seek the same server in the future. This feature allows the name server to resolve queries on that portion of the domain space quickly and without having to contact other name servers. When a name server gets the results of a query, it caches the query result for a specific amount of time that's called the *Time To Live (TTL)*. The zone providing the results specifies the TTL. By default, the TTL is 60 minutes. Upon caching the results, the name server begins counting down the TTL from its original value. When the server has fully counted down, the TTL expires and the name server deletes the result from the cache.

Instead of waiting for the TTLs to expire, you can clear the DNS Server Cache by selecting the DNS server in the DNS Console and selecting Clear Cache from the Action menu.

on the *Job* — *Determining a value to set for TTLs is a trade-off. Shorter TTLs ensure that data about a domain is more current. Longer TTL values allow name resolution to be performed faster, because information on that portion of the domain namespace is kept in case it is needed again.*

Managing the Domain Name Service

To start or stop the DNS server, select the DNS server from the left window of the console. Right-clicking it to bring up the context menu or using the Action menu, you then move your pointer over All Tasks. This displays a submenu of items:

- Start, which starts DNS
- Stop, which stops DNS
- Pause, which interrupts DNS
- Resume, which causes DNS to continue again after Pause has been selected
- Restart, which stops and automatically restarts DNS

You can perform most of these actions from the command prompt using the following commands:

- **NET START DNS**, which starts DNS
- **NET STOP DNS**, which stops DNS
- **NET PAUSE DNS**, which interrupts DNS
- **NET CONTINUE DNS**, which causes DNS to resume after the NET PAUSE DNS command has been used

Creating Records

When a zone is selected in DNS Console, the Action menu displays a number of commands that allow you to create various elements that make up your zone. When these commands are used, they make up different *resource records,* which are entries in the zone's database file to provide information on various network resources. For example, a resource record for a host computer provides information on that computer's IP address.

When a zone is created using the New Zone Wizard, two resource records are automatically created: the Start of Authority (SOA) record and the Name Server (NS) record. The *SOA resource record* is used to identify the name server that has authority over the data in your domain. In other words, it says which name server provides name resolution services for your zone. This is the first record in your zone database. The *NS resource record* follows the SOA record, identifying the name servers that are assigned to your domain.

In addition to these records, other records can be created using the various commands found on the Action menu. These commands are

- **New Host,** which is used to create a new host resource record. This record type is called Host (A) and lists a host's name-to-IP address mapping for a forward lookup zone.

- **New Alias,** a command that's used to create a new alias resource record. This record type is called Alias (CNAME). It is used to create an alternate name for a host. The CNAME record—short for *canonical name*—can be used to have more than one name point to a single IP address. This allows an FTP server and a Web server to run on the same computer and use a single IP address.

- **New Mail Exchanger** is a command used to make a new mail exchanger record. This record type is called Mail Exchanger (MX), and is used to identify which mail exchanger is to be contacted for different domains. It also specifies the order to use mail hosts.

- **New Domain** is a command that's used to create new domains under your current domain.

- **New Delegation** is a command that's used to create new delegated domains under a currently selected domain.

- **Other New Records** is used to add a variety of other resource record types to a domain. Common record types you can add here include HINFO, which provides host information and is used to identify the operating system and CPU of a host. It is a tool for resource tracking. PTR is used to create pointers, which point to another domain namespace. In a reverse lookup zone, a PTR record is used to provide IP address-to-computer name mappings. SRV is a resource record for a service. It identifies which servers are running certain services on a network.

EXERCISE 5-2

Viewing Resource Records Through DNS Console

1. In DNS Console, select the zone containing resource records you want to view.

2. In the details pane (the right window) of the console, click the record you want to view.

3. On the Action menu, click Properties.

4. When the dialog box for that record's properties appears, you see various information contained within that resource record. The properties appearing here constitute the data contained in the resource record. The properties that appear depend upon the type of resource record you are viewing. The types of properties may include such things as the Time To Live (TTL), IP address, or security associated with that record.

SCENARIO & SOLUTION

My network uses Microsoft Windows 2000 DNS and other platforms running their own DNS software. Can I use DNS Console to manage all DNS servers on my network?	No. DNS Console works only with Windows 2000 DNS servers. You have to manage other DNS servers with software for the DNS software designed to manage DNS running on other platforms.
Is there a difference between Microsoft Management Console with the DNS snap-in and the DNS program that's started from the Programs | Administrative Tools folder in the Windows Start menu?	No. Except for some minor cosmetic appearances, there is no functional difference between starting DNS by starting MMC and adding the snap-in yourself and starting DNS by selecting DNS from the Programs | Administrative Tools folder on the Windows Start menu.
What determines how long a cached result of a query is kept?	The Time-To-Live determines how long a cached result is kept. It counts down from its initial value until it expires and is removed. You can also clear cached results using the Clear Cache command on the Action menu of DNS Console.

The Performance Console

Performance is always an issue on any network. To monitor DNS servers, you use the Performance Console, which provides the functionality of a program called Performance Monitor in Windows NT 4.0. Performance Console allows you to add counters that are service specific so that you can monitor and measure how well or poorly DNS Server is running.

The Performance Console can be started by clicking the item called Performance that's found in the Programs | Administrative Tools folder of the Windows Start menu. It can also be started through the Run command on the Windows Start menu. If you choose to start Performance Console via the Run command, you enter the word **perfmon**, and then click OK. Although Performance Console is the Microsoft Management Console with the System Monitor and Performance Logs and Alerts snap-ins added to it, you cannot start Performance Console by adding these two snap-ins to MMC. Performance Logs and Alerts is available as a snap-in, but System Monitor is not.

FROM THE CLASSROOM

Using Performance Console to Monitor and Troubleshoot Domain Name Service

Performance Console is a powerful tool in determining possible problems in DNS, but IT professionals and students who are new to using Performance Console often miss an important step in its use. When a problem is suspected, they start Performance Console, add the counters associated with DNS, and watch the display to see if anything odd is happening. However, they have no idea what value these counters had during normal hours of use when DNS was believed to be working properly.

When DNS is first installed on a server and hosts on your network begin using it, you should log the values of DNS counters. This log creates a baseline. Once the baseline has been created, you then have a basis for comparison. If a problem occurs, you then use Performance Console to check DNS counters and compare their values to those in the baseline. If you see dramatic changes to certain values, you'll be able to identify where a DNS problem is occurring.

—*Michael Cross, MCSE, MCP+I, MCPS, CNA*

As shown in Figure 5-7, the Performance Console has two components. System Monitor is used to add counters related to DNS so that charts and graphs detailing DNS server performance can be created for analysis purposes. This feature allows you to see trends in performance so that you can determine benchmarks and decide whether DNS needs to be optimized. The Performance Logs and Alerts snap-in is used to log counter data and set alerts so that if a counter's value exceeds or drops below a certain point, you can be notified.

When you first select System Monitor, you see a pane on the right of the console that is dormant. This is because no counters have been added. *Performance counters* monitor specific aspects of your system and provide a value that corresponds to the object being monitored. This system provides you with real-time data, so you can see how your system is doing.

To add a counter, right-click the details pane and select Add Counters from the context menu that appears. You can also add counters by clicking the button on the toolbar that has the plus symbol (+). This displays the Add Counters dialog box, shown in Figure 5-8.

FIGURE 5-7

Performance
Console

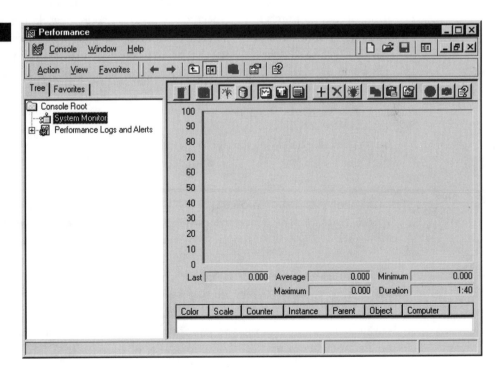

The Add
Counters
dialog box

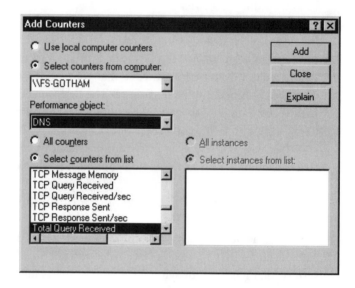

At the top of this dialog box, you are given two options regarding what computer should be monitored. You can use counters for the local computer you're currently using or select counters from a specific computer on your network. Below these options is a drop-down list of performance objects. These are elements of your systems (CPU, DHCP, DNS, and so on) that have counters associated with them, which you can use in the Performance Console. To use counters for DNS Server, select DNS from the listing. Once you do so, counters appear in the listing at the bottom. If you select the "All counters" option, all counters are used by Performance Console. If you want to view specific counters, select the counter you want to use, and click the Add button. When you click Close, graphical data derived from the counter is displayed in the Details pane (the right pane) of the Performance Console.

on the

ⓙob   *Don't worry about memorizing each and every counter for use in the real world. You can select a counter and click the Explain button in the Add Counters dialog box to see an explanation of what that counter does.*

As you use Performance Console, it's important to realize that different counters are used to measure different areas of performance. Some are used to measure memory, others dynamic updates, and still others to measure the overall performance of the DNS server. As shown in Table 5-1, various counters can be used together to measure the performance of your server.

TABLE 5-1	DNS Counters Used with Performance Console

Counter	Description	Related Performance Issue
AXFR Request Received	Measures the total number of full zone transfer requests your DNS server receives when it is operating as a master server for a zone.	All zone transfer (AXFR)
AXFR Request Sent	Measures the total number of full zone transfer requests your DNS server sends when it is running as a secondary server for a zone.	All zone transfer (AXFR)
AXFR Response Received	Measures the total number of full zone transfer requests your DNS server receives when it is running as a secondary server for a zone.	All zone transfer (AXFR)
AXFR Success Received	Measures the total number of full zone transfers your DNS server receives when it is running as a secondary server for a zone.	All zone transfer (AXFR)
AXFR Success Sent	Measures the total number of full zone transfers your DNS server sends successfully when it is running as a master server for a zone.	All zone transfer (AXFR)
Caching Memory	Measures the total amount of system memory used by your DNS server for caching.	DNS server memory
Database Node Memory	Measures the total amount of system memory in use by your DNS server for database nodes.	DNS server memory
Dynamic Update NoOperation	Measures the total number of No-operation/Empty dynamic update requests received by your DNS server.	Dynamic Updates
Dynamic Update NoOperation/sec	Measures the average number of No-operation/Empty dynamic update requests received by your DNS server each second.	Dynamic Updates
Dynamic Update Queued	Measures the total number of dynamic updates queued by your DNS server.	Dynamic Updates
Dynamic Update Received	Measures the total number of dynamic update requests your DNS server receives.	Dynamic Updates

TABLE 5-1 DNS Counters Used with Performance Console *(Continued)*

Counter	Description	Related Performance Issue
Dynamic Update Received/sec	Measures the average number of dynamic update requests your DNS server receives each second.	Dynamic Updates
Dynamic Update Rejected	Measures the total number of dynamic updates rejected by your DNS server.	Dynamic Updates
Dynamic Update TimeOuts	Measures the total number of dynamic update time-outs of your DNS server.	Dynamic Updates
Dynamic Update Written to Database	Measures the total number of dynamic updates written to the database by your DNS server.	Dynamic Updates
Dynamic Update Written to Database/sec	Measures the average number of dynamic updates written to the database by your DNS server each second.	Dynamic Updates
IXFR Request Received	Measures the total number of incremental zone transfer requests received by the master DNS server.	Incremental zone transfer (IXFR)
IXFR Request Sent	Measures the total number of incremental zone transfer requests sent by the secondary DNS server.	Incremental zone transfer (IXFR)
IXFR Response Received	Measures the total number of incremental zone transfer responses received by the secondary DNS server.	Incremental zone transfer (IXFR)
IXFR Success Received	Measures the total number of successful incremental zone transfers received by the secondary DNS server.	Incremental zone transfer (IXFR)
IXFR Success Sent	Measures the total number of successful incremental zone transfers of the master DNS server.	Incremental zone transfer (IXFR)
IXFR TCP Success Received	Measures the total number of successful TCP incremental zone transfers received by the secondary DNS server.	Incremental zone transfer (IXFR)
IXFR UDP Success Received	Measures the total number of successful UDP incremental zone transfers received by the secondary DNS server.	Incremental zone transfer (IXFR)

TABLE 5-1   DNS Counters Used with Performance Console *(Continued)*

Counter	Description	Related Performance Issue
Nbtstat Memory	Measures the total amount of system memory in use by the DNS Server for Nbtstat.	DNS server memory
Notify Received	Measures the total number of notifies received by the secondary DNS server.	Notification
Notify Sent	Measures the total number of notifies sent by the master DNS server.	Notification
Record Flow Memory	Measures the total amount of system memory in use by the DNS server for record flow.	DNS server memory
Recursive Queries	The total number of recursive queries received by the DNS server.	Recursion
Recursive Queries/sec	Measures the average number of recursive queries the DNS server receives each second.	Recursion
Recursive Query Failure	Measures the total number of recursive query failures.	Recursion
Recursive Query Failure/sec	Measures the average number of recursive query failures each second.	Recursion
Recursive TimeOuts	Measures the total number of recursive query sending time-outs.	Recursion
Recursive TimeOuts/sec	Measures the average number of recursive queries sending time-outs each second.	Recursion
Secure Update Failure	Measures the total number of secure updates that have failed on the DNS server.	Secure dynamic update
Secure Update Received	Measures the total number of secure update requests that the DNS server has received.	Secure dynamic update
Secure Update Received/sec	Measures the average number of secure update requests that the DNS server has received each second.	Secure dynamic update

TABLE 5-1   DNS Counters Used with Performance Console *(Continued)*

Counter	Description	Related Performance Issue
TCP Message Memory	Measures the total TCP message memory used by the DNS server.	TCP
TCP Query Received	Measures the total number of TCP queries received by the DNS server.	TCP
TCP Query Received/sec	Measures the average number of TCP queries that the DNS server receives each second.	TCP
TCP Response Sent	Measures the total number of TCP responses sent by the DNS server.	TCP
TCP Response Sent/sec	Measures the average number of TCP responses sent by the DNS server each second.	TCP
Total Query Received	Measures the total number of queries that the DNS server receives.	Overall Performance
Total Query Received/sec	Measures the average number of queries the DNS server receives each second.	Overall Performance
Total Response Sent	Measures the total number of responses sent by the DNS server.	Overall Performance
Total Response Sent/sec	Measures the average number of responses the DNS server sends each second.	Overall Performance
UDP Message Memory	Measures the total UDP message memory that the DNS server uses.	UDP
UDP Query Received	Measures the total number of UDP queries the DNS server receives.	UDP
UDP Query Received/sec	Measures the average number of UDP queries the DNS server receives each second.	UDP
UDP Response Sent	Measures the total number of UDP responses the DNS server sends.	UDP
UDP Response Sent/sec	Measures the average number of UDP responses the DNS server sends each second.	UDP

TABLE 5-1 DNS Counters Used with Performance Console *(Continued)*

Counter	Description	Related Performance Issue
WINS Lookup Received	Measures the total number of WINS lookup requests the server receives.	WINS
WINS Lookup Received/sec	Measures the average number of WINS lookup requests the server receives each second.	WINS
WINS Response Sent	Measures the total number of WINS lookup responses the server sends.	WINS
WINS Response Sent/sec	Measures the average number of WINS lookup responses the server sends each second.	WINS
WINS Reverse Lookup Received	Measures the total number of WINS reverse lookup requests the server receives.	WINS
WINS Reverse Lookup Received/sec	Measures the average number of WINS reverse lookup requests the server receives each second.	WINS
WINS Reverse Response Sent	Measures the total number of WINS reverse lookup responses the server sends.	WINS
WINS Reverse Response Sent/sec	Measures the average number of WINS reverse lookup responses the server sends per second.	WINS
Zone Transfer Failure	Measures the total number of failed zone transfers of the master DNS server.	Zone Transfers
Zone Transfer Request Received	Measures the total number of zone transfer requests the master DNS server receives.	Zone Transfers
Zone Transfer SOA Request Sent	Measures the total number of zone transfer SOA requests the secondary DNS server sends.	Zone Transfers
Zone Transfer Success	Measures the total number of successful zone transfers of the master DNS server.	Zone Transfers

Domain Name Service Event Log

Event Viewer is another snap-in that can be added to Microsoft Management Console. It can be started with the snap-in by selecting the Event Viewer item from the Programs | Administrative Tools folder of the Windows Start menu. Event Viewer allows you to view events raised by DNS and other applications and services of your Windows 2000 Server.

When Event Viewer is started, the tree pane (the left pane) of the console shows a number of logs from which you can choose. To view the log on DNS, you need to select DNS Server from this listing. DNS event messages are logged separately from other applications and services and contain such events as the times at which DNS Server was started and stopped.

To view more detailed events beyond these basic ones, you need to configure DNS Console to log various activities. Logging options are set through the DNS Console by selecting a DNS server from the tree pane. From the Action menu, you then select Properties. When the Properties dialog box for this server appears, click the Logging dialog box. Here you see a number of logging options used in debugging DNS Server, which are listed in Table 5-2.

When logging options are set in DNS Console, a temporary trace log is created to log server activity. This is a text-based file that, by default, is stored in the directory %SystemRoot%\system32\dns and is called DNS.LOG. Because this file consumes server resources (such as disk space), you should use these debugging options only when you're concerned about problems with DNS Server.

Additional Troubleshooting Tools

NSLookup is a command-line utility that can be used to test the DNS domain namespace. NSLookup is installed with TCP/IP. Using NSLookup, you can query DNS to display information from name servers and find the IP address of computers in a domain. For example, let's say you wanted to find the IP address of a computer named LT101. From the command prompt, you could type

```
NSLOOKUP LT101
```

Querying the name server, NSLookup returns the address of that computer. If you want to perform a reverse lookup and find the computer name of a computer with an IP address, you type **NSLOOKUP** followed by the IP address you want to resolve. Although DNS doesn't require reverse lookup zones, you need to configure reverse lookup zones if you want to run NSLookup in this way.

| **TABLE 5-2** | DNS Server Debug Logging Options |

Debug Logging Option	Description
Query	Used to log queries received by your DNS server from clients.
Notify	Used to log notification messages received by your DNS server from other servers.
Update	Used to log dynamic updates received from other computers.
Questions	Used to log the contents of the question section of each DNS query message that your DNS server has processed.
Answers	Used to log the contents of the answer section of each DNS query message that your DNS server has processed.
Send	Used to log the number of DNS query messages that have been sent by DNS.
Receive	Used to log the number of DNS query messages that have been received by DNS.
UDP	Used to log the number of DNS requests received by DNS over a UDP port.
TCP	Used to log the number of DNS requests received by DNS over a TCP port.
Full Packets	Used to log the number of full packets that have been written and sent by DNS.
Write Through	Used to log the number of packets that have been written through DNS and back to the zone.

IPConfig is another command-line tool that can be used to view and modify IP configuration for a computer. By simply typing **IPCONFIG** at the command prompt, you can view configuration information about the server or client you're currently working on. However, in Windows 2000, IPConfig has command-line options that can be used to troubleshoot DNS clients.

When dynamic registration is used, you can use IPConfig to manually initiate dynamic registration. This ability is helpful when you are troubleshooting failed dynamic registration or update problems between clients and DNS servers. To manually initiate dynamic registration, type the following at the command prompt of the client:

```
IPCONFIG /REGISTERDNS
```

This command refreshes all DHCP address leases and reregisters all DNS names configured and used by the client.

Managing Replication of Domain Name Service Data

Zones are vital to DNS, so it makes sense that you'd want to take precautions against name resolution for a zone that is unavailable. After all, there might be times when you have to take down a Windows 2000 server running DNS. If this were the only DNS server on your network, queries for names in that zone would fail. To deal with such problems, it makes sense to have multiple name servers in each zone. Not only does this configuration reduce loads on a primary server and possibly reduce network traffic, but adding more than one DNS server provides redundancy and protection against DNS server failures.

When multiple name servers are on a network, there is a need for DNS data to be replicated. This ensures that secondary servers have the same information as primary servers. As we see in this section, when changes occur, this data needs to be updated, so replication again needs to occur between the DNS servers.

How Domain Name Service Data Is Replicated

DNS data is replicated when one of the following situations occurs:

- When DNS is started on a secondary server
- When a zone's refresh interval time expires
- When the primary zone has experienced changes and configuration changes are made to the notify list
- When replication is initiated manually

If any of these conditions apply, the data on the primary name server needs to be replicated to other secondary servers in the zone.

Zone transfers are never initiated by the primary server but, in fact, are initiated by secondary servers. When this occurs, the secondary server contacts the DNS server that has source data for that particular zone. The DNS server that's contacted can be either a primary server or another secondary server. When a secondary server contacts another name server for zone data, the source server responds by performing a full or incremental transfer of the zone.

A full zone transfer copies all resource records for a zone to a secondary server. In previous versions of DNS, this was the only type of zone transfer that could be made. This is also the only type of transfer that occurs when a secondary server is added to a network running DNS. When it first starts, it needs to perform a full zone transfer (AXFR) to obtain all the information that is available on the zone it is servicing.

In Windows 2000 DNS Server, incremental zone transfers are available. Incremental zone transfers (IXFR) are more efficient because the entire zone database is not copied across the network. This type of transfer allows the secondary server to pull changes that have occurred since it last synchronized. Incremental zone transfers send only the differences between the source and replicated versions of a zone. A serial number contained in the zone database is how the two servers determine these changes. If a serial number on the source server is higher than the requesting server, a transfer of every resource record with a higher version number is sent.

on the **Job**

If your network is a mixture of Windows 2000 DNS Server and servers running BIND, it is good to realize that recent versions of BIND also support incremental zone transfers (IXFRs).

To prevent unauthorized servers from pulling zone updates from name servers, you can use DNS Console to set zone security. In DNS Console, select the zone on which you want to configure zone transfers, and then select Properties from the Action menu. When the Properties screen appears, select the Zone Transfers tab. On this tab, you will see a check box labeled "Allow zone transfers." Ensure that this check box appears with a check mark in it. If it does not, click the check box. Below this check box, you will see three options:

- To any server, which allows zone transfers to occur with any server that makes a request.

- Only to servers listed on the Name Servers Tab, which allows zone transfers only to name servers listed on this Property screen's Name Servers tab. This list contains all secondary servers for the zone.

- Only to the following servers, which requires you to enter the IP address of servers permitted to receive zone transfers from this server.

Also on this tab is a button labeled Notify. If this button is selected, you can set DNS notification, which implements a push mechanism that sends out a message to servers, letting them know when a zone has been updated. When other servers receive this notification, they can request a zone transfer and pull the changes from this server.

When you click the Notify button, another dialog box appears. To automatically notify other servers of changes, ensure that the check box labeled "Automatically notify" is selected. You can then set one of two options: "Servers listed on the Name Servers tab" and "The following address." If the first option is selected, only servers listed on the Name Servers tab of Properties are contacted about changes. If the second is selected, you need to add IP addresses of servers you want contacted when changes occur.

For servers to participate in notification, they must support the Notify directive (RFC 1996). Windows 2000 DNS supports this directive; but if your networking environment uses a mixture of DNS servers, you should check to ensure that the other servers do support RFC 1996. If they do not, notification does not work.

Active Directory-Integrated Zone Considerations

You don't need to configure DNS notification if you are running Active Directory-integrated zones. This is because servers running AD-integrated zones load zone information directly from Active Directory. These servers then poll the directory every 15 minutes to update and refresh the zone. If you add an AD-integrated server to a notification list, it causes that server to make unnecessary requests for zone transfers. This creates extra network traffic and can degrade performance.

SCENARIO & SOLUTION

I want to check the performance of a DNS server running on Windows 2000 Server. What should I use?	Performance Console. This tool allows you to add counters that allow you to measure DNS server performance.
I am troubleshooting my Windows 2000 DNS server. What can I use to view DNS events for debugging?	Debugging logging options can be set through DNS Console. Once these are set, logging can be viewed through Event Viewer.

CERTIFICATION SUMMARY

In this chapter, we discussed the importance of Windows 2000 DNS and saw how DNS is installed on Windows 2000 Server. We also saw how Windows 2000 DNS is configured. We discussed how to create and configure zones and the importance of the domain namespace, and we compared the various zone types.

We also saw how Windows 2000 DNS is managed and monitored and discussed tools that can be used to troubleshoot potential problems. We discussed how the primary tool used to manage DNS is the DNS Console and that Performance Console uses a number of counters to monitor DNS performance. The DNS Event Log provides information on Windows 2000 DNS, and we also saw that there are command-line tools available for troubleshooting.

TWO-MINUTE DRILL

Installing, Configuring, and Troubleshooting Domain Name Service for Active Directory

❑ DNS can be installed by itself through the Add/Remove Programs applet in Control Panel or as part of the process of installing Active Directory.

❑ Forward lookup queries resolve a name to an IP address; reverse lookup queries resolve an IP address to a name.

❑ A name server cannot resolve a query for a zone over which it doesn't have authority. If a name server can't resolve a query, it passes the query to other name servers. The name server then caches the results to reduce traffic, should the same name resolution be required in the future.

❑ There are three types of zones you can choose to configure: Active Directory-integrated, standard primary, and standard secondary. The type of zone chosen determines how zone information is obtained and stored.

❑ New zones can be created through Microsoft Management Console with the DNS snap-in. By right-clicking the DNS server name, you can select New Zone (to invoke the New Zone Wizard) or Configure the Server (to start the Configure DNS Server Wizard).

❑ Active Directory-integrated zones have a master copy of the zone integrated in Active Directory. Information on the zone is stored in Active Directory.

❑ Rather than updating DNS zone information manually, you can implement dynamic DNS (DDNS). This feature allows client computers to register and dynamically update resource records with DNS servers when changes occur.

Managing, Monitoring, and Troubleshooting Domain Name Service

❑ DNS Console is the core tool used to manage Windows 2000 DNS servers. Using DNS Console, you can make a number of modifications to DNS. These include configuring new DNS servers, adding and removing forward and reverse lookup zones, modifying how zones are stored and replicated, and modifying query processing and whether dynamic updates are used.

❏ In standard primary zones, aging and scavenging need to be enabled for each zone. If you don't manually enable "Scavenge stale resource records" for each standard primary zone, this feature remains disabled for those zones.

❏ The Clear Cache command on the Action menu is used to clear the contents of the DNS Server Cache. The other—and most common way—that a cached result is removed from the name server is when the result's Time-To-Live (TTL) value expires.

❏ Resource records are entries in the zone's database file and are used to provide information on various network resources.

❏ Performance Console is the Microsoft Management Console with the System Monitor and Performance Logs and Alerts snap-ins added. It allows you to measure the performance of your Windows 2000 DNS server.

❏ DNS events are logged separately and can be viewed through the Event Viewer. DNS Console can be used to view the properties of a DNS server and set debug logging options that allow more comprehensive events to be viewed.

❏ NSLookup and IPConfig are two command-line utilities that can be used in troubleshooting DNS.

❏ Zone transfers occur when DNS is started on a secondary server, a zone's refresh interval time expires, changes are made to the primary zone and configuration changes are made to the notify list, or when replication is initiated manually.

SELF TEST

The following questions will help you measure your understanding of the material presented in this chapter. Read all the choices carefully because there might be more than one correct answer. Choose all correct answers for each question.

Installing, Configuring, and Troubleshooting Domain Name Service for Active Directory

1. Which of the following best describes the difference between zones and namespaces?

    A. The namespace is a logical representation of your network resources, whereas zones provide physical storage of those resources.

    B. The namespace provides physical storage of network resources, whereas the zones provide a logical representation of network resources.

    C. Zones are used in name resolution, whereas the namespace is used to manage files on server hard disks.

    D. Zones apply to local area networks, whereas the namespace does not. The namespace is used for the Internet.

2. Which of the following is used to query a name server to obtain the IP address of a computer?

    A. Forward lookup query

    B. Backward lookup query

    C. Reverse lookup query

    D. Zone query

3. A client queries a name server to resolve the name of a server. This server is not in the zone over which the local name server has authority. Which of the following will occur?

    A. The local name server will check its DNS database and respond to the client with the IP address of the server.

    B. The local name server will pass the query to other name servers. Once another name server finds the name-to-address mapping, it will provide it to the local name server. The local name server will then provide the client with the IP address of the server it's looking for.

    C. The local name server will cache the request. An IP address will be sent to the client once the local name server has been provided with this address-to-name mapping.

    D. The local name server will respond to the client with an error.

4. Which of the following is used to obtain the name of a computer by providing that computer's IP address?

A. Forward lookup query

B. Reverse lookup query

C. Backward lookup query

D. DNS cannot resolve IP addresses to computer names; this is because DNS is indexed by computer names

5. You are creating a new zone using the New Zone Wizard. Which of the following zone types would you select if you wanted to create a replica of an existing zone?

A. Active Directory-integrated

B. Standard primary

C. Standard secondary

D. Active Directory-secondary

6. You are running standard primary and standard secondary zones on Windows 2000 DNS servers. The primary server crashes and is unavailable to process requests and updates. Which of the following will occur?

A. Because a master copy is stored in Active Directory and this is fully replicated to every domain controller, every DNS server has a duplicate of the data. Therefore, any domain controller with DNS can perform updates and process requests from clients to perform updates.

B. DNS servers with secondary standard zones will perform updates. Each secondary server will act as the primary authoritative source for the zone.

C. DNS servers with secondary standard zones will be able to fulfill client requests for lookups but will be unable to send requests to update their copies of the database.

D. Forward and reverse lookups will be completely unavailable.

7. Your network uses a mix of Windows 2000 DNS Servers and UNIX BIND 4.9.4 DNS Servers. You find that you are unable to deploy Active Directory because the UNIX server running BIND doesn't support Active Directory. Why is this, and what can you do about it? Choose all that apply.

A. BIND doesn't support Active Directory. You need to re-create all the zones in Windows 2000 DNS Server and stop using BIND.

B. Windows 2000 Server doesn't support BIND or UNIX.

C. This version of BIND is too old to support Active Directory. Upgrade to the most recent version.

D. This version of BIND is too old to support Active Directory. Migrate current DNS zones to Windows 2000 DNS servers and stop using the DNS servers running older versions of BIND.

8. Which of the following describes DDNS, and how is it configured?

A. DDNS automatically assigns IP addresses to clients and is automatically configured when DNS is used on a machine acting as a DHCP server.

B. DDNS is automatically set up when DNS is installed. DDNS is a type of resource record.

C. DDNS is configured through the DNS console. It is a type of resource record.

D. DDNS allows computers to register and dynamically update resource records. It is configured through DNS Console.

Managing, Monitoring, and Troubleshooting Domain Name Service

9. In DNS Console, you select a DNS server from the left pane. In the right pane, you see items for forward and reverse lookup zones, but you don't see any item for cached lookups. Why?

A. You haven't selected Details as the view style from the View menu.

B. You haven't selected List as the view style from the View menu.

C. You haven't toggled Advanced View Mode by selecting Advanced from the View menu.

D. You haven't toggled Advanced View Mode by selecting Customize from the View menu.

10. You want to set aging/scavenging for all zones on a DNS server that uses standard primary zones. You select the DNS server in DNS Console and select Set Aging/Scavenging for All Zones from the Action menu. On the dialog box that appears, you ensure that the "Scavenge stale resource records" check box has been selected, and then confirm your changes. However, you later notice that scavenging isn't taking place. Why?

A. Setting aging/scavenging applies only to Active Directory-integrated zones. You can't set aging/scavenging for standard primary zones.

B. You need to configure aging/scavenging for each standard primary zone.

C. Scavenging won't take place automatically.

D. These settings weren't accepted. Go through this procedure again.

11. Which of the following determines whether a cached result is cleared from a name server? Choose all that apply.

    A. The Time-To-Live value set by the server that caches the results

    B. The Time-To-Live value set by the server that sent the results

    C. The Clear Cache command available from the Action menu

    D. The Time-To-Live command available from the Action menu

12. You have paused the DNS server running on your Windows 2000 server. Which of the following would you do to resume the name server? Choose all that apply.

    A. In Control Panel, open the Services applet. Select DNS from the listing, and then click the Continue button.

    B. In DNS Console, right-click the DNS Server, and then select Resume from the All Tasks folder on the context menu.

    C. In DNS Console, select the DNS server. From the Action menu, select Continue from the All Tasks folder.

    D. From the command prompt, run the following command: NET CONTINUE DNS.

13. Which of the following resource record types contains the name-to-IP mappings of a host computer?

    A. Host (A)

    B. HINFO

    C. PTR

    D. SRV

14. You need to find out whether any computers on your network are using a particular IP address. If so, you need to know what computer name has been configured with that address. Which of the following could you do to find this information?

    A. Use the NSLookup tool to perform a forward lookup query.

    B. Use the NSLookup tool to perform a reverse lookup query.

    C. Use Microsoft Management Console with the DNS snap-in to create an Active Directory-integrated zone type.

    D. Use the DNSLookup tool to perform a backward lookup query.

15. Which of the following are command-line utilities that can be used in troubleshooting DNS? Choose all that apply.

    A. IPCONFIG

    B. Event Viewer

    C. DNS Console

    D. NSLOOKUP

16. Under what conditions do zone replication and transfer occur? Choose all that apply.

    A. When the DNS service is started on the primary server

    B. When the DNS service is started on a secondary server

    C. When a zone's refresh interval time expires

    D. When changes are made to the primary zone and configuration changes are made to the notify list

17. A Windows 2000 server running DNS Server requests a zone transfer. The server making the request is a secondary server. What occurs when the transfer is requested?

    A. A primary server responds with either a partial or full zone transfer.

    B. A primary server responds with an incremental zone transfer. Secondary servers are unable to respond to these requests.

    C. A primary or secondary server responds with a full zone transfer. Windows 2000 DNS Server cannot do partial replication.

    D. Nothing. Secondary servers don't initiate zone transfers.

LAB QUESTION

In this lab, you use DNS Console to create a forward lookup zone and a reverse lookup zone for your network. These zones enable computers to look up other computers by querying the name server to resolve a computer name to an IP address, or vice versa. Should you fall into trouble, refer to the section of this chapter that describes creating forward and reverse lookup zones. In the lab, you also convert the zone you create to a different zone type.

1. On the Windows Start menu, click the Start button. Select Programs, and when this folder expands, point to Administrative Tools; finally, click DNS.

2. When the DNS Console opens, select the folder called Forward Lookup Zone, and then click New Zone on the Action menu.

3. When the New Zone Wizard opens, follow the instructions in this chapter and in the wizard to create a new forward lookup zone. Choose "Standard primary" as the zone type for your new zone, and choose to create a new zone file when using the wizard.

4. When you have finished following the instructions on creating a new forward lookup zone, create a reverse lookup zone. This is done by selecting Reverse Lookup Zone, and then invoking the New Zone Wizard. Select "Standard primary" as the zone type, and create a new zone file.

5. When the new zone has been created, configure the newly created forward lookup zone so that dynamic updates are allowed.

6. Change the zone type of the newly created forward lookup zone so that it is Active Directory-integrated.

7. Enable scavenging of stale resource records for this zone.

SELF TEST ANSWERS

Installing, Configuring, and Troubleshooting Domain Name Service for Active Directory

1. ☑ A. The namespace is a logical representation of your network resources, whereas zones provide physical storage of those resources. In the domain name system, the namespace is a logical representation of your network and its resources. Upon installing DNS, you have the option of dividing these namespaces into "zones." The namespace represents the logical structure of network resources; zones are used to provide physical storage of resources. Name servers store information for resolving names in a hierarchical database. In this hierarchy, called a *tree,* there can be subtrees called *zones* that act as administrative units. These zones can consist of a domain or a domain with subdomains.

   ☒ **B** is incorrect because the definition is reversed. The namespace is a logical representation of your network resources, whereas zones provide physical storage of those resources. **C** is incorrect because the namespace isn't used to manage files on server hard disks. **D** is incorrect because Windows 2000 DNS uses the namespace and zones in name resolution.

2. ☑ A. Forward lookup queries resolve a name to an IP address. A forward lookup query is the type of query most often performed by DNS. A computer asks the name server where a computer is located on a network by asking for its IP address.

   ☒ **B** and **D** are both incorrect because there are no lookup queries called backward or zone. **C** is also incorrect because reverse lookup queries are used to resolve IP addresses to computer names.

3. ☑ B. The local name server will pass the query to other name servers. Once another name server finds the name-to-address mapping, it will provide it to the local name server. The local name server will then provide the client with the IP address of the server it's looking for.

   ☒ **A** is incorrect because a name server cannot resolve a query for a zone over which it doesn't have authority. If a name server can't resolve a query, it passes the query to other name servers. **C** is incorrect for two reasons. First, requests aren't cached for future use on a name server. The name server caches the results of a query to reduce traffic, should the same name resolution be required in the future. Second, a forward lookup has the server checking it's name-to-address mappings. An address-to-name mapping is part of a reverse lookup. **D** is incorrect because an error is not automatically returned to the client. First, the local name server passes the request to other name servers.

4. ☑ **B.** Reverse lookup queries are used to resolve IP addresses to computer names. Reverse lookup queries use address-to-name mappings in reverse lookup zones.

 ☒ **A** is incorrect because forward lookup queries resolve computer names to IP addresses. **C** is incorrect because there is no such query as a backward lookup query. **D** is incorrect because DNS resolves IP addresses to computer names through reverse lookup zones and reverse lookup queries.

5. ☑ **C.** Standard secondary is a zone type that creates a replica of the existing zone. Data for this copy of an existing zone is stored in a read-only, standard text file.

 ☒ **A** is incorrect because when Active Directory-integrated is chosen as the zone type, a master copy of the new zone is created and integrated in Active Directory. Information on the zone is stored in the Active Directory. **B** is incorrect because when standard primary is selected as the zone type, a master copy of the new zone is also created. Like the standard secondary zone type, data in a standard primary is stored in a text file. This allows you to exchange DNS data with other DNS servers that use text-based storage methods. **D** is incorrect because there is no zone type called Active Directory-secondary.

6. ☑ **C.** DNS servers with secondary standard zones will be able to fulfill client requests for lookups but will be unable to send update requests to update their copies of the database. In a standard zone, DNS updates are performed using a single-master update model. In this model, a single DNS server acts as the primary authoritative source for the zone. It maintains a master copy of the zone, and other secondary servers send requests to update their copies of the database. If the primary server experiences problems and becomes unavailable, these updates can't be processed.

 ☒ **A** is incorrect because this choice explains what occurs when an Active Directory-integrated zone is used. Because a master copy is stored in Active Directory and this is fully replicated to every domain controller, every DNS server has a duplicate of the data. Therefore, any domain controller with DNS can perform updates and process requests from clients to perform updates. **B** is incorrect because standard zones use a single-master update model. In this model, a single DNS server acts as the primary authoritative source for the zone and maintains a master copy of the zone. Secondary servers send requests to update their copies of the database. If the primary server experiences problems and becomes unavailable, these updates can't be processed. **D** is incorrect because forward and reverse lookups will be available for computers currently in the DNS database. However, updates will be unavailable as new systems join the network.

7. ☑ **C and D.** This version of BIND is too old to support Active Directory. You have two options available. First, you can upgrade to a more recent version of BIND. Versions 8.1.2 and higher of BIND meet the requirements for Active Directory. Second, you can migrate current DNS zones to Windows 2000 DNS servers and stop using the DNS servers running older versions of BIND.

   ☒ **A** is incorrect because newer versions of BIND do support the requirements for deploying Active Directory. It is also incorrect because you could migrate current DNS zones to Windows 2000 DNS servers and stop using the DNS servers running older versions of BIND. **B** is incorrect because Windows 2000 DNS works alongside UNIX servers running BIND.

8. ☑ **D.** DDNS is dynamic DNS and is used to allow client computers to perform dynamic updates. Dynamic updates allow client computers to register and dynamically update resource records with DNS servers when changes occur. To configure your DNS server to use DDNS, use the DNS Console.

   ☒ **A** is incorrect because DHCP automatically assigns IP addresses to clients. DDNS is configured through the DNS console. **B** is incorrect because DDNS is Dynamic DNS. It is not a type of resource record and isn't automatically set up when DNS is installed. **C** is incorrect because DDNS is not a type of resource record.

Managing, Monitoring, and Troubleshooting Domain Name Service

9. ☑ **C.** You haven't toggled Advanced View Mode by selecting Advanced from the View menu. Advanced allows you to toggle Advanced View Mode on and off. This mode allows you to see items that are for advanced users. If Advanced View Mode is on, you are able to see a folder for cached lookups under the DNS Server. These contain DNS requests that have been fulfilled and cached for future use.

   ☒ **A** is incorrect because Details shows a listing of items that have detailed information beside them, organized in a range of columns. **B** is incorrect because List is used to show items in the console window as a listing, without details. **D** is incorrect because Customize allows you to determine what options will be shown or hidden in the console.

10. ☑ **B.** Even though the Set Aging/Scavenging for All Zones has been configured, and you've ensured that the "Scavenge stale resource material" check box has been selected, aging/scavenging is enabled only for Active Directory-integrated zones. It's important to remember that standard primary zones need to have this feature manually enabled. If you don't manually enable "Scavenge stale resource material" for each standard primary zone, this feature remains disabled for those zones.

☒ **A** is incorrect because you can set aging/scavenging for standard primary zones. **C** is incorrect because although you can manually or automatically scavenge and remove resource records, aging/scavenging won't occur in standard primary zones unless aging/scavenging has been configured for each zone. **D** is incorrect because each zone needs to have its properties configured. You can ensure that Set Aging/Scavenging for All Zones has been configured, but until each zone is configured, scavenging won't take place for standard primary zones.

11. ☑ **B and C.** The Time-To-Live value set by the server that sent the results and the Clear Cache command available from the Action menu determine whether cached results are cleared. The zone that provides a query result sets the TTL. Upon caching the results, the name server begins counting down the TTL from its original value. When it has fully counted down, the TTL expires, and the name server deletes the result from the cache. If the Clear Cache command is used from the Action menu, results stored in the cache are cleared.
☒ **A** is incorrect because the zone providing the results specifies the Time To Live. By default, the TTL is 60 minutes. **D** is incorrect because no Time-To-Live command is available on the Action menu.

12. ☑ **B and D.** After the DNS server has been paused, you can have it resume its work in two ways. In DNS Console, right-click the DNS Server, and then select Resume from the All Tasks folder on the context menu. You can also run the command NET CONTINUE DNS from the command prompt to have DNS server resume.
☒ **A** is incorrect because there is no Services applet in the Windows 2000 Control Panel. This was an applet found in NT 4.*x* Control Panels. **C** is incorrect because there is no Continue command in the All Tasks folder of the Action menu. The correct command here would be Resume.

13. ☑ **A.** The record type Host (A) lists a host's name-to-IP address mapping for a forward lookup zone. Using the New Host command on DNS Console's Action menu, you can create a Host (A) resource record.
☒ **B** is incorrect because HINFO provides host information and is used to identify the operating system and CPU of a host. It is a tool used for resource tracking. **C** is incorrect because PTR is used to create pointers, which point to another domain namespace. In a reverse lookup zone, a PTR record is used to provide IP address-to-computer name mappings. **D** is incorrect because SRV is a resource record for a service. It identifies the servers that are running certain services on a network.

14. ☑ **B.** NSLookup is a tool that allows you to work with DNS to perform forward and reverse lookup queries. Since you have only the IP address of the computer you're searching for, you could only use NSLookup to look for the IP address and resolve it to a computer name. This is a reverse lookup query.

☒ **A** is incorrect because a forward lookup query resolves computer names to IP addresses. Since you don't have the computer name, you would be unable to perform a forward lookup query. **C** is also incorrect because creating an Active Directory-integrated zone type would have a new zone created in Active Directory. You wouldn't be able to determine any information from simply performing this task. **D** is incorrect because there is no such thing as a backup lookup query or a tool called DNSLookup.

15. ☑ **A and D.** IPCONFIG and NSLOOKUP are two command-line utilities that can be used in troubleshooting DNS. Each of these tools have command-line switches that provide abilities that are helpful in determining problems with DNS.

☒ **B and C** are incorrect. Although Event Viewer and DNS Console are necessary to solving problems with DNS, neither of these are command-line utilities.

16. ☑ **B, C, and D.** Zone replication and transfer occur when the DNS service is started on a secondary server, a zone's refresh interval time expires, or changes are made to the primary zone and configuration changes are made to the notify list. Although it was not offered as a choice, you can also initiate replication manually.

☒ **A** is incorrect. Zone replication does not occur when the DNS service is started on the primary server. It does, however, occur if this service is started on a secondary server.

17. ☑ **A.** A primary server responds with either a partial or full zone transfer. A primary or a secondary server responds with either a partial or full zone transfer. Only secondary servers can initiate zone transfers, but the DNS server that's contacted can be either a primary server or another secondary server. When a secondary server contacts another name server for zone data, the source server responds by performing a full or incremental transfer of the zone.

☒ **C** is incorrect because Windows 2000 DNS Server can perform full or incremental transfers of data. **B** is incorrect because secondary servers and primary servers can reply to a request by a secondary server with either a partial or full zone transfer. **D** is incorrect because secondary servers always initiate zone transfers. It is primary servers that don't initiate a zone transfer.

LAB ANSWER

1. On the Windows Start menu, click the Start button. Select Programs, and when this folder expands, point to Administrative Tools; finally click DNS.

2. When the DNS Console opens, select the folder called Forward Lookup Zone, and then click New Zone on the Action menu.

3. When the New Zone Wizard appears, you will see a welcome screen. Click Next.

4. Select "Standard primary" as the zone type you want to create. Click Next.

5. Enter a name for the new zone. An example of a new zone is example.exampledns.com. Click Next.

6. The screen that appears allows you to specify whether you want to create a new zone file or use an existing zone file. If you were to use an existing file, you would need to copy it to the %systemroot%\system32\dns folder. If this file were from a BIND server, you would need to change that file's extension to .DNS. Select "Create a new file with this file name," and then click Next.

7. The final screen appears. Click Finish to create the new zone.

8. Select the folder called Forward Lookup Zone. This folder is found in the tree pane of the DNS Console. Once the folder is selected, click New Zone on the Action menu.

9. A welcome screen appears. Click Next

10. Select "Standard primary" as the zone type, and then click Next.

11. Enter the network ID for your zone. This is your IP address, without the host ID portion of the address. As the network ID is entered, the zone name is automatically entered in the field below. Click Next.

12. As we saw when creating a forward lookup zone, you have the option of creating a new file or using an existing file. Choose the default option of creating a new zone file, and then click Next.

13. The final screen appears. Click Finish to create the new zone.

14. In DNS Console, select the new forward lookup zone you created. The name of this new zone appears in the tree pane, beneath the folder named Forward Lookup Zones. Once the zone is selected, click Properties on the Action menu.

15. On the General tab of your zone's Properties sheet, you will see a drop-down list entitled "Allow dynamic updates?" Click this drop-down list, and select Yes as its value. Dynamic updates are now configured for use.

16. On the General tab of your zone's Properties sheet, you will see an upper section. In this section, you will see the word "Type:" followed by "Primary." This indicates the zone is a standard primary zone. Click the Change button to invoke the Change Zone Type dialog box.

17. When the Change Zone Type dialog box appears, select "Active Directory-integrated" as your new zone type. Click OK. This converts your zone to Active Directory-integrated. A message box then appears, asking you to confirm this change. Click OK.

18. Click OK to exit the Properties sheet for this zone. This causes the changes you've made to take place. Once done, bring up the Properties sheet for this zone again so that you can make further changes to the zone.

19. On the General tab, click the Aging button to invoke the Zone Aging/Scavenging Properties. Click the check box labeled "Scavenge stale resource records" to enable scavenging for this zone. Click OK.

20. Click OK again to exit the Properties sheet for this zone.

6

Implementing and Troubleshooting Group Policy

CERTIFICATION OBJECTIVES

6.01	Creating a Group Policy Object
6.02	Linking an Existing Group Policy Object
6.03	Delegating Administrative Control of Group Policy
6.04	Modifying Group Policy Inheritance
6.05	Filtering Group Policy Settings
6.06	Modifying Group Policy
6.07	Controlling User Environments Using Administrative Templates
6.08	Assigning Script Policies to Users and Computers
✓	Two-Minute Drill
Q&A	Self Test

This chapter discusses Group Policy objects (GPOs) in-depth, covering all aspects of GPOs, from creation, delegation, and modification of GPOs to assigning, filtering, and controlling users and computers. As you will see, GPOs allow you to control just about anything—from desktop settings to installation of new software.

GPOs are descendants of the System Policy Editor in Windows NT 4.0. In NT 4.0, you could create system policies that were enforceable when a user logged onto your domain. If you were smart enough, you could also tailor system policies by scripting your own custom policy. By adding the elements that you could not find in standard policies, you could control just about anything with policies in the Windows NT environment.

Today, GPOs have evolved. They have been modified, expanded, and integrated into Windows 2000 to allow a tighter, more flexible means of easily managing Windows 2000 users and computers on your network. As you see later in the chapter, GPOs greatly simplify the management of Windows 2000 systems.

on the Job

Before reading too far into this chapter and getting excited about the great things you can do with GPOs, keep in mind one very limiting factor: GPOs can be applied to Windows 2000 systems only. GPOs are not supported for legacy systems (Windows NT 4.0, Windows 95/98, and the like).

CERTIFICATION OBJECTIVE 6.01

Creating a Group Policy Object

One of the biggest problems you face as an administrator is the management of users and computers. Settings such as user interface options (background colors, wallpaper), running logon scripts, location of user home directories, and the like are only a fraction of the items that need to be managed on a daily basis. You need a tool to help configure and manage these systems. Group Policy is that tool.

What Are GPOs?

What are Group Policy objects, anyway? GPOs are collections of common
configurations that can be applied to a single user or computer or a group of
users or computers. GPOs consist of Software Settings, Windows Settings, and an
Administrative Templates section for both computers and users (see Figure 6-1).

The Default Domain Policy GPO

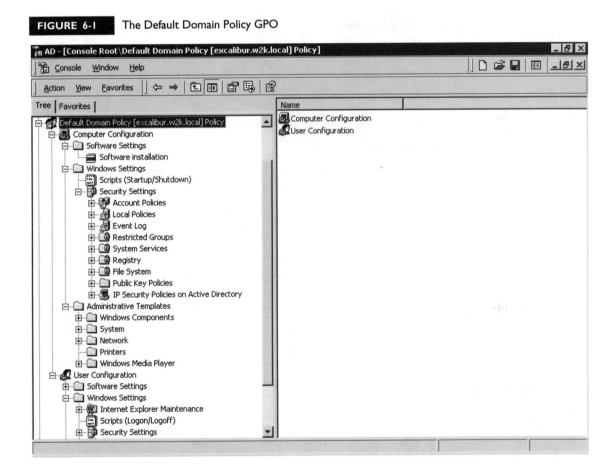

Using these settings, you can dynamically control the computers and users on your network. Software settings allow you to distribute packaged software to target users and computers. Imagine the ability to install a set of applications on a new system without ever having to touch the keyboard! Just turn on the system and the applications are installed automatically.

Windows settings are probably the most powerful in a GPO. With Windows settings, you can add or modify key parts of Windows 2000, such as:

- Restricted user groups
- Startup/shutdown script enforcement
- System services
- Registry settings
- Public key policies (such as Encrypting File System recovery agents)
- IP Security (IPSec) policies
- Other local security settings (such as Event Log settings, audit and account policies, and user right assignments)

Windows settings are what really make GPOs so powerful in Windows 2000.

Finally, there are the Administrative Templates. Administrative Templates give GPOs their flexibility. Administrative Templates are very close to what System Policies are in Windows NT 4.0. Basically, Administrative Templates are registry settings that can further control a user or computer and are grouped together in folders (such as Network, System, Printers). Administrative Templates can control users and computers, whereas other parts of a GPO cannot. By creating your own templates and importing them into Administrative Templates, you can modify your users and computers beyond what can be managed by the default templates provided with Windows 2000. The rule of thumb here is, if it has a registry setting, it can be modified.

Deciding Where to Apply a Group Policy Object in the Organizational Unit Structure

Deciding where to apply your GPO(s) can be hard. Many factors must play a role in the decision as to where to apply your GPOs. As you see later in this chapter, you can selectively apply your GPOs in several different ways:

- Assigning GPOs based on a location such as a site, domain, or OU
- Filtering the assignment of GPOs using security groups
- Modifying the inheritance of a GPO by using the Block Inheritance and No Override switches for group policies

Although there are many ways to apply GPOs within Windows 2000, it is a good idea to select a method in which you apply the majority of your GPOs. You might not be able to apply all your GPOs with the method you choose, but at least you have a *default* method. This helps your organization eliminate some confusion that is bound to arise when there is doubt as to what GPO has been applied to a user or computer.

on the **job**

Keep some of the best practices for Group Policy in the back of your mind when reading this chapter. They are as follows: Disable unused parts of a GPO for faster processing and application of GPOs, use Block Policy Inheritance and No Override sparingly to avoid confusion over the enforcement of GPOs, and minimize use of GPOs in order to allow for faster logons. Following these best practices will help you understand how to properly use GPOs.

How to Create the Policy

Creating group policies within Windows 2000 is pretty simple. Open the Microsoft Management Console (MMC) by clicking Start | Run and typing **MMC**. Click OK, and the MMC console appears. To work with Group Policy, click Console | Add/Remove Snap-in. In the Add/Remove Snap-in window, click the Add button, and select Group Policy from the Add Standalone Snap-in window (see Figure 6-2).

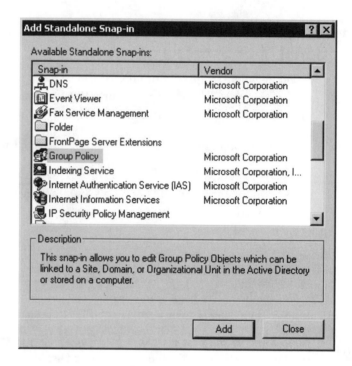

FIGURE 6-2

Selecting the
Group Policy
snap-in

Click the Add button again, and the Select Group Policy Object window appears (see Figure 6-3). Here you must select the group policy you want to put in the MMC. By default, the Group Policy snap-in selects the Local Computer GPO, but you can select another GPO by clicking the Browse button.

Clicking the Browse button creates a Browse for Group Policy Object window, as shown in Figure 6-4. Here you can browse for a GPO that is stored in Active Directory, or you can create a new object by right-clicking in the Browse for Group Policy Object window (see Figure 6-4). Notice that you have a broad range from which to select, or you can create a new GPO. You can browse any domain, OU, or site or select a local computer GPO from another computer.

Once you have either selected or created your GPO, click OK, close the Add Standalone snap-in window, and click OK in the Add/Remove Snap-in window to add the selected or created GPOs to the MMC.

FIGURE 6-3

Selecting the
Group Policy
object

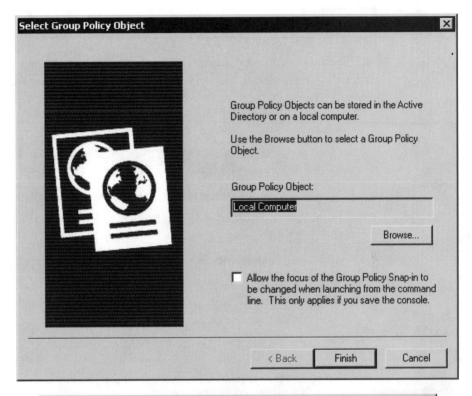

FIGURE 6-4

Browsing for a
Group Policy
object

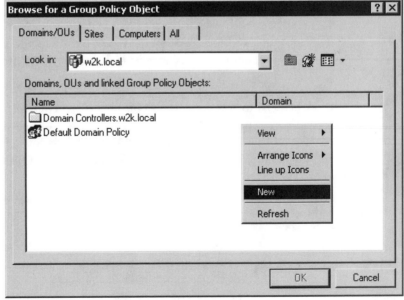

CertCam 6-1

EXERCISE 6-1

Creating a Group Policy Object

For this exercise, you need Active Directory installed through the DCPROMO process. To create a group policy, we use the domain name that was used to install Active Directory.

1. Verify that you are logged on as Administrator.

2. Open the Group Policy MMC snap-in by clicking Start | Run. Type **MMC**. Click OK to run the MMC.

3. To add the Group Policy snap-in, click Console | Add/Remove snap-ins.

4. In the Add/Remove snap-in window, click the Standalone tab, and then click the Add button.

5. In the Add Standalone snap-in window, select the Group Policy snap-in, and click Add.

6. When the Select Group Policy Object window appears (refer back to Figure 6-3), click Browse.

7. When the Browse for a Group Policy Object window appears (refer back to Figure 6-4), select either the Domain/OUs or Sites tabs shown in Figure 6-4, right-click the tab, and select New from the pop-up context menu. This series of actions creates a new GPO in the tab. Name the new GPO **ABCFUTURES**. You will use this GPO in later exercises.

8. Click OK, and then click on the Finish button to add the ABCFUTURES GPO to the list of snap-ins to be included in the MMC.

9. Click Close to close the Add Standalone snap-in window.

10. Click OK to add the new GPO to the MMC console.

Note that this GPO is stored in the object in which you created it. In other words, if you created a new GPO in the Sites tab, the GPO is stored in the Sites object.

CERTIFICATION OBJECTIVE 6.02

Linking an Existing Group Policy Object

Linking an existing GPO to a site, domain, or OU is the way to assign a GPO in order to apply the selected policies within the GPO. By linking the GPO to the site, domain, or OU, you make it possible to apply the policies within the GPO to all or part of the group that exists within the site, domain, or OU. Later in the chapter, you will see that just because you assign a GPO to a site, domain, or OU, that does not actually mean that all the computers or users within the site, domain, or OU have the GPO applied to them. You see later in the chapter how to selectively apply GPOs to computers and users.

An Overview of Group Policy Object Location in Active Directory

When GPOs are created, they exist in the container in which they were created. In another words, when you create a GPO in a site, the GPO can be found in that site by browsing for GPOs in Active Directory. To browse for GPOs, open the MMC and select the Group Policy snap-in. When the Select Group Policy Objects window appears, click the Browse button. In the Browse for a Group Policy Object window, you can see that GPOs can be found in sites, domains, OUs, and local computers (see Figure 6-5).

Once the browsing window is open, select the GPO from the proper container. If you do not find the appropriate existing GPO, you can create your own GPOs in any container (sites, domains, or OUs), just by right-clicking in the window and selecting the New context menu item. This action creates a new GPO in the container with which you are working.

Although you can browse for GPOs, you can also see what GPOs are assigned to a specific container (i.e., site, domain, or OU). By viewing a container's properties and selecting the container's Group Policy tab, you can see exactly what GPOs are assigned to that container.

Finally, although GPOs are logically located in the container in which they are created, they physically reside in one location on all domain controllers in the %SystemRoot%\SYSVOL\sysvol\<domain name>\Policies folder.

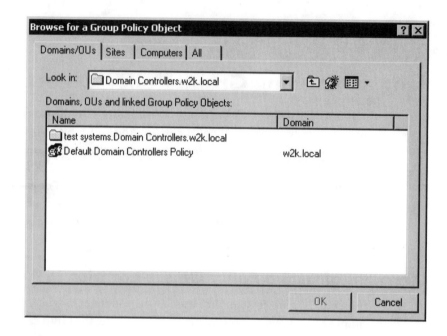

FIGURE 6-3

Browsing for
GPOs in Active
Directory

How to Link a Group Policy Object, and Why

Once you have your GPOs created, you will want to link them to the appropriate containers to start managing users and computers in your network. To link a GPO to a container (site, domain, or OU), right-click the receiving container, and click the Properties context menu item. The Properties window for the container object appears. Click the Group Policy tab, and you will see the list of currently assigned GPOs for the container object (see Figure 6-6).

To create a new GPO, you can click the New button. When creating a new GPO, you have to modify the GPO according to the policies you want to apply. To add an existing GPO, click Add. Once all GPOs have been created or added to the container object, click Apply, and then click OK to apply all the changes.

One thing to keep in mind is that once a GPO is created, it can be applied again to any other container object in Active Directory. By clicking the Add button, as shown in Figure 6-6, you can apply a GPO that has already been created to any container object. GPOs can be applied any number of times, since they are not solely dedicated to the container object to which they are applied.

Once GPOs are linked to a container object, you will want to assign the proper security groups to the GPO in order to correctly apply the GPO settings to all the desired computers and users in the container object. Later in the chapter, we discuss the need to assign the proper security groups for filtering GPOs in container objects.

FIGURE 6-4

Viewing GPOs
assigned to a
container object

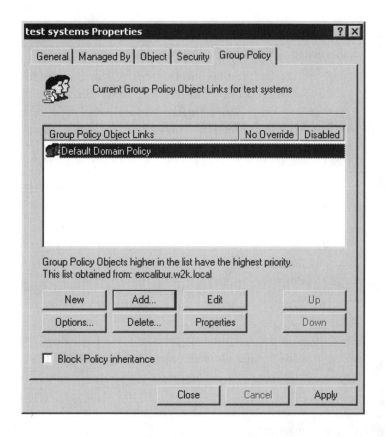

Question	Answer
Are group policies anything like my user profile?	No. Your user profile contains your personal settings, such as desktop configurations. A group policy has a wider scope, covering not only the user but also the computer. Group Policy overrides user profiles by applying its own policies.
Where exactly are group policies stored?	When GPOs are created, they are stored in the domain in which they were created. When browsing for GPOs, you can find your GPO in the object in which it was created. GPOs can be found in several containers: sites, domains, or OUs.
Can I reuse my GPOs? Can I reuse my GPOs in different Active Directory container objects (such as a site and a OU)?	GPOs can be reused as many times as desired. GPOs are not "hard-coded" to a single Active Directory container object, so they can be reused as needed. GPOs can also be assigned to different types of container objects without problems.

SCENARIO & SOLUTION

CertCam 6-2

EXERCISE 6-2

Linking a Group Policy Object

For this exercise, you need to have Active Directory installed through the DCPROMO process. To link a GPO to an object, we use the Domain object that was created when Active Directory was installed. We also use the ABCFUTURES GPO that you created in the previous exercise and link it to the Domain object.

1. Verify that you are logged on as Administrator.

2. Open the Control Panel by clicking Start | Settings | Control Panel. Open the Administrative Tools applet, and click the Active Directory Users and Computers administrative tool.

3. When the Active Directory Users and Computers tool opens, it shows the domain name of your network. Right-click the domain name, and select Properties from the pop-up context menu.

4. When the <domain name> Properties window appears, click the Group Policy tab. Your window will be the same as the one shown in Figure 6-6, with the exception that you will find the ABCFUTURES GPO already added to the Domain object. Select the ABCFUTURES GPO, and click the Delete button to remove the link from the list. Make sure that you select the option to remove the GPO from the list only; do not delete the GPO from Active Directory! Click OK, and the ABCFUTURES GPO is removed from the list.

5. To link the ABCFUTURES GPO to the Domain object, click Add. In the Add a Group Policy Object Link window, select the All tab, and make sure the Look In drop-down window has your domain selected. The ABCFUTURES GPO is listed here.

6. Click the ABCFUTURES GPO, and click OK. The ABCFUTURES GPO is added to the Domain object. The ABCFUTURES GPO is now linked to the Domain object. Leave the ABCFUTURES GPO linked; we use this linked GPO for exercises later in the chapter.

Delegating Administrative Control of Group Policy

One of the first observations you will make regarding Windows 2000 is that it is complex. One of the features that makes Windows 2000 complex is Group Policy. The nature of Group Policy and its flexibility, which allows easy configuration of computers and users, also makes it extremely hard for only one person to manage all the configurations. You will find that Group Policy, along with several other tasks, needs to be broken into pieces and managed by a few select individuals for each task. Breaking up the burden not only allows administrators to approach management of Windows 2000 with a "divide and conquer" attitude with respect to the amount of work, but it also allows administrators to delegate parts of Windows 2000 to certain administrators and be able to secure the assigned part of Windows 2000 so that only those assigned to work with a specific section are allowed to do so.

Why Delegate Control?

Why delegate control of Group Policy? The answer to that question is easy to see when you open a default group policy, such as the Default Domain Policy. By browsing through this policy, you can get a feel for just how powerful group policies are. Delegating control of group policies allows administrators to control exactly who enforces and modifies a group policy. Strict control of *all* group policies is necessary for a large enterprise network because a poorly configured group policy, placed on the wrong Active Directory object, can spell disaster for your network.

How to Delegate Control of Group Policy Objects

Delegating control over GPOs is a little complicated, so we take it step-by-step. First, open the Active Directory Sites and Services snap-in, and navigate to the Sites object. From the Sites object, expand the object and select a site. In Figure 6-7, we selected the London site to use as our example, but keep in mind that any Active

FIGURE 6-5   Selecting the London site to view its Properties page

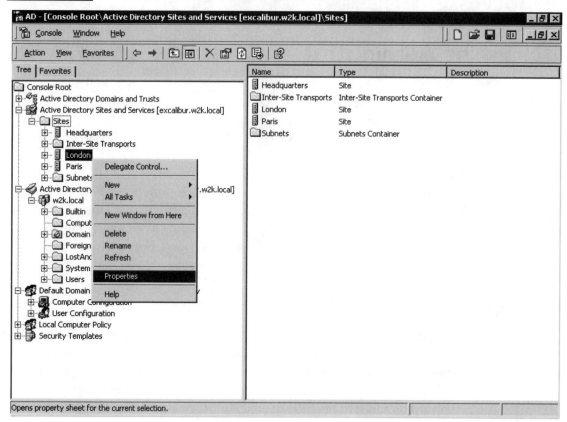

Directory container object (such as a site or OU) could be used. When you right-click London and select Properties, a London Properties window appears, as shown in Figure 6-8. Do *not* select the Delegate Control context menu item by mistake. This menu item controls the delegation of control over the London object, not the GPOs for London.

In the London Properties window, click the New button, which creates a new GPO. A newly created GPO is initially named New Group Policy Object, but as shown in Figure 6-8, we renamed the GPO *GPO Control.*

FIGURE 6-6

London
Properties
window and the
new group policy,
GPO Control

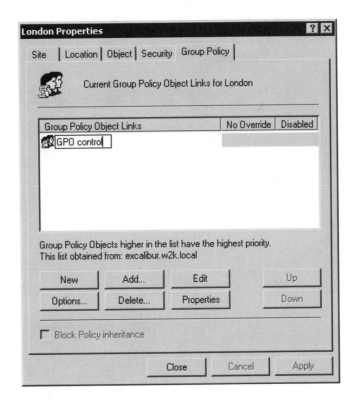

Continuing on, click the Properties button, which opens the GPO Control Properties window. By clicking on the Security tab, as shown in Figure 6-9, you can view the access control list (ACL) for Control GPO. This ACL is where you delegate the control over any GPO. Clicking each access control entry (ACE) reveals its permissions in the Permissions text box. Notice that Authenticated Users has only Read and Apply Group Policy permissions—just enough permission to allow any authenticated user to read and apply the GPO in question.

To delegate new users or groups to work with this GPO, click Add to add the necessary users or groups. Once all users and/or groups have been delegated,

FIGURE 6-7

Viewing the ACL
for GPO Control

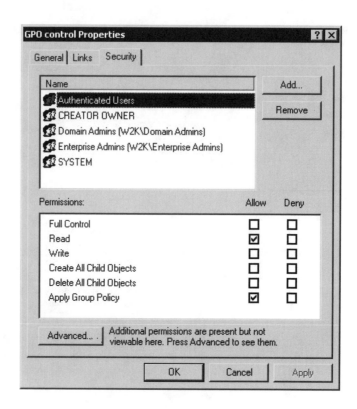

remember to assign the necessary permissions for each user and group, and click OK to save your changes. These permissions are:

■ **Full Control** Allows assigned users or groups to have full control over the object specified. Users or groups have all permissions that are listed below.

■ **Read** Users or groups are only allowed to open and read the specified object. They are not allowed to write to the object, nor are they permitted to apply the object.

- **Write**   Users or groups are only allowed to write to the specified object. They cannot read the object, nor are they permitted to apply the object.

- **Create All Child Objects**   Users or groups can create objects that are children to the object in question.

- **Delete All Child Objects**   Users or groups can delete objects that are children to the object in question.

- **Apply Group Policy**   Allows users or groups to apply the GPO that is linked to the Active Directory container. This permission is always assigned along with the Read permission because users or groups must be able to read the GPO in order to apply it.

on the **Job**

Another way of controlling access to Group Policy is through the assignment of a group policy. By creating a new group policy and navigating down the GPO to the User Configuration\Administrative Templates\Windows Components\ Microsoft Management Console\Restricted/Permitted Snap-ins\Group Policy object, you will see in the right-hand window several policies, shown in Figure 6-10. These policies control how Group Policy is enforced when the GPO is applied to users. As shown in Figure 6-10, the Group Policy snap-in and Group Policy Tab for Active Directory Tools policies are disabled. When this policy is applied to a set of users, all users who are affected by the GPO are unable to add the Group Policy snap-in to the Microsoft Management Console. Furthermore, all affected users do not see Group Policy tabs on any sites, domains, or OUs when viewing their Properties pages.

WARNING! If you implement this method as a security measure, make sure that you do not apply it to any Administrator equivalent accounts (such as Administrator). Doing so will disable Group Policy for Administrators! Make sure that you remove Authenticated Users from the ACL on the GPO because Administrators are members of this group once they are authenticated by Windows 2000.

FIGURE 6-8   Configuring a GPO to disable the Group Policy snap-in

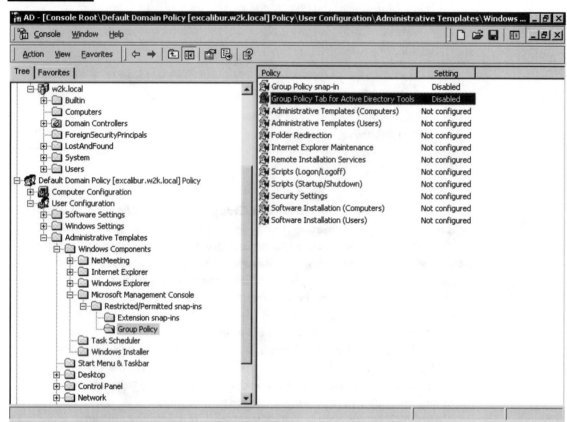

exam
ⓦ a t c h   *Make sure that you understand how to delegate control of Group Policy by giving users and groups specific permissions, such as read only, read-write, or apply the group policy.*

CertCam 6-3

Delegating Control of a Group Policy Object

EXERCISE 6-3

In this exercise, you create a security group, ABCFUTURES-ADMIN, and delegate control of the GPO, ABCFUTURES, to this security group.

1. Verify that you are logged on as Administrator.

2. Open the Control Panel by clicking Start | Settings | Control Panel. Open the Administrative Tools applet, and click the Active Directory Users and Computers administrative tool.

3. When the Active Directory Users and Computers tool opens, it shows the domain name of your network. Right-click the domain name, and select Properties from the pop-up context menu.

4. When the <domain name> Properties window appears, click the Group Policy tab. The ABCFUTURES GPO is listed as the only GPO linked to this domain object.

5. Click the ABCFUTURES GPO, and then click the Properties button. The ABCFUTURES Properties window appears. Click the Security tab to view all the groups linked to this GPO.

6. To delegate exclusive control over this GPO, remove the Domain Admins, Enterprise Admins, and Creator Owner security groups. This leaves the Authenticated Users and SYSTEM security groups only. The Authenticated Users group remains so that it can apply the GPO once it is finished. *Note:* Make positively sure that the administrator account that you are using is a member of the ABCFUTURES-ADMIN security group. If it is not, you will *not* be able to access the GPO for later exercises!

7. Add the ABCFUTURES-ADMIN security group, and give this group Full Control access to the GPO. Click OK to make your changes effective.

Make sure you keep the ABCFUTURES-ADMIN security group and the ABCFUTURES GPO because we use them for later exercises.

CERTIFICATION OBJECTIVE 6.04

Modifying Group Policy Inheritance

One of the most important concepts that you need to clearly understand is the concept of GPO inheritance. *Inheritance* is the acceptance of GPO settings as designated by group policies assigned higher in the chain of Group Policy processing.

Group policies, as stated earlier in the chapter, can be assigned to local computers, sites, domains, and OUs. Processing of group policies occurs in this order while, at the same time, multiple GPOs for objects are applied in order from *bottom to top*. As shown in Figure 6-11, it is stated below the GPO links that GPOs higher in the GPO list have the highest priority.

Looking even deeper into how GPOs are applied, once a GPO is selected to be applied, it applies all sections within the Computer configuration section first, including the execution of any startup scripts, followed by the application of all sections within the User Configuration section. Again, all sections are applied, including any logon scripts. One thing to keep in mind is that if there are computer and user policies that specify contradictory settings and/or behavior, the computer policy generally wins out over the user policy.

Looking at Figure 6-11, you can see that for the W2K.LOCAL domain object, several GPOs are assigned. Note that the Default Domain Controllers Policy GPO is highlighted, and the Up and Down buttons are enabled to allow the GPO to be moved up or down the list of GPOs in order to change its processing order.

What Is Inheritance?

Inheritance, as explained previously, is the acceptance of GPO settings that were applied by a previous GPO. Take the example of desktop settings. The ABC Company decides that it wants to place its logo as the wallpaper for all company workstations and change the mouse pointer to an animated mouse. The GPO for this policy is placed in the ABC Company's only site, ABC. The ABC Company has a marketing organization that deals with external kiosks and cannot have the company's logo for wallpaper, but the staff like the animated mouse for marketing

FIGURE 6-9

Multiple GPOs
assigned to the
W2K.LOCAL
domain object

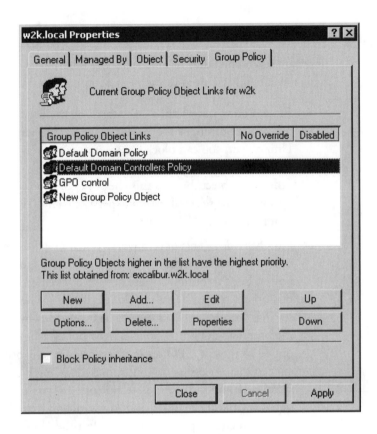

purposes. They create a GPO that changes the wallpaper to a blue background, but they leave the animated mouse pointer. They assign this new GPO to the OU that handles marketing. When the marketing systems are rebooted, the Sites GPO is processed first, which assigns the wallpaper logo and the animated mouse pointer. Next, the marketing GPO is applied and, because there is a new configuration for the wallpaper, the wallpaper is set to a blue background. Since there is no new configuration for the mouse pointer, the workstation inherits the GPO setting that was last applied to the workstation. In this case, the last applied mouse pointer setting was the animated mouse pointer.

Managing Inheritance

There are several methods of modifying the inheritance of GPO changes in order to apply the settings you need to the right computers or users. You can:

- **Block Policy Inheritance** By checking the Block Policy Inheritance check box at the bottom of the Group Policy tab for any Domain or Organizational Unit object, you can block the inheritance of any group policies for this object. Instead of inheriting policies applied higher in the GPO processing order, the object that has this check box selected ignores all policies. This option can be selected without specifying any GPOs for an object (such as a Domain or Organizational Unit object).

- **No Override** This option works much like the Block Policy Inheritance option in that it blocks the inheritance of any group policies for a container object, but this option applies only to a specific GPO. Not only that, but this option is considered the "king" of options because it specifies that all settings within the GPO cannot be overridden by any other GPO during the processing of group policies. Any policy assigned the No Override option assigns its GPO settings regardless of any other settings found later in the processing of GPOs, including any Block Policy Inheritance settings. To select the No Override option, you must click the GPO in question, and then click the Options button (refer back to Figure 6-11). Once you click Options, you can select the No Override check box, as shown in Figure 6-12.

Note that if Windows 2000 is forced to apply both No Override and Block Policy Inheritance settings, No Override always "wins."

exam
⑩atch

Know the order of GPO processing by heart because this topic will certainly be a key point Microsoft emphasizes in the certification exam. Remember that the Local Computer GPO is processed first, then all GPOs assigned to sites, domains, and OUs are processed, in that order. The acronym that is taught in Microsoft Official Curriculum classes is LSDOU: Local Computer, Site, Domain, Organizational Unit.

In addition, keep in mind that OUs can be nested, which means that each OU is traversed until the object in question is reached. Lastly, remember that a list of GPOs assigned to an object is processed from bottom to top.

FIGURE 6-10

Modifying the
inheritance of
GPOs

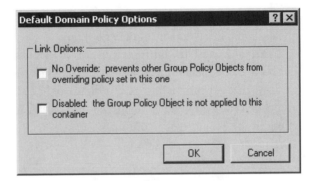

How to Change the Group Policy Object Inheritance

To change the GPO inheritance, you first must open a GPO. Open the Active
Directory Users and Computers snap-in and navigate to the <domain name> | Domain
Controllers Organizational Unit object. Right-click the Domain Controllers object, and
select the Properties context menu item. A Domain Controllers Properties window
appears. Click the Group Policy tab. To block policy inheritance, click the Block Policy
Inheritance check box at the bottom of the tab (refer back to Figure 6-11). Again, any

FROM THE CLASSROOM

Group Policy: The Cornerstone of Windows 2000 Management

Hopefully, by now you understand how
important group policies are to the
management of Windows 2000. Group Policy
is the key to effectively managing *all* aspects of
Windows 2000 on your network. Group
Policy is probably the hardest concept to
understand, and that is why a significant
amount of time is spent in Windows 2000
training classes trying to teach this concept.

Unfortunately, Group Policy is such a hard
concept to understand because there is really

no equivalent to it on any other platform.
Before you take your certification test, make
sure that you have gone through group
policies, part by part, so that you have an
in-depth understanding of Group Policy. Do
not ignore the exercises in this chapter! These
will help you get the experience with working
with Group Policy that you need for the
certification test.

—*Michael Seamans, MCSE*

other Active Directory container object could be used, but for this example, we have chosen to use the Domain container object.

Next, click the New button to create a new Group Policy object. Once the object has been created, click the object, and then click the Options button. In the Options window that appears (refer back to Figure 6-12), select the No Override check box, and click OK. You will be able to see that New Group Policy Object now has a check in the No Override column.

CertCam 6-4

EXERCISE 6-4

Modifying Group Policy Inheritance

In this exercise, you learn how modifying inheritance can affect GPO processing.

1. Verify that you are logged on as Administrator.

2. Open the Control Panel by clicking Start | Settings | Control Panel. Open the Administrative Tools applet, and click the Active Directory Users and Computers administrative tool.

3. When Active Directory Users and Computers opens, it shows the domain name of your network. Right-click the domain name, and select Properties from the pop-up context menu.

4. When the <domain name> Properties window appears, click the Group Policy tab. The ABCFUTURES GPO is listed as the only GPO linked to this Domain object.

5. Click New to add another GPO to the Domain object. You can name this GPO anything you want. Ensure that the new GPO was created and placed second in the list of policies for the domain.

6. Modify both GPOs with the following User Configuration setting: Administrative Templates/Desktop | Hide all icons on Desktop. Configure the ABCFUTURES GPO as Enabled and the new GPO with Disabled. Make no other modifications. Save your settings and log off.

7. Log on to your system. What happened? Was it what you expected? What should have happened was that the desktop icons were hidden on your desktop. This is because GPOs are applied in order, and since you specifically enabled and disabled the policy Hide all Icons on Desktop for both GPOs, the policy was applied in both GPOs. Since the new GPO was

created and placed second in the list, its policy was applied first (remember, bottom to top). Since the ABCFUTURES GPOs policy was set to Enabled, it has the effect of hiding the desktop icons, since it was applied last.

8. Go back to the <domain name> Properties window and modify the new GPO by clicking the Options button. When the Options window appears for the new GPO, check the No Override check box, click OK, and then click Close.

9. Log off the system and then log on again. What happened? Was it what you expected?
   What should have happened was that the desktop icons became visible on your desktop. Since the No Override option was enabled on the new GPO, no other GPO policies could be inherited. The new GPO policy stated that Hide all Icons on Desktop was disabled. Since no other GPO policy could be inherited, this policy remained disabled through the processing of all GPOs, which, in turn, allowed the desktop icons to remain visible.

10. Go back to the <domain name> Properties window and delete the new GPO. Change the ABCFUTURES GPO back to its original state by resetting the User Configuration at Administrative Templates/Desktop | Hide all icons on Desktop. This choice enables you to use this GPO for exercises later in the chapter.

CERTIFICATION OBJECTIVE 6.05

Filtering Group Policy Settings

You can filter group policies using various Active Directory objects, but it is very difficult to do this when you have a large enterprise. A finer granularity is needed when dealing with smaller groups that must have certain settings. Using Active Directory objects then becomes impractical. Using security groups with group policies, you can achieve a finer granularity by applying a GPO only to those computers or users that require it, even though these computers or users might belong to a larger group within an OU or domain.

Why Filter a Group Policy Object?

Why filter GPOs? As stated previously, you might need to apply unique computer or user GPO settings to a small group within a company. This need could grow with the size of your company. The larger the company, the greater the possibility that you will need to treat certain groups of computers or users uniquely. This is where you can filter the application of GPOs to certain groups of computers and users through the use of security groups.

Take, for example, a small company of 100 people. All computers and users are in the same site because of the size of the company. The human resources (HR) department, however, needs to have several policies enforced on both their computers and for each user, along with having a couple of HR-specific applications installed to their computers. We call the GPO needed for the HR group HRTWEAKS. No other group in the company needs this configuration. Once the HRTWEAKS GPO is linked to the company's site, an administrator can create a security group called HR and place all the computers and users from HR within this group.

on the
ⓙob   *Remember, with Windows 2000, you can use computers as well as users within security groups. In Windows NT, you had only the ability to use users within security groups. Windows 2000 has been expanded to allow administrators to place computers into security groups, mostly to allow the filtering of GPOs.*

Once the HRTWEAKS GPO is linked to the site, the administrator applies the HR security group to the GPO and sets the Read and Apply Group Policy permissions to allow all the computers and users within this security group to apply the HRTWEAKS GPO (see Figure 6-13). The Authenticated Users group must also be removed to correctly apply the GPO. Remember that this GPO is in a site, so not only are there users in the HR group in this site, but there are also the rest of the domain users in this site. Without removing the Authenticated Users group, you apply the GPO to all users in this site.

When the HR computers are rebooted and HR users log on, the settings within the HRTWEAKS GPO are applied.

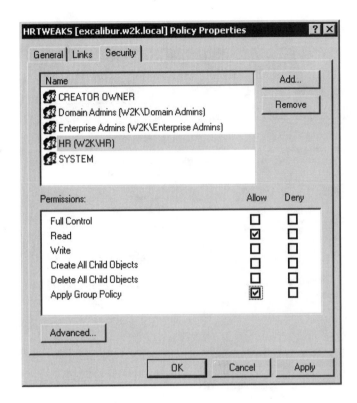

FIGURE 6-11

Applying the security group HR to the HRTWEAKS GPO

How to Apply a Filter to a Group Policy Object

Applying a filter to a GPO is relatively simple. If you have applied security permissions to files or folders on NTFS drives, you will be able to apply filters to a GPO, because the two are very similar procedures.

As a simple example, we apply a new GPO to the W2K.LOCAL domain and apply the previously used HR security group to the new GPO.

First, for our example, the Active Directory Users and Computers MMC snap-in must be opened. Underneath Active Directory Users and Computers, the Windows 2000 domain can be found. For our example, we use the W2K.LOCAL domain, as

FIGURE 6-12   Selecting the W2K.LOCAL domain in order to apply a GPO

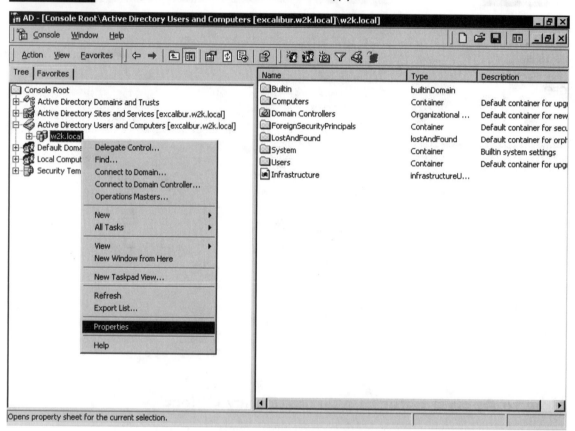

shown in Figure 6-14. When you right-click the W2K.LOCAL domain and select the Properties context menu item, the W2K.LOCAL Properties windows appears. To apply a GPO and filter, click the Group Policy tab to show all the GPOs currently assigned to the W2K.LOCAL Domain object. For this example, we use the GPO Control GPO, as shown in Figure 6-15.

By clicking the Control GPO and then clicking the Properties button, we can view the security groups assigned to the GPO by clicking the Security tab in the

FIGURE 6-13

List of GPOs
assigned to the
W2K.LOCAL
Domain object

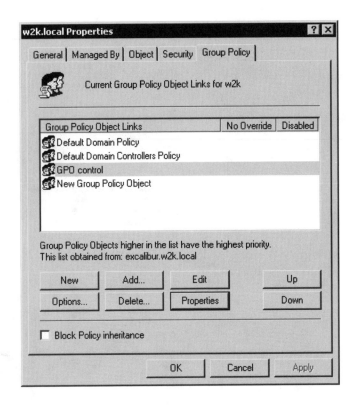

GPO Control Properties window, as shown in Figure 6-16. To add the HR security group, click Add, scroll down the W2K.LOCAL list, select the HR security group, and click OK.

Once the HR security group is added to the GPO Control object, click HR to be able to modify the permissions for the HR security group. As shown in Figure 6-16, you want to assign Read and Apply Group Policy permissions to the HR security group. This assignment gives the minimum amount of permission in order for the HR security group to apply the GPO correctly. Again, note that the Authenticated Users group has been removed because the GPO is being applied to a specific set of users. Once you have applied permissions to the security group, you have successfully applied a GPO filter using security groups.

FIGURE 6-14

Applying the HR
security group to
the GPO Control
GPO

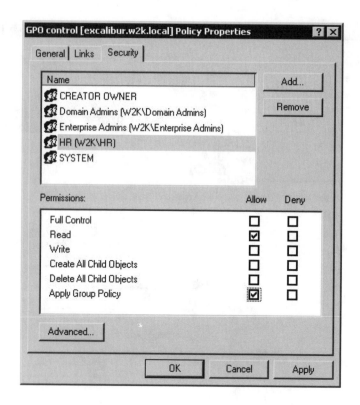

exam

watch

Know filtering of group policies like "the back of your hand." In the Microsoft certification exams, you are bound to run into questions regarding the application of group policies. Some questions will center around the application of GPOs by the order of processing from sites, domains, and OUs, while other questions will focus on applying GPOs through the use of security groups. This is definitely a topic area in which paying close attention to the wording of questions, along with strong knowledge of filtering GPOs, is necessary.

SCENARIO & SOLUTION

What is the purpose for delegating control of GPOs?	Delegating control allows for management of GPOs on a much finer scale. Delegating control allows administrators to designate a user or group of users to administer either a single GPO or several GPOs. GPOs are very complex and powerful objects within Active Directory; open management of GPOs can lead to enterprisewide problems.
I am confused with the order of GPO processing. What is the order of processing?	The order of processing for GPOs is local computer, sites, domains, and organizational units (from parent to child OUs). Remember LSDOU, as mentioned earlier in the chapter. Because any object can have several GPOs applied to it, you must remember when using a list of GPOs that GPOs are also applied from bottom to top before moving onto the next object in the processing order.
What is the difference between Block Policy Inheritance and No Override? These two items seem to do the same thing.	Using Block Policy Inheritance prevents the inheritance of *any* Group Policy settings from GPOs higher in the order of processing, whereas No Override specifies GPO settings never to be overridden during the processing of other GPOs later in the sequence. Note that a No Override setting overrides a Block Policy Inheritance setting for an Active Directory object. Block Policy Inheritance blocks inheritance from a point in the processing order down the processing tree, depending on where it is implemented. No Override does not care where it is implemented. Once No Override is used, the GPO that is using it is not overridden with any other GPO. Period.
I have linked a GPO to an Active Directory object (a site), but the GPO does not seem to be working correctly. What is wrong?	Remember that one of the final steps to linking a GPO to an Active Directory object is to assign the proper security permissions. When you link a GPO, you have to make sure that the proper security groups are added so that the GPO can be applied correctly. Authenticated Users is added by default, and the Apply Group Policy permission is automatically given. This should be enough to enforce any GPO. You might have to modify the security groups in order to properly apply your GPO.

CertCam 6-5

Filtering Group Policy Using Security Groups

In this exercise, you learn how to apply GPOs through the use of security groups. You use the security group ABCFUTURES-ADMIN to filter GPOs.

1. Verify that you are logged on as Administrator.

2. Create a new user account, **TEST1**, and place it in the global group ABCFUTURES-ADMIN.

3. Open the Control Panel by clicking Start | Settings | Control Panel. Open the Administrative Tools applet, and click the Active Directory Users and Computers administrative tool.

4. When the Active Directory Users and Computers tool opens, it shows the domain name of your network. Right-click the domain name, and select Properties from the pop-up context menu.

5. When the <domain name> Properties window appears, click the Group Policy tab. The ABCFUTURES GPO is listed as the only GPO linked to this domain object.

6. Click the ABCFUTURES GPO, and then click the Properties button.

7. In the ABCFUTURES Properties window, modify permissions for ABCFUTURES by adding Domain Admins and Enterprise Admins as Full Control, remove Authenticated Users, and modify the ABCFUTURES-ADMIN security group so that it has only Read and Apply Group Policy permissions.

8. Next, click ABCFUTURES, and then click Edit. In the Group Policy window, navigate to the User Configuration/Administrative Templates/Desktop | Hide all icons on Desktop entry. Modify the entry from Not Configured to Enabled. Click OK to save the modification.

9. Close the GPO windows and log off. Log back on to the system with the TEST1 account. What happens? Was this expected? Why or why not? What should have happened is that all desktop icons were removed from the desktop. Because TEST1 is a member of the ABCFUTURES-ADMIN security group and this group was given Read and Apply Group Policy permissions, TEST1 was able to apply the Hide all icons on Desktop policy.

10. Log off and log on with the Administrator account. Remove TEST1 from the ABCFUTURES-ADMIN security group.

11. Log off the system and log on with TEST1. What happens? Was this expected? Why or why not?

 What should have happened is that all desktop icons became visible on the desktop. Since TEST1 was removed as a member of the ABCFUTURES-ADMIN security group, it could not apply the ABCFUTURES GPO.

CERTIFICATION OBJECTIVE 6.06

Modifying Group Policy

So far in this chapter, we have talked about what GPOs are, linking GPOs to objects, and even how GPOs work, but we have not yet closely looked at or talked about GPOs in detail. In this section, we do just that.

GPOs consist of two main sections, the Computer Configuration section and the User Configuration section. Within these two sections is another set of three main folders: Software Settings, Windows Settings, and Administrative Templates (see Figure 6-17). These folders contain settings for such items as software installation(s), security configurations (such as account policy, event log, and IP Security policy settings), and registry settings to control the configuration of Windows 2000 systems.

Digging even deeper into GPOs, you will find many hidden gems via which to control and manage your Windows 2000 system.

 on the *Job*

You are encouraged to open a default GPO and examine the contents that lie within. Only by exploring, analyzing, and understanding GPOs will you be able to get a feel for exactly how they work and how they can be applied. This exploration is extremely valuable in conjunction with the study of any Windows 2000 textbook.

FIGURE 6-15 A view of the Default Domain GPO, showing the various settings sections

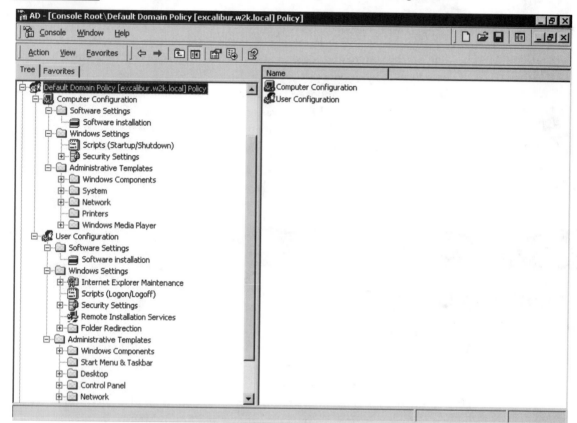

Changing the Policy

Changing a policy is relatively easy. Using the MMC, you can add any group policy by clicking Console | Add/Remove Snap-in in the MMC and adding the Group Policy snap-in. You are prompted to select a group policy, as shown in Figure 6-3; by clicking Browse, you can select any Group Policy in the Active Directory, or you can create a new policy, as shown in Figure 6-4.

Once you have your group policy selected, you can open and modify it as needed. Remember that there is no saving mechanism, so any changes you make are applied immediately. Anyone rebooting a computer or a user logging onto the network that uses the group policy you are modifying will receive these changes.

When changing a policy, you must pay close attention to how each setting is configured. Leaving a setting Not Defined or Not Configured is basically akin to instructing Group Policy to ignore the setting and to use the last setting that was applied. (This is where the concept of inheritance comes into play; however, inheritance applies to all objects, whether they are configured or not.) Group Policy using the last applied setting might or might not be what you want. Having policies set as Not Defined or Not Configured allows GPOs to be processed faster. This is true because the system can see that each individual policy is not configured, so it can move onto the next individual policy. If there is an individual policy that is configured as Enabled or Disabled, there is extra processing time involved with making the correct configurations to enforce this individual policy setting.

You must understand both of these settings in order to correctly set up group policies, because these settings can affect not only how a group policy is applied to a computer or user, but how fast group policies are processed on a system. For example, look at Figure 6-18, which is a policy that defines the Slow Network Connection Timeout for User Profiles. As shown, the policy is Not Defined. This individual policy will be ignored when the group policy is processed.

FIGURE 6-16

Policy defining
slow network
timeout for user
profile processing

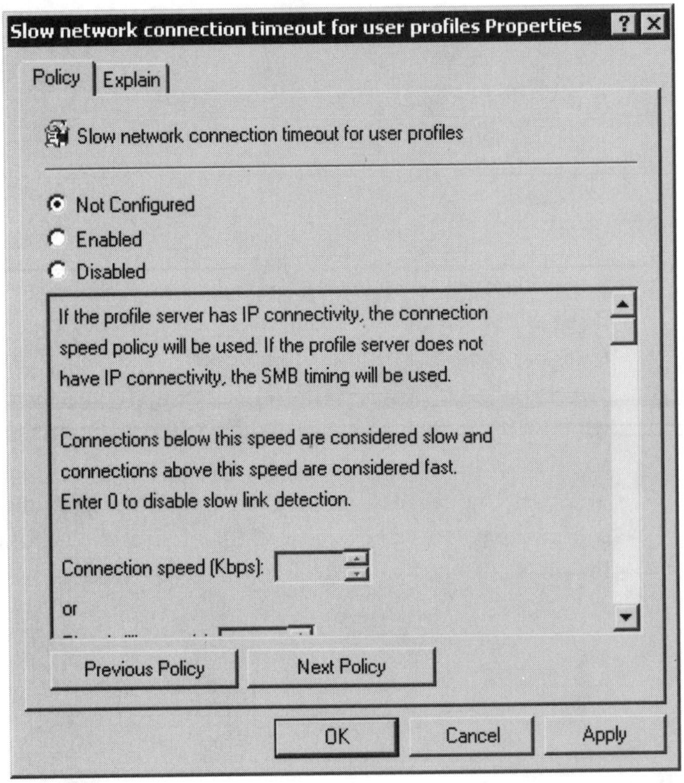

FIGURE 6-17

Disabling the
Computer
Configuration
section within a
GPO

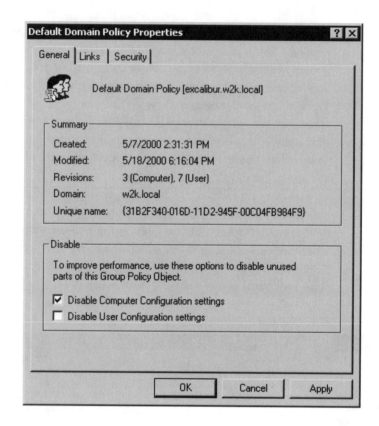

FIGURE 6-17

Disabling the
Computer
Configuration
section within a
GPO

Another way of changing a GPO is to disable some of its parts. If you are not using either the User or Computer Configurations within a GPO, you can disable them in order to speed GPO processing in Windows 2000 (see Figure 6-19). You can also disable a whole GPO by selecting the Disabled check box in the Options window (refer back to Figure 6-12). You usually disable GPOs in order to help troubleshoot their application.

When you disable Computer or User Configuration settings, you are asked to confirm that you want to disable that part of the GPO that you have selected (see Figure 6-20).

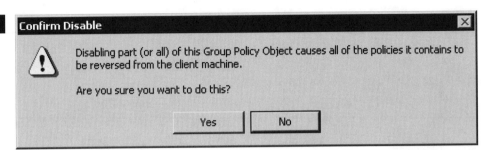

FIGURE 6-18

Confirming the
disabling of a
section within
a GPO

CertCam 6-6

EXERCISE 6-6

Deleting a Group Policy

In this exercise, we look at deleting GPOs from Active Directory. We also look at
the options to remove a GPO from a container object and to actually delete a GPO
from the Active Directory.

1. Verify that you are logged on as Administrator.

2. Open the Control Panel by clicking Start | Settings | Control Panel. Open
   the Administrative Tools applet, and click the Active Directory Users and
   Computers administrative tool.

3. When the Active Directory Users and Computers tool opens, it shows the
   domain name of your network. Right-click the domain name, and select
   Properties from the pop-up context menu.

4. When the <domain name> Properties window appears, click the Group
   Policy tab. The ABCFUTURES GPO is listed as one of the GPOs linked to
   this Domain object.

5. Click the ABCFUTURES GPO, and then click the Delete button. A Delete
   window appears, asking whether you want to remove the GPO link from the
   list of linked GPOs or if you want to remove the GPO link from the list and
   delete the GPO permanently from Active Directory. Make sure that you
   select the option to remove the GPO link from the list of linked GPOs, and
   click OK. The GPO link is removed from the domain container.

6. Add the ABCFUTURES GPO back to the domain object by clicking the Add button and selecting the ABCFUTURES GPO. You need to use this GPO for later exercises.

7. Next, click the New button to create a new GPO. Name this new GPO **ABC123**. To confirm that the GPO has been created and it exists in Active Directory, click Add. You should be able to see the ABC123 GPO by looking in either the Domains/OUs or All tabs.

8. Once you have verified that the ABC123 GPO exists in the Active Directory, click the Cancel button to return to the <domain name> Properties window.

9. Click the ABC123 GPO, and then click Delete. When the Delete window appears, select the option to remove the GPO link and permanently delete the GPO from Active Directory. Click OK.

10. A Delete Group Policy Object window appears, asking you to confirm that you want to delete the GPO. Click Yes.

11. To confirm that the ABC123 GPO has not only been removed from the GPO list but has also been deleted from Active Directory, click Add.

12. If you look under the Domains/OUs or All tabs, you will not find the ABC123 GPO, which confirms that it was deleted from Active Directory.

13. Click Cancel to close the Add a Group Policy Object Link window. Click Close button to close the <domain name> Properties window.

CERTIFICATION OBJECTIVE 6.07

Controlling User Environments Using Administrative Templates

Although each part of Group Policy (Software Settings, Windows Settings, and Administrative Templates) is very powerful, only one, Administrative Templates, can be modified through the addition or deletion of templates. Software Settings and Windows Settings are dependent on modifications to change (through modified settings), and you cannot actually add to either part, whereas Administrative Templates allows administrators to add to the section for adding templates. These templates consist of new registry settings that allow administrators to control certain computer or user settings, depending on which section the template focuses.

Although Windows 2000 includes several default templates, administrators can create their own custom templates and import these templates into group policies, to be applied as needed. This feature makes Group Policy an even more powerful management tool because it gives administrators more flexibility to manage Windows 2000.

on the **Job** *Creating your own administrative templates is one of the most challenging and rewarding tasks that you can do in Group Policy. By creating your own custom templates, you can control just about anything dealing with computer or user settings. To learn more about creating your own administrative templates, see Appendix B: Administrative Templates, in Microsoft's* **Group Policy White Paper.** *This white paper fully explains how to create custom templates, including a full list of keywords and syntax examples. This white paper can be found at www.microsoft.com/TechNet/win2000/win2ksrv/ technote/nt5polcy.asp.*

on the **Job** *A migration issue you might run into is the use of Windows NT 4.0 system policies on Windows 2000 systems. It is possible to import these policies into Administrative Templates, but it is not recommended. The reason that importing them is not recommended is that the use of Windows NT 4.0 system policies "tattoos" the registry, making the policy settings permanent wherever they are applied. All modifications made with Administrative Templates are removed when the user logs off or the computer shuts down, leaving the original registry settings intact. To properly use your custom policies, you need to rewrite these policies using guidance from Microsoft's* **Group Policy White Paper.**

What Can the Administrator Control?

What can the administrator control? With all the talk about creating custom administrative templates, what can you really control with the Administrative Templates feature?

Administrative templates are templates that can modify registry settings for a computer or user. For a computer, the Administrative Templates component can only modify registry settings within the HKEY_LOCAL_MACHINE (HKLM) registry hive. For a user, Administrative Templates can only modify registry settings within the HKEY_CURRENT_USER (HKCU) registry hive. Although these limitations might seem restrictive, think about exactly what is covered within these two hives. All software configurations (HKLM\Software) and all aspects of desktop settings for users (HKCU\Control Panel) are a couple of broad examples of the functions covered within these registry hives.

How to Create and Import Templates

As previously discussed, you can create your own custom administrative templates to use in group policies. Once created, custom administrative templates should be saved with the .ADM file extension and saved to the %SystemRoot%\INF folder. This is the target/default folder for all template files. Although this is the default folder for storing administrative templates, when you add custom templates to a GPO, the custom template is copied to the GPO's ADM folder in the SYSVOL folder (i.e.%SystemRoot%\SYSVOL\Sysvol\<domain name>\Policies\<GPO GUID>\ADM). The reason for this difference is that the GPO is replicated to all other domain controllers in the domain, and this custom template must also be replicated to all domain controllers in order to properly apply it.

To import templates, simply navigate to either Computer Configuration | Administrative Templates or User Configuration | Administrative Templates in the target GPO, right-click Administrative Templates, and select Add/Remove Templates from the pop-up context menu (see Figure 6-21). Make sure that if your template has both User and Computer policies, you select both Computer Configuration and User Configuration to import the appropriate policies. If your template has both User and Computer policies and you import from only one configuration (such as the User configuration), you will not import the other section's policies. You *must* import the policy in both User and Computer configurations.

Once you have clicked Add/Remove Templates, the Add/Remove Templates window appears with a list of currently installed templates in the Administrative Templates section of your GPO (see Figure 6-22).

FIGURE 6-19 Adding a template to the Administrative Templates section of a GPO

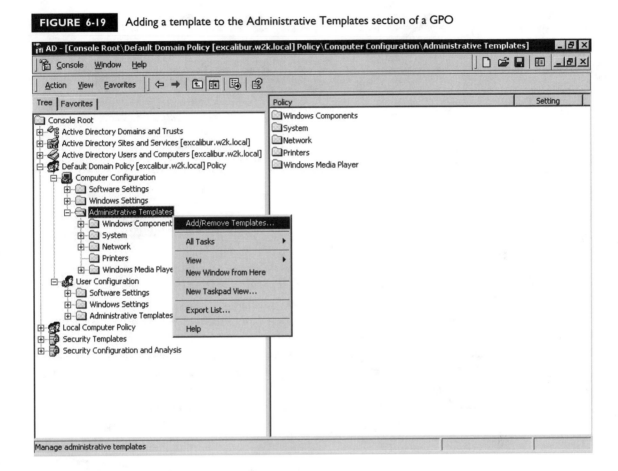

To add a template, click Add. A window appears to select a template to add to the current list of templates. Select a template file, and click Open to add it to the list of installed templates. Once you are finished, click Close. Once you click Close, all new templates are checked for syntax and, if no errors are found, they are added to the correct Computer or User Configuration section of Administrative Templates.

FIGURE 6-20

Current list of
templates
installed in
Administrative
Templates

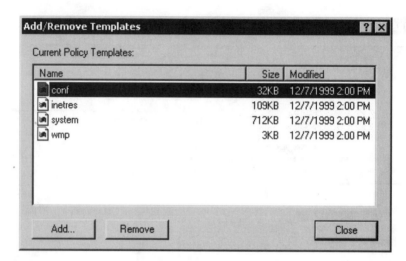

exam

⚆atch

Understand the function administrative templates perform and the difference between using Administrative Templates and setting registry settings through the Registry section in the Windows Settings section of Group Policy. Using Administrative Templates, you can control computer or user settings through an easy-to-use, graphical template rather than trying to apply registry settings through the Registry section of Windows Settings. This section is reserved to make individual registry settings when necessary, not to make computer or user changes on a regular basis. In addition, remember that Administrative Templates makes modifications to the HKEY_LOCAL_MACHINE for computer configurations and HKEY_CURRENT_USERS for user configurations.

CertCam 6-7

EXERCISE 6-7

Controlling Environments with Administrative Templates

In this exercise, you learn how to change the desktop environment by importing and configuring templates in Administrative Templates.

1. Verify that you are logged on as Administrator.

2. Open the Control Panel by clicking Start | Settings | Control Panel. Open the Administrative Tools applet, and click the Active Directory Users and Computers administrative tool.

3. When the Active Directory Users and Computers tool opens, it shows the domain name of your network. Right-click the domain name, and select Properties from the pop-up context menu.

4. When the <domain name> Properties window appears, click the Group Policy tab. The ABCFUTURES GPO is listed as the only GPO linked to this Domain object.

5. Click the ABCFUTURES GPO, and then click Edit. When the Group Policy window appears, navigate to the User Configuration/Administrative Templates of the GPO.

6. Right-click the Administrative Templates section, and select Add/Remove Templates from the pop-up context menu.

7. In the Add/Remove Templates window, click Add to add a new template to the list of imported templates already in the GPO.

8. Search the %SystemRoot%\INF folder for Administrative Templates (look for .ADM extension files). Once all these files are found, select the WMP.ADM template (the Windows Media Player template), and click Open to import this template.

9. Once the template is imported, click Close to return to the Group Policy window.

10. The GPO then takes the template, scans the template for syntax and other errors, and, if no problems are detected, the template is added to the GPO. You will see a Windows Media Player entry added beneath the Administrative Templates section.

11. Navigate to the Windows Media Player/Windows Media Player Configurations section. Double-click the Customize the Windows Media Player entry to modify the entry.

12. In the Customize the Windows Media Player window, click the Policy tab, click the Enabled radio button to enable this entry, and then type **This is the Windows Media Player** in the text box for the Title Bar for the Windows Media Player. Click OK to accept the changes.

13. Modify the ABCFUTURES GPO security groups by adding the Authenticated Users group back and giving the group Read and Apply Group Policy permissions.

14. Log off and log on again. Start the Windows Media Player and check the Title Bar. You will see that it has changed.

CERTIFICATION OBJECTIVE 6.08

Assigning Script Policies to Users and Computers

Another new feature of Windows 2000 that is implemented in Group Policy is the ability to assign scripts, not only to users but also to computers. Furthermore, you can also assign the scripts to run during computer startup or shutdown or user logon or logoff.

As for the order of processing, when a computer boots, the Computer Configuration section of a Group Policy is processed first, which includes any startup scripts, followed by the processing of the User Configuration section within any group policies, when a user logs on. This includes the execution of any logon scripts found in the GPO. On shutdown, however, the reverse is true. First, all user

---

FIGURE 6-21   User scripts (Logon/Logoff) in the Default Domain Policy GPO

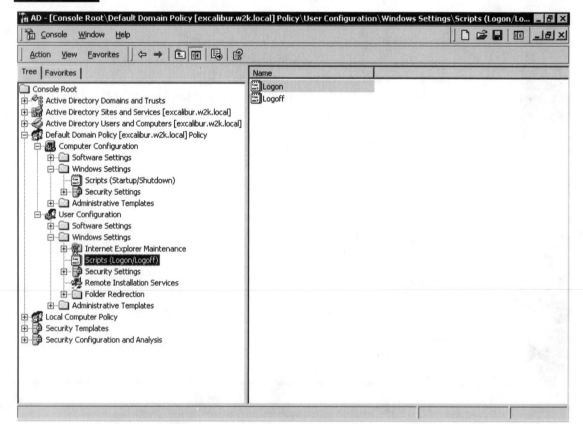

configurations in group policies are processed, including logoff scripts, followed by the processing of all Computer Configuration sections, including shutdown scripts.

With the inclusion of startup or shutdown scripts for computers, along with logoff scripts for users, Windows 2000 makes workstation and user configurations much more flexible.

User vs. Computer Scripts

What is the difference between user and computer scripts? The main difference between the two, as explained previously, is that user scripts are processed at logon and logoff, whereas computer scripts are processed only at startup or shutdown. Computer scripts are not processed every time a user logs on or off a computer. Looking at Figure 6-23 (on the preceding page) and Figure 6-24, you can see the difference between user scripts and computer scripts.

FIGURE 6-22   Computer scripts (Startup/Shutdown) in the Default Domain Policy GPO

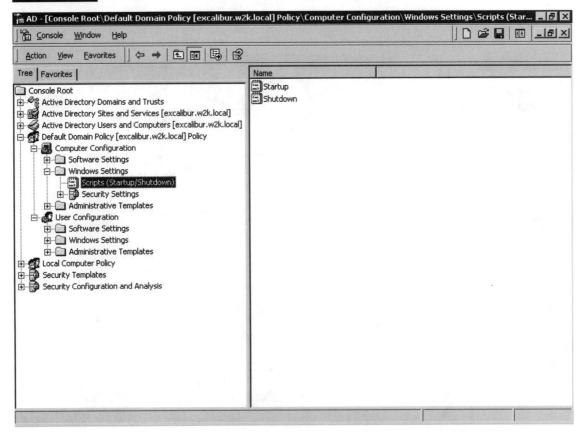

To have a script processed in either section, you must place it in the spot where you want it processed. Take the example of a logon script that needs to be processed by all employees within a company. This script assigns three drive letters, one each for a home directory (H:), an application directory (R:), and a projects directory (P:). Without these drives, users cannot use applications, store their personal data, or work on company projects. To assign these drives, you must place the logon script in a group policy so that all users run the script when they log on. The script, LOGON.BAT, must be placed in the User Configuration section of Group Policy.

To set up the script correctly, an administrator must navigate to the User Configuration | Windows Settings | Scripts (Logon/Logoff) section of the GPO. Once there, double-click the Logon section, and a Logon Properties window appears, as shown in Figure 6-25.

To add a script, click Add and add the script(s) needed. In our example, we need to add only one script, LOGON.BAT, to the Logon section. Once the script is added, click OK to accept all the additions. Note that in Figure 6-25 there are Up and Down buttons, which allow you to change the processing of logon scripts. Remember that scripts are processed in order from top to bottom.

FIGURE 6-23

Adding the script LOGON.BAT to the Logon section of Scripts

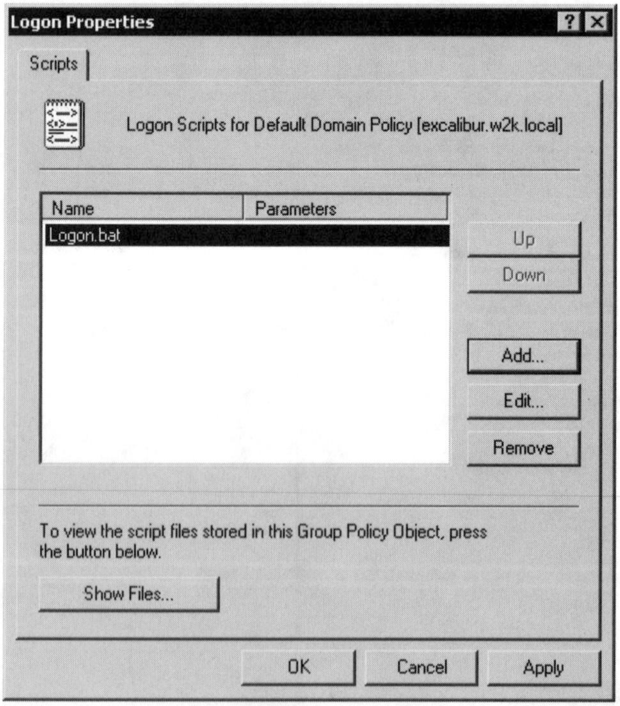

SCENARIO & SOLUTION

I have a large enterprise environment. How can my company effectively deploy Group Policy without having a large performance hit?	Since GPOs can be deployed at the Local Computer, Site, Domain, and Organizational Unit object level, along with the ability to deploy multiple GPOs at each level, you should not place many GPOs in objects to be processed when a computer is booted or a user logs on. To speed the processing of GPOs, you need to not only look at limiting the amount of GPOs you use in your infrastructure; you also need to use the disable User/Computer Configuration check boxes for each GPO. If your GPO deploys only user configurations, there is no need to have the computer configurations enabled; it wastes time processing an unused part of a GPO.
Should I go through and define or configure all my GPO settings, or should I leave them set as Not Defined or Not Configured?	Unless you have a definite need to change a GPO setting from Not Defined or Not Configured to a valid setting, leave all settings as Not Defined or Not Configured. The reason is, again, processing speed of the GPO. Configuring every GPO setting takes an excessive amount of time to process. Configure *only* what is necessary for the GPO.
I want to control several desktop settings, but there are no Administrative Templates available to do this. What can I do?	First, see if there are other GPO settings that can perform the settings that you need. If none exists, you have no other choice than to write your own administrative template and import it into the GPO. Once the template is imported, you can select the new template settings and apply them as needed.
We heavily use system policies in Windows NT 4.0. How can we use our policies in Windows 2000?	Remember that Windows NT 4.0 system policies can be used by importing them into the Administrative Templates section of a GPO, but also keep in mind exactly how these policies work. These policies "tattoo" the registry with their settings, which means that these settings are not removed when a user logs off or a computer is shut down. For Windows NT 4.0 policies to work correctly, they should be rewritten.

CertCam 6-8

EXERCISE 6-8

Assigning Script Policies

In this exercise, you learn how to assign scripts through the use of GPOs.

1. Verify that you are logged on as Administrator.

2. Create a sample logon script called LOGON.BAT. The only line of text should be NET SEND ADMINISTRATOR "HELLO." Save the script under the %SystemRoot%\SYSVOL\<domain name>\SCRIPTS\ folder.

Saving the script here not only places the script in a place to be used by other GPOs, it also allows the script to be replicated to all other domain controllers and makes it available to down-level clients (i.e., Windows NT 4.0 clients) so that they can run the logon script(s), since this folder is the NETLOGON share for all domain controllers. You can place the script anywhere, but remember that the script needs to be placed in the same location on all domain controllers. For example, if you choose to place scripts in a folder called SCRIPTS on your D: drive, you need to place this folder on each of your domain controllers. If you do not, your scripts will fail because the script is pulled from the domain controller that authenticates you.

3. Open the Control Panel by clicking Start | Settings | Control Panel. Open the Administrative Tools applet, and click the Active Directory Users and Computers administrative tool.

4. When the Active Directory Users and Computers tool opens, it shows the domain name of your network. Right-click the domain name, and select Properties from the pop-up context menu.

5. When the <domain name> Properties window appears, click the Group Policy tab. The ABCFUTURES GPO is listed as the only GPO linked to this Domain object.

6. Click the ABCFUTURES GPO, and then click Edit. When the Group Policy window appears, navigate to User Configuration/Windows Settings/Scripts (Logon/Logoff).

7. Double-click Logon, and in the Logon Properties window, click Add to add the LOGON.BAT file. Click OK to exit.

8. Log off and log on again with the Administrator account. Once your logon is complete, you get a pop-up window that states HELLO. This message signifies that the sample logon script ran. *Note:* You need to use the Administrator account in order to see the notification when you log on.

CERTIFICATION SUMMARY

In the first two objectives, we talked about creating and linking GPOs. We covered what GPOs are, the value they give to administrators for management purposes, and how to link GPOs to Site, Domain, and Organizational Unit objects within Active Directory.

Next we covered how to manipulate GPOs by delegating control, modifying inheritance of Group Policy, and filtering the application of GPOs through the use of security groups. We talked about delegating control of GPOs to individuals because of the complexity and power of group policies. Because GPOs are so powerful and complex, they need to be strictly controlled by only a select group of individuals. Furthermore, we covered the need to manipulate how group policies are applied. Modifying the application of GPOs through the use of the Block Inheritance and No Override fields, along with filtering the application of GPOs through the use of security groups, proved that GPOs could be applied in almost any type of situation without problems.

Lastly, we talked about modifying group policies, along with discussing specific sections within Group Policy: Administrative Templates and assigning script policies to computers and users. We covered how to modify GPOs, what Not Defined or Not Configured meant when processing GPOs, and, along with learning how to add and remove templates to GPOs in order to more easily manage computers and users, we learned about adding scripts within GPOs for computers and users to run during startup and shutdown as well as logon and logoff.

✓ TWO-MINUTE DRILL

Creating a Group Policy Object

❑ Group Policy is highly flexible; it allows the configuration and management of just about any computer or user setting.

Linking an Existing Group Policy Object

❑ When GPOs are created, they can be assigned only to a Local Computer, Site, Domain, or OU Active Directory object. They cannot be assigned to an object such as the built-in folders in Active Directory.

Delegating Administrative Control of Group Policy

❑ Delegating control of group policies allows administrators to divide the task of managing group policies into an IT support group that manages only Group Policy or assignment of GPOs to specific individuals for security purposes.

❑ Delegating control of GPOs is different from delegating authority to objects in Active Directory; delegation is very much like assigning permissions to a folder within NTFS.

Modifying Group Policy Inheritance

❑ Remember that group policies follow the inheritance path of Local Computer | Sites | Domains | Organizational Units (OUs).

❑ Remember that GPOs are processed from the bottom to the top due to the fact that the top of a GPO link list has higher priority when enforcing individual policy settings.

❑ You can affect the application of GPOs using Block Inheritance and No Override settings.

❑ No Override *always* overrides a Block Inheritance GPO setting.

Filtering Group Policy Settings

❑ Filtering GPOs should always be performed using security groups and not using Active Directory objects such as OUs.

❑ Filtering GPOs gives administrators the flexibility to apply GPO settings to a subset of computers or users within a site, domain, or organizational unit.

Modifying Group Policy

❏ GPOs consist of two main sections, Computer Configuration and User Configuration. Each section has three subsections: Software Settings, Windows Settings, and Administrative Templates. Remember not to confuse settings between Computer and User Configurations, which could lead to improper application of GPOs.

❏ Most policies have either an Enabled/Disabled/Not Configured setting or a Not Defined/Not Configured setting. These settings are used to let Windows 2000 ignore the processing of individual policy settings in order to speed the processing of GPOs. Make sure you know the impact of using or not using these settings.

Controlling User Environments Using Administrative Templates

❏ Administrative Templates is the only section in a GPO that can be added to or removed from a GPO. The Software and Windows Settings sections can be modified, but not through the addition or removal of templates such as administrative templates.

❏ Administrative Templates can be expanded through the use of customized templates.

❏ The only parts of the registry that Administrative Templates can modify through customized or default templates are the HKEY_LOCAL_MACHINE (for computer) and HKEY_CURRENT_USER (for user) registry hives.

Assigning Script Policies to Users and Computers

❏ Scripts can now be assigned to computers along with users.

❏ Users have scripts applied at logon and logoff; computers have scripts applied at startup and shutdown.

❏ The order of processing for scripts is computer startup, user logon, user logoff, and computer shutdown. During the course of using a computer, you can execute user scripts several times during logon and logoff.

❏ Script policies are processed from the top of the scripts list to the bottom.

SELF TEST

The following questions will help you measure your understanding of the material presented in this chapter. Read all the choices carefully because there might be more than one correct answer. Choose all correct answers for each question.

Creating a Group Policy Object

1. Which one is not a section of a Group Policy object?

   A. Software Settings

   B. Windows Settings

   C. Administrative Templates

   D. Computer Settings

2. How is a new GPO added? Choose all that apply.

   A. From the Sites and Services snap-in

   B. From the Users and Computers snap-in

   C. From the Group Policy snap-in

   D. From the Computer Management snap-in

Linking an Existing Group Policy Object

3. What Active Directory object cannot have a GPO linked to it?

   A. Domain

   B. Computer

   C. Organizational Unit

   D. Site

4. Why would you link a GPO?

   A. To activate the GPO

   B. So the GPO is applied to the correct security group

   C. To reuse an existing GPO and apply it to another OU, domain, or site

   D. Because domains and sites can only have predefined GPOs applied to them

Delegating Administrative Control of Group Policy

5. What is the purpose of delegating control of a GPO?

    A. To control who can work with GPOs within an organization

    B. To control the application of the GPO to a site, domain, or OU

    C. To put the control of the GPO in the hands of those who are designated to work with and manage the GPO

    D. To assign the correct security groups to properly apply the GPO to an object

Modifying Group Policy Inheritance

6. What is the order of processing for GPOs?

    A. There is no order; Group Policy inheritance ensures that all policies are applied correctly

    B. Sites, Domains, and Organizational Units

    C. Local Computer, Sites, Domains, and Organizational Units

    D. The order of processing does not matter, because GPO processing can be altered by the use of Block Policy Inheritance and/or No Override settings for GPOs

7. When several GPOs are linked to an object, what is the order of processing?

    A. Bottom to top

    B. Top to bottom

    C. Top to bottom, processing the Block Policy Inheritance option for each GPO

    D. Top to bottom, processing the No Override option for each GPO

8. Which GPO setting has the greatest power in terms of policy enforcement?

    A. No Override

    B. Block Policy Inheritance

    C. Apply Group Policy

    D. Not Defined

9. What should you do when using only a part of GPO (such as User Configuration) in order to efficiently use the GPO?

    A. Disable the configuration that is not being used.

    B. Apply the GPO to only the object(s) to which it needs to be applied.

C. Assign the GPO to only one object at a time; create multiple GPOs if the same GPO configurations are needed.

D. Limit the number of individual policies applied in each GPO. Spreading individual policy settings over several GPOs increases the speed of processing a GPO.

Filtering Group Policy Settings

10. How are GPOs filtered?

A. GPOs are filtered through the use of Block Policy Inheritance and No Override settings for GPOs and objects.

B. GPOs are processed in order, and policies are filtered through inheritance of previously processed GPOs.

C. GPOs are not filtered at all. They rely on policy inheritance to provide the filtering of policies to Active Directory objects.

D. You use security groups and application of permissions to apply GPOs to Active Directory objects.

11. Jack has created two GPOs that are linked to his domain. The first GPO is for a set of code developers who need several mapped network drives for their development tools. The other GPO is for Web developers and contains another set of mapped drives for their tool sets. The development GPO is processed first, followed by the Web developers' GPO. Jack's problem is that no matter in what order he puts the GPOs, everybody gets both policies. What is the reason for Jack's problem?

A. Jack has placed his GPOs in the wrong place in Active Directory. He needs to place his GPOs in an OU and put his Web developers and code developers in separate OUs to properly enforce his GPOs.

B. Jack has forgotten to filter his GPOs through the use of security groups. He needs to create two security groups and apply them to the proper GPOs.

C. Jack has the No Override option enabled for both the GPOs he is using.

D. Jack has the Block Policy Inheritance option enabled for the Domain object.

12. What is the purpose of filtering GPOs?

A. To properly assign GPOs to users and or/computers as desired

B. To determine which policies are applied to users and/or computers

C. To properly apply GPOs to groups of users and/or computers and security groups as desired

Modifying Group Policy

13. What is the purpose of configuring individual policy settings in a GPO with Not Configured or Not Defined?

    A. They are default settings chosen in order to save administrators time in configuring GPOs. They prevent administrators from having to configure each individual policy.

    B. They speed up processing of the GPO.

    C. They make sure that the individual policy is not applied.

    D. They make sure that the individual policy is removed from the GPO because it is not used.

14. What section does *not* make up the User or Computer Configuration section of a GPO?

    A. Windows Settings

    B. Administrative Templates

    C. Software Settings

    D. Administrative Settings

Controlling User Environments Using Administrative Templates

15. You have several computer configurations that you need to enforce on computers, but there are no default policies defined for what you need. What is a possible solution?

    A. Create a custom administrative template and import the template into a GPO in order to apply the new settings to computers.

    B. There is no solution. Unless you can find a policy already included in your GPO, you cannot configure your systems with the settings you need.

    C. Modify a current template to include your new computer configurations.

    D. Check other areas of your GPO to see if the settings you need are not already covered there. If you cannot find an adequate solution, you may not be able to modify computer configurations as needed.

16. What two registry hives can be controlled through the use of Administrative Templates? Choose two.

    A. HKEY_LOCAL_MACHINE

    B. HKEY_USERS

    C. HKEY_CURRENT_CONFIG

    D. HKEY_CURRENT_USER

Assigning Script Policies to Users and Computers

17. What is the order in which scripts are processed?

    A. Startup, logon, logoff, shutdown.

    B. Logon, startup, logoff, shutdown.

    C. Logon, startup, shutdown, logoff.

    D. Startup, logon, shutdown, logoff.

LAB QUESTION

The ABCFUTURES Company from Chapter 2 has completed its split from the ABC Company. ABCFUTURES has migrated all its servers to Windows 2000, but the company needs to configure its systems with Group Policy. Several desktop settings need to be set (such as a company logo for the desktops' wallpaper, color scheme, and so on), distribution of several applications, some basic security settings, and the assignment of some mapped network drives for all users, depending on who they are. Lastly, one system administrator is dedicated to the HR department. This person should have any pertinent HR sensitive information delegated to him or her for management purposes. Your task is to prepare Group Policy to handle all the requirements as follows. The requirements are:

■ All 100 systems must have the desktop settings and basic security settings applied.

■ All personnel in the HR department need to have two applications installed on their systems for personnel management.

■ One systems administrator must be assigned to all HR resources to manage them because of the sensitive nature of HR data.

■ All personnel in software development need to have P:, Q:, and R: network drives mapped when they log on.

■ You must deploy all of these settings with minimum processing overhead (i.e., the group policies must run as fast as possible).

■ You only have one domain, ABCFUTURES.COM, and one site, ABCFUTURES. You must deploy your group policies so that they are centrally located and manipulated from one location.

Explain, in detail, the configurations you would use for this situation and why you would use the selected configurations.

SELF TEST ANSWERS

Creating a Group Policy Object

1. ☑ **D. Computer Settings.** There is no Computer Settings section within a GPO, although there is a Computer Configuration section that further breaks down to Software Settings, Windows Settings, and Administrative Templates.

   ☒ **A, B,** and **C** are all incorrect because Software Settings, Windows Settings, and Administrative Templates are sections beneath the User or Computer Configuration section of a GPO.

2. ☑ **A, B,** and **C.** GPOs may be added to a domain or OU from the User and Computers snap-in. GPOs may be added to a site from the Sites and Services snap-in. GPOs may also be added directly from the Group Policy snap-in interface.

   ☒ **D** is incorrect because the Computer Management snap-in is used to manage the components and services running on a computer.

Linking an Existing Group Policy Object

3. ☑ **B. Computer.** A computer, although an object in Active Directory, is not designed to be linked to a GPO. A GPO can be *applied* to a computer, but it cannot have a GPO *linked* to it.

   ☒ **A, C,** and **D** are all incorrect because they are the only three objects in Active Directory that can have a GPO linked to them.

4. ☑ **C. To reuse an existing GPO and apply it to another OU, domain, or site.** A GPO is linked to an OU, site, or domain if it has been previously created and needs to be applied at another place in the directory.

   ☒ **A** is incorrect because GPOs are "active" unless disabled; linking a GPO will not re-enable a GPO if it is disabled. **B** is incorrect because GPOs are applied to security groups via filters. Only a specific group of GPOs is granted Read and Apply GPO rights to the GPO. **D** is incorrect because domains and sites can have user-defined policies applied to them as well as predefined policies.

Delegating Administrative Control of Group Policy

5. ☑ **C. To put the control of the GPO in the hands of those who are designated to work with and manage the GPO.** Delegating control of a GPO means exactly what it says; you are specifying exactly who you want to control the GPO. This could mean the removal of all

groups with the exception of a small group of users because the GPO is sensitive. It could mean that an organization has so many GPOs, it has an independent group of IT professionals whose primary function is GPO management.

☒ **A** is incorrect because delegating control is based on a GPO, not Group Policy as an overall concept. **B** is incorrect because delegation of control does not control how a GPO is applied to a site, domain, or OU. This is a function of filtering a GPO for an Active Directory object such as a site. **D** is incorrect because assigning the correct security groups to properly apply a GPO is another function of filtering a GPO for an Active Directory object.

Modifying Group Policy Inheritance

6. ☑ **C. Local Computer, Sites, Domains, and Organizational Units.** This is the order that Windows 2000 uses to process GPOs. If an Active Directory object (such as an OU) contains a list of GPOs, those GPOs are also processed, in order, from the top of the list to the bottom.

   ☒ **A** is incorrect because there is a structured order, as shown above, that is followed when applying GPOs. **B** is incorrect because it fails to list the local computer as the first place where a GPO is processed. **D** is incorrect because, although Block Policy Inheritance and No Override do alter the processing of GPOs, they do *not* alter the order in which they are processed.

7. ☑ **A. Bottom to top.** GPOs are processed from bottom to top because it is stated on Group Policy tabs for objects that GPOs higher in the list of GPOs have higher priority. This means that GPOs higher in the list are applied after other GPOs that are lower in the list.

   ☒ **B** is incorrect because top to bottom is the opposite of how GPOs are processed. **C**, top to bottom, processing the Block Policy Inheritance option for each GPO, is incorrect because not only is this the opposite of how GPOs are processed, but using Block Policy Inheritance has nothing to do with the processing order of GPOs. **D**, top to bottom, processing the No Override option for each GPO, is incorrect because not only is this the opposite of how GPOs are processed, but using No Override also has nothing to do with the processing order of GPOs.

8. ☑ **A. No Override.** When No Override is specified, all other policy settings are ignored.

   ☒ **B** is incorrect because Block Policy Inheritance is ignored when a policy with No Override set is inherited. **C** is incorrect because this is a permission assigned to a security group, computer, or user. It is a security mechanism and has nothing to do with GPO enforcement. **D** is incorrect because, although Not Defined is an individual policy setting, along with Enabled and Disabled, it is not as powerful as No Override because it can be easily overridden with a policy in the No Override option set.

9. ☑ **A.** Disable the configuration that is not being used. If you are using only the computer or user configuration section of a GPO, disable the section that is not being used in order to speed up the processing of the GPO. If it is disabled, it is not processed.

☒ **B** is incorrect because, although applying the GPO to only the object to which it needs to be applied would be a best practice, this choice does not apply. If you were to apply a GPO using only User Configuration and then apply the GPO to a group of computers, the GPO simply would not apply. **C** is incorrect because you do not need to create multiple GPOs for performance reasons. GPOs are designed to be used for multiple Active Directory objects. **D** is incorrect because spreading your individual policies over several GPOs actually *increases* processing time because each GPO needs to be processed, which takes more time than processing only one GPO.

Filtering Group Policy Settings

10. ☑ **D.** You use security groups and application of permissions to apply GPOs to Active Directory objects. Security groups provide the containers to place the users or computers in order to apply the correct GPO. A security group is created, then the desired permissions (such as Read or Apply Group Policy) are applied to the security group. Security groups also play a role when delegating control of a GPO. Security groups are the only method of applying a GPO.

☒ **A** is incorrect because Block Policy Inheritance and No Override settings do not affect how policies are filtered to Active Directory objects. They do affect how policies are processed, but not how a certain policy is applied to a user or computer. **B** is incorrect because inheritance has nothing to do with the filtering of GPOs. Inheritance deals with the inheritance of previous policy settings, not what or who has a policy applied to an Active Directory object. **C** is totally false because GPOs are filtered and, as shown, inheritance has nothing to do with the filtering of GPOs to users and computers.

11. ☑ **B.** Jack has forgotten to filter his GPOs through the use of security groups. He needs to create two security groups and apply them to the proper GPOs. Filtering is the only way Jack will be able to selectively apply these GPOs to the groups needed. What is happening is that the Authenticated Users group, which is added by default, has the Apply Group Policy permission added, which causes all users to apply the GPOs in question.

☒ **A** is incorrect because it does not matter to Active Directory where the GPOs are located. You can use a GPO from anywhere in Active Directory, as long as you have the permission to do so. **C** is incorrect because the No Override option, when applied to both GPOs, would still cause one GPO to not be applied. **D** is incorrect because Block Policy Inheritance would prevent at least one policy from being applied. It would not product the results as explained in the question.

12. ☑ C. To properly apply GPOs to groups of users and/or computers and security groups as desired. By filtering GPOs through the use of security groups, administrators can selectively apply policies as needed.

☒ A is incorrect because assigning GPOs to users and/or computers is accomplished through the delegation of control. You delegate certain people to a GPO in order for them to manage the GPO. **B** is incorrect because determining which policies are applied to users and/or computers is what inheritance of policies accomplishes.

Modifying Group Policy

13. ☑ B. To speed up processing of the GPO. If an individual policy is configured with the Not Configured or Not Defined option, the individual policy is ignored during the processing of the GPO, which, in turn, helps to speed the processing of the GPO.

☒ A is incorrect because, although Not Configured and Not Defined are default settings for GPOs, they are not used in order to save administrators time with configuring GPOs. **C** is incorrect because Not Configured or Not Defined settings ensure that the policy is ignored. Setting an individual policy to Disabled ensures that an individual policy is not applied. **D** is incorrect because individual policies are not removed from a GPO, no matter what setting the individual policy is configured with.

14. ☑ D. Administrative Settings. There is no such section within the User or Computer Configuration section of a GPO.

☒ A, B, and C are incorrect because Windows Settings, Administrative Templates, and Software Settings are the three sections that can be found within a User or Computer Configuration section of a GPO.

Controlling User Environments Using Administrative Templates

15. ☑ A. Create a custom administrative template and import the template into a GPO in order to apply the new settings to computers. This is the best solution because the new template that is created can be shared to other GPOs.

☒ B is incorrect because there is a viable solution to customize GPOs through the use of Administrative Templates. **C** is not correct because it would be a very bad decision to modify a default template to accept your new computer configurations. If this solution is used, you will not be able to share the changes as easily as if the changes were separate. **D** is incorrect because there are limited capabilities in other areas of a GPO. Administrative templates are the most flexible way of applying new user and computer policies.

16. ☑ **A and D.** HKEY_LOCAL_MACHINE and HKEY_CURRENT_USER. These registry hives are the hives that are used when administrative templates are applied. No other registry hives can be modified using Administrative Templates. If other hives must be modified, an administrator must use another method of modifying these hives.

    ☒ **B and C** are both incorrect because, as stated, only the HKEY_LOCAL_MACHINE and the HKEY_CURRENT_USER registry hives can be modified through Administrative Templates.

Assigning Script Policies to Users and Computers

17. ☑ **A.** Startup, logon, logoff, shutdown. This is the proper order in which scripts are processed in GPOs.

    ☒ **B, C, and D** are all incorrect because they use the wrong order of processing. B and C are incorrect because they start off by processing logon scripts first, which is wrong; startup scripts are processed first. D is incorrect because, although the startup script is processed first, followed by the logon script, logoff scripts, not shutdown scripts, are processed next.

LAB ANSWER

First, we fulfill the last requirement by stating that all group policies could be created and linked to the Windows 2000 domain, ABCFUTURES.COM, or the ABCFUTURES site. You could split up the group policies and distribute the GPOs between both, but it will be easier to manage if all GPOs are linked to one central object.

Next, create three separate GPOs in either the ABCFUTURES.COM domain or the ABCFUTURES site and name these GPOs ABCFUTURES-HW (for computer configurations), ABCFUTURES-HR (for HR computer configurations), and ABCFUTURES-DEV (for developer user configurations).

Add all the desktop and basic security settings to the Computer Configuration | Administrative Templates section of the GPO ABCFUTURES-HW. Add the two HR applications to the Computer Configuration | Software Settings section of the GPO ABCFUTURES-HR. Finally, create a logon script called LOGON.BAT to map the P:, Q:, and R: drives for all software developers. Place the logon script in the User Configuration | Windows Settings | Scripts (Logon/Logoff) section of the GPO ABCFUTURES-DEV.

Before filtering the GPOs, you need to "streamline" the GPOs for faster processing. For the ABCFUTURES-HW and ABCFUTURES-HR GPOs, disable the User Configuration sections. Also disable the Computer Configuration section of the ABCFUTURES-DEV GPO. Disabling these sections within the GPOs minimizes the processing time for these GPOs to be applied. In addition, make sure that each enabled section has no configured policies that need to be configured. Remember, any policy configured as enabled or disabled will be processed, thus adding processing time for the GPO.

Once the three GPOs are assigned to either the ABCFUTURES.COM domain or the ABCFUTURES site, you must properly filter these GPOs so that they are properly applied.

Create two security groups, HR and DEVS. Populate these two security groups with the appropriate users and/or computers. Once you have created and populated these two groups, you must apply these groups to ABCFUTURES-HR and ABCFUTURES-DEV GPOs appropriately so that they receive the policies configured for them. You do not need to create a security group for the ABCFUTURES-HW GPO, because you can use the Authenticated Users group (which is added by default) to apply the GPO, since everyone in the company needs these configurations applied.

Remember that the ABCFUTURES-HR group members need software applied to their computers, so you actually populate the HR security group with computers instead of users.

Lastly, you must delegate control of the ABCFUTURES-HR GPO to one system administrator for security purposes. Click the ABCFUTURES-HR GPO and look at the GPO's security configuration. Remove all the security groups (such as Domain Admins and Enterprise Admins) and add only the designated systems administrator.

Once you have delegated control of the ABCFUTURES-HR GPO, you have properly configured GPOs for the ABCFUTURES Company.

7

Managing Software and Network Configuration Using Group Policy

CERTIFICATION OBJECTIVES

7.01   Deploying Software Using Group Policy

7.02   Maintaining Software Using Group Policy

7.03   Configuring Deployment Options

7.04   Troubleshooting During Software Deployment

7.05   Managing Network Configuration Using Group Policy

✓   Two-Minute Drill

Q&A   Self Test

I n the previous chapter, you learned how to set Group Policy, administer permissions on group policy objects (GPOs), and use Group Policy to administer change to and place restrictions on users' desktops and accounts. You did this through the use of administrative templates and the assignment of logon, logoff, startup, and shutdown scripts. In this chapter, you learn how you can use Group Policy to distribute, maintain, and remove software throughout your organization automatically. You also see how to administer change to many of the resources remotely throughout your network.

Microsoft Windows 2000 includes several technologies under the blanket name *IntelliMirror;* these technologies are intended to decrease total cost of ownership (TCO) of the product by providing the ability to remotely implement change throughout an enterprise. Among the IntelliMirror features we inspect in this chapter are the *Windows Installer service,* which allows automated, hands-off installation of self-repairing software packages, and the *Software Installation and Maintenance technology,* which uses GPOs to deploy and administer these software packages. We also look at *Folder Redirection,* which allows us to automatically send files in user folders such as My Documents to a central location for backup and security.

exam

ⓦatch

IntelliMirror is based on users' need to have data, applications, and settings follow them around the network. It includes the features, benefits, and technologies outlined in Table 7-1. IntelliMirror, together with Remote Installation Service (covered in Chapter 8), forms the basis for Windows 2000 Change and Configuration Management.

TABLE 7-1 IntelliMirror's Features, Benefits, and Technologies

Feature	Benefit	Technologies
User Data Management	"My documents follow me."	Active Directory, Group Policy, Offline Folders, Synchronization Manager, Disk Quotas
Software Installation and Maintenance	"My applications follow me."	Active Directory, Group Policy, Windows Installer Service
User and Computer Settings Management	"My preferences follow me."	Active Directory, Group Policy, Roaming Profiles

CERTIFICATION OBJECTIVE 7.01

Deploying Software Using Group Policy

It used to be that deployment of software to a few, several hundred, or several thousand machines meant that an administrator had to visit each and every desktop at various points throughout the life cycle of an application. Since ordinary users did not (and probably should not) have the ability to install software on their own workstations by default, an administrator had to visit each individual desktop whenever any of the following occurred:

- Initial software deployment
- Upgrades to software, such as service packs
- Corruption of software
- Unknown file types encountered by user
- Removal of software

By use of Software Installation and Maintenance in conjunction with Windows Installer and Group Policy, the entire process is now automated and performed remotely from an administrator's desktop, resulting in a great savings of time, effort, and money.

The software deployment process essentially consists of two steps: preparation or acquisition of a Microsoft Windows Installer (.MSI) package and, optionally, the construction of a MSI transform file (.MST) as well as the publication or assignment of that package through a GPO. To fully understand the deployment process, we must first take a look at what is being deployed.

Windows Installer and .MSI Files

The *Windows Installer Service*, available for Windows 95, 98, 2000, and NT 4.0, is a local service on each workstation that allows for the automated installation of software through the use of *Microsoft Software Installation (.MSI)* files. Windows Installer and .MSI files replace the traditional SETUP.EXE file that required a good deal of user input during the installation process. With Windows Installer, an application is installed and configured on a test computer and then repackaged into an .MSI file by a third-party application. Once an .MSI is created, a user needs only to find and invoke the application in order to install it, possibly without answering any configuration questions during the installation. Additionally, a user needs no sort of administrative privileges in order to install software using an .MSI file. This is in contrast to the old SETUP.EXE file, for which a user needed to have administrative privileges on his or her own machine in order to run the setup program. Using .MSI files, it is very easy for the administrator to deploy a preconfigured application and assure that it appears and behaves the same for all users.

There are essentially two ways to acquire a package. *Native packages* usually come packaged with the software. Office 2000, for example, contains .MSI packages for various operating systems. If no native package exists, you can *repackage* the application to create a package. We first take a brief look at the repackaging process, and then we look at one example of how a third-party repackaging tool works to create and modify Microsoft Installer packages.

The Repackaging Process

If you do not have a native .MSI file available with the software or if you decide you need to create a custom package to meet your organization's needs, you need to use third-party repackaging software. Fortunately, Windows 2000 Server includes such software on its CD. The program, called Veritas WinINSTALL LE, is located in %CDROOT%\VALUEADD\MGMT\WINSTLE. Once you have WinINSTALL or your software loaded and placed into a shared folder, it is a four-step process to create a package:

1. You need a clean computer with only Windows 2000 Professional installed. From that machine, you connect to the share with your repackaging software and run the program, taking a "before" snapshot, per your application's instructions.

2. You then install and configure the application for which you want to create an installation package.

3. You need to reconnect to the repackaging software and take an "after" snapshot. This creates a package based on the differences your test computer found between the before and after snapshots.

4. Finally, you need to test and tweak the application as necessary before full-scale deployment.

EXERCISE 7-1

Creating an .MSI Package Using WinINSTALL LE

1. From the Windows 2000 Professional, Server, or Advanced Server compact disc, run \VALUADD\3RDPARTY\MGMT\WINSTLE\SWIADMLE.MSI and follow any prompts. This installs WinINSTALL LE.

2. Share C:\PROGRAMFILES\VERITAS SOFTWARE\WINSTALL with its default settings (or giving only administrators full control).

3. Install Windows 2000 Professional on a source machine.

4. Choose Start | Run, then type *servername*\winstall\discoz.exe and click Next.

5. Type a name for the application to be packaged and a location in which it will be stored. This location should be a UNC path to a server.

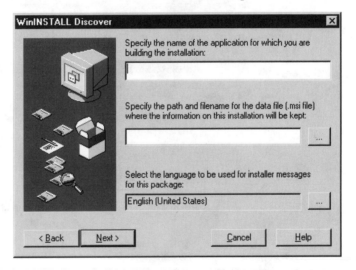

6. Click Next to accept the default temporary file drive letter.

7. Choose the source computer drive or drives to scan while making the "before" snapshot. Choose any drives that might be affected by the installation. Click Next.

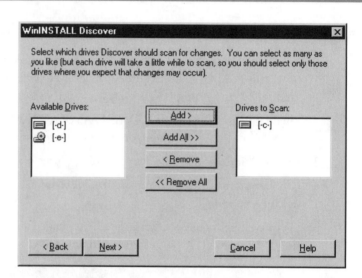

8. Choose any files or types of files to be left out of the directory. Click Next.

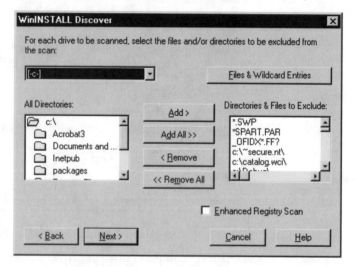

9. When Discover indicates it is through taking the "before" snapshot, click OK.

10. Discover asks you to launch a setup program. Choose the program for which you want to create a package, and click OK.

11. Install and configure the application on the source computer. *Do not reboot if prompted.*

12. Choose Start | Run, then type *servername*\winstall\discoz.exe. You see a screen similar to the one shown here:

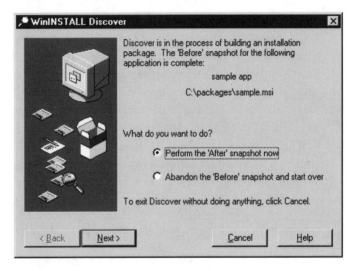

13. Click Next to choose the default Perform the 'After' Snapshot Now.

14. Discover takes an "after" snapshot and create an .MSI file. Place it and any other support files created into a shared folder.

It is critically important to make sure you are starting with a clean machine before beginning the package creation process. Otherwise, some files that are needed by the application might not be included in the package. Remember that we are using a "before/after" snapshot process to create our package. The Discover program is simply concerned with finding the differences between the two snapshots, regardless of what they are.

Consider what would happen if we were to take a "before" snapshot on a machine running Word 2000, and then we were to install Excel 2000 and take our "after" snapshot. The package would include only files that were installed with Excel but were not a part of the Word installation. As you likely know, many files are shared by the two programs. The result would be that the package would work only on machines that already had Word installed and would fail on any others.

Modifying Packages

Once a package has been created, it can be opened up and modified at any time using the Veritas Software Console (see Figure 7-1). With this utility, you have the ability to view and edit all aspects of the package that was created. You can add or remove files, create new shortcuts, determine exactly how different portions of the registry will be affected by the package, configure how services and .INI files will be changed, and configure the advertising attributes of the package. All of this can be done after the actual creation of the package takes place, eliminating the need to redo the "before" and "after" snapshots, should a change need to be made after the fact. (For more information regarding changing the characteristics of a package, refer to the Veritas help files or the help files that came with your third-party repackaging software.)

When to Use GPOs to Deploy Software, and Why

Now that we have created or acquired our Microsoft Software Installer package, we need to look at how to get this package to the user. With their dynamic nature and ease of administration, Active Directory and Group Policy Objects make the distribution of packages simple and flexible. Whenever we need to be sure that a software package is available to a large number of users or computers, we use Group Policy to distribute the package. The following is a review of some of the key benefits of Group Policy and a look at how it can aid in the distribution of software:

- GPOs can be placed in any organizational unit (OU) and through the use of filtering applied to any user, group, or computer you want.

- Because they can be placed in any OU, the administration of GPOs can be delegated to a user or group without giving that user or group full-fledged administrative privileges.

FIGURE 7-1 Veritas Software Console

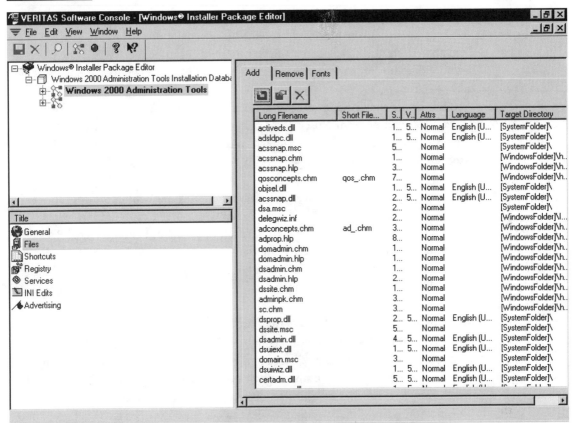

■ When a package is applied with a GPO, you have several options regarding how to distribute it, such as whether to make it mandatory or optional for the user.

■ As is usually the case with Group Policy, if a policy can be assigned, it can easily be unassigned, although with software distribution, the process is slightly different than in most other cases.

■ When software is distributed as .MSI files through the use of GPOs, users do not need to have administrative control of their own machines. They need to have only that particular package assigned or published to them.

Applying the Package to an Organizational Unit

Once we have our package ready to go, we need to associate it with one or more GPOs at the site, domain, or OU level. This is usually done through Active Directory Users and Computers. Any existing GPO can be modified to include a software distribution package, but you might want to create a separate one for the sake of clarity.

Once inside the GPO, you need to decide whether to associate the software package to a computer or a user. If you assign it to a computer, you work with the Software Settings under the Computer Configuration section of the policy. If you associate with a user, you again work with Software Settings, but this time under the User Configuration section.

Either way, the actual association is very simple. After opening the appropriate Software Settings section under either User or Computer Configuration, you see an icon labeled Software Packages. Right-click this icon and choose New | Packages, browse to find the package, specify whether it will be assigned or published, and you're done. The real trick lies in understanding the differences between assigning and publishing software and assigning it to users, as opposed to assigning it to computers.

Assigning Packages to Computers

If you need to make sure that every computer in a certain department has access to an application, assigning that package to a group of computers is the most foolproof way to do it. When you *assign* a package to a computer, that package is automatically installed the next time the machine reboots, no matter who is sitting at that machine. This method is useful if, for example, all your accountants need to have Excel 2000 on their desktops.

When a package is assigned in this way, it is installed as a *self-repairing* application. Every time the computer is restarted and the policy is applied, the package is checked to see if it has been run on that machine. If any files are missing from the original installation, they are replaced. Likewise, future changes to the original package are very easy to distribute.

To assign a package to a computer or group of computers, apply the package under Software Settings in the Computer Configuration section of the GPO. When asked whether you want the package published or assigned, choose Assigned (see Figure 7-2). You are not able to choose Published in this case. Assuming you have not filtered out the rights of any computers in this OU to receive the GPO, the software is automatically installed the next time the computer boots up.

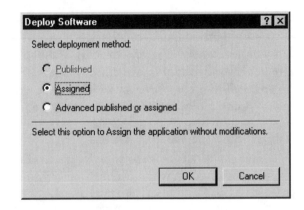

FIGURE 7-2

Choosing
Assigned, rather
than Published,
in the Deploy
Software screen

Assigning Packages to Users

When you assign a package to users, you are essentially advertising to the users that the package is there for them when they need it. A package that has been deployed in this way appears to the user as though it has been installed, but in reality it is installed only when the user calls on the application in one way or another.

When you assign a package to a user or group of users, the GPO that contains that package assigns that package when the user logs on. At that time, the application appears on the user's Start menu, but it is not actually installed. In addition, any files that were of a previously unknown type but that now have extensions associated with the assigned application now show the application's icon instead of the "flying window" for the unknown file type.

The first time a user calls on an application, either by choosing it from the Start menu or through *document invocation* (double-clicking a file of that type), it is installed automatically on the user's computer. If the user logs on to a different machine, the same process occurs on that machine as well.

This method of software deployment is useful when you have a group of users, most of whom need to use an application but some of whom might not. Via this method, the application is readily available to the users who need it but does not take up precious disk space on the machines of the users who do not need it. As is the case when you assign a package to a computer, software is self-repairing when you assign it to a user. Each time the user calls on that application, the package is checked for changes or missing files.

To assign a package to users, associate the package with the User Configuration side of the GPO and, when asked, assign the software instead of publishing it.

on the Job

Take care when assigning large packages to users. Imagine innocently clicking on an e-mail attachment, thinking you have Word installed, only to realize that you have now begun the process of dumping the entire Office 2000 suite onto your workstation! In this situation, it is probably better to either assign the package to a computer, in which case it would install on startup, or publish it and make the user intentionally go find it if he or she wants it.

Publishing Software to Users

When you *publish* a package to a user or group of users, you give the user or group permission to install it, without actually advertising its presence. On the surface, a package deployed in this way does not appear to the user at all. It is only when the user goes to Add/Remove Programs that he or she discovers its availability.

When a user logs on after a package has been published to that user, the package is not installed, nor is it placed on the Start menu, nor do any icons change. Instead, it simply appears in Add/Remove Programs as a program that is available to the user. Choosing the program from here starts the appropriate .MSI file, and automated installation occurs.

Document invocation also installs a published package. When a user double-clicks on a file of an unknown type, Active Directory is searched for a published package that will open files of that type. If any exist, the associated GPOs are checked for the necessary permissions. If the package has been published to the user, it is installed. (Incidentally, this makes for some interesting trivia for your next slow cocktail party. The reason it takes a few seconds longer for the Open With dialog box to appear than it did in NT 4.0 is that all of Active Directory is being searched for published software first.)

To publish a package to users, associate the package with the User Configuration side of the GPO and, when asked, publish the software instead of assigning it. Note that packages can be published only to users, not to computers.

exam
ⓦatch

This is both a confusing topic and one that is featured quite prominently on the exam. Perhaps an analogy will help. Let's say that I have written an article that I want very much for you to read. I assign that article to you in one of two ways, depending on how desperately I want you to read it. If it is mandatory, utterly critical, end-of-the-world material, I sit you down and read it to you. This is similar to assigning software to a computer. If it is required reading, an assignment such as you might have gotten in school, I might hand the article to you, tell you to read it, and leave "helpful" sticky notes all over your desk as a reminder. This is similar to what happens when you assign a package to users; it's there for the taking, and they are encouraged to use it. On the other hand, if this is completely optional stuff in which you might or might not be interested, I publish it and put it on file at the library. If you want it, you have my permission to go get it. This is what publishing to a user does. The package is out there but not advertised, so to speak.

CertCam 7-2

EXERCISE 7-2

Creating a Group Policy Object to Deploy Software

In this exercise, we walk through the steps involved in creating a GPO to deploy software.

1. Open Active Directory Users and Computers.

2. Expand your domain, and find the OU to which you want to deploy the software (Software Users, in my case).

3. Right-click on the OU and choose Properties.

4. Click the Group Policy tab.

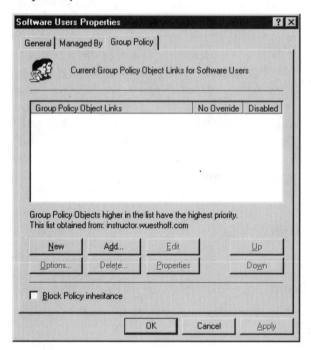

5. Click New, and give your GPO a title (Software Distribution, in my case).
6. Click Edit.

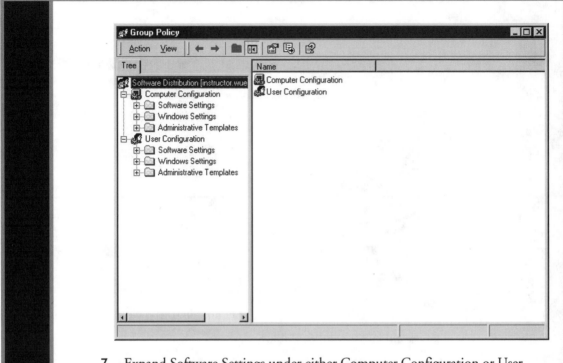

7. Expand Software Settings under either Computer Configuration or User Configuration, depending on your distribution method. (Note: You might want to repeat this exercise using each of the three deployment methods.)

8. Right-click Software Installation and choose New | Package.

9. Navigate to the shared package location, and double-click the .MSI file.

10. Choose either Assigned or Published, if available.

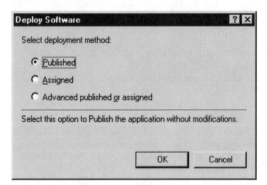

11. If successful, you see the new package in the GPO.

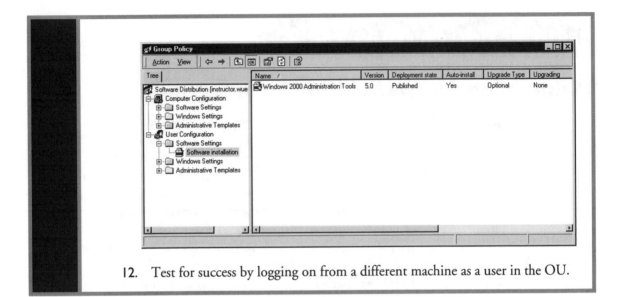

12. Test for success by logging on from a different machine as a user in the OU.

SCENARIO & SOLUTION

All users in the graphics department need to have PhotoShop 5.5 installed and available on their desktops when they get to work on Monday morning. How do I take care of this task?	Assign the package to computers. This solution automatically puts the application on users' desktops when they boot up in the morning.
Most of my training staff needs Excel installed on their machines to develop new courses. Not all of them will need it right away. What should I do?	Assign the package to the users. This solution advertises its presence on the network but does not actually install it until it is needed.
I want to make WinZip available on the network so users can access it if they need to unzip downloaded files.	Publish the package to users. They are then able to invoke the program when they need it by double-clicking on a compressed file.

CERTIFICATION OBJECTIVE 7.02

Maintaining Software Using Group Policy

Just as Group Policy in conjunction with Software Installation and Maintenance allowed us to deploy software to users and computers easily and automatically, it also provides us flexibility and simplicity when it is time to upgrade, change, or remove the software. When we want to upgrade version 1 to version 2, for example, we can decide whether we want that upgrade to happen automatically to all users of version 1 or whether we want the user of the software in question to be able to decide whether or not he or she wants the upgrade. If version 2 is installed, we also have options regarding what to do with version 1. Likewise, when we want to remove a package, we can decide whether we want current users to be able to continue to use the software or whether it should be removed from their machines.

Software Upgrades

There are two types of software upgrades we can deploy: mandatory and optional. With a *mandatory upgrade*, the new version of the software is automatically installed the next time the user calls the application. With an *optional upgrade*, the user has the option of going to Add/Remove Programs to get the new software.

Mandatory Upgrades

A mandatory upgrade automatically installs the new version of the software and optionally removes the old version. This is useful if you want to roll out the new version of the software fairly quickly and universally. It is important to be sure that the new version is completely compatible with everyone's hardware, existing software, and current needs. If there are users whose productivity could be hampered by the installation of the new software or if you just don't feel comfortable running the latest and greatest version of your graphics software on some of your less powerful machines, this might not be the proper option for you.

A mandatory upgrade is a very simple process. You need to come up with an .MSI for the new version of the software and share it out. You then publish it or assign it in a GPO. You can pull up a property sheet for the new package by right-clicking it in the GPO. When you do this and click the Upgrades tab, you see a sheet like the following (see Figure 7-3).

FIGURE 7-3

The Upgrades tab
in a package's
Properties sheet

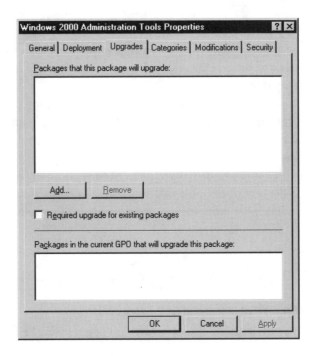

In the Add Upgrade Package dialog box, click Add, and find version 1 of the software. You can also decide at this point whether to remove the first package or upgrade over it. Checking the "Required upgrade for existing packages" box makes this a mandatory upgrade.

Incidentally, if versions 1 and 2 of the software are both *native* .MSI packages—that is, if they were both provided by the manufacturer with the software—you do not need to specify which package you are upgrading. The new package automatically finds and replaces the old. When the user runs the application the next time, it replaces version 1 with version 2.

on the **job**

It is interesting to note that any package can be used to "update" any other package. The two packages do not necessarily need to be related. This feature comes in handy if you want to replace one vendor's word processor with that of another vendor. For that matter, you could replace your accounting department's spreadsheets with a game if you wanted to really send them into a tizzy.

Optional Upgrades

With an optional upgrade, you give users the choice of whether to install the new package or leave the old one intact, giving users more flexibility over the packages they think they need.

Optional upgrades are done in almost the same manner as mandatory ones. You create the new package, share it, deploy it using Group Policy, and go to the Properties sheet for that package in the GPO. This time, you simply clear the Required Upgrade for Existing Packages: box.

If a user already has version 1 of an application, version 2 is installed automatically if the user opens a file that requires the new version of the software. If this does not happen, the user must go to Add/Remove Programs to apply the upgrade.

Deploying a Software Upgrade

In this exercise, we deploy a software upgrade via the following steps.

1. Acquire or create a new Windows Installer package and deploy it through Group Policy, as you did before.

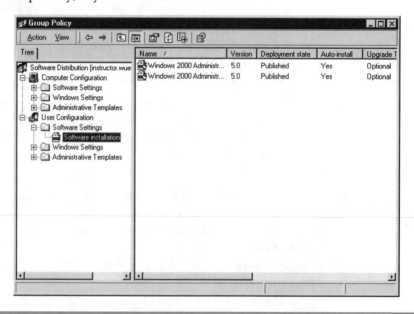

2. Right-click the new package, and choose Properties.

3. Click the Upgrades tab.

4. Find the package you want to upgrade, and decide whether to have it remove the old package or install over it.

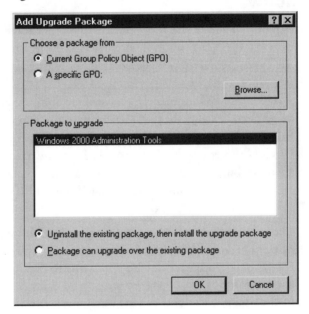

5. Click OK.

6. Choose whether you want mandatory or optional upgrade, and click OK.

7. Test the upgrade on a few systems.

Redeploying Software

Software Installation and Maintenance allows you to easily redeploy software to users when there are a few changes to be made to the installation. Perhaps you want to install a service pack onto everyone's installation of Microsoft Office, or maybe everyone in your marketing department all suddenly decided to start speaking Swahili, so they now need new dictionaries for their word processors. These changes can be easily deployed throughout your network, assuming that the original installation as done using Group Policy.

To redeploy, simply include the new files with the original package, go to the package in the GPO, right-click, and choose All Tasks | Redeploy. You get a warning that redeployment will occur on all machines that already have the package. Bypass the warning, and you have finished the process.

Removing Software

Windows 2000 makes it just as easy to remove software that was originally installed through a GPO. You simply need to right-click the package in the GPO, and choose All Tasks | Remove. You get a dialog box asking you to choose a removal method (see Figure 7-4).

If you choose Immediately Uninstall the Software From Users and Computers, also called *forced removal*, the GPO sends the instruction to physically remove the software from users' desktops. If you choose Allow User to Continue to Use the Software, But Prevent Further Installations, also called *optional removal*, it does not physically remove anything, but no new users get the software distributed to them. Furthermore, the users are no longer able to install the software from Add/Remove Programs.

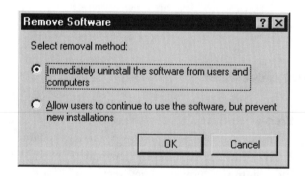

exam
Watch

There is one bothersome quirk in the removal process. If you choose an optional removal, the package disappears because it is no longer needed. However, if you later decide you want to forcibly remove the package from users' desktops, you have no way to go back and change the removal status. In that case, you need to visit each workstation individually to remove the software. You could also redeploy the application to everyone, wait until it has had a chance to be applied, and then force removal.

FIGURE 7-4

Software removal options

Remove Software   [?] [X]

Select removal method:

(•) Immediately uninstall the software from users and computers

( ) Allow users to continue to use the software, but prevent new installations

[OK]   [Cancel]

If an order to uninstall has been received by a computer, it checks an information cache on the local machine. If software was installed through Group Policy, uninstall directions are listed in the cache. If no such directions are found, the software is not installed. This feature prevents you from inadvertently uninstalling software from machines that had it manually installed.

FROM THE CLASSROOM

Uninstalling Packages

Be sure you understand that the process to "undo" a software installation is very different than the process to undo most Group Policy Object effects. Usually, you simply need to remove or disable a Group Policy Object in order to undo it. Here, that will not do the trick. You must physically tell the package to uninstall itself.

If you were to delete a Group Policy Object that had been used to distribute a software package, you would make it impossible to use Group Policy to automatically uninstall the package. In this case, you would physically have to visit each machine and manually uninstall the software. As with many other aspects of Windows 2000, you are far better spending a few extra moments contemplating the results of an action before performing the action.

—*Martin Wuesthoff, MCSE/MCT/CNE/A+/N+*

CERTIFICATION OBJECTIVE 7.03

Configuring Deployment Options

We have looked at how to how to distribute, upgrade, redeploy, and uninstall a package to all the users or computers in an OU. Sometimes, however, you do not want the same action performed on all members of an OU. In this section, we review the process of filtering GPOs so that only specific users or computers receive a policy. We also look at some other options that are available for tweaking the deployment process. Finally, we look at transforms, which allow us to create customized packages for groups of users with slightly different needs.

Filtering the Package

If you have your OUs set up so perfectly that everyone in each OU should receive exactly the same software all the time, more power to you. Most of us, however, need to pick and choose to whom certain software is distributed. *Filtering* is the process of determining exactly who will and who will not receive policy.

Filtering is done on the Security tab of the Properties sheet of a GPO (see Figure 7-5). Remember from the previous chapter that the Read and Apply Group Policy permissions are needed to have a group policy applied to you, meaning that software packages in the policy will also apply to you. If we want to prohibit some users or computers in the OU from receiving the software distribution, we need to remove the Apply Group Policy permission from the Authenticated Users group and explicitly grant it to whomever we want to have it.

It is also important to remember that the package is stored in a shared folder. Users need read permission to access the folder where the package is shared.

Remember, too, that you can choose how you want permissions to flow from site to domain, domain to OU, and parent OU to child OU. If you click the Advanced button in the Security sheet, you have the ability to determine whether permissions should be propagated to child containers and whether to allow parent container permissions to propagate onto this one.

SCENARIO & SOLUTION

Propagation	Allows the permissions from one OU to flow down on another OU.
Block Permission Inheritance	Check this option if you want to prevent permissions from flowing onto a child OU.
User and Group Permissions	Keep in mind that this is a separate topic from parent/child inheritance. Users get permissions from the groups they are in, regardless of any OU properties.
No Override	Prevents one GPO from overriding the settings of another in the same OU.

FIGURE 7-5

Group policy object Security settings

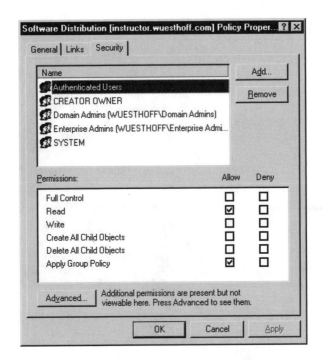

Miscellaneous Deployment Options

We can choose from among several other options when we deploy our package; these options affect naming, deployment, and how the package is displayed to the user. These options are reached by choosing Properties of the software package from within the GPO. For these examples, you see a standard deployment of the Administrative Tools package that is available automatically when you install Windows 2000 Server.

In the General tab (see Figure 7-6), you can change the display name of the application. This option changes the way the application name is displayed in the GPO, as well as the way it is displayed to users in Add/Remove Programs. The other information either comes with a native package or can be placed in a package when the package is being created.

The Deployment tab (see Figure 7-7) contains three sections. The "Deployment type" section simply allows you to switch between a published and an assigned package. In the "Deployment options" section are three options from which to choose. "Auto-install this application by file extension activation" (selected by default and not available if Assigned) indicates whether you want document

FIGURE 7-6

Changing the
name of the
package

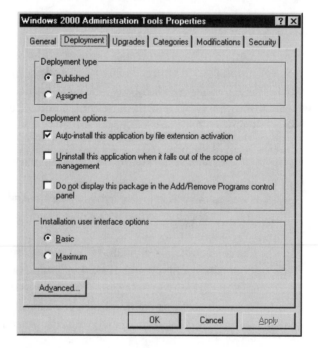

FIGURE 7-7

Changing
deployment
options

invocation to be used to call a package. If this option is not selected, users must call the application through, for example, the Start menu or Add/Remove Programs. "Uninstall this application when it falls out of the scope of management" indicates whether you want an application to be removed when a user or computer moves out of the group or OU to which it is assigned. For example, if only accountants in your company need your spreadsheet program, you can select this box. Then when Betty moves from the accounting department to sales, the application is automatically removed from her machine. "Do not display this package in the Add/Remove Programs control panel" (not available if Assigned) means just that. "Installation user interface options" specifies whether a user sees installation screens, messages, and settings when the program is being installed (Maximum) or simply a basic message that the application is being installed (Basic).

Clicking the Advanced button displays two other options (see Figure 7-8). Ignore Language When Deploying This Package allows you to deploy a package, even if its language conflicts with the language of the machine. Remove Previous Installs of This Product for Users, if The Product Was Not Installed by Group Policy-based Software Installation allows you to deploy the package to users, even if they already have the software installed on their machines. This option allows you to control users' installation through Group Policy when it comes time to upgrade or remove the software.

FIGURE 7-8

The Advanced
Deployment
Options screen

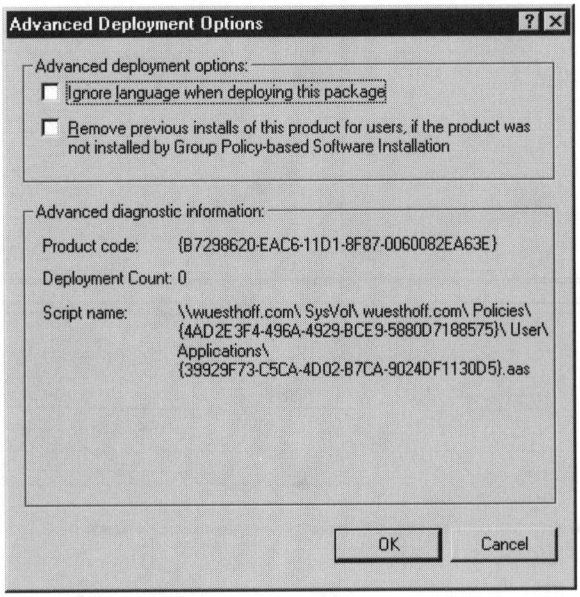

Advanced Deployment Options

Advanced deployment options:
☐ Ignore language when deploying this package
☐ Remove previous installs of this product for users, if the product was not installed by Group Policy-based Software Installation

Advanced diagnostic information:
Product code: {B7298620-EAC6-11D1-8F87-0060082EA63E}
Deployment Count: 0
Script name: \\wuesthoff.com\ SysVol\ wuesthoff.com\ Policies\ {4AD2E3F4-496A-4929-BCE9-5880D7188575}\ User\ Applications\ {39929F73-C5CA-4D02-B7CA-9024DF1130D5}.aas

OK   Cancel

The Categories tab of Administration Tools Properties allows you to place packages into categories in Add/Remove Programs. This option helps users identify the software that is available to them and might help prevent them from installing more software than they actually need.

Changing Categories

Now let's take a look at the process of changing categories.

1. Open Active Directory Users and Computers.

2. Right-click your domain name, and choose Properties.

3. On the Group Policy tab, double-click your Default Domain Policy.

4. Under Computer Configuration, expand Software Settings.

5. Right-click Software Installation, and choose PROPERTIES.

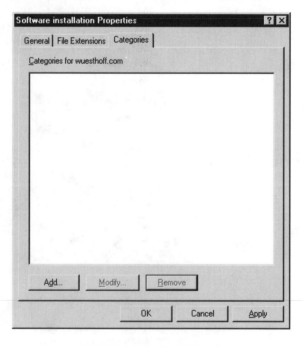

6. On the Categories tab, click Add.

7. Type the name of a category that you want to appear in Add/Remove Programs.

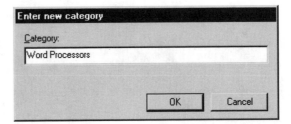

8. Repeat Steps 6 and 7 for all categories you want to add. (I added Spreadsheets, Games, and Graphics.)

9. Click OK to close Software Installation Properties, and close the Group Policy window.

Categorizing Packages

Now that we have some categories, let's categorize our packages for users.

1. In Active Directory Users and Computers, right-click the OU that contains your GPO with your package.

2. On the Group Policy tab, double-click your software Installation GPO.

3. Under Computer Configuration or User Configuration (wherever your package lives), expand Software Settings, and click Software Installation to view your packages.

EXERCISE 7-5

4. Double-click a package, and choose the Categories tab.

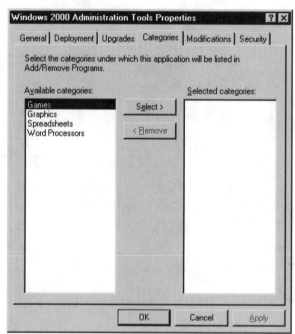

5. Select the category under which you want the package to appear, and click Select. Repeat this step if you want the package to appear in more than one category.

The published package now appears in users' Add/Remove Programs under the appropriate categories.

Using Transforms

As more software companies begin including Windows Installer packages with their applications, the same companies might also include tools that allow you to customize the package for different groups of users. Office 2000 already includes such a tool, which you could use to include different language dictionaries to groups of users in an international or multilingual corporation. These customizations are stored as .MST files (the T stands for *Transform*) and are associated with the main package.

A transform can be added to the package only before it is actually deployed; the transform is done from the Modifications tab of the package's Properties sheet. You can add multiple modifications to a package, but they must all be added at the same time.

To assign different modifications to different groups of users, you must assign the package multiple times and add a different modification to each instance of the package. For example, suppose you have an Austria OU and a Brazil OU. In the former, you would add the German dictionary as a modification to the Word 2000 package in that OU's GPO. For the latter, you would create a GPO in the Brazil OU with the Word 2000 package and add an .MST that installs the Portuguese dictionary.

CERTIFICATION OBJECTIVE 7.04

Troubleshooting During Software Deployment

Even though Software Installation and Maintenance greatly simplifies the process of deploying software throughout your organization, there are still times when things do not work exactly as you planned. In this section, we look at a few of the most common problems that could occur. We also take a quick look at using the Event Viewer snap-in to help diagnose software installation problems.

Common Deployment Problems

Most deployment problems fall into one of three categories: packages that do not install at all on a machine or for a user, packages that install with unexpected or unintended results (such as the incorrect files), or packages that are deployed in an improper way.

Package Fails to Install

If you expect a package to be installed on a machine, advertised for a user, or appear in Add/Remove Programs and it does not, the problem most likely lies somewhere within Group Policy. As noted in the previous chapter, there are many ways that the assignment of Group Policy can fail. Remember that for Group Policy to be assigned to a user, the user must be given the Read and Apply Group Policy permissions (see Figure 7-9). By default, these permissions are assigned to Authenticated Users in the OU. However, if the user or any group of which the user is a member has the Deny box checked for either of those permissions, the software overrides the default policy, and the Group Policy, in this case the package distribution, does not apply. In this case, you do not receive any warning message to tell you the process did not complete correctly.

If you get a message along the lines of "The Network Path could not be found," you likely either have some sort of a connectivity issue (incorrect protocol, address conflict, or the like) or you have shared the package to an invalid share name. Make sure the two machines can "see" each other, the package has been installed and shared on the network, the path to the object in the GPO has been entered correctly, and the user or computer has read access to the shared folder and files.

The Package Installs Incompletely or with Unexpected Results

A message telling you that the package installed incompletely or with unexpected results usually indicates a problem in the initial repackaging process. Remember the example of creating a package to install Excel on a source computer that already

FIGURE 7-9

The Security tab of a group policy object

contains the Word files? The package would not be enough to install Excel on many machines. It would have no files that are shared between the two applications. Likewise, if something else other than software installation was done on the source computer between snapshots, the extra changes are reflected in the package.

The Package Does Not Install Itself But Appears on the Add/Remove Programs Control Panel

If the package fails to install but appears on the Add/Remove Programs Control Panel, you are not deploying the package in the correct manner. If you definitely want to install software, assign it. Published software is not automatically installed or even advertised except through Add/Remove Programs. Check the Deployment tab of the package's Properties sheet to make sure you have chosen the proper method.

If the package fails to install upon document invocation, be sure you have selected Auto-install on the same Deployment tab. Auto-install turns on or off a user's ability to double-click a document's icon to install the related package.

on the **Job** *The* Windows 2000 Server Resource Kit *contains an extensive list of possible package installation errors and their solutions.*

Event Viewer

Whenever a new package is installed, whether successfully or not, it is logged as an event in Event Viewer. You find this information in the application log of Event Viewer. In most cases, if there was an error, enough information is given inside the log entry to help you begin an investigation as to why the installation failed. For example, if you see an entry that indicates that the desired package or some of its files could not be found, you need to check the network placement of the package as well as connectivity issues.

To view these events, open Event Viewer from Administrative Tools or type **EVENTVWR** at a Run command. You are looking for two types of entries under Source: Application Management or MSInstaller. Application Management shows events related to Software Installation and Maintenance. MSInstaller shows the status of package installation—in other words, the success or failure of .MSI files to properly install.

exam **Watch** *Remember, the software installation events are logged to the application log, not the system log.*

CertCam 7-6

EXERCISE 7-6

Checking the Windows Installer Service in Event Viewer

Now let's take a quick look at the Installer Service through Event Viewer.

1. Go to Start | Programs | Administrative Tools | Event Viewer.

2. In Event Viewer, select Application Log.

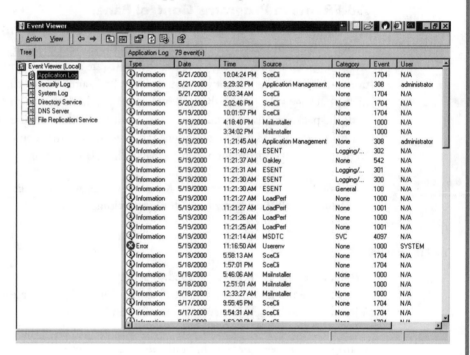

3. Select View | Filter.

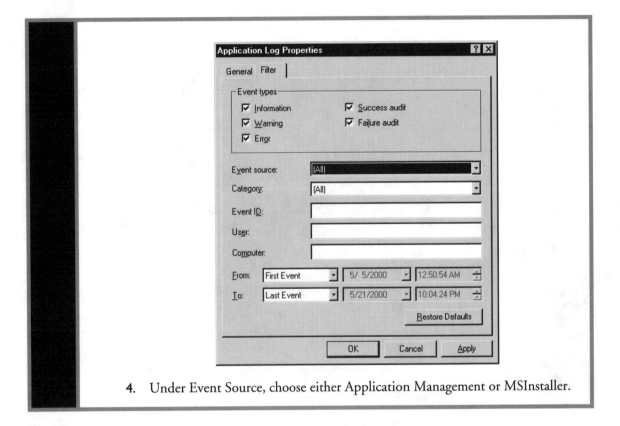

4. Under Event Source, choose either Application Management or MSInstaller.

5. In the resulting filtered list, double-click one of the entries to view the details.

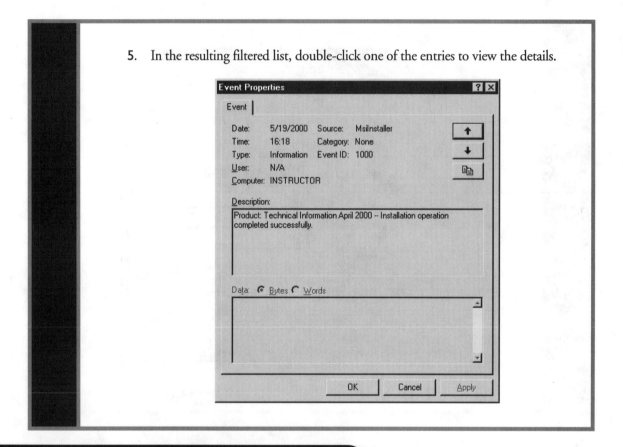

CERTIFICATION OBJECTIVE 7.05

Managing Network Configuration Using Group Policy

A handful of software-related settings can be configured using Group Policy but do not fit neatly into the category of Software Installation and Maintenance. In this next section, we look at how to deploy configuration changes to Internet Explorer. We also inspect how GPOs can be used to configure login scripts, printers, offline files, and network and dial-up connections.

Configuring Internet Explorer

Using Group Policy, you can remotely configure Internet Explorer on desktops throughout your organization. You can determine everything from what will appear in users' Favorites folders to what type of content they are able to view on the Internet and what logo you want to appear in the upper-right corner of their browsers. To do this, go to Windows Settings in the GPO for a site, domain, or OU. Here we look at the five categories of settings you can change in this manner: browser user interface, connection, URL, security, and programs.

Browser User Interface

In the Browser User Interface section of Windows Settings, you can customize the look of the browser. For example, you can create your own logo to replace the standard Internet Explorer logo or change the text on the title bar (see Figure 7-10). If you are deploying these changes throughout a network, be sure to save the logos and images to a network path rather than a local one.

Connection

Here you can configure Internet connectivity settings for computers in your network. You have the ability to set proxy servers, specify a shared file to automatically set browser configuration, import connection settings, and set a custom string of data to be appended to the browser's identification of itself on the Internet (see Figure 7-11).

URLs

In the Important URLs section, you have the ability to set certain pages as favorites, define important sites such as a home URL, and define channels (see Figure 7-12). The Favorites and Links setting allows you define an entire hierarchy of favorite pages and links, as well as allowing you to keep or delete existing favorites and links. The section allows you to set a home page, define a search URL, and direct users to a URL when they choose Help | Support in the browser. Channels allows you to define channels and categories, as well as to remove existing channels.

FIGURE 7-10 Choosing a custom logo

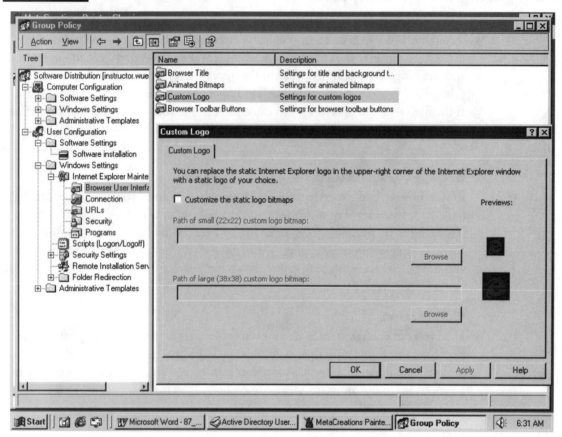

Security

Here you can define the kind of content you want to allow users to see on their browsers, as well as what publishers you want to have browsers trust (see Figure 7-13). Security Zones and Content Ratings options allow you to determine the types of content users can view, the specific sites they may or may not display, and the types of ratings system you use. You can also set an administrator password to prevent others from changing their individual settings. The Authenticode Settings option allows you to determine a list of publishers and certificate agencies that you want to be identified as trustworthy by your browsers.

FIGURE 7-11   Setting proxy servers

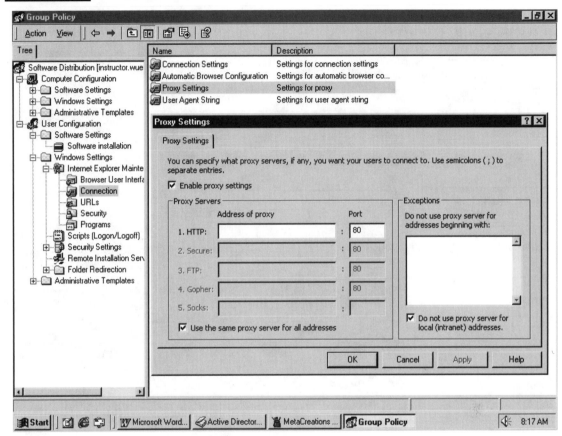

Programs

Under Programs, you can define the applications that automatically open when you invoke certain tasks. For example, if you use GroupWise instead of Outlook for your company's e-mail, you can set up that choice here (see Figure 7-14).

Other Configurable Options

A handful of other software options can be configured with Group Policy. They are found in various locations in the GPOs. Let's take a look at them now.

FIGURE 7-12   Setting a home page

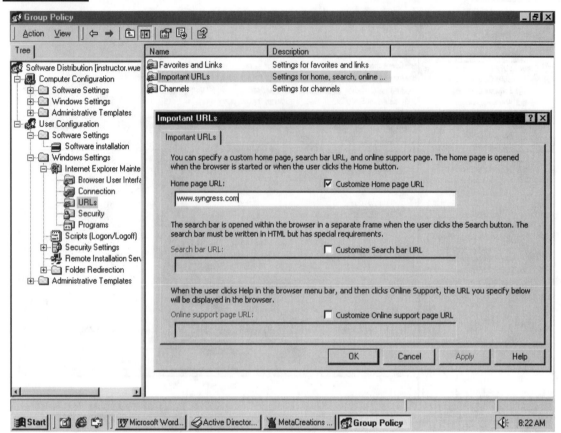

Logon Scripts

With Windows 2000, we have the ability to run four types of scripts. Under the Computer Management section of the GPO, you have the ability to set startup and shutdown scripts. As the names imply, these scripts can be written in a variety of scripting languages and perform some sort of configuration or tasks on the machine when it boots up or shuts down. Logon and logoff scripts are set up under User Management and run when the user logs on or off.

FIGURE 7-13   Approving and disapproving sites

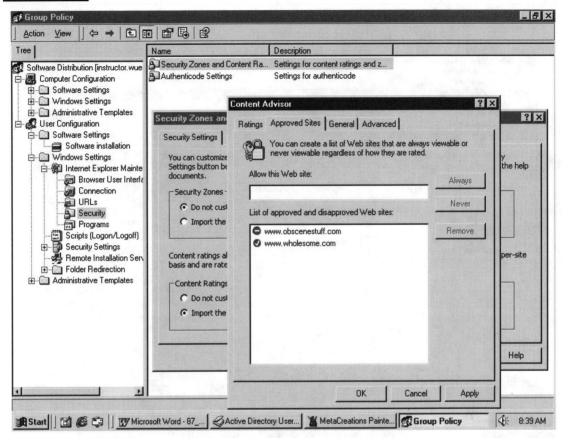

To set these scripts, go to Windows Settings under the appropriate section of the GPO, choose Scripts, and double-click the type of script you want to set. Click Add, and type or browse to the network location for the script (see Figure 7-15).

If you have scripts in different GPOs, they run in the same order as the GPOs. That is, any scripts on the site level run first, followed by those on the domain level and then those at the OU level. If you have nested OUs, the GPOs in the children run after those in the parent, thus taking precedence. If there are two or more scripts of one kind in one GPO, you can configure which script takes precedence by moving it to the bottom of the list, thus running it last (see Figure 7-16).

FIGURE 7-14   Changing default programs

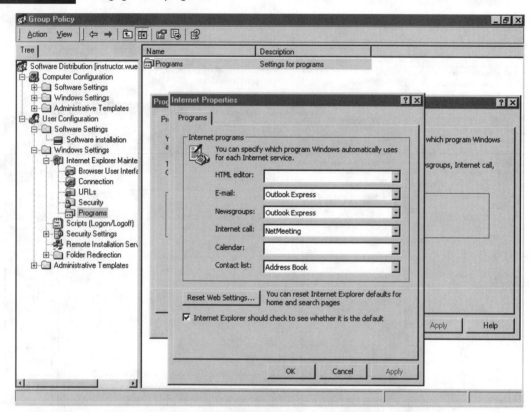

FIGURE 7-15

Adding a
shutdown script

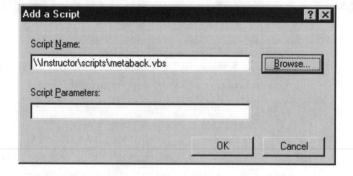

FIGURE 7-16

Changing script
execution order

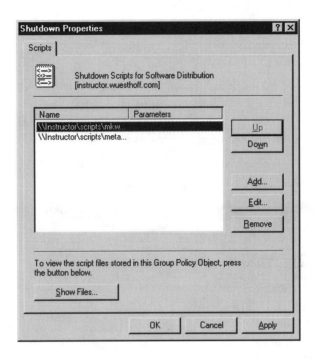

SCENARIO & SOLUTION	
Logon	Runs at each user logon. Can be used to map drives, attach to printers, and so on.
Logoff	Runs at user logoff. Could be used, for example, to generate a report of the user's activities.
Startup	Runs when Windows 2000 starts. Could be used for virus checking or diagnostics.
Shutdown	Runs at Windows 2000 shutdown. Could send warning message to connected users or back up certain files.

Printers

With Group Policy, you are able to set how users can search for and install printers. For example, you can allow or disallow users to add, remove, or browse the network to find printers. You can additionally configure where users will default to when they search Active Directory for printers, and you can automatically direct them to a Web site for printer support and installation (see Figure 7-17). These settings are under Administrative Templates | Control Panel | Printers in the GPO.

FIGURE 7-17   Directing users to a URL for printer support

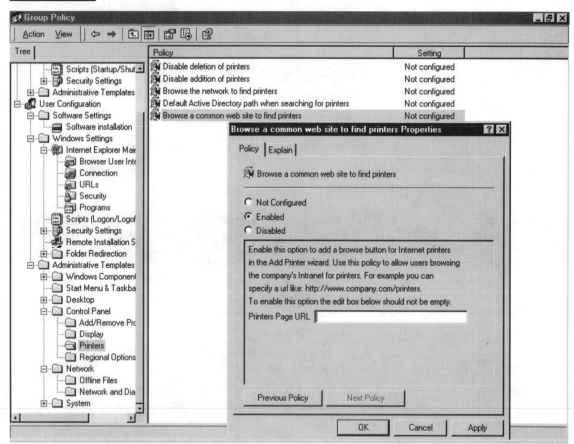

Offline Files

The ability to use offline files is set up at the shared folder itself, but we can configure the way users are able to use them in Group Policy. We can configure synchronization, reminder balloons, server actions, and logging options. These options are available under Administrative Templates | Network | Offline Files.

Network and Dial-up Connections

In the same Network portion of the GPO, where we found the Offline Files options, we can find some options for configuring network and dial-up connections. Again, we give permission to use RAS and dial-up in another place, but here we can configure how it behaves and what users can do in a RAS context (see Figure 7-18).

FIGURE 7-18   Network and dial-up options

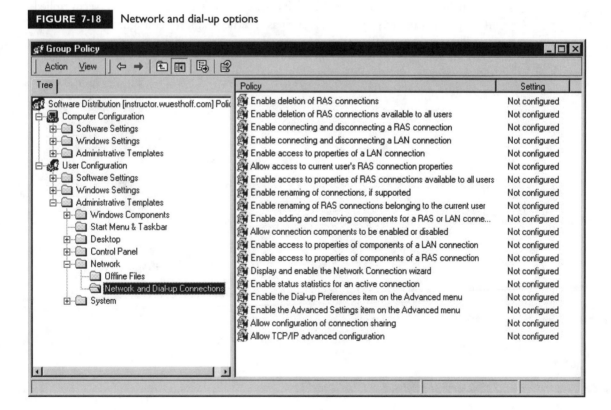

CERTIFICATION SUMMARY

In this chapter, we looked at some of the new software deployment and installation features present in Windows 2000. Most of our discussion revolved around Group Policy and how it can be used to deploy and maintain applications.

We inspected the Windows Installer Service, which is used to ease the installation of software through the use of a new file type, the .MSI package. We then looked at how we could assign these packages to users or computers or publish them to users and how we could modify them or remove them through Group Policy.

Troubleshooting is mostly going to involve inspecting the assignment of GPOs, as well as making sure our packages are created properly. With the Event Viewer, we can start to diagnose troubles as they appear.

Finally, we looked at some miscellaneous software settings that could be controlled through the use of Group Policy, such as Internet Explorer configuration, printer installation issues, offline file settings, and network and dial-up configurations.

✓ TWO-MINUTE DRILL

Deploying Software Using Group Policy

❑ Windows Installer Service allows you to use .MSI files to automate and simplify the software installation process.

❑ Windows Installer Service is available for Windows 95, 98, NT, and 2000.

❑ Repackaging an application involves taking a "before" snapshot of a clean machine, installing software, and taking an "after" snapshot to create a package of differences.

❑ Software Installation and Maintenance is a new technology that allows for the automated deployment of software through the use of Group Policy.

❑ Packages can be assigned to users or computers or published to users.

❑ Assigning a package to a computer automatically installs the package on that machine.

❑ Assigning a package to a user advertises it to the user and installs it when the user calls on it.

❑ Publishing a package to a user places it in Add/Remove Programs but does not advertise it or install it automatically.

❑ You cannot publish a package to a computer.

Maintaining Software Using Group Policy

❑ When you upgrade a package, it replaces an existing one.

❑ A mandatory upgrade replaces the package the next time a user uses it or the computer reboots.

❑ With an optional upgrade, a user can decide whether to upgrade or keep his or her existing package.

❑ When you remove a package, you can decide whether to remove existing installations or simply stop deploying it.

Configuring Deployment Options

❑ A user needs Read and Apply Group Policy permissions for a GPO to be applied to that user.

❑ Clear the Auto-install This Application by File Extension Activation option to disable document invocation installation.

❑ Categories help users find the packages they need in Add/Remove Programs.

❑ Modifications take the form of .MST files and allow for customized deployments of the same package to different groups of users.

Troubleshooting During Software Deployment

❑ The first thing to check in any troubleshooting situation is the application of Group Policy.

❑ The Event Viewer can be used to help diagnose installation and distribution problems.

❑ Be sure to place a package in a shared network location, accessible to users.

Managing Network Configuration Using Group Policy

❑ Internet Explorer configuration options can be set in Group Policy.

❑ Scripts run in the following order: site, domain, parent OU, child OU.

❑ Move the script that should take precedence to the bottom of the list so that it runs last.

SELF TEST

The following questions will help you measure your understanding of the material presented in this chapter. Read all the choices carefully because there might be more than one correct answer. Choose all correct answers for each question.

Deploying Software Using Group Policy

1. You are deploying a custom bookkeeping application to certain parts of your organization. All members of the accounting department should have the application at their desktops. You want members of the training staff to have access to the application, too, in case they should need to develop custom training for the program in the future. The application package takes up a significant amount of disk space, so you do not want it installed on trainers' machines until they feel they need it. What is the most efficient method of deployment for this application? Assume that each user stays at his or her own desktop and that the application has already been repackaged into an .MSI file and copied to a shared location.

    A. Create a GPO at the domain level. Under Computer Configuration, publish the package and apply it to the Accounting group. As individual trainers need the package, apply it to them as well.

    B. Create a GPO in the Trainers OU. Assign the package under Computer Configuration. Leave the default permissions. Create another GPO in the Accounting OU. Publish the package under User Configuration, leaving the default permissions.

    C. Create a GPO in the Accounting OU. Assign the package under Computer Configuration. Leave the default permissions. Create another GPO in the Trainers OU. Publish the package under User Configuration, leaving the default permissions.

    D. Create a GPO in the Accounting OU. Assign the package under Computer Configuration. Leave the default permissions. Manually install the package to the trainers' machines as they need it.

2. What is the difference between Windows Installer Service and Software Installation and Maintenance?

    A. Windows Installer Service deals with publishing software, whereas Software Installation and Maintenance deals with assigning software.

    B. Windows Installer Service is a technology that simplifies software installation through the use of .MSI files. Software Installation and Maintenance allows you to distribute the packages through Group Policy.

C. There is no real difference. They are two different ways to describe the same technology.

D. Windows Installer Service is available only for Windows 2000, whereas Software Installation and Maintenance can be used with Windows 95, 98, NT 4.0, or 2000.

3. "Before" snapshots and "after" snapshots are associated with which of the following?

A. Repackaging software

B. Publishing packages

C. Assigning packages

D. Filtering permissions

Maintaining Software Using Group Policy

4. What would happen by default if you chose to perform a mandatory upgrade from Word to Excel?

A. You would get an error message and the upgrade would fail.

B. Excel would install and Word would be left alone.

C. Excel would install and Word would be removed.

D. The user would be prompted whether he or she wanted to complete the removal of Word.

5. You want to remove a custom application, which was installed by Group Policy, from users' desktops. How can you do this?

A. Delete the GPO that contains the package.

B. Stop sharing the folder that contains the package.

C. Run the Discover program to create a removal package.

D. Right-click the package, choose All Tasks | Remove, and choose to automatically uninstall the package from users' desktops.

6. How can you remove software through Group Policy if it was installed manually?

A. You cannot do this.

B. Add a package to a Group Policy Object with the same name as the application to be removed. Right-click on the package and choose Remove.

C. Add a package to a Group Policy Object with the same name as the application to be removed. Deny access to the package for authenticated users.

D. Publish a removal package to all computers.

7. How would a user perform an optional upgrade?

 A. It will happen automatically the next time the user logs in.

 B. Go to File | Upgrade.

 C. Go to Add/Remove Programs.

 D. Find the package in Active Directory.

Configuring Deployment Options

 8. What do you need to do to prevent users from installing a package through document invocation?

 A. Clear the Auto-install This Application Through File Extension Activity option.

 B. Publish the package to users.

 C. Remove the users' Apply Group Policy permission.

 D. Clear the Invoke Documents check box in the users' accounts.

 9. Why would you categorize packages?

 A. To make sure users can install only one of each type of package

 B. To apply them to different OUs

 C. To associate them with .MST files

 D. To make it easier for users to find the software they need

10. How do you change the name of an already deployed package?

 A. The name of a package cannot be changed without redeploying the package

 B. On the General tab of the package's Properties sheet

 C. Right-click the package in Windows Explorer and choose Rename

 D. You need to open the package with your third-party repackaging tool

Troubleshooting During Software Deployment

11. Which log records Windows Installer activity in the Event Viewer?

 A. System

 B. Application

 C. Security

 D. Installation

12. What would be the result of an incorrect share name associated with a package?

    A. A "Network path not found" message

    B. A prompt for location of files

    C. Failure of installation with no warning message

    D. An "Insufficient rights" message

13. What will happen if users try to install an .MSI package with missing files?

    A. The installation will fail and an error message will be generated.

    B. The installation will fail and no error message will be generated.

    C. The installation will succeed with errors and an error message will be generated.

    D. The installation will succeed with errors and no error message will be generated.

Managing Network Configuration Using Group Policy

14. You have two logon scripts in a GPO. By default, how will they run?

    A. The top script will run first. The bottom script will override any conflicting settings.

    B. The top script will run first. The user will be prompted for any conflicting settings.

    C. The bottom script will run first. The top script will override any conflicting settings.

    D. The bottom script will run first. The user will be prompted for any conflicting settings.

15. Which of the following Internet Explorer options can be configured through Group Policy? Choose all that apply.

    A. Proxy servers

    B. Home page

    C. Favorites folder

    D. Title bar

16. What is the most efficient way to provide printer support to all users in a network?

    A. Publish the support page in Add/Remove Programs.

    B. Configure Internet Explorer to display the support phone number in the title bar.

    C. In the Printers section of a GPO, configure the browser to a common Web site to find the printers parameter.

    D. Give all users Manage Print Document permission.

17. What is another name for client-side caching?

    A. Offline Files

    B. User Configuration

    C. Folder Redirection

    D. Group Policy

LAB QUESTION

Software Installation and Maintenance provides us with several methods to deploy applications to large numbers of users. In this exercise, you will try to reconstruct the best method to deploy software, given a certain scenario.

Assume that you have a custom accounting application that you need to make available to all users in the accounting department. This application has no associated .MSI file. All users in the accounting department have their own computers and never need to use computers outside the department. Document the steps to deploy this application in the most effective manner possible.

SELF TEST ANSWERS

Deploying Software Using Group Policy

1. ☑ **C.** By assigning the application to the accountants' computers, you are sure that they have a copy of the software available to them. By publishing the package to the trainers, you give them the option of going to get the application whenever they deem it necessary, but it will not take up valuable disk space until then.

   ☒ **A** is incorrect because there is no such thing as publishing to computers. **B** is simply a reversal of the correct process. **D** makes more work for you than is necessary by not taking advantage of Group Policy software distribution.

2. ☑ **B.** Software Installation and Maintenance is the method of deploying packages created for the Windows Installer Service.

   ☒ **A** is incorrect because publishing and assigning software are both terms associated with Software Installation and Maintenance. **C** is incorrect because the two technologies are different. **D** is actually reversed. Windows Installer Service does have versions available for different operating systems, whereas the use of Group Policy makes Software Installation and Maintenance available only on Windows 2000.

3. ☑ **A.** When you are repackaging applications, you create a "before" and an "after" snapshot of a source machine.

   ☒ **A, B,** and **C** are all incorrect because filtering permissions, publishing packages, and assigning packages are all done after the "before" and "after" snapshots have been created.

Maintaining Software Using Group Policy

4. ☑ **C.** Excel would install and Word would be removed. When you perform a mandatory upgrade, the second package replaces the first, regardless of what the two packages actually contain.

   ☒ **A** is incorrect because it is valid to upgrade one package with an unrelated package. In its default configuration, an upgrade removes the old package, making **B** incorrect. **D** is incorrect because a user is not prompted about an upgrade.

5. ☑ **D.** Right-click the package, choose All Tasks | Remove, and choose to automatically uninstall the package from users' desktops.

   ☒ **A,** delete the GPO that contains the package, is incorrect because software does not follow the same removal process as other policy changes. **B,** stop sharing the folder that contains the package, does nothing. There is no such thing as option **C,** run the Discover program to create a removal package.

6. ☑ **A.** Only software which was installed using Group Policy can be removed using Group Policy.
☒ **B** and **C** would not remove a software package. **D** is incorrect because there is no such thing as a removal package.

7. ☑ **C.** For optional upgrades, the user must indicate in Add/Remove Programs that they want the upgrade.
☒ **A** is incorrect because it is a mandatory, not an optional, upgrade that is automatic.
B is incorrect because there is no such menu option as File | Upgrade. With Software Installation and Maintenance, a user does not have to go to Active Directory to find packages. Thus, **D** is incorrect.

Configuring Deployment Options

8. ☑ **A.** In the Properties of the package, you can clear the Auto-install This Application Through File Extension Activity check box, which disables document invocation.
☒ **B** is incorrect because published packages can still be called by document invocation.
C is incorrect because removing the users' Apply Group Policy permission would prevent the package from being assigned to the user at all. **D**, clear the "Invoke documents" check box in the users' accounts, is completely fabricated and thus is incorrect.

9. ☑ **D.** Categorizing packages makes it easier for users to locate what they need in Add/Remove Programs.
☒ **A, B** and **C** are unrelated to categories.

10. ☑ **B.** You can change the name of a package on the General tab of its Properties sheet.
☒ **A** and **D** both describe unnecessary steps to rename an application. **C**, right-click the package in Windows Explorer and choose Rename, would not be effective.

Troubleshooting During Software Deployment

11. ☑ **B.** The application log is where installation errors are recorded.
☒ **A, C,** and **D** are incorrect because the system, security, and installation logs do not record Windows Installer activity.

12. ☑ **A.** "Network path not found" indicates the policy was appropriately applied, but the files could not be found.
☒ **B, C,** and **D** describe error messages that would occur at other times.

13. ☑ **D.** An .MSI package will install, whether it has missing files or not. The program might not work, but the installation will take place.
☒ **A** and **B** incorrectly imply that the installation will fail. **C** implies that an error message will be generated and thus is wrong.

Managing Network Configuration Using Group Policy

14. ☑ **A.** Scripts are by default run from the top of the list to the bottom, and settings are automatically overridden as the scripts run.

☒ **C** is in the incorrect order. **B** and **D** are incorrect because settings are overridden automatically.

15. ☑ **A, B, C,** and **D.** All are options that can be configured through Group Policy.

16. ☑ **C.** Setting a default Web page for printers allows users to easily connect to a Web page for printer installation and support, right from the Printers folder.

☒ **A** describes publishing software, not information. **B** describes a different function of an Internet Explorer configuration. **D** hands out much higher levels of permission than you need.

17. ☑ **A.** Offline Files and client-side caching both refer to a user's ability to cache networked files to their local machines. This feature can be configured through Group Policy.

☒ **B, C,** and **D,** User Configuration, Folder Redirection, and Group Policy, refer to other aspects of Active Directory.

LAB ANSWER

Because there is no existing package, we need to create a Windows Installer package using a third-party repackaging application. This requires us to set up a source machine with a fresh installation of Windows 2000 Professional, connect to the server running our repackaging application, and take a "before" snapshot. We must then install and configure the application, reconnect to the server, and take an "after" snapshot to create the package.

After sharing the package and all related files with at least Read permission, we then need to use Group Policy to deploy it. Assigning this application to computers is the best choice in this situation, for two reasons. First, the application needs to be available to all users. Second, the application does not need to follow the users to any different machines. Therefore, assigning to computers works well in this situation.

To assign the package to computers in the accounting department, we create a GPO in the appropriate OU. Under the Computer Configuration section of the GPO, we choose Software Settings, right-click Software Installation, and choose New | Package. We choose Assigned as the deployment method. Finally, we need to make sure that the appropriate computers have Read and Apply Group Policy permissions to the GPO.

8

Installing and Configuring the RIS Service

CERTIFICATION OBJECTIVES

8.01   What Is Remote Installation Services?

8.02   Creating a RIS Server

8.03   Authorizing a RIS Server

8.04   Configuring a RIS Server

8.05   Troubleshooting RIS

✓   Two-Minute Drill

Q&A   Self Test

Ome of the most time-consuming parts of network administration involves deploying and replacing operating systems. There have been many attempts to simplify and automate the process through the years, each with a varying amount of success, but all of them requiring some amount of training in order to get them to work properly.

With Remote Installation Services (RIS), we have the ability to deploy an automated and virtually foolproof installation of an operating system, applications, and profile information. If we plan well, we can send a user who needs a new computer back to her workstation with a floppy disk if needed, tell her to boot from the floppy, press a couple of keys, go to lunch, and enjoy her completely configured and personalized computer when she returns.

This chapter looks at the Remote Installation Services (RIS) from a server standpoint. We will learn what RIS is, when we can and should use it, how to install and configure the RIS service, how to create images to deploy to clients, and how to troubleshoot issues as they arise.

CERTIFICATION OBJECTIVE 8.01

What Is Remote Installation Services?

Remote Installation Services, or *RIS,* is an optional component that runs as a service on the Windows 2000 Server operating system. RIS takes advantage of the new Pre-Boot Execution Environment (PXE)–based remote-boot technology to allow a user to boot his or her workstation and have it automatically find and connect to a RIS server to download a fully configured Windows 2000 Professional image, complete with user profile and applications.

Once the operating system and basic applications have been installed through RIS, various IntelliMirror technologies can be used to further customize the desktop for the user. For example, Software Installation and Maintenance (see Chapter 7, "Managing Software and Network Configuration Using Group Policy") can be used to deploy additional, customized applications to individual users. Group Policy Objects can be put into place that can implement Folder Redirection, Offline Files, and Logon Scripts. In short, RIS and Window 2000 IntelliMirror technologies, when used together, can make for a completely automated installation and configuration of a new or replacement machine, saving administrative time and providing for a reduced Total Cost of Ownership (TCO).

PXE and Supported Hardware

In order for a client machine to be able to get an image from a RIS server, it must have one of the two following options:

- PXE-based remote boot ROM version .99c or later
- PCI-based network card that is supported by the RIS remote boot disk

In a nutshell, your client machine needs to be able to boot up either from the ROM or the RIS boot disk, obtain an address from a DHCP server, find a RIS server, ask it for an image, and receive it from the RIS server. Computers that are designated to be PC98 compliant should have PXE Remote Boot ROM. In addition, Net PCs will have a bootable ROM, as most of them do not have a disk drive to boot from.

If you do not have machines with PXE-bootable ROM, you need to supply a boot disk to kick off the process. Windows 2000 RIS Server includes a utility called the Remote Boot Disk Generator, or RBFG.EXE (the "F" stands for "Floppy"—the display name of the application was changed, but they left the actual command alone). This utility creates a single floppy that can be used to start the Remote Operating System Installation on any machines with a supported drive. The good point is that one floppy can be used for all of your supported machines, so you don't need to carry around a pocketful of boot floppies if you have different network adapters—one disk fits all (or, more accurately, "one disk fits all who are invited"). You see, as of this writing, only 25 network adapters are supported by RBFG.EXE. If yours isn't on the list, you are out of luck. Fortunately, the 25 adapters are 25 of the most popular adapters on the market.

on the
Job

There is also the chance that the floppy may work with your adapters even if they are not on the list. The only way to find out for sure is to try it out on one. Do not, however, expect Microsoft to support your decision to use a nonsanctioned network card.

In Exercise 8-1, you will install the Remote Boot Disk Generator and use it to check to see if your network cards are supported. You will then create a boot floppy. Note: This exercise is included here in the text to coincide with the discussion of supported cards. It assumes that you have RIS installed on the D drive. If you do not, perform Exercise 8-1 after Exercise 8-2.

CertCam 8-1

EXERCISE 8-1

Installing RBFG.EXE and Checking Network Card Compatibility

1. Click Start | Run, and type **D:\RemoteInstall\Admin\i386\rbfg.exe**. Press ENTER.

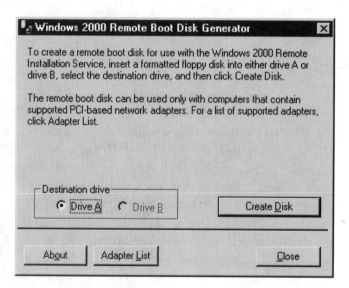

2. Click Adapter List to view a list of supported adapters.

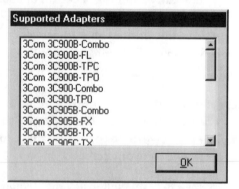

3. Click OK to close the list, and click Create Disk to make the floppy.
4. Close RBFG.

The Remote Boot Floppy will only work with Plug-and-Play PCI cards. This means that they will not work will laptop machines, with the exception of certain docked machines. Even a docked machine will only work if the docking station has a supported PCI network card.

How RIS Works

When a potential RIS client boots up, either through the use of a RIS boot disk or straight from the boot ROM, a DHCP discover packet (with PXE client extension tags) is sent to get an IP address from a DHCP server and to find the address of a RIS server. In addition, the client at that time sends its Globally Unique Identifier, or GUID. A GUID is a 32-digit hexadecimal number that all PXE devices have assigned to them. After a DHCP server has sent an address (with PXE server extension tags) and a RIS server has identified itself, a message is displayed to the user to press the F12 key in order to initiate the Remote Installation.

The RIS server checks Active Directory to see if the client computer's GUID has been prestaged for any RIS servers. If so, that particular RIS server would take over the process. This is done using the Boot Information Negotiation Layer, or BINL, service. This service was added to the server upon RIS installation and is responsible for most of the communications in the RIS process.

After the RIS server knows whether there is a prestaged client account, it sends the client a small application called the Client Installation Wizard, or CIW. This asks for the user's name and password, which is then checked against Active Directory. The user's account is verified, and the RIS policy settings are checked to determine which images and options are available to the user. If there is more than one installation available, it will present a list to choose from. If only one installation is available to the user, and no options are available, the choices will not be offered. Rather, the user will be asked to confirm the installation and the reformatting of his or her hard drive.

After the user has selected or confirmed an installation, his or her account will be checked for permissions to create a new computer account, if the client machine was not prestaged. The computer will be assigned a name from the RIS server, and the transfer of files begins. From this point, the process is completely hands-off to the user.

RIS Components

To fully understand the RIS process and how to configure it for use, we need a basic understanding of the different components that work together to complete the RIS picture. We will look at five components, which require at least three computers to execute fully.

Remote Installation Services Setup, or RISetup.exe, prepares a RIS server for use by preparing a partition for installation storage and creating the initial CD-based image. One important feature of RIS involves the Single Instance Store, or SIS. If two or more images are stored on the same RIS server, there are obviously going to be many files shared among the images. Rather than having each image store its own copy of each file, SIS will inspect a new image for files that have already been stored with a different image, and will replace the second instance of the file with a pointer to the initial instance of the file. This method will dramatically reduce the amount of drive space taken up by multiple images.

When RIS is installed on a server, that server will have a Remote Install tab added to its Properties sheet in Active Directory Users and Computers. This tab gives administrators the ability to configure what images to hand out, naming schemes and placement of new computer accounts, and the ability to prestage computers. Administrators also have the ability to control what RIS servers are allowed to hand out images on the network by authorizing them in Active Directory. This all falls under the scope of Remote Installation Services Administration and Configuration Options.

The Remote Installation Preparation Wizard, or RIPrep.exe, is used to create RIPrep images. It is run from a *source computer,* or a computer from which an image will be generated. After Windows 2000 Professional has been installed, and all applications that are to be a part of the image have also been installed and configured, the source computer will connect to the RIS server and run RIPrep. This will dump the contents of the C drive of the source computer onto the RIS server as a RIPrep image. This image will not contain any user-specific settings.

The Remote Boot Disk Generator, or rbfg.exe, creates boot floppies for any machines without PXE-enabled BIOS but with RIS-supported network cards. Unlike the boot floppies of the past, one Remote Boot Floppy will work for any of the currently 25 supported network cards.

The Client Installation Wizard, or OSChooser.exe, is sent to the client machine from the RIS server. It allows the user to interact with the RIS server by giving logon name and password, choosing an installation if more than one is available, and displaying installation options if appropriate for that user.

Now that we've discussed the RIS components, here is a quick reference to help you keep these programs straight:

RISetup.exe	Claims a drive for RIS, creates the first image, and sets up the Single Instance Store.
Active Directory Users and Computers	Configures the RIS server for client requests.
RIPrep.exe	Creates RIPrep images.
Rbfg.exe	Creates the boot floppy.
Oschooser.exe	Sent to client computer to allow a user to choose an image to download.

CERTIFICATION OBJECTIVE 8.02

Creating a RIS Server

Setting up a RIS server is a simple process. First, Remote Installation Services needs to be installed. The server must then be authorized in Active Directory. RISetup must be run to create an initial image. RIS must be set up to allow users to create accounts in Active Directory. Additional images may also be created and placed on the RIS server for distribution. These steps are discussed in more detail later in this chapter.

Prerequisites

A number of things must be present on your network in order for the RIS process to be able to distribute an image to a client machine. First, a client machine is going to need an IP address in order to communicate on the network and find the RIS server. The idea behind RIS is that a user should be able to get an image without any special knowledge or skills, other than the ability to press F12 and type in a username and password. Configuring IP would definitely be considered a special skill. Thus, we have the need for a DHCP server somewhere on the network, accessible to the client machine.

A user will need to be granted permission to create a computer account. This permission is given out in Active Directory. Thus, we need an Active Directory server available. Of course, in order to find an Active Directory server, the client machine needs to ask DNS. So, our third service that must be available is DNS.

There is one server-specific requirement that must be met as well. In order to store images on the server, you must have a partition with at least 2GB of space dedicated to the RIS process. It will not allow you to install images on your system or boot partition. The partition used must be formatted with the NTFS file system.

Installing RIS

Once we have an established DHCP, DNS, and Active Directory server in place on our network, we need to install the Remote Installation Services. This is done through Add/Remove Programs. When you are there, choose Add/Remove Windows Components. Select Remote Installation Services, follow prompts, and RIS is installed. We discuss installation in Exercise 8-2.

SCENARIO & SOLUTION

Why do we need a DHCP server somewhere on the network?	The DHCP server gives the client computer an IP address so it can communicate with the RIS server.
Why do we need DNS?	DNS allows the RIS server to find and use Active Directory.
Why do we need Active Directory?	Active Directory allows a RIS server to determine user rights and permissions.

CertCam 8-2

EXERCISE 8-2

Installing RIS

1. Click Start | Settings | Control Panel.

2. Double-click Change or Remove Programs.

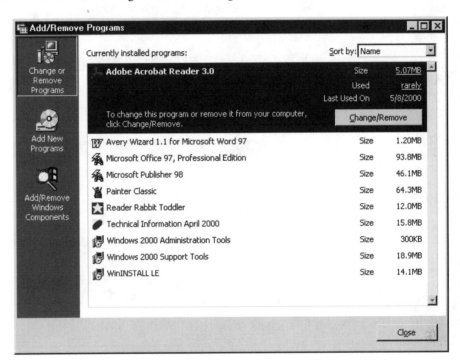

3. Click Add/Remove Windows Components.

4. Check Remote Installation Services, and click Next.

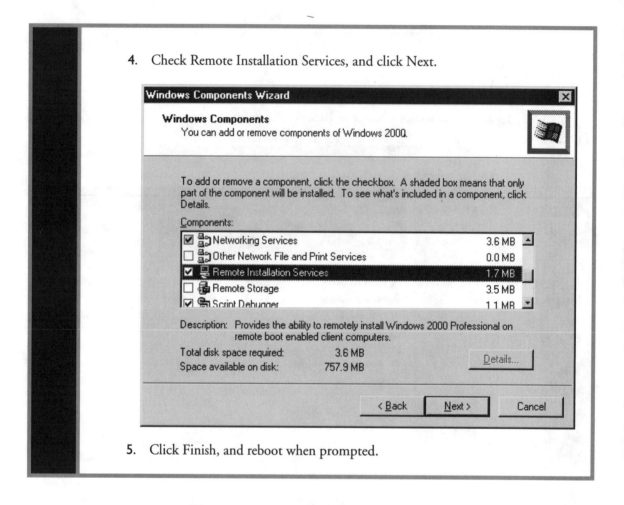

5. Click Finish, and reboot when prompted.

CERTIFICATION OBJECTIVE 8.03

Authorizing a RIS Server

Before a RIS server can deploy images, it must be *authorized* in Active Directory. The authorization process is described in more detail next.

Why Authorize a RIS Server?

A DHCP server needs to be authorized in Active Directory before it starts handing out IP addresses. This helps to prevent someone from setting up another server with either duplicate or invalid addresses on your network, potentially causing you a great deal of headaches trying to troubleshoot all of the new bad addresses that start popping up. Likewise, it would be relatively simple for someone to install Windows 2000 Server on a machine, set it up as a RIS server with some bad images (possibly virus-ridden images?), and start letting it serve. Unless you were prestaging computers, you would have no guarantee that a user would get his or her image from your RIS server rather than the imposter's. For this reason, we need to have a way to guarantee that we approve of all RIS servers that are handing out images. This guarantee is the *authorization process.*

Only a user with Enterprise Administrator privileges can authorize a machine in Active Directory. A RIS server will not give out images unless it is authorized in Active Directory. As a result, only a user with Enterprise Administrator privileges has the ability to start deploying RIS images.

The Authorization Process

The funny thing about the authorization process is that you have to pretend that your RIS server is a DHCP server, even if it is not. There is no interface to authorize a server from within RIS, so we "borrow" the interface from DHCP.

exam
ⓦatch

If your intended RIS server is already an authorized DHCP server, you do not need to do this step. Read exam questions regarding authorization very carefully. If you are asked what the requirements are for a RIS server, one of them is that it must be authorized in Active Directory. However, if you are asked what the steps are to prepare a RIS server, you may not need to authorize it if it is already a DHCP server.

To authorize your RIS server, you need to make sure you are logged on under an account with Enterprise Administrator privilege. You then need to go to the DHCP snap-in, right-click DHCP, and choose Manage Authorized Servers. When you click Authorize, you will give the IP address of the RIS server. You will perform this in Exercise 8-3.

Authorizing a RIS Server

1. Click Start | Programs | Administrative Tools | DHCP.

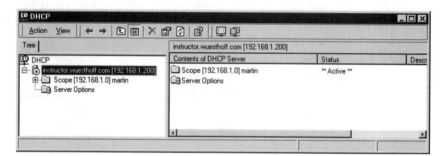

2. Right-click DHCP, and choose Manage Authorized Servers. . . .

3. Click Authorize. . . .

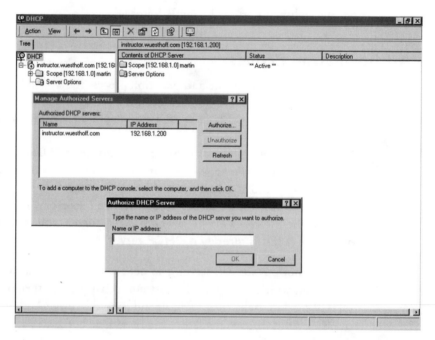

4. Type the IP address or server name of the RIS server. Click OK, then click Yes, and then click OK again.

5. Exit DHCP.

CERTIFICATION OBJECTIVE 8.04

Configuring a RIS Server

Now that we have our prerequisites taken care of and we have installed and authorized our RIS server, it is time to get down to the process of creating images, and then making sure users can get them from the server when needed. Before we can create images, we need to have an understanding of the types of images we can create.

Types of Images

There are two types of images we can deploy: CD-based and RIPrep images. A *CD-based image* is simply a copy of the i386 folder off the Windows 2000 Professional CD-ROM, associated with an answer file. When you create your first CD-based image using RISetup, it creates a standard answer file called RIStandard.sif. This answer file will allow you to install a bare-bones default operating system. You can create your own answer files, which will allow for more customized installation. This is the simplest method to set up and administer, although it is certainly not the fastest method to deploy or the most powerful.

If you want to deploy applications with the operating system, or you want to get the image onto target machines in the quickest method possible, you will want to create a *RIPrep image*. This image is derived by copying a preconfigured computer. It will allow you to deploy applications along with the operating system.

Here is a review of the two types of images:

CD based	Uses answer files to customize an installation. Contains the Windows 2000 Professional source files.
RIPrep	Contains a complete image of a computer, including applications and configuration.

RISetup and CD-Based Images

Before you can install any other images, you must run the RISetup program, which will claim a drive for RIS, set up the Single Instance Store, and create the first image with a default answer file.

Running RISetup

Before you run RISetup to set up RIS and install your first image, there are a few things you need to do:

- Make sure you have a nonsystem drive with at least 2GB of disk space formatted with NTFS.
- Put your Windows 2000 Professional CD in the CD-ROM drive.
- Decide on a name and description for your first image.

exam
ⓦatch

Make sure you know that the images must be copied to an NTFS partition. Real world says that you will get an error message if you try to put them on a FAT partition (Figure 8-1), but you don't get to see that message when you're in the exam room!

Once these steps are completed, running RISetup is a simple process of starting the program, following the prompts, and waiting. The only thing you need to be aware of is that you might want to wait until all of your images have been created and your configuration is done before allowing your server to respond to client requests.

on the
Ⓙob

Remember that this initial image is required on the RIS server, even if you have no intention of ever using it.

Modifying CD-Based Images

Once you have created the default image, you will probably want to customize it through the use of answer files. An *answer file* is a text file that pre-answers some or all of the information a user would normally provide during installation. Answer files can be created manually or by using the Windows 2000 Server's Setup Manager Wizard. Once you have an answer file created, the process of applying it involves going to the RIS server's properties in Active Directory Users and Computers and

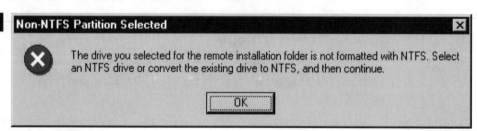

FIGURE 8-1

Non-NTFS error message

Non-NTFS Partition Selected ✕

The drive you selected for the remote installation folder is not formatted with NTFS. Select an NTFS drive or convert the existing drive to NTFS, and then continue.

OK

Running RISetup

1. Click Start | Run, type **risetup**, and press ENTER.

2. Click Next. RIS will scan your drives and suggest a location for its Installation Folder.

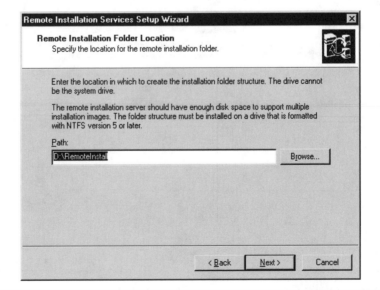

3. Choose a location, or click Next to choose the default. RIS will ask if you want to start responding to client requests.

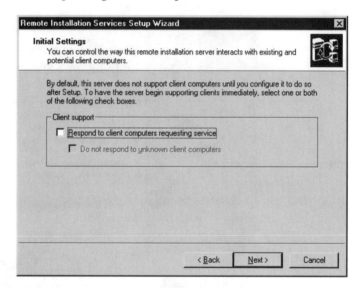

4. You do not want to respond to clients until you have created your images, so leave this unselected, and click Next. RIS will ask for the location of the Source Files.

5. Type *%cdroot%\i386*, and click Next. You will be asked for a folder name for the initial image.

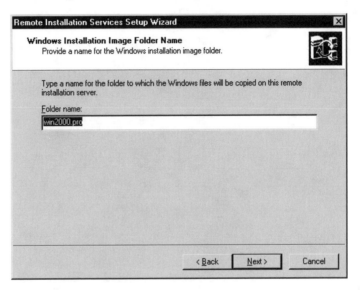

6. Accept the default name, and click Next. You will be asked to type a friendly description and help text for the installation. These will appear to users as they boot to a RIS server and try to choose an installation.

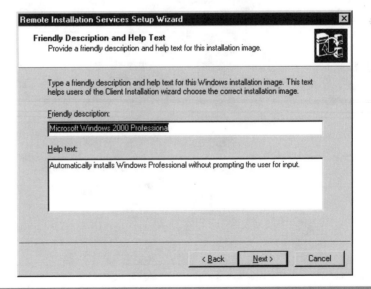

7. Type the appropriate text, and click Next. You will be asked to confirm your choices.

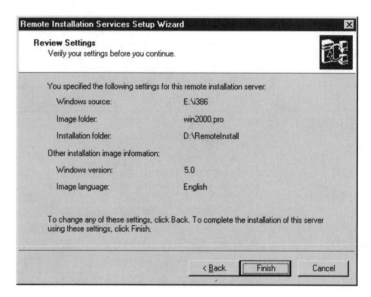

8. Click Finish. You will see a progress indicator. Get a cup of coffee; this will take 10 to 20 minutes or so. When it is finished, your first image is ready.

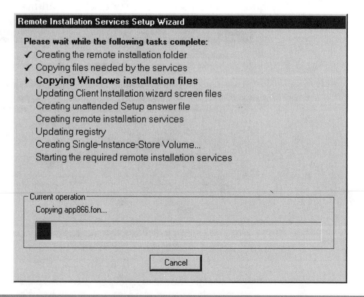

installing a new image from the Remote Install tab. You will have the option of using your own text file, or taking one of the samples that is included with RIS. One sample file instructs RIS not to repartition the client's drives automatically.

exam
ⓦatch

By default, RIS will wipe out all existing partitions on a client machine and reformat everything as one large drive with NTFS. If you do not want this to happen, you need to include a parameter in your answer file. Under the [RemoteInstall] section of the file, add a parameter that reads "repartition=no." RIS will then read the answer file to see how to partition the drives.

Once you have created and associated the new answer file with your CD-based image, you can restrict who is able to use it through ordinary NTFS permissions. Simply go to the properties of the file itself and give Read and Read & Execute permission to the users who should be able to install the image.

In Exercise 8-5, you will create a second CD-based image by associating a sample answer file with it.

exam
ⓦatch

Remember, at this point it is simply NTFS permissions applied to the answer file itself that restricts this installation. It has nothing to do with the Remote Install properties.

Computer Account Creation

At some point in the Remote OS Installation process, a computer account needs to be created in Active Directory. By default, the account will be created upon installation, and a computer name will be generated by the RIS server, following parameters that were preconfigured by the administrator. In order for this method to work, the user who is starting the RIS process needs to have the appropriate permissions to create a computer account. This may not always be desirable. For this reason, and to give more control to the administrators over computer names, there is another option called *prestaging* computer accounts. In this method, you use a number that is unique to each piece of hardware, a Globally Unique ID, or GUID, and you tell Active Directory to create a computer account with a specific name when a request comes from that particular machine. In this section, we will compare the two methods.

EXERCISE 8-5

Associating an Answer File with a CD-Based Image

1. Go to Start | Programs | Administrative Tools | Active Directory Users and Computers.

2. Find your RIS server, right-click it, and choose Properties.

3. Click the Remote Install tab.

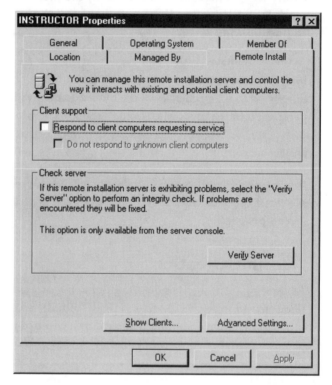

4. Click Advanced Settings. . . .

5. Click the Images tab. (Note: You should only have one image at this point. I happen to have two on my machine.)

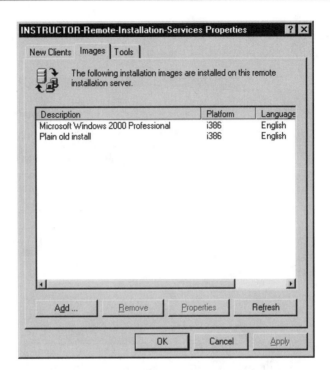

6. Click Add. You will be asked if you want to create a new image, or associate an answer file with an existing image.

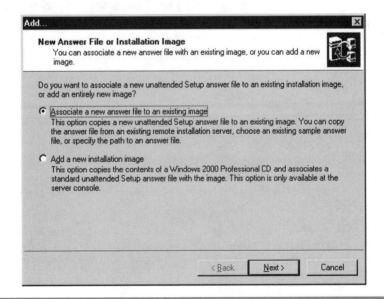

7. Select "Associate a new answer file to an existing image," and click Next. You will be asked for the source of the answer file.

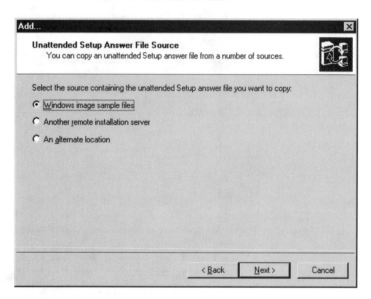

8. Choose "Windows image sample files," and click Next. You will be asked to choose which image to attach this answer file to.

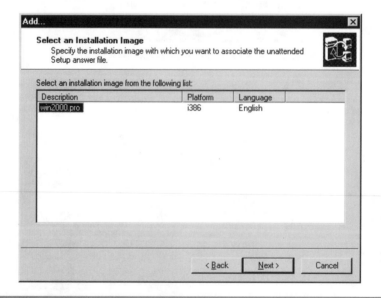

9. Choose the appropriate image, and click Next. You will be asked to select a sample answer file.

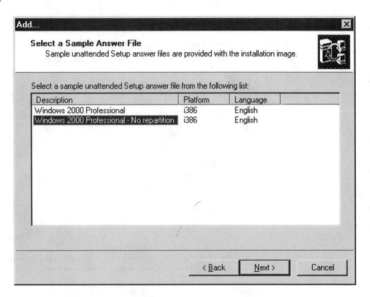

10. Select "Windows 2000 Professional – No repartition," and click Next. You will be asked how you want this installation choice to appear to users.

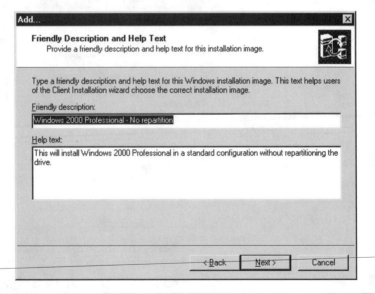

11. Type some text, or leave the default. Click Next. You will have a chance to review your settings.

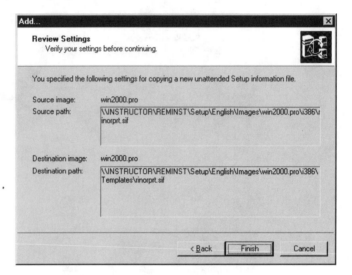

12. Review your settings, and click Finish. You should see the new image on the Properties sheet.

Default Installation and Computer Naming

If you do not wish to prestage client computers, you need to decide on a naming convention and choose where in Active Directory new computer accounts will be placed. You then need to be sure to give the user who is going to start the RIS process on a client machine permission to create a computer account in the appropriate Organizational Unit. The former is done in Active Directory Users and Computers on the Remote Install tab of the RIS server's Properties sheet. The latter is done through Group Policy.

In the Advanced section of the Remote Install tab, you have the option of choosing a predefined naming scheme or developing a custom scheme of your own. These schemes involve either the user's name or the MAC address of the client computer. From the same place, you can also define a single OU for new computer accounts to be created, or specify that the account will be created in the user's OU.

Exercise 8-6 will give you practice configuring naming schemes and placing computer accounts for RIS installs

Choosing a Naming and Placement Scheme

1. Open Active Directory Users and Computers.

2. Right-click the RIS server, and choose Properties.

3. Click the Remote Install tab

4. Click Advanced Settings.

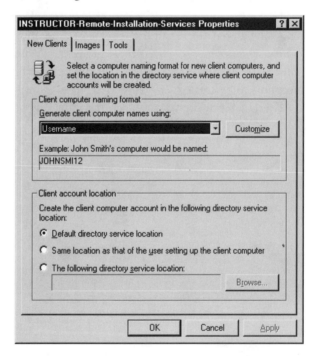

5. Click the drop-down arrow to choose a naming convention, or click Customize.

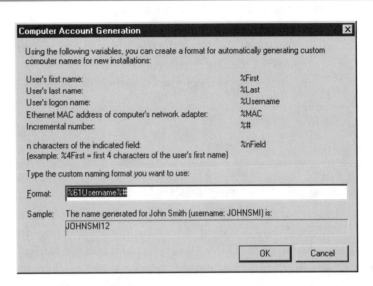

6. Click OK. Once a naming scheme has been chosen, choose the new computer account placement. You can choose to place new accounts in the same OU as the RIS server, the same OU as the user who is starting the installation, or a specified default location. In this case, we will choose the center option, "Same location as that of the user setting up the client computer." Click OK to close the Advanced settings, and OK again to close the server's Properties sheet.

Assigning Permissions to Users

If you are not going to prestage client computers, you need to make sure that the user who is going to begin the client installation process has the right to add computers to the Organizational Unit that the new account will be placed in. This can be done through the Delegation of Control Wizard.

Assigning Permissions to Users

In this exercise, we will assume that Joe User has approached you with complaints that his computer is dead. After some questioning, you determine that a fresh installation of the OS and all applications is called for. You hand Joe a RIS floppy, give him instructions, and send him on his way. You now need to give him permission to add a computer account to his domain.

1. In Active Directory Users and Computers, right-click Joe's Organizational Unit (in this case, Trainers) and choose Delegate Control.

2. Click Next. You will be asked to choose users to delegate control to.

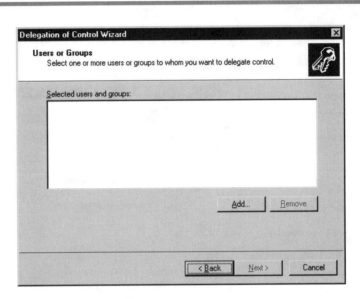

3. Click Add to choose a new user or group.

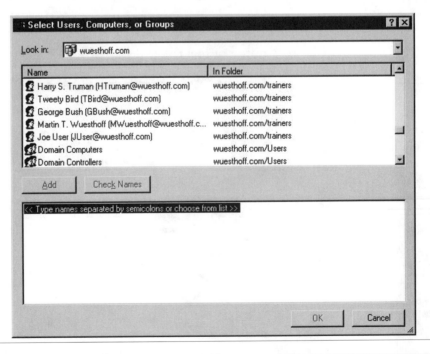

4. Double-click the user or group to add (in this case, Joe User), click Add, and click Next. You will be asked which tasks you wish to delegate.

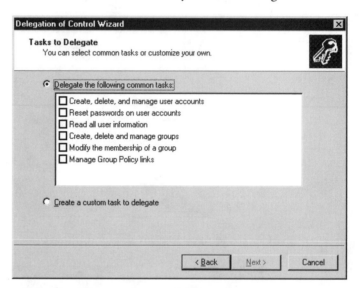

5. Choose "Create a custom task to delegate," and click Next.

6. Choose "Only the following objects in the folder," check "Computer objects," and click Next. You will be asked what level of permission to delegate.

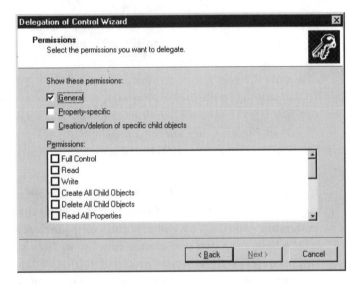

7. Choose General, then click "Create All Child Objects," and click Next. You will be asked to review your choices.

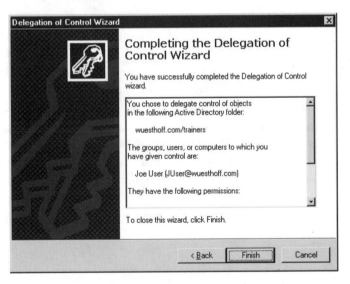

8. Click Finish to confirm choices.

Prestaging Client Computers

As an alternative to giving users the right to add computer accounts and choosing a default naming scheme, you can set up computer accounts ahead of time and designate them as RIS accounts. *Prestaging* is the process of creating an account ahead of time and associating it with a particular machine's network card or BIOS. Besides eliminating the need to give users permissions we may not wish to hand out and giving us control of computer names, prestaging computers will also allow us to distribute the load across multiple RIS servers if we wish.

Before you can prestage a computer, you need to know its Globally Unique ID, or GUID. A *GUID* is a 32-digit hex number that is given to all PXE-based devices. It is usually located on a sticker somewhere on the computer or inside the case. For non-PXE machines, the GUID is 20 zeros followed by the computer's MAC address.

on the **Job**

If you are having difficulty determining a computer's GUID, the following suggestions may help. For a non-PXE machine, type ipconfig /all from a command prompt. You will find the computer's MAC address. Add 20 zeros to the beginning and you have a functional GUID. For a PXE-based machine, the process is a little more difficult if you can't find the number printed on the case or in the machine somewhere. One method is to run a network sniffer such as Network Monitor and issue an ipconfig /renew command. If you look inside the captured DHCP Discover packet, you will find the client's GUID.

To prestage a computer, you must first create the account in Active Directory Users and Computers. Right-click the Organizational Unit into which you wish to place the new account, and choose New | Computer. Give the account a name as usual, and click Next. You will be asked whether this is a managed computer or not. Indicate that it is, and type in the GUID for the computer that will receive the account (Figure 8-2).

When you click Next, you will have the opportunity to designate a particular RIS server to service this machine if you wish. This will allow you to spread the work across multiple RIS servers (Figure 8-3).

Clicking Next will allow you to review your choices. Review, press Finish, and you have a prestaged computer (Figure 8-4).

FIGURE 8-2

Prestaging a
computer

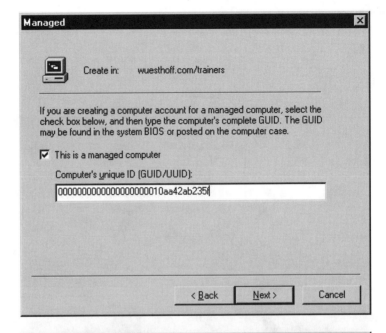

FIGURE 8-3

Designating a
RIS server

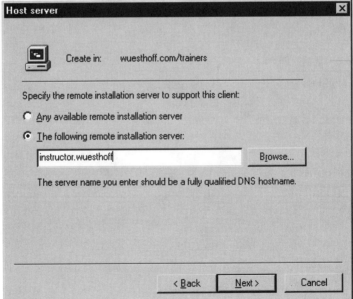

FIGURE 8-4

Confirming the prestaging

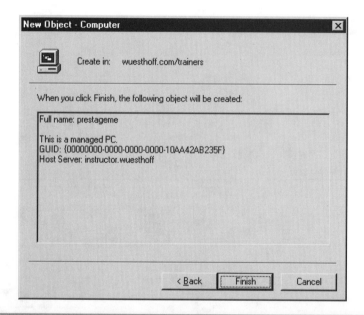

New Object - Computer

Create in: wuesthoff.com/trainers

When you click Finish, the following object will be created:

Full name: prestageme

This is a managed PC.
GUID: {00000000-0000-0000-0000-10AA42AB235F}
Host Server: instructor.wuesthoff

< Back   Finish   Cancel

FROM THE CLASSROOM

Prestaging or Not?

The issue of how to create accounts using RIS can be a tricky one to deal with. There is no perfect method that combines total automation and simplicity of setup with tight security and flexibility.

On the one end of the spectrum, we have prestaging. This offers the best security, since we don't need to give administrative-type privileges to ordinary users. We also have complete control and flexibility over computer names and placement. However, it can be time consuming, especially if you have a number of machines to deploy with RIS.

On the other end, you could give all authenticated users the ability to add computers to their own Organizational Unit at all times. This would be the most automated method, but would give an obvious potential breach of security.

A compromise may be to create a group called RISInstallers, and give that group permission to add computers anywhere in the domain. As you hand a user a RIS floppy, you can quickly add his account to the RISInstallers group, thus giving him the ability to kick off the RIS process. After successful installation, remove the user from the RISInstallers group. This way, the user has the permissions needed to perform an install, but only for a brief period of time.

—*Martin Wuesthoff, MCSE/MCT/CNE/A+/N+*

CERTIFICATION OBJECTIVE 8.05

Troubleshooting RIS

There are many places where a RIS installation can fail. At the simplest level, a typo in any one of the many dialog boxes can lead to a failed installation. This is particularly common when typing GUIDs to prestage computers. It is also common to have nonsupported hardware, or to have a problem with one of the network services. Fortunately, Microsoft provides good tools and documentation to aid your troubleshooting efforts. We will look first at some common errors you will encounter. and will then look at the RIS Troubleshooter.

Common Errors

There are different points in the boot process where the RIS installation might fail. By inspecting how far you are able to get in the process before an error, you can get some idea of what problem you might be having.

The Troubleshooter

Windows 2000 Help includes many troubleshooters to assist you when you run into trouble. There is a troubleshooter for the Remote Installation Services as well. The troubleshooters are presented in a problem/solution format. Common problems are

SCENARIO & SOLUTION

Client computers cannot boot to the RIS server.	The client may not be on the list of supported adapters.
Clients get a BootP message, but go no further.	The DHCP server is likely unavailable.
Clients get a DHCP message and then stop.	RIS server is either offline or not authorized.
Clients get a BINL message and then stop.	The BINLSVC service on the RIS server may be stalled. Try stopping and restarting the service on the RIS server.
Installation options or images not available to user.	Most likely a permissions problem somewhere, or an incorrectly set Group Policy Object.

listed, and when you select a problem, a discussion on solutions appears. Many of the solutions have hyperlinks to bring you to the tools that you will need to perform a task. Some of the troubleshooters present error messages you may encounter. As with all other Windows 2000 errors, details of all error messages will be stored in the Event Log, which you can access using the Event Viewer. Most of the RIS-based errors will be found in the Application or System logs.

Make use of the troubleshooters in Windows 2000. They are more useful and in depth than they have been in the past.

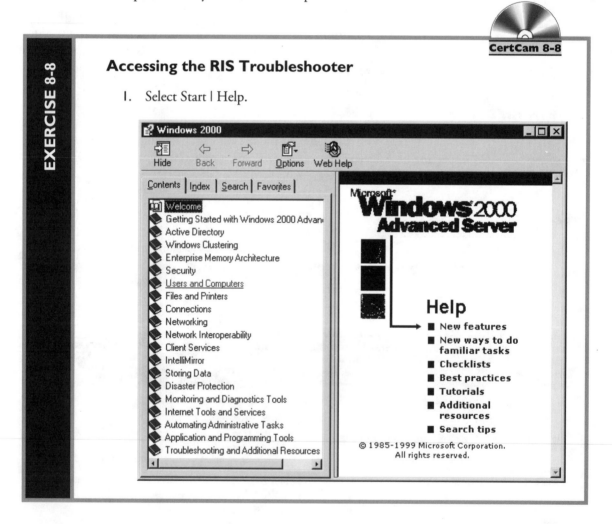

CertCam 8-8

EXERCISE 8-8

Accessing the RIS Troubleshooter

1. Select Start | Help.

2. Choose IntelliMirror | Remote installation services.

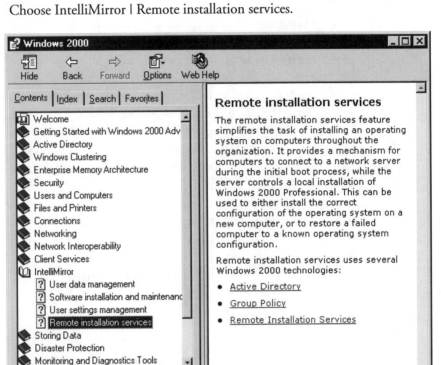

3. On the right-hand side, choose Remote Installation Services, and then Troubleshooting. You will see a number of topics on the right. Choose one and follow the directions given.

CERTIFICATION SUMMARY

Remote Installation Services gives us the ability to automate the installation of Windows 2000 Professional on client computers. Using RIS, we are able to allow an average user to do his or her own installation without fear of getting any configuration options incorrect.

We began this chapter by looking at RIS, inspecting cases when it may be useful, and studying the RIS process. Next, we looked at how to set up and install a RIS server. We discussed the network prerequisites and the fact that you need to have DNS, DHCP, and Active Directory running on your network before you can set up RIS. We saw that a RIS server needs to be authorized in Active Directory, whether or not it is already a DHCP server.

In the next section, we discussed how to configure the RIS server, particularly how to create images for deployment. We learned the difference between CD-based images and RIPrep images. We looked at how to create computer accounts for your RIS-installed clients, and whether to prestage client machines or not. Finally, we looked at the Troubleshooter, a tool you can turn to when RIS installations do not work.

✓ TWO-MINUTE DRILL

What Is Remote Installation Services?

❑ Remote Installation Services allows you to deploy images from a RIS server to compatible client machines.

❑ RIS can only deploy images based on Windows 2000 Professional.

❑ A RIS image contains the preconfigured OS, plus any applications that may need to go on all client machines.

❑ A client computer wishing to use RIS for image deployment must either be PXE based or supported by the Remote Boot Floppy.

❑ A client starting up will first contact a DHCP server to get an address, and will then find a RIS server to get an image.

Creating a RIS Server

❑ DHCP, DNS, and Active Directory must be running and available somewhere on your network for RIS to work.

❑ RIS runs and is installed as a service within Windows 2000 Server.

❑ A RIS server must have a partition other than the system and boot partitions to store images. The partition should have 2GB of free space and be formatted with the NTFS file system.

Authorizing a RIS Server

❑ A RIS server will not respond to client requests unless it has received permission to do so. That permission is granted by authorizing the server in Active Directory.

❑ The server must be authorized in the DHCP manager as an authorized DHCP server, even if we have no intention of ever running DHCP on this machine.

Configuring a RIS Server

❑ There are two types of images: CD based and RIPrep.

❑ CD-based images are derived from a simple copy of the Windows 2000 Professional files from the CD, and use answer files for customization purposes.

❑ RIPrep images are snapshots of an entire source machine's configuration. With these issues, you can deploy applications along with a fully configured OS.

❑ Prestaging computers allows you to have full control over the RIS process and the naming structure.

❑ If you do not prestage clients, you must give the user the ability to create computer objects in the appropriate OU.

Troubleshooting RIS

❑ Troubleshooting involves two main tools: Event logs and the Troubleshooter.

❑ The Event log will help us track down the reasons for RIS failure by keeping track of and recording all error messages.

❑ The RIS Troubleshooter is included with Windows 2000 Server help, and will help you solve problems.

SELF TEST

The following questions will help you measure your understanding of the material presented in this chapter. Read all the choices carefully because there might be more than one correct answer. Choose all correct answers for each question.

What Is Remote Installation Services?

1. I have a non-PXE enabled desktop. How can I find out whether it will work as a RIS client?

   A. Check to see whether the BIOS is RIS compatible.

   B. Check to see whether the network card is supported by the Remote Boot Floppy.

   C. You cannot use a non-PXE enabled machine with RIS.

   D. Check to see whether your client machine is on the Windows 2000 Professional HCL.

2. Where do you get a Remote Boot Floppy?

   A. Run rbfg.exe from a RIS server.

   B. Run makeboot.exe from the Windows 2000 CD.

   C. Run the Network Client Administrator program.

   D. Format a floppy at a RIS server.

3. Why is RIS unlikely to work with a laptop?

   A. The laptop will not have enough drive space for the image.

   B. The laptop is likely not on the Windows 2000 HCL.

   C. Laptops cannot be DHCP clients.

   D. The Remote Boot Floppy only supports plug-and-play–compatible PCI network cards.

4. You have three different configurations of client computers that you want to set up using Remote OS installation. All three have different network cards that are supported by the Remote Boot Floppy. How many different boot disks will you need?

   A. None. If a computer is supported, you do not need a boot floppy.

   B. One. If all network cards are supported by the floppy, you only need one disk.

   C. Three. You will need one disk for each network card.

   D. This cannot be done without PXE-supported clients.

Creating a RIS Server

5. What services must be running on your network in order to install RIS? (Choose all that apply.)

    A. DHCP

    B. DNS

    C. WINS

    D. Active Directory

6. Which program is run to install RIS on a server?

    A. RIPrep from a client machine.

    B. RISetup from a client machine.

    C. RIPrep from the server.

    D. RISetup from the server.

7. Why do you need DNS on your network for RIS to succeed?

    A. Active Directory depends on DNS for name resolution.

    B. DHCP depends on DNS for name resolution.

    C. You need to be able to reach the Microsoft Web site for occasional updates to RIS.

    D. You do not need DNS.

Authorizing a RIS Server

8. What do you need to do if you want to authorize a RIS server and it is already authorized?

    A. Remove DHCP and reauthorize. DHCP and RIS cannot exist on the same server.

    B. Unauthorize the computer and then reauthorize it. You must be able to authorize while running RIS.

    C. Authorize the server a second time.

    D. Do nothing. The server is fine the way it is.

9. Who can authorize a RIS server?

    A. Any Domain Administrator.

    B. Anyone who has been given the DHCP Authorization right.

    C. Only an Enterprise Administrator.

    D. Only the original Administrator account.

10. What will happen if a RIS server is not authorized?

    A. Users will not be able to get an IP address.

    B. You will not be able to create any images.

    C. Users will not be able to get an image from the RIS server.

    D. Users will get an unauthorized image on their machines.

Configuring a RIS Server

11. You have two different CD-based images. How do you make sure users in the accounting department can load only the accounting image and not the management image?

    A. In the properties of the RIS server, give permissions to the accounting group for the accounting image only.

    B. In Active Directory Users and Computers, open the Accounting group's properties, go to Remote Install, and assign the appropriate image.

    C. Set up a Group Policy Object that distributes the appropriate image.

    D. Assign appropriate NTFS permissions to the answer file associated with each image.

12. What are some of the potential benefits of prestaging client computers? (Choose all that apply.)

    A. Eliminates the need to hand out administrative privileges to ordinary users.

    B. Gives greater control of naming conventions.

    C. Allows for load balancing among RIS servers.

    D. Saves administrative setup time.

13. What is an advantage of a RIPrep image over a CD-based image?

    A. A RIPrep image is created by default upon RIS setup.

    B. A RIPrep image distributes an entire desktop, complete with applications.

    C. A RIPrep image allows for user interaction.

    D. A RIPrep image is easier to create.

14. If you are not prestaging computers, what is one necessary step you must take in order to use the RIS process?

    A. Create a computer account ahead of time.

    B. Put the user running the RIS process into the administrators' group.

    C. Give the user in question the password for the RIS process.

    D. Temporarily give the user beginning the RIS process the ability to add new computer accounts.

Troubleshooting RIS

15. What would happen if a DHCP server were unavailable at the time of client startup?

    A. The boot process would fail, and no image would be delivered.

    B. The boot process would continue, but the image would be corrupt.

    C. The installation would succeed, but a new IP address would need to be assigned.

    D. The user would be prompted for a static IP address.

16. Where can you go to start the troubleshooting process?

    A. The Remote Install tab of the computer's properties.

    B. The Help menu of the RISetup program.

    C. Windows 2000 Help.

    D. Right-click any RIS server and choose Help.

17. What special requirements are there for the hard drive on a RIS server? (Choose all that apply.)

    A. It must have a 2GB free partition.

    B. The partition for the images must be formatted with NTFS.

    C. The disk must be dynamic.

    D. The disk must be a SCSI interface.

LAB QUESTION

You have decided to implement two RIS servers on your network. You have two geographically separate locations, and you want to avoid as much costly WAN traffic as possible. You also want security to be as tight as possible.

Along with Windows 2000 Professional, you want to distribute several custom applications with the image, and you want to be able to configure users' desktops as quickly and efficiently as possible. In short, should a user's computer fail, you want to provide him or her with a new desktop identical to the old one with as little manual intervention as possible.

Devise a plan to implement RIS in your network given the above criteria. Pay close attention to areas such as whether or not to prestage client computers, and what kind of images to use.

SELF TEST ANSWERS

What Is Remote Installation Services?

1. ☑ **B.** If a computer is not PXE enabled, you can still make it a RIS client if its network card is supported by the Remote Boot Floppy.
☒ **A** is incorrect because there is no such thing as a RIS-compatible BIOS. **C** is incorrect because you can use RIS with some non-PXE machines. **D** is incorrect because the HCL only lists Windows 2000 compatibility, not RIS compatibility.

2. ☑ **A.** Rbfg.exe is a program that creates Remote Boot Floppies.
☒ **B, C,** and **D** are incorrect because they do not successfully create boot floppies. **C** is not even available with Windows 2000.

3. ☑ **D.** Laptop machines will not have PCI network cards.
☒ **A, B,** and **C** are all potentially untrue statements about laptops.

4. ☑ **B.** One of the benefits of RIS is that one boot floppy will work for all supported machines.
☒ **A** is incorrect because a boot floppy is needed without PXE-supported computers. **C** is incorrect because one disk is sufficient for all three cards. **D** is incorrect because a Remote Boot Floppy can be used to start the RIS process on non-PXE enabled computers.

Creating a RIS Server

5. ☑ **A, B,** and **D.** DHCP, DNS, and Active Directory must all be running in order to successfully run RIS.
☒ **C** is incorrect because WINS is not required for RIS operation.

6. ☑ **D.** To install RIS, you need to run RISetup from the server itself.
☒ **A, B,** and **C** are all incorrect because these will not install RIS on a server.

7. ☑ **A.** Active Directory is required for RIS, and DNS is required for Active Directory.
☒ **B** is incorrect because DHCP does not need DNS to work. **C** is incorrect because Internet access is irrelevant to RIS. **D** is incorrect because DNS is required for RIS to function.

Authorizing a RIS Server

8. ☑ **D.** If a server is already authorized as a DHCP server in Active Directory, you do not need to do it again.
☒ **A** is incorrect because DHCP and RIS can exist on the same computer. **B** and **C** both describe actions that are unnecessary.

9. ☑ **C.** You must have Enterprise Administrator status to authorize a RIS or DHCP server.
   ☒ **A** is incorrect because it is not enough to have Domain Admin privileges. **B** is incorrect because there is no such right to be granted. **D** is too restrictive.

10. ☑ **C.** An unauthorized RIS server will not distribute images.
   ☒ **A** would be the effect on a DHCP server, not a RIS server. **B** is incorrect because you would be able to create images, not distribute them. **D** is incorrect because there is no such thing as an unauthorized image.

Configuring a RIS Server

11. ☑ **D.** CD-based images are assigned by assigning NTFS permissions to the answer file.
   ☒ **A, B,** and **C** all define fictitious processes.

12. ☑ **A, B,** and **C** are correct. These are all legitimate potential benefits of prestaging computers.
   ☒ **D** is incorrect because prestaging usually takes more time than not prestaging.

13. ☑ **B.** A RIPrep image delivers the entire desktop environment, complete with applications.
   ☒ **A, C,** and **D** are all true of CD-based images, not RIPrep.

14. ☑ **D.** A user starting the Remote OS install process on a nonstaged computer must have the permissions necessary to add new computer accounts in the appropriate OU.
   ☒ **A** is incorrect because it defines a step in the prestaging process. **B** gives a user far more permissions than are actually needed. **C** is fictitious.

Troubleshooting RIS

15. ☑ **A.** If a computer does not get an address from a DHCP server, it cannot find the RIS server, and the process will stop.
   ☒ **B** and **C** are incorrect because they incorrectly imply that the process can continue without an IP address. **D** is incorrect because the user never gets prompted for an IP address during the boot process.

16. **C.** Windows 2000 Help is where the troubleshooters are located.
   ☒ **A, B,** and **D** are incorrect because there is no extensive RIS-based help available in any of the other three locations listed.

17. ☑ **A** and **B.** A RIS server must have an NTFS partition with at least 2GB of free space.
   ☒ **C** and **D** are not requirements for a RIS server and are incorrect.

LAB ANSWER

First, you want to make sure that the prerequisites are in place. That means making sure you have a DNS, DHCP, and Active Directory server on your network. After installing RIS, you want to make sure the server is authorized in Active Directory. You also want to check your client machines to find which are compatible with RIS.

RISetup will install a CD-based image by default, but we are going to want to create at least one RIPrep image. This is because we do not simply want to deploy the OS, but also configure it and distribute software with the image as well. This means that we will have to set up a test machine, completely configured and with applications, and run RIPrep on the server from the source machine to create the image.

Because we want to be able to assign client computers to local RIS servers, and because security is an issue, you will want to prestage computers as needed. This will allow you to assign a RIS server to an individual computer, preventing WAN traffic from occurring. You will also not need to give users the ability to add computers given this scenario.

9

Using Remote Installation Service to Install the Client Machine

CERTIFICATION OBJECTIVES

9.01   Preparing for Installation

9.02   Installing an Image to a Client
        Machine

9.03   Troubleshooting

✓   Two-Minute Drill

Q&A   Self Test

I n the previous chapter, you learned about installation and configuration of Remote Installation Service (RIS), which is included in the Windows 2000 Server operating system. RIS is a low-cost deployment tool for implementing a standardized desktop environment throughout an organization. With careful planning, you can minimize both the time and the effort required to implement a desktop environment.

This chapter discusses the details of installing a desktop operating system using RIS. We start with preparation and discuss the various requirements for using RIS once it has been installed and configured on a Windows 2000 server. We then move on to a variety of scenarios in which this service can be best utilized. We also examine the Remote Installation Preparation (RIPrep) utility, which is used to prepare an image of a fully configured desktop machine.

RIS requires a proper setup and a favorable network environment. If any of the components are not running or not responding when you start client installations, you could very well encounter one or more problems. Later in this chapter, we discuss some of the common problems you can face while running RIS installations, as well as their possible causes and resolutions.

CERTIFICATION OBJECTIVE 9.01

Preparing for Installation

Utilizing RIS for large-scale deployment of the Windows 2000 Professional operating system on a desktop needs careful planning and preparation. In order to gather full benefits from RIS, you must consider certain planning issues and make some important decisions in advance. For example, you need to check your client hardware, check the RIS server configuration, check network adapters, plan which images to install, and decide who will perform RIS installations.

■ **Check Hardware** Check whether or not the hardware of the client machines meets the minimum requirements for using RIS. It is not recommended that you stick to the minimum requirements. For example, if the documents say that you need a minimum of 32MB RAM, you should use 64MB or more RAM so that you get the best results. The next section details the minimum hardware requirements for client desktop machines.

- **Check RIS Server Configuration** Before you start installing a client machine, you must check that the RIS server is up and running. In addition, the Domain Name Service (DNS) and the Dynamic Host Configuration Protocol (DHCP) services must be running. There must be a scope created and activated on the DHCP server so that client computers can get IP addresses. The DHCP must be authorized in Active Directory. You must also ensure that if there are routers being used in the network for segmentation, they are not blocking any BootP broadcasts. The client machines depend on BootP protocol to get an IP address from the DHCP server.

- **Check Network Adapters** Make a thorough check of all the desktop machines that will use RIS for installation to ensure they have supported network adapters or a PXE-based Boot ROM. In order to use RIS, a machine with a PXE boot ROM must be configured to boot from this ROM. If the desktops have supported PCI adapters, you need to create remote installation boot disks, a process that is discussed later in this chapter.

- **Plan Which Images to Install** If you are using prepared images to install the operating system and application software, you must decide in advance which desktop will receive which image. For example, a desktop in the accounting department might not have the same image as that of a desktop in the marketing department.

- **Decide Who Will Perform RIS Installations** It is important to decide who will perform installations. In most large organizations, the help desk staff is responsible for desktop installations. If that is the case in your organization, you need to give the members of the help desk group proper rights in the domain so that they can do their jobs without running into problems. If you decide to let users perform the installations, you must configure the RIS server in such a way that a user does not pick up a wrong image to install.

With proper planning, you can achieve a trouble-free deployment of Windows 2000 Professional in your organization. At the same time, you can implement organization-wide desktop policies. Make sure that you document each and every aspect of planning and implementation for your installation.

Supported Hardware

In the last chapter, you learned about various requirements for Windows 2000 Server machines on which RIS is installed. This chapter gives you a brief idea of client hardware requirements so that clients are able to utilize RIS for quick and hassle-free installation of operating system and applications. RIS is different from several disk-imaging utilities available in the marketplace today in that it does not require that all the desktop machines be identical in each and every hardware configuration. This flexibility frees your company's staff involved in purchasing hardware from depending on a single vendor.

Even so, certain requirements must be met before you start using RIS. The client computers requesting RIS must have the following minimum hardware:

- A Pentium processor of 166MHz or faster
- A minimum of 32MB RAM; 64MB is recommended
- A hard disk with a minimum capacity of 800MB
- A PCI plug-and-play adapter supported by RIS or a PXE-based remote boot ROM version .99 or later; desktops that are Net PC compliant can also be RIS clients

There are certain other requirements for Net PC-compliant desktops. These are as follows:

- The Net PC BIOS must be configured such that the network adapter is the primary boot device.
- The user account that is used to run the remote installation must be given "Logon as batch job" rights.
- Users must have sufficient privileges to create computer accounts in the domain.

For desktops that either do not have a PXE-based boot ROM or are not Net PC compliant, RIS includes a *Remote Installation Boot Disk Generator utility, RBFG.EXE.* This utility can create a remote boot disk that supports a number of PCI plug-and-play network adapters. When you create a boot disk using the RBFG.EXE utility, as discussed later in this section, you are able to view a list of the supported network adapters.

exam
ⓌatcH
For running RIS-based installation on a Net PC, you must ensure that the user account used during the installation has "Logon as batch job" rights. These rights must be given even if the administrator account is used for this purpose, because the administrator's group does not have these rights by default.

Unsupported Hardware

The RBFG.EXE utility does not support any ISA, EISA, or Token Ring network cards. It is also not possible to add support for additional network adapters because the included drivers are hard coded in the RBGF.EXE utility. Laptops usually have PC Cards or PCMCIA cards and are not supported as RIS clients. One exception is laptop computers in their docking stations that have a supported network adapter.

Group Policy Settings

When you have a large network with hundreds of computers and many images, you need to restrict access to the options that are presented to users when the Client Installation Wizard runs. You can actually restrict clients from choosing an incorrect installation option by applying a group policy for the RIS server. This restriction is accomplished via the Active Directory Users and Computers snap-in.

exam
ⓦatch

In the following exercise, the don't-care option is the default setting for all four types of Client Installation Wizard choice options.

EXERCISE 9-1

Restricting Client Installation Options

1. Log on to the RIS server as domain administrator.

2. Choose Start | Programs | Administrative Tools | Active Directory Users and Computers.

3. Select the container for the RIS policy settings. By default, these settings are at the domain container level, in the Default Domain Group Policy.

4. In the left pane, right-click the domain name and click Properties. Click the Group Policy tab in the Properties window.

5. Click the Default Domain Policy and click Edit. Double-click the User Configuration. Double-click the Windows Settings.

6. Click Remote Installation Services. An icon for Choice Options appears on the right-side pane.

7. Double-click the Choice Options icon. Three choice options are displayed, as shown here.

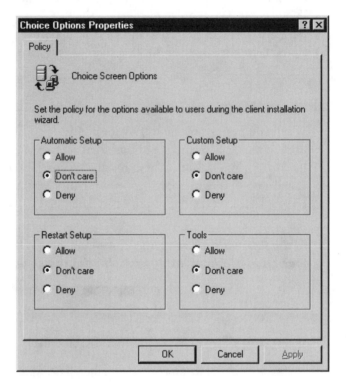

The options are as follows:

- **Allow**   This option allows users to choose an installation option.

- **Don't care**   In this option, the predefined group policy is applied to all users. This is the default setting for all choice options.

- **Deny**   When selected, this option does not allow users to access a particular installation option.

8. After making a selection, click OK. Close all the windows. Close the Active Directory window as well.

Restricting the Operating System Image Options

The next step is to specify which client or user will use which image. This is an important step to ensure that each user installs a correct operating system image. If this step is not done, the client could choose a wrong image, and all the efforts for saving time on unattended installations would be wasted. By applying user or group security policies, we can specify which image the user can see and install. You can either choose to show all the images to the user or you can restrict the user from seeing any images that are available on the RIS server but not meant for him or her.

EXERCISE 9-2

Restricting the Operating System Image Options

1. Log on to the RIS server as a domain administrator.

2. Choose Start | Programs | Accessories | Windows Explorer

3. Locate the win2000.pro folder and double-click it to expand it. Double-click the i386 folder.

4. Right-click the Templates subfolder and click Properties, as shown here.

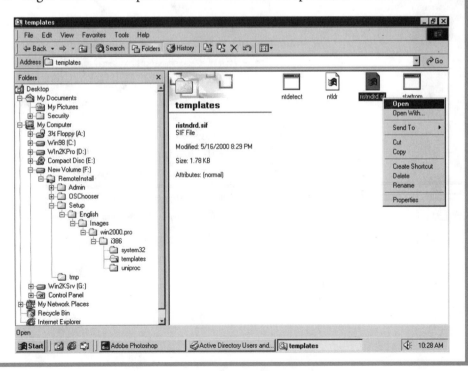

5. The Properties window for the templates opens. Click the Security tab. This is where you can select a user or group of users and set permissions. Select the Everyone group in the upper part of the dialog box, and click Remove.

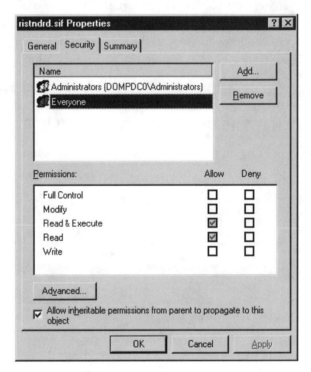

6. To add a particular user or group that will have access to this image, click Add. Select the user or the group, and click OK. It is recommended that you set permissions for groups rather than individual users.

7. Click OK to exit. Close all windows.

To ensure that users pick up a correct image, the following steps are recommended: 1) Determine the client requirements and make groups of users with identical requirements, 2) Prepare images based on the group requirements, 3) Set permissions on images based on the user groups. Do not allow all user groups access to all images, and 4) Although we selected only one .SIF file for setting permissions in Exercise 9-2, it is recommended that you set permissions on the Templates folder.

Now that you have read about various requirements for RIS-based client installations, take a look at some real-life questions.

SCENARIO & SOLUTION

My network has a mix of desktop computers supplied by different vendors. Can I use RIS for installing Windows 2000 Professional?	Yes. RIS-based installations can be performed, provided the desktops meet the minimum hardware requirements.
I have already implemented NTFS security on all the servers. Why do I need separate Group Policies for the RIS images?	The Group Policy settings are different from NTFS security. These policies ensure that users choose a correct image to install.
Some of the managers in my office use laptops in the office and at home. Can I use RIS to install Windows 2000 Professional on these laptops?	Yes and no—yes because you can use RIS if the laptops are used in docking stations and these docking stations have supported network adapters; no because, unless the said condition is met, laptops are not supported as RIS clients.

CERTIFICATION OBJECTIVE 9.02

Installing an Image to a Client Machine

Installation of an operating system image to client computers requires significant planning and preparation, as discussed earlier in this chapter. This preparation effort can include setting up and configuring a RIS server, creating and activating a DHCP scope for client computers on the DHCP server, and configuration of group policies that affect the behavior of RIS server. When the client computers are not Net PC compliant or do not have PXE-based boot ROMs, another task is added to the list: creation of a remote boot disk so that all such clients that have supported PCI network adapters are able to boot from the RIS server.

The following sections describe the creation of a remote boot disk and cover various installation scenarios.

Creating the RIS Boot Disk

When the client computer starts, it needs to contact the RIS server. There are two ways to accomplish this contact: either the client must have a PXE-based boot ROM on the network adapter, or the client must boot using a remote installation boot disk. The *remote installation boot disk* simulates the PXE boot process, helping the client get an IP address from any DHCP server on the network. Once the client gets an IP address, it can communicate with other computers on the network.

For the client computers that do not have a PXE boot ROM, the RIS includes a boot disk generator utility, as mentioned earlier. This RBGF.EXE disk can be used to initiate the remote installation process.

The Remote Installation Boot Disk Generator currently supports only a limited number of PCI-based network adapters. Because many of the popular adapters are supported, there is no need to purchase new adapters for hundreds of client computers. The RBGF.EXE utility can be run from any of the following computers:

- The RIS server
- A client computer that has a connection to the RIS server
- Any client connected to the RIS server on which the Windows 2000 Server Administrative Tools are installed

exam
⚠️atch

The Remote Installation Boot Disk Generator program supports only PCI plug-and-play network adapters. ISA, EISA, or Token Ring network adapters are not supported. It also does not support PC Cards and PCMCIA cards that are used in laptop computers.

EXERCISE 9-3

Creating a Remote Installation Boot Disk

1. Ensure that the RIS server is up and running. Log on as an administrator.

2. Click Start | Run and type in RBGF.EXE. Click OK. If you are running this command from another computer, type the following command and click OK:

   ```
   \\RISServer_name\RemoteInstall\Admin\i386\RBGF.exe
   ```

3. The Windows 2000 Remote Installation Boot Disk Generator window opens, shown here.

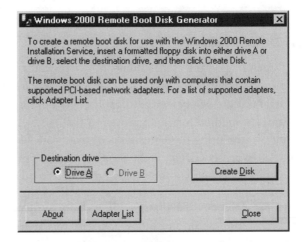

4. Check the path of the destination disk. It is usually drive A:. The Drive B radio button remains disabled if a second floppy disk drive is not found on the computer. Insert a blank, formatted 3.5-inch high-density floppy disk in drive A:.

5. To see a list of supported adapters, click the Adapter List button. Make sure that the adapters you have are in the list.

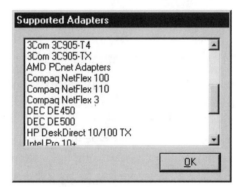

6. Click Create Disk. Doing so creates a remote installation boot disk. Remove the disk and close the Windows 2000 Remote Boot Disk Generator window.

Installation Scenarios

Depending on the requirements of a particular organization, a number of methods can be employed for installation of a desktop operating system throughout the organization. Many factors affect the selection of a deployment method. The simplest method for an organization that has 5–10 desktops is to perform a manual installation using the setup disks or a network file server. However, this method can be an expensive choice if the number of desktops is large. The following alternative methods can be used for deploying a desktop operating system:

- **Attended installation**   This is the simplest method when you have only a few desktop machines. You can use the setup CD-ROM for this installation and answer every question posed by the setup program. This method should not be used for multiple installations due to the time consumed and the cost involved in terms of person-hours.

- **Unattended installation**   This method involves creation of setup scripts for automated or unattended installation. This script is also known as an *answer file*. This script contains answers to all or most of the setup queries that otherwise have to be answered by the user. A network file server can be employed to distribute the setup files. This method is, again, an expensive one because it requires good technical expertise.

- ■ **Imaging utilities** A number of disk-imaging utilities are available in the marketplace today. All of them have their own advantages and limitations. These utilities save deployment time and involved costs. One of the factors that does not favor many such utilities is that they require the source and destination computers to be identical in all respects.

When you decide to use Windows 2000 Remote Installation Service for deployment of Windows 2000 Professional in your organization, it saves you from many troubles such as time spent on deployment, costs incurred, and buying a third-party imaging utility. RIS includes the RIPrep utility, which can be used to prepare the disk image of a fully configured computer. In addition, the source and destination computers need not have identical hardware. The next section describes how RIS can be employed for desktop installations.

Fresh Installations

RIS can be employed for installation of a fresh operating system on desktop computers. The RIS client computers can be desktops that are already running operating systems, or they can be newly purchased desktops. All desktops that have either network adapters supported by RIS or network adapters with PXE-based boot ROMs can utilize RIS for a fresh installation. RIS can be used to create a remote boot disk for supported network adapters using the RBGF.EXE utility.

Many desktop hardware vendors supply computers with preinstalled operating systems. This operating system might or might not meet the requirements of a particular organization. Sometimes the bundled operating system and any applications do not fall within the standards of an organization and need to be removed. This can be a cumbersome process. RIS can help administrators save time and costs in installing fresh Windows 2000 Professional operating systems on these desktops.

You can also use the included imaging RIPrep utility, which can further help in duplicating and distributing disk images. The only limitation of RIPrep is that it can be used on single disks and single partitions. However, because most desktops do not have multiple disk partitions, this RIPrep limitation does not outweigh its advantages. A source desktop machine is first installed with the base Windows 2000

Professional. Any required application software is installed on this desktop and thoroughly tested in all respects. RIPrep is run on this desktop to prepare an image of the hard disk, which is stored on the RIS server. Other desktops run the Client Installation Wizard to select and install an image. The RIS-based installation reformats the destination computer's hard disk and installs a fresh operating system. This process is discussed in more detail later in this chapter.

OS Recovery

One of the best features of RIS is that it can be used to recover even desktops in which the hard drive fails. In a very short time, you can replace the hard drive of a failed desktop and use an existing operating system image from the RIS server to rebuild the desktop. This method works in conjunction with the IntelliMirror technology that can be used to recover the user-specific settings and data from the network.

When a desktop reports a failed hard drive problem, you can replace the disk and boot the desktop using the remote boot disk. The Client Installation Wizard gives you an option of selecting an image from the available OS images on the RIS server. You can select the required image so that the basic operating system and application software are installed on the desktop. After this installation is complete, other user-specific settings, such as user profile and user data in the My Documents folder, can be made available to the user from the network when he or she logs on for the first time after installation. This feature saves you the trouble of reinstalling the operating system and each application separately and performing a number of other user-specific configuration operations.

Preinstall vs. Prestage

Preinstall and *prestage* are altogether different terms. Most of the hardware vendors supply desktop computers with an operating system that is bundled with the hardware. Often, the desktop also has other unwanted software packages installed that might not be required at all. The installed operating system either might be totally useless for your organization or, if required, might not be in accordance with the desktop standards that you have implemented in the organization.

In some cases, the hardware vendor installs the operating system and the applications specified by you when an order is placed. This is known as *preinstalled* software. Preinstalled software saves you time that you might otherwise spend installing the OS and the applications on each desktop. In large organizations that have thousand of desktops already in place, new desktops usually number in the hundreds, and installations on these new entrants can be a costly process. Once the vendor has done a base preinstallation, you might need to perform minimal further configuration so as to utilize Windows 2000 features, such as specifying computer names and configuring Active Directory.

Prestaging a computer is a term that is used in the context of RIS. Prestaging a computer in RIS is the process of creating computer accounts in the Active Directory before an attempt is made to use RIS. This process ensures that only those computers that have been prestaged can use the RIS server for installation. You might recall that the RIS server can be configured not to respond to unknown client computers. If you have a very large network with more than one RIS server, prestaging also allows you to specify which RIS server will respond to a particular client requesting the service.

on the
Job

Two practical issues relate to prestaging of client computers in the RIS server:
1) If more than one RIS server exists on the network, prestaging ensures that
clients get a response from only the RIS server that is configured to respond to
that particular client, and 2) If you have multiple images spread across multiple
RIS servers, prestaging ensures that a client does not get a wrong image.

Exercise 9-4 explains the steps necessary to prestage a client computer in Active Directory.

Using RIPrep

Remote Installation Preparation (RIPrep) is a disk duplication tool included with Windows 2000 Server. It is an ideal tool for creating images of fully prepared client computers. Having fully prepared clients helps in fast deployment of the operating system and applications on a large number of client computers using the RIS of a Windows 2000 Server. It is notable that RIPrep can only prepare the images of fully configured client computers that are running the Windows 2000 Professional operating system. The deployment of images created by RIPrep does not need the client computer hardware to be identical, but the *Hardware Abstraction Layer (HAL)* on both the source and destination computers must be identical.

CertCam 9-4

Prestaging a Client Computer

1. Log on to the RIS server as an administrator.

2. Choose Start | Programs | Administrative Tools | Active Directory Users and Computers.

3. Locate the Computers container on the left-hand pane. For the purpose of this exercise, this container contains the name of the client computers account. You can, however, use any container.

4. Right-click Computers and select New. Click Computer. This opens the New Object-Computer dialog box, shown here.

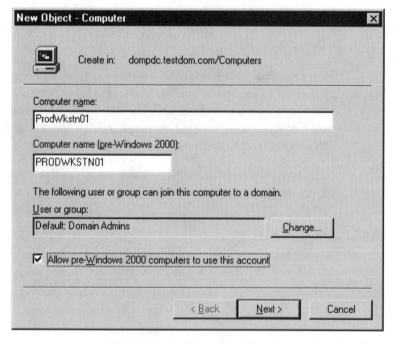

5. Type the name of the computer in the Computer name box.

6. Click the Change tab in order to grant permissions to a user or group to join this computer to the domain. It is important to note that at least one user must be granted permissions to perform installation on the selected machine. Click Next.

7. The next screen prompts you to enter the 32-character unique ID of the computer that is supplied by the manufacturer. This ID is known as the computer's *GUID/UUID*. You can check the computer BIOS or the label on the computer box to get this ID number.

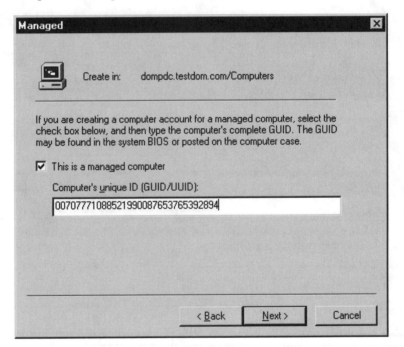

8. Click This Is a Managed Computer check box when you have entered the GUID. Click Next.

9. The Host Server screen appears, as shown in the following illustration. Here you can specify the name of the RIS server that will respond to this client computer. Click The Following Remote Installation Server: radio button and type the name of the RIS server. If you have more than one RIS server on the network and want any server to respond to this client, leave the option blank. Check the top radio button Any Available Remote Installation Server, if you do not want to specify a particular server to respond to this client. Click Next.

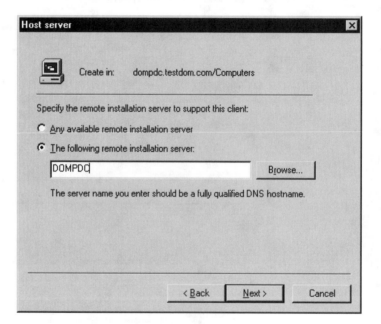

10. You will notice that the computer account has been created in the Computers container of the Active Directory. This completes the prestaging of the client computer.

To have a look at the properties of this computer account, right-click the account and select Properties. Click the Remote Install tab. The following illustration shows the information that you get from this Properties sheet.

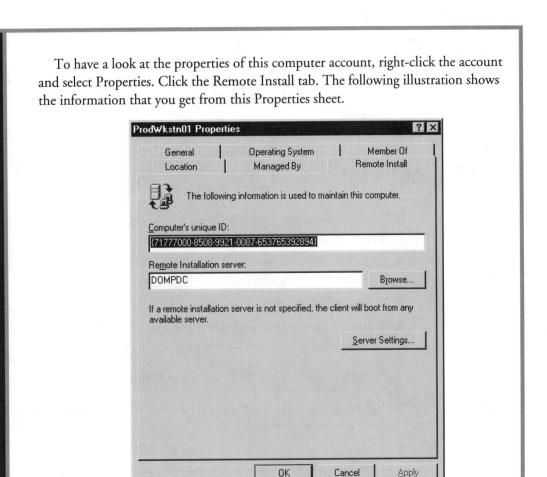

RIPrep requires that RIS and its associated services are configured and running on one or more servers on the network. The client computers are first configured with an operating system and all standard or custom-built business applications. The Remote Installation Preparation Wizard is run on the client computer to create an image of the computer. This image is uploaded to a Windows 2000 server running RIS for further distribution to other client computers. During the RIPrep process, the client computer loses all its user-specific settings, such as security IDs. This loss allows computers with different hardware configurations to use the same image.

Advantages and Disadvantages of RIPrep RIPrep is another method of preparing images of computers running Windows 2000 Professional. The following advantages and disadvantages are important to study before deciding to use RIPrep. Some of the advantages of using RIPrep are as follows:

■ The RIPrep utility is bundled with Windows 2000 Server, and no third-party tool is required for creation or delivery of images.

■ RIPrep uses Single-Instance Store (SIS), a feature that saves a good deal of hard drive space by eliminating duplicate copies of setup files.

■ RIPrep is independent of hardware configuration.

■ RIPrep helps in standardizing a Windows 2000 Professional-based desktop environment in an organization.

The following points highlight some disadvantages of using RIPrep:

■ RIPrep incurs high administrative costs because it requires trained professionals to implement.

■ RIPrep is dependent on several other services, such as RIS, Active Directory, DNS, and DHCP. These must be running on the network.

■ RIPrep can be used for clean installations only. Upgrades are not supported.

■ RIPrep can be used to prepare images of Windows 2000 Professional only.

■ RIPrep can duplicate images of a single hard drive consisting of a single partition only.

■ Only a limited number of PCI-based network adapters or PXE-ROM version .99 or later are supported for booting the remote client.

exam
ⓦatch

RIS can be used only to deliver the Windows 2000 Professional operating system. RIPrep runs only on computers that have the Windows 2000 Professional operating system installed.

Preparations for Using RIPrep   To use the RIPrep utility, you must select one of the desktop computers that will be treated as a source computer for preparing the image. Windows 2000 Professional is installed on this desktop using RIS. Any standard application software such as Office 2000 or custom-built software that you want to use is installed on this desktop. The source desktop is tested in all respects of functionality. It might be necessary to configure more than one source computer to prepare multiple images, depending on the requirements of the organization's departments. The RIPrep utility is run on this desktop to prepare an image of the hard disk that is uploaded to the RIS server. This image can then be distributed to other desktops that are to be configured with a similar image.

When you decide to use RIPrep, you must test the source computer thoroughly. Any configuration you skip will result in replication of the same to all the destination desktops that receive the image. Testing is very important because failing to do so could cause you a great deal of rework later. You must also ensure that you are not violating any software agreement while distributing images of the operating system or any application software.

CertCam 9-5

EXERCISE 9-5

Running the Remote Installation Preparation Wizard

1. Select a client computer as a model and install Windows 2000 Professional from an existing RIS server on the network.

2. Install on this computer any applications that meet the requirements of your desktop standards. Configure the operating system and the applications. Test all aspects of the client computer for reliability. Before proceeding, ensure that no applications are running on this desktop.

3. Connect to the RIS server to run the Remote Installation Preparation Wizard. Choose Start | Run and type the correct path of the RIPREP.EXE file as follows:

```
\\RISserver_name\RemoteInstallshare_name\Admin\i386\RIPrep.exe
```

4. The Remote Installation Preparation Wizard starts with a welcome screen, as shown here. Click Next.

5. When prompted, type in the name of the RIS server from which the image is intended to be copied. By default, this is the same RIS server from which RIPrep was run, as shown here. Click Next.

6. Next, you are prompted for the name of the directory to which the image is to be copied. Type the name and click Next.

7. The next screen is the Friendly Description and Help Text window. In the Friendly Description box, type a friendly description for the image. Additionally, you can type some useful text that describes the image details, such as applications it includes, in the Help Text box. Click Next.

8. The next window displays a summary of the selections you have made. If you need to change any setting, click Back and review the settings.

9. If everything seems fine, click Next.

The image preparation and replication to the RIS server take a few minutes. The time taken to prepare the image and upload it to the RIS server depends on several factors, such as number of applications included in the image, processing speed of the desktop, and the available network bandwidth. Once the image is copied to the RIS server, any remote boot client can use the image for installation.

SCENARIO & SOLUTION

How do I know which of the network adapters are supported by RIS?	Run the RBFG.EXE utility and click the Adapter List tab to view the supported adapters.
The desktop that I want to use as a source computer has two hard disk partitions. Will there be any problems using RIPrep on this desktop for creating an image?	Yes. RIPrep supports images of only a single partition.
I have desktop hardware that is supplied by two different vendors. Can I use the RIPrep image created on one for duplicating on the other?	Yes. So long as the desktops supplied by the two vendors have an identical HAL, you can use the image created on one to duplicate on the other.
Can I configure the RIS server not to respond to any curious users who might try to use RIS just to see how it works?	Yes. Prestage the client computers that need RIS installations. Configure the RIS server to "Do not respond to unknown client computers."

Installation Options

It's time now to turn to the client side. When a client computer boots using either the remote boot disk or the PXE-based boot ROM, it tries to establish a connection to the DHCP server. A BootP message is displayed on the client computer during this time. If the DHCP server is preconfigured to service the RIS clients, it allocates an IP address from the DHCP scope. Once the client is successful in getting an IP address, it tries to connect to the RIS server. At that time, the BootP message changes to DHCP. This is because the client uses the DHCP broadcasts to connect to the RIS server.

Once the RIS server is contacted, the client computer shows a Boot Installation Negotiation Layer (BINL) message. It might also prompt the user to press the F12 key to proceed. The BINL message indicates that the client is waiting for the RIS server to download the initial boot files, which include the Client Installation Wizard (CIW). The RIS server uses the Trivial File Transfer Protocol (TFTP) to download initial boot files to the client. On some machines, the BINL or TFTP message might not be noticed because it flashes very quickly.

The Client Installation Wizard

The *Client Installation Wizard* has four installation options. The options that are presented to the user depend on the group policy set in the Active Directory. Starting an automatic setup, a user might get all four options or might not get any of the options. The four installation options are as follows:

- Automatic Setup
- Custom Setup
- Restart a Previous Setup Attempt
- Maintenance and Troubleshooting

Each of these options is discussed in the following sections.

Automatic Setup

Automatic Setup is the default option. This is also the easiest installation method that is available to all users. The various configuration parameters are predetermined. The automatic installation option can be configured in such a way that the user is not prompted for even a single question during the installation process.

You might also configure the Automatic Setup option in such a way that users are given an option to select an image from the available images on the RIS server.

Because each RIS image has an attached friendly help and description section, the users can select the appropriate image. It is recommended, however, that when you have multiple images on the RIS server, you restrict users from choosing an incorrect image. This is particularly helpful when you have images relevant to the requirements of various departments in the organization.

The following are the main points to consider when using the Automatic Setup method:

- Users are able to see only those images that have been configured in Group Policy. If only one image exists, a user is not given an option to select the image. In this case, the installation starts as soon as the user logs on.

- You must ensure that in case of multiple images, the user is shown only the relevant images in order to avoid the user selecting an incorrect image.

- Permissions set on images should preferably be based on user groups instead of individual users. This policy helps reduce administrative efforts.

- Use security options on the Templates folder instead of individual .SIF files.

Custom Setup

Custom Setup is a flexible option that allows the user to override the process of automatically naming a computer. It also allows users to select a location in Active Directory where the computer account will be created. This option requires significant administrative efforts because almost every aspect of the installation can be customized. The following are the main points to remember when using this option:

- This option is usually helpful when the help desk staff is involved in the deployment process. Using Custom Setup, you can prestage a client computer. This ensures that only those computers that have been predetermined can request the RIS service.

- The Custom Setup option is usually selected when end users are not involved in the setup process. This is a flexible setup option and can be utilized in the best way by either the help desk staff of the administrators. Custom Setup also allows you to override the default naming format.

Restart a Previous Setup Attempt

As its name suggests, the Restart a Previous Setup Attempt option enables the user to restart a failed setup attempt. The user is not prompted for any input that he has already entered. This option is particularly useful when for some reason the user loses connection to the RIS server during setup or in case there is accidental shutdown of the client computer.

If the remote installation on a desktop computer fails for some reason, this option gives users the ability to restart the installation. The following are the main points to remember while using this option:

- The Restart a Previous Setup Attempt option does not restart installation from the point where the installation aborted. It starts from the beginning but does not prompt the user for any questions that have already been answered.

- This option is best utilized in an unstable network that frequently has networking problems. Another scenario in which it is helpful is when unstable power sources cause frequent failures.

- This option should not be given to end users. Rather, keep this option for the help desk staff or for yourself.

- If the previous setup was aborted due to some problem with the client hardware, it cannot be fixed using this option. You might have to contact the hardware vendor for assistance resolving specific hardware problems.

Maintenance and Troubleshooting

The Maintenance and Troubleshooting option provides access to any third-party maintenance tools that you may want to use before the installation starts. Because this option is not meant for every user, the administrator can restrict access to it in the Group Policy set in the Active Directory.

The tools that can be used range from updating BIOS to memory virus scanners. By default, RIS does not install any maintenance tools. The following are the main points to keep in mind when using this option:

- This is an advanced option and preferably should not be available to end users performing remote installations. You might, however, want to delegate the help desk staff to use these tools, if a need arises.

- By default, RIS does not install any maintenance tools. You might have to contact hardware vendors to acquire Windows 2000-compatible maintenance tools.

After making a selection from among these options, the user sees a displayed list of available image options. When a selection has been made, the user is presented with a summary screen. The installation begins immediately afterward.

exam
ⓦatch

If the domain administrator has authorized a user for only one image, the user is not prompted for image selection and the installation starts as soon as the user selects the Automatic Setup option.

CERTIFICATION OBJECTIVE 9.03

Troubleshooting

RIS is dependent on a number of other network services, such as AD, DNS, and DHCP. It also requires that the RIS server and the desktops meet the specified hardware requirements in terms of hard drive space and network adapters. Failure of any network service while starting to perform an RIS-based installation or anytime during the installation process can result in many problems. A careful study of various problems that can occur can help reduce the chances of failed installations.

The following sections describe various issues that can cause trouble during RIS-based installations. If any step is missed or any requirement is overlooked, you might end up in an endless loop of trouble. The flip side of this is that if all issues are taken care of before you start RIS-based installations, you might actually enjoy the job assigned to you.

Before you actually start an RIS-based installation, you must ensure the following:

- The RIS server is up and running.
- The RIS server has been configured in the Active Directory to service remote clients requesting the service.
- A scope has been created in the DHCP server for the remote clients, and the scope is active. Ensure that the DHCP service is running.
- The user accounts exist for performing remote installations, and each user is assigned rights to create computer accounts in the domain.

The other issues related to network and hardware are discussed in the next section.

Network Errors

It is important to have a look at the sequence of processes that take place on the network when a client computer starts using the remote installation boot disk. RIS, AD, DNS, and the DHCP server all team up to provide a workable operating system to the desktop machine. This sequence of events is more or less similar in all desktops, regardless of the fact that the desktop is a Net PC or has a network adapter with PXE-based boot ROM. The sequence holds true for those desktops that start using the remote boot disk generated by the RBFG.EXE utility.

Sequence of Events when the Client Computer Starts

When the client computer is started using the remote boot disk, it displays a DHCP message. This message indicates that the client is trying to contact the DHCP server to get an IP address. The message stays there, even when the client has received the IP address and is trying to connect to the RIS server.

Step 1: DHCP   If the client does not move further and keeps displaying the DHCP message, this could mean there is a problem. Either the client is not able to get an IP address or the RIS server is not responding. The RIS server service that is relevant here is BINL. Perform the following checks:

1. The DHCP server is available.

2. The DHCP scope is activated, and it has an IP address available for the client.

3. If there is a router between the client and the DHCP server, it is configured to forward BootP broadcasts.

4. Other clients on the same segment of the network are getting IPs from the DHCP server.

5. You might also want to have a look at the system event logs on the DHCP server.

Step 2: BINL   When the client has received an IP address successfully, the client computer message changes to BINL. This indicates that the client is trying to connect to the RIS server. If no RIS server is available or there are some network connectivity problems between the RIS server and the client, the BINL times out and the following error message is displayed: "No Boot File received from DHCP, BINL, or BootP."

To get around this problem, perform the following checks:

1. Ensure that there is no connectivity problem between the client computer and the RIS server.

2. Ensure that the BINL service is running. This problem is also caused if the RIS server is not authorized in Active Directory.

3. Ensure that the RIS and DHCP servers are authorized in Active Directory.

4. Check to see whether the other RIS clients are facing the same problem. If the problem is with this client only, check that the client has a supported network adapter.

5. If there is a router on the network, check that it is not blocking any BootP broadcasts.

6. You can also check the system event log to find any DHCP, BINL, or AD-related errors or warnings.

on the
job

When you get some error message during an RIS-based installation on one client computer, you must check one or two other clients to see whether or not they are exhibiting similar behavior. This check helps pinpoint the source of the problem. For example, if the remote boot disk works well with one computer but causes a DHCP error on the other, the possible cause could be an unsupported network adapter.

Step 3: TFTP When the client computer is successful in connecting to the RIS server, the message on the client screen changes from BINL to TFTP. This is the *Trivial File Transfer Protocol,* which is used to download initial boot files to the client computer. At this time, the user is prompted to press the F12 function key. The TFTP message indicates that the client is waiting for the initial files to be downloaded. These files start the Client Installation Wizard on the client. If the process is successful, you might not be able to see this message because it flashes too quickly on some fast computers.

Continuous display of TFTP messages could again mean a problem. No response from the RIS server causes these messages. If you run into this problem, perform the following checks:

1. Stop and restart the BINL service on the RIS server. Exercise 9-6 explains how to stop and start the BINL service from Computer Management. This can be done from the command prompt. Start the command prompt on the RIS server and type the following commands:

```
net stop BINLSVC
net start BINLSVC
```

   If the problem is due to a misbehaving BINL service on the RIS server, these commands will hopefully resolve it.

2. Ensure that the RIS server is configured to "Respond to Known Client Computers." Also clear the "Do Not Respond to Unknown Client Computers" check box if it is checked. If the latter option is checked, make sure that the client computer on which installation is being performed is prestaged in the Active Directory.

3. You might also want to check the system log for any error or warning messages concerning the DHCP, DNS, or BINL and AD.

exam
ⓦatch

The correct sequence of events is DHCP, BINL, and TFTP. Make sure you do not forget this sequence; you could get exam questions based on it.

Step 4: CIW Welcome Screen When the client computer gets through all the stages discussed, the Client Installation Wizard is downloaded to the client machine. A welcome screen is shown to the user; here, he or she can select an installation option and start the installation process.

CertCam 9-6

EXERCISE 9-6

Stopping and Restarting the BINL Service

If the BINL service is not responding on the RIS server, it could cause a continuous display of TFTP message on the client machine that is attempting to perform an RIS-based installation. Stopping and restarting the BINL service can help resolve the problem. In this exercise, we stop and restart the BINL service on the RIS server from Computer Management:

1. Log on to the RIS server as an administrator.

2. Right-click on the My Computer icon on the desktop, and select Manage. This opens the Computer Management console.

3. Click the plus (+) sign before Services and Applications to expand the tree. Click Services. Notice that the currently installed services are shown on the right-hand pane.

4. Click Boot Information Negotiation Layer service as shown in the following illustration. Click Stop from the Action menu.

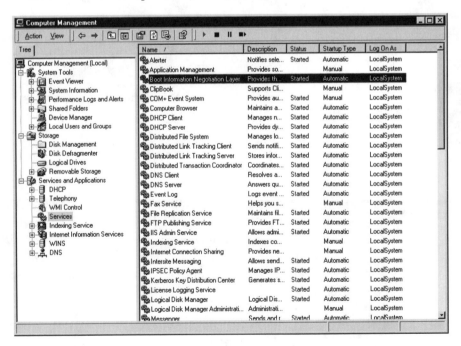

5. The computer attempts to stop the service, which takes only a few moments. A message is displayed, as shown here:

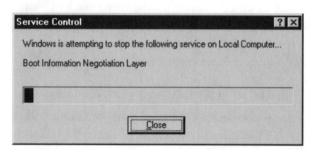

6. Click Start from the Action menu. This time the computer displays the following message while attempting to restart the service.

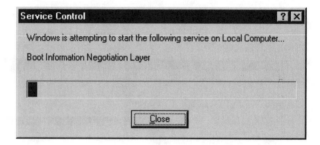

7. Close the Computer Management console.

Stopping and restarting the BINL service, or any other service, from the command prompt is a quick method used by many network administrators. It requires that you know the correct name of the service as it should appear in the command. The BINL service is written as BINLSVC, and you can use the following two commands from the command prompt to stop and start the service, respectively:

```
net stop BINLSVC
net start BINLSVC
```

It is not mandatory to write BINLSVC in all capital letters, because the command is not case sensitive.

Hardware Issues

RIS-based desktop installations require certain minimum hardware, as described earlier in this chapter. The RIS-based installation process can be an enjoyable project to work on when the present desktops or the newly purchased ones have specified recommended hardware. The following issues are very important to consider while installing RIS-based operating system images.

Check Hardware Requirements

Before you start any RIS-based installation, make sure you have all hardware specified as the minimum recommended. For example, the hard drive must have a capacity of 800MB for receiving an RIS image.

Using RIPrep Images

For an image created by RIPrep, the capacity of the hard disk on destination computers must be either equal to or larger than that of the computer on which the image is created. Distributing RIPrep images also requires that at least the HAL of the source and destination computers be identical. Again, there must not be any partitions on the hard disk; the RIPrep utility can be used for only single-drive and single-partition computers. An attempt to install a RIPrep image of a client that has a different HAL from the source will not be successful.

Network Adapters

Requirements for the network adapters were discussed in detail earlier in this chapter. As a reminder: The client computer must either be a Net PC-compliant computer or have a network adapter with PXE-based Boot ROM. The network adapter must be configured in the computer BIOS to boot from the network. Otherwise, the client must have one of the supported PCI plug-and-play adapters. Failure of the client computer to comply with these network adapter requirements can lead to installation troubles. The computer will not be able to connect to the network and will display a DHCP message indefinitely.

Laptop Computer Considerations

Laptop computers usually have PC Cards or PCMCIA cards. These are not supported by RIS. An exception is laptops that are in docking stations that have a supported network adapter.

PXE Boot ROM Version

RIS supports PXE Boot ROM version .99 or later. Any version prior to .99 can cause problems in using RIS. To check which version is used by your network adapter boot ROM, read the messages that appear on the client screen when the client starts booting up.

After a detailed study of various troubleshooting scenarios, let's take a quick look at some practical problems.

SCENARIO & SOLUTION

I am getting the same DHCP error from all client computers when I try to start them using the remote boot disk. Is the floppy disk corrupted?	Yes, that might be a problem. However, if the error persists with a second good remote boot disk, look for other reasons.
When I installed Windows 2000 Professional on my desktop, I was not given any option to select an image. What could be the problem?	This is not a problem. RIS is configured for an automatic installation when your user account is used.
I created an image using RIPrep on a desktop with a 6.4GB hard disk. I am unable to distribute the image to other desktops that have 4.3GB hard drives. Why is it so?	You made a mistake. The hard disk on the destination computers must be either equal to or larger than the source computer where the image is created. The solution is to re-create the image, keeping that specification in mind.
Are there any event logs for RIS?	Yes. Check the system log for any error or warning messages regarding AD, DHCP, DNS, or BINL services.

FROM THE CLASSROOM

Getting Ready for Remote Installations

The details of employing RIS for rolling out Windows 2000 Professional and using RIPrep to prepare Windows 2000 Professional-based disk images have been discussed in this and the preceding chapter. The brief discussion here is on some of the best practices that you can adopt while implementing your RIS-based deployment plans. Consider the following practical points, which are generally overlooked:

1. The hardware required is the minimum recommended for the RIS server and the clients. Most of the present-day servers and desktops meet these requirements. The only thing you must be very careful about is the disk space requirement. On the server side, make sure you have a separate partition dedicated to RIS images of large capacity. This must be an NTFS partition.

2. When using RIPrep, make sure the source and the destination computers have identical HALs. Disk space on the destination computers must be either equal to or larger than that of the source computer.

3. When planning for RIS-based or any other imaging solution, you must ensure that you have a sufficient number of licenses for the operating system and the application software. Remember, because you are the one in charge of deployment, you will be the first to be questioned if there are any license agreement violations.

4. Document each and every aspect of RIS configuration. Doing so helps ensure that you are not going wrong at any time. If you are delegating the deployment responsibilities to help desk personnel, create a detailed document explaining how to use RIS. Make sure you also include some of the common troubleshooting scenarios so that help desk staff do not keep calling you for every little problem.

5. The RIS-based deployment option needs careful planning, so make a thorough study of the requirements of your organization. This is particularly important if you were hired recently and are not familiar with the desktop policies or standards of the organization.

—Pawan K. Bhardwaj, MCSE, MCP+I, CCNA

CERTIFICATION SUMMARY

Remote Installation Service (RIS) can be employed for large-scale deployment of the Windows 2000 Professional operating system in the organization. The RIS-based deployment calls for careful planning, keeping in mind all the requirements of this service and the requirements of a particular organization. You must check hardware compatibility and various factors regarding RIS server configuration and decide on the users or user groups that will be responsible for installations. Accordingly, group policies must be set so that a trouble-free installation can take place.

RIS supports desktop clients that are Net PC compliant; these machines have the network adapter configured to boot from the network. Desktops that have network adapters with a PXE-based boot ROM can also be RIS clients. For other desktops, RIS provides the RGFG.EXE utility that can create a remote installation boot disk. This disk contains drivers for several popular PCI-based network adapters.

When a client computer boots using the remote boot disk or using the PXE-based boot ROM, it looks for the DHCP server for getting an IP address. After getting the IP address, it requests the RIS server to download startup files. The startup files start the Client Installation Wizard (CIW) on the client machine, giving four different installation options, depending on the Group Policy set for the user who is performing the installation. The administrator could set client choice options, and Group Policy is a method by which the user does not have to intervene in the installation process. Otherwise, the administrator can also choose to show some or all the image options. RIPrep is used on a fully configured client computer to prepare an image of the disk. This image can be distributed to other clients that have an identical Hardware Abstraction Layer (HAL).

With proper planning and careful inspection of various requirements of RIS-based installations, many problems can be eliminated. Most of the problems occur during the time when the client computer boots. The problems related to DHCP, BINL, and TFTP services display self-explanatory error messages on the client machine. You can also check the system logs for any errors related to AD, DHCP, DNS, and BINL services to find a resolution to a problem.

✓ TWO-MINUTE DRILL

Preparing for Installation

❑ RIS-based installations require that the RIS server is installed and authorized in the Active Directory to service the clients requesting this service. A DHCP scope must be created and activated for clients.

❑ RIS-based installations can be performed on any client machines that meet the minimum hardware requirements. At a minimum, the client machines must have a Pentium 166MHz processor, 32MB RAM, and hard disk capacity of 800MB.

❑ The client computer must be either Net PC compliant or have a network adapter with a PXE-based boot ROM set as a primary boot device in the BIOS. The user performing the installation should have "Log on as batch job" rights in the domain. The RBFG.EXE utility can be used to create a remote boot disk for other clients that have supported network adapters.

❑ Because laptops use either PC Cards or PCMCIA cards, they are not supported as RIS clients. An exception is laptops in their docking stations that have a supported network adapter.

❑ Group Policy settings for the RIS service are done from the Active Directory Users and Computers snap-in to restrict client installation options. The "Don't care" option is the default choice. Client image options can also be set using the security permissions on the Templates folder.

Installing an Image to a Client Machine

❑ The RBFG.EXE utility can be run from the RIS server, a client that has connection to the RIS server, or any client that is connected to the RIS server on which Windows 2000 Server Administrative Tools are installed. A remote boot disk can be generated for client computers that have one of the supported PCI-based network adapters. A list of adapters can be viewed by clicking the Adapter List tab.

❑ The RBFG.EXE utility does not support ISA, EISA, or Token Ring cards. Furthermore, you cannot add support for any additional adapters, because the drivers are hard-coded in the RBFG.EXE utility.

❑ Prestaging of client computers is done to create computer accounts in the domain and to ensure that client computers are serviced by a predetermined RIS server. This also ensures that client machines obtain a correct image.

❑ The RIPrep utility is run on a client computer that is fully configured with the operating system and applications to prepare an image of the hard disk. This image is stored on the RIS server and can be distributed to other clients. Only single disk and single partition machines are supported for duplication.

❑ The Client Installation Wizard runs on a client computer giving four installation options: Automatic Setup, Custom Setup, Restart a Previous Setup Attempt, and Maintenance and Troubleshooting. A failed setup attempt can be resumed using the Restart a Previous Setup Attempt option.

Troubleshooting

❑ To avoid any possible problems during RIS installations, you must ensure that the RIS server is up and running and a DHCP scope is active for the RIS clients.

❑ User accounts must exist for users who will perform RIS installations. To make sure the installation process runs smoothly, these users must have rights to create computer accounts in the domain.

❑ The client machine runs a sequence of events when it boots using the remote boot disk. DHCP, BINL, and TFTP messages are displayed on the client machine when it tries to get an IP address and download startup files from the RIS server. If the RIS server is not responding, you can stop and restart the BINL service in an attempt to resolve the problem.

❑ If there is a router between the client computer and the RIS and DHCP servers, it must be configured to forward BootP messages. This configuration ensures that the client computer receives an IP address.

❑ If you meet all the hardware requirements in regard to the RIS installations and the RIPrep-based image distribution, you will probably encounter no errors during the installation process. You can check the system event log for any AD, DHCP, or BINL errors or warning messages if you have trouble running the installation.

SELF TEST

The following questions will help you measure your understanding of the material presented in this chapter. Read all of the choices carefully because there may be more than one correct answer. Choose all correct answers for each question.

Preparing for Installation

1. You have ensured that all the desktop clients that will use the RIS server for installation have network adapters with a PXE-based boot ROM. These PXE boot ROMs have the correct version, as required by RIS. Which of the following will ensure that clients are able to boot from the network?

    A. The network adapter must be the primary boot device.

    B. The BIOS must be configured to use a RIS server as the preferred server.

    C. The user performing the installation must have "Log on as service" rights.

    D. All of the above.

2. You have been told to prepare a list of computers in your office network that can be upgraded to Windows 2000 Professional using RIS. Which of the following will you include in your list? Choose all that apply.

    A. All Intel-based computers and laptops running Windows NT 4.0 Workstation

    B. Computers with a single network adapter supported by RIS

    C. Computers with network adapters that have PXE-based boot ROM

    D. Net PCs with network adapters configured as the primary boot device

    E. None of the above

3. Some of the users in your office started installations on their desktops using RIS. Two of the users selected incorrect images, and you had to reformat their hard drives, increasing your workload. Looking at the possible problems caused by more users selecting wrong images available on the RIS server, you immediately change the RIS policy and set restrictions on clients in the Active Directory Users and Computers snap-in so as to avoid any more such problems. After half an hour, two more users approach you with the same problem. Why did this happen? How can you ensure that no more users come to you with the same problem?

    A. Stop and restart RIS so that the changes take effect immediately.

    B. Choose Start | Run and type **secedit** in the open box. Press ENTER to refresh group policy.

    C. Restart the RIS server to make the changes effective.

    D. Ask the users to restart their computers, and start installation again.

4. A senior network administrator wants you to take charge of RIS-based installations on 20 desktop machines on your company's network. This requires you to make some changes to the RIS configuration and set some group policies. What privileges do you need to accomplish the task successfully?

    A. Log on as a batch job

    B. Create computer accounts in the domain

    C. Local administrator rights on the domain controller

    D. Domain administrator

5. You want to restrict access to certain images stored on your company server so that users do not select a wrong image. Which of the following is a recommended folder in which you should set NTFS permissions?

    A. The i386 folder

    B. The Templates folder

    C. The RemoteInstall folder

    D. The SIF folder

6. You have set up RIS on one of the servers running the Windows 2000 Server operating system. Windows 2000 Professional will be installed on nearly one-fourth of the office desktops in the first phase. You know that due to curiosity, many other users might attempt to install Windows 2000 on their desktops using RIS. How can you prevent these desktop users from making unscheduled installations?

    A. By setting group policy

    B. By setting NTFS permissions on RIS images

    C. By blocking traffic from their desktops to the RIS server

    D. By prestaging client computers in the RIS server

7. You have created five images and stored them on the RIS server. You want your help desk department technicians to handle remote installations for all five departments in the office. Some users want to perform the installation themselves. How will you ensure that the help desk technicians are able to see all the available images but restrict other users from viewing or selecting any image other than the one intended for their use?

    A. By configuring Group Policy settings

    B. By setting NTFS permissions on image files

    C. By configuring shared folder permissions

    D. Any of the above

8. What options would you choose for the RIS policy in the Default Domain Policy when you do not want the Custom Setup option to be displayed to a user when the Client Installation Wizard starts?

   A. Deny for the Automatic Setup

   B. Don't care for the Custom Setup

   C. Allow for the Restart Setup

   D. Deny for the Custom Setup

Installing an Image to a Client Machine

9. Which of the following commands is used to run the remote boot disk generator utility?

   A. OSCHOOSER.EXE

   B. RBFG.EXE

   C. MAKEBOOT.EXE

   D. RISETUP.EXE

10. You have a mix of makes of desktop computers in your office; some of these have network adapters that are not supported by RIS. You have created three remote boot disks for the desktops that have supported adapters. How can you add other adapters to the remote boot disks?

    A. Copy the INF files and the driver files to the boot disk.

    B. Install additional drivers for the unsupported adapters in the RIS server.

    C. Use some third-party software to add drivers.

    D. None of the above.

11. After preparing one of the Windows 2000 Professional computers to transfer the image of the operating system and the applications using the RIPrep tool, you reboot it as required by the procedure. What you see now is that the system is running setup again. What could be the reason?

    A. The RIPrep utility has to be run on the RIS server, and you did it on the client by mistake.

    B. The RIPrep utility deletes the current installation after making the image.

    C. While RIPrep is running, it takes off all the computer-specific configuration and security ID of the client, which has to be restored.

    D. You must not have rebooted the client manually after running RIPrep.

12. Which of the following options is used to install third-party maintenance utilities from the Client Installation Wizard?

    A. Automatic Setup

    B. Custom Setup

    C. Restart a Previous Setup Attempt

    D. Maintenance and Troubleshooting

13. You want to use RIS for deployment of the Windows 2000 Professional operating system on your network, but you are not sure whether all the client computers have network adapters supported by RIS. Which of the following will enable you to view all supported adapters?

    A. Run the remote boot disk generator utility and click Adapter List.

    B. Check the adapter documentation.

    C. Run RISETUP.EXE on the RIS server and click View Supported Adapters.

    D. Any of the above.

Troubleshooting

14. A client computer has been powered on using a remote boot disk. This computer is supposed to contact a preconfigured RIS server for installation of Windows 2000 Professional. What is the correct sequence of activities that should take place on initialization?

    A. DHCP, BINL, and TFTP

    B. BINL, DHCP, and TFTP

    C. TFTP, BINL, and DHCP

    D. TFTP, DHCP, and BINL

15. One of your junior administrators has selected a desktop as reference computer for running RIPrep. The image will be uploaded to a running RIS server on the network. The desktop has a 233MHz microprocessor, 128MB RAM, a 6.4GB hard drive with two partitions, and a 10/100Mbps plug-and-play network adapter. The administrator has installed and tested the hardware on the system and found it to be working fine. Windows 2000 Professional and all applications are installed on the C: drive, which is 2GB and formatted using NTFS partition. The custom-built applications meant for distribution are installed on drive D:, which is 4.4GB and is also in NTFS format. Can you identify what problem she might be facing?

A. Drive C: is too small to run RIPrep.

B. The two partitions must be of equal size.

C. There must be exactly one partition.

D. All applications must be on the D: drive because the C: drive contains system and boot files.

16. While trying to boot from the RIS boot disk after preparing the RIS server, you find that it is not responding. The computer times out, displaying an error message: "No boot file received from DHCP, BINL or BootP." You know that the RIS server is online. What must you do to resolve the problem?

A. Restart the client computer.

B. Restart the RIS server.

C. Stop and restart the BINL service.

D. Restart the DHCP server.

17. One of your users started remote installation on his desktop computer with the remote boot disk created earlier using the RBGF.EXE utility. After the initial boot, the system displayed some BootP messages and seems to be hung. What is indicated by this error?

A. The client computer is not able to connect to the RIS server.

B. The client computer is unable to get an IP address from the DHCP server.

C. A router between the client and the RIS server or the DHCP server is preventing the BootP broadcast.

D. All of the above.

LAB QUESTION

Current Situation

You are the network administrator of a company called My Company, Inc. The company has six Windows 2000 servers that were upgraded from Windows NT 4.0 last month. There are seven departments within the company, and the total number of client computers is nearly 240 at a single location, all running Windows NT 4.0 Workstation on different hardware configurations.

Your current project requires you to install Windows 2000 Professional and business applications on all 240 workstations. The software configuration is almost the same on all departmental computers except the accounts and business development departments, which have some custom-built software for accounting and business analysis, respectively. For data security reasons, management would not like to hire anyone from outside to do the upgrade. Here is what you have to accomplish.

Required Result

Use Remote Installation Service to roll out of Windows 2000 Professional and any applications that are used in the organization on all desktop computers.

Desired Optional Results

1. Each department must get appropriate working software after the rollout is over.

2. Users must be involved in the rollout project in order to reduce the administrative burden.

Suggested Solution

We list some steps that could help you perform a successful RIS-based deployment of Windows 2000 Professional. You are to find out whether some steps are missing or are incorrect:

- Install RIS on one of the servers. Authorize the RIS server in Active Directory to "Respond to known client computers requesting service." Do not check the "Do not respond to unknown client computers" option.

- Ensure that you have a DNS server running on the network.

- Create a DHCP scope on the DHCP server and activate it.

- Install Windows 2000 Professional on a computer using RIS.

- Install all business and custom applications on this computer and test them.

- Run RIPrep on the test computer to make an image of the system and copy it to the RIS server.

- Make remote boot disks for the clients using the RBGF.EXE utility.

- Ask the users to boot their desktops using the remote boot disk to run the Client Installation Wizard.

- When given a choice select the image appropriate to the department.

SELF TEST ANSWERS

Preparing for Installation

1. ☑ **A.** The network adapter must be the primary boot device. When client computers have network adapters with a PXE-based boot ROM, you must ensure that the BIOS of all such clients is configured to use the network adapter as a primary boot device. Otherwise, the computer looks for an operating system from either the floppy disk or the hard disk, and booting fails.

   ☒ **B** is incorrect because you cannot configure a preferred boot server in the BIOS of any computer. **C** is incorrect because "Log on as service" rights are insufficient for the user performing the installation. These make **D** an incorrect choice.

2. ☑ **E.** None of the above. The question statement says that you must make a list of computers that will be upgraded. RIS cannot be used to upgrade any of the computers mentioned.

   ☒ **A** is incorrect because it lists all Intel-based and laptop computers. Laptops are not supported by RIS, even for clean installations. Even though the computers listed in **B**, **C**, and **D** can utilize RIS, they can use it only for a clean installation. This explanation makes **A**, **B**, **C**, and **D** incorrect.

3. ☑ **C.** Restart the RIS server to make the changes effective. The best way to immediately apply the security changes from RIS is to restart the server. Otherwise, you must wait for automatic policy propagation that occurs every eight hours.

   ☒ **A** is incorrect because stopping and restarting only RIS will not resolve the problem. **B** is incorrect because the SECEDIT command must be used with the /refreshpolicy switch, specifying the user policy that has been modified. **D** is incorrect because even after restarting their computers, users can still pick up a wrong image.

4. ☑ **D.** Domain administrator. In order to install and configure one or more RIS components and set group policies, you must have domain administrator rights.

   ☒ **A** is incorrect because "Log on as batch job" rights are usually required for the user who is performing an RIS-based installation on a Net PC. **B** is incorrect because "Create computer accounts in the domain" is not enough to set group policies. **C** is incorrect because local accounts do not exist on the domain controllers.

5. ☑ **B.** The Templates folder. The permissions to images should preferably be set on the templates folder. However, you can set permissions on individual files within the Templates folder.

☒   **A** is incorrect because the i386 folder contains all the images. **C** is incorrect because the RemoteInstall folder is not the right folder for restricting access to images. **D** is incorrect because there is no such folder as SIF.

6. ☑   **D.** By prestaging client computers in the RIS server. This policy will ensure that the RIS server does not respond to the unknown client computers that might request service. Any desktop user who tries to contact the server will be denied access to the RIS server if his or her desktop is not already prestaged.

☒   **A** is incorrect because Group Policy settings are helpful in preventing such curious desktop users. **B** is incorrect because setting NTFS permissions will not help and will merely add to your administrative efforts. **C** is incorrect because blocking traffic from these desktops will cause other problems for these users while they are performing other work. Moreover, it will add to your efforts.

7. ☑   **A.** By configuring Group Policy settings. The requirements given in the question can be satisfied using the Group Policy settings. You can configure the Automatic Setup option for ordinary users so that the image intended for them is installed automatically when they log on to the RIS server. The group policy settings for the help desk technicians can be set so that they are able to select appropriate images for specific departments and perform maintenance work if an installation attempt fails.

☒   **B** is incorrect because setting NTFS permissions on images is not the correct way to restrict images. **C** is incorrect because shared folder permissions are not effective for RIS. These explanations make **D** an incorrect choice.

8. ☑   **D.** Deny for the Custom Setup. This choice ensures that the user is not able to see the Custom Setup option when the Client Installation Wizard runs on his or her computer.

☒   **A** is incorrect because this setting is for the Automatic Setup option and does not affect Custom Setup. **B** is incorrect because if the "Don't care" option is selected for Custom Setup, the CIW option display will depend on the predefined group policy, which might or might not allow the Custom Setup option to be displayed. **C** is incorrect because this setting is for the Restart a Previous Setup Attempt option and does not affect Custom Setup.

Installing an Image to a Client Machine

9. ☑   **B.** RBGF.EXE. It is evident from the name of the executable file that it stands for Remote Boot Generator Floppy utility.

☒   **A** is incorrect because the OSCHOOSER file is the Client Installation Wizard executable file. **C** is incorrect because the MAKEBOOT command is used to create Windows 2000 setup disk set. **D** is an inappropriate choice because the RISETUP command is used to configure RIS.

10.   ☑   **D.** None of the above. This task cannot be accomplished. The drivers for supported network adapters are hard-coded into the remote boot disk generator utility. It is not possible to add more drivers to the remote boot disk.

☒   **A** is incorrect because simply adding INF and driver files will not enable the remote boot disk to work. **B** is incorrect because there is no option in RIS to add network adapters for the remote boot disk. **C** is an invalid choice because no third-party software can be used to add adapters to the remote boot disk.

11.   ☑   **C.** While RIPrep is running, it takes off all the computer-specific configuration and security ID of the client, which has to be restored. The RIPrep tool is run on the client computer that is fully configured with operating system and applications. When you run this utility, it removes the user-specific settings from the client computer. On restart, it runs a mini-setup wizard so that you can restore your earlier settings.

☒   **A** is incorrect because RIPrep is always run on the fully configured client computer, not on the RIS server. The RIS server only stores the image. **B** is incorrect because RIPrep does not delete the current installation on the client. **D** is incorrect because the removal of user-specific settings from the client computer is not affected, even if you choose to reboot the computer manually.

12.   ☑   **D.** Maintenance and Troubleshooting. When the Client Installation Wizard starts on a client computer, the user is given four setup options. The Maintenance and Troubleshooting option enables access to installing third-party tools that could be helpful to the user.

☒   **A** is incorrect because the Automatic Setup option is used for a fully automated setup. **B** is incorrect because the Custom Setup option cannot be selected to install any third-party utility. This option enables the user to configure the operating system in a desired way. **C** is also incorrect because the Restart a Previous Setup Attempt option is used when a setup attempt has failed or aborted for any reason. When selected, this option does not prompt the user for any answers that were previously provided.

13.   ☑   **A.** Run the remote boot disk generator utility and click Adapter List. This way, you can view a list of all network adapters that are supported by RIS.

☒   **B** is incorrect because the adapter documentation does not give the required information. **C** is an invalid choice because the RISetup utility is for configuration of RIS. There is no option to check a list of supported adapters. These explanations make **D** incorrect.

Troubleshooting

14. ☑ **A**. DHCP, BINL, and TFTP. When a computer is started using a remote boot disk, it first tries to contact the DHCP server to obtain an IP address. After getting an IP address, the computer contacts the RIS server to obtain the boot file. This is accomplished by the BINL service running on the RIS server. TFTP is then utilized to transfer the necessary boot files from the RIS server to the client computer.
    ☒ **B** and **C** are incorrect because BINL and TFTP do not initialize before the DHCP. DHCP must first provide an IP address to the client. **D** is incorrect because TFTP works after DHCP and BINL.

15. ☑ **C**. There must be exactly one partition. The RIPrep utility works for only a single drive with single partitions. It is not possible to create an image of a hard disk that has multiple partitions.
    ☒ **A** is incorrect because drive C: has sufficient space, and this is not a reason for the problem. **B** is an inappropriate choice because there must not be any partitions at all. **D** is incorrect because RIPrep works only for single hard disk with a single partition, even if it contains system and boot files.

16. ☑ **C**. Stop and restart the BINL service. The possible cause of this timing out is that the BINL service on the RIS server is not responding. This happens after the computer has received an IP address from the DHCP server. Stopping and restarting the BINL service on the RIS server will help resolve the problem.
    ☒ **A** is incorrect because restarting the client computer will not help; the problem is not at the client end. **B** is not a good choice because if stopping and restarting only the BINL service can help resolve the problem, there is no need to restart the RIS server. **D** is incorrect because the DHCP server is not an issue; the client has already got the IP address.

17. ☑ **D**. All of the above. The reason for the client computer to display a BootP message and hang there could be any or all of the listed reasons. This client uses this protocol to get an IP address from the DHCP server. The client is not able to connect to either the RIS server or the DHCP server. The DHCP might also not be configured to provide an IP address to the client. There is also the possibility of a router on the network that is not configured to relay BootP broadcasts. If you have any routers on the network between the RIS client and the RIS or DHCP servers, the client must be configured to relay BootP broadcasts.
    ☒ **A**, **B**, and **C** are incorrect choices due to the preceding explanation.

LAB ANSWER

The steps given seem to be perfect, but in fact, they are not. They produce the required result but fail to produce any of the optional results. If you follow the previously given steps, you will end up with several problems during the installation process. The following important steps are missing.

1. The first important missing step is that you did not check whether RIS or the client desktops meet the minimum hardware requirements for RIS-based installations. Second, you did not check whether or not the client computers have supported network adapters. Run the RGBF.EXE utility and click Adapter List tab to view a list of supported adapters.

2. The next missing step is that there must be three different images. The steps in the question do not mention creation of any image. This is incorrect.

3. The above procedure assumes that you have the domain administrator rights and are the only one performing remote installations. The optional results demand that users must be able to perform the installations in order to reduce the administrative burden. If you want users to perform installations, you need to give them rights so that they can create computer accounts in the domain.

4. It is not stated anywhere in the suggested solution that you are applying any group policies for setting restrictions on image selection by users. If you want users to perform automated installations, you must apply appropriate group policies to ensure that users do not install incorrect images.

10

Managing, Monitoring, and Optimizing Active Directory Components

CERTIFICATION OBJECTIVES

10.01	Managing Active Directory Objects
10.02	Managing Active Directory Performance
✓	Two-Minute Drill
Q&A	Self Test

S o far, you have learned about such various aspects of Active Directory as installation of domain controllers, configuration of sites and services, and DNS. Any running network needs regular monitoring and maintenance; a Windows 2000–based network is no exception. Several administrative tasks in Windows 2000 Active Directory require administrative effort to keep the system running and performing seamlessly.

Windows 2000 comes with many utilities that help you in monitoring the network performance and resolving problems related to Active Directory. The built-in management features of Windows 2000 Server make many otherwise complex jobs easier for you. Active Directory consoles such as Schema, Users and Computers, Sites and Services, and Domains and Trusts provide interactive interfaces to handle day-to-day maintenance functions. Active Directory performance is monitored using the Performance Monitor console. The Event Viewer console now includes additional event logs such as Directory Service, DNS Server, and File Replication Service.

CERTIFICATION OBJECTIVE 10.01

Managing Active Directory Objects

Each of the components of Active Directory is known as an *object*. Different objects can be spread physically at diverse locations on the network. Management of Active Directory objects includes creating, publishing, moving, and removing objects in the AD database. The AD consoles enable administrators to manage various objects efficiently and effectively. This results in reduced administrative efforts and minimized total cost of ownership (TCO). In addition, AD makes it easy for users to locate and use network resources regardless of their physical location. At the same time, administrators can enforce group policies throughout the organization without having to manage each network resource from its individual computer.

The AD design that you implement in your organization today is most likely based on the organization's current requirements. These requirements can change with time and due to changes in organizational hierarchy. Growth of the company or its diversification into other business areas can also contribute to changes in Active Directory structure.

Moving Active Directory Objects

Active Directory objects include users, groups, computers, shared folders, printers, and other network services that need regular maintenance. Moving objects from one OU to another is a common administrative function required to keep the AD database in synchronization with organizational changes.

Why Move Objects?

When some changes take place at the organization level, you might have to make corresponding changes in the network setup. An organization that is using AD definitely must incorporate the changes at different levels of AD setup. Moving AD objects contributes to such changes. The objects you create today might not be suitable to the needs of the organization after six months. Hardware upgrades, failures of network components, and regular maintenance could also require movement of objects.

The movement of objects can take place within the domain or between different domains, depending on the size of the organization. The following are some of the reasons for moving AD objects:

- Changes or growth in company hierarchy
- Creation of new domains
- Movement of users from one location to another
- Hardware upgrades
- Network maintenance

Depending on the reason for the movement of objects, you might have to move only one user from one group to another or a whole group to become part of a larger group at another location of the company. The basic methods for moving objects, however, remain the same. The next section describes various methods to implement movement of AD objects.

How to Move Objects

Moving objects from one container in the AD to another is an easy process. Two methods can be employed to move AD objects. The choice of a method to move objects depends on whether you want to move an object within a domain or from one domain to another. Certain restrictions apply to object movement in AD. These restrictions are discussed in the following sections.

Moving Objects Within a Domain You can move one or more objects at a time from one OU to another within the domain. Depending on the situation, you might have to move a user's account when he or she is shifted to a different department or office location, or you might need to move a computer account when the computer is reconfigured for a different function. When you move objects within a domain, you must remember the following points:

■ Any original permissions that were set directly for the objects do not change. You need not apply a new set of permissions after moving the object. This feature reduces your administrative burden.

■ When you move an object from one OU to another, the permissions set for the destination OU apply. The inherited permissions from the old OU are lost. Make sure when you move objects from one OU to another that the network functions are not affected.

Exercise 10-1 illustrates the steps to move user objects from one OU container to another OU container within a domain.

exam
Ⓦatch
When you move objects within a domain, the permissions set directly on the objects do not change. When you move objects from one OU to another, the permissions set on the destination OU apply. In simple words, the original object permissions are retained and the destination OU permissions are inherited.

Moving Objects Across Domains The process described to move objects works when objects are moved within a domain. To move objects across domains, use the *MOVETREE* and *NETDOM* utilities. These utilities are located in the \Support\Tools folder on the Windows 2000 Server setup CD-ROM. You can use these utilities to move objects such as users, computers, and OUs from one domain to another. Member servers and workstations are moved across domains using the NETDOM command-line utility.

Moving User Accounts Within a Domain

1. Log on to the domain controller with domain administrative privileges.

2. Choose Start | Programs | Administrative Tools, and select Active Directory Users and Computers. This choice opens the Active Directory Users and Computers console.

3. Click Users from the console tree on the left-side pane. Notice that a list of users is displayed on the results pane in the right side.

4. Select the Users that you want to move from this OU. Right-click and select Move from the drop-down menu. You can also click Move from the Action menu.

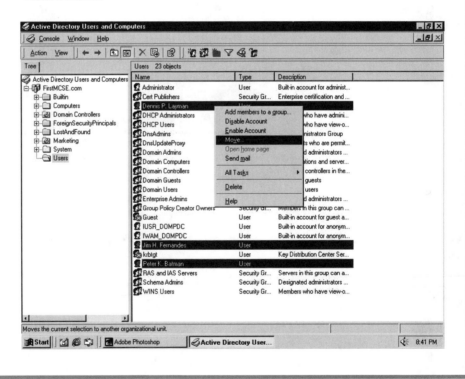

5. A Move dialog box appears. Select the container to which you want to move the User objects, as shown here:

6. Select OK to close the Move dialog box. Notice that the users you moved are no longer displayed in the Users container.

7. To verify the Move operation, open the container to which you moved the users. The users are now listed there.

8. Close the Active Directory Users and Computers console.

A similar procedure can be followed to move other objects such as computers or printers within the same domain. Printers do not normally appear as Active Directory objects in the same way as users or computers do. However, in essence, any object visible from the snap-in can be moved in a similar way. Printer objects appear within computer objects and can be viewed only by selecting View | Users, Groups and Computers as Containers.

Users and groups have a security ID (SID) that is unique in the domain. When you move any users from one domain to another, the SID changes. The SIDHistory feature of Windows 2000 preserves security settings that enable users to enjoy their original privileges. This option is available only when the network is functioning in Windows 2000 native mode.

You must be familiar with certain important points before you can use the MOVETREE tool effectively. The following conditions and restrictions apply for moving objects between domains using the MOVETREE command:

- MOVETREE can move only objects between domains in the same forest. If this condition is not met, the move operation will not succeed.

- Locked objects cannot be moved. If a folder is locked by a user, you cannot move it without first unlocking it.

- Replication delays can cause a move operation to fail. For example, if a printer is deleted from the source domain but is still shown in the source domain, and the destination domain has updated its records to show the printer as deleted, you will not be able to move it.

- If there are capacity problems at the destination domain, such as hard disk space limitations, the MOVETREE command will not work.

Besides these restrictions, the following operations are not supported when you use the MOVETREE command to move objects between domains:

- Global groups that reside at the domain level and have member user accounts cannot be moved. Similarly, local groups with members cannot be moved.

- The group policies associated with an object do not move with the object. You might have to apply new policies after the move operation. This caveat holds true for users, groups, and computers.

- System objects cannot be moved using the MOVETREE command.

- You cannot move objects that reside in the special-purpose containers such as LostAndFound, Built-in, ForeignSecurityPrincipals, and System.

- And of course, as a simple rule, you cannot move an object that has a namesake at the destination domain. Two objects with an identical name cannot co-exist.

■ Domain controllers and objects whose parent is a domain controller cannot be moved.

■ Users with global group membership cannot be moved. If a user is moved, its object attributes/properties must meet the criteria imposed by the destination domain (for example, password length).

Using MOVETREE to Move an Organizational Unit from One Domain to Another The MOVETREE command is used from the DOS prompt or can be run from the Start menu. If you are good at scripting, you can also choose to write a batch file to run this command. Figure 10-1 displays the syntax of the MOVETREE command.

FIGURE 10-1 MOVETREE command syntax

```
G:\WINNT\System32\cmd.exe

G:\>movetree /?

THE SYNTAX OF THIS COMMAND IS:

MoveTree [/start | /continue | /check] [/s SrcDSA] [/d DstDSA]
         [/sdn SrcDN] [/ddn DstDN] [/u Domain\Username] [/p Password] [/verbose]

  /start         : Start a move tree operation with /check option by default.
                 : Instead, you could be able to use /startnocheck to start a move
                 : tree operation without any check.
  /continue      : Continue a failed move tree operation.
  /check         : Check the whole tree before actually move any object.
  /s <SrcDSA>    : Source server's fully qualified primary DNS name. Required
  /d <DstDSA>    : Destination server's fully qualified primary DNS name. Required
  /sdn <SrcDN>   : Source sub-tree's root DN.
                 : Required in Start and Check case. Optional in Continue case
  /ddn <DstDN>   : Destination sub-tree's root DN. RDN plus Destinaton Parent DN. Requ
ired
  /u <Domain\UserName>  : Domain Name and User Account Name. Optional
  /p <Password> : Password. Optional
  /verbose       : Verbose Mode. Pipe anything onto screen. Optional

EXAMPLES:

  movetree /check /s Server1.Dom1.Com /d Server2.Dom2.Com /sdn OU=foo,DC=Dom1,DC=Com
           /ddn OU=foo,DC=Dom2,DC=Com /u Dom1\administrator /p *

  movetree /start /s Server1.Dom1.Com /d Server2.Dom2.Com /sdn OU=foo,DC=Dom1,DC=Com
           /ddn OU=foo,DC=Dom2,DC=Com /u Dom1\administrator /p MySecretPwd

  movetree /startnocheck /s Server1.Dom1.Com /d Server2.Dom2.Com /sdn OU=foo,DC=Dom1,
DC=Com
           /ddn OU=foo,DC=Dom2,DC=Com /u Dom1\administrator /p MySecretPwd

  movetree /continue /s Server1.Dom1.Com /d Server2.Dom2.Com /ddn OU=foo,DC=Dom1,DC=C
om
           /u Dom1\administrator /p * /verbose

G:\>
```

Exercise 10-2 explains how an OU can be moved from one domain to another using the MOVETREE command. In this exercise, we move an OU named Onlinesales from Server1 in the Marketing domain to Server2 in the Support domain and rename the new OU *Records*.

When the MOVETREE command completes the move operation, it creates some log files. These files are very useful for verifying details of the move operation. These log files are named MOVETREE.ERR, MOVETREE.LOG, and MOVETREE.CHK, and they are located in the same directory from which you run the MOVETREE command.

on the Job

AD provides many functions to make your administrative jobs easy, but that does not mean that you can take it for granted that everything is done. The easier-to-perform jobs are also easier to spoil. Moving objects is one such action that needs proper planning. In particular, the computer objects that correspond to servers must be moved only after careful planning.

EXERCISE 10-2

Moving an Organizational Unit from One Domain to Another

1. Log on to the domain controller with domain administrative privileges.

2. Choose Start | Run, and type **cmd** in the Open box. This command opens the MS-DOS window.

3. Type the following command at the prompt:

```
Movetree /check /start /s:Server1.Marketing.Firstmcse.com
/d:Server2.Support.Firstmcse.com /sdn:OU=Onlinesales,DC=
Marketing,DC=Firstmcse,DC=com
/ddn:OU=Records,DC=Support,DC=Firstmcse,DC=com
```

4. The given command includes the /check switch, which performs a test run without moving any object. If the test does not encounter any errors, the command is executed.

5. If you are sure that everything is fine with the move operation, you can add the /startnocheck switch in place of the /start switch. Using this switch completes the move operation without performing any check. Make sure that you use only one switch because it is not possible to use both /start and /startnocheck in a single MOVETREE command.

The NETDOM Utility *NETDOM* is a Windows 2000 domain manager support utility that is used to move member servers and workstations from one domain to another. NETDOM is also a command-line tool. As we saw, a limitation of the MOVETREE command is that it cannot be used to move member servers and workstations between domains. The reason is that the MOVETREE command cannot disjoin a computer object from the original source domain and join it with the destination domain. We use NETDOM for these tasks instead.

The following is a simple example of a NETDOM command:

```
netdom move /d:destination_domain server1 /ud:sourcedomain\admin /pd:password
```

This command moves a member server named Server1 to the specified destination domain. The /ud switch is used to specify the user who is performing the move operation. The /pd specifies the password of the user.

You can use the NETDOM /? command to view a list of syntax and switch options for this command. The full syntax for the NETDOM command is

```
netdom move /D:domain [/OU:ou_path] [/Ud:User /Pd:{password|*}] [/Uo:User /
Po:{password|*}] [/Reboot:[time_in_seconds]]
```

where

- **/domain** is the name of the destination domain to which the member server or workstation is being moved.

- **/OU:ou_path** is the name of the destination organizational unit in the domain specified by the /domain argument.

- **/Ud:User** is the user account used to connect to the destination domain specified in the /domain argument. If no user account is specified, the current user account is used.

- **/Pd:{password|*}** is the password of the user account specified in the /Ud argument. When the asterisk (*) is used, the user is prompted for the password.

- **/Uo:User** is the user account that will make a connection to the object on which the move action is being performed. If the account is not specified, the current user account is used.

- **/Po:{password|*}** is the password of the user account specified in the /Uo argument. If the asterisk (*) is used, the user is prompted for the password.

- **/Reboot:[time_in_seconds]** specifies that the computer being moved should be shut down and restarted after the move operation is complete. If the time is not specified, a default time of 20 seconds is used.

Publishing Resources in Active Directory

Active Directory provides a centralized database for all network resources. This setup makes administration and maintenance easy for network administrators. In addition, network users can easily look for a desired resource such as shared folder or printer from a single search engine. Resources on the network, such as users, computers, printers, and network services, need to be published in AD so that network users can easily locate them. Many of the network resources on Windows 2000 computers are published automatically when installed.

Active Directory allows you to publish these resources and set appropriate security attributes to these resources. AD also enables you to set various administrative controls on the published resources so that you can ensure that users gain access to only those resources that they need to perform their job functions. AD also ensures that the data security is not at stake at any time. The published resources can be made available to network users irrespective of physical location.

What Are Published Resources?

The network resources that can be searched in AD are known as *published resources*. The network users can use AD search tools to find any published resource. Access to these resources is provided to users based on their credentials and security settings for each user or group. The following are examples of some of the resources that can be published in AD:

- Users and groups
- Shared folders
- Shared printers
- Computers
- Network services

The next section discusses various methods that can be employed to publish resources in Active Directory.

How to Publish a Resource

Users, groups, and computer accounts are published in Active Directory when they are created. Similarly, Windows 2000 printers are published automatically when installed and shared using the Add Printer Wizard. A List in the Directory check box is enabled by default in the Sharing tab of the Printer Properties dialog box.

Non–Windows 2000 printers, such as those on Windows NT computers, need to be published manually.

The Active Directory Users and Computers console is the centralized place to view and create published network resources. The creation of AD objects can also be scripted using the Active Directory Services Interface (ADSI) application programming interfaces (APIs). This is a nice alternative to user interfaces. Later in this chapter, we discuss creation of user accounts using the scripting method.

Publishing Users, Groups, and Computers   When you use the Active Directory Users and Computers console to create a user or a user group, it is published in the directory automatically. Similarly, computers, including servers and domain controllers, need not be published manually. The Active Directory database makes it easy for users to search for other users on the network. AD ensures that only the information that is relevant to the user is displayed. For example, a malicious user trying to change security credentials of another user or trying to create a bogus user account cannot succeed in doing so.

Publishing a Shared Folder   Publishing shared folders in AD is done from the Active Directory Users and Computers console. Once published, the AD-enabled clients can search for these shared folders using the Find option. The shared folders that are published in AD basically reside in their original locations. AD maintains a link to these folders so that users do not have to search for the share anywhere else on the network.

Exercise 10-3 explains the steps to publish a shared folder in Active Directory. Before you proceed, you must ensure that the folder you want to publish is shared on the network.

Publishing a Shared Printer   Printers that are shared on the network can be published in Active Directory from the Users and Computers console. The printers installed on non–Windows 2000 computers, such as Windows NT printers, must be installed manually. Windows 2000 allows you to publish printers automatically when they are created and shared using the Add Printer Wizard. The Sharing tab of the Windows 2000 Printer Properties dialog box has a List in the Directory check box that is selected by default. This can be verified from the Printer Properties sheet, as shown in Figure 10-2. When this check box is selected for a shared Windows 2000 Printer, it is automatically published in the Active Directory. You must deselect this check box if you do not want to publish the printer.

Publishing a Shared Folder in Active Directory

1. Log on to the domain controller with domain administrative privileges.

2. Choose Start | Programs | Administrative Tools, and select Active Directory Users and Computers. This choice opens the Active Directory Users and Computers console.

3. Click the Domain container from the console tree on the left-side pane. The existing OU containers are displayed on the results pane in the right side.

4. Select the container to which you want to publish the shared folder. Right-click the container, click New, and select Shared Folder.

5. The New Object-Shared Folder appears. Type the share name of the folder.

6. Type the location of the shared folder in the Path box. Ensure that you follow the Universal Naming Convention (UNC)—that is, \\server_name\share_name.

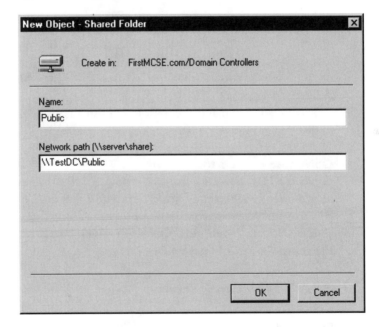

7. Click OK to close the dialog box. Notice that the new Shared Folder object is now listed in the container that you selected.

8. Close the Active Directory Users and Computers console.

FIGURE 10-2

Windows 2000
printers are
published
automatically in
Active Directory

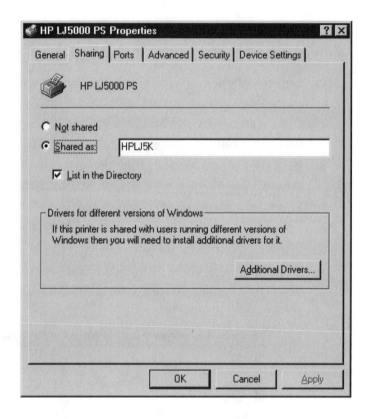

Exercise 10-4 explains the steps to publish a non–Windows 2000 printer in
Active Directory.

*Only those printers that are on non-Windows 2000 servers need to be
published in Active Directory. Windows 2000 printers are published
automatically when they are created and shared. The Sharing tab of the
Windows 2000 Properties dialog box has a List in the Directory check box
that is selected by default. Clear this check box if you do not want to publish
the shared printer in Active Directory.*

Publishing Network Services When published in Active Directory, network
services can be easily managed from a centralized location by administrators rather
than being managed from individual computers. In Windows NT, it was rather a
tedious job to check the status information or to start and stop services on a

Publishing a Non-Windows Printer in Active Directory

1. Log on to the domain controller with domain administrative privileges.

2. Choose Start | Programs | Administrative Tools, and select Active Directory Users and Computers. This step opens the Active Directory Users and Computers console.

3. Right-click the Computers object and click New. Select Printer from the drop-down menu that appears.

4. Type the share name and UNC path of the printer. Ensure that you type the printer name in UNC convention, \\Printserver_name\Printer_name.

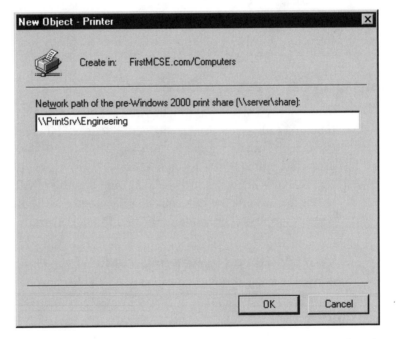

5. Click OK to close the New Object—Printer dialog box. Notice that the printer is listed in the Computers OU.

6. Close the Active Directory Users and Computers console.

particular server. Active Directory can be used as a single location for all these network maintenance activities. You need not use any third-party software or bother about the physical location of the server.

The Active Directory Sites and Services console is used to publish and manage network services. This somewhat advanced operation requires experience and knowledge. The following are some of the services that can be published:

■ **Binding information**   Allows client desktops to automatically establish connections to services.

■ **Configuration information**   Allows administrators to distribute configuration information for a particular application to all network clients.

Exercise 10-5 explains how to view a published service.

Other types of network services can be published in Active Directory, but most frequently you deal with only the Binding and Configuration information.

Locating Objects in Active Directory

When Active Directory is installed and configured properly in a large organization, it becomes a huge database of network resources and useful information. This database becomes a centralized location for finding information on the resources, users, and computers in the organization. As we've seen, each Active Directory component is known as an *object* that can be spread physically at diverse locations on the network. Active Directory enables users to find objects on the network without having to bother about the location of the object.

What Is Stored in Active Directory?

Active Directory contains information on all the network objects in a centralized database. The Find option in Active Directory allows you to search for the following objects:

■ **User accounts**   Active Directory stores information on all users created on the domain. This information includes user logon name, first name, last name, and other information such as the user's contact telephone number and e-mail address. You can also store the home-page address of the user.

■ **Contacts**   Information on anyone who has business connections with the organization can be listed in Active Directory. This information can include name, address, telephone number, and e-mail address.

EXERCISE 10-5

Viewing Published Network Services in Active Directory

1. Log on to the domain controller with domain administrative privileges.

2. Choose Start | Programs | Administrative Tools, and select Active Directory Sites and Services. This step opens the Active Directory Sites and Services console.

3. Click Show Services Node from the View menu. Click Active Directory Sites and Services.

4. Click Services from the Console menu. Expand each service tree. The published services look like the ones shown here:

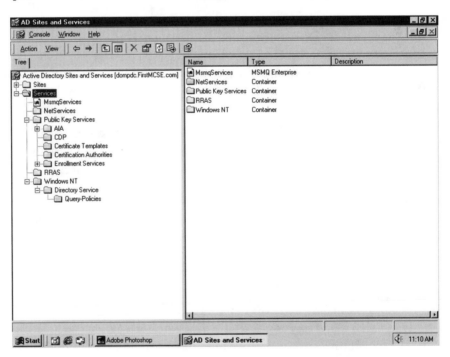

5. Close the Active Directory Sites and Services console.

- **User and computer groups**   Groups are collections of user accounts, computers, or other user groups. Information on user and computer groups is important for administrative purposes.

- **Shared folders**   Information on shared folders that are published in Active Directory includes the actual location of the folder; the server name and share name tell you on which server the folder is actually located.

- **Printers**   This object contains information on printers that are published in the Active Directory either automatically or manually. (Only non-Windows 2000 printers need to be published manually.)

- **Computers**   Any computer that is a member of the domain is listed in the Active Directory database. You can search for a particular computer using its host name.

- **Domain controllers**   Information on Windows 2000 domain controllers includes its host name, its DNS name, its pre-Windows 2000 name, the OS version used, and its location, as well as other information such as the person who is in charge of a particular domain controller.

- **Organizational units**   Organizational units are basic Active Directory components that store other OUs. However, an OU doesn't have to contain other OUs. OUs can also store users, groups, shared folders, and so on. Active Directory stores information about all the OUs in the domain.

When you create new objects in Active Directory, they either become a part of the existing containers or can form a new OU. You must be careful to include every piece of important information about the object that you create so that finding an object is easy at a later date.

Searching Active Directory

Searching for network resources or looking for particular users or computers was never as easy as it is with Active Directory. When you are looking for an object on the network, the Active Directory Users and Computers console is the right place to search, provided the object is published and listed in AD. Figure 10-3 shows the objects that you can search for using the Find option.

The Find option is used to locate objects in the Active Directory database. This is a powerful command that has many advanced search options. You can search for an object using any of the search criteria, and you can use a condition list to limit your search. If the number of objects is very large and you have found a particular object

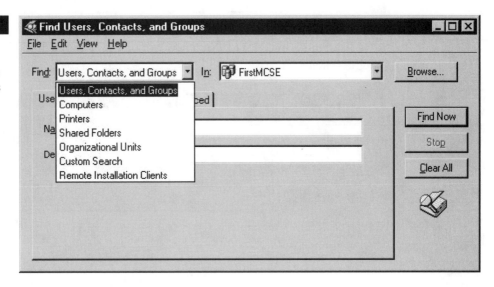

FIGURE 10-3

Using the Find option in Active Directory Users and Computers

you are looking for, you can terminate the search using the Stop tab at any time during the search process. The Clear All button is used to clear previously specified search criteria so that you can start a new search.

Exercise 10-6 explains the steps to search for a shared folder on the network.

Using the same procedure, you can locate any network resource, such as users, groups, computers, domain controllers, or printers. You can use any of the object

EXERCISE 10-6

Searching for a Shared Folder in Active Directory

1. Log on to the domain controller with domain administrative privileges.

2. Choose Start | Programs | Administrative Tools, and select Active Directory Users and Computers. This choice opens the Active Directory Users and Computers console.

3. Right-click the domain on which you want to search for the shared folder. Select Find from the menu that appears. The Find dialog box appears.

4. Select Shared Folders from the Find drop-down menu. Type the share name of the folder in the Named box.

5. Click Find Now. Notice that a new section opens in the dialog box and lists the search results:

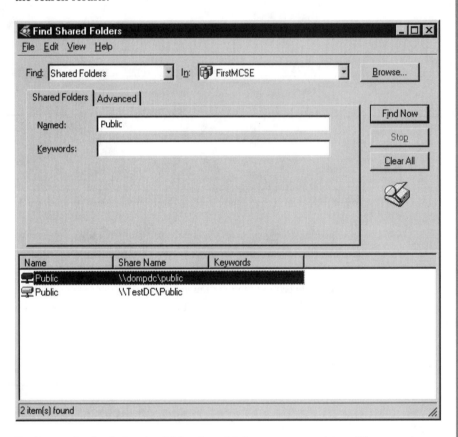

6. In the results, look for the folder for which you are searching. If you are successful in locating the folder, click Clear All. This choice closes the search results section of the dialog box.

7. Select a different name for another shared folder. Click the Advanced tab to specify advanced search criteria. When you have finished, close the Find dialog box from the File menu.

8. Close the Active Directory Users and Computers console.

properties as your search criteria. For example, if you know only the last name of a user, you can get a list of all users who have similar last names. You can use other conditions such as "5th floor" to limit your search to those users who have the same last name and whose offices are located on the fifth floor.

on the
job

When you try to locate objects in Active Directory based on some search criteria, the same criteria must have been previously included in the Object properties. For example, if you are looking for a printer on the 11th floor and use "11th Floor" as a search criterion, the Find command is able to locate it only if the printer properties contain "11th Floor" in their description.

Creating and Managing Accounts Manually or by Scripting

When you create new OUs in Active Directory, the next important job is to create accounts for users. You will probably create user groups first and then create user accounts in those groups. Creating a user account is a simple process that can be done manually or by writing scripts. The next section details the process of creating user accounts in a domain.

Manual Creation vs. Scripting

Creation of user or group accounts can be handled either manually or by writing scripts that run as batch files. When you use the Active Directory Users and Computers console to create accounts, the process is manual. This process does not require very expert skill, but the person creating accounts must have sufficient rights to create accounts in the domain.

Scripting the creation of user accounts, on the other hand, requires you to be familiar with at least one scripting language such as VBScript or Jscript. If you know how to write scripts and know various parameters of the account that you will create, scripting is a fast process. It does not involve interaction with any of the interfaces, and you need not provide each and every answer to the Windows 2000 wizards manually. All answers are included in the script file.

Creating an Account Manually

User and group accounts are created manually using the Active Directory Users and Computers console. When you have made plans regarding user groups and users that will become members of each group, you are ready to proceed.

The process is straightforward. As a domain administrator, you can create the accounts yourself, as can any other person to whom you have delegated control of the specific Active Directory container, and you can create new objects. All accounts created using Active Directory are domain accounts.

Exercise 10-7 explains the procedure of creating a user account.

EXERCISE 10-7

Creating User Accounts in a Domain

1. Log on to the domain controller with domain administrative privileges.

2. Choose Start | Programs | Administrative Tools, and select Active Directory Users and Computers. This step opens the Active Directory Users and Computers console.

3. Select the container in which you want to create the account. Right-click it, select click New, and select User. Refer to the following illustration:

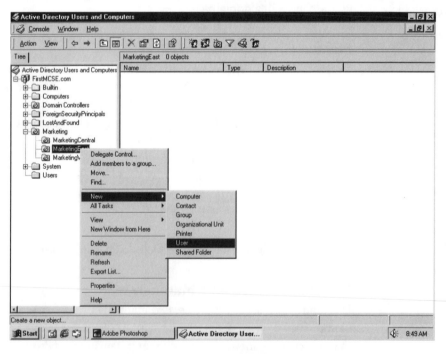

4. The New Object—User dialog box appears. Type the user's first, middle, and last names in the appropriate boxes. Type a logon name in the User

Logon Name box. Notice that a pre-Windows 2000 logon name is automatically created. Click Next.

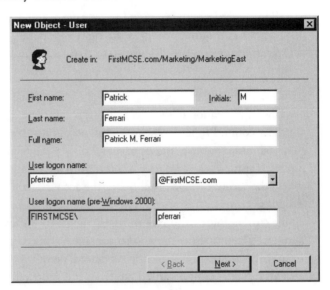

5. The next screen prompts for the user's initial password. Type a password in the Password box and retype it in the Confirm Password box. Select User Must Change Password at Next Logon. Click Next.

6. The next screen displays a summary of parameters that you entered for the new user account. If everything is fine, click Finish.

7. This completes the process for creating a user account manually. Notice that the new account appears in the right-side pane of the container in which you created the account. Repeat steps 3–6 for creating more user accounts.

When the creation of the user account is complete, the next step is to set properties for the account. Properties include user's account properties, group memberships, personal information, a user profile, and dial-in properties. To view or set properties for a particular user, select the user account from the right-side pane of the container in which the account resides. Right-click the account name, and select Properties from the drop-down menu. A Properties sheet for the selected account opens; the sheet contains all the current information for the user. Figure 10-4 shows Account properties for a user account. The properties shown also contain Advanced properties that can be enabled from the View menu by selecting Advanced View.

You can select any required tab from the Properties dialog box and set other user account properties. Whenever you want to view or change any user properties, you access this dialog box and view or make necessary changes to the account.

Scripting the Creation of Accounts

Scripting of user account creation is a fast process that needs no interaction with Windows 2000 account creation interfaces. This process is also faster than manually creating accounts. The script you write is saved as a batch file and run from the command line.

To write a script, you need to collect the following information regarding a user account:

■ Name of OU

■ Fully qualified domain name (FQDN)

■ User's full name

■ Account name

■ Initial password

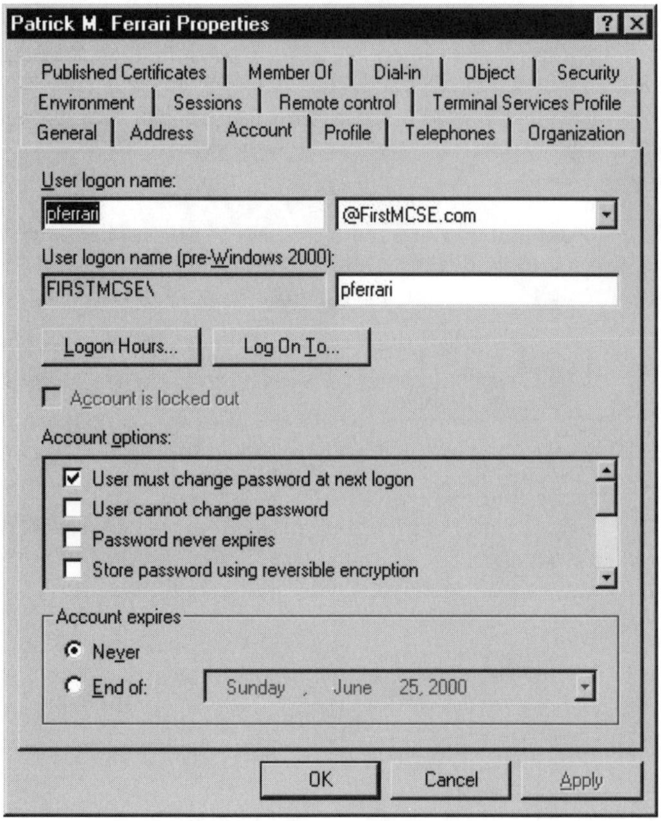

FIGURE 10-4

Account
properties for the
selected user

You also need additional, optional information such as the user's telephone number, his or her title, and the name of the department. When you have collected all this information, you are ready to write a script.

Windows 2000 Active Directory Services Interface (ADSI) comes with a set of interfaces that are called by the scripts written in Windows Scripting Host, VBScript, Jscript, and the like. You can use any other scripting language in which you are proficient; but if the network is running in Windows 2000 native mode only, Windows Scripting Host, VBScript, and Jscript languages are supported.

The following script is an example of script that can be modified to suit your requirements:

```
'----The following script creates a user account for Peter
Ferrari in the Marketing East object in Marketing OU. The domain
name is FirstMCSE.com-----------

Set ou = GetObject("LDAP://OU=Marketing,OU=MerketingEast,
DC=dompdc,DC=FirstMCSE,DC=com")
Set usr = ou.Create("user", "CN=Patrick Ferrari")

'--- The following line must be included. It is mandatory.----
usr.Put "samAccountName", "pferrari"

'---- The following steps are optional and can be skipped----
usr.Put "sn", "Ferrari"
usr.Put "givenName", "Patrick"
usr.Put "userPrincipalName", "pferrari@firstmcse.com"
usr.Put "telephoneNumber", "(732) 424 8974"
usr.Put "title", "Marketing Supervisor, New York"
usr.SetInfo

'—This completes account creation. The next lines reset the
password and enable it.
usr.SetPassword "pass321"
usr.AccountDisabled = False
usr.SetInfo
```

Various functions used in the given script are as follows:

- **GetObject**   The specific OU is bound to the Lightweight Directory Access Protocol (LDAP) using the GetObject function.

- **Create**   The Create function is used to create the new user object in the OU.

- **Object type (user) and canonical name (CN)**   These are parameters of the Create Function.

- **SamAccountName**   This is a mandatory property of the account and must be specified. Other properties are specified using the Put function.

- **SetPassword**   This function specifies the initial password of the user.

- **SetInfo**   This function is used to save the settings in the OU.

e x a m
ⓦa t c h *When you use the scripting method to create new accounts in an Active Directory container, it is important to note that the user running the script must have sufficient rights to create new objects in the OU.*

Controlling Access to Active Directory Objects

You might be familiar with *access control lists (ACLs)* in Windows NT, which are used to define how a user or a group can get access to the network and existing resources. The same ACLs are used in Windows 2000 to describe permissions of users to various objects in Active Directory. Every object in AD has attached to it an ACL that defines which users or groups have access to it and what level of access is granted.

AD permissions enable you to control access to objects. The objects can be computers, printers, and other network resources such as shared folders. You can define a user's or group's level of access to a particular object. The discussion that follows details various aspects of controlling access to AD objects.

SCENARIO & SOLUTION

We want to move two servers from this location to another location of the company within the same domain. Should I delete the servers in Active Directory and create them again in a different container?	No. You can move the servers from one container to another.
I am not sure about the syntax of the MOVETREE command. Do I have to consult the Resource Kit?	No. Use the MOVETREE /? command. This command lists the command syntax and the switches available for the command.
I installed a printer on a Windows 2000 server last week, but it does not show up in Active Directory. What could be the reason?	Check the Sharing properties of the printer. Make sure that the List in the Directory check box is enabled.
I am installing several servers in my company, which is spread over four floors of our building. How do I make sure that I am able to know the location of a particular server in Active Directory at a later date?	Fill in the server information in detail when you set its properties. Use location details so that you can find it in Active Directory later.

Degrees of Granularity

The *degree of granularity* that you want to achieve by assigning permissions to AD objects depends basically on the needs of your organization and policies that have been set for the entire corporation. Many companies prefer to limit administrative access to senior people in the company and give only as much access to general users as is required for them to perform their job functions. This strategy has several benefits, including ease of administration and security of sensitive data.

AD permissions allow you to go as far as possible to secure access to objects. Careful planning is required in deciding the permissions that you assign to users or groups. You must remember that many users are members of multiple groups, which can change their effective permissions on some objects.

Object and Attribute Permissions

As described earlier, AD object permissions work in the same way as the usual NTFS permissions. Each object in the AD database has an associated ACL. If a user is a member of multiple groups, his or her effective permissions are the combination of permissions for all the groups. However, this assignment is subject to whether or not any group of which the user is a member has Deny permission, which overrides all other permissions.

For example, if John is a member of one group that gives him Read permissions on a folder and a member of another group that gives him Modify permissions on the same folder, his effective permissions on the folder are Modify. Certain permissions cannot be assigned to specific objects. Obviously, you cannot assign Reset Password permission for a printer object.

Besides Standard and Special Active Directory permissions, there are two other main sets of permissions. These are Allow and Deny. The Deny permission always overrides all other individual or combined permissions of a user. You should use the Deny permission only in certain cases. Otherwise, use the most restrictive permissions that still allow users to perform their job functions with the utmost ease.

Standard Active Directory Permissions   The following are the standard Active Directory object permissions that can be set to Allow or Deny:

- **Full Control**   This permission allows users to take ownership of the AD object, change its permissions, and perform all actions permitted by other permissions.

- **Read**   Allows users to view only the objects and associated attributes.
- **Write**   The Write permission allows specified users to change object attributes.
- **Create All Child Objects**   This permission allows users to create child objects in an existing OU.
- **Delete All Child Objects**   Users given this permission can delete objects from the OU.

exam
ⓦatch

Permissions for Active Directory objects work exactly as standard NTFS permissions. The effective permissions for a user who is a member of multiple groups are the combination of permissions in each group. The Deny permission, however, takes precedence over all other permissions.

Special Active Directory Permissions   In practice, you will find the standard permissions sufficient to control access to Active Directory objects. However, when these permissions are not enough and you want to achieve finer control on some objects, you can use the *special permissions*. The special permissions are viewed and set from the Advanced tab of the Security properties of an object.

Inheritance of Active Directory Object Permissions   The AD object permissions inheritance works in the same way as standard NTFS permission inheritance. While setting permissions on an object, you can deselect the Allow Inheritable Permissions from Parent to Propagate to This Object check box.

Exercise 10-8 explains the procedure to set permissions on Active Directory objects.

EXERCISE 10-8

Setting Permissions on Active Directory Objects

1. Log on to the domain controller with domain administrative privileges.

2. Choose Start | Programs | Administrative Tools, and select Active Directory Users and Computers. This choice opens the Active Directory Users and Computers console.

3. Select the object for which you want to set permissions. Right-click and select Properties. This choice opens the Properties window for the selected object.

4. Click the Security tab. The standard security properties are displayed:

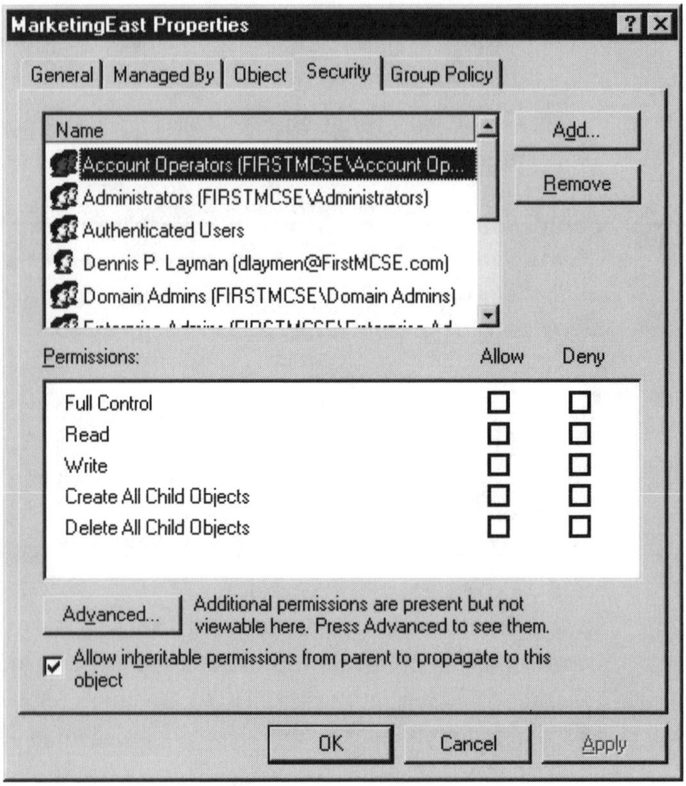

5. From the list in the upper portion of the dialog box, select the users to which you want to give access. Select the access type you want to assign from the lower portion of the dialog box.

6. If you want to set Access special permissions, click the Advanced tab. The Advanced Security permissions are displayed, as shown next.

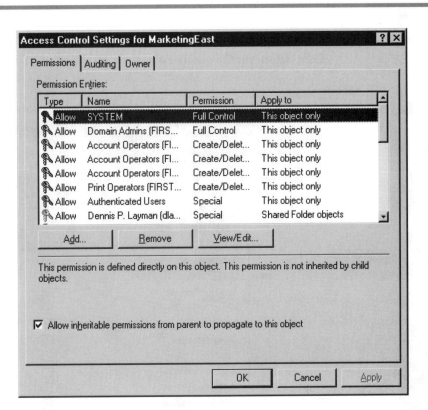

7. To add a user, click Add. The next screen is Select User, Computer, or Group:

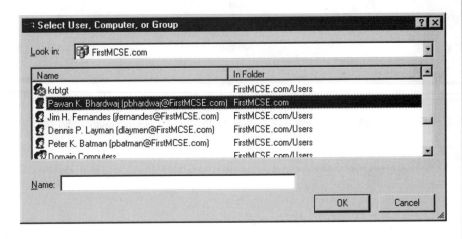

8. Select a user from the list, and click OK. This action opens the Permission Entry screen for the selected object. Select the appropriate object from the Apply Onto the drop-down box. The default is This Object and All Child Objects.

9. Check the permissions that you want to assign, and click OK. Close the Active Directory Users and Computers console.

exam
ⓦatch

The permissions on Active Directory objects are automatically inherited from the parent container to the child container. You must deselect the Allow Inheritable Permissions from Parent to Propagate to This Object check box to disable the propagation of inheritance.

Delegating Administrative Control of Objects in Active Directory

If the organization is small, you can handle the administrative responsibilities yourself, without any help from anyone. But when the network is an enterprise-level network spread across various parts of the country or the globe, you will definitely like to share the administrative tasks among other administrators. Giving permissions to other users or departmental administrators on AD objects is known as *delegation of control.* Delegating control helps you off-load some of your administrative tasks so that the administration functions run smoothly.

Why Delegate Control?

Many factors call for delegation of control; size of the organization is first among them. A single network administrator cannot handle all network-related functions. These tasks must be divided among many other administrators or users, depending on the policies of the organization.

For example, if your organization has 12 branches across the country, one person cannot look after the maintenance needs of all locations single-handedly. There must be local administrators with full or limited privileges to handle day-to-day administrative tasks. If you are at the top of the network administrator hierarchy, you are responsible for delegation of administrative tasks. Even when the network is at a single location, you may want to delegate control of many network resources to selected users.

This stands true for AD components, too. The organizations that use Windows 2000 Active Directory are using this wonderful feature to manage network resources effectively. Delegation of control is required for Active Directory components such as OUs and specific containers to distribute administrative functions. The following discussion helps you understand the process of delegating control of AD components.

How to Delegate Control

Administrative control of Active Directory is delegated by assigning permissions to objects so that other administrators, users, or groups of users can handle their functions more effectively and according to their needs. This delegation helps achieve more granular control of function-based OUs. You could also call it *decentralization of administration* at various levels of the organization, which lessens the centralized administrative burden.

Delegation of control of AD objects works equally well at both the OU level and the container level. This again depends on the organization's hierarchy and how you want to distribute various administrative functions. This method of delegation ensures that you are able to track permissions in a better way than tracking permissions on an individual object level. You can also easily maintain documentation of permission assignments.

The Delegation of Control Wizard is the best way of assigning permissions. This wizard is helpful in simplifying the delegation process. Figure 10-5 shows the Delegation of Control Wizard welcome screen.

FIGURE 10-5

Delegation of
Control Wizard
Welcome screen

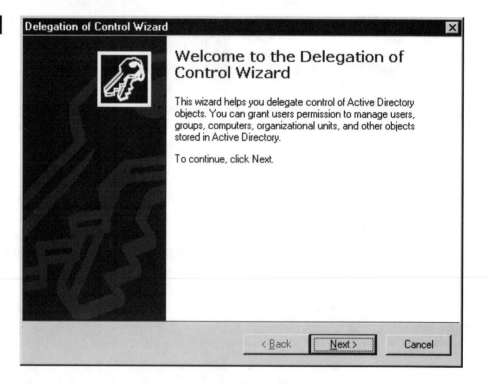

Once you have decided about the users or groups that will be assigned permissions to handle AD objects, you are all set to use the Active Directory Delegation of Control Wizard to complete the job. Exercise 10-9 explains the steps that will help you understand the procedure.

CertCam 10-9

EXERCISE 10-9

Delegating Control of Active Directory Objects

1. Log on to the domain controller with domain administrative privileges.

2. Choose Start | Programs | Administrative Tools, and select Active Directory Users and Computers. This choice opens the Active Directory Users and Computers console.

3. Select the OU object for which you want to delegate control. Right-click and select Delegate Control from the menu that appears. The Delegation of Control Wizard Welcome screen appears (refer back to Figure 10-5).

4. Click Next, and then click Add. The Select Users, Computers, or Groups screen appears:

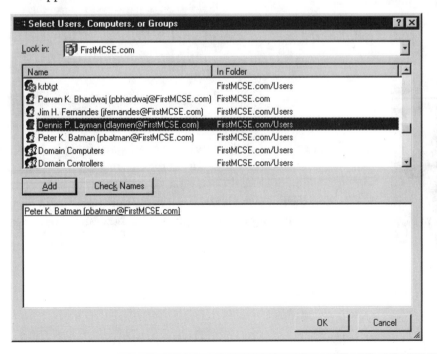

5. Select the user(s) and/or group(s) to which you want to delegate control of the previously selected object. The Look In drop-down list allows you to select a user or group from any domain in the forest. Click Add. Click OK.

6. Click Next. The next screen that appears is Tasks to Delegate. The common list of tasks is displayed:

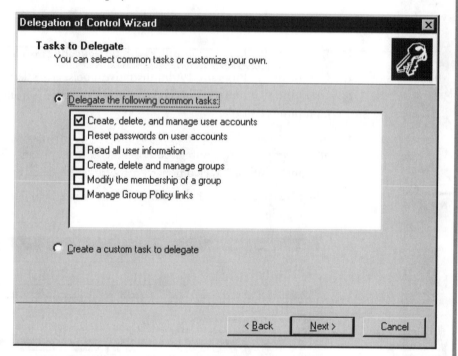

7. If you want to delegate custom tasks that include Active Directory–related tasks, click the radio button for Create a Custom Task to Delegate. This action disables the common tasks list, and the next screen appears, as shown in the following illustration. If the uppermost radio button is selected, along with appropriate check boxes, click Next and skip to step 12.

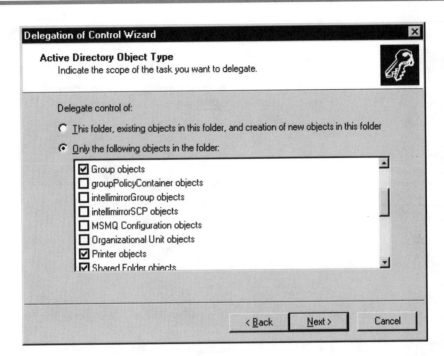

8. In this screen, you can select one of the following options:

   ■ This folder, existing objects in this folder, and creation of new objects in this folder

   ■ Only the following objects in this folder

   The latter choice gives you the option to select objects from a given list. Choose the Only the Following Objects in This Folder option.

9. Select each object you want. Click Next.

10. The Permissions screen appears. Select the permissions that you want to delegate, as shown next.

11. Click Next. The summary screen appears. Check that your configuration is correct.

12. Click Finish to close the Delegation of Control Wizard.

13. Close the Active Directory Users and Computers console.

SCENARIO & SOLUTION

I have set permissions on some objects in Active Directory. Does that mean that the original NTFS permissions are lost?	No. Setting permissions on Active Directory objects does not affect original NTFS permissions.
How do I decide what permissions should be set on Active Directory objects?	Consult users about their requirements and follow the policies of the company. Be as restrictive as possible, but ensure that users have enough privileges to perform their jobs.
My company has several locations, each of which has a network administrator. Is there a way to give these administrators some responsibilities to manage those Active Directory objects that fall in their locations?	Yes. Use the Delegation of Control Wizard and distribute control of Active Directory objects among local administrators.

exam
⚠atch

When configuring the Delegation of Control Wizard, you must select the Create a Custom Task to Delegate option in order to customize the list of tasks for which you want to delegate control for Active Directory maintenance.

FROM THE CLASSROOM

A Word About Active Directory Administration

Delegation of control and controlling access to AD objects are very important functions of Active Directory administration. Delegation of control helps you off-load many of your administrative responsibilities. When working in a large organization, it is not possible to handle all network functions alone. Even if a team of administrators is involved in network activities, some of the functions are distributed among users to help reduce administrative burdens. Controlling access to AD objects is necessary to secure configuration and AD data. The following are some guidelines for delegating control of AD objects:

■ Wherever possible, delegate control on containers instead of individual objects.

■ Consult other people involved in administrative activities to understand their requirements. In addition, follow the policies of your organization.

■ Delegation of control requires that the users whom you select for delegation are familiar with Active Directory and its

functions. If necessary, arrange training for users.

■ When controlling access of AD objects, do not forget that at least one person must have Full Control permissions.

■ Use the Deny permission with caution. Be as restrictive as possible, but ensure that you do not prevent users from performing their duties.

■ When you have finished with configuration of distributing control activities, never forget to track the assignment of permissions. Tracking assignments requires a bit of extra work, but it helps you keep tighter control on AD objects.

Finally, do not forget documentation. Documenting your AD object control decisions not only helps your fellow administrators understand the configuration, but it also could help you at a later date. Sometimes you will forget the configuration parameters yourself, so do keep notes.

—Pawan K. Bhardwaj MCSE, MCP+I, CCNA

CERTIFICATION OBJECTIVE 10.02

Managing Active Directory Performance

Performance monitoring and optimization are important aspects of Active Directory administration. As an administrator, you must have an idea of various performance-monitoring tools that are included with Windows 2000 Server. The Performance Monitor console and Event Viewer are the tools administrators most frequently use to find performance bottlenecks. These tools help you resolve many performance-related problems. This section discusses how to monitor the performance of domain controllers with regard to Active Directory.

Monitoring, Maintaining, and Troubleshooting Domain Controller Performance

Active Directory administrative functions include monitoring, maintaining, and troubleshooting domain controllers that are basic storage places for its components. The Event Viewer console gives you a view of various events that happen in separate sections of the domain controller. The Performance Monitor console gives a real-time display of the system performance based on the counters that you select for monitoring. Both of these utilities allow you to save your data so that you can analyze it at a later time.

Event Logs

Most of the domain controller's activities are recorded in the event logs. You can access the event log files from the Administrative Tools Event Viewer console. The event logs are helpful in locating information on various system and application problems that are running on the domain controller. The Event Viewer on a domain controller has the following types of logs:

- **Application logs** These event logs display information generated by applications.

- **Security logs** Security events are recorded only if the administrator sets some auditing on security events, such as success or failure of logon or access to shared resources.

■ **System logs**   These events display information on services that are used by the Windows 2000 operating system.

■ **Directory service logs**   These events relate to Active Directory services.

■ **DNS server logs**   The Domain Name Service (DNS) server generates these events.

■ **File Replication Service logs**   The File Replication Service events are displayed in this section.

Each of the given event types contain information, warning, and error messages. The event logs that should concern you while you track problems in Active Directory are the Directory Service logs. These logs are the first place to check for any problems or bottlenecks with Active Directory. Figure 10-6 shows the Event Viewer console with Directory Services events in the results pane. You can double-click any event to get detailed information on it.

If you have more than one domain controller on the network, each participating in Active Directory data replication, the File Replication System logs give you details of events that occur during replication. The event logs enable you to understand each event as it happens on the domain controller and help you diagnose the problems quickly.

Performance Counters

The Performance Monitor console gives a real-time analysis of domain controller performance. You can configure the Performance Monitor console by adding only those counters that you want to monitor. You can also monitor performance of the remote domain controllers.

There are two snap-ins within the Performance Monitor console. These are System Monitor and Performance Logs and Alerts. The System Monitor snap-in is used to monitor system performance by adding counters for specific objects. The Performance Logs and Alerts snap-in allows you to create counter logs, trace logs, and system alerts.

The monitored events can be saved in log files. For example, you can configure some Active Directory counters to monitor a particular domain controller, set the intervals for monitoring events, and configure the System Monitor to save the results in a file. You can analyze this file later to find any problems with the Active Directory services.

FIGURE 10-6 Directory Service events in the Event Viewer

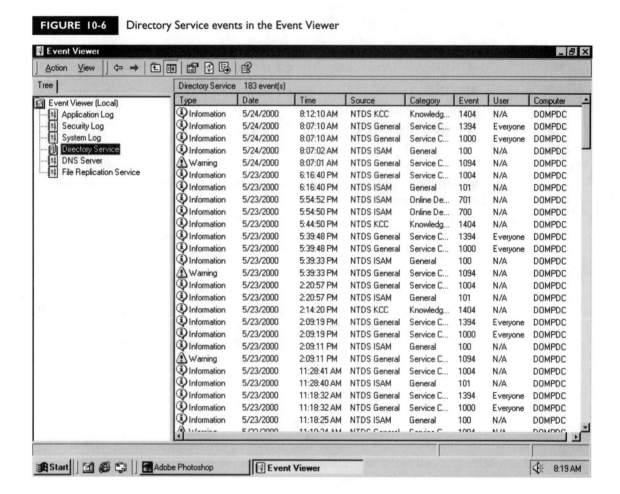

System Monitor The System Monitor snap-in enables you to view, collect, and print real-time performance data on selected performance counters. You can view performance for local as well as remote domain controllers. The formats available for viewing data are graph, histogram, or report. A previously saved performance log file can also be viewed. The Active Directory performance counters are included in the System Monitor snap-in. Figure 10-7 shows the System Monitor with counters selected from NTDS, which refer to Active Directory and Processor objects.

You can configure the System Monitor to display Active Directory data by selecting the performance objects and counters available for that object. The source of data can be the local or any remote domain controller on the network. The

FIGURE 10-7   The System Monitor snap-in of the Performance Monitor console

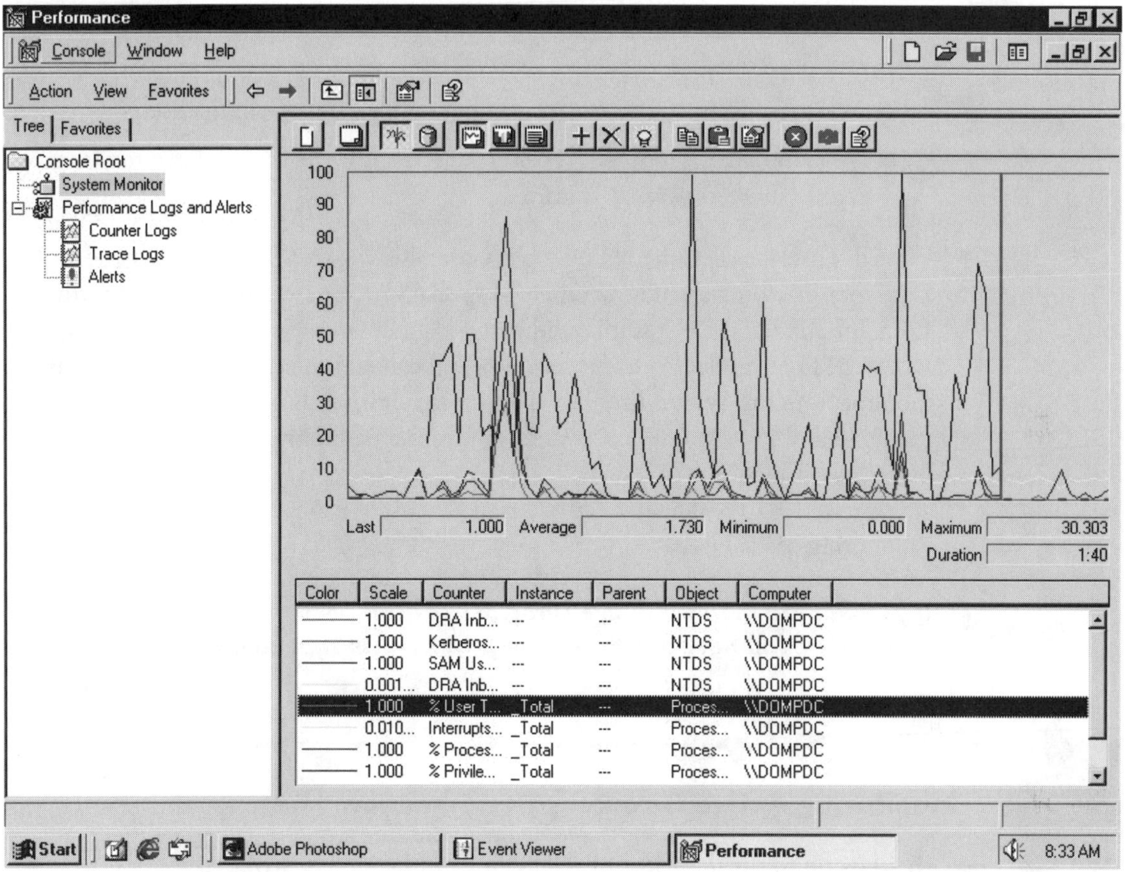

System Monitor enables you to collect samples of data by specifying time intervals. The System Monitor view can also be configured to display any specified colors, fonts, or characteristics.

When you open the Performance Monitor console from the Administrative Tools menu, by default, no objects or counters are selected. You must select objects and specific counters for that object that have to be monitored. The Active Directory object that concerns us while monitoring a domain controller is NTDS. Before you can get any useful statistics from the System Monitor, you must decide on what objects and counters to monitor.

Under any specified object are three types of counters of importance:

- **Statistics counters** These counters show the totals per second for the specific counter.

- **Ratio counters** These counters show the percentage of the total.

- **Accumulative counters** These counters show the accumulated total since Active Directory was last started.

As discussed earlier, the NTDS object contains counters for monitoring Active Directory performance. The counters of special interest are those that start with DRA Inbound and DRA Outbound names. Other counters are those with DS, LDAP, NTLM, and XDS client sessions. You can add the counters that you want to monitor from the System Monitor snap-in. In addition to NTDS object counters, the DNS and Processor object counters must also be monitored to keep watch on overall performance.

Exercise 10-10 will help you understand the Active Directory performance-monitoring procedure.

exam
ⓦatch

If you want to monitor Active Directory performance on a remote computer, ensure that you have administrative privileges on that computer.

CertCam 10-10

EXERCISE 10-10

Monitoring Active Directory Performance

1. Log on to the domain controller with administrative privileges.

2. Choose Start | Programs | Administrative Tools, and select Performance. This action opens an empty Performance console

3. Click System Monitor. Notice that the right-side pane of the console shows nothing.

4. Right-click the free area in the right-side results pane. Select Add Counters from the menu that appears.

5. The Add Counters dialog box appears. Select the computer from which you want to collect performance data. You can choose the local computer or a remote computer.

6. Select NTDS in the Performance Objects box. Click the Explain button to open another box that explains the purpose of the selected counter. The counters for NTDS objects are displayed in the Select Counters from List box:

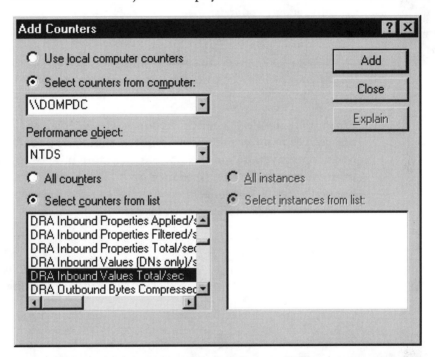

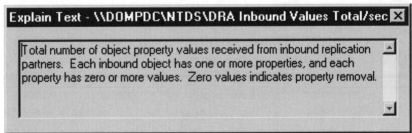

7. You can click the Select All Counters button if you want to monitor all counters from the NTDS object. Otherwise, skip to the next step.

8. Click Add. You can add as many counters as you want. Click Close to close the Add Counters dialog box.

9. Notice that the console has started collecting and displaying a graph of the data for the selected counters. The selected counters appear in the box on the bottom of the console. Refer back to Figure 10-7 for a view of the console after adding counters.

10. Close the Performance Monitor console.

on the job

When using the Performance Monitor console, you must decide what object(s) to monitor and which counters should be added. The more objects and counters you add in the console, the more processing power is needed from the system. The Performance Monitor console is run only when there are performance bottlenecks, so be sure you don't overburden the system with performance-monitoring activities.

Performance Logs and Alerts   The Performance Logs and Alerts snap-in is used to create counter logs, trace logs, and system alerts. You must have Full Control permissions on the following registry key for creating or modifying these logs:

`HKEY_LOCAL_MACHINE\System\CurrentControlSet\Services\SysmonLog\Log Queries`

The Security menu from the registry editor can be used to grant these permissions to other users. Administrators have these rights by default.

Counter logs enable you to specify counters that you want to collect and save to a file. These logs can also be exported to a spreadsheet or a database application. The database program can read these logs because they are written in tab-separated format. Interpreting the data collected by trace logs requires special tools.

With both counter and trace logs, you can set the start and stop times, name of the file, file size, and other parameters for creation of logs. The logging can also be scheduled for a specific time slot. The logs can be viewed during the time the data is collected or after the data collection is complete. Figure 10-8 shows the Log Files tab of the Counter Log dialog box of the counters log. You can schedule the log data collection from the Schedule tab.

Performance alerts enable you to monitor hardware and system services for specified periods of time. Alerts use the performance objects and counters to scan

The Log Files tab
of the counter log

the collected data. When a specified performance threshold, such as percentage processor time, is reached, an alert is sent to a computer on the network and an event is written to the application event log. Alert scans can be either run manually or configured to run automatically.

Monitoring, Maintaining, and Troubleshooting Active Directory Components

Some Active Directory components need consistent monitoring of performance and error messages generated by them. This section of the chapter deals with monitoring, maintaining, and troubleshooting services such as DNS service and schema.

Domain Name Service

DNS is one of the most important components of Active Directory. All domain-related functions are dependent on proper configuration and maintenance of DNS. Windows 2000 Server comes with built-in tools for monitoring, maintaining, and troubleshooting DNS. As an administrator, you should be familiar with all maintenance tools available.

The DNS events are written to the DNS server log, which is stored separately from other applications and services running on a Windows 2000 server. You might recall that these logs are classified as DNS server logs under the Event Viewer console. Events written in these logs are predefined in the operating system. Figure 10-9 shows a DNS server event log. You can double-click any event log name to get detailed information on a particular event.

FIGURE 10-9 DNS server events in the Event Viewer

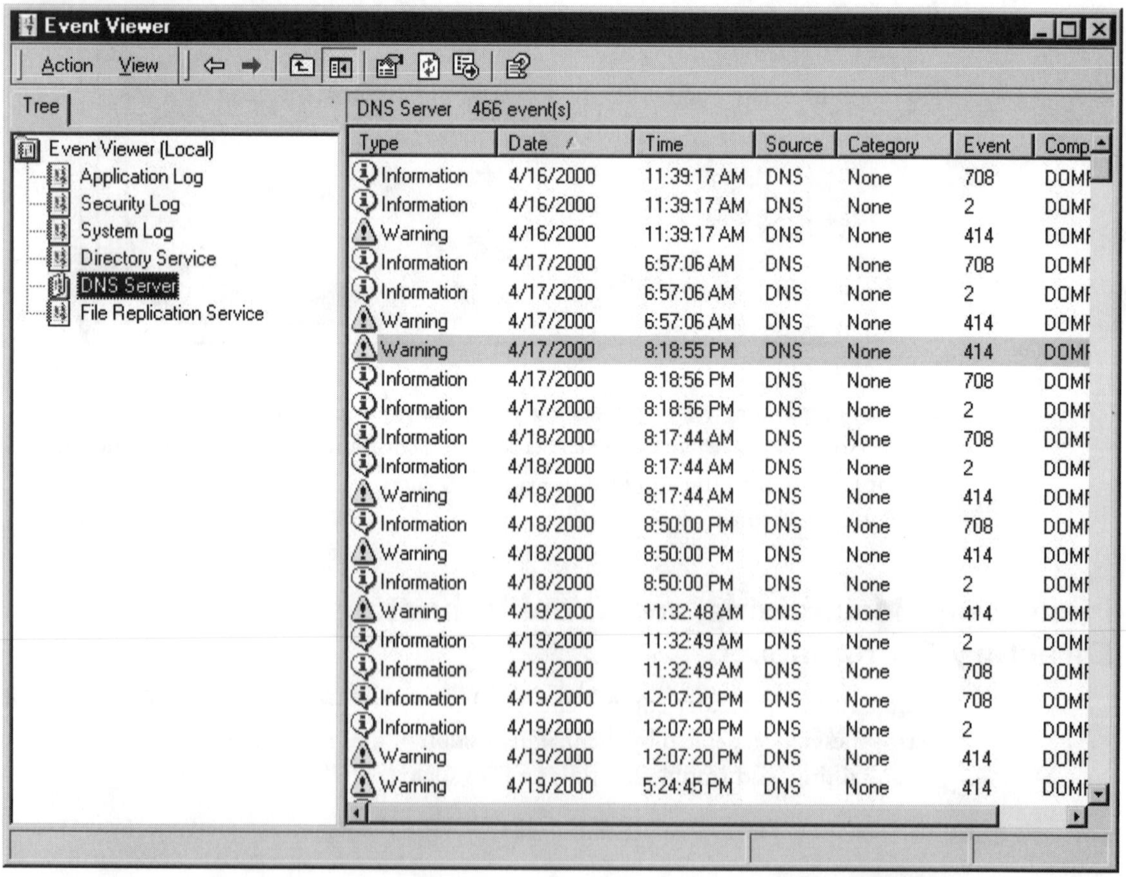

It is important to note that the DNS server in the Event Viewer keeps a history of only DNS server-related events. The client-related DNS events go to the system logs, and these client events are collected from only Windows 2000 clients. The DNS logs are stored in the file DNS.LOG in the \Systemroot\System32\Dns folder.

DNS Debug Logging Options There are several logging options for a Windows 2000 DNS server. By default, all debug logging options are disabled for reasons of DNS server performance. Enabling all debug logging options puts a significant load on the DNS server.

You can set any number of debug logging options from the DNS console. Open the DNS console from the Administrative Tools menu, select the DNS server from the console root, and open its Properties sheet. Click the Logging tab, and select the debug options, as shown in Figure 10-10. Click OK.

FIGURE 10-10

Selecting DNS debug logging options

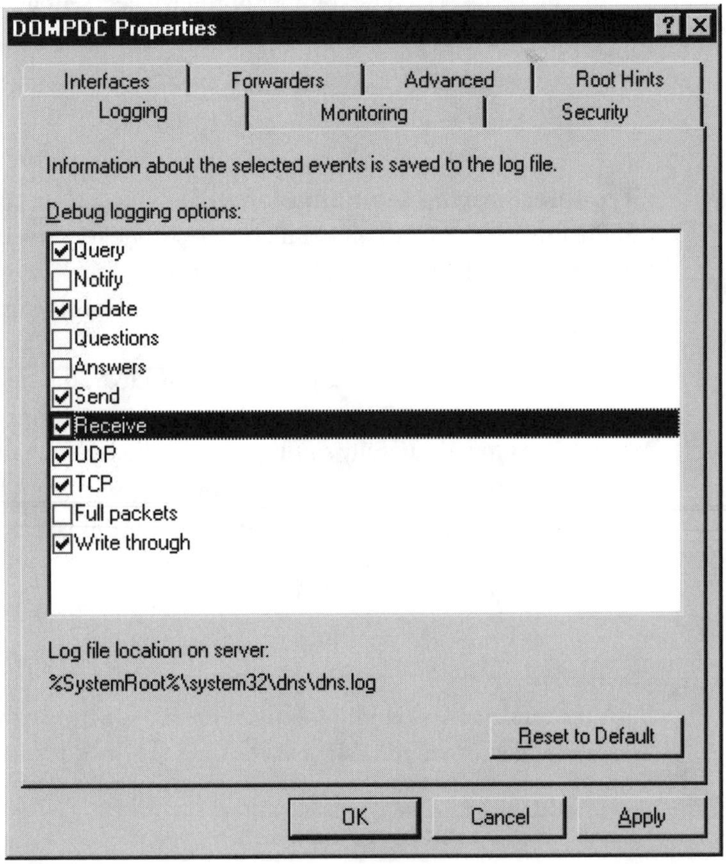

The following is the description of the debug logging options:

- **Query**   The queries sent by the clients to the DNS server.
- **Notify**   Notification received by the DNS server from other servers.
- **Update**   A record of DNS updates received from other servers.
- **Questions**   Contents of the questions section of a DNS query.
- **Answers**   Contents of the answers section of a DNS query.
- **Send**   The number of DNS query messages sent by the DNS server.
- **Receive**   The number of DNS query messages received by the DNS server.
- **UDP**   The number of DNS requests received on the UDP port.
- **TCP**   The number of DNS requests received on the TCP port.
- **Full packets**   The number of full packets sent and received by the DNS server.
- **Write-through**   The number of packets written through by the DNS server back to the DNS zone.

Troubleshooting Domain Name Service   You could experience problems in the DNS if the DNS on the master or secondary servers is stopped. There might be problems if the DNS zone is paused on any of these servers. Network connectivity among DNS servers can also cause DNS update problems. You can use the PING command to verify connectivity.

Whenever you experience problems with DNS, the first thing you should check is the DNS server logs in the Event Viewer. Any warning or error entry in the log must be examined carefully so that you can discover the cause of the problem and find a resolution. In case the Event Viewer console is not helpful in diagnosing the DNS server problem, you could monitor DNS counters in the Performance Monitor console. (For more information on DNS performance, refer back to Chapter 5, "DNS for Active Directory.")

Schema

Schema reside at the center of Active Directory. Schema store information about the types of objects that you can create in Active Directory and their locations. There is only a single schema in one forest. *Classes* and *attributes* are two types of schema subsets. Several classes and attributes are included in schema by default. Maintenance of schema requires you to make modifications to schema classes and attributes.

The domain controller hosting the schema operations master role keeps the master copy of schema. All modifications are made on this domain controller. There are at least two copies of schema in the forest. The domain controller that hosts the schema master replicates the changes in schema to other domain controllers after a default five-minute interval.

Modifications in schema allow you to extend the types of objects and the information that can be stored for each object in the directory. By default, the schema console is not included in the Active Directory administration tools. (Refer to Chapter 3, "Configuring Active Directory," for details on how to add this console.)

Note that once an attribute has been added, it can never be deleted. You can, however, disable the attribute. The disabled attribute cannot be added to any class. The same rule applies to classes; once a class is created, it cannot be deleted, but it can be disabled. A disabled class is replicated in the domain. Hence, proper planning is a must for any modifications in schema.

We must also mention here that if you ever need to merge two forests, both of them must have identical schema. Forest mergers are seldom required, but due to business expansion, companies do merge to form a larger organization. This change might require modifications in the existing schema.

Adding and Modifying Attributes A new attribute is required when you need to extend the attributes used by an existing class. A new attribute is also needed when you want to add a new class. Before you extend the Active Directory schema, however, you must have a unique object ID (OID) for each object you want to create.

Schema attributes can be added from the Active Directory Schema console. Exercise 10-11 explains the steps.

Modifications in schema attributes are required when you have to change the syntax and range, for indexing the attribute, to include the attribute in the global catalog, or to change the description of an object. To modify an existing attribute, open the Active Directory Schema console and select the attribute you want to modify. Right-click the attribute, and select Properties. Here you can make any changes that are required.

Adding a New Schema Attribute

1. Log on to the domain controller with domain administrative privileges.

2. Choose Start | Programs | Administrative Tools, and select Active Directory Schema.

3. Right-click Attributes in the left-side pane, and select Create Attribute.

4. A warning message is displayed, telling you that if you add a new attribute, you will not be able to delete it. Click Continue.

5. The Create New Attribute dialog box appears:

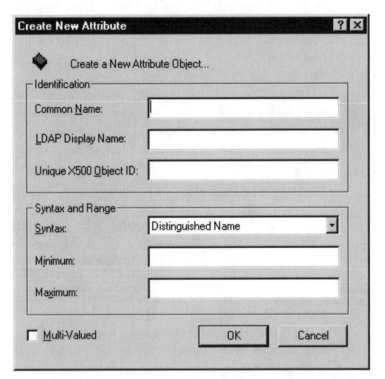

6. Fill in the required information—Common Name, LDAP Directory, Unique X500 Object ID—and set the minimum and maximum range values.

7. Click OK. Close the Active Directory Schema console.

Adding and Modifying Classes   Every object in Active Directory has an instance of *class*. Several classes are included in the schema by default. Each class is defined by the set of attributes used by that class. A new class is added when no existing class meets your requirements. An existing class can also be modified.

The addition and modification of schema classes is done from the Active Directory Schema console. Exercise 10-12 explains how to add a new class.

Modifications in an existing class are required when you need to add one or more mandatory or optional attributes to the class. You can add an existing attribute in the class or remove any existing attribute. An attribute or class that you create in Active Directory Schema can never be deleted, but it can be deactivated. A *deactivated class* is no longer replicated to other domain controllers. It is not possible to create new objects in a class that has been deactivated. Similarly, a deactivated attribute cannot be added to any class. A class that has been deactivated can be activated again at any time.

exam
Watch

Once you add an attribute or a class to the schema, it can never be deleted. You can, however, deactivate it. A deactivated class is never replicated to other domain controllers. A deactivated attribute cannot be added to a class.

Additional Tools for Active Directory Support

The Windows 2000 Server CD-ROM contains several tools that can help you monitor, manage, and maintain Active Directory. These tools are optional and are

---

EXERCISE 10-12

Adding a New Schema Class

1. Log on to the domain controller with domain administrative privileges.

2. Choose Start | Programs | Administrative Tools, and select Active Directory Schema.

3. Right-click Classes in the left-side pane, and select Create Class.

4. A warning message is displayed, telling you that if you add a new class, you will not be able to delete it. Click Continue.

5. The Create New Schema Class dialog box appears:

Create New Schema Class   ☒

┌─ Identification ──────────────────────────────────────┐
│   │
│   Common Name: [_____]   │
│   │
│   LDAP Display Name: [_____]   │
│   │
│   Unique X500 Object ID: [_____]   │
│   │
└──┘

┌─ Inheritance and Type ────────────────────────────────┐
│   │
│   Parent Class: [_____]   │
│   │
│   Class Type: [Structural   ▼]   │
│   │
└──┘

                        [< Back] [Next >] [Cancel]

---

6. Fill in the required information, including Common Name, LDAP Display, Unique X500 Object ID, and Parent Class. Select Class Type.

7. Click Next. The Attributes window appears. Click Add in the Mandatory section.

8. Highlight the displayed attribute in the list. Click OK.

9. Notice that an OID for the new class is listed. Click Finish.

10. Close the Active Directory Schema console.

not installed by default. To install these tools, run the SETUP.EXE file from the \Support\Tools folder of the Windows 2000 Server CD-ROM. This installation adds a Resource Kit folder in the \Systemroot\Program Files directory. The following tools are installed; they can be helpful in maintaining Active Directory components:

- **LDP** This is the Active Directory Administration tool that is helpful in carrying out Lightweight Active Directory Protocol (LDAP) operations.

- **REPLMON** This tool is used to monitor replication of Active Directory. It can also force a synchronization between various domain controllers on the network.

- **REPADMIN** This tool is used to diagnose replication problems in Windows 2000 domain controllers. REPADMIN is a command-line tool.

- **DSASTAT** DSASAT is another command-line tool; it is used to compare and detect differences between naming contexts on domain controllers.

- **SDCHECK** This command-line tool shows the security descriptor for any selected object in Active Directory. In other words, this tool shows the ACL for the selected object.

- **NLTEST** NLTEST is a command-line tool that tests and forces synchronization of trust relationships. It can also be used to force shutdown of a Windows 2000 domain controller.

- **ACLDIAG** ACLDIAG is used to diagnose problems with permissions set on Active Directory objects.

- **DSACLS** DSACLS is used to view and change security permissions on AD objects (command line only).

on the
①ob

The additional Active Directory tools discussed here are advanced-level tools and must be used with caution. Microsoft has included these tools on the Windows 2000 setup CD-ROM for use by its support personnel and experienced administrators.

SCENARIO & SOLUTION

I am having trouble with my domain controller. How can I find the problem?	The Event Viewer is the first place you should look for any errors or warning messages.
I have added several counters to the Performance Monitor console on the domain controller. Does that make any difference?	Yes. It affects the performance of the domain controller. Add only those counters that are necessary.
I am having trouble with the DNS server. Is there a way to log DNS events that are helpful in debugging the problem?	Yes. Use the Logging tab of the DNS server Properties sheet to enable debug logging options. Enable only those options that are necessary.
I want to monitor the performance of my domain controller but cannot do it during office hours. Is there any solution?	Yes. Schedule Performance Monitor to log events to a log file. Specify the time interval when the performance should be monitored.
I created many classes in the Active Directory Schema console, but now I find that these are useless. Can I delete them?	No. The classes created in Active Directory Schema cannot be deleted. If they are not used, deactivate them.

CERTIFICATION SUMMARY

The built-in management features of Windows 2000 Active Directory enable administrators to efficiently maintain a Windows 2000 network. Active Directory maintenance includes tasks such as creating, configuring, monitoring, and troubleshooting its components. The Active Directory administrative consoles provide the administrator a centralized location to perform these functions.

Active Directory objects such as servers, users, and computers can be moved within a domain or across domains. Movement of objects can be required due to changes in the organization or network maintenance. The MOVETREE command is used to move objects from one domain to another, with certain restrictions. Users, computers, shared folders, and printers are published in Active Directory from the Users and Computers console. The network resources that are published in Active Directory can be located using the Find option.

Accounts are created in Active Directory manually using the Users and Computers console. Scripts can also be written to create accounts; this method requires knowledge of a scripting language. Access to AD objects is configured by setting permissions, which work like standard NTFS permissions. The Delegation of Control Wizard is used to delegate control of objects to other users to reduce administrative burdens.

Active Directory performance is monitored from the Performance Monitor console. Performance Monitor has two snap-ins: System Monitor and Performance Logs and Alerts. Counters related to AD are located under the NTDS object in the System Monitor. Network performance can be monitored on a real-time basis, or you can create a schedule to record performance events to a log file. The Event Viewer console is used to trace events on the domain controller. It contains logs for applications, security, system, directory service, DNS, and file replication. DNS server events are recorded in a DNS.LOG file that is separate from other system and application logs. DNS.LOG is the place to check DNS server-related events in case of a problem.

Schema modifications are done from the Active Directory Schema console. New classes and attributes can be added but cannot be deleted. Classes and attributes can be modified and deactivated. Deactivated classes are not replicated to other domain controllers. Deactivated attributes cannot be added to any class.

TWO-MINUTE DRILL

Managing Active Directory Objects

❑ Managing Active Directory includes tasks such as creating, moving, and removing objects, as well as troubleshooting problems with AD components.

❑ Active Directory objects can be moved from one container to another within and across domains. Users or computers need to be moved within or between domains due to changing requirements of an organization.

❑ The MOVETREE command is used to move objects from one domain to another. When moving objects between domains, you must have sufficient permissions to complete the move operation.

❑ Network resources such as users, computers, shared folders, and printers are published in AD using the Users and Computers console. Only non-Windows 2000 printers need to be published.

❑ Information contained in the properties of an AD object can be used to locate an object via the Find option. You can narrow your search by setting conditions on search.

❑ New accounts in AD are created from the Users and Computers console. You can also use scripts to create new accounts.

❑ Access to AD objects is controlled by setting permissions on objects. These permissions work in the same fashion as standard NTFS permissions. Permissions are inherited from parent object to child object by default.

❑ Delegation of control of AD objects is done to distribute administrative responsibilities among users. Other reasons for delegation are decentralization of administration at various locations of an organization.

Managing Active Directory Performance

❑ It is important to monitor and maintain AD performance on a regular basis to keep your network running smoothly. The performance of the domain controller is vital in providing Active Directory services.

❑ The Event Viewer console is the centralized location for getting information on system events. Event logs are classified into application, system security, directory services, DNS server, and file replication service categories.

❑ The directory services events contain information on AD events. The DNS server logs contain events on the DNS server.

❑ The Performance Monitor console is used to monitor domain controller performance. It has two snap-ins: System Monitor and Performance Logs and Alerts. You can monitor performance on a local or a remote computer.

❑ Active Directory performance counters are located under the NTDS object in the System Monitor snap-in of the Performance Monitor console. You can perform real-time monitoring of Active Directory performance or schedule it and save the results in a log file.

❑ Care must be taken while running the Performance Monitor console because it can put a significant load on system resources. You should add only counters that are absolutely necessary.

❑ The DNS server has debug logging options that are disabled by default. To troubleshoot a DNS server, use the DNS console to enable debug counters. The log file is named DNS.LOG.

❑ Schema classes and attributes can be added or modified. Classes and attributes once created cannot be deleted, but they can be deactivated. A deactivated class is not replicated. Deactivated attributes cannot be added to a class.

SELF TEST

The following questions will help you measure your understanding of the material presented in this chapter. Read all of the choices carefully because there could be more than one correct answer. Choose all correct answers for each question.

Managing Active Directory Objects

1. Which of the following methods can be employed to publish shared printers in Active Directory that are installed on computers running the Windows 2000 Professional operating system?

   A. Using the create New Object option in Active Directory Users and Computers.

   B. Using create New Object in Active Directory Sites and Services.

   C. Using the NET PRINTER command.

   D. Do nothing; the shared printer is published automatically.

2. You are trying to locate a user who works in the production department of your company from the Users and Computers console of Active Directory. All you know about that user is that his first name is George. How can you quickly find all information about this user?

   A. Use the Find option in Active Directory.

   B. Browse the list of all users.

   C. Browse the mailing lists.

   D. Send an e-mail to him.

3. Your boss has asked about the search capabilities of Active Directory. You know many of the published objects can be searched using the Find option. Which of the following is not a valid choice to answer your boss's question?

   A. Organizational units

   B. Mailing lists

   C. Shared printers

   D. Remote installation clients

4. Which of the following Active Directory permissions allows a user to create new accounts in an Active Directory object? Choose all that apply.

   A. Create All Child Objects

   B. Delete All Child Objects

   C. Write

   D. Full Control

5. You have been put in charge of one of the branch offices of the company. A separate organizational unit has been created in Active Directory for this unit and it is your responsibility to manage the unit. The first thing you have to do is create user accounts in the OU. Which of the following tools can you employ to accomplish the job?

   A. User Manager for Domains

   B. Server Manager

   C. Active Directory Users and Computers

   D. By using the NET ACCOUNTS command

6. Which of the following are not standard Active Directory permissions? Choose all that apply.

   A. Full Control

   B. Delete All Child Objects

   C. Read All Properties

   D. Write

   E. Modify Permissions

7. In order to have a more strict control on network resources, you have set permissions on printers and shared folder objects in Active Directory. Earlier, these objects had only NTFS and share permissions set for them. What happened to the original permissions of these objects when a new set of permissions is created on them?

   A. The original permissions are retained.

   B. The original permissions are lost.

   C. Only one set of permissions is selected at a time.

   D. None of the above.

8. An organizational unit object in Active Directory is named Marketing. Mariah is a member of the Marketing users group, which allows her Read permissions for this object. She is also a member of the Marketing Representatives group, which gives her Write permissions on the object. A third group membership allows her Create All Child Objects permissions in the OU. What are her effective permissions on the Marketing OU?

   A. Read

   B. Read and Write

   C. Read and Create All Child Objects

   D. Read, Write, and Create All Child Objects

9. You have set permissions on some objects in Active Directory using the Security tab of the object properties. How can you make sure that the permissions you have set on the parent container are not applied to other child objects in the container?

   A. By setting separate permissions for the child objects

   B. By clearing the Inheritance check box

   C. By denying Inheritance permissions

   D. By allowing Full Control on all child objects

10. You are configuring the Delegation of Control Wizard to share your administrative duties with some users. You are not able to access the tasks related to Active Directory administration in the wizard. The only tasks shown are related to managing users, groups, and passwords. How can you configure delegation of Active Directory components?

    A. Configure properties of each object in the Users and Computers console.

    B. Click the Create a Custom Task to Delegate option in the Delegation of Control Wizard.

    C. Set NTFS permissions as Full Control on each object.

    D. Create a separate administrative group for these users and give them Domain Administrative privileges.

Managing Active Directory Performance

11. You are the administrator of a large network. Users on the network complain that sometimes they get error messages when they try to access Active Directory objects. To quickly find a resolution, what should be your first action when you receive such a complaint?

    A. Use Performance Monitor console.

    B. Configure logging of Active Directory events.

    C. Generate alerts for resource access problems.

    D. Check the Event Viewer.

12. Which of the following object counters must be added to the Performance Monitor console for monitoring Active Directory service performance?

    A. NTDS

    B. Processor

    C. Physical disk

    D. Logical disk

13. Your boss has asked you to measure performance of all domain controllers because he is working on increasing the capacity. You want to monitor performance of all domain controllers but are worried about the extra processing power the system required for this purpose. Which of the following is a solution to the problem?

    A. Add extra RAM in the domain controllers.

    B. Log only those counters that are required.

    C. Schedule the Performance Monitor console to collect data after office hours.

    D. View the Log files after office hours.

14. You want to monitor performance of one of your domain controllers and need to configure alerts so that whenever a specific threshold is reached, you can get a message on your computer. Which of the following can you configure to generate performance alert messages?

    A. File Replication Service

    B. Application failure events

    C. Excessive usage of processor time

    D. All of the above

15. The DNS server in your network has not been behaving for the last week, and you want to check the events that are generated by the DNS clients. Which of the following logs will you check in the Event Viewer to find this information?

    A. The system log

    B. The DNS server log

    C. The directory service log

    D. The application log

16. You are experiencing some problems with the DNS server on one of your domain controllers. You want to log and debug some activities that take place on the DNS server. Which of the following tools can you use to log the number of packets received on the UDP and TCP ports of the DNS server?

    A. Event Viewer

    B. Performance Monitor console

    C. Debug logging options

    D. Any of the above

17. Which of the following tools is used to diagnose problems in Active Directory replication from one domain controller to another in the network? Choose all that apply.

    A. REPADMIN

    B. DSASTAT

    C. REPLMON

    D. NLTEST

LAB QUESTION

Current Situation

You have a Windows 2000 network and are using Active Directory services. When implementing Active Directory, you did no planning to control access to various objects in Active Directory. Anyone can make modifications to the objects. Your boss is not happy with this situation and wants to control access to objects and delegate control of some objects to selected users.

Required Result

Control Access to Active Directory objects so that users have only as much access as required by their jobs.

Optional Desired Results

1. Delegate creation and deletion of child objects to selected users.

2. Users must not be able to make changes to the OU structure.

   Proposed Solution: We propose some steps to produce the required and optional results. Go through each step and see if any step is missing or incorrect.

1. Open the Active Directory Users and Computers console.

2. Select the objects to which you want to control access. Right-click the object and select Properties.

3. Click the Security tab. Ensure that no one has Full Control permission on any object.

4. Select Users or User Groups. Select the Create All Child Objects and Delete All Child Objects check boxes. In addition, select the Write permission check box.

5. Click OK. Close the Object Properties sheet.

   What results do these steps produce?

SELF TEST ANSWERS

Managing Active Directory Objects

1. ☑ **D. Do nothing; the shared printer is published automatically.** You need not do anything to publish shared printers in Active Directory if they are installed on Windows 2000 computers. The condition is that the Active Directory services must be running on the network when the printer is installed and the List in the Directory check box should not be disabled from the Sharing properties of the printer.

   ☒ **A** is incorrect because the Users and Computers console is used to publish those shared printers in Active Directory that are installed on non-Windows 2000 computers. **B** is incorrect because the Sites and Services console is used to manage Active Directory sites. **C** is incorrect because the NET PRINTER command is used to connect to a shared printer.

2. ☑ **A. Using the Find option in Active Directory.** The Find option in Active Directory is helpful for locating users and other network resources that are published in Active Directory.

   ☒ **B and C** are incorrect because browsing a user or mailing list is a time-consuming job. **D** is incorrect because you might not be able to send e-mail to the user unless you know his full name or e-mail address. When there is an option in Active Directory to find users or groups, you need not waste time on other time-consuming options.

3. ☑ **B. Mailing lists.** Mailing lists cannot be searched in Active Directory. Printers and other shared resources can be searched using the Find option. Search can also be done for organizational units and remote installation clients that are prestaged in Active Directory.

   ☒ **A, C, and D** are incorrect options because these objects can be searched using the Find option.

4. ☑ **A and D. Create All Child Objects and Full Control.** These two Active Directory permissions allow a user to create new accounts in Active Directory.

   ☒ **B and C** are incorrect because these permissions do not allow a user to create new accounts in Active Directory.

5. ☑ **C. Active Directory Users and Computers.** The Active Directory Users and Computers console is used to create new user accounts in the OU. Another way of creating new accounts is by writing scripts that require knowledge of some scripting language.

   ☒ **A** is incorrect because the User Manager for Domains is used in Windows NT for creating user accounts. **B** is incorrect because the Server Manager cannot be used to create user accounts. **D** is incorrect because the NET ACCOUNTS command is used in Windows NT to manage user accounts and cannot be used to create new accounts in Active Directory.

6. ☑ **C and E.** The Read All Properties and Modify Properties permissions are special-access permissions in Active Directory and are not visible when setting permissions on objects. These permissions must be accessed from the Advanced tab of the Security configuration dialog box.
   ☒ **A, B, and D** are incorrect because these are standard Active Directory permissions.

7. ☑ **A.** The original permissions are retained. Setting access control permissions on Active Directory objects does not affect the original permissions set on the objects and these are retained.
   ☒ **B** is incorrect because the original permissions on the objects are not lost but retained. **C** is incorrect because both sets of permissions are effective. **D** is an incorrect option because a correct answer option exists.

8. ☑ **D.** Read, Write, and Create All Child Objects. When a user is a member of multiple groups, his effective permissions are a combination of the permissions defined by her individual group membership. In this case, Mariah gets Read permission from one group, Write permission from the second, and Create All Child Objects permission from the third group.
   ☒ **A, B, and C** are incorrect because permissions from all her group memberships combine to give her Read, Write, and Create All Child Objects permissions on the object.

9. ☑ **B.** By clearing the Inheritance check box. Access permissions on the Active Directory objects are propagated from the parent container to the child containers by default. To disable inheritance, you must clear the Inheritance check box.
   ☒ **A** is incorrect because setting separate permissions on a child does not disable propagation of permissions inheritance. **C** is incorrect because there is no Inheritance permission. **D** is an invalid choice because setting Full-Control permissions is not a solution to disable propagation of permissions inheritance.

10. ☑ **B.** Click the Create a Custom Task to Delegate option in the Delegation of Control Wizard. The Delegation of Control Wizard configuration for Active Directory–related tasks is done from the Active Directory Object Type screen of the Delegation of Control Wizard by clicking the option.
    ☒ **A** is incorrect because configuring properties of each object in the Users and Computers console is a complex process. **C** is incorrect because setting Full Control permissions for every object is an undesired action. **D** is incorrect because giving Domain Administrative privileges to other users is not recommended when other options are available.

Managing Active Directory Performance

11. ☑ **D.** Check the Event Viewer. The Event Viewer should be checked immediately when you experience problems with any Active Directory objects. The Event Viewer gives you a quick view of the events related to AD and other system and application services running on domain controllers.

☒ **A** is incorrect because Performance Monitor console is used to monitor performance and not to check events. **B** is incorrect because you need not log Active Directory events since most of the events are preconfigured. **C** is invalid because alerts are usually generated for performance-related problems.

12. ☑ **A.** NTDS. The performance counters for the Active Directory service are found under the NTDS object in the Performance Monitor console. The counters of interest start with names such as DRA Inbound and DRA Outbound.

☒ **B, C,** and **D,** processor, physical disk, and logical disk, are incorrect because none of these objects contain counters for monitoring Active Directory performance.

13. ☑ **B.** Log only those counters that are required. Monitoring performance for a large number of object counters might cause excessive loading of the domain controller system resources. Only those counters that are absolutely necessary should be enabled.

☒ **A** is not the best answer because adding RAM is not a solution. The purpose of the exercise is capacity planning, which is defeated if individual components are added. **C** is incorrect because the data collected after office hours might not be as useful because the domain controllers might not be working with peak loads after office hours. **D** is not correct because viewing log files does not matter. The fact that matters is the collection of performance data.

14. ☑ **C.** Excessive usage of processor time. Performance alerts are configured from the Performance Logs and Alerts snap-in of the Performance Monitor console for generating alerts when a specified performance threshold is reached for a system service or hardware.

☒ **A** is incorrect because you cannot generate alerts on File Replication Service performance. **B** is incorrect because the application failures cannot be configured to generate alert notices. **D** is incorrect because we have only one correct answer.

15. ☑ **A.** The system log. The events relating to the DNS clients are recoded and displayed under the system log section of the Event Viewer.

☒ **B** is incorrect because the DNS server log section contains only those events that are related to the DNS server. **C** is an inappropriate choice because the directory service log does not contain events for the DNS server or DNS clients. **D** is inappropriate because the application logs do not collect information on the DNS server or DNS clients.

16. ☑ **C.** Debug logging options. The debug logging options can be enabled from the DNS Server properties to create a log of packets received on the UDP and TCP ports of the DNS server.

    ☒ **A** is incorrect because the Event Viewer cannot be used for this purpose. **B** is incorrect because the Performance Monitor console does not enable you to collect debug information. **D** is also not an appropriate choice because there is only one correct answer.

17. ☑ **A and C.** REPADMIN and REPLMON. The REPADMIN tool is an advanced command-line troubleshooting tool used to diagnose problems in Active Directory replication. The REPLMON tool is used to monitor replication and force synchronization between domain controllers.

    ☒ **B** is incorrect because DSASTAT cannot be used to troubleshoot Active Directory replication. **D** is incorrect because the NLTEST tool is used for testing trust relationships.

LAB ANSWER

The suggested steps do not produce any required or optional results. The suggested step 3 will land you in a more difficult situation because you are removing the Full Control permission for everyone. You must remember that at least one user or the administrator must have Full Control permissions on an object.

There are several missing steps, since none has been suggested to configure delegation of control. First, you must select the users that will be delegated control of Active Directory objects. Next, the Delegation of Control Wizard should be used to delegate control of objects to selected users.

11

Managing Active Directory and Domain Name Service Replication

CERTIFICATION OBJECTIVES

11.01	Managing and Troubleshooting Active Directory Replication
11.02	Managing and Troubleshooting Domain Name Service Replication
✓	Two-Minute Drill
Q&A	Self Test

Windows 2000 Active Directory was designed to meet the scalability needs of the large enterprise through the concept of a domain forest. AD spans the entire forest, regardless of whether the forest contains a single domain or a multitude of domains. The forest is also the boundary to AD; it cannot span multiple-domain forests. AD "lives" on domain controllers, which are often distributed throughout the enterprise network to provide high availability and redundancy. Windows 2000 uses an advanced topology that allows changes to objects in a domain to be performed by any domain controller that belongs to that domain. This means that it is possible for domain controllers within a domain to have a different or even conflicting view of the domain data at any given time. *Replication* is the process that migrates these changes between domain controllers and resolves conflicts when they occur.

Replication in Windows 2000 is managed automatically by default, but the feature allows for administrative intervention to customize or optimize the replication process. A thorough understanding of how replication works is needed to grasp the capabilities and impact of manual configuration of replication.

Windows 2000 relies heavily on DNS service for proper domain operation, and the same issues of high availability and redundancy that apply to domain controllers apply to DNS servers. Microsoft provides a DNS server as part of the Windows 2000 Server operating systems but also supports the use of non-Microsoft DNS servers. Many organizations have an existing DNS infrastructure and want to leverage their existing equipment and expertise. To provide interoperability with these other DNS servers, Microsoft has provided Windows 2000 with the capability to replicate and interoperate with any RFC-compliant DNS server but added new features unique to Windows 2000 DNS, such as the ability to store DNS records in Active Directory. DNS information stored in AD is replicated between domain controllers using the AD replication model and inherits the replication efficiency and scalability that AD provides.

CERTIFICATION OBJECTIVE 11.01

Managing and Troubleshooting Active Directory Replication

AD replication is highly automated in Windows 2000 to minimize administration. The default settings have been designed to work well in most network environments. Replication is a very important part of maintaining a properly functioning and secure AD installation, and a good understanding of how the replication process functions is vital to troubleshooting and correcting problems with replication. This section assumes that the reader is familiar with general AD concepts such as domains, forests, and organizational units (OUs).

What Is Active Directory Replication?

Replication is the process of keeping data stored in Active Directory synchronized on all domain controllers. Each domain controller in a Windows 2000 domain is able to function independently and therefore must contain a complete copy of the domain information for which it is responsible. AD is not static, and entries change with use. When a change is made, it is written to the directory by a single domain controller. Changes made on each domain controller must be distributed to other domain controllers. The replication process efficiently distributes these changes to the other domain controllers in the forest that maintain the same information, and it resolves any conflicts that occur.

In a Windows 2000 domain forest, there are many reasons for choosing to deploy multiple domain controllers. A small office network configured as a single Windows 2000 domain requires only one domain controller to establish the domain. The resulting domain is fully functional but has no redundancy. If the domain controller fails, network operations are interrupted until it is repaired or replaced. In this scenario, additional domain controllers are often used for fault tolerance. If one domain controller fails, others are available to keep the network running. Of course, each additional domain in the forest requires at least one additional domain controller to establish the new domain.

Performance is often another reason to add additional domain controllers. When the number of accesses to Active Directory increases to a point where the existing domain controllers are overwhelmed, additional controllers can be added to distribute the load. Because all domain controllers operate independently, a client can contact anyone with the required information to perform a query or submit a change to the directory.

When a network becomes distributed over a wide area, the network links between those areas are typically expensive and provide limited bandwidth. If we place a domain controller on each side of a wide area network (WAN) link, client traffic for directory access can utilize the local domain controller over the local area network (LAN), increasing client performance. It is generally much more efficient to add a domain controller to a LAN rather than have all client traffic cross a slow WAN link to access a domain controller. Client accesses to the directory are often interactive, and the time it takes for a user to log on or get a response to a query is an important part of a network's performance.

The goal of AD replication is to maintain a *loose consistency* of the database information on all domain controllers by utilizing a minimum of domain resources. Loose consistency means that there might be a period of time after a change is made during which other domain controllers will not have the updated data immediately available. Network bandwidth is the most critical resource to replication because it provides the path for the replicated data to travel. In order to reduce the amount of bandwidth required by replication, Windows 2000 makes use of data compression and replication when possible. In addition, Windows 2000 uses store-and-forward technology, which avoids duplicate replication when possible and ensures that only the minimum amount of information needed to make the change is transmitted across the network.

Active Directory contains objects of many types. A Container object such as an organizational unit or domain can contain other objects such as User or Computer objects. All objects have properties, or *attributes,* that specify information such as the name of the object and describe properties of the object. A User object, as shown in Figure 11-1, has the attributes display name, e-mail address, and telephone number, to name a few. Active Directory is able to replicate changes at the attribute level. If only the e-mail address of a user is changed in AD, only the change in that attribute, not the entire User object, needs to be replicated to other domain controllers. This significantly reduces the amount of bandwidth used in replication.

Naming Contexts

The data that makes up AD is divided into multiple partitions, or *naming contexts.* These containers are logical partitions; all AD information on a domain controller is physically stored in a file named NTDS.DIT. Two naming contexts are shared among all domain controllers in the forest: the *schema* naming context, which is essentially a blueprint for all containers, objects, and attributes that make up Active Directory, and the *configuration* naming context, which contains information that describes the physical layout of the enterprise network. Each domain in the forest also has its own naming context that is a Parent object for all the Child objects that exist in that domain. Replication for each naming context is performed separately; information in the naming context for a domain is replicated only between domain controllers responsible for that domain. However, both the schema and the configuration container must be replicated to every domain controller in the forest,

FIGURE 11-1

User objects have many attributes. AD replication is extremely efficient in that it can replicate a change for a single attribute without having to replicate the whole object.

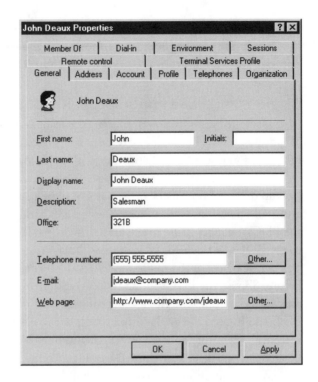

regardless of the domain to which they belong. A complete copy of a naming context stored on a domain controller is called a *full replica* of the information.

Global catalog servers participate in the replication process for their own domain and can also replicate with domain controllers from other domains and/or other global catalog servers to maintain the global catalog. Since the data used by the global catalog is read only and contains only a small subset of attributes, the global catalog information is considered a *partial replica*. A partial replica cannot be used to update a full replica, but it can be used to update a partial replica on another global catalog server. The following table summarizes the replication scopes for the various naming contexts.

Naming Context	Replication Scope
Configuration	All domain controllers in the forest.
Schema	All domain controllers in the forest.
Domain (one for each domain)	Only domain controllers within the domain and global catalog servers within the forest.

The global catalog contains information about objects from all domains in the forest and can replicate information in the domain naming context with domain controllers from domains other than its own.

Single-Master and Multimaster Replication

Microsoft used a *single-master directory model* in versions of Windows NT prior to Windows 2000. The single master was designated as the primary domain controller, or PDC, and it was the only computer in the domain that was able to both read and write to the directory services database. Additional domain controllers, designated backup domain controllers, or BDCs, could be deployed to assist with validation and read operations from clients, but changes had to be written to the directory by the PDC. Changes made to the directory on the PDC were eventually passed down to the BDCs through the process of replication.

One weakness of the single-master model is the existence of a single point of failure. Should the PDC fail, no writes could be made to the directory database; passwords could not be changed, accounts could not be added or deleted. A single PDC also limited the availability of write access to the database. Since the PDC was the only system that allowed writes, the number of changes and updates that could be made at one time were limited by the performance of that system.

Another limitation is when large NT 4 domains span several physical locations that are connected by slow network links. With a single PDC in a domain, changes that originated at remote sites have to cross these slow links to be made on the PDC. If BDCs are located at these sites, the changes made on the PDC have to be replicated back over the link, once for each BDC. These limitations needed to be overcome to improve scalability and acceptance of Windows in large enterprise environments.

With Windows 2000, Microsoft implemented a *multimaster directory model.* In a multimaster configuration, all domain controllers hold a copy of the directory database information for which they are responsible and are allowed to perform both reads and writes to their databases. Whereas this solves many of the scalability problems with previous versions of Windows NT, the process of replication, in which changes are propagated to all the other domain controllers in the enterprise, becomes more complex.

Store and Forward

Windows NT replication was further limited by the fact that the PDC was a single point for updates. Every BDC, regardless of its location, had to receive updates to the database directly from the PDC. In the case in which four NT 4 BDCs were located across a slow WAN link from the PDC, a single change on the PDC results in that change being replicated over the WAN link four times, once to each BDC. AD replication in Windows 2000 is transitive and uses a *store-and-forward model,* in which a domain controller that learns about changes from one domain controller is able to pass the learned changes to other domain controllers. In a properly configured Windows 2000 network, a change made on a domain controller on one side of a WAN link is replicated across the link to a single domain controller on the other side. That domain controller then distributes the changes to all the other domain controllers at that site. This results in much lower utilization of the WAN link for directory replication.

How Domain Controllers Track Changes

In order to provide the most efficient replication possible, domain controllers must keep track of each change made to Active Directory and differentiate between changes made by themselves as opposed to changes they have learned about through replication with other domain controllers.

Update Sequence Numbers

Each domain controller maintains a counter for each naming context that is used to assign a unique numeric identifier to every change made to the replica stored on that particular domain controller. These numbers are known as *update sequence numbers (USNs).* When a write occurs (either an originating write or one due to replication), the USN counter is incremented and the new value is attached to the objects or attributes that were changed as a result of the write. If the write operation fails for any reason, those changes are not made to the database, and that USN goes unused. It is important to realize that each domain controller maintains its own USN counters for changes written to its own replica of the directory. The USN counters for other domain controllers in the domain will very likely be different.

High-Watermark Vector

The *high-watermark vector* is used to determine whether changes are available to be replicated. Each domain controller maintains a high-watermark vector for each naming context. This is a two-column table (shown below) that contains the globally unique identifier (GUID) of each domain controller to which it has a Connection object in one column and the highest USN seen from those systems. During replication, the domain controller receiving updates passes the high-watermark vector to the domain controller providing updates as part of the pull request. By examining the high-watermark vector, the domain controller providing updates is able to determine which information the receiving domain controller already knows about. Any updates with a USN greater than the one in the high-watermark vector of the receiving computer are potential candidates for replication.

Server Globally Unique Identifier	Highest USN Seen from that Server
362BEB43-0433-4B2F-9CF7-A0981865AF49	6284
2324C2A1-B41C-4BED-A4AA-Cce3E27A145B	4976

There is, however, the possibility that both the receiving systems have already received some or all of the updated information through replication with another domain controller. If this is the case, some of the information planned for replication might not have to be replicated. The up-to-dateness vector is what further allows replication traffic to be reduced.

Up-to-Dateness Vector

In addition to the high-watermark vector, each domain controller also maintains an *up-to-dateness vector* for each naming context. Like the high-watermark vector, it is a two-column table (shown in following table) with the GUID of a domain controller on the left side and a USN on the right side. The difference is that the up-to-dateness vector tracks *originating updates*. Originating updates are those that are accepted from a user or program and written to the directory for the first time on a particular domain controller. The up-to-dateness vector for a naming context on a domain controller has an entry for every system that it knows has made an originating write. The USN entry is the highest USN seen for an originating write from that particular domain controller.

Server Globally Unique Identifier	Highest Originating Write Seen from Server
362BEB43-0433-4B2F-9CF7-A0981865AF49	6280
A2AA5A76-E8D5-4D8C-8868-02E445D460E9	3201
2324C2A1-B41C-4BED-A4AA-CCE3E27A145B	4976

As before, the up-to-dateness vector is passed to the sending computer when the receiving computer initiates pull replication. The sending computer uses this information to further reduce the list of updates sent to the receiving computer. If a change marked for replication has an originating USN of 2033 and the up-to-dateness vector shows that the destination computer has already seen a USN of 2033 from the computer that performed the originating write, the change does not have to be replicated.

Making Changes to Active Directory

When a domain controller writes changes to the Active Directory, those changes can be classified into one of four types: addition, change, move, or deletion. A domain controller further distinguishes these changes into *originating updates*, or *replicated updates*. Originating updates are those that are accepted from a user or program and written to the directory for the first time on a particular domain controller; replicated updates are those that originate on other domain controllers and are learned through the replication process.

When a new object is created on a domain controller by a user or process (other than by replication), it is marked as an originating update and is assigned a version number of one, as well as a time stamp and the GUID of the originating domain controller. There are two USN entries for the object and every attribute of that object, one to track when the object was initially created and another to track the last change to the object. Both are set to the same USN during object creation. Each subsequent change to the object increases the version number by one in order to determine the most current version of the object, and the USN entry that tracks changes is updated. Moving an object works in the same way as a change, because a move is essentially a change to the name attribute of the object.

Of the possible changes to AD, deletions are by far the most problematic in replication. In order to remove an object from AD and update the removal to other domain controllers, a special kind of change operation is used. Instead of actually deleting an object, a special attribute is set to mark the object as a tombstone or deleted object. Most of the nonessential attributes of the object are changed to null values to reduce the amount of space the object takes up in the directory. This Tombstone object can be replicated to all other domain controllers.

Tombstone objects continue to take up space in AD, and a method for removing them must be implemented to prevent AD from continuously increasing in size over time. After a certain age, tombstones are permanently deleted from AD through a process known as *garbage collection*. A garbage collection process runs by default every 12 hours on each individual domain controller, checks for tombstones that have expired, and deletes them. The garbage collection process is also responsible for removing unused log files and the defragmentation of the database.

By default, tombstones have a lifetime of 60 days. Tombstone lifetime can have some serious consequences for restoring a domain controller from backup. Backups of AD that are older than the tombstone lifetime can no longer be used for nonauthoritative restores. If such a backup restored an object, such as a user account, that had been deleted, and the Tombstone object no longer existed in the database, there would be no replication conflict and the deleted object would become fully restored. Tombstone lifetime must be set to a period that is longer than the time it takes for AD to replicate completely. If set to too short an interval, garbage collection could remove tombstones on domain controllers before they were replicated to other domain controllers, leaving AD in an inconsistent state.

Conflict Resolution

Since it is possible that a conflicting change to the same object could be made on two different domain controllers at the same time, the resulting replication forces the domain controller that receives the updates to resolve these conflicts. Each domain controller is able to follow a simple consistent set of rules to resolve these conflicts without having to query or otherwise discuss the conflict with any other domain controllers.

In order to implement this process, an originating write tags an object with a version number, a time stamp, and the GUID of the domain controller that originated the write. This information is replicated with the object. Each object has its own version number, which starts at one when it is created. These version numbers are replicated with the objects. Every time the object is changed or updated, the version number is increased by one, and the time stamp and originating domain controller GUID are refreshed. When conflicts occur, the object or attribute with the highest version number is written, and others are discarded. If two conflicting attributes have the same version number, the time stamps of the changes are compared and the most recent change is written. In the very unlikely event that the changes occurred at the exact same time, the GUID of the originating domain controller is used to break the tie.

The significance of the version number is that time alone does not dictate the changes that are made to the directory. If time was the primary deciding factor for resolving a conflict, differences in time between domain controllers could cause serious problems. For example, suppose a change is made and time stamped 1:59 AM. At 2:00 AM, daylight savings time ends and the clocks are all rolled back to 1:00 AM. Any changes made during the next hour would be immediately overwritten by the change time stamped at 1:59 AM. Imagine what could happen if the date was inadvertently set forward 10 years on a domain controller and objects were written. Once the correct time was restored, those objects with origination dates in the future would override any new updates or deletions! By making the version number the primary decision maker, you avoid a dependence on time synchronization.

In order to delete a container from AD, it cannot contain any Child object; but consider what happens when an empty OU that has replicated to multiple domain controllers is part of a conflicting change. On one domain controller, an administrator adds a user to the empty OU. On another domain controller, an administrator deletes the empty OU. When changes replicate, the Tombstone object for the OU replicates and the new User object remains without a parent container. A special container called "lost and found" exists in Active Directory for this reason, and the orphaned User object is relocated there.

Network and Knowledge Consistency Checker Topology

In most cases, Windows 2000 handles replication automatically. The *Knowledge Consistency Checker (KCC)* generates the virtual replication topology within a site. The KCC runs on all domain controllers every 15 minutes by default. It examines the information in the Active Directory configuration container to generate the replication topology. To provide a level of fault tolerance to the replication process within a site, a bidirectional ring configuration is used. This configuration allows for multiple replication paths to any domain controller in the ring, and if a domain controller fails, replication can still occur to all the other domain controllers in the ring. In fact, the KCC maintains the ring such that any domain controller is no more than three hops from any other domain controller in the domain.

The KCC on each domain controller uses the unique GUIDs of all the domain controllers installed at a site to sort them into an ordered list and virtually connects the first domain controller in the list to the last domain controller in the list to create the bidirectional ring. Each domain controller determines the replication topology independently, and since they are operating under the same rules with the same data, all can come to the same conclusion without any network traffic being sent. A separate bidirectional ring is created for each naming context in the forest. A forest with a single domain has three naming contexts and thus three replication rings, one for the domain naming context, one for the configuration naming context, and a third for the schema naming context. Each additional domain in the forest introduces a new naming context and a new replication path. Since both the schema naming context and the configuration naming context replicate to all domain controllers in a forest, they share the same replication path, regardless of the number of domains in the forest.

After creating the virtual topology for AD replication, the KCC creates *Connection objects*. A Connection object is a unidirectional path along which replication can take place. Connection objects are created between domain controllers that the KCC has determined to be neighbors in the virtual topology. The Connection objects on a domain controller point to other domain controllers that can be the source for replicated data. Because Connection objects are one-way, a domain controller can use a Connection object to obtain information from another domain controller. Each domain controller creates connection objects to its neighbors in order to receive updates from other domain controllers. The KCC automatically regenerates the site topology and creates and removes Connection objects if domain controllers fail or if they are added or removed from the forest. A Connection object is not tied to a particular naming context and can be used by multiple naming contexts.

Administrators can create their own Connection objects in addition to the ones created by the KCC. Connection objects are owned by the user or process that creates them. The KCC does not manipulate any Connection objects that it did not create. If an administrator modifies a KCC-created Connection object, that object is no longer owned by the KCC and it no longer maintains it. Figure 11-2 shows an example of using the Active Directory Sites and Services snap-in to view the KCC-generated Connection objects.

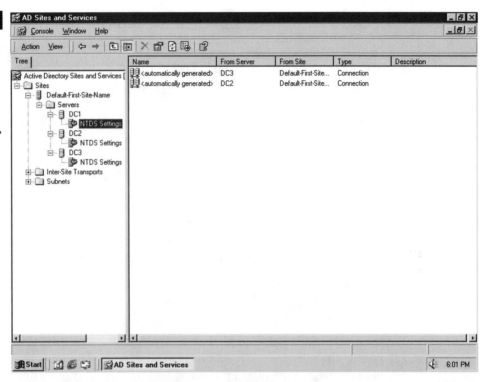

FIGURE 11-2

In this site with three domain controllers, DC1 has a Connection object to each of its ring neighbors, DC2 and DC3

SCENARIO & SOLUTION

Which Windows 2000 process generates the replication topology?	The Knowledge Consistency Checker (KCC) generates the replication topology.
What best describes the virtual replication topology within a site?	A bidirectional ring.
Can an administrator manually create or change the replication topology?	Yes. An administrator can create new Connection objects or modify those created by the KCC.
When conflicting changes are made to the directory on different domain controllers, where are those changes resolved?	Each domain controller individually resolves conflicts obtained through replication.
When resolving conflicting updates, what information does a domain controller use to determine which change to keep?	Domain controllers compare the version number, the time stamp, and the GUID of the domain controller that performed an originating write.

Overview of Sites, Subnets, Links, and Replication

A *Site object* in Active Directory represents a group of computers networked together with a reliable high-speed network. Logically, a site is a Container object with attributes that is stored in the configuration container. Most sites contain one or more domain controllers, but that is not a requirement for a site. Sites are required to use TCP/IP as their network protocol, and a site can contain multiple TCP/IP subnets. Subnets cannot span sites, however. When you define multiple sites in AD, there must be some type of network link to interconnect the sites so that replication traffic can be passed. These network links are represented in AD by a site link or site link bridge object.

exam
ⓦatch

Replication within a site is called **intrasite replication,** *and replication between sites is called* **intersite replication.** *If you have trouble remembering which is which, it might help to think of the terms intranet and Internet, which describe internal and external networks, respectively.*

In order to utilize network bandwidth efficiently, Windows 2000 differentiates between two types of connectivity, within a site (or intrasite) and between sites (or intersite). When you install the first domain controller in a forest, an initial default site is created. In addition, a Server object is created for your domain controller and placed in that site. This Server object should not be confused with the Computer object created in the Domain Controllers OU. The Computer object is part of the domain naming context. The Server object is created within a site, which is part of the configuration naming context for the forest. The site is called Default-First-Site-Name, which can, of course, be renamed. If you don't plan on configuring any additional sites, Windows 2000 assumes that you have good network connectivity and will configure and perform intrasite replication between all domain controllers in the forest, regardless of where they are physically located.

Sites are configured by using the Active Directory Sites and Services snap-in. Figure 11-3 shows the configuration for a single domain forest within a single site. Domain controllers DC1 and DC2 have Server objects that have been created in the site named Default-First-Site-Name.

Creating New Sites

When a site is created, it must have a *site link*. A site link defines a connection to another site or sites. A site link is a logical representation of the physical network that connects sites. A site link named DEFAULTIPSITELINK is created along with the default site when a forest is created, as shown in Figure 11-4. Site links have two important attributes that can be used to manipulate replication: cost and replication schedule.

FROM THE CLASSROOM

Physical and Logical Sites

There is a big difference between physical sites and the logical sites that are configured in Active Directory. Some physical network designs map to the logical idea of sites very well. A company with an office in New York and an office in Los Angeles that has a T1 line connecting the 100MBps Ethernet network at each office is a textbook example of where you could create two sites and a site link in Active Directory. On the other hand, if the company has a lot of available bandwidth on its T1 connection, makes few changes to AD, and

needs low latency for those updates, using a single logical site is a reasonable option. Alternatively, an office that shares two floors of a building could have a 155MBps ATM link between the floors, but, due to high utilization of the bandwidth, large numbers of changes to AD that can easily wait a day to propagate to the other floor, and a need to schedule replication between floors after business hours, each floor of its office is configured as a logical site to meet employees' requirements.

—*Brian K. Doré, MCSE, MCT*

FIGURE 11-3

The Active Directory Sites and Services Snap-in. Notice the Connection object for DC1 points to DC2 as a source for directory updates.

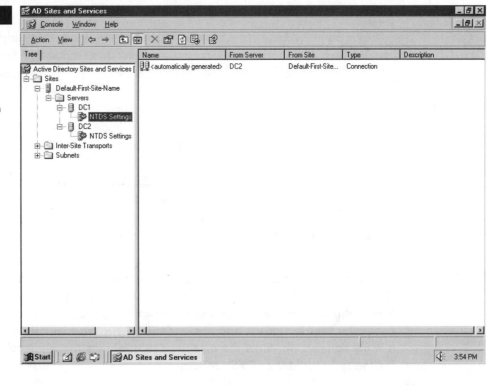

FIGURE 11-4

The Default IP
site link

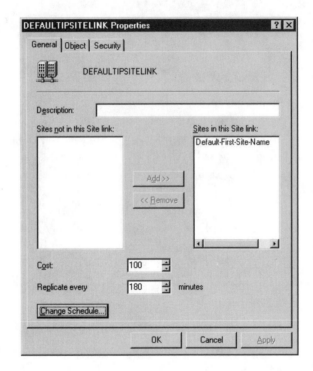

Cost is expressed by assigning a value to a site link. If there are multiple paths between sites, the intersite topology generator configures replication to occur on the path with the lowest cost. In general, slow links are configured with a higher cost than fast links.

The times that replication is allowed to occur over a link are determined by the replication schedule, which is set on the site link Properties sheet. Clicking the Change Schedule button opens the window shown in Figure 11-5. By default, links are available seven days a week, 24 hours a day.

You can also create subnet objects within the Active Directory Sites and Services snap-in and assign these subnets to sites. Multiple subnets can be assigned to the same site. Assigning subnets to sites is important for placing new domain controllers in the correct site when they are first installed as well as for clients to locate resources in their own sites.

exam
ⓦatch

Sites are used for more than merely configuring replication. Windows 2000 clients requesting services such as logon validation or password changes from a domain controller use site information to locate the domain controller that is nearest and prevent this traffic from having to cross a WAN connection. Sites are also used to minimize file replication traffic for the sysvol folder or DFS replicas.

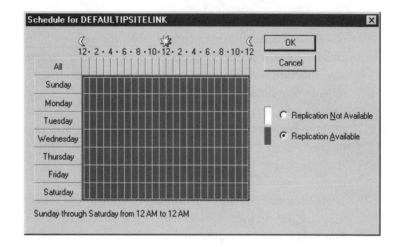

FIGURE 11-5

Site link schedules can be set to allow replication only at certain times and only on certain days of the week.

Site link bridges form the basis for very advanced network topologies. These objects can be used to describe a connection between site links. Site links are transitive by default, but this state can be turned off via the site link Properties sheet. Once transitivity is disabled, site link bridges can be used to create a replication through multiple site links. Like site links, site link bridges have cost and replication schedule attributes. (For more information on sites, site links, and site link bridges, see Chapter 2, "Installing the Components of Active Directory," in this book.)

Managing Intrasite Replication

Network connectivity within a site is assumed to be fast and reliable. This high bandwidth allows for frequent replication, which results in low latency within the site. When replicating within a site, domain controllers do not use compression to save bandwidth.

Replication within sites occurs when a domain controller performs a write to Active Directory and needs to inform other domain controllers that changes have been made. The domain controller waits for five minutes before announcing that updates are available. The five-minute wait allows time for additional changes to be made to the database before replication starts so that a group of changes made close together can be replicated together in one efficient cycle. When the replication partners receive notification of an update, they initiate the pull replication sequence by sending their high-watermark and up-to-dateness vectors, the maximum number of updates they will accept at a time, and other information. After determining the data that needs to be replicated, the source domain controller sends the data.

For domain controllers within a site, the KCC attempts to create Connection objects so that replication needs to travel through no more than three domain controllers to replicate to all points in the network. When a small number of domain controllers are present in a site, simply creating Connection objects to neighboring domain controllers in the ring is sufficient, but when more than seven domain controllers are present, the KCC creates additional Connection objects in order to keep the replication path between any two domain controllers to three hops or fewer. Since the default replication period within a site is 5 minutes, this means that any change made on a domain controller should fully replicate to all other domain controllers in a site within 15 minutes.

As a backup procedure, a domain controller also attempts to replicate on schedule. By default, this replication is scheduled to occur every hour. This system helps reduce replication latency in conditions where update notifications were missed due to network or system outages.

Urgent Replication

Some changes to Active Directory, such as account lockouts, are critical in nature and must be replicated to all domain controllers immediately. Otherwise, if an administrator locked a user's account, it could take up to 15 minutes for that change to replicate to all domain controllers through normal replication and could result in a major security problem. Urgent replication immediately replicates an account lockout to the PDC emulator and then to all domain controllers within a site. By default, site links do not pass change notifications but can be configured to do so. If site links are configured to allow change notifications to cross them, the changes propagate to domain controllers within those connected sites as well. Sites connected by links that do not support change notification receive the lockout through normal intersite replication.

Managing Intersite Replication

When you are replicating data between sites, it is important to use as little bandwidth as possible. Replication between sites is heavily compressed before it is sent and must be uncompressed at the destination. The trade-off for this reduction in bandwidth utilization is higher CPU utilization on both domain controllers while the compression or decompression is taking place.

Replication Protocols

When Active Directory information is replicating between sites, the RPC protocol used for intrasite replication is normally used. Windows 2000 also provides the ability to use SMTP to transfer replication information in certain circumstances. SMTP replication requires an SMTP service configured such as the one included with IIS 5.0 on the Windows 2000 Server CD. It also requires a Certificate Authority configured to verify the authenticity of SMTP replication messages. SMTP requires more network bandwidth than RPC replication because the protocol uses message headers that cannot be compressed. SMTP is valuable in that it supports very slow connections, intermittent connections, and intrasite connections that might not be based on the IP protocol but can pass SMTP messages.

on the
job

For optimal replication performance, use RPC as your replication protocol whenever possible.

Unlike replication within a site, update notifications are not sent across intersite links. Instead, replication between sites is scheduled to occur on a periodic basis. These schedules can further be controlled by limiting replication between sites to occur only during certain times of the day. This method allows an administrator to schedule updates between sites to occur during periods of low network utilization. For redundancy, it is common that sites are connected by multiple paths. A cost factor can be applied to these links individually to set a preferential path for replication. By default, intersite replication occurs every 15 minutes, 24 hours a day.

The replication topology between sites is the responsibility of the *Intersite Topology Generator.* Each site has one domain controller that is responsible for examining the WAN connections between sites and determining the replication path.

A *bridgehead server* is the domain controller at a site that is responsible for replication with the bridgehead servers at other sites. The Intersite Topology Generator designates a single bridgehead server in a site automatically. A single domain controller can be the bridgehead server for multiple protocols, or a separate bridgehead server can be chosen for each protocol. Should the automatically determined bridgehead server fail, the Intersite Topology Generator automatically recovers and chooses another one.

Administrators have the ability to *designate preferred bridgehead servers,* as shown in Figure 11-6. This allows the administrator to choose a domain controller that has the extra capacity to handle intersite traffic. Since all intersite traffic must be

FIGURE 11-6

The Server
Properties sheet
for the domain
controller DC2
from the Active
Directory Sites
and Services
snap-in

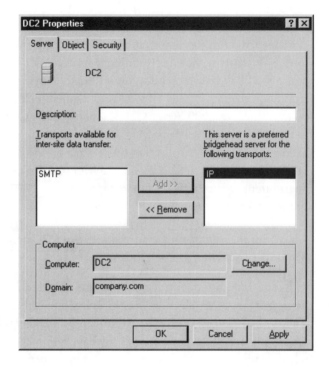

compressed before it is sent and uncompressed when it is received, bridgehead
servers experience higher CPU utilization due to replication. Multiple domain
controllers can be designated as preferred bridgeheads, but only one is used at any
given time. If a preferred bridgehead server fails, another preferred bridgehead server
is selected to replace it. If a preferred bridgehead server fails and no other preferred
bridgehead servers are available in that site, intersite replication ceases.

exam
ⓦ*atch*

***Bridgehead servers are selected and maintained automatically by default.
An administrator can intervene in this process by designating one or
more preferred bridgehead servers. Once a preferred bridgehead server
is designated, only domain controllers that are marked as preferred
bridgehead servers can become bridgehead servers.***

Replication with NT 4.0 Backup Domain Controllers

There are some operations critical to domain operation that, when implemented as
multimaster operations, could cause complicated conflicts that could not be easily
resolved. For these special cases, Microsoft has resorted to using single-master
operations. Domain controllers devoted to these operations are known as *operations
masters*. Operations masters are not covered in depth here, but a specific operations
master, the PDC emulator, is of particular interest to replication.

Windows 2000 domains can operate in two modes: Mixed Mode or Native Mode. The primary purpose of Mixed Mode is to provide backward compatibility with Windows NT 4.0 BDCs. Domains in Mixed Mode cannot use features of Windows 2000 such as nested groups that could not be replicated to an NT 4.0 BDC. Conversion to Native Mode is a one-way operation because, once a domain is operating in Native Mode, it is a difficult operation to remove all objects from the domain that are not backward compatible with NT 4.0.

Windows NT 4 BDCs are designed to exist in a single-master domain and therefore look for a PDC to provide directory updates. NT 4 BDCs can replicate with a single Windows 2000 domain controller. The PDC emulator is the domain controller responsible for replication. All Windows NT 4.0 BDCs in a domain receive their updates from the PDC emulator, regardless of which site they are in.

The NT 4.0 SAM database is stored in the registry, and due to maximum size limitations on the NT registry, the SAM database is limited to approximately 40,000 objects. It is important that domains operating in Mixed Mode and replicating to NT 4 BDCs keep the number of Domain objects below this number to avoid replication problems.

Password Changes

Password changes within a Windows 2000 domain are immediately replicated to the PDC emulator for the domain, regardless of which domain controller originated the change and regardless of the site in which the PDC emulator is located. Other domain controllers in the domain obtain these changes through normal replication.

The reason for replicating password changes to the PDC emulator immediately is that pre-Windows 2000 clients that are not able to access the Active Directory Services always contact the PDC emulator for authentication. When a domain controller gets a logon request from a Windows 2000 or other Active Directory-aware client, it first attempts to validate that client using the data stored in its replica of the domain information. If the logon fails, the domain controller contacts the PDC emulator for the domain to make another attempt to validate the logon in case the password was recently changed and the change had not yet replicated.

Domain Controller and Global Catalog Placement

The decision of whether or not to place a domain controller or global catalog server at a site is determined by a number of issues, including the speed and reliability of network connectivity to that site, the number of clients that access the directory at that location, and the size and number of changes made to the enterprise directory as a whole. A primary design goal is to choose the approach that minimizes the amount of directory traffic sent over the WAN during times when users are working, freeing that bandwidth for use by applications. Since Active Directory replication traffic can be scheduled to occur outside normal working hours, whereas logons and queries are interactive, it is not a simple situation of choosing which approach uses the least amount of bandwidth.

In most cases, the need for low response times for client logons and queries means that you should have at least one global catalog server in a site. However, it is better not to place a domain controller or global catalog server at a small site, operating 24 hours a day, seven days a week, that is part of a large enterprise forest. Suppose this site had 5 or 10 users who made minimal accesses to the directory, perhaps a logon and a couple of queries per user per day, but used the WAN link heavily for application traffic. Furthermore, at other sites the enterprise directory for this large organization is very dynamic, with thousands of additions and changes made to the directory daily. In this situation, the replication traffic that occurs to a domain controller or global catalog server located at the small, remote site is significantly higher than the bandwidth required by the client logon, query operations, and group policy application traffic.

on the
job

When deploying a group policy, it is important to realize that the links to Group Policy are stored in Active Directory and replicate using Active Directory replication. However, the group policy templates themselves are stored in sysvol and replicate separately using file replication. The group policy does not take effect until both pieces of the group policy have replicated.

Troubleshooting Active Directory Replication

When Active Directory replication fails to occur, inconsistencies in the database usually manifest themselves as inconsistent behavior. Different domain controllers in a domain have different information, and depending on the domain controller used for a particular operation, the results can vary. Replication is dependent on reliable network connectivity, which should be the first thing checked in the case of Active Directory replication failures. Network connectivity and TCP/IP configuration can be verified using the PING command-line utility between the domain controllers that are not replicating data. After verifying connectivity, use the Active Directory Sites and Services tool on each domain controller and verify that each has proper site configuration and that Connection objects exist between the domain controllers.

Several tools are included in the Support Tools folder of the Windows 2000 Server CD-ROM that can further assist in troubleshooting replication issues such as REPLMON, which is described in an upcoming section.

Event Logs

Replication events are logged into the Directory Services log and can be monitored using Event Viewer. An administrator should monitor these logs regularly to spot potential problems with replication or other aspects of Active Directory.

Many normal informational messages are logged regularly. For example, event IDs 700 and 701 are logged every 12 hours when the garbage collection process defragments the directory. Some other common events and their descriptions are:

- **1009**   The KCC is updating the replication topology for this domain controller.
- **1013**   The KCC has completed updating the replication topology.
- **1265**   Replication with a specific replication partner failed.
- **1404**   The server has assumed the role of the intersite topology generator.

Monitoring Replication

Active Directory replication can be monitored through the use of the Windows 2000 Performance Monitor which includes counters for replication traffic under the NTDS object. Counters are available to measure total bytes of inbound and outbound replication traffic, the number of bytes replicated per second, and counters that differentiate between compressed (intersite) and uncompressed (intrasite) replication traffic. Performance Monitor can be a useful tool in spotting problems, but it is very important to monitor normal operation of the system to establish a baseline value. In other words you must know what normal performance is for your system in order to determine if activity captured by Performance Monitor is indicative of a problem. AD is periodic and replication performance will vary greatly depending on performance of the domain controller, the network, and the number of changes made to the directory.

Windows 2000 Server also includes an Active Directory replication monitor tool in the support tools folder on the CD that can be used to monitor and verify the replication process. Exercise 11-1 will introduce this tool and give an overview of the capabilities.

EXERCISE 11-1

Using the Active Directory Replication Monitor

The Active Directory Replication Monitor is a tool provided on the Windows 2000 Server CD in the Support Tools folder. It provides an interface to monitor the replication processes on individual or multiple domain controllers. In order to complete this exercise, you must have at least two domain controllers in the same domain and have installed on one of them the Replication Monitor from the Support Tools folder on the Windows 2000 Server CD.

1. Log into one domain controller as Administrator.

2. Start the Active Directory Replication Monitor. Click Start | Programs | Windows 2000 Support Tools | Tools | Active Directory Replication Monitor.

3. In the left pane, right-click Monitored Servers, and choose Add Monitored Server from the context-sensitive menu. The Add Monitored Server Wizard starts.

4. Choose "Add server explicitly by name," and click Next.

5. Type the name of the server you are logged on to as the server you want to monitor. Click Finish. You can add additional servers as shown in the following illustration.

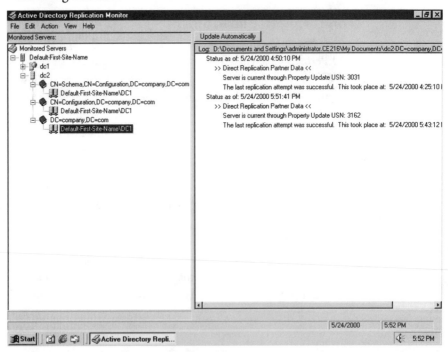

6. Your server should now be added to the left pane. If the pane is not already expanded, click the plus sign (+) next to your server to expose the naming contexts for which it is responsible.

7. Right-click the Server object and choose Check Replication Topology from the context-sensitive menu, as shown in the following illustration. This choice forces the KCC to run. Click OK in the resulting dialog box.

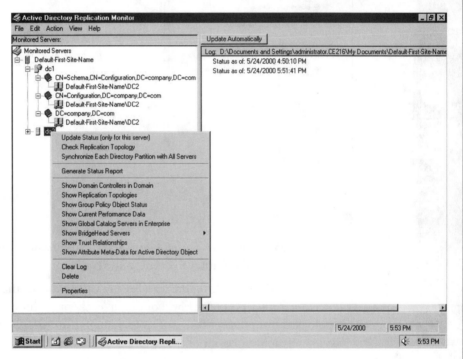

8. Expand the schema naming context. This step exposes the Connection objects, as shown in the next illustration.

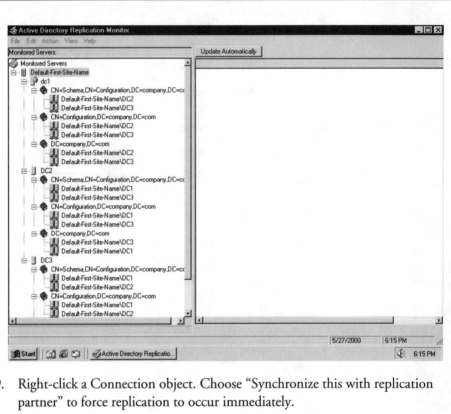

9. Right-click a Connection object. Choose "Synchronize this with replication partner" to force replication to occur immediately.

10. Spend some time exploring the features and capabilities of the Active Directory Replication Monitor. For example, choose "Show replication topologies" from the context-sensitive menu of a Domain Controller object to view a graphical layout of the replication topology.

11. Close the Active Directory Replication Monitor and log off.

SCENARIO & SOLUTION

What tool would you use to change the replication schedule between sites?	The AD Sites and Services snap-in.
How is replication bandwidth between sites minimized?	Intrasite replication is compressed to save bandwidth, and replication traffic can be scheduled to occur at off-peak times.
What is a tombstone?	A tombstone is a deleted object in the Active Directory. Tombstones must replicate to other domain controllers for the object to be fully deleted. Tombstone objects are eventually removed from Active Directory through the process of garbage collection.
In a meeting, your boss instructs your team to change information about a user. Both you and your co-worker change this information at the same time on different domain controllers. Which change will take effect?	The change with the highest version number will take effect. If both users started with a fully replicated directory and made only a single change, the two changes will likely have the same version number and the change with the later time stamp will take effect. If by some chance the time stamps are exactly the same, the change made on the domain controller with the higher GUID will take effect.

CERTIFICATION OBJECTIVE 11.02

Managing and Troubleshooting Domain Name Service Replication

Domain Name Service (DNS) is an Internet Directory Service that allows mapping of IP addresses to names. DNS is designed as a distributed system and is based on a single-master model. DNS is an Internet standard protocol that is part of the TCP/IP protocol stack and is defined by RFCs. Like most Internet protocols, it has been changed and extended over time to provide new functionality. Windows 2000 DNS provides an implementation of DNS that is fully interoperable with any Internet-standard compliant name servers yet provides new functionalities that have been submitted as draft standards.

exam
🕲 *atch*

A common Unix-based DNS server is BIND, which is an acronym for Berkeley Internet Naming Daemon.

FIGURE 11-7

The DNS snap-in can be used to administer DNS servers

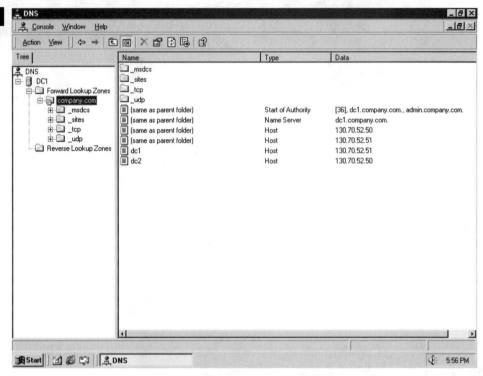

The basic unit of DNS storage is a *zone*. A DNS zone contains resource records for the zone. DNS zones can be either forward lookup zones or reverse lookup zones. A *forward lookup zone* is used to resolve a name to an IP address; a *reverse lookup zone* is used to retrieve a DNS name from an IP address. Windows 2000 DNS zones are configured and managed through the DNS snap-in shown in Figure 11-7.

Windows 2000 DNS Features

Traditional DNS servers use a single-master configuration in which one DNS server is designated as the *primary* DNS server for a zone. The primary DNS server is the only system that can add or change resource records in the zone. All changes and updates are made on the primary DNS server. For redundancy and load balancing, DNS provides for *secondary* DNS servers that maintain a read-only copy of the zone files and can answer queries against the database. A DNS server that provides zone information to a secondary DNS server is called a *master DNS server*. Either a primary or secondary DNS server can be a master DNS server and provide records to a secondary server. The process of replicating DNS data from a master name server to a secondary name server is called a *zone transfer*.

A single DNS server can host multiple zone files. The DNS server can serve as the primary or secondary server for any combination of zones. Within the DNS snap-in, Standard Primary, Standard Secondary, or Active Directory-integrated zones can be created using the New Zone Wizard, which is shown in Figure 11-8.

Windows 2000 DNS is fully interoperable with the "traditional" DNS server and can store the DNS zone information in standard files and participate in zone transfers. Windows 2000 also allows Active Directory-integrated zones, which store the DNS records in Active Directory. There are several benefits to this method, including support for secure dynamic updates, aging, and scavenging of the zone records. By integrating the DNS zone into Active Directory, DNS is able to take advantage of the multimaster nature of AD and dynamic updates to DNS can be made by any domain controller. DNS records stored in an AD-integrated zone replicate automatically to all domain controllers within the domain according to existing replication rules and schedules.

Replication of Non-Active Directory-Integrated Zones

Early DNS standards specified that a zone transfer from a master to a secondary DNS server would be done by moving the entire zone database. These full zone transfers were initially limited to transmitting one record per packet, but later the system was improved to allow multiple records per packet. As zone files got larger, the inefficiency

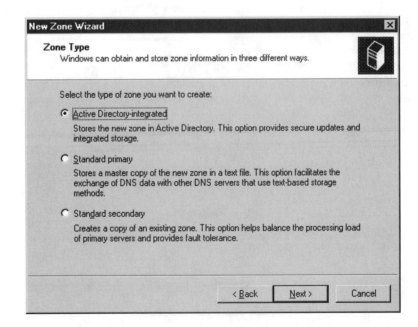

FIGURE 11-8

New DNS zones can be created with the New Zone Wizard

of transferring the entire zone was realized, and improvements defined in RFC 1995 defined an *incremental zone transfer,* in which only the changed records are transferred during a zone transfer. In order to implement incremental zone transfers, both the master and the secondary server must support them.

A master DNS server uses a *serial number,* as shown in Figure 11-9, which is part of the Start of Authority (SOA) record to track changes to the DNS database. When a zone transfer is initiated, the secondary DNS server sends a copy of the SOA record for the copy of the database it is using. By comparing serial numbers, the master DNS server can determine whether there are updates available. If both the master and secondary servers both support incremental zone transfers, the master can also determine which changes need to be replicated to the secondary.

When a secondary zone is created, a reference is provided to the master name server that is providing the zone records, and a refresh interval indicates how often the secondary server should request a zone transfer. Secondary name servers first request a zone transfer when the DNS server is started, and then again regularly at each refresh interval. By default, the refresh interval is set to 15 minutes. Master name servers can be configured to provide zone transfers to any secondary server or only specific secondary servers, as shown in Figure 11-10.

FIGURE 11-9	

The DNS serial number and refresh interval are part of the SOA record in a DNS zone

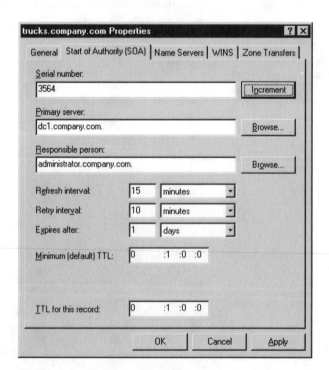

FIGURE 11-10

The Properties
sheet for an
Active Directory-
integrated zone
can be configured
to provide zone
transfers to any
or selected
secondary DNS
servers

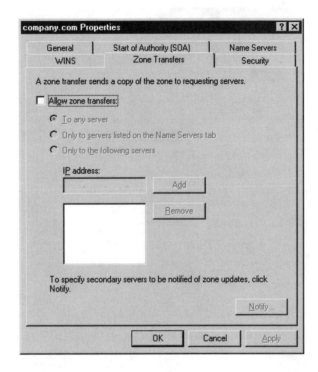

A small refresh interval provides for quick updates from the master zones to the secondary zones, but at the expense of network traffic. Longer refresh intervals can be used to reduce the replication, but changes take longer to propagate. RFC 1996 defined a method of update notification in which a master name server could inform a secondary server that changes were available. The notification provided another situation in which the secondary server initiates a zone transfer.

Replication of Active Directory-Integrated Zones

DNS zones that are stored in Active Directory replicate to all domain controllers in a domain through normal Active Directory replication. An Active Directory-integrated zone can be used to provide DNS records to a standard secondary name server through full or incremental zone transfers. Figure 11-11 shows the objects in an Active Directory-integrated zone viewed with the Active Directory Users and Computers snap-in. It is important to notice that Active Directory-integrated DNS zone information is stored in the domain naming context. Active Directory-integrated zone information is replicated only within a domain using Active Directory replication.

FIGURE 11-11

Viewing
AD-integrated
zones using
Active Directory
Users and
Computers.

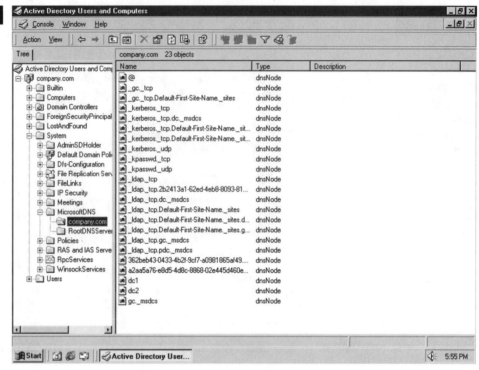

on the job *Windows 2000 DNS supports notification of secondary servers when DNS records are changed. You can enable this feature on the Transfer tab of the Zone Properties sheet. This feature can reduce latency in DNS update replication and can be used to reduce network traffic by allowing the refresh interval to be raised.*

SCENARIO & SOLUTION

What types of DNS zones does Windows 2000 DNS support?	Primary, secondary, and Active Directory integrated.
What is the term that describes a server that provides information to a secondary?	Master name server.
Which types of DNS zones can a secondary name server receive data from through a zone transfer?	A secondary DNS server can receive data from a Standard Primary, Standard Secondary, or Active Directory Integrated zones through a zone transfer.

Troubleshooting Domain Name Service Replication

Replication failure in an Active Directory-integrated zone can be identified by the same symptoms as Active Directory replication failure, because the process used to replicate them is the same. Troubleshooting and resolution of replication failures with Active Directory-integrated zones is therefore also the same as general Active Directory replication troubleshooting, described in the previous section. With standard DNS zones, the failure of a primary DNS server might not be noticed until the expiration interval defined in the SOA records has passed. At this point, secondary DNS servers no longer maintain their DNS records, and clients configured to use those DNS servers fail to resolve queries.

DNS replication problems can occur for a variety of reasons. Failure of network connectivity between the master and secondary servers is a common source of replication problems. When troubleshooting DNS replication problems, begin by ensuring TCP/IP connectivity between the master and secondary zone servers using the PING or TRACERT TCP/IP utilities. Ensure that TCP/IP connectivity exists between the master and secondary servers. If connectivity is found to be satisfactory, you should check the DNS server logs for errors using the Event Viewer.

Verify the configuration of both the primary server and secondary server. On the secondary, ensure that the IP address of the master name server is correct. On the master name server, ensure that zone transfers are allowed and that the secondary is allowed to retrieve the zone data by checking the zone transfers tab on the zone Properties sheet. If the master name server is also a secondary name server for the zone, verify that replication is occurring from the primary name server. When using secondary servers that are not running Windows 2000, verify that they are able to accept the records you are providing. Some BIND servers, for example, might not accept WINS resource records or Unicode DNS names.

Finally, verify that the DNS server service is operating properly on both the master and secondary servers. You can use the NSLOOKUP command from the Windows 2000 command prompt to perform DNS queries against both the master and secondary servers to see if they are responding and to verify the records have replicated properly. If the service does not respond, attempt to stop and restart the service. In cases in which the DNS service fails regularly, you can configure it to automatically restart using the Recovery tab on the DNS Properties sheet accessed through the Services snap-in.

CertCam 11-2

Creating Primary and Secondary DNS Zones

In this exercise, you create primary and secondary DNS zones and force a zone transfer to occur. You need two networked Windows 2000 servers (we refer to them as Server1 and Server2, but their computer names are not important for this exercise) running the Windows 2000 DNS. You should complete these exercises while logged in as an Administrator.

First, create the primary zone on Server1.

1. Start the DNS Administrative Console from the Administrative tools menu.

2. Expand Server1 in the left pane (click the + next to it). Select Forward Lookup Zones in the left pane. Right-click Forward Lookup Zones, and choose New Zone from the context-sensitive menu.

3. The New Zone Wizard appears. After reading the introductory information, click Next.

4. On the Zone Type Panel, select the radio button used to create a Standard Primary Zone. (This screen was shown in Figure 11-8.) Click Next.

5. Name your new zone **school.edu** and click Next.

6. Accept the default name for the zone file (school.edu.dns) and click Next.

7. Click Finish. You have successfully created a new zone file for SCHOOL.EDU. Now you add a new host record and configure the refresh interval for your new zone.

8. In the left pane, expand the list of forward lookup zones. Right-click SCHOOL.EDU in the left pane and choose New Host from the context-sensitive menu.

9. In the new host dialog box, enter **www** for the host name and **10.0.0.1** as the IP address for the new record. Choose not to create a reverse lookup record by making sure the check box is not marked. Use the default TTL. Click the Add Host button to create the record.

10. Click OK in the confirmation dialog box. Click Done to close the New Host dialog box.

11. Right-click the SCHOOL.DNS zone in the left pane. Choose Properties from the context-sensitive menu.

12. Choose the Start of Authority (SOA) tab. Change the refresh interval to 1 minute. Click OK.

Next we configure a secondary zone on Server2.

1. On Server2, start the DNS Administrative Console from the Administrative Tools menu.

2. Expand Server2. Select Forward Lookup Zones. Right-click Forward Lookup Zones, and choose New Zone from the context-sensitive menu.

3. The New Zone Wizard appears. Click Next.

4. On the Zone Type Panel, choose to create a Standard Secondary Zone. Click Next.

5. Enter **school.edu** as the name for your secondary zone, and click Next.

6. Add the IP address of your first DNS server as the IP address of the master name server, and click Next.

7. Click Finish to create your secondary zone.

8. Expand the Forward Lookup Zones entry in the left pane.

9. Right-click on the SCHOOL.EDU secondary zone, and choose Transfer from Master to initiate a zone transfer.

10. Select the SCHOOL.EDU zone in the left pane, and verify that the host record for www has transferred from the master to the secondary server by looking for it in the results (right) pane.

11. The exercise is now complete. You may want to experiment further by making changes to the primary zone and waiting for them to replicate to the secondary. Because the refresh interval was set to 1 minute in Step 12, your changes should be available on the secondary zone in about a minute without forcing a manual zone transfer.

CERTIFICATION SUMMARY

Multimaster replication in Active Directory provides the foundation for large-scale deployment of Windows 2000 domains. With no single point of failure as in single-master domain models, the Active Directory forest is more reliable. The ability to allow writes to any domain controller increases performance, especially for enterprises that span multiple sites.

Whereas traditional DNS is single master and uses inefficient zone transfers, Windows 2000 DNS supports storing DNS records in Active Directory, which provides for multimaster update capability, efficient replication for DNS records through the Active Directory replication process, secure dynamic updates, and support for aging and scavenging of DNS records.

TWO-MINUTE DRILL

Here are some of the key points from each certification objective in Chapter 11.

Managing and Troubleshooting Active Directory Replication

❑ Use the Active Directory Sites and Services Snap-in to create sites, site links (including site link bridges), and subnets.

❑ The KCC runs on each domain controller and generates the replication topology automatically.

❑ Replication traffic within a site uses the RPC protocol and is uncompressed.

❑ Replication between sites is compressed. RPC is used for all replication traffic within a domain naming context. In some cases, SMTP can be used to replicate the global catalog, schema, or configuration naming contexts.

❑ A high-watermark vector and the up-to-dateness vector are maintained individually by each domain controller to identify updates they have received through replication.

❑ A bridgehead server is a domain controller in a site that can replicate with other sites.

❑ Replication to NT 4.0 BDCs is possible only in Mixed Mode.

Managing and Troubleshooting Domain Name Service Replication

❑ A zone transfer is the process of replicating a standard DNS zone.

❑ A single Windows 2000 DNS server can host multiple zones, which can be any combination of primary, secondary, or Active Directory-integrated zones.

❑ Active Directory-integrated zones can exist only on Windows 2000 domain controllers.

❑ Standard DNS zones are single master, whereby only one DNS server has write access to the zone file.

❑ A secondary DNS server holds a read-only copy of the DNS zone file and can be used to resolve queries and provide a copy of the zone file to other secondary servers.

❏ A master name server is a replication source for a zone. Either a primary or a secondary server can be a master DNS server.

❏ Windows 2000 Active Directory-integrated zones take advantage of multimaster updates and replication.

❏ DNS information stored in Active Directory replicates to all domain controllers in the domain, regardless of whether they are running the DNS server or not.

❏ Active Directory-integrated zones are stored in the domain naming context and replicate only to domain controllers in that domain.

SELF TEST

The following questions will help you measure your understanding of the material presented in this chapter. Read all of the choices carefully because there might be more than one correct answer. Choose all correct answers for each question.

Managing and Troubleshooting Active Directory Replication

1. What is the primary advantage of a multimaster domain model over a single-master domain model?

   A. Any domain controller in the domain can validate logons.

   B. Any domain controller can write changes to the directory.

   C. Data can be stored much more efficiently in multimaster configurations.

   D. Single-master models use pull replication, whereas multimaster models use push replication.

2. Which of the following replication traffic is compressed? Choose all that apply.

   A. RPC within a site

   B. RPC between sites

   C. SMTP within a site

   D. SMTP between sites

3. In a forest with two domains (A and B) at a single site, which of the following replicates with a domain controller in Domain A? Choose all that apply.

   A. A global catalog server in Domain A

   B. A domain controller in Domain B

   C. A stand-alone server in Domain A

   D. A stand-alone server in Domain B

4. How does the KCC on a domain controller determine the path replication takes within a site?

   A. The KCC service on all domain controllers elects a bridgehead server that decides on the topology and replicates it to all other domain controllers.

   B. The KCC orders domain controllers alphabetically by name.

   C. Each KCC independently determines the replication path using the site information in the configuration container of Active Directory.

   D. The KCC generates Connection objects to those servers that are in physical proximity to each other.

5. After making originating write operations on the BLUE.COMPANY.COM domain controller, domain controller WHITE.COMPANY.COM has a USN of 2932 for the domain naming context. Domain controller RED.COMPANY.COM has an up-to-dateness vector for the domain naming context for the domain controller WHITE.COMPANY.COM of 2927. Which of the following statements are true? Choose all that apply.

    A. The domain controllers RED.COMPANY.COM and WHITE.COMPANY.COM are direct replication partners.

    B. Originating changes have been made on WHITE.COMPANY.COM that have not yet replicated to RED.COMPANY.COM.

    C. RED.COMPANY.COM has changes that WHITE.COMPANY.COM does not have.

    D. There is the possibility that no changes need to be replicated between RED.COMPANY.COM and WHITE.COMPANY.COM.

6. You are managing three sites, A, B, and C. A pair of T3 connections are installed, linking site A to Site B, and Site B to Site C, which are represented in Active Directory by a single site link configured with the default cost. A T1 link is installed between Sites A and C to provide redundancy. When creating a new site link for the T1, what cost would you assign to ensure that replication traffic between A and C uses the T3 links, if possible?

    A. 1.4

    B. 45

    C. 100

    D. 150

7. You have configured two sites in Active Directory and assigned subnets 128.1.40.0/21 to Site Lafayette and 128.1.48.0/21 to Site Baton Rouge. Which IP address can you assign to a domain controller in Site Baton Rouge? Choose all that apply.

    A. 128.1.40.71

    B. 128.1.48.71

    C. 128.1.54.254

    D. 128.1.50.0

8. Using the Active Directory Users and Computers snap-in, you add an e-mail address and Web page address to the existing user Carol. What information must be replicated to other domain controllers?

    A. The User object for Carol

    B. The parent container for Carol and all objects in it

C. The NTDS.DIT file

D. The e-mail and Web page address attributes

9. Your company offices are maintained in three adjacent buildings. Two of the offices are adjacent and are linked by a fiber-optic ATM backbone. The third building is located across the street from the other two and is connected by a 1MBps wireless bridge that experiences high utilization during the workday. Windows 2000 domain controllers and client computers are located in all buildings. All computers in your company belong to a single domain. A different IP subnet is used in each building. How many sites would you configure?

A. One

B. Two

C. Three

D. Four

10. It is the beginning of a new semester at your school. You support a remote campus that is connected to the main campus by a T1 line. The main campus and remote campus are configured as separate sites in Active Directory, and the T1 is represented by a site link with default cost. Users at this remote location are complaining that network performance to servers on the main campus is slow. You discover that a large amount of replication traffic is taking place between domain controllers at the main campus and the remote site because of the large number of user accounts recently created for incoming freshmen. What can you do to improve network performance for users at the remote site?

A. Schedule replication for the site link to occur only outside of working hours.

B. Raise the cost of the site link.

C. Lower the cost of the site link.

D. Pause the KCC process. Restart the KCC after working hours to complete replication.

Managing and Troubleshooting Domain Name Service Replication

11. What is the name for the process that moves records from a master DNS server to a secondary DNS server?

A. Replication

B. Zone transfer

C. Intermediate copy

D. Notification

12. What DNS improvement made it unnecessary to transfer the entire zone file during DNS replication?

    A. Dynamic updates

    B. Incremental zone transfer

    C. Update notification

    D. Reverse lookup

13. Which of the following is required of a Windows 2000 DNS server to host an Active Directory-integrated zone?

    A. It must run DHCP.

    B. It must run WINS.

    C. It must be configured with a standard primary zone first.

    D. It must be a domain controller.

14. You are adding a new domain controller to your domain. You are currently using an Active Directory-integrated zone for your enterprise. After assigning the IP address of the new server to be the DNS server for your clients though DHCP, what steps must you take so that clients can utilize your new domain controller as a DNS server for the existing zone? Choose all that apply.

    A. Install the DNS server service on your domain controller.

    B. Create a secondary Active Directory-integrated zone on the new domain controller.

    C. Configure a standard primary zone on your new domain controller.

    D. Copy the zone database files from an existing domain controller to the new domain controller.

15. The root domain (COMPANY.COM) of your enterprise uses an Active Directory-integrated zone on a Windows 2000 domain controller for DNS. You are setting up a child domain (CHILD.COMPANY.COM) and want to utilize a domain controller in the child domain (DC.CHILD.COMPANY.COM) as a backup DNS server for the root zone. You have installed the DNS service on DC.CHILD.COMPANY.COM. How would you configure DC.CHILD.COMPANY.COM? Choose all that apply.

    A. Do nothing. The Active Directory-integrated zone replicates to DC.CHILD.COMPANY.COM automatically.

    B. Set up a secondary Active Directory-integrated zone on DC.CHILD.COM. The zone records are then replicated automatically.

C. Set up a new primary zone for COMPANY.COM on DC.CHILD.COMPANY.COM. Dynamic registration populates the zone automatically.

D. Set up a secondary zone for COMPANY.COM on DC.CHILD.COMPANY.COM. Pick a single DC from the COMPANY.COM domain as the master DNS server.

16. Which of the following events immediately initiates a zone transfer?

A. Restarting the server on which the primary zone resides

B. Restarting the server on which the secondary zone resides

C. Choosing 'transfer from master' in the DNS console for the secondary zone

D. Making a change to the zone file on a secondary name server

17. For which of the following RFC-compliant servers can a Windows 2000 DNS host a secondary zone?

A. BIND running on Linux

B. BIND running on SUN Solaris

C. IBM DNS running on MVS/ESA

D. Windows NT 4 DNS

18. Which of the following systems can receive updates from an Active Directory-integrated zone through Active Directory replication?

A. All domain controllers in the same domain

B. All domain controllers in the same forest (regardless to which domain they belong)

C. All Windows 2000 secondary DNS servers

D. All RFC-compliant DNS servers

LAB QUESTION

You are creating an Active Directory forest comprising two domains at a single site. There will be three domain controllers for each domain. Sketch a diagram showing the Connection objects that will be used to replicate the domain naming contexts within the forest. Sketch a second diagram that shows the replication path for the schema and configuration naming contexts.

SELF TEST ANSWERS

Managing and Troubleshooting Active Directory Replication

1. ☑ **B.** With multimaster replication, any domain controller can write changes to the database, unlike the single-master model, where changes can be made at only one point.
   ☒ **A** is incorrect because it is true of both single- and multimaster configurations. **C** is incorrect because the efficiency of data storage has nothing to do with the configuration. **D** is incorrect because both single-master and multimaster models can use either push or pull replication.

2. ☑ **B and D.** Only replication traffic between sites is compressed.
   ☒ **A and C** are incorrect because RPC traffic within a site is not compressed and SMTP is not an option for carrying intersite replication traffic.

3. ☑ **A and B.** By definition, a global catalog server must be a domain controller and replicates with other domain controllers in Domain A. A domain controller in Domain B also replicates the schema and configuration information with a domain controller in Domain A.
   ☒ **C and D** are incorrect because stand-alone servers do not maintain Active Directory information and do not participate in Active Directory replication.

4. ☑ **C** is correct because each domain controller in a domain runs a KCC process. The KCC examines information stored in the local replica of the configuration naming context to determine which domain controllers are located at a site and uses that information to generate the virtual ring topology and connection objects used for intrasite replication.
   ☒ **A** is incorrect because a bridgehead server is used for replication between sites, not within a site. **B** is incorrect because, when determining the replication topology, the KCC orders systems by GUID, not by name. **D** is incorrect because the KCC does not have any information on the physical location or orientation of machines within a site.

5. ☑ **A and D. A** is correct because a domain controller keeps an up-to-dateness vector only for domain controllers that are direct replication partners. **D** is correct because the changes made to BLUE might have already replicated to RED.COMPANY.COM.
   ☒ **B** is incorrect because you cannot be sure that any originating writes were performed on WHITE.COMPANY.COM. **C** is incorrect because you cannot determine what changes they have from the information given.

6. ☑ **D.** The default cost is 100, so you must assign a higher cost to the new site link, since replication traffic attempts to use the lowest-cost link.

   ☒ **A** and **B** are incorrect because they have a lower cost than the default and replication would prefer that route. **A** is also incorrect because cost values must be integers between 1 and 32,767. **C** is incorrect because it would be the same cost as the previous site link and replication would not favor the T3 as required because the T3 cost would not be lower.

7. ☑ **B, C,** and **D.** These choices—128.1.48.71, 128.1.54.254, and 128.1.50.0—are all valid IP addresses in the 128.1.48.0/21 subnet.

   ☒ The IP address in **A** is part of the 128.1.40.0/21 subnet; if the address were assigned to a host, that host would be placed in the Lafayette site.

8. ☑ **D.** Active Directory replicates changes at the attribute level; only the changed attributes need to be replicated.

   ☒ **A** is incorrect because the user object for Carol would include all attributes for the user object Carol, including many which were not changed. Replication of all of the attributes when only two have changed would not be efficient. **B** is incorrect because the parent container for Carol and all other objects in it would comprise a great deal more data than is needed to replicate the changes. **C** is incorrect because the NTDS.DIT file contains all of the Active Directory replicas stored on a domain controller and the file is not replicated between domain controllers.

9. ☑ **B.** Two. By configuring the two buildings connected by ATM into one site and the third building into a site of its own, replication traffic over the wireless link can be scheduled to occur when the slow wireless link is not experiencing high utilization.

   ☒ **A, C,** and **D** are the incorrect number of sites.

10. ☑ **A.** Schedule replication for the site link to occur only outside of working hours. **A** is correct because by setting an appropriate site link schedule, Active Directory replication will take place only after working hours, allowing the network bandwidth to be used for other purposes during working hours..

   ☒ **B** and **C** are incorrect because there is only one replication path between the sites, so the cost has no effect. **D** is incorrect because the KCC does not run as a service and cannot be paused.

Managing and Troubleshooting Domain Name Service Replication

11. ☑ **B.** A zone transfer is the name of the process through which DNS records are moved from a master name server to a secondary name server.

☒ **A** is incorrect because replication in the context of this chapter refers specifically to Active Directory replication, which does include transfers of Active Directory-integrated zones but only to other domain controllers in the domain, not to secondary DNS servers. **C** is incorrect because "Intermediate copy" is a made-up term that does not apply to DNS. **D** is incorrect because notification is the process by which a master name server can inform a secondary server that changes are available. Notification is an event that initiates a zone transfer on servers that support it, but it does not describe a zone transfer.

12. ☑ **B.** Incremental updates were defined in RFC 1995 as an improvement to DNS so that only new or changed DNS records needed to be moved from the master name server to the secondary name server as part of the zone transfer.

☒ **A** is incorrect because *Dynamic updates* describes a DNS feature that allows systems to register their own DNS information on a server instead of requiring an administrator to manually add the records. **C** is incorrect because update notification is the process by which a master name server can inform a secondary server that changes are available. **D** is incorrect because reverse lookup occurs when DNS is used to resolve an IP address to a DNS name.

13. ☑ **D.** It must be a domain controller. Since Active Directory-integrated zones are stored in Active Directory, and Active Directory exists only on domain controllers, a Windows 2000 DNS server must be a domain controller.

☒ **A** and **B** are incorrect because DHCP and WINS are not required on a server for any DNS functions. **C** is incorrect because, although a domain controller that runs DNS can be configured to host both Active Directory-integrated zones and standard primary zones, these zones can be created independently. Active Directory-integrated, standard primary, and standard secondary zones can also be used together, in any combination, for different DNS zones.

14. ☑ **A.** Active Directory-integrated zones are automatically replicated to all domain controllers within a domain. When you install the DNS server, the new domain controller is able to resolve client requests.

☒ **B** is incorrect because there is no such thing as a secondary Active Directory-integrated zone. **C** is incorrect because an Active Directory-integrated zone for your domain automatically exists on your new domain controller, and you are unable to create a standard primary zone with the same name. **D** is incorrect because an Active Directory-integrated zone stores the zone records in Active Directory; there are no physical files containing the DNS records for the zone.

15. ☑ **D.** Set up a secondary zone for COMPANY.COM on DC.CHILD.COMPANY.COM. Pick a single DC from the COMPANY.COM domain as the master DNS server. **D** is correct because a zone transfer is required to replicate Active Directory integrated zones to Domain Controllers in other domains.

☒ **A** is incorrect because Active Directory-integrated zones are stored in the domain naming context and replicate only to other domain controllers in the same domain. **B** is incorrect because there is no such thing as a secondary Active Directory-integrated zone. **C** is incorrect because this action creates a new duplicate primary zone. Dynamic updates from clients and servers configured to use this server would register records into this database, but these records would be independent of and inconsistent with those in the AD-integrated zone. Note that when you create a secondary zone, only one DNS server can serve as the master, and if the source is an Active Directory-integrated zone, any domain controller running DNS services in that domain can serve as the master.

16. ☑ **B and C.** Restarting the server on which the primary zone resides, and restarting the server on which the secondary zone resides. **B** is correct because restarting a secondary server will force that server to request a new copy of the zone file from the master name server. **C** is correct because it is a procedure for manually initiating a zone transfer.

☒ **A** is incorrect because restarting the master name server does not force a zone transfer. **D** is incorrect because a secondary zone cannot be changed.

17. ☑ **A, B, C,** and **D.** Windows 2000 can host a secondary zone for any RFC-compliant master name server.

☒ There are no incorrect options.

18. ☑ **A.** Because Active Directory-integrated zones are stored in the domain naming context, only domain controllers in the same forest can receive updates through Active Directory replication.

☒ **B** is incorrect because the domain naming context is not replicated to domain controllers in other domains. **C** is incorrect because secondary name servers can receive updates only through zone transfers, not Active Directory replication. **D** is incorrect because Active Directory replication is not an RFC-compliant way of transferring DNS zone information.

LAB ANSWER

For the domain naming contexts, each domain will replicate separately. The domain controllers for each domain will replicate in a bidirectional ring, as shown in Figure 11-12.

FIGURE 11-12 Each domain naming context replicates in a bidirectional ring

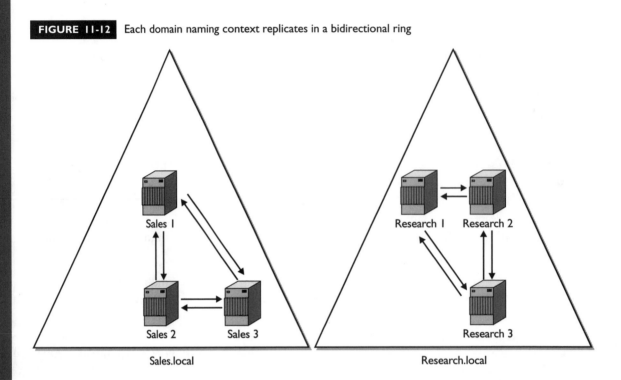

The schema and configuration naming contexts will replicate together in a forestwide bidirectional ring, as shown in Figure 11-13.

FIGURE 11-13 The schema and configuration naming contexts replicate to all domain controllers in the forest

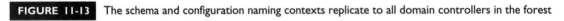

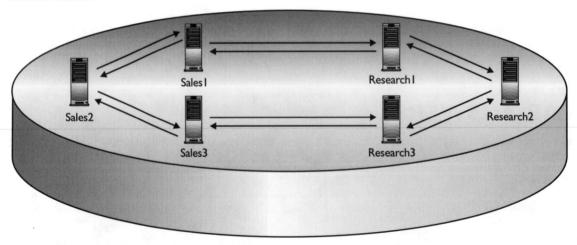

MICROSOFT CERTIFIED SYSTEMS ENGINEER

12

Active Directory Security Solutions

CERTIFICATION OBJECTIVES

12.01	Configuring and Troubleshooting Security in a Directory Services Infrastructure
12.02	Monitoring and Analyzing Security Events
✓	Two-Minute Drill
Q&A	Self Test

By this time you must be quite familiar with Active Directory, configuration of sites, group policies, replication, and DNS integration with Active Directory. The components of Active Directory such as objects, organizational units, and containers have been discussed in detail in the previous chapters. This chapter deals with options included with the Windows 2000 operating system to configure security for domain controllers and server computers.

Security is important for every organization. Windows 2000 offers more options for configuring security than its previous counterpart, Windows NT. The built-in features, which include group policies, the Security Configuration and Analysis tool, and auditing, make it easy for the administrator to implement organizationwide security. The Event Viewer gives you a detailed look at the security events when auditing is enabled.

CERTIFICATION OBJECTIVE 12.01

Configuring and Troubleshooting Security in a Directory Services Infrastructure

Security is one of the most important aspects of any operating system, and Windows 2000 is no exception. The built-in security features of Windows 2000 include several tools to keep the network secure from undesired actions of users. Security is not only applied to data files but is also applicable to user actions, such as misuse of the rights assigned to them.

Using group policies, you can apply required security policies at the local level, site level, domain level, or OU level. This section discusses how to implement useful and manageable security policies in a Windows 2000 network.

Applying Security Policies Using Group Policy

In Windows 2000, group policies are defined using the Group Policy snap-in and its extensions. Group policies are used to restrict users' rights and control what actions users can perform. Active Directory enables Group Policy and Group Policy objects (GPOs) to store policy information. Group Policy has built-in features for setting policies. The data created by Group Policy is stored in a GPO and is replicated to all domain controllers in the domain.

The following security areas can be configured using the Group Policy snap-in:

- **Account Policies.** This area includes Password Policy, Account Lockout Policy, and Kerberos Policy.

- **Local Policies.** These policies affect the local computer only. These policies include Audit Policy, User Rights Assignment, and Security Options.

- **Event Log.** The Event Log area defines such settings for event log files as maximum log file size, rights given to users on each log file, and the like.

- **Restricted Groups.** The Restricted Group area defines policies for built-in user groups such as power users, backup operators, and domain administrators.

- **System Services.** These policies are used to define startup types for system services and user rights on these services.

- **Registry.** These policies define user rights on registry keys.

- **File System.** The File System policies are used to configure security on files and folders.

- **Public Key Policies.** These policies are used to define encrypted data recovery agents and trusted certificate authorities.

- **IP Security Policies.** These policies are used to define network Internet Protocol Security (IPSec).

Figure 12-1 shows, for example, the User Rights assignment policies for a particular domain controller computer. You might notice that the policy set to back up files and folders is set for server operators, backup operators, and administrators.

There are three basic parts of Group Policy:

- **Group Policy objects.** GPOs contain configuration settings for Group Policy. A group policy is applied to an entire site or domain or an entire OU.

- **Group Policy containers.** The Group Policy container (GPC) is the Active Directory object and contains Group Policy object properties.

- **Group Policy templates.** Group Policy information that changes frequently is stored in a Group Policy template (GPT). Templates are stored in the SYSVOL folder.

FIGURE 12-1

Group Policy for
security settings

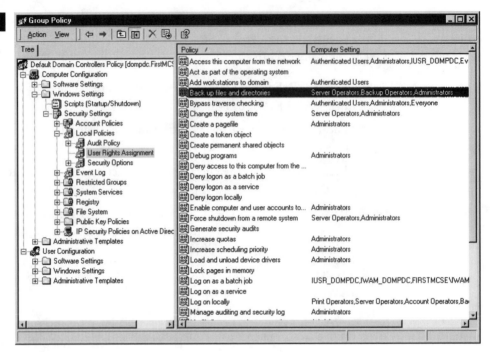

When to Use Security Policies

The security policies in a Windows 2000 domain can be set at the domain level,
site level, or OU level. If the network is small and has only one or two domain
controllers, planning security might not be a big issue. When you are responsible
for implementing security policies for larger networks, it is important to understand
when and how to use the security policies of Windows 2000.

The local security policies are effective only on the local computer. These policies
include the audit policy, which determines the events that are written to the security
logs. User policies determine the assignment of user rights and privileges on the
computer and become effective only after a user logs in. As the name implies, these
policies are local to the computer. The policies must be imported to a GPO in
Active Directory. Computer policies are effective whether or not a user is logged
on to the computer and are executed when the computer starts.

Security policies are used when you want to have a set of standard policies throughout the organization. These policies allow you to configure security at a centralized place in the network; you do not have to configure every server manually. The policies defined at the root of the domain become applicable automatically to all domain controllers and member servers in the network. This functionality greatly reduces administrative efforts and time required to implement security. Once defined and configured, these policies are your primary tool for controlling the network.

exam
ⓦatch

Windows 2000 allows you to have only one account policy throughout the domain; that account policy is applied to the root of the domain.

How to Create Security Policies

Security policies are created using the Group Policy editor. In Exercise 12-1, you create a Group Policy object and then configure its settings.

When a new GPO is created, all security settings for this GPO are undefined until configuration is complete. Assignment of security settings is accomplished using the Group Policy Editor. Exercise 12-2 explains the necessary steps. This exercise serves as example for setting all or most security policies.

Security Configuration and Analysis

Windows 2000 includes a powerful tool to manage security in a domain. The Security Configuration and Analysis tool helps you configure security, analyze the results, and resolve any problems that concern system and resource security. This tool uses a database to perform these functions. This database is computer specific and allows you to use personalized databases, import and export templates, and create new security templates that suit your requirements.

Since the Security Configuration and Analysis tool is computer specific, you can collect and analyze data on a local computer only. This tool allows you to make quick analysis of the system security. The tool also gives you its recommendations based on your settings in comparison to what is proposed by the operating system.

Creating a New Group Policy Object

1. Log on to the domain controller with Administrative privileges.

2. To create a GPO in a domain or an OU, choose Start | Programs | Administrative Tools, and select Active Directory Users and Computers. This sequence opens the Active Directory Users and Computers Console. To create a GPO that is linked to a site, open the Active Directory Sites and Services Console.

3. From the View menu, click Advanced View. Select the AD object for which you want to create a GPO. Right-click the selected object, and click Properties. Click the Group Policy tab from the Properties window.

4. Click New, and type a name for the GPO. The new GPO is linked to the selected object by default.

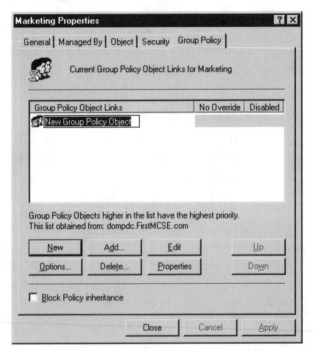

5. Click Close. Close the Active Directory Users and Computers Console.

EXERCISE 12-2

Using Group Policy Editor to Change Security Settings

1. Log on to the domain controller with Administrative privileges.

2. Choose Start | Programs | Administrative Tools, and select Active Directory Users and Computers. This choice opens the Active Directory Users and Computers Console.

3. Right-click the OU for which you created the new GPO in the previous exercise, and select Properties from the drop-down menu.

4. The Properties sheet appears. From the View menu, click Advanced View. Click the Group Policy tab. Notice that New Group Policy Object (or the name you might have given to the GPO) appears in the Group Policy Object Links list, as shown in the following illustration.

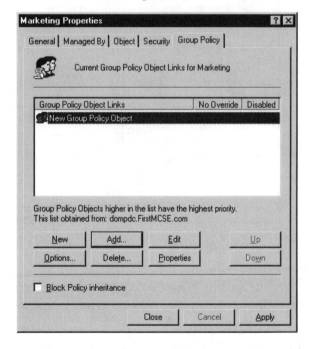

5. Click New Group Policy Object. Click Edit. This step opens the Group Policy Console.

6. Double-click Computer Configuration, double-click Windows Settings, double-click Security Settings, and double-click Local Policies.

7. Click User Rights Assignments. Notice that a list of user rights is displayed as Not Defined in the results pane, as shown here.

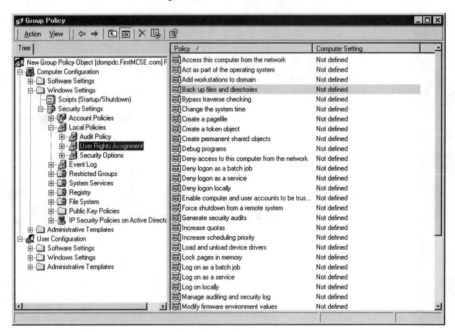

8. Select a user right that you want to configure. For the purpose of this exercise, double-click "Back up files and directories."

9. The Security Policy Setting dialog box appears. Click the check box for "Define these policy settings." This choice enables the Add and Remove buttons. Click Add.

10. The Add User or Group box appears next. Click Browse.

11. The Select Users or Groups dialog box appears. Select Everyone (or any other user or group appropriate to your requirements), as shown here.

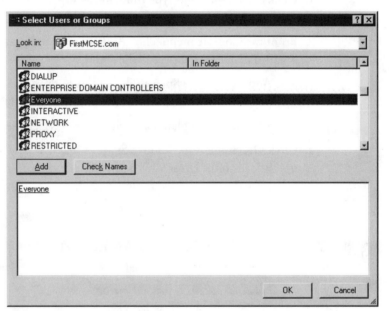

12. Click Add. Click OK. The Add User or Group dialog box shows the group you selected. Click OK.

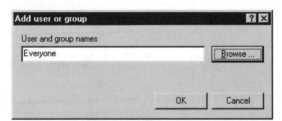

13. Click OK to close the Security Policy Settings window. Close the Group Policy Editor window.

14. Close the Active Directory Users and Computers Console.

The Security Configuration and Analysis tool can be installed using the following steps:

1. Click Start | Run, and type **mmc** in the Open box. This step opens an empty console.

2. From the Console menu, click Add/Remove Snap-in. The Add/Remove Snap-in dialog box appears. Click Add.

3. The Add Standalone Snap-in dialog box appears. Select Security Configuration and Analysis from the list. Click Add. See Figure 12-2.

4. Select Security Templates, and click Add. Click Close.

5. Click OK in the Add/Remove Snap-in dialog box. The selected snap-ins are now added to the console. When you open the console for the first time, it looks like the one shown in Figure 12-3.

FIGURE 12-2

Adding security
snap-ins to
the MMC

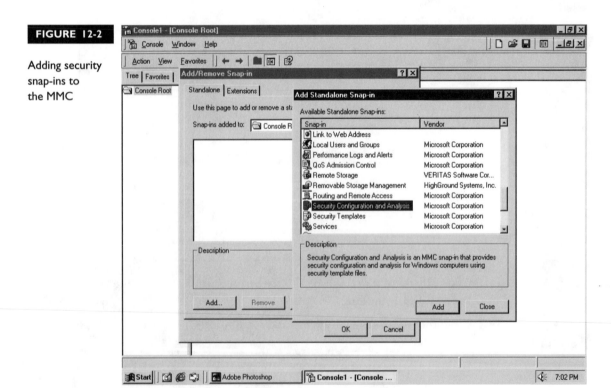

FIGURE 12-3

Initial Security
Configuration and
Analysis Console

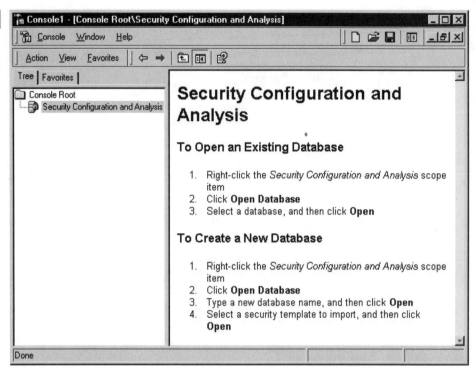

6. Click Save As from the Console menu. Notice that the path shown in the Save As dialog box defaults to Administrative Tools. Type **Security Configuration and Analysis** in the File Name box, and click Save. You can open this console later from the Administrative Tools menu.

Security Templates

The Security Templates Console allows you to set up security templates for one or more of the following areas:

- **Account policies.** These policies include local account policies such as minimum password length, account lockout duration, and Kerberos settings. For example, you can set a minimum password length of ten characters to discourage "crackers."

- **Local policies.** These policies include audit policy, user rights, and other policies that affect the local system.

■ **Event log.** The security settings include configuration of log files for the system, applications, and security. You can set the minimum size of log files, overriding the default size of 512KB.

■ **Restricted groups.** These groups are predefined user groups in Windows 2000.

■ **System services.** The system services include a list of services on the local system. Some of these are file and print services and network and telephony services.

■ **Registry.** You can configure security descriptors on the system registry from these templates.

■ **File system.** This template allows you to access the hard drive partitions as a single tree and apply security settings for files and folders.

Figure 12-4 shows the Security Templates Console.

Any of the security templates can be imported into the Security Configurations and Analysis Console. Some predefined security template files are included with the

FIGURE 12-4	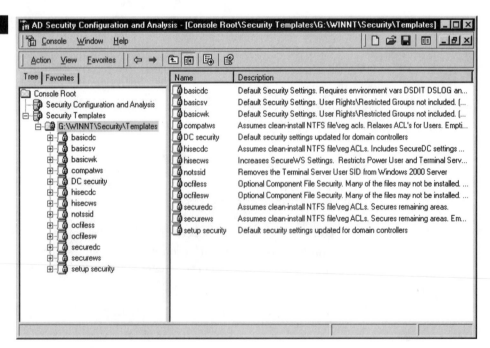
The Security Templates Console	

operating system, as outlined in the following list. These files are stored in the \Systemroot\Security\Templates folder:

- **BASICWK.INF**   Default workstation
- **BASICSV.INF**   Default server
- **BASICDC.INF**   Default domain controller
- **COMPATSWS.INF**   Compatible workstation or server
- **SECUREWS.INF**   Secure workstation or server
- **HISECWS.INF**   Highly secure workstation or server
- **DCSECURITY.INF**   Default security settings updated for domain controller
- **SECUREDC.INF**   Secure domain controller
- **HISECDC.INF**   Highly secure domain controller
- **OCFILESS.INF**   Optional component file security for servers
- **OCFILESW.INF**   Optional component file security for workstations
- **SETUP SECURITY**   Default security settings for domain controllers
- **NOTSSID**   Removes Terminal Server security ID from Windows 2000 Server

These templates can be grouped in categories—for example, Basic, Secure, Highly Secure, Optional, and so on.

Exercise 12-3 explains the steps to import a security template into the Security Analysis and Configuration Console to set up a working security database.

Microsoft does not recommend using the Security Configuration and Analysis tool to analyze security of domain-based clients, because you would then have to visit each client computer individually. A solution to this problem is to modify the Security Template from the Security Templates Console and reapply it to the GPO.

Why Perform a Security Analysis?   The security templates included with Windows 2000 enable systems administrators to perform a quick inspection of security settings for a Windows 2000 computer by comparing configured security against settings recommended by Microsoft. After the security analysis is performed, the administrator is informed of any discrepancies in the configured security settings compared with the settings proposed by the system.

Setting Up a Working Security Database

EXERCISE 12-3

1. Log on to the computer as Administrator.

2. Click Start | Programs | Administrative Tools, and select Security Configuration and Analysis. You might recall that you saved this console in Exercise 12-2.

3. Right-click Security Configuration and Analysis. Click Open Database. The Open Database dialog box appears.

4. Type a filename in the filename box. This step opens the Import Template dialog box.

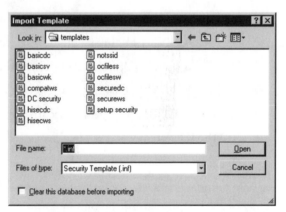

5. Select a security template. Click Open. The template database becomes your working security database.

After the exercise is complete, you might perform one or more of the following operations:

■ If you want to import another template database into the Security Configuration and Analysis Console, click Import Template instead of Open Database in step 3 of the exercise.

■ To immediately analyze system security, right-click Security Configuration and Analysis, and click Analyze Computer Now. This step opens a Perform Analysis dialog box, where you verify the name and path of the log file in which to store the results. Click OK. The various security areas are analyzed and results appear.

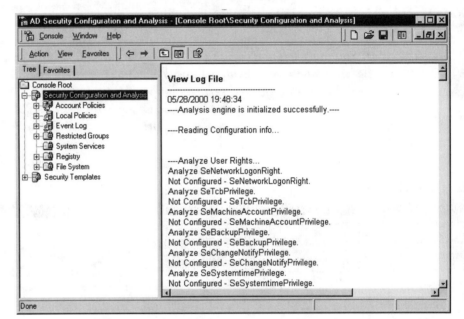

■ To view the analyzed results sorted by category, double-click a category to expand the node. Click a policy for which you want to see the analysis results. The right-side pane shows the results.

By regular security analysis, individual Windows 2000 computers can be tuned to an acceptable level of security. The security analysis tool also allows administrators to reset the security settings so that they conform to the recommended level. This is a great help in overcoming any flaws that might creep into a system over time.

Setting Rights on System Services

The System Configuration and Analysis Console allows you to set user rights and privileges on system services. These services include file and print services, network services, and telephony services. Figure 12-5 shows System Services when no settings are defined.

Exercise 12-4 explains the steps to set security on system services.

on the
job

There are two important things you must remember when setting security using the built-in security templates:

1. You must select a security template database based on your requirements. Before you apply a security template in your working environment, it must be tested to ensure that no security loopholes are left.

2. When you import a template, the changes that you make are stored in the new database that you create. The original template remains unchanged.

FIGURE 12-5

The System Services in the Security Configuration and Analysis Console

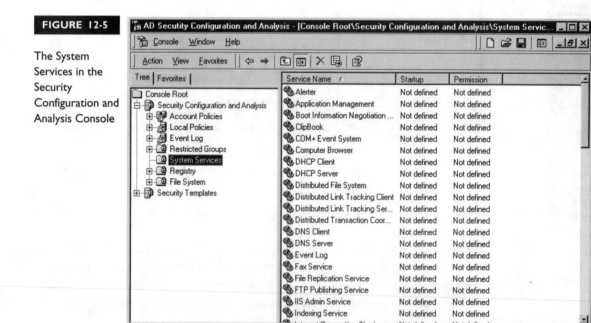

Setting Security on System Services

1. Click Start | Programs |Administrative Tools, and select Security Configuration and Analysis. This sequence opens the Security Configuration and Analysis Console.

2. Double-click Security Configuration and Analysis to expand the node. Double-click System Services.

3. In the right-side pane, right-click the system service for which you want to edit security. Click Security. For example, if you click DNS server, you will see an Analyzed Security Policy Setting dialog box, as shown here.

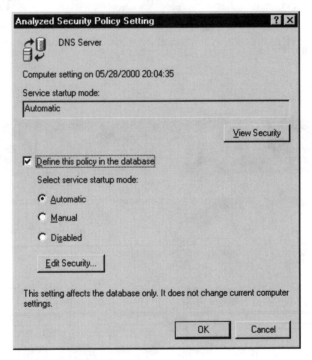

4. Click the "Define this policy in the database" check box. Select a startup type for the service, if required.

5. Click Edit Security button to further configure security parameters.

6. Repeat these steps for each system service for which you want to set security.

7. Click OK to exit.

Setting Rights on a File System

The Security Configuration and Analysis Console allows you to set security policies for the local file system. The procedure is similar to setting security for system services. Exercise 12-5 explains the steps to configure file system security.

exam
Ⓦatch

The rights on file systems can be configured only on NTFS volumes. It is not possible to set rights or enable security on file allocation table (FAT) volumes.

Implementing an Audit Policy

Auditing user and system activities in a Windows 2000 computer involves recording events that happen to log files on the system. These logs help you analyze various events that happen on local systems and on domain resources. Auditing is an efficient tool to track user activities that concern security.

SCENARIO & SOLUTION

I want to create a new group policy for an OU. What is the first step in creating a new group policy?	Use the Active Directory Users and Computers Console. Select the object for which you want to set up a new group policy, and create a new Group Policy object from the Group Policy tab.
What is the next step in configuring a security policy for the new GPO?	Edit the new GPO using the Group Policy Editor.
How can I use the Security Configuration and Analysis tool to analyze security on domain controllers?	Open the Security Configuration and Analysis Console and import a suitable template database to set up a working security database. Make changes to the template database.
I have modified the Security template file that I imported using the Security Configuration and Analysis tool. Is the original database file lost?	No. The original template file is not lost or modified. The changes you made are stored in a separate database file.

Setting Security on a File System

1. Click Start | Programs |Administrative Tools, and select Security Configuration and Analysis. This choice opens the Security Configuration and Analysis Console.

2. Double-click Security Configuration and Analysis to expand the node. Double-click File Systems to expand the node.

3. A list of existing drives is displayed. Double-click the drive to view a list of folders.

4. Right-click a folder for which you want to set up security. Choose Security from the menu.

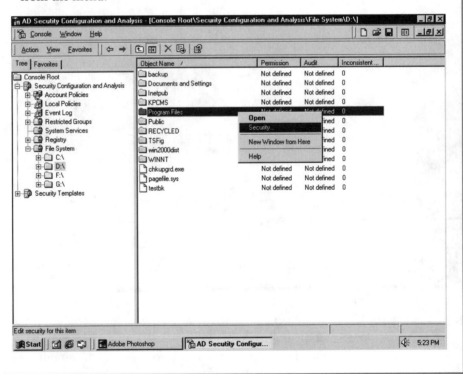

5. The Analyzed Security Policy Setting dialog box appears. Notice that by default the computer setting is not defined. Click the "Define this policy in the database" check box.

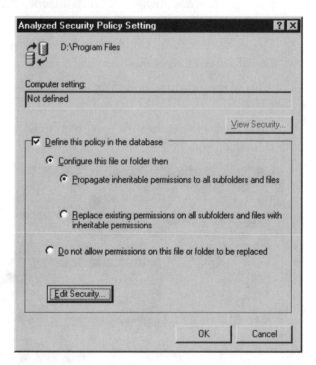

6. Click Edit Security button to configure policies for users and computers. This step opens the database security dialog box for the selected folder.

7. Click OK. Close the Security Configuration and Analysis Console.

Once you have completed setting up permissions on network resources, it is important to keep track of access to these resources by setting up audit policies. Auditing can be set up to track user logon and logoff, computer startup and shutdown, and changes made to Active Directory objects. Attempts to access secure company data files and folders can also be logged.

The events that occur on a Windows 2000 domain are recorded on the domain controller computers, except those for which auditing is set up locally. The recorded events are read using the security log of the Event Viewer.

Why Audit Events?

As a systems administrator, it is your responsibility to secure network resources. You must have some solid plans to minimize the risk of unauthorized access to the secure data. Network resources include network components and data. These resources are equally important. *Network resources* include domain controllers, system services, shared printers, and shared data files. Each resource is vital in keeping the organization working smoothly. Unless you have some means of determining who is using what resources and how these resources are accessed, there is no way to track what is going on with the secure data or resources.

Security configuration in Windows 2000 helps you secure data and resources; auditing helps you find out what kind of activities are being performed on these resources. In order to keep a check on user and system activities, it is necessary to log the events to log files. Logging helps in tracking authorized or unauthorized attempts to access network resources. Examples of such events are logon attempts of users to restricted computers or attempts to read, delete, or modify secure data. Auditing helps you track information by recording events in the system security log files. These events include the action that was initiated, the user who initiated the action, and whether the attempt succeeded or failed.

Auditing configuration tools allow you to specify which events must be written to the security event logs. With careful planning, you can secure the system and network resources in the domain by implementing domainwide audit policies.

By default, auditing is disabled on all Windows 2000 computers. Without using audit policies, however, it is very difficult to track network security events

How to Implement an Audit Policy

Audit policies can be set only on those resources that reside on NTFS drives. Setting up audit policies requires either administrative rights in the domain or the Manage Auditing and Security Log right. The Administrators group on each machine has this auditing right, by default. The following are important points to remember:

- Auditing is disabled by default. A domain administrator must enable auditing.
- The administrator must specify the resources and events that should be audited.
- The events that occur on a Windows 2000 computer are logged to the security log files.
- The recorded events must be scanned and interpreted on a regular basis to get the results of auditing.

There are several types of objects on which you can set up auditing. Auditing each and every event and access to each and every shared resource would result in collection of large amounts of data. A decision must be taken to specify the computers on which auditing will be set up. In addition, it is also important to decide which events will be audited.

Auditing is disabled on all objects by default. In order to set up auditing, you must be a domain administrator or have Manage Audits and Security Log rights in the domain.

Configuring Auditing   Configuration of auditing is a two-step process. First, you must set up the audit policy. Second, the auditing must be enabled on specified computers on events that you need to track. These events can be related to files, folders, network printers, and other Active Directory objects. You must select the categories of events that should be audited. The size of the security log file is limited, so you must take care that unnecessary events are not logged.

The events audited in Windows 2000 computers are classified into the following categories:

- **Account logon events.** Logon requests received by the domain controller.

- **Account management.** Actions that concern attempts to create, remove, or modify user and group accounts.

- **Directory Service access.** Attempts to access objects in the Active Directory.

- **Logon events.** Attempts to log on and log off in the domain.

- **Object access.** Attempts to access files, folders, or printers.

- **Policy change.** Attempts to change user security options, user rights, or audit policies.

- **Privilege use:** Attempts to exercise privileges given to a user.

- **Process tracking.** Attempts by program files to perform an action.

- **System events.** Shutdown/startup of computer or events that affect system security.

Exercise 12-6 explains the procedure to implement audit policies.

EXERCISE 12-6

Setting Up Audit Policy on a Domain Controller

1. Log on to the domain controller as an Administrator.

2. Click Start | Programs | Administrative Tools, and select Active Directory Users and Computers.

3. Right-click Domain Controllers, and select Properties. This step opens the Properties sheet of the Domain Controllers object.

4. Click the Group Policy tab. Select the policy for which auditing is to be enabled, and click Edit. This step opens the Group Policy snap-in.

5. Double-click Computer Configuration to expand it. Double-click Windows Settings. Double-click Security Settings. Double-click Local Policies. Double-click Audit Policy.

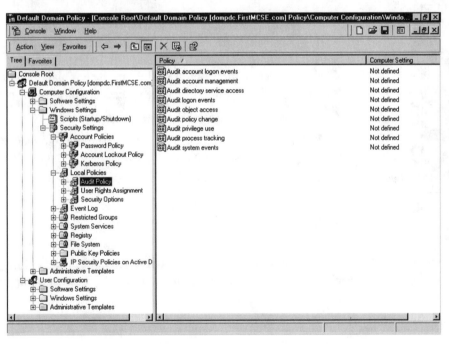

6. From the right-side pane, right-click the event that you want to audit, and click Security. This action opens the Template Security Policy Setting dialog box.

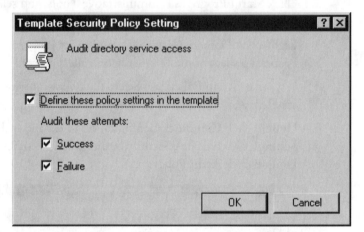

7. Click the "Define these policy settings in the template" check box. This choice allows you to select the success or failure attempts.

8. Click Success or Failure check boxes, as required.

9. Click OK. Notice that Group Policy now shows these events as "Success," "Failure," or "Success, Failure."

If you want to set audit policy on a stand-alone server that is not a part of the domain, you need to access the Local Security Policy from Administrative Tools. Exercise 12-7 explains how to set up audit policy on such a computer.

Setting Up Audit Policies on a Stand-Alone Computer

1. Log on to the computer as Administrator.

2. Click Start | Programs | Administrative Tools, and select Local Security Policy. This step opens the Local Security Policy Console.

3. Click the plus (+) sign before Local Policies to expand it. Double-click Audit Policy.

4. Right-click the event that you want to audit from the right-side pane. Click Security. This choice opens the Local Security Policy Settings dialog box. Notice that No Auditing is the effective policy setting by default.

5. Click Success or Failure, as required, in the Local Security Policy Setting dialog box for the account logon events.

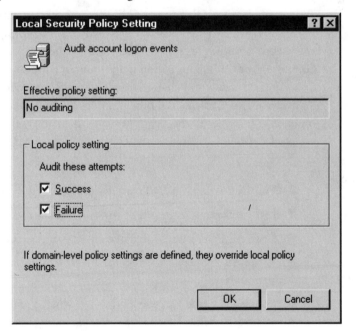

6. Click OK.

Making the Security Policy Changes Effective The changes you make to the security policies do not take effect immediately but wait for the policies to propagate. The automatic propagation of policies occurs every eight hours by default. If you cannot wait for such a long duration, there are two ways to make the policy changes effective immediately:

- Restart the computer. However, this action is not recommended when the computer is active in the domain.

- Type **secedit /refreshpolicy machine_policy** at the command prompt, and press ENTER. This option does not require restarting.

To force the changed security policies, you must select an appropriate method for your environment.

Auditing Active Directory Objects Auditing access to Active Directory objects is also a two-step process. First, you have to configure the audit policy and then set up auditing for the specific objects. These objects can be users, groups, computers, or OUs. This action helps you track events that concern authorized or unauthorized access and changes made to the Active Directory objects.

Exercise 12-8 explains the procedure for enabling auditing on Active Directory objects.

The following list details some of the auditing event entries and when they are triggered.

- **Full Control.** Triggered by performing any type of access to the object.
- **List Contents.** Triggered by viewing the objects.
- **Read All Properties.** Triggered by viewing object attributes.
- **Write All Properties.** Triggered by making some change to the object attributes.
- **Create All Child Objects.** Triggered when a child object is created within the audited object.
- **Delete All Child Objects.** Triggered when a child object is deleted within the audited object.
- **Modify Permissions.** Triggered when the permissions of the audited object are changed.
- **Modify Owner.** Triggered when someone takes ownership of the audited object.

Auditing Active Directory Objects

1. Log on to the domain controller as an Administrator.

2. Click Start | Programs | Administrative Tools, and select Active Directory Users and Computers.

3. From the View menu, select Advanced Features.

4. Select the container where the object is located. Right-click the object, and select Properties. This step opens the Properties sheet of the object.

5. Click the Security tab. Click Advanced.

6. The Access Control Settings dialog box appears. Click the Auditing tab.

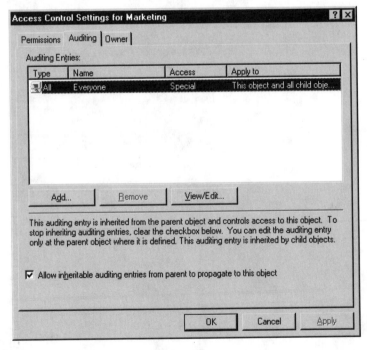

7. Click Add. This step opens the Select User, Computer, or Group dialog box.

8. Select the users for whom auditing is required. Click OK.

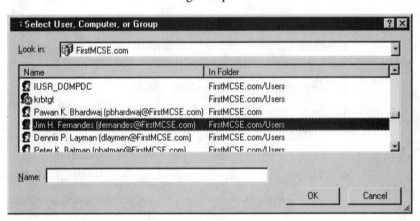

9. The Auditing Entry dialog box appears. Select the Successful or Failed check boxes, or both, as required for the events that you want to audit.

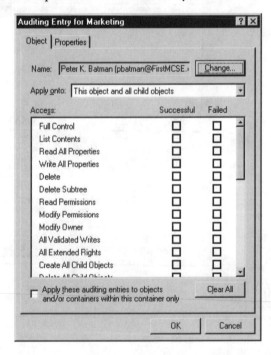

10. The Auditing Entry dialog box has an Apply Onto list box. From this list you can select where the auditing is applicable. The default setting is "This object and all child objects."

11. Click OK to return to the Access Control dialog box.

12. By default, the changes that you make to the parent object are set to propagate to the child objects. You can clear the "Allow inheritance auditing entries from parent to propagate to this object" check box.

13. Click OK to exit.

It might not be necessary to enable auditing for all events. Since auditing degrades system performance, you must study your requirements carefully and decide which events you need to audit to maintain an acceptable balance between security and performance.

When setting up auditing on Active Directory objects, you sometimes might notice that the check boxes under Access are disabled or grayed out. The Remove button is also not available sometimes in the Access Control Settings dialog box. These settings simply mean that the auditing setup on the parent container is being propagated to this container or object.

Auditing Files, Folders, and Printers   Access to files, folders, and printers can be set up following the procedure given in the exercises. You must take care that you audit only those events that are absolutely necessary to track. Enabling auditing for a large number of events not only fills up log files quickly, but it also affects the performance of computers on which the events are being recorded. You might recall that auditing can be enabled on only those files and folders that reside on NTFS volumes.

Exercise 12-9 explains the steps necessary to audit file and folder access.

Auditing Access to Files and Folders

1. Click Start | Programs | Accessories, and select Windows Explorer.

2. In Windows Explorer, right-click the file or folder for which you want to enable auditing, and select Properties.

3. Click the Security tab from the Properties dialog box. Click Advanced. This step opens the Access Control Settings dialog box for the selected file or folder.

4. Click the Auditing tab. Click Add, and from the next dialog box, select the users or groups for whom auditing of the selected file or folder access is required. Click OK.

5. The Auditing Entry dialog box appears. Check the Failure or Success boxes for the events that you want to audit. Refer to the list of event details following this exercise.

6. In the Apply Onto list, you can specify where the objects are audited. The default is "This folder, subfolders and files." Click OK.

7. If you want to prevent the audit settings from the parent folder of the selected file or folder to propagate to this file or folder, clear the "Allow inheritable auditing entry from parent folder to propagate to this object" check box.

8. Click OK.

The following list explains some of the events that you can audit for file and folder access and what triggers them:

- **Traverse Folder/Execute File.** This event is triggered when a user tries to move through folders to find a particular file or tries to execute a file, even though the user does not have permissions for such an action.

- **List Folder/Read Data.** This event is triggered when a user tries to list folder contents or read data from a file.

- **Read Attributes and Read Extended Attributes.** This event is triggered when the attributes of a file or folder are displayed.

- **Create Files/Write Data.** This event is triggered when a file is created within a folder or the contents of a file are changed.

- **Create Folders/Append Data.** This event is triggered when a folder is created within the audited folder or data is appended to the audited file. This does not apply to deleting or changing the data in a file.

- **Write Attributes and Write Extended Attributes.** This event is triggered when the attributes are changed.

- **Delete Subfolders and Files.** This event is triggered when a subfolder or a file within a folder is deleted.

- **Change Permissions.** This event is triggered when file or folder permissions are changed.

- **Take Ownership.** This event is triggered when a user takes ownership of the audited file or folder.

Best Practices   Implementation of audit policies is effective when you make a concrete plan as to how to implement and which events to record in the event logs. The following points will help you implement the audit policies effectively:

- Logon and logoff failure audits help you track who is attempting to log on to the domain but is not granted access.

- Auditing success events for user and group management, system shutdown and restart, and changes in security policies help you track misuse of privileges.

- Success or failure of access to files, folders, and read/write access helps track suspected users who attempt to access secure data.

- Success/failure audits for printer management help track attempts to change network printers.

- Auditing success/failure of process tracking events helps track attacks from virus programs.

exam
Watch

In order to track access to a particular object by any person on the network, you need to audit the Everyone group. The Everyone group contains all users and groups in the network.

SCENARIO & SOLUTION

What is the first step in configuration of auditing on Windows 2000 computers?	The first step in setting up auditing is to set up audit policy. Then you have to enable auditing for the objects that you want to monitor.
I want to set up the strongest audit policy on all domain controllers. Should I enable auditing on all objects and all types of events?	No. Enabling auditing for all objects and all types of events is not recommended, because auditing is a resource-hungry process. You need to decide which security events you must audit.
I want to track access to secure folders by all users. Is there any simple method to enable auditing so that all users who get access are monitored?	Yes. Enable auditing for the Everyone group. The Everyone group contains all users.

CERTIFICATION OBJECTIVE 12.02

Monitoring and Analyzing Security Events

Configuration of Windows 2000 security, such as auditing of events, is only half the job of making your network secure. To exercise complete control of system and data security, you must monitor and analyze data collected by security configuration. You must check security events on a regular basis. The previous section of the chapter detailed how to configure security of Active Directory objects. This section details how to monitor and analyze the events that are recorded in the security log files.

Events to Monitor

It is not possible to view and interpret each and every event in the security log files. When you are looking at the events to monitor system and data security, you must have a clear idea of what types of events should be monitored. Viewing all events is not only undesirable, it is also a time-consuming job.

The decision of which events to monitor largely depends on what type of network environment you have and what type of security breaches you fear from outside or within the organization. Data is always valuable. The importance of a single file lost, altered, or viewed by undesired personnel can cause unpredictable loss. Depending on your network environment and the business needs of the company, you might find helpful these suggestions for monitoring security events:

- **Logon attempts.** You must monitor users' unsuccessful attempts to log on to secure systems. If any such attempts are found in the security logs, the responsible users must be warned.

- **Access to confidential files and folders.** Files and folders that contain confidential business data must be monitored regularly. Any users found attempting to view, alter, or delete data must be warned of legal consequences of his or her action. You must ensure proper access rights to these confidential files and folders from the beginning.

- **Undesired use of user rights and privileges.** You might have delegated some of your responsibilities to some users to lessen your administrative burdens. You must ensure that the delegated privileges are being exercised in the desired way. You must keep a check on user and group management. This check also ensures that company policies are followed properly.

The Security Event Log

The Event Viewer in Windows 2000 Administrative Tools is your ultimate tool for tracking the events occurring on the system and the network. The Event Viewer displays events, depending on the configuration of a Windows 2000 computer. The computer acting as a domain controller essentially has the Directory Services, DNS server, and file replication logs, in addition to application, system, and security logs that are standard in any Windows 2000 computer. Only administrators can view the security logs. All other users can view the application and system logs.

In order for you to monitor security events on a Windows 2000 computer, auditing of files, folders, and other Active Directory objects must be enabled. Group policies must be configured to ensure that the system and data security is maintained at all times. Figure 12-6 shows the security log of the Event Viewer, with no events. This is because auditing has not been configured; hence, no security events have been written to the security log files.

exam
Ⓦⓐⓣⓒⓗ

By default, only administrators have the right to view security events. The application and system logs are available to all users.

FIGURE 12-6

The empty
security log when
no auditing is
enabled

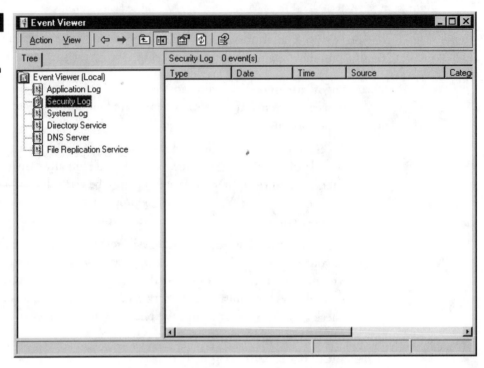

Locating Events in the Security Log When a large number of events are in the security snap-in, it becomes difficult to look for a particular event. To search for a particular event, click the Find option in the View menu of the security log. The Find in Local Security Log dialog box appears, as shown in Figure 12-7.

The Find dialog box has the following options:

- **Event types.** You can find only audit events in the security log.
- **Event source.** The source of the event, either a software or driver component.
- **Category:** Category of the event.
- **Event ID.** An event ID number.
- **User.** The name of the user who is logged on.
- **Computer.** The name of the computer.
- **Description.** Detailed text of the event.
- **Search direction:** To search the log in an up or down direction.

Locating events in
the security log

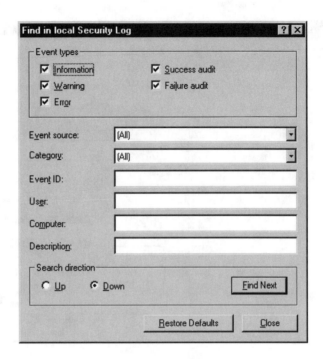

Filtering Events   The Filter option in the Event Viewer enables you to specify
how the events are displayed. Via filtering, you do not have to look at all the events.
To filter the event display, click Filter in the View menu. This opens the Filter tab
of the Security Log Properties sheet, as shown in Figure 12-8.

As with the Find option, the Filter option can be configured on the basis of event
type, event source, event ID, and so on to display only those events that fulfill the
conditions set in the Filter option. You can also specify the start and end dates of
the events.

Security Log Settings   It is essential to configure the security logs in order to
ensure that important information is not missed due to full security log files or
overwritten events. When you have configured auditing, the next step is to configure
the security log settings so that these do not become constrained by security event

FIGURE 12-8

Event Viewer
display filtering

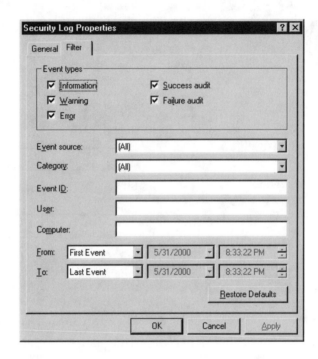

monitoring. It is important to note that when the security log file is full, further
security events are not recorded. In this case, an error is written to the application log.
To avoid this situation, you must configure the security log options. Exercise 12-10
explains the steps to configure a security log.

Archiving Security Logs

Security logs can be archived in the Event Viewer for later viewing. This allows you
to maintain a history of security-related events. The logs can be archived in log-file
format (*.EVT file) that retains the binary format. If the logs are saved in text
format, you can use a word processor to view the events later. Furthermore, the log
can be saved in comma-separated format; that way, a spreadsheet can then be used
to view and manipulate the saved log file. Some organizations have a policy to
archive security logs for a specified period.

Configuring a Security Log

1. Log on to the computer as Administrator.

2. Click Start | Programs | Administrative Tools, and select Event Viewer. This step opens the Event Viewer.

3. Click Security Log on the left-side pane. The security logs are displayed on the right-side results pane.

4. Right-click Security Log, and select Properties. This sequence opens the Properties sheet of the security log, as shown here. Notice that the name of the security log file is SecEvent.Evt and it is stored in the \Systemrooot\System32\Config folder.

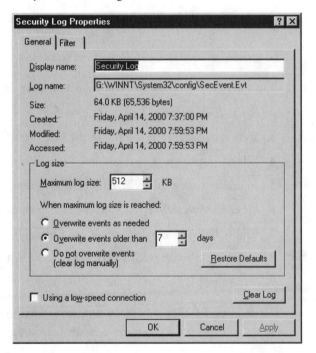

5. In the "Maximum log size" box, either select one of the file size options or type in the required size of the file. The log file size must be a multiple of 64KB. If you reduce the size of the log file, the new size takes effect only after the log has been cleared. The log file size can vary from 64KB (minimum) to 4,194,240KB or 4GB (maximum).

6. Select one of the following options from the "When maximum log size is reached" section:

   ■ "Overwrite events as needed" allows the system to delete the older events in favor of the newer ones when the log file is full.

   ■ Specify the number of days to keep the events in the log file in "Overwrite events older than" box. Default is seven days.

   ■ Select "Do not overwrite events" if you want to clear the events manually. Select "Using a low-speed connection" if the log is located on a computer connected by a slow link, such as a modem.

   ■ Click Apply. Close the Security Log Properties sheet.

To archive a security log, follow these steps:

1. Open the Event Viewer from the Administrative Tools menu.

2. Right-click Security Log, and select Save Log File As.

3. Type a name for the log file in the File Name box.

4. Select a format for the file. Click Save.

5. In order to view an archived file, follow these steps:

6. Open the Event Viewer from the Administrative Tools menu.

7. Right-click Security Log, and click Open Log File.

8. Select the file you want to open. Click Security from the Log Type list.

9. Type a display name for the log file in the Display Name box. Click Open.

The archived log files are usually kept for a certain period of time that is decided by company policies. After the specified time period expires, these files can be deleted.

Clearing Security Logs

You might have noticed a Clear Log button in the Security Log Properties sheet. When you select "Do not overwrite events," you can click the Clear Log button to clear the security log manually. You are given a warning before clearing the log. The cleared logs are permanently removed from the system.

You can also clear the security logs from the console tree in the Event Viewer. Follow these steps to clear the security log manually:

1. Open the Event Viewer from the Administrative Tools menu.

2. Right-click the Security Log, and select Clear All Events.

3. A message dialog box appears. Click Yes if you want to archive the security logs before clearing. Click No of you want to clear the events without archiving.

4. If you click Yes from the message box, you are prompted to type a filename for the archive file. You can also select a format for the archive log file. After typing a name and selecting a format, click Save.

5. If you select No from the message box, the security logs are deleted permanently.

When you configure the security logs not to overwrite the events and want to clear the logs manually, you must check the size of the log files. Depending on the number of events you are recording, it is quite possible that the log files have filled up very quickly. Once the log files are full, no more events are recorded and you might no longer be able to monitor security events.

Interpreting Security Events

As described earlier in this chapter, the security-related events are not written to the security log files unless audit policies are configured and auditing is enabled on the selected objects. The events that are monitored by the system after auditing is enabled are recorded in the security log files. The events are displayed in the Security Events category in the Event Viewer.

Follow the steps given ahead to view the security log on a computer.

1. Log on to the Windows 2000 computer as administrator or as a user with the right to manage Auditing and Security Logs

2. Click Start | Programs | Administrative Tools, and select Event Viewer. This step opens the Event Viewer.

3. Click the Security Log. Notice that the security events are displayed in the results pane on the right side.

SCENARIO & SOLUTION

I do not have time to monitor all the security events written to the security log files. Can I delegate someone to do this job for me?	Yes. Make sure that the other user has Manage Auditing and Security Logs rights.
I enabled auditing on several objects and several types of events, and now the security log file is full of events. Is there a way to look for a particular event based on the source of the event or the event category?	Yes. Use the Find option in the Event Viewer. You can specify what kind of events you want to locate.
I have given rights to a user to manage user accounts in the domain. How can I keep a check on his activities?	Enable auditing for User Rights assignments for this user.
How do I ensure that the security events do not fill up the security log file? Should I make the security log file as large as possible?	No. Making the security log file large is not recommended. You must monitor the events regularly and clear the log files if the system is configured not to overwrite events. When you have checked the events, you can either save the file or simply clear the events.

The display depends on how the Event Viewer is configured. The security events that should be of interest to you are especially those that indicate violation of the organizationwide security policies. Examples of such events are

- Logon attempts by unauthorized users

- Logon attempts by authorized users in off hours when access is restricted

- Attempts by users to access confidential files or folders

- Misuse of administrative privileges, such as opening of undesired user accounts or giving rights to undesired users

- Attempts to alter security settings on Active Directory objects, such as changing attributes of an object

Tracking security events can lead you to find solutions to security problems, even before they happen. In order to understand the severity of an event, you must first interpret the event. Each event listed in the security log has plenty of information that can be helpful in complete interpretation of what actually happened.

The events listed in the security log display only summary information of the event, such as event ID, event type, date, and time. When you double-click a particular event, the details of the event are displayed in a separate box.

Events with Similar IDs

It is important to note that many events get a common event ID and might look similar, but in fact, they are not. Microsoft recommends that you read the details of the event to completely understand it. For an example, when a user logs on interactively or from the network, the events generated get the same event ID in both instance.

In any case, the events that you ignore at first view, considering that they have similar event IDs, might in fact be distinct ones. Another example of such events is a user connecting to a shared resource. The event ID is generated when the user first connects to the resource, but the ID does not explain how the resource was accessed.

on the job

Many organizations use the auditing feature to monitor the usage of network resources such as network printers. By generating log files and analyzing them, you can find out how the resources are currently being used and how demand for the resources grows over a period of time. This ability helps in evaluating future needs for network resources and in planning ahead so that resource requirements do not become a problem.

FROM THE CLASSROOM

Your Audit Plans

This chapter includes some discussion on enabling and configuring auditing on Windows 2000 computers. As you know now, auditing is disabled by default on all Windows 2000 computers in favor of system performance. If you have decided to set up auditing security events on the network, the following are some of the practical key points that you must remember:

- It is not necessary that all domain controllers should have auditing enabled. Decide the computers that are important from a security point of view and need auditing.

- Decide whether you need to audit success events or failure events, or both. Enable auditing for only those objects that you think are necessary to monitor.

- Do not forget to audit use or misuse of administrative privileges given to other users. Remember, anyone in the Administrators group can disable auditing and effectively remove any audit trails.

- Configuring auditing is only part of the job. You must view the security logs regularly to find out any breaches in your security setup.

- Decide if you want to clear the security logs after the log files are full or you want to archive them. Archiving security logs is useful if anyone in the organization wants to check the events at a later date.

In addition, several other factors, including the policies of your organization, might contribute to your auditing plans. Your auditing plan must be a concrete one so that there is no threat to system security. At the same time, you must ensure that only essential events are monitored, because auditing can become a performance problem in busy computers.

—*Pawan K. Bhardwaj, MCSE, MCP+I, CCNA.*

CERTIFICATION SUMMARY

In this chapter, you studied various tools included with the Windows 2000 operating system for configuration and analysis of security. Security is important for every organization. Security in Windows 2000 is applied using group policies. Group Policy enables you to configure security for account policies, local policies, event logs, system services, registry, and many other areas. Security policies are usually defined at the domain level. The three constituents of Group Policy are Group Policy objects, Group Policy containers, and Group Policy templates.

The Security Configuration and Analysis tool is used to manage security via the security database files. Several template data files are included with Windows 2000, and a suitable template can be imported to set up a working security database that meets your requirements. The Security Configuration and Analysis tool allows you to analyze your security settings immediately by comparing them with the predefined settings.

Audit policies are used to monitor usage of network resources and maintain applied security policies. In order to view security events happening on the network, auditing must be enabled. Auditing helps you track authorized or unauthorized access to resources, which helps ensure that user rights and privileges are not misused.

The security-related events are written to security log files. The events can be viewed from the security log of the Event Viewer. It is important to check the security logs at regular intervals. The logs contain detailed information on all events. You must check events related to logon attempts, access to confidential folders, and undesired use of user rights. The Event Viewer allows you to filter events and save log files. The log settings can be configured to strike a balance between disk space and recording of all required events.

TWO-MINUTE DRILL

Configuring and Troubleshooting Security in a Directory Services Infrastructure

❑ Using group policies, you can implement a manageable security policy in Windows 2000 networks. The data created by Group Policy is stored in Group Policy objects.

❑ The three elements of Group Policy are GPOs, GPCs, and GPTs. The GPTs are stored in the SYSVOL folder.

❑ New security policies are created using Group Policy, which is a two-step process. First, you create a new GPO; second, you use the Group Policy Editor to configure security settings.

❑ The Security Configuration and Analysis tool is used to manage security on a computer. By default, this tool is not installed. You can add this snap-in to an empty MMC using the Add/Remove Snap-in option.

❑ Security templates are included with Windows 2000 and contain predefined security settings stored in database files. Any template file can be imported to the Security Configuration and Analysis tool. Changes can be made to the template file to set up a working security database.

❑ Rights on system services, Active Directory objects, and file systems can be configured using the Security Configuration and Analysis tool. Rights on file systems can be set only on NTFS volumes.

❑ Auditing is disabled by default. Configuring auditing enables you to specify which security events must be monitored to maintain security. You must be an administrator or have Manage Auditing and Security Logs rights in order to audit security events.

❑ Configuration of auditing is a two-step process. First, an audit policy is set with the Group Policy, and then auditing is configured on required objects using the Active Directory Users and Computers Console.

Monitoring and Analyzing Security Events

❑ Security events happening in a Windows 2000 network must be monitored in order to maintain security. The most important events that must be monitored are logon attempts, access to confidential folders, and misuse of user rights.

❑ The Event Viewer contains security events in the Security Events category. You must be an administrator or have the user right to manage auditing and security logs. All users can view the application and system logs.

❑ It is necessary to configure audit policies and enable auditing on resources in order to log security events to log files. The security logs must be checked regularly.

❑ Each event recorded in the security log has an event ID, event source, name of computer, and user and event category.

❑ The displayed events in the security logs can be filtered to view only desired events, such as events classified by category or originating from a particular source.

❑ The security log files can be configured with regard to its size and whether or not to overwrite events when the file is full. You can also clear the log files manually if you do not want the system to overwrite events automatically.

❑ Security events must be interpreted carefully to analyze and maintain security. Several events can have similar event IDs, but the actual event might be different. Proper interpretation of events enables you to know the cause and source of a security breach.

SELF TEST

The following questions will help you measure your understanding of the material presented in this chapter. Read all the choices carefully because there might be more than one correct answer. Choose all correct answers for each question.

Configuring and Troubleshooting Security in a Directory Services Infrastructure

1. Your boss has asked you about some essential elements of Group Policy. Which of the following is not a part of Windows 2000 Group Policy?

   A. Group Policy administrator

   B. Group Policy objects

   C. Group Policy containers

   D. Group Policy templates

2. You have been assigned the responsibility of creating new policies for one of the locations of your company. This location has been configured as a separate OU in Active Directory. The first thing you want to do is to create new Group Policy object for the OU. Which of the following methods can you use to create a new GPO?

   A. From the Security tab of the OU Properties sheet

   B. From the Group Policy tab of the OU Properties sheet

   C. From the Default Domain Policy Console of Administrative Tools

   D. From the Local Security Policy Console

3. You have a Windows 2000 domain that is spread over five locations across the country. You want to set up account policies for the domain. Which of the following statements are true regarding account policies? Choose all correct answers.

   A. There must be an account policy for each location.

   B. There can be only one policy at the domain level.

   C. There can be an account policy for each user group.

   D. The users always take account policy from the domain root.

4. When using the Security Configurations and Analysis tool, you imported a template database file. You then made several changes to the security configuration and saved the changes. What happened to the original template file after the security changes become effective?

   A. The template file is changed.

   B. The template file remains unchanged.

   C. The template file is removed from the original location.

   D. None of the above.

5. Which of the Active Directory Consoles is used to set up security on objects such as folders, printers, and computers that are located on a single site, considering that the file replication system is working on all domain controllers?

   A. Sites and Services

   B. Domains and Trusts

   C. Users and Computers

   D. Security Configuration and Analysis

6. You are the domain administrator of your Windows 2000 office network. You want to implement audit policies to track security events happening in the network. Which of the following two steps are necessary to have a working audit policy in order to enable you to monitor security events? Select all correct answers.

   A. Enable auditing by setting audit policy

   B. Configure objects that must be audited

   C. Copy security templates to all domain controllers

   D. Install the Security Configuration and Analysis tool

7. You want to delegate one of your users to check security logs on some domain controller computers. You do not want to make him a domain administrator for this purpose alone. Which of the following rights will enable the user to monitor security events?

   A. Log on Locally

   B. Manage Auditing and Security Logs

   C. Local Administrator

   D. Log on as a Batch Job

8. Which of the following types of auditing would be helpful to monitor users who are not authorized but make attempts to access secure data folders? Select the best answer.

    A. Folder access success events

    B. User management failure events

    C. Process-tracking failure events

    D. Folder access failure events

9. You have made some changes to the security policies on a domain controller computer. You need these policies to become effective immediately without disturbing the working of the network. Which of the following is your best option to accomplish this task?

    A. Restart the computer.

    B. Use the SECEDIT /MACHINE_POLICY command.

    C. Use the SECEDIT /REFRESHPOLICY MACHINE_POLICY command.

    D. Log off from the computer and log on again.

10. You opened the Active Directory Users and Computers Console to enable auditing for certain objects on a domain controller. What you notice is that all the check boxes under Access in the Auditing dialog box are disabled. The Remove button is also not visible in the Access Control Settings dialog box. Which of the following could be the reason for this?

    A. You do not have rights to enable auditing.

    B. The audit policy of the parent container is propagated to this object.

    C. You need to set up a separate audit policy.

    D. Group Policy does not allow you to configure auditing on the objects.

11. You and your other administrator colleagues have created a security document and stored it in a folder on the file server. The document describes the security policies of the organization and is considered highly confidential. Several user groups have been given Read access to the folder, as you do not want anyone to modify the folder. You want to track all users who access this folder. Which of the user groups should you enable auditing to accomplish this task?

    A. Everyone group

    B. Users group

    C. Guests group

    D. All of the above

Monitoring and Analyzing Security Events

12. Which of the following options would you use in the security log to display events that contain only success audit events and that happened between specific dates?

    A. By using the Find option

    B. By configuring audit policy

    C. By using the Filter option

    D. By setting a group policy

13. You are the domain administrator of your network. Last week you had added a new domain controller to the network. When you connected to this domain controller remotely and opened the security log, you found that the log was empty. What is the reason that you did not see any security events in the log?

    A. Security events cannot be viewed remotely.

    B. You do not have sufficient privileges to view the security log.

    C. The security log configuration is not done.

    D. Auditing is not enabled.

14. Which of the following users or groups can view security event logs by default on remote domain controllers?

    A. Domain administrators

    B. Server operators group

    C. Backup operators group

    D. All of the above

15. Your weekly schedule in office includes spending nearly two hours for checking security logs on all domain controllers on Monday mornings. You do not want to clear your security logs manually on each domain controller. Which of the following would be the best configuration option for security logs, considering that you do not want to lose any unchecked events?

    A. Keep the log size to accommodate a week's events.

    B. Click Restore Defaults every time you check the logs.

    C. Increase log size and select "Overwrite events older than 7 days."

    D. Select "Overwrite events as needed."

16. When you logged on to one of your domain controllers, you noticed a message, "Security log is full." Which of the following is a true statement regarding the security events after the log file became full?

    A. No events were written.

    B. Further events were written to the system log.

    C. Further events were written to the application log.

    D. None of the above.

17. Which of the following options is used to clear a log file in security log properties manually?

    A. Select "Do not overwrite events."

    B. Specify the minimum possible log file size.

    C. Click the Restore Defaults button.

    D. Click the Clear Log button.

LAB QUESTION

Current Situation: You have a medium-sized network with five Windows 2000 domain controllers. You want to monitor security events on these domain controllers.

Required Result: Set up auditing on Active Directory objects and monitor security events.

Desired Optional Results:

1. Auditing should not affect the performance of domain controllers.

2. The security events must be monitored regularly.

3. The security log files should not be automatically deleted.

We suggest some steps to accomplish some or all of these results mentioned. Read the following steps carefully and look for any missing step or incorrect information.

Proposed Solution: Perform the following steps:

1. Open the default domain policy on each domain controller.

2. Expand Computer Configuration, Security Settings, Local Policies, and select Audit Policies. Configure Audit Policies as per your requirements.

3. Open the Active Directory Users and Computers Console. Select the first object that you want to audit.

4. Open the Properties sheet of the selected object, and click the Group Policy tab.

5. Click Auditing. Select the User, Computer, or Group for which auditing is required. Select all the events in the Access list.

6. Repeat steps 4 and 5 for all the Active Directory objects.

7. Open the Event Viewer. Click Security Log. Open the log Properties sheet.

8. Select "Do not overwrite events" from the "When maximum log size is reached."

This should complete the process in our view. Let us see what is accomplished by performing the given steps.

SELF TEST ANSWERS

Configuring and Troubleshooting Security in a Directory Services Infrastructure

1. ☑ **A. Group Policy administrator.** The Group Policy administrator is not a constituent element of the Windows 2000 Group Policy. This is a position that is responsible for setting up and maintaining Group Policy in the organization.
   ☒ **B, C, and D** are incorrect because objects, containers, and templates are essential elements of Windows 2000 Group Policy.

2. ☑ **B. From the Group Policy tab of the OU Properties sheet.** A new Group Policy object at the OU level is created from the Group Policy tab of the OU Properties sheet.
   ☒ **A** is incorrect because the security tab of the OU Properties sheet is not used for creating new Group Policy object. **C and D** are incorrect because neither Default Domain Policy nor the Local Security Policy Console is used to create Group Policy for any OU.

3. ☑ **B and D.** Windows 2000 allows only one account policy for the entire domain, with the exception of individual account policies set for the OUs in Active Directory.
   ☒ **A** is incorrect because you cannot have a separate account policy for each location unless each location is regarded as a separate OU in Active Directory. **C** is incorrect because there cannot be an account policy for each user group.

4. ☑ **B. The template file remains unchanged.** When you import a template security database file into the Security Configuration and Analysis tool, the changes that you make to this template are saved in a separate database.
   ☒ **A** is incorrect because the original template file remains unchanged. **C** is incorrect because the template file is not removed from its original location. The templates are located in the \Systemroot\Security\Templates folder. This makes **D** an incorrect option.

5. ☑ **C. Users and Computers.** The Active Directory Users and Computers Console is used for setting security on all objects of Active Directory, irrespective of the site location.
   ☒ **A, B, and D** are incorrect because none of these consoles is appropriate for setting up security on Active Directory objects. *Be careful because sites, locations, and file replication system might be included in the question statement just to confuse you.*

6. ☑ **A and B.** In order to implement a working audit policy in the domain, you must first enable audit policy and then configure the objects that you want to audit. Auditing is a two-step process.

   ☒ **C** is incorrect because the Security Configuration and Analysis tool need not be installed in order to have a working audit policy. This tool is used to configure and analyze security on local computers. **D** is incorrect because the security templates are not required to set up and configure auditing.

7. ☑ **B.** Manage auditing and security logs. If you want someone to monitor security events on a computer, the user must have Manage Auditing and Security Logs rights.

   ☒ **A** is incorrect because logging on locally will not allow the user to view security events. **C** is incorrect because there is no local administrator account on domain controller computers. **D** is an invalid choice because the Log on as a Batch Job right is usually given to application specific accounts.

8. ☑ **D.** Folder access failure events. When you want to track events related to users' unsuccessful attempts to access secure data folders, you must set up auditing of access failure events.

   ☒ **A** is incorrect because when the users are not granted access to secure data folders, their access attempts will not be successful. **B** is incorrect because auditing of user management rights has no link to object access events. **C** is inappropriate because process-tracking events are usually generated by application programs, not by user activities.

9. ☑ **C.** Use the SECEDIT /REFRESHPOLICY MACHINE_POLICY command. This command ensures that the policy becomes effective immediately.

   ☒ **A** is not the best option because the computer is a domain controller and cannot be restarted without disturbing the network. **B** is incorrect because the given command is incorrect. **D** is incorrect because logging off from the computer and logging on again will make the new policy effective.

10. ☑ **B.** The audit policy of the parent container is propagated to this object. The auditing options are disabled on certain objects in Active Directory because the audit policies set on the parent container are propagated to the objects.

    ☒ **A** is incorrect because rights is not a problem; if you are able to access the Auditing Properties dialog box, it means you have sufficient rights to alter audit properties. **C** is incorrect because you need not set a separate audit policy. **D** is incorrect because the Group Policy settings are not causing the problem.

11. ☑ **A. Everyone group.** You must enable auditing for the Everyone group in order to track access to the folder by any user. The Everyone group contains all users and groups in the network.

☒ **B** is incorrect because the Users group does not contain all users in the network, and you might miss events related to access by all those users who are not members of the users group. **C** is incorrect because the Guests group is disabled by default and, even if enabled, does not contain all users. This makes **D** incorrect, since we have one correct answer.

Monitoring and Analyzing Security Events

12. ☑ **C. By using the Filter option.** The security log display can be filtered to display events on the basis of the specified criteria given in the question.

☒ **A** is incorrect because the Find option is used to locate events in the security log file. **B** and **D** are inappropriate choices because the audit and group policies are not used for such a simple operation.

13. ☑ **D. Auditing is not enabled.** Auditing must be enabled on the domain controller in order to record security events in the security log files. No events are recorded in security log files unless auditing is enabled.

☒ **A** is incorrect because it is possible to view security and other events on remote computers. **B** is incorrect because the statement says you are domain administrator and thus have sufficient privileges to view security logs. If you do not have sufficient privileges, you would rather get an "Access denied" error message. **C** is incorrect because even when the security log configuration is not done, the default settings exist.

14. ☑ **A. Domain administrators.** You must be a member of Domain Administrators group or have the Manage Auditing and Security Logs right to view security logs on local and remote domain controller computers.

☒ **B** and **C** are incorrect because neither server operators nor backup operators group can view security logs on remote domain controllers. **D** is incorrect because there is only one correct answer.

15. ☑ **C. Increase log size and select "Overwrite events older than 7 days."** This is your best option because this way, you will not have to clear the logs manually and you will be able to view security events for the previous week.

☒ **A** is incorrect because it is very difficult to predict the size of the log file to accommodate a week's events. **B** is incorrect because clicking Restore Defaults does not clear the logs. **D** is incorrect because selecting "Overwrite events as needed" when the log file is full could delete even those events that might have happened during the previous week.

16. ☑ **A.** No events were written. When the security log file is full, no further events can be written to it, and one event is written to the application log that describes that the security log is full.

☒ **B** and **C** are incorrect because the security events are not written to either system or application log files if the security log is full. **D** is incorrect because we have a correct answer.

17. ☑ **D.** Click the Clear Log button. The Clear Log button is used to clear the security log. This becomes necessary when you have configured the security logs not to overwrite events. Another way to clear the security event logs is to right-click Security Log, and click Clear All Events. This option also allows you to archive the file before clearing the logs.

☒ **A** is incorrect because the log file cannot be cleared automatically by selecting "Do not overwrite events." You must clear the logs manually. **B** is incorrect because setting the log file size to minimum will further create problems because a small file will not be able to record many events before it becomes full. **C** is incorrect because when you click the Restore Defaults button, all configured log file settings are returned to their original defaults.

LAB ANSWER

The suggested steps will not produce either the required result or any of the optional results due to the following missing or incorrect steps:

1. In step 2, some information is missing. You must expand the Windows Settings in order to access the Security Settings node.

2. In order to make the audit policy effective, you must use the SECEDIT /REFRESHPOLICY MACHINE_POLICY command. This step is missing.

3. Step 4 suggests an incorrect action. You must click the Security tab instead of the Group Policy tab in order to enable auditing.

4. Steps 3, 4, 5, and 6 together suggest that you must enable auditing for every Active Directory object and audit every event. This method is not recommended because auditing all objects and all events will eat up all system resources on the domain controllers. You must enable auditing on only required objects, and only selected events should be monitored.

A

About the CD

This CD-ROM contains the CertTrainer software. CertTrainer comes complete with ExamSim, Skill Assessment tests, CertCam movie clips, the e-book (electronic version of the book), and Drive Time. CertTrainer is easy to install on any Windows 98/NT/2000 computer and must be installed to access these features. You may, however, browse the e-book directly from the CD without installation.

Installing CertTrainer

If your computer CD-ROM drive is configured to autorun, the CD-ROM will automatically start up upon inserting the disk. From the opening screen you may either browse the e-book or install CertTrainer by pressing the *Install Now* button. This will begin the installation process and create a program group named "CertTrainer." To run CertTrainer use START | PROGRAMS | CERTTRAINER.

System Requirements

CertTrainer requires Windows 98 or higher and Internet Explorer 4.0 or above and 600MB of hard disk space for full installation.

CertTrainer

CertTrainer provides a complete review of each exam objective, organized by chapter. You should read each objective summary and make certain that you understand it before proceeding to the SkillAssessor. If you still need more practice on the concepts of any objective, use the "In Depth" button to link to the corresponding section from the Study Guide or use the CertCam button to view a short .AVI clip illustrating various exercises from within the chapter.

Once you have completed the review(s) and feel comfortable with the material, launch the SkillAssessor quiz to test your grasp of each objective. Once you complete the quiz, you will be presented with your score for that chapter.

ExamSim

As its name implies, ExamSim provides you with a simulation of the actual exam. The number of questions, the type of questions, and the time allowed are intended to be an accurate representation of the exam environment. You will see the following screen when you are ready to begin ExamSim:

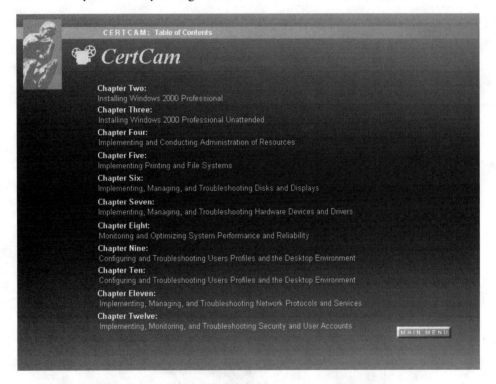

When you launch ExamSim, a digital clock display will appear in the upper left-hand corner of your screen. The clock will continue to count down to zero unless you choose to end the exam before the time expires.

There are three types of questions on the exam:

■ **Multiple Choice**   These questions have a single correct answer that you indicate by selecting the appropriate check box.

- **Multiple-Multiple Choice** These questions require more than one correct answer. Indicate each correct answer by selecting the appropriate check boxes.
- **Simulations** These questions simulate actual Windows 2000 menus and dialog boxes. After reading the question, you are required to select the appropriate settings to most accurately meet the objectives for that question.

Saving Scores as Cookies

Your ExamSim score is stored as a browser cookie. If you've configured your browser to accept cookies, your score will be stored in a file named *History*. If your browser is not configured to accept cookies, you cannot permanently save your scores. If you delete this History cookie, the scores will be deleted permanently.

E-Book

The entire contents of the Study Guide are provided in HTML form, as shown in the following screen. Although the files are optimized for Internet Explorer, they can also be viewed with other browsers including Netscape.

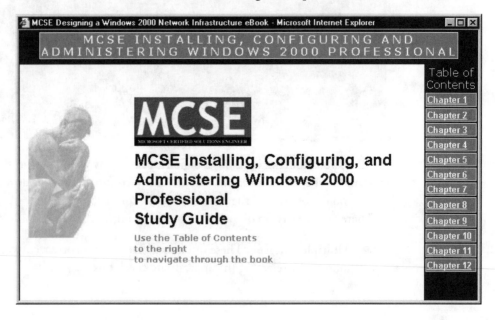

CertCam

CertCam .AVI clips provide detailed examples of key certification objectives. These clips walk you step-by-step through various system configurations and are narrated by Thomas Shinder, M.D., MCSE, MCT. You can access the clips directly from the CertCam table of contents (shown in the following screen) or through the CertTrainer objectives.

The CertCam .AVI clips are recorded and produced using TechSmith's Camtasia Producer. Since .AVI clips can be very large, ExamSim uses TechSmith's special AVI Codec to compress the clips. The file named **tsccvid.dll** is copied to your Windows\System folder when you install CertTrainer. If the .AVI clip runs with audio but no video, you may need to reinstall the file from the CD-ROM. Browse to the "bin" folder, and run TSCC.EXE.

DriveTime

DriveTime audio tracks will automatically play when you insert the CD-ROM into a standard CD-ROM player, such as the one in your car or stereo. There is one track for each chapter. These tracks provide you with certification summaries for each chapter and are the perfect way to study while commuting.

Help

A help file is provided through a help button on the main CertTrainer screen in the lower right hand corner.

Upgrading

A button is provided on the main ExamSim screen for upgrades. This button will take you to www.syngress.com where you can download any available upgrades.

MICROSOFT CERTIFIED SYSTEMS ENGINEER

B

About the Web Site

A t Access.Globalknowledge, the premier online information source for IT professionals (http://access.globalknowledge.com), you'll enter a Global Knowledge information portal designed to inform, educate, and update visitors on issues regarding IT and IT education.

Get *What* You Want *When* You Want It

At the Access.Globalknowledge site, you can:

- Choose personalized technology articles related to your interests. Access a news article, a review, or a tutorial, customized to what you want to see, regularly throughout the week.

- Continue your education, in between Global courses, by taking advantage of chat sessions with other users or instructors. Get the tips, tricks, and advice that you need today!

- Make your point in the Access.Globalknowledge community by participating in threaded discussion groups related to technologies and certification.

- Get instant course information at your fingertips. Customized course calendars show you the courses you want, and when and where you want them.

- Obtain the resources you need with online tools, trivia, skills assessment, and more!

All this and more is available now on the Web at http://access.globalknowledge.com. Visit today!

Glossary

Account Lockout Policy   The Account Lockout Policy dictates the behavior for locking and unlocking user accounts. There are two configurable parameters: Account lockout threshold determines how many times users can attempt to log on before their accounts are locked. This can range from low (five attempts) to high (one or two attempts). The Account lockout duration parameter controls how long an account is locked after the Account lockout threshold parameter is triggered.

ACPI   *See* Advanced Configuration and Power Interface

Active Directory   The Active Directory is implemented on Windows 2000 domain controllers, and the directory can be accessed from Windows 2000 Professional as an Active Directory client. The Active Directory arranges objects—including computer information, user and group information, shared folders, printers, and other resources—in a hierarchical structure, in which domains can be joined into trees (groups of domains that share a contiguous namespace). Trees can be joined into forests (groups of domain trees that share a common schema, configuration, and global catalog).

Active Directory Service   This service provides the means for locating the Remote Installation Service (RIS) servers and the client computers on the network. The RIS server must have access to the Active Directory.

Administration   The word *administer* is generally used as a synonym for *manage,* which in turn means to exert control. One of the many enhancements to Windows 2000—both the Professional and Server incarnations—is the ability Microsoft has given administrators to apply the degree of control desired, in a flexible and granular manner.

Add Printer Wizard   All clients running a version of the Windows operating system (Windows 2000, Windows NT, Windows 98, and Windows 95) can use the Add Printer Wizard to create a printer entry on the client. This Add Printer Wizard can create and share a printer on a print server. The Windows 2000 version of the Add Printer Wizard has more options than the wizard in other versions of Windows, but many of the same methods can be used to get the printer set up on the client.

Address Resolution Protocol (ARP)   The Address Resolution Protocol (ARP) is used to resolve Internet Protocol (IP) logical addresses to Media Access Control (MAC) physical hardware addresses. ARP uses broadcasts to discover the hardware addresses and stores the information in its ARP cache.

Advanced Configuration and Power Interface (ACPI)   ACPI combines Plug and Play (PnP) capability with Power Management, and places these functions under complete control of the operating system.

Advanced Power Management (APM)   An Intel/Microsoft application programming interface (API) that allows programs to indicate their requirements for power to regulate the speed of components.

Alerts   Alerts allow an action to be performed when a performance counter reaches a particular threshold. A common action is to log the event in the application event log. You can also send a network message to a specified computer. You can have the alert start a performance log to start logging when the alert occurs. And finally, you can configure the alert to start a program.

Algorithm   An algorithm is a procedure or formula used to solve a problem.

Analysis   Analysis is the process of comparison, contrast, diagnosis, diagramming, discrimination, and/or drawing conclusions.

Answer file   An answer file is a file containing the information you would normally have to key in during the setup process. Answer files help automate the installation process, as all the queries presented to you during installation are answered by the answer files. With careful planning, you can prepare answers that eliminate the possibility of incorrect answers typed in by the person performing the installation, thus reducing the chances of setup failure. You can use the Setup Manager Wizard to create a customized answer file. This technique minimizes the chances of committing syntax-related errors while manually creating or editing the sample answer files.

APIPA   *See* Automatic Private Internet Protocol Addressing.

APM   *See* Advanced Power Management.

AppleTalk   The AppleTalk protocol suite was developed by Apple Computer for use in its Macintosh line of personal computers. AppleTalk is a local area networking system that was developed by Apple Computer, Inc. AppleTalk networks can run over a variety of networks that include Ethernet, FDDI, and Token Ring, as well as Apple's proprietary media system LocalTalk. Macintosh computers are very popular in the education and art industries, so familiarity with the way they communicate using their native protocol is very useful.

AppleTalk printing device   Another type of remote printer is the AppleTalk printing device. Like a Transmission Control Protocol/Internet Protocol (TCP/IP) printer, an AppleTalk printer can be connected directly to an AppleTalk network or shared across the network through an AppleShare print server. Like the TCP/IP printers, a large number of modern, high-capacity PostScript printers can be configured to communicate with an AppleTalk network as well as a TCP/IP network. In fact, many Hewlett-Packard LaserJet printers have JetDirect cards that will speak TCP/IP and AppleTalk at the same time.

Application   A program designed to perform a specific function directly for the user or for another application program. Examples of an application would be, for example, word processors, database programs, graphics/drawing programs, Web browsers, and e-mail programs.

Application   The process of choice, demonstration, performing a procedure, solving, plotting, calculation, changing, interpretation, and operation.

Application Service Provider (ASP)   ASPs are companies that manage applications and provide organizations with application hosting services. Analysts expect the ASP market will be a six-billion-dollar industry by the year 2001. The application-hosting model offers organizations the option of outsourcing application support and maintenance.

Application System Border Router (ASBR)   An AS Border Router is a router that connects together different ASs. When the ASBR exchanges routing information with an external network, the routing information received from outside the AS are referred to as external routes.

ARP   *See* Address Resolution Protocol.

ARPAnet   ARPAnet, the predecessor of the Internet was begun by the U.S. Department of Defense (DoD), in conjunction with major universities. The DoD developed the nationwide system (which then was extended throughout the world) to provide highly reliable, redundant communications links that could withstand even a nuclear war.

ASBR   *See* Application System Border Router.

ASP   *See* Application Service Provider.

Asymmetric algorithm   A cryptographic algorithm that utilizes a different key for encrypting data than the one used to decrypt the data.

Asynchronous Transfer Mode over Asymmetric Digital Subscriber Line (ATM over ADSL)   ADSL offers a new technology aimed at small businesses and residential customers. It offers a higher throughput than Public Switched Telephone Network (PSTN) and Integrated Services Digital Network (ISDN) connections, but the bit rate is higher downstream than upstream—typically 384 Kbps when going out and 384 Kbps–1.544 Mbps when coming in (this usually suits Internet traffic usage where users download a much higher percentage of data than they upload). ADSL equipment can appear to a Windows 2000 server as one of two interfaces: Ethernet or dial-up. When seen as an Ethernet interface, the ASDL behaves in the same way as a standard network adapter connected to the Internet. When seen as a dial-up interface, ADSL provides the physical connection for ATM traffic.

Auditing   Windows 2000 gives the ability to audit security-related events, track access to objects and use of user rights, and detect attempted and successful access (authorized and unauthorized) to the network. Auditing is not enabled by default, but once enabled, a security log is generated that provides information in regard to specific activities performed on the computer.

Authenticated data exchange   The only problem with confidential data exchange is that there is no assurance that the person who used your public key to encrypt and send you a message is really whomever he or she claims to be. How can we ensure that? What if the sender encrypted the message using his or her private key, and then you decrypted it using his or her public key? What would this accomplish? We get the same confidentiality of the data as with the first method, but since presumably only the sender has the private key, we can be confident of his identity. Now we have an authenticated data exchange.

Authentication   Authentication is when a user is identified (usually by means of a username and password). If this is done in an encrypted form, an authentication protocol is used. A successful authentication proves that users are who they say they are, but has nothing to do with what resources they can access.

Authentication Header (AH)   The Authentication Header ensures data integrity and authentication. The AH does not encrypt data, and therefore provides no confidentiality, but does protect the data from modification. When the AH protocol is applied in transport mode, the Authentication Header is inserted between the original Internet Protocol (IP) header and the Transmission Control Protocol (TCP) or User Datagram Protocol (UDP) header.

Authorization   Authorization is the process of determining whether users can have access to requested resources based on their identity. By definition, this can only happen after a successful authentication. In the context of Routing and Remote Access (RRAS), remote users' connection attempts can be authenticated (because they have proved who they are), but their connection can still be denied because their authorization failed if they did not have permission to dial in, for example.

Automatic Partner Discovery   You can configure your Windows Internet Name Server (WINS) servers to find other WINS servers on the network and create a replication partnership with them automatically. When you enable Automatic Partner Discovery, WINS servers use the multicast address 224.0.1.24 to discover or find other WINS servers.

Automatic Private Internet Protocol Addressing (APIPA)   APIPA, or Automatic Client Configuration, is a new feature initially available in Windows 98. The feature has been extended to Windows 2000 and allows Dynamic Host Control Protocol (DHCP) client computers to self-configure their IP addressing information in the event a DHCP server is not available when the computer issues a DHCPDISCOVER message. It also allows self-configuration when it senses that it has been moved from a previous network via Windows 2000 media sensing capabilities.

Backup Domain Controller (BDC)   A backup file or copy of the Primary Domain Controller (PDC). Periodically, the BDC is synchronized with the PDC.

Backup Logs   Windows Backup generates a backup log file for every backup job. These files are the best place to review the backup process in case some problem is encountered by the program. The backup log is a text file that records all the events during the backup process.

BACP   *See* Bandwidth Allocation Control Protocol.

Bandwidth Allocation Control Protocol (BACP)   BACP polices multiple peers using Multilink Point-to-Point Protocol (MP); for example, electing a favored peer when more than one PPP peer requests to add or remove a connection at the same time. The sole job of this protocol is to elect a favored peer when necessary. If both peers of an MP- and BAP-enabled connection send a BAP Call Request or BAP Link Drop Query Request message at the same time, only one request can succeed, and it is the responsibility of this protocol to elect which peer wins.

Bandwidth Allocation Protocol (BAP)   BAP is a Point-to-Point Protocol (PPP) that is used to add or remove additional links to an MP connection dynamically.

BAP   *See* Bandwidth Allocation Protocol.

Basic Input/Output System (BIOS)   A set of programs encoded in ROM on IBM PC-compatible computers programs handle startup operations such as

Power On Self Test (POST) and low-level control for hardware such as disk drives and keyboards.

BDC   *See* Backup Domain Controller.

BIOS   *See* Basic Input/Output System.

Black holes   Because the Routing Information Protocol (RIP) is a distance vector-based routing protocol that uses unacknowledged delivery, data can often be lost without trace. One router could realize that its neighboring router was unavailable and send out information to broadcast this—but if the information is never received, other routers can continue to send data to the downed router in the mistaken belief it is still available. This is a "black hole" because there is nowhere for the packets to go, but the sending system hasn't realized this. Link state routing protocols that use directed and acknowledged announcements are not vulnerable to this problem.

B-node   A b-node (broadcast node) client uses broadcasts instead of a WINS server. A Windows NetBIOS client computer without a configured WINS server is a b-node client.

Boot   The process of loading an operating system into the computer's memory (RAM) so those applications can be run on it.

Boot ROM   A boot ROM is a chip on the network adapter that helps the computer boot from the network. Such a computer need not have a previously installed operating system. The BIOS of the computer that has a PXE-based boot ROM must be configured to boot from the network. Windows 2000 Server RIS supports PXE ROM versions 99 or later.

BOOTP   *See* Bootstrap Protocol.

Bootstrap Protocol (BOOTP)   Bootstrap Protocol (BOOTP) is the predecessor to DHCP. It was originally designed to provide IP address configuration to diskless workstations, which not only received IP addressing information from a

BOOTP server, but also received information regarding where to download its operating system image. DHCP was developed to improve on the host configuration services offered by BOOTP, and address some of the problems encountered in using it.

Bottleneck   A bottleneck in computer terms is a component of the system as a whole that restricts the system from operating at its peak. When a bottleneck occurs, the component that is a bottleneck will have a high rate of usage and other components will have a low rate of usage. A lack of memory is a common cause of bottleneck when your computer doesn't have enough memory for the applications and services that are running.

Burst mode   When the Windows Internet Name Server (WINS) server is in burst mode, any name registration requests received over a predefined number receive immediate acknowledgement. However, the WINS server does not check the NetBIOS against the WINS database; it does not issue a challenge against duplicate names, and it does not write an entry to the WINS database.

CA   *See* Certificate Authority.

Caching resolver   The caching resolver not only caches queries that have been answered positively, but also caches negative results. When a Domain Name System (DNS) query fails, this failed result is placed in cache for five minutes, by default. If the machines issues a DNS query for the same object within five minutes, no query will be sent, and a failure message will be retrieved from cache. This can significantly reduce the overall DNS query traffic on a large network.

Caching-only DNS server   The caching-only Domain Name System (DNS) server does not contain any zone information; it only stores (caches) the results of previous queries it has issued. You might want to place a caching-only server on the other side of a slow Wide Area Network (WAN) link, since they do not generate zone transfer traffic.

Caching-only server   All Domain Name System (DNS) servers cache results of queries they have resolved. The caching-only DNS server does not contain zone information or a zone file. The caching-only server builds its database of host name and domain mappings over time from successful DNS queries it has resolved for DNS clients.

CAL   *See* Client Access License.

Callback   Callback is when the remote user dials in and requests the server to call back, so the connection cost of the remote access session is charged to the server's line and not the user.

Canonical Name (CNAME)   This is an alias for a computer with an existing A Address record. For example, if you have a computer called "bigserver" that is going to be your Web server, you could create a CNAME for it, such as "www". It is important to note that you must have an A record for the host that you intend to create the alias for, since the CNAME record requests that you include the host name of the computer for which you wish to create the alias.

CAPI   *See* CryptoAPI.

Capture filter   A capture filter works somewhat like a database query; you can use it to specify the types of network information you want to monitor. For example, you can capture packets based on the protocol or based on the addresses of two computers whose interactions you wish to monitor. When a capture filter is applied, all packets are examined and compared to the filter's parameters; those that do not fulfill the filter requirements are dropped. This can be a processor-intensive activity during periods of moderate or high network utilization when the network card is placed in promiscuous mode.

Centralized model   This model consolidates administrative control of group policies. A single team of administrators is responsible for managing all Group Policy Objects (GPOs) no matter where they are. This is usually applied by giving all the top-level Organizational Unit (OU) administrators full control to all GPOs no matter where they are located. They give each second-level OU administrator Read permission only to each GPO. You can also decentralize other resources or keep all resources centralized, depending on the environment.

Certificate   A message that contains the digital signature of a trusted third party, called a certificate authority, which ensures that a specific public key belongs to a specific user or device.

Certificate Authority (CA)   An authority/organization that produces digital certificates with its available public key. A Certificate Authority (CA) is a public key certificate issuer (for example, VeriSign). To use a public key certificate, you must trust the issuer (CA). This means that you have faith in the CA's authentication policies. The CA is used for doing things such as authorizing certification authenticity, revoking expired certificates, and responding to certification requests. Windows 2000 offers an alternative to a third-party CA. You can become a CA within your own Intranet. Thus you can manage your own certificates rather than relying on a third-party Certification Authority.

Certificate service   Provides security and authentication support, including secure e-mail, Web-based authentication, and smart card authentication.

Challenge Handshake Authentication Protocol (CHAP)   A protocol (Point-to-Point Protocol or PPP) in which a password is required to begin a connection as well as during the connection. If the password fails any of these requirements, the system breaks the connection.

Change Permission   You can use this permission to allow users the ability to change permissions on files and folders without giving them the Full Control permission. You can use this permission to give a user or group access to modify permissions on file or folder objects without giving them the ability to have complete control over the object.

CHAP   *See* Challenge Handshake Authentication Protocol.

Cipher   The process that turns readable text data into ciphertext, which is encrypted data that must be deciphered before it is readable.

Cipher Block Chaining (CBC)   Because the blocks of data are encrypted in 64-bit chunks, there must be a way to "chain" these blocks together. The chaining algorithm will define how the combination of the unencrypted text, the secret key, and the encrypted text (also known as ciphertext) will be combined to send to the destination host. Data Encryption Standard (DES) can be combined with Cipher Block Chaining (CBC) to prevent identical messages from looking the same. This DES-CBC algorithm will make each ciphertext message appear different by using a different "initialization vector" (IV).

Cipher command   The cipher command is another way to encrypt and decrypt data. You can use it from the command line, and it has many switches, so that you can define exactly what you want to have done. The Cipher.exe command syntax is simply CIPHER, followed by the switches that you would like to use, followed by the path and directory/file name. The most common switches are the /E switch (encrypts the specified directories) and the /D switch (decrypts the specified directories). You can also use wildcards with the cipher command. For example, C:\>cipher /e /s *win* will encrypt all files and folders with "win" in the name and all files within them.

CIW   *See* Client Installation Wizard.

Class A addresses   Class A addresses are for the "large size" networks, those that have a tremendous number of computers, and thus a need for many host addresses. Class A addresses always begin with a 0 in the first octet (also called the W octet). This will be the first bit on the left. This leaves seven bits for the individual network ID, and 24 bits to identify the host computers. When we convert to decimal, we see that this means a Class A address will have a decimal value in the first octet of 127 or less. Class A addresses, because they use only the first octet to identify the network, are limited in number. However, each Class A network can have a huge number of host computers, over 16 million. The Class A network numbers were all used up some time ago; they have been assigned to very large organizations such as IBM, MIT, and General Electric.

Class B addresses   Class B networks are the "medium size" networks. Class B networks use the first two octets (the 16 leftmost bits) to identify the network, and the last two octets (or the 16 rightmost bits) to identify the host computers. This means there can be far more Class B networks than Class As (over 16,000), but each can have fewer hosts ("only" 65,535 each). Class B addresses always begin with a 10 for the two leftmost bits in the W octet, and the network is defined by the first two octets, which translates to decimal values of 128 through 191 for the first octet. Sixteen bits identify the Network ID, and the remaining 16 bits identify the Host ID. Microsoft's network is an example of a Class B network.

Class C addresses   The smallest sized block of addresses designated by a class is the Class C network, each of which can have only 254 hosts. However, there can be over 2 million Class C networks. A Class C network always has 110 as its first three bits. This leaves 24 bits to identify the network, with only 8 bits to use for host IDs. A Class C network, in decimal notation, will have a first octet decimal value of 192 through 223.

Class D addresses   Class D addresses, whose four high-order (leftmost) bits in the W octet are 1110, are used for multicasting. This is a method of sending a message to multiple computers simultaneously.

Class E addresses   Class E addresses, with four high order bits of 1111, are reserved to be used for experimental and testing purposes.

Classless addressing (CIDR)   The use of address classes is the traditional way of working with Internet Protocol (IP) addressing and subnetting. A more recent development is called Classless InterDomain Routing (CIDR). CIDR networks are referred to as "slash x" networks, with the "x" representing the number of bits assigned originally as the network ID (before subnetting). Think of this as the number of bits that don't "belong" to you. With CIDR, the subnet mask actually becomes part of the routing tables. CIDR allows us to break networks into subnets and combine networks into supernets.

Client Access License (CAL)   The CAL allows clients to access the Windows 2000's network services, shared folders, and printers. There are two types of CAL modes: Per Seat and Per Server. It important to understand the difference between the two modes: Per Seat and Per Server. When you use the Per Seat mode, each computer that accesses the server must have a CAL. The Per Server mode requires a CAL for each connection to the server. This is a subtle but significant difference. In addition, the CAL allows clients to access the Windows 2000 Server's network services, shared folders, and printers. The licensing modes are the same as under Windows NT 4.0.

Client impersonation   This is when somebody takes over an existing authenticated connection by obtaining connection parameters from a successfully authenticated client, disconnecting the client, and then taking control of the original connection.

Client Installation Wizard (CIW)   When a client computer boots using either the Remote Boot Disk or the PXE-based Boot ROM, it tries to establish a connection to the Remote Installation Service (RIS) server. If the RIS server is preconfigured to service the RIS clients, it helps the client get an Internet Protocol (IP) address from the Dynamic Host Control Protocol (DHCP) service. The CIW is then downloaded from the RIS server. This wizard has four installation options. The options that are presented to the user depend on the group policy set in the Active Directory. A user may get all four options, or may not get any of the options starting an automatic setup.

Client reservations   Client reservations allow you to manage virtually the entirety of your Internet Protocol (IP) addresses space centrally, with the exception being your Dynamic Host Control Protocol (DHCP) servers.

Cloning   *See* Disk imaging/cloning.

CNAME   *See* Canonical Name.

Comprehension   The process of distinguishing between situations, discussing, estimation, explaining, indicating, paraphrasing, and giving examples.

Computer account   A computer account is an account that is created by a domain administrator and uniquely identifies the computer on the domain. A newly created account is used so that a computer may be brought into a Windows 2000 Domain.

Confidential data exchange   Think of the method used to secure safety deposit boxes at banks. When you rent a box, you have a key to it—but your key alone won't unlock it. The bank officer also has a key, but again, that key by itself isn't of much value. When both keys are used, however, the authorized person can access the box. Likewise, with public key encryption technologies, it takes two keys to tango. One is the public key, which is made available to all those who want to send you an encrypted message. They can all use that public key to encrypt their messages, but they cannot use it to decrypt them—only your private key, which you keep secret, can do that. This is called a confidential data exchange.

Configuration   Configuration of an operating system involves specifying settings that will govern how the system behaves.

Container object   Container objects can contain other objects. A special type of container object you can create in the Active Directory is the Organizational Unit (OU).

Containers   Containers are used to describe any group of related items, whether they are objects, containers, domains, or an entire network.

Control Panel accessibility options   These options include StickyKeys, FilterKeys, ToggleKeys, SoundSentry, ShowSounds, High Contrast, MouseKeys, and SerialKeys.

Convergence   When all the routers on the internetwork have the correct routing information in their routing tables, the internetwork is said to have converged. When convergence is achieved, the internetwork is in a stable state and all routing occurs along optimal paths. When a link or router fails, the internetwork must reconfigure itself to reflect the new topology and to achieve this, routing tables must be updated. Until the internetwork has converged once again, routing will be vulnerable to loops and black holes. The time it takes for the internetwork to reconverge is known as the convergence time, and the optimal aim is for the shortest convergence time with minimum traffic.

Cooperative multitasking   An environment in which application relinquishes its use of the computer's Central Processing Unit (CPU) so that another application can use the CPU.

Copy backup   This type of backup simply copies the selected files. It neither looks for any markers set on the files nor does it clear them. The Copy backup does not affect the other Incremental or Differential backup jobs and can be performed along with the other types of backup jobs.

Counter logs   Counter logs are maintained in a similar fashion as they were in Windows NT 4.0, but the procedure for configuring the Counter logs is a bit different. Trace logs are much easier to configure in Windows 2000 because you now can set them up from the console, rather than having to edit the registry as you had to do in Windows NT 4.0.

CryptoAPI (CAPI)   CryptoAPI (CAPI) architecture is a collection of tasks that permit applications to digitally sign or encrypt data while providing security for the user's private key data.

Cryptography   The science of encrypting and decrypting data. The science (and art) of breaking cryptographic code is called cryptanalysis.

Daily backup   This type of backup does not use any markers to back up selected files and folders. The files that have changed during the day are backed up every day at a specified time. This backup will not affect other backup schedules.

Data backup   A backup and disaster protection plan is an essential part of a network administrator's duties. Windows 2000 provides a built-in backup utility used to back up data to tape or file, or to create an Emergency Repair Disk (ERD). An ERD can be used to repair a computer with damaged system files.

Data compression   Windows 2000 offers the capability of compressing data on a file-level basis, so long as the files and folders are located on an NT File System (NTFS) formatted partition or volume. Compression saves disk space; however, NTFS compression cannot be used in conjunction with file encryption.

Data Encryption Standard (DES)   The most commonly used encryption algorithm used with Internet Protocol Security (IPSec) is the Data Encryption Standard (DES) algorithm. The widely used Data Encryption Standard (DES) uses secret key algorithms. Standard DES operates on 64-bit blocks of data, and uses a series of complex steps (even more complex than our Bible-assisted method) to transform the original input bits to encoded output bits. DES is the current U.S. government standard for encryption. The DES algorithm is an example of a symmetric encryption algorithm.

Data Link Control (DLC)   DLC is a nonroutable protocol used for connecting to IBM mainframes and some network-connected laser printers.

Debugging Mode   This is the most advanced startup option of all. To use this option you will need to connect another computer to the problematic computer through a serial cable. With proper configuration, the debug information is sent to the second computer.

Decentralized model   This model is appropriate for companies that rely on delegated levels of administration. They decentralize the management of Group Policy Objects (GPOs), which distributes the workload to a number of domains. To apply this model, simply give all Organizational Unit (OU) administrators full control of their respective GPOs.

Dedicated server   A dedicated printer server is a Windows 2000 server whose only role is to provide printing services. The server does not provide directory space for users other than storage for spooled print jobs. It does not provide authentication services, does not host database services, does not act as a Domain Name System (DNS) server, and so on. A dedicated print server can host several hundred printers and print queues, however. Though it may not be obvious, the printing process does have an impact on the performance of the server providing the printing services. An environment with a large number of printers or print jobs should strongly consider using at least one dedicated print server.

Defragmentation   The task of finding fragmented files and moving them into contiguous space is called defragmentation.

Demand-dial routing   Dial-on demand connections are normally used when a permanent connection is not available, so demand-dial routing is used connect your router to the required host or router when there is no permanent connection to do this. They can be used as a backup to a permanent connection or if no permanent connection is possible. Because dial-up connections are usually charged on a time basis, a demand-dial connection is an efficient method of only paying for a connection when you have data to transfer. An idle timeout value allows the connection to automatically terminate when there is no more data to transfer.

Deny permission   Unlike the Allow permission, the Deny permission overrides all other permissions set for a file or folder. If a user is a member of one group with a Deny Write permission for a folder and is a member of another group with a Allow Full Control permission, the user will be unable to perform any of the Write permission tasks allows because it has been denied. The Deny permission should be used with extreme caution, as it can actually lock out all users, even administrators, from a file or folder. The proper way to remove a permission from a user or group on a file or folder is to uncheck the Allow permission for that user or group, not to check the Deny permission.

DER Encoded Binary X.509   This is the format used for non-Windows 2000 certification authorities. Since the Internet is still dominated by non-Windows servers, it is supported for interoperability. DER certificate files use the .cer file extension.

DES   *See* Data Encryption Standard.

Dfs   *See* Distributed File System.

DHCP   *See* Dynamic Host Control Protocol.

Dictionary attack   Dictionary attack is when a malicious user attempts to gain access by "cracking" a password by automatically trying a list of words or commonly used phrases.

Differential backup   The Differential backup checks and performs a backup of only those files that are marked. It does not clear the markers after the backup, which means that any consecutive differential backups will back up the marked files again. When you need to restore from a differential backup, you will need the most current full backup and the differential backup performed after that.

Diffie-Hellman key exchange　Provides a method for two parties to construct a shared secret (key) that is known only to two of them, even though they are communicating via an insecure channel.

Digital signature　A string of bits that is added to a message (an encrypted hash), which provides for data integrity and authentication.

Digital Subscriber Line (DSL)　There are many variants of digital subscriber line (xDSL). All versions utilize the existing copper loop between a home and the local telco's Central Office (CO). Doing so allows them to be deployed rapidly and inexpensively. However, all DSL variants suffer from attenuation, and speeds drop as the loop length increases. Asymmetrical DSL (ADSL) and Symmetrical DSL (SDSL) may be deployed only within 17,500 feet of a CO, and Integrated Services Digital Network emulation over DSL (IDSL) will work only up to 30,500 feet. All DSL variants use Asynchronous Transfer Mode (ATM) as the data-link layer.

Direct Memory Access (DMA)　DMA is a microprocessor capable of transferring data between memory units without the aid of the Central Processing Unit (CPU). Occasionally, built-in circuitry can do this same function.

Directory　A directory is a database that contains information about objects and their attributes.

Directory service　The directory service is the component that organizes the objects into a logical and accessible structure, and provides for a means of searching and locating objects within the directory. The directory service includes the entire directory and the method of storing it on the network.

Directory Services Restore Mode　This startup mode is available on Windows 2000 Server domain controller computers only. This mode can be used to restore the SYSVOL directory and Active Directory on the domain controller.

Discover   A Dynamic Host Control Protocol (DHCP) client begins the lease process with a DHCPDISCOVER message. The client broadcasts this message after loading a minimal Transmission Control Protocol/Internet Protocol (TCP/IP) environment. The client does not know the address of the DHCP server, so it sends the message using a TCP/IP broadcast, with 0.0.0.0 as the source address and 255.255.255.255 as the destination address. The DHCPDISCOVER message contains the clients network hardware address, its computer name, a list of DHCP options the client supports, and a message ID that will be used in all messages between the client and server to identify the particular request.

Disk compression   This compression allows you to compress folders, subfolders, and files to increase the amount of file storage, but slow down access to the files.

Disk Defragmenter   Disk Defragmenter can analyze your volumes and make a recommendation as to whether or not you should defragment it. It will also give you a graphical display showing you the fragmented files, contiguous files, system files and free space. Disk Defragmenter does not always completely defragment free space; instead, it often moves it into just a few contiguous areas of the disk, which will still improve performance. Making the free space one contiguous space would have little added benefit.

Disk imaging/cloning   The deployment of a new operating system is one of the most challenging and time-consuming tasks that a network administrator has to perform. The disk duplication methods are particularly useful when you need to deploy Windows 2000 Professional on a large number of computers. This is also known as disk imaging or cloning. These tools make the rollout fast and easy.

Disk quota   Windows 2000 comes with a disk quota feature that allows you to control users' disk consumption on a per user/per partition basis. To begin setting disk quotas for your users, right-click any partition in either Windows Explorer or the My Computer object. Click Properties and then click the Quota tab. Also, a disk quota allows you to limit the amount of disk space used by each user.

Distance vector protocol   Routing Information Protocol (RIP) is known as a distance vector protocol. This means that it has a maximum path length of 15 hops. If a packet must pass through more than 15 routers (gateways) to reach its destination, RIP considers the destination "unreachable."

Distinguished Name (DN))   DN, in Active Directory parlance, is a Lightweight Directory Access Protocol (LDAP) way of uniquely identifying an object.

Distributed File System (Dfs)   The Windows 2000 Distributed File System provides you a method to centralize the organization of the shared resources on your network. In the past, shared resources were most often accessed via the Network Neighborhood applet, and users would have to wade through a number of domains and servers in order to access the shared folder or printer that they sought. Network users also had to remember where the obscure bit of information was stored, including both a cryptic server name and share name. The Distributed File System (Dfs) allows you to simplify the organization of your network resources by placing them in central shares accessed via a single server. Also, the Dfs allows you to create a central share point for shared resources located through the organization on a number of different servers.

Distribution Server   This is a server on which the Windows 2000 installation files reside. When you install the operating system over the network, the client machine does not need a CD-ROM drive. The first requirement for network installation is a distribution server that contains the installation files. The distribution server can be any computer on the network to which the clients have access.

DLC   *See* Data Link Control.

DMA   *See* Direct Memory Access.

DN   *See* Distinguished Name.

DNM   *See* Domain Naming Master.

DNS   *See* Domain Name System.

Domain   A collection of connected areas. Routing domains provide full connectivity to all end systems within them. Also, a domain is a collection of accounts and network resources that are grouped together using a single domain name and security boundary.

Domain controller   Domain controllers validate logons, participate in replication of logon scripts and policies, and synchronize the user account database. This means that domain controllers have an extra amount of work to perform. Since the Terminal Server already requires such heavy resources, it is not a good idea to burden a Terminal Server with the extra work of being a domain controller. Also, all user accounts, permissions, and other network details are all stored in a centralized database on the domain controllers.

Domain Local Groups   Domain Local Groups are used for granting access rights to resources such as file systems or printers that are located on any computer in the domain in which common access permissions are required. The advantage of Domain Local Groups being used to protect resources is that a member of the Domain Local Group can come from both inside the same domain and from outside as well.

Domain Name System (DNS)   Because the actual unique Internet Protocol (IP) address of a web server is in the form of a number difficult for humans to work with, text labels separated by dots (domain names) are used instead. DNS is responsible for mapping these domain names to the actual Internet Protocol (IP) numbers in a process called resolution. Sometimes called a Domain Name Server.

Domain Naming Master (DNM)   A Domain Naming Master is one of the operations masters roles played by domain controllers in a Windows 2000 network.

Domain restructure   Domain restructure, or domain consolidation, is the method of changing the structure of your domains. Restructuring your domains can allow you to take advantage of the new features of Windows 2000, such as greater scalability. Windows 2000 does not have the same limitation as the Security Accounts Manager (SAM) account database in Windows NT. Without this limitation, you can merge domains into one larger domain. Using Windows 2000 Organizational Units (OUs), you have finer granularity in delegating administrative tasks.

Domain tree   A domain tree is a hierarchical collection of the child and parent domains within a network. The domains in a domain tree have contiguous namespaces. Domain trees in a domain forest do not share common security rights, but can access one another through the global catalog.

Downlevel clients Downlevel clients with static Internet Protocol (IP) addresses are not able to communicate directly with the Dynamic Domain Name System (DDNS) server. DDNS entries for these clients must be manually reconfigured at the DDNS server. Downlevel clients are not able to communicate directly with a DDNS server.

Driver signing One of the most frustrating things about Windows operating systems is that any software vendors can overwrite critical system level files with their own versions. Sometimes the vendor's version of a system level file is buggy or flawed, and it prevents the operating system from functioning correctly, or in the worst case, prevents it from starting at all. Windows 2000 uses a procedure called Driver Signing that allows the operating system to recognize functional, high-quality files approved by Microsoft. With this seal of approval, you should be confident that installing applications containing signed files will not disable your computer. Windows 98 was the first Microsoft operating system to use digital signatures, but Windows 2000 marks the first Microsoft operating system based on NT technology to do this.

DSL *See* Digital Subscriber Line.

Dynamic compulsory tunnels Dynamic compulsory tunnels are where a connection is dynamically assessed and the tunnel directed accordingly. For example, based on certain criteria, the same user may be directed to different Virtual Private Network (VPN) servers, depending on what time of day the connection is made. Realms can be further divided into usernames, departments, the telephone number being used, and so forth. In this way, dynamic compulsory tunnels offer the highest degree of flexibility and granularity. An additional advantage for the owner of the Network Access Server is that it can simultaneously support both tunneling and nontunneling connections.

Dynamic disks Dynamic disks introduce conceptual and technical changes from traditional basic disk structure. Partitions are now called volumes, and these can be created or changed without losing existing data on the disk. Recall that when using basic disks, you must first create primary partitions (up to a maximum of four), then extended partitions (a maximum of one) with logical drives. Dynamic disks allow you to create volume after volume, with no limit on the number or type that can exist on a single disk; you are limited only by the capacity of the disk itself.

Dynamic Host Configuration Protocol (DHCP)   A software utility that is designed to assign Internet Protocol (IP) addresses to clients and their stations logging onto a Transmission Control Protocol/Internet Protocol (TCP/IP) and eliminates manual IP address assignments.

Dynamic Host Control Protocol (DHCP) allocator   A Dynamic Host Control Protocol (DHCP) allocator is a simplified DHCP service without the database or configurable options. Invoking the DHCP allocator means that the computer will automatically assign Internet Protocol (IP) addresses to other workstations on the same subnet using a private address range, and it will assign the default gateway and the DNS server to be the same IP address as the computer running Internet Connection Sharing (ICS). Note there is no Windows Internet Name Server (WINS) server allocation.

Dynamic routing   Dynamic routing uses routing protocols such as the Routing Information Protocol (RIP) or Open Shortest Path First (OSPF) to allow routers to communicate with one another and automatically, dynamically update their routing tables without human intervention.

EAP   *See* Extensible Authentication Protocol.

EFS   *See* Encrypting File System.

Encapsulating Security Payload (ESP)   A header used by Internet Protocol Security (IPSec) when encrypting the contents of a packet.

Encrypting File System (EFS)   Unlike Windows NT 4.0, Windows 2000 provides the Encrypting File System (EFS), which allows you to encrypt and decrypt data on a file-by-file basis without the need for third-party software, as long as it is stored on an NTFS formatted partition or volume.

Encryption   Scrambling of data so as to be unreadable; therefore, an unauthorized person cannot decipher the data.

ESP   *See* Encapsulating Security Payload.

Ethernet   A networking protocol and shared media (or switched) Local Area Network (LAN) access method linking up to 1K nodes in a bus topology.

Evaluation   Evaluation is the process of assessing, summarizing, weighing, deciding, and applying standards.

Event Viewer   The Windows 2000 Event Viewer has a dedicated log for DNS-specific information. The Event Viewer can provide you information on when zone transfers have taken place, if there was a problem with a zone transfer, when changes have taken place within the zone, or even report that an excessive number of changes have occurred to the zone for a specific period of time.

Extended partitions   Although extended partitions cannot be used to host operating systems, they can store other types of data and provide an excellent way to create more drives above the four-partition limit. Extended partitions do not represent one drive; rather, they can be subdivided into as many logical drives as there are letters in the alphabet. Therefore, one extended partition can contain several logical drives, each of which appears as a separate drive letter to the user.

Extensible Authentication Protocol (EAP)   The Extensible Authentication Protocol is an extension to Point-to-Point Protocol (PPP) that allows for arbitrary authentication mechanisms to be used to validate a PPP connection. Its design is such that it allows authentication plug-in modules at both the client and server. One example is using security token cards ("smart cards"), where the remote access server queries the client for a name, PIN, and card token value. Another example is using biometrics; for example, a retina scan or finger print match to uniquely identify an individual. Once the connection authentication phase is reached, the client negotiates which EAP authentication it wants to use, which is known as the EAP type. Once the EAP type is agreed upon, the server can issue multiple authentication requests to the client (as in the client name, then PIN, then card token value).

Fast transfer   The Windows 2000 Domain Name System (DNS) Server supports a method of zone transfer that allows multiple records to be included in a single message. This compressed form of zone file transfer is referred to as a fast transfer. Not all DNS servers support the fast transfer mode, although most of the popular ones do. One popular DNS server that does not support fast transfers is

Berkeley Internet Name Domain (BIND) versions before 4.9.4. Subsequent versions of BIND do support the fast transfer mode. If you do maintain BIND versions earlier than 4.9.4, you can use the Advanced Options in the DNS server to indicate you have BIND Secondaries, and this disabled the fast transfer mode.

FAT *See* File Allocation Table.

Fault tolerance Fault tolerance is high-system availability with enough resources to accommodate unexpected failure. Fault tolerance is also the design of a computer to maintain its system's performance when some internal hardware problems occur. This is done through the use of backup systems.

FEK *See* File Encryption Key.

File Allocation Table (FAT) A FAT is an area on a disk that indicates the arrangement of files in the sectors. Because of the multiuser nature of Terminal Server, it is strongly recommended that the NTFS file system be used rather than the FAT file system. FAT does not offer file and directory security, whereas with NTFS you can limit access to subdirectories and files to certain users or groups of users.

File Allocation Table 16 (FAT16) The earlier version of the FAT file system implemented in MS-DOS is known as FAT16, to differentiate it from the improved FAT32.

File Allocation Table 32 (FAT32) FAT32 is the default file system for Windows 95 OSR2 and Windows 98. The FAT32 file system was first implemented in Windows 95 OSR2, and was supported by Windows 98 and now Windows 2000. While FAT16 cannot support partitions larger than 4GB in Windows 2000, FAT32 can support partitions up to 2TB (Terabytes) in size. However, for performance reasons, the creation of FAT32 partitions is limited to 32GB in Windows 2000. The second major benefit of FAT32 in comparison to FAT16 is that it supports a significantly smaller cluster size—as low as 4K for partitions up to 8GB. This results in more efficient use of disk space, with a 15 to 30 percent utilization improvement in comparison to FAT16.

File Encryption Key (FEK)   A random key called a file encryption key (FEK) is used to encrypt each file and is then itself encrypted using the user's public key. At least two FEKs are created for every encrypted file. One FEK is created with the user's public key, and one is created with the public key of each recovery agent. There could be more than one recovery agent certificate used to encrypt each file, resulting in more than two FEKs. The user's public key can decrypt FEKs created with the public key.

File Transfer Protocol (FTP)   Transfers files to and from a computer running an FTP server service (sometimes called a daemon).

Filter actions   Filter actions define the type of security and the methods in which security is established. The primary methods are: Permit, Block, and Negotiate security.

FireWire   Also known as IEEE 1394. An Apple/Texas Instruments high-speed serial bus allowing up to 63 devices to connect; this bus supports hot swapping and isochronous data transfer.

Forest   A forest is a grouping of one or more domain trees that do not share a common namespace but do share a common schema, configuration, and global catalog; in fact, it forms a noncontiguous (or discontiguous) namespace. The users in one tree do not have global access to resources in other trees, but trusts can be created that allow users to access resources in another tree.

Forward lookup query   A forward lookup query occurs when a computer needs to get the Internet Protocol (IP) address for a computer with an Internet name. The local computer sends a query to a local Domain Name System (DNS) name server, which resolves the name or passes the request on to another server for resolution.

Forward lookup zones   Forward lookup zones are used to provide a mechanism to resolve host names to IP addresses for DNS clients. A forward lookup zone will contain what are known as resource records. These resource records contain the actual information about the resources available in the zone.

Forwarder   A DNS forwarder accepts requests to resolve host names from another DNS server. A forwarder can be used to protect your internal DNS server from access by Internet users.

FQDN   *See* Fully Qualified Domain Name.

FTP   *See* File Transfer Protocol.

Fully Qualified Domain Name (FQDN)   A full site name of a system, rather than just its host name. The FQDN of each child domain is made up of the combination of its own name and the FQDN of the parent domain. The FQDN includes the host name and the domain membership of that computer.

Gateway   In networking, gateway refers to a router or a computer functioning as one, the "way out" of the network or subnet, to get to another network. You also use gateways for software that connects a system using one protocol to a system using a different protocol, such as the Systems Network Architecture (SNA) software (allows a Local Area Network (LAN) to connect to an IBM mainframe). You can also use Gateway Services for NetWare to provide a way for Microsoft clients to go through a Windows NT or Windows 2000 server to access files on a Novell file server.

Global Groups   Global Groups are used for combining users who share a common access profile based on job function or business role. Typically organizations use Global Groups for all groups in which membership is expected to change frequently. These groups can have as members only user accounts defined in the same domain as the Global Group.

Globally Unique IDentifier (GUID)   The Globally Unique IDentifier (GUID) is a unique numerical identification created at the time the object is created. An analogy would be a person's social security number, which is assigned once and never changes, even if the person changes his or her name, or moves.

Glue record   The Host (A) Address record is referred to as a glue record. It is called a glue record because it associates the host name in the Name Server (NS) record with an Internet Protocol (IP) address of the machine noted in the NS record. It glues together the name server's host name and IP address in this way.

GPC   *See* Group Policy Container.

GPO   *See* Group Policy Object.

GPT   *See* Group Policy Template.

Graphical User Interface (GUI)   An overall and consistent system for the interactive and visual program that interacts (or interfaces) with the user. GUI can involve pull-down menus, dialog boxes, on-screen graphics, and a variety of icons.

Group policy   Group Policy provides for change management and desktop control on the Windows 2000 platform. You are familiar with the control you had in Windows NT 4.0 using System Policies. Group Policy is similar to System Policies but allows you a much higher level of granular configuration management over your network. Some of the confusion comes from the change of names applied to different groups in Windows 2000. You can apply Group Policy to sites, domains, and organizational units. Each of these represents a group of objects, so Group Policy is applied to the group of objects contained in each of these entities. Group Policy cannot be directly applied to Security Groups that are similar to the groups you are used to working with in Windows NT 4.0. However, by using Group Policy Filtering, you can successfully apply Group Policy to individual Security Groups.

Group Policy Container (GPC)   The Active Directory object Group Policy Containers (GPCs) store the information for the Folder Redirection snap-in and the Software Deployment snap-in. GPCs do not apply to local group policies. They contain component lists and status information, which indicate whether Group Policy Objects (GPOs) are enabled or disabled. They also contain version information, which ensures that the information is synchronized with the Group Policy Template (GPT) information. GPCs also contain the class store in which GPO group policy extensions have settings.

Group Policy Object (GPO)   After you create a group policy, it is stored in a Group Policy Object (GPO) and applied to the site, domain, or Organizational Unit (OU). GPOs are used to keep the group policy information; essentially, it is a collection of policies. You can apply single or multiple GPOs to each site, domain or OU. Group policies are not inherited across domains, and users must have Read permission for the GPO that you want to have applied to them. This way, you can filter the scope of GPOs by adjusting who has read access to each GPO.

Group Policy Template (GPT)   The subset of folders created on each domain controller that store Group Policy Object (GPO) information for specific GPOs are called Group Policy Templates (GPTs). GPTs are stored in the SysVol (System Volume) folder, on the domain controller. GPTs store data for Software Policies, Scripts, Desktop File and Folder Management, Software Deployment, and Security settings. GPTs can be defined in computer or user configurations. Consequently, they take effect either when the computer starts or when the user logs on.

GUI   *See* Graphical User Interface.

GUID   *See* Globally Unique IDentifier.

HAL   *See* Hardware Abstraction Layer.

Hardware Abstraction Layer (HAL)   Windows NT's translation layer existing between the hardware, kernel, and input/output (I/O) system.

Hardware Compatibility List (HCL)   The Hardware Compatibility List is published by Microsoft for each of its operating systems, and is updated on a monthly basis. There is a copy of the HCL on the Windows 2000 Professional CD, located in the Support folder and named Hcl.txt.

Hardware profile   A hardware profile is a set of instructions that tells your computer how to boot the system properly, based on the setup of your hardware. Hardware profiles are most commonly used with laptops. This is because laptops are frequently used in at least two different settings: stand-alone and in a docking station on a network. For example, when the laptop is being used at a docking station, it requires a network adapter. However, when the laptop is used away from the network, it does not. The hardware profile dialog manages these configuration changes. If a profile is created for each situation, the user will automatically be presented these choices on Windows startup.

Hash function   A mathematical calculation that produces a fixed-length string of bits, which cannot be reverse-engineered to produce the original.

HCL   *See* Hardware Compatibility List.

HINFO   *See* Host Information.

HKEY_CLASSES_ROOT   Contains information used for software configuration and object linking and embedding (OLE), as well as file association information.

HKEY_CURRENT_CONFIG   Holds data about the current hardware profile that is in use.

HKEY_CURRENT_USER   Has information about the user who is currently logged on.

HKEY_LOCAL_MACHINE   Stores information about the hardware, software, system devices, and security information for the local computer.

HKEY_USERS   Holds information and settings for the environments of all users of the computer.

H-node   H-node (hybrid node) Windows Internet Name Server (WINS) clients are similar to M-node, but use WINS NetBIOS name resolution first, before initiating a NetBIOS broadcast message.

Host Information (HINFO)   HINFO records provide information about the Domain Name System (DNS) server itself. Information about the CPU and operating system on the host can be included in the HINFO record. This information is used by application protocols, such as File Transfer Protocol (FTP), that can use special procedures when communicating between computers of the same CPU and OS type (RFC 1035).

Host routing   Host routing occurs when a computer forwards a packet to a router, rather than sending the packet directly on its own network.

Host-to-host layer   This layer is basically the same as the Transport layer in the OSI model. It is responsible for flow control, acknowledgments, sequencing (ordering) of packets, and establishment of end-to-end communications. Transmission Control Protocol (TCP) and the User Datagram Protocol (UDP) operate at this level.

HTML   *See* HyperText Markup Language.

HTTP   *See* HyperText Transfer Protocol.

HyperText Markup Language (HTML)   The format used to create documents viewed on the World Wide Web (WWW) by the use of tags (codes) embedded within the text.

HyperText Transfer Protocol (HTTP)   HTTP is an Internet standard supporting World Wide Web (WWW) exchanges. By creating the definitions of Universal Resource Locators (URLs) and their retrieval usage throughout the Internet.

IAS   *See* Internet Authentication Services.

ICS   *See* Internet Connection Sharing.

IDE   *See* Integrated Drive Electronics.

IIS   *See* Internet Information Service.

IKE   *See* Internet Key Exchange.

in-addr.arpa domain   The in-addr.arpa domain indexes host names based on Network IDs and makes reverse lookups much more efficient and speedy.

Incremental backup   This backup process is similar to the Differential backup, but it clears the markers from the selected files after the process. Because it clears the markers, an incremental backup will not back up any files that have not changed since the last incremental backup. This type of backup is fast during the backup but is very slow while restoring the files. You will need the last full backup and all of the subsequent incremental backups to fully restore data. The positive side of this backup type is that it is fast and consumes very little media space.

Indexing service   Provides indexing functions for documents stored on disk, allowing users to search for specific document text or properties.

Industry Standard Architecture (ISA)   A PC's expansion bus used for peripherals plug-in boards.

Infrastructure   Infrastructure of a computer network consists of the basic components upon which it is built.

Initialization Vector (IV)   The IV is a random block of encrypted data that begins each chain. In this fashion, we are able to make each message's ciphertext appear different, even if we were to send the exact same message a hundred times.

Integrated Drive Electronics (IDE) drive   An IDE drive is a hard disk drive for processors containing most controller circuitry within the drive. IDE drives combine Enhanced System Device Interface (ESDI) speed with Small Computer System Interface (SCSI) hard drive interface intelligence.

Integrated Services Digital Network (ISDN)   Integrated Services indicates the provider offers voice and data services over the same medium. Digital Network is a reminder that ISDN was born out of the digital nature of the intercarrier and intracarrier networks. ISDN runs across the same copper wiring that carries regular telephone service. Before attenuation and noise cause the signal to be unintelligible, an ISDN circuit can run a maximum of 18,000 feet. A repeater doubles this distance to 36,000 feet.

Internal Router (IR)   An Internal Router as its name suggests, is a router that sits in its area, and only in its area and handles intra-area routing.

Internet Authentication Services (IAS)   IAS performs authentication, authorization, and accounting of dial-up and Virtual Private Networking (VPN) users. IAS supports the Remote Access Dial-In User Service (RADIUS) protocol.

Internet Connection Sharing (ICS)   ICS can be thought of as a less robust version of Network Address Translation (NAT lite). ICS uses the same address translation technology. ICS is a simpler version of NAT useful for connecting a few computers on a small Local Area Network (LAN) to the Internet or useful for a remote server through a single phone line and account.

Internet Control Message Protocol (ICMP)   The Internet Control Message Protocol (ICMP) is a Transmission Control Protocol/Internet Protocol (TCP/IP) standard that allows hosts and routers that use IP communication to report errors and exchange limited control and status information. The PING utility works by sending an ICMP echo request message and recording the response of echo replies.

Internet Group Management Protocol (IGMP)   The Internet Group Management Protocol is used for multicasting, which is a method of sending a message to multiple hosts but only addressing it to a single address. Members of a multicast group can be defined, and then when a message is sent to the group address, only those computers that belong to the group will receive it. IGMP is used to exchange membership status information between IP routers that support multicasting and members of multicast groups.

Internet Information Service (IIS)   Windows NT Web browser software that supports Secure Sockets Layer (SSL) security protocol from Netscape. IIS provides support for Web site creation, configuration, and management, along with Network News Transfer Protocol (NNTP), File Transfer Protocol (FTP), and Simple Mail Transfer Protocol (SMTP).

Internet Key Exchange (IKE)   Automated Key Management uses a combination of the Internet Security Association Key Management Protocol and the Oakley Protocol (ISAKMP/Oakley). This combination of protocols is often referred to collectively as the Internet Key Exchange (IKE). The IKE is responsible for exchange of "key material" (groups of numbers that will form the basis of new key), session keys, SA negotiation, and authentication of peers participating in an Internet Protocol Security (IPSec) interaction. During this exchange, the Oakley protocol protects the identities of the negotiating parties.

Internet Packet eXchange (IPX)   Novell NetWare's built-in networking protocol for Local Area Network (LAN) communication derived from the Xerox Network System protocol. IPX moves data between a server and/or workstation programs from different network nodes. Sometimes called an Internetnetwork Packet eXchange.

Internet Protocol Security (IPSec)   IPSec is a new feature included in Windows 2000 and provides for encryption of data as it travels between two computers, protecting it from modification and interpretation if anyone were to see it on the network.

Internet Security Association and Key Management Protocol (ISAKMP)   An Internet Protocol Security (IPSec) protocol required as part of the IPSec implementation, which provides a framework for Internet key management.

Internet Service Provider (ISP) The organization allowing users to connect to its computers and then to the Internet. ISPs provider the software to connect and sometimes a portal site and/or internal browsing capability.

Internetwork layer This layer matches the Network layer in the OSI model. The Internet Protocol (IP) works here to route and deliver packets to the correct destination address. Other protocols that operate at this layer include the Address Resolution Protocol (ARP), Reverse Address Resolution Protocol (RARP), and the Internet Control Message Protocol (ICMP).

Interrupt ReQuest (IRQ) An electronic signal that is sent to the computer's processor requiring the processor's attention. Also, a computer instruction designed to interrupt a program for an Input/Output (I/O).

IPCONFIG command-line utility IPCONFIG is used to gather information about the Transmission Control Protocol/Internet Protocol (TCP/IP) configuration on the computer. Typing IPCONFIG at the command line will display the computer's Internet Protocol (IP) address, subnet mask, and default gateway. Adding the /all switch will display additional information such as the host name, Media Access Control (MAC) address, node type, and much more. IPCONFIG includes new switches that increase its usefulness beyond a great tool for getting IP addressing information about your machines.

IPSec *See* Internet Protocol Security.

IPX *See* Internet Packet eXchange.

IR *See* Internal Router.

IRQ *See* Interrupt ReQuest.

ISA *See* Industry Standard Architecture.

ISDN *See* Integrated Services Digital Network.

ISP   *See* Internet Service Provider.

Iterative query   Iterative queries allow the Domain Name System (DNS) server responding to the request to make a best-effort attempt at resolving the DNS query. If the DNS server receiving an iterative query is not authoritative for the domain included in the query, it can return a Referral response.

JetBEUI   Microsoft had intended NetBEUI to become even more robust, and even routable. They were working on a networking protocol dubbed "JetBEUI" that would have been a routable implementation of NetBEUI.

Kerberos   Kerberos guards against this username and password safety vulnerability by using tickets (temporary electronic credentials) to authenticate. Tickets have a limited life span and can be used in place of usernames and passwords (if the software supports this). Kerberos encrypts the password into the ticket. It uses a trusted server called the Key Distribution Center (KDC) to handle authentication requests. Kerberos speeds up network processes by integrating security and rights across network domains and also eliminates workstations' need to authenticate themselves repeatedly at every domain they access. Kerberos security also makes maneuvering around networks using multiple platforms such as UNIX or NetWare easier.

Knowledge   Knowledge is the very lowest level of learning. It is, of course, important that a network administrator have this knowledge. Knowledge involves the processes of defining, location, recall, recognition, stating, matching, labeling, and identification.

L2TP   *See* Layer-Two Tunneling Protocol.

Last Known Good Configuration   This mode starts the system using the configuration that was saved in the registry during the last system shutdown. This startup option is useful when you have changed some configuration parameters and the system fails to boot. When you use this mode to start the system, all changes that were made after the last successful logon are lost. Use this option when you suspect that some incorrect configuration changes are causing the system startup failure.

This mode does not help if any of the installed drivers have been corrupted or any driver files are deleted by mistake.

Layer Two Tunneling Protocol (L2TP)   L2TP offers better security through the use of IPSec and creates Virtual Private Networks (VPNs). Windows 2000 uses L2TP to provide tunneling services over Internet Protocol Security (IPSec)-based communications. L2TP tunnels can be set up to traverse data across intervening networks that are not part of the VPN being created. L2TP is used to send information across intervening and nonsecure networks.

LDAP   *See* Lightweight Directory Access Protocol.

Lease   A lease is an agreement to let someone use something for a defined length of time. The Dynamic Host Control Protocol (DHCP) client leases Internet Protocol (IP) addressing information from the DHCP server. The DHCP client does not own this information, and does not get to keep it forever.

Legend   The legend displays information about the counters that are being measured. It is the set of columns at the bottom of System Monitor.

Lifetime   This is the "shelf-life" of a route—how long it is considered valid. Static routes automatically have an infinite lifetime, but dynamic routes have a finite lifetime and the route must be refreshed before the lifetime expires in order to be retained in the routing table.

Lightweight Directory Access Protocol (LDAP)   A simplified Directory Access Protocol (DAP) accessing a computer's directory listing. LDAP is able to access to X.500 directories.

Line Printer Daemon (LPD)   LPD is the server process that advertises printer queues and accepts incoming print submissions, which are then routed to the print device.

Line Printer Remote (LPR)   LPR is a process that spools a print job to a remote print spool that is advertised by the Line Printer Daemon (LPD).

Link State Routing   Link state routing was designed specifically to overcome some of the shortcomings of the older distance vector routing protocol, which was never designed for today's wide-scale enterprise internetworks.

LMHOSTS   An LMHOSTS file is a plain-text file that contains NetBIOS names to IP address mappings. LMHOSTS can be useful as a backup method of resolving names of especially important computers when other methods fail.

Load balancing   The fine tuning process of a system (computer, network, etc.) to allow the data to be distributed more efficiently and evenly. Load balancing is an add-on feature of MetaFrame that must be purchased separately from the base product. Load balancing allows the administrator to group servers in a server farm which can act as a single point of access for clients accessing published applications.

Local policy   A group policy stored locally on a Windows 2000 member server or a Windows 2000 professional computer is called a local policy. The local policy is used to set up the configuration settings for each computer and for each user. Local policies are stored in the \%systemroot%\system32\grouppolicy folder on the local computer. Local policies include the auditing policy, user rights and privilege assignment, and various security options.

Local printer   A print device that is directly attached, via a parallel or serial cable, to the computer that is providing the printing services. For a Windows 2000 Professional workstation, a local printer is one that is connected to the workstation. For a Windows 2000 Server, a local printer is one that is connected to the server. Drivers for the print device must reside on the computer that connects to the printer.

Local user profiles (local profiles)   Local user profiles are kept on one local computer hard drive. When a user initially logs on to a computer, a local profile is created for them in the \%systemdrive%\Documents and Settings\<username> folder. When users log off the computer, the changes that they made while they were logged on will be saved to their local profile on that client computer. This way, subsequent logons to that computer will bring up their personal settings. When users log on to a different computer, they will not receive these settings, as they are local to the computer in which they made the changes. Therefore, each user that logs on to that computer receives individual desktop settings. Local profiles are ideal for users who only use one computer. For users that require access to multiple computers, the Roaming profile would be the better choice.

Logical infrastructure   Logical infrastructure is the networking protocols, the Domain Name System (DNS) namespace and services, the Internet Protocol (IP) addressing scheme and Dynamic Host Control Protocol (DHCP) strategy, the remote access services, and security protocols. Components of the logical infrastructure includes Network Protocols, IP Addressing Schemes, Name Resolution Services, Remote Access, Routing and Network Address Translation, and Security Infrastructure (Certificate Services)

LogicalDisk object   The LogicalDisk object measures the transfer of data for a logical drive (such as C: or D:) or storage volumes. You can use the PhysicalDisk object to determine which hard disk is causing the bottleneck. Then, to narrow the cause of the bottleneck, you can use the LogicalDisk object to determine which, if any, partition is the specific cause of the bottleneck. By default, the PhysicalDisk object is enabled and the LogicalDisk object is disabled on Windows 2000 Server.

LPD   *See* Line Printer Daemon.

LPR   *See* Line Printer Remote.

MAC   *See* Media Access Control; Message Authentication Code.

Mail eXchanger (MX)   Identifies the preferred mail servers on the network. If you have several mail servers, an order of precedence will be run. Note that the MX record has similar requirements to the Canonical Name (CNAME) record. You must have an existing A record for the machine that you wish to create a MX record for.

Mandatory Roaming profiles   Mandatory roaming profiles are mandatory user profiles the user cannot change. They are usually created to define desktop configuration settings for groups of users in order to simplify administration and support. Users can make changes to their desktop settings while they are logged on, but these changes will not be saved to the profile, as Mandatory profiles are read-only. The next time they log on, their desktop will be set back to the original Mandatory profile settings.

Many-to-one certificate mapping   This involves mapping many certificates to a single user account. This is particularly convenient when organizations need to share specific information with each other. An administrator must install the Root Certificate Authority (CA) certificates of all the desired CA's as trusted Root CAs in their enterprise. The administrator can then set a rule that maps all certificates installed by the trusted CAs to a single Windows 2000 account. Users using these mapped certificates possess access rights defined by the rights set on the mapped account.

Master File Table (MFT)   The MFT stores the information needed by the operating system to retrieve files from the volume. Part of the MFT is stored at the beginning of the volume and cannot be moved. Also, if the volume contains a large number of directories, it can prevent the free space from being defragmented.

Master image   After configuring one computer with the operating system and all the applications, Sysprep is run to create an image of the hard disk. This computer serves as the master or model computer that will have the complete setup of the operating system, application software, and any service packs. This hard disk image is the master image and is copied to a CD or put on a network share for distribution to many computers. Any third-party disk-imaging tool can then be used to replicate the image to other identical computers.

MCSE   *See* Microsoft Certified Systems Engineer.

Media Access Control (MAC)   A sublayer in the Open System Interconnection (OSI) data link layer that controls access, control, procedures, and format for a Local Area Network (LAN), for example, Institute of Electronic and Electrical Engineers (IEEE) 802.3, 802.5, and 802.5 standards.

Message Authentication Code (MAC)   A cryptographically generated fixed-length code associated with a message in order to ensure the authenticity of the message (a digital signature is a public key MAC).

Message queuing service   Provides a communication infrastructure and a development tool for creating distributed messaging applications. Such applications can communicate across heterogeneous networks and with computers that might be offline. Message queuing provides guaranteed message delivery, efficient routing, security, transactional support, and priority-based messaging.

Metric   A metric is the cost of using a particular route from one destination to another. Generally this will be the number of hops to the Internet Protocol (IP) destination. Anything on the local subnet is one hop, and every time a router is crossed, this adds 1 to the hop count. The value of this is that it lets Windows 2000 select the route with the lowest metric if there are multiple routes to the same destination.

MFT   *See* Master File Table.

Microsoft Certified Systems Engineer (MCSE)   An engineer who is a technical specialist in advanced Microsoft products, specifically NT Server and NT Workstation.

Microsoft Challenge Handshake Authentication Protocol (MS-CHAP)   This is Microsoft's version of the Challenge Handshake Authentication Protocol, and offers the same features as CHAP, with some additional advantages. It is supported on all versions of Windows, and as such, makes a suitable default authentication protocol. However, where you have the choice, you should instead use the later version, MS-CHAPv2, which is a more secure protocol that protects against server impersonation. If mutual authentication (where both sides can verify they are who they say they are) is important to your security policies, then you should ensure that Microsoft clients have the latest MS-CHAPv2 and disable MS-CHAP on the server.

Microsoft Management Console (MMC)   The MMC provides a standardized interface for using administrative tools and utilities. The management applications contained in an MMC are called snap-ins, and custom MMCs hold the snap-ins required to perform specific tasks. Custom consoles can be saved as files with the .msc file extension. The MMC was first introduced with NT Option Pack. Using the MMC leverages the familiarity you have with the other snap-ins available within MMC, such as SQL Server 7 and Internet Information Server 4. With the MMC, all your administrative tasks can be done in one place.

Mini-Setup Wizard   The purpose of this wizard is to add some user-specific parameters on the destination computer. These parameters include: End-user license agreement (EULA); Product key (serial number); Username, company name, and administrator password; Network configuration; Domain or workgroup name; and Date and time zone selection.

Mirror set   In a mirror set, all data on a selected partition or drive are automatically duplicated onto another physical disk. The main purpose of a mirror set is to provide fault tolerance in the event of missing or corrupt data. If one disk fails or contains corrupt files, the data is simply retrieved and rebuilt from the other disk.

Mirrored volume   Like basic disks, dynamic disks can also be mirrored, and are called mirrored volumes. A continuous and automatic backup of all data in a mirrored volume is saved to a separate disk to provide fault tolerance in the event of a disk failure or corrupt file. Note that you cannot mirror a spanned or striped volume.

Mirroring   Also called RAID 1. RAID 1 consists of two drives that are identical matches, or mirrors, of each other. If one drive fails, you have another drive to boot up and keep the server going.

Mixed Mode   When in Mixed Mode, the domain still uses master replication with a Windows 2000 DC. The Windows NT Backup Domain Controllers (BDCs) replicate from the Windows 2000 server, as did the Windows NT Primary Domain Controller (PDC). When you are operating in Mixed Mode, some Windows 2000 functionality will not be available. You will not be able to use group nesting or transitive trusts. Mixed Mode is the default mode.

MMC   *See* Microsoft Management Console.

M-node   M-node (mixed node) Windows Internet Name Server (WINS) clients use both broadcasts and WINS servers to resolve NetBIOS names to Internet Protocol (IP) addresses. The mixed-node client preferentially uses broadcasts before querying a WINS server.

MP *See* Multilink Point-to-Point Protocol.

MSCHAP *See* Microsoft Challenge Handshake Authentication Protocol.

MX *See* Mail eXchanger.

Multilink Point-to-Point Protocol (MP) MP allows multiple physical links to appear as a single local link over which data can be sent and received at a higher throughput than if going over a single physical link.

Name collision When a machine tries to update its name in the zone database, and finds that its name is already there with a different IP address, it has experienced a name collision. The default behavior of the DNS client is to overwrite the existing record with its own information.

Name Server (NS) An NS record lists the Domain Name System (DNS) servers that can return authoritative answers for the domain. This includes the Primary DNS server for the zone, and any other DNS servers to which you delegate authority for the zone. The NS record is also used to direct DNS client requests to other DNS servers when the server is not authoritative for a zone. For example, when you issue a query for the microsoft.com domain, the .com domain DNS server is not authoritative for the microsoft.com domain. However, an NS record is contained on the .com DNS server that can return a referral answer to the requesting client, which will direct it to the microsoft.com DNS server.

NAT *See* Network Address Translation.

Native Mode Native Mode allows only Windows 2000 domain controllers to operate in the domain. When all domain controllers for the domain are upgraded to Windows 2000 Server, you can switch to Native Mode. This allows you to use transitive trusts and the group-nesting features of Windows 2000. When switching to Native Mode, ensure that you no longer need to operate in Mixed Mode, because you cannot switch back to Mixed Mode once you are in Native Mode.

NBMA *See* Non-Broadcast Multiple Access.

NBNS   *See* NETwork Basic Input/Output System Name Server.

NBTSTAT   NBTSTAT is used to display the local NetBIOS name table, a table of NetBIOS names registered by local applications, and the NetBIOS name cache, a local cache listing of NetBIOS computer names that have been resolved to IP addresses.

NDS   *See* NetWare Directory Service.

Net Shell (Netsh)   Net Shell (Netsh) is a command-line and scripting tool for both local and remote Windows 2000 servers running Routing and Remote Access. It can be used in conjunction with remote access settings, but is also for routing, Dynamic Host Control Protocol (DHCP) Relay, and Network Address Translation (NAT).

NetBEUI   *See* NETwork Basic Input/Output System Extended User Interface.

NetBIOS   *See* Network Basic Input/Output System.

NETDIAG   The Resource Kit for Windows 2000 Professional includes the NETDIAG utility. This is a command-line diagnostic tool that helps isolate networking and connectivity problems. It does this by performing a series of tests designed to determine the state of the network client software, and ascertain whether it is functional. This tool does not require that parameters or switches be specified, which means support personnel and network administrators can focus on analyzing the output, rather than training users on how to use the tool.

NETSTAT command-line utility   NETSTAT is used to display protocol statistics and current TCP/IP network connections.

NetWare Directory Service (NDS)   NDS (created by Novell) has a hierarchical information database allowing the user to log on to a network with NDS capable of calculating the user's access rights.

Network   Two or more computers connected together by cable or wireless media for the purpose of sharing data, hardware peripherals, and other resources.

Network Address Translation (NAT)   With NAT, you can allow internal users to have access to important external resources while still preventing unauthorized access from the outside world.

NETwork Basic Input/Output System (NetBIOS)   A program in Microsoft's operating system that links personal computers to a Local Area Network (LAN).

NETwork Basic Input/Output System Extended User Interface (NetBEUI)   The transport layer for the Disk Operating System (DOS) networking protocol called Network Basic Input/Output System (NetBIOS).

NETwork Basic Input/Output System Name Server   A NetBIOS Name Server (NBNS) is a machine that runs server software dedicated to resolving NetBIOS names to IP addresses. The NBNS contains a database file that can accept dynamic NetBIOS name registrations and answer queries for NetBIOS name resolution.

Network Interface Card (NIC)   A board with encoding and decoding circuitry and a receptacle for a network cable connection that, bypassing the serial ports and operating through the internal bus, allows computers to be connected at higher speeds to media for communications between stations.

Network interface layer   This bottom layer of the U.S. Department of Defense (DoD) model corresponds to both the Data Link and Physical layers of OSI. It provides the interface between the network architecture (Ethernet, Token Ring, AppleTalk, and so on) and the upper layers, as well as the physical (hardware) issues.

Network News Transfer Protocol (NNTP)   The Network News Transfer Protocol is used for managing messages posted to private and public newsgroups. NNTP servers provide for storage of newsgroup posts that can be downloaded by client software called a newsreader. Windows 2000 Server includes an NNTP server with IIS, and Outlook Explorer version 5, which is part of the Internet Explorer software included with Windows 2000, provides both an e-mail client and a newsreader

Network protocol   Network protocol usually refers to the network and transport layer protocols (often part of a protocol "stack" or "suite") used for communication over a Local Area Network (LAN).

Network printer   A print device that has a built-in network interface or connects directly to a dedicated network interface. Both workstations and servers can be configured to print directly to the network printer, and the network printer controls its own printer queue, determining which jobs from which clients will print in which order. Printing clients have no direct control over the printer queue and cannot see other print jobs being submitted to the printer. Administration of a network printer is difficult. Drivers for the print device must reside on the computer that connects to the printer.

NIC   *See* Network Interface Card.

NNTP   *See* Network News Transfer Protocol

Non-Broadcast Multiple Access (NBMA)   This represents a network that can connect more than two routers, but which cannot support hardware broadcasts. In this particular case, because multicasts cannot be used, Open Shortest Path First (OSPF) must be configured to use unicast to the specific IP addresses of the routers on the NBMA network.

Nondedicated server   A nondedicated print server is a Windows 2000 server that hosts printing services in addition to other services. A domain controller, database server, or Domain Name System (DNS) server can provide printing services as well, but should be used only for a smaller number of printers or for printers that are not heavily used. Anyone setting up a nondedicated print server should monitor the performance of the printing process and the other tasks running on the server and be prepared to modify the server configuration if the performance drops below acceptable levels.

Nonmandatory Roaming profiles   Roaming user profiles are stored on the network file server and are the perfect solution for users who have access to multiple computers. This way their profile is accessible, no matter where they log on in the domain. When users log on to a computer within their domain, their Roaming profile will be copied from the network server to the client computer, and the settings will be applied to the computer while they are logged on. Subsequent logins will compare the Roaming profile files to the local profile files. The file server then copies only any files that have been altered since the user last logged on locally, significantly decreasing the time required to log on. When the user logs off, any changes that the user made on the local computer will be copied back to the profile on the network file server.

Normal backup   This is the most common type and is also known as a full backup. The Normal backup operation backs up all files and folders that are selected, irrespective of the archive attributes of the files. This provides the easiest way to restore the files and folders but is expensive in terms of the time it takes to complete the backup job and the storage space it consumes. The restore process from a Normal backup is less complex because you do not have to use multiple tape sets to restore data completely.

NS   *See* Name Server.

NSLOOKUP command-line utility   NSLOOKUP is used to check records, domain host aliases, domain host services, and operating system information by querying Domain Name System (DNS) servers. NSLOOKUP works in two modes: interactive mode and command mode. Command mode is used when you only want to do a single query.

NT File System (NTFS)   The NT File System (with filenames up to 255 characters) is a system created to aid the computer and its components recover from hard disk crashes.

NTFS   *See* NT File System.

NWLink IPX/SPX/NetBIOS Compatible Transport Protocol (NWLink)   Microsoft's implementation of Novell's Internet Packet eXchange/Sequenced Packet eXchange (IPX/SPX) protocol stack, required for connecting to NetWare servers prior to version 5. NWLink can also be used on small networks that use only Windows 2000 and other Microsoft client software. NWLink is a Network Driver Interface Specification (NDIS) compliant, native 32-bit protocol. The NWLink protocol supports Windows sockets and NetBIOS.

ODBC   *See* Open DataBase Connectivity.

Offer   After the Dynamic Host Control Protocol (DHCP) server receives the DHCPDISCOVER message, it looks at the request to see if the client configuration request is valid. If so, it sends back a DHCPOFFER message with the client's network hardware address, an IP address, a subnet mask, the length of time the lease is valid, and the IP address of the server that provided the DHCP information. This message is also a Transmission Control Protocol/Internet Protocol (TCP/IP) broadcast, as the client does not yet have an Internet Protocol (IP) address. The server then reserves the address it sent to the client so that it is not offered to another client making a request. If there are more than one DHCP servers on the network, all servers respond to the DHCPDISCOVER message with a DHCPOFFER message.

Off-subnet addressing   When the Dynamic Host Control Protocol (DHCP) server allocates an Internet Protocol (IP) address that is on a different subnet to the remote access server itself; this is called off-subnet addressing.

One-to-one certificate mapping   This type of mapping simply involves mapping a single user certificate to a single Windows 2000 user account. Certificates may be issued from your own Enterprise CA or from a trusted CA. These certificates are then manually mapped to their respective user accounts.

One-way initiated demand-dial connections   A one-way initiated connection restricts one router to being the calling router and the other to being an answering router. In many ways, this is the easiest of configurations because there is less to configure. It also offers a more secure routing environment from the perspective of the calling router because it has complete control over when a connection is made.

On-subnet addressing   When the allocated addresses are on the same subnet as the remote access server, this is called on-subnet addressing and is by far the more common setup.

Open DataBase Connectivity (ODBC)   A database programming interface that allows applications a way to access network databases.

Open Shortest Path First (OSPF)   Open Shortest Path First is a link-state routing protocol designed for use in large scale internetworks and seeks to redress some of the shortcomings associated with traditional distance vector-based routing protocols. OSPF is a new and unfamiliar routing protocol. It is outside the scope of this chapter to give a complete and detailed description on every aspect of OSPF, but it does aim to provide the basic understanding and provide a framework of concepts and terminology to get you started. Without this, the OSPF configuration options themselves will make little sense, let alone understanding the consequences of setting their values.

Open Systems Interconnection (OSI) model   This is a model of breaking networking tasks into layers. Each layer is responsible for a specific set of functionality. There are performance objects available in System Monitor for analyzing network performance.

Organizational Units (OUs)   OUs in Windows 2000 are objects that are containers for other objects, such as users, groups, or other organizational units. Objects cannot be placed in another domain's OUs. The whole purpose of an OU is to have a hierarchical structure to organize your network objects. You can assign a group policy to an OU. Generally, the OU will follow a structure from your company. It may be a location, if you have multiple locations. It can even be a department-level organization. Also, OUs are units used to organize objects within a domain. These objects can include user accounts, groups, computers, printers, and even other OUs. The hierarchy of OUs is independent of other domains.

OSI   *See* Open Systems Interconnection.

OSPF   *See* Open Shortest Path First.

OU *See* Organizational Unit.

Paging When enough memory is not available for the running applications, pages of memory can be swapped from physical memory to the hard disk too much and slow the system down. This is also known as paging because pages of memory are swapped at a time. Windows 2000 separates memory into 4KB pages of memory to help prevent fragmentation of memory. Swapping can even get bad enough that you can hear your hard disk running constantly.

Paging file A file on the hard disk (or spanning multiple disks) that stores some of the program code that is normally in the computer's RAM. This is called virtual memory, and allows the programs to function as if the computer had more memory than is physically installed.

PAP *See* Password Authentication Protocol.

Password Authentication Protocol (PAP) The Password Authentication Protocol is the least secure of the authentication protocols provided using a simple, plain-text authentication. It offers no protection against replay attacks, client impersonation, or server impersonation. However, it is offered in Windows 2000 Routing and Remote Access for downward compatibility for older clients and non-Microsoft clients that cannot support a stronger authentication protocol.

Password policy A password policy regulates how your users must establish and manage their passwords. This includes password complexity requirements and how often passwords must change. There are several settings that can be used to implement a successful password policy. You can enforce password uniqueness so those users cannot simply switch back and forth between a few easy to remember passwords. This can be set to low, medium, or high security. With low security, the system remembers the user's last 1–8 passwords (it is your choice as administrator to decide how many); with medium, it remembers the last 9–16 passwords; with high, it remembers the last 17–24 passwords.

PathPing This is new to Windows 2000 and combines features from both Ping and Tracert by sending packets to each router in the source to destination route, and then computing results based on the information returned from each discovered router. It helps to indicate the degree of packet loss at each link of the route, which allows you to identify, which routers or links might be causing problems in the way of packet loss and delays.

PATHPING command-line utility   PATHPING is used to verify configurations and test IP connectivity by name or IP address. PATHPING combines features of PING and TRACERT with added functionality, and is used to trace the route a packet takes to a destination and display information on packet losses for each router in the path. PATHPING can also be used to troubleshoot Quality of Service (QoS) connectivity.

PCMCIA   *See* Personal Computer Memory Card Interface Adapter.

PDC   *See* Primary Domain Controller.

Peer-to-peer network   A workgroup is also referred to as a peer-to-peer network, because all the computers connected together and communicating with one another are created equal. That is, there is no central computer that manages security and controls access to the network.

Performance logging   Performance logging has many features. The data collected are stored in a comma-delimited or tab-delimited format, which allows for exportation to spreadsheet and database applications for a variety of tasks such as charting and reports. The data can also be viewed as collected. You can configure the logging by specifying start and stop times, the name of the log files and the maximum size of the log. You can start and stop the logging of data manually or create a schedule for logging. You can even specify a program to run automatically when logging stops. You can also create trace logs. Trace logs track events that occur rather than measuring performance counters.

Permissions inheritance   By default, all permissions set for a folder are inherited by the files in the folder, the subfolders in the folder, and the contents of the subfolders. When the permissions on a folder are viewed in the Security tab of the file or folder Permissions window, inherited permissions are indicated with a gray checkbox.

Personal Computer Memory Card Interface Adapter (PCMCIA)
An interface standard for plug-in cards for portable computers; devices meeting the standard (for example, fax cards, modems) are theoretically interchangeable.

Personal Information Exchange   The Personal Information Exchange format is an industry format that facilitates backup and restoration of a certificate and its private key. This vendor-independent certificate format enables certificates and their corresponding private keys to be transferred from one computer to another or from a computer to removable media. Personal Information Exchange format is the only format used by Windows 2000 when exporting certificates and private keys because it avoids exposing the keys to unintended parties.

Physical infrastructure   Physical infrastructure compromises the machines themselves, along with the cables, network interface cards, hubs, and routers.

Physical layer protocols   Physical layer protocols consist of specifications or standards governing the hardware components.

Physical memory   Physical memory is the actual Random Access Memory (RAM) on the computer. When the physical memory becomes full, the operating system can also use space on the hard disk as virtual memory. When memory becomes full, rather than locking up the computer, the operating system stores unused data on the hard disk in a page file (also called paging or swap file). Data are swapped back and forth between the hard disk and physical memory as needed for running applications. If memory is needed that is in virtual memory, it is swapped back into physical memory.

PhysicalDisk object   The PhysicalDisk object measures the transfer of data for the entire hard disk. You can use the PhysicalDisk object to determine which hard disk is causing the bottleneck. By default, the PhysicalDisk object is enabled and the LogicalDisk object is disabled on Windows 2000 Server.

PKI   *See* Public Key Infrastructure.

Plug and Play (PnP)   A standard requiring add-in hardware to carry the software to configure itself in a given way supported by Microsoft Windows 95. Plug and Play can make peripheral configuration software, jumper settings, and Dual In-line Package (DIP) switches unnecessary. PnP allows the operating system to load device drivers automatically and assign system resources dynamically to computer components and peripherals. Windows 2000 moves away from this older technology with its use of Kernel-mode and User-mode PnP architecture. PnP autodetects, configures, and installs the necessary drivers in order to minimize user interaction with hardware configuration. Users no longer have to tinker with IRQ and I/O settings.

P-node   A p-node (peer node) Windows Internet Name Server (WINS) client uses a WINS server and does not issue broadcasts. When a WINS client is configured as a p-node WINS client, it will *not* broadcast to resolve a NetBIOS name to an IP address. The advantage of configuring WINS clients as p-nodes is that there is no possibility of NetBIOS broadcast traffic using up valuable network bandwidth. On the other hand, if the p-node client is not able to access a WINS server, it will have to use alternative methods to resolve the NetBIOS name to an IP address, even if the destination host is local. This can lead to strange things, like the p-node client accessing a remote Domain Name System (DNS) server to resolve the Internet Protocol (IP) address of a host on the local segment.

PnP   *See* Plug and Play.

Pointer record (PTR)   The Pointer record is created to allow for reverse lookups. Reverse lookups are valuable when doing security analysis and checking authenticity of source domains for e-mail.

Point-to-Point Protocol (PPP)   A serial communication protocol most commonly used to connect a personal computer to an Internet Service Provider (ISP). PPP is the successor to Serial Line Internet Protocol (SLIP) and may be used over both synchronous and asynchronous circuits. Also, PPP is a full-duplex, connectionless protocol that supports many different types of links. The advantages of PPP made it de facto standard for dial-up connections.

Point-to-Point Tunneling Protocol (PPTP)   One of two standards for dial-up telephone connection of computers to the Internet, with better data negotiation, compression, and error corrections than the other Serial Line Internet Protocol (SLIP), but costing more to transmit data and unnecessary when both sending and receiving modems can handle some of the procedures.

Policy inheritance   Group policies have an order of inheritance in which the policies are applied. Local policies are applied first, then group policies are applied to the site, then the domain, and finally the Organizational Unit (OU). Policies applied first are overwritten by policies applied later. Therefore, group policies applied to a site overwrite the local policies and so on. When there are multiple Group Policy Objects (GPOs) for a site, domain, or OU, the order in which they appear in the Properties list applies. This policy inheritance order works well for small companies, but a more complex inheritance strategy may be essential for larger corporations.

Ports   A channel of a device that can support single point-to-point connections is known as a port. Devices can be single port, as in a modem.

Power options   Power options are dependent on the particular hardware. Power options include Standby and Hibernation modes. Standby mode turns off the monitor and hard disks to save power. Hibernation mode turns off the monitor and disks, saves everything in memory to disk, turns off the computer, and then restores the desktop to the state in which you left it when the computer is turned on.

PPP   *See* Point-to-Point Protocol.

PPTP   *See* Point-to-Point Tunneling Protocol.

Preboot eXecution Environment (PXE)   The PXE is a new Dynamic Host Control Protocol (DHCP)-based technology used to help client computers boot from the network. The Windows 2000 Remote Installation Service (RIS) uses the PXE technology and the existing Transmission Control Protocol/Internet Protocol (TCP/IP) network infrastructure to implement the RIS-based deployment of Windows 2000 Professional. The client computer that has the PXE-based ROM uses its Basic Input/Output System (BIOS) to contact an existing RIS server and get an Internet Protocol (IP) address from the DHCP server running on the network. The RIS server then initializes the installation process on the client computer.

Preemptive multitasking   An environment in which timesharing controls the programs in use by exploiting a scheduled time usage of the computer's Central Processing Unit (CPU).

Preshared keys   A preshared key is a secret key agreed upon previously by two users conducting the transaction. This method, like the public key certificate, has the advantage of working with computers that are not running Kerberos v5. The disadvantage is that Internet Protocol Security (IPSec) must be configured on both sides to use the specified preshared key. However, this simple method is also appropriate for non-Windows 2000 computers, and works well in cases where only authentication protection is required.

Primary Domain Controller (PDC)   An NT security management for its local domain. The PDC is periodically synchronized to its copy, the Backup Domain Controller (BDC). Only one PDC can exist in a domain. In an NT 4.0 single domain model, any user having a valid domain user account and password in the user accounts database of the PDC has the ability to log onto any computer that is a member of the domain, including MetaFrame servers.

Primary Domain Name System (DNS) server   The Primary DNS server maintains the master copy of the DNS database for the zone. This copy of the database is the only one that can be modified, and any changes made to its database are distributed to secondary servers in the zone during a zone transfer process. The server can cache resolution requests locally so a lookup query does not have to be sent across the network for a duplicate request. The primary server contains the address mappings for the Internet root DNS servers. Primary servers can also act as secondary servers for other zones.

Primary partitions   Primary partitions are typically used to create bootable drives. Each primary partition represents one drive letter, up to a maximum of four on a single hard disk. One primary partition must be marked as active in order to boot the system, and most operating systems must be loaded on a primary partition to work.

Print device   The hardware that actually does the printing. A print device is one of two types as defined in Windows 2000: local or network interface. A local print device connects directly to the print server with a serial or parallel interface. A network-interface print device connects to the printer across the network and must have its own network interface or be connected to an external network adapter.

Print driver   A software program used by Windows 2000 and other computer programs to connect with printers and plotters. It translates information sent to it into commands that the print device can understand.

Print server   A print server is a computer that manages printing on the network. A print server can be a dedicated computer hosting multiple printers, or it can run as one of many processes on a nondedicated computer.

Printer permissions   Printer permissions are established through the Security tab in the printer's Properties dialog. The security settings for printer objects are similar to the security settings for folder shares.

Private key   A digital code used to decrypt data, which is kept secret and works in conjunction with a published public key.

Protocol stack   A protocol stack consists of two or more protocols working together to accomplish a purpose (communication with another computer across a network). Transmission Control Protocol (TCP) and Internet Protocol (IP) make up the stack, which handles the most important tasks of communication such as handling addressing and routing issues, error checking, and flow control.

Protocol suite   A protocol suite is a more elaborate collection of communication protocols, utilities, tools, and applications. The suite includes a large number of additional protocols, used in various situations and for different purposes. Different vendors may include different tools and utilities in their implementations of the Transmission Control Protocol/Internet Protocol (TCP/IP) suite.

Protocols   Protocols are sets of rules that computers use to communicate with one another. Protocols usually work together in stacks, so called because in a layered networking model, they operate at different layers or levels. These protocols govern the logic, formatting, and timing of information exchange between layers.

Proxy autodiscovery   Proxy autodiscovery is used only by clients that have Internet Explorer 5.0. This option informs the client of the location of the Internet Explorer 5.0 automatic configuration file.

PSTN   *See* Public Switched Telephone Network.

PTR   *See* Pointer record.

Public key   A digital code used to encrypt or decrypt data, which is published and made available to the public, used in conjunction with a secret private key.

Public Key Certificate   A Public Key Certificate is a security token that is passed between a certificate server and a client that causes data exchanged between the two to be encrypted. Public encryption keys include the public key certificates and are responsible for encoding the data. Certificates can be either single use (such as secure e-mail (S/MIME) only) or multi- use (such as secure e-mail (S/MIME, Encrypting File System, and client authentication). So, we can easily see the certificates can be applied in various scenarios.

Public Key Infrastructure (PKI)   A key and certificate management system that is trusted.

Public Switched Telephone Network (PSTN)   Also known as POTS (Plain Old Telephone Service), this is the analog telephone system originally designed to transfer human voice. The dial-up equipment consists of an analog modem at the client and at the server. The maximum bit rate is low.

Publishing resources   Resources, such as folders and printers, which are available to be shared on the network, can be published to the Active Directory. The resources are published to the directory and can be located by users, who can query the directory based on the resource's properties (for example, to locate all color printers).

Push replication Push replication causes the push partner to send changes based on the number of changes made in the Windows Internet Name Server (WINS) database. After the minimum number of changes have been made, the push partner sends a pull notification to the WINS server to request the changes. Windows 2000 WINS Servers are able to maintain persistent connections, which allow push partners to push changes as soon as they take place.

PXE *See* Preboot eXecution Environment.

QoS *See* Quality of Service.

Quality of Service (QoS) Admission Control Admission control allows you to control how applications are allotted network bandwidth. You can give important applications more bandwidth, less important applications less bandwidth.

RADIUS *See* Remote Access Dial-In User Service.

RAID *See* Redundant Array of Inexpensive Disks.

RARP *See* Reverse Address Resolution Protocol.

RAS *See* Remote Access Service.

RDP *See* Remote Desktop Protocol.

Realm-based tunneling Realm-based tunneling is where the access concentrator makes decisions on the tunnel's final destination (Virtual Private Network—VPN—server) based on additional group information about the user (referred to as the realm).

Rebinding Time Value The Rebinding Time Value represents 87.5 percent of the lease period. If the lease period is eight days, then the rebinding interval is 168 hours. The client will attempt to rebind its IP address at this time only if it was not able to renew its lease at the Renewal Time (T1). The client broadcasts a DHCPREQUEST message. If the server that granted the Internet Protocol (IP) address does not respond, the client will enter the Rebinding State and begin the DHCPDISCOVER process, attempting to renew its IP address with any Dynamic Host Control Protocol (DHCP) server. If it cannot renew its IP address, it will try to receive a new one from any responding DHCP server. If unsuccessful, TCP/IP services are shut down on that computer.

Recovery agent   The recovery agent restores the encrypted file on a secure computer with its private recovery keys. The agent decrypts it using the cipher command line and then returns the plain text file to the user. The recovery agent goes to the computer with the encrypted file, loads the recovery certificate and private key, and performs the recovery. It is not as safe as the first option because the recovery agent's private key may remain on the user's computer.

Recovery Console   The Recovery Console is a new command-line interpreter program feature in Windows 2000 that helps in system maintenance activities and resolving system problems. This program is separate from the Windows 2000 command prompt.

Recursive query   The Domain Name System (DNS) client most often will send a recursive query. When a recursive query is sent to the client's Preferred DNS server, the server must respond to the query either positively or negatively. A positive response returns the Internet Protocol (IP) address; a negative response returns a "host not found" or similar error. A recursive query is one that requires a definitive response, either affirmative or negative.

Redundant Array of Inexpensive Disks (RAID)   Although mirroring and duplexing are forms of RAID, most people think of RAID as involving more than two drives. The most common form of RAID is RAID-5, which is the striping of data across three or more drives, providing fault tolerance if one drive fails. For the best disk performance, consider using a SCSI RAID (Redundant Array of Independent Disks) controller. RAID controllers automatically place data on multiple disk drives and can increase disk performance. Using the software implementation of RAID provided by NT would increase performance if designed properly, but the best performance is always realized through hardware RAID controllers.

Redundant Array of Inexpensive Disks 5 (RAID-5) Volume   A RAID-5 volume on a dynamic drive provides disk striping with parity, and is similar to a basic stripe set with parity. This disk configuration provides both increased storage capacity and fault tolerance. Data in a dynamic RAID-5 volume are interleaved across three or more disks (up to 32 disks), and parity information is included to rebuild lost data in the event of an individual disk failure. Like a spanned or striped volume, a RAID-5 volume cannot be mirrored.

Referral response   The Referral response contains the Internet Protocol (IP) address of another Domain Name System (DNS) server that may be able to service the query. The Referral is based on information contained in delegations (NS records) on the DNS server being queried.

Registry   The Registry is the hierarchical database that stores operating system and application configuration information. It was introduced in Windows 9*x* and NT and replaced much of the functionality of the old initialization, system, and command files used in the early versions of Windows (.ini, .sys, and .com extensions). The registry is also a Microsoft Windows program allowing the user to choose options for configuration and applications to set them; it replaces confusing text-based .INI files.

Remote   The word "remote" can take on a number of different meanings, depending on the context. In the case of an individual computer, the computer you are sitting in front of is sometimes referred to as being "local," while any other computer is considered "remote." In this context any machine but your own is considered a remote computer. In discussions related to network configuration and design, "remote" may refer to segments and machines that are on the far side of a router. In this context, all machines on your physical segment are considered "local," and machines located on other physical segments are referred to as remote.

Remote access   Remote access is when a workstation connects to a remote network so that remote resources can be transparently accessed. All applications are still run on the workstation—the only processing done on the remote access server involves the connection process (such as routing, authentication, and encryption) rather than running any applications for the remote client.

Remote Access Dial-In User Service (RADIUS)   RADIUS is an industry-standard protocol providing that's often referred to as the three "A"s—Authentication, Authorization, and Accounting services for distributed dial-up networking. RADIUS is actually a client/server protocol. In the context of Windows 2000 Routing and Remote Access, the RAS server is actually the RADIUS client because although it physically accepts the incoming connections, it passes all connection requests and information about the connections to the RADIUS server. That RADIUS server is usually devoted to running a large user account database against which it can identify remote users.

Remote access policy   Remote access policies allow you to create demand-dial connections to use specific authentication and encryption methods. In Windows NT versions 3.5*x* and Windows NT 4.0, authorization was much simpler. The administrator simply granted dial-in permission to the user. The callback options were configured on a per-user basis.

Remote Access Service (RAS)   Remote Access Service is a built-in feature of the Microsoft NT operating system. It allows users to dial establish a connection to an NT network over a standard phone line. Remote Access allows users to access files on a network or transfer files from a remote PC, over a Dial-Up Networking connection. The performance of transferring files over a dial-up connection is very similar to the performance you would get if you were downloading a file from the Internet.

Remote control   Remote control is when a workstation shares (controls) a remote machine's resources (screen, keyboard, mouse, processor) over a remote link. This means that the remote machine can run applications for the client workstation because the CPU is shared. In this case, the workstation effectively becomes a dumb terminal because it is not running applications itself, but is using the CPU on the remote machine.

Remote Desktop Protocol (RDP)   Remote Desktop Protocol (RDP) is the application protocol between the client and the server. It informs the server of the keystrokes and mouse movement of the client and returns to the client the Windows 2000 graphical display from the server. RDP is a multichannel, standard protocol that provides various levels of compression so that it can adapt to different connection speeds and encryption levels from 40 to 128 bit. Transmission Control Protocol/Internet Protocol (TCP/IP) carries the messages, and RDP is the language in which the messages are written. Both are needed to use Microsoft's implementation of Terminal Services.

Remote Installation Preparation (RIPrep)   RIPrep is a disk duplication tool included with Windows 2000 Server. It is an ideal tool for creating images of fully prepared client computers. These images are the customized images made from the base operating system, local installation of applications such as Microsoft Office, and customized configurations.

Remote Installation Preparation (RIPrep) Wizard   The RIPrep Wizard enables the network administrator to distribute to a large number of client computers a standard desktop configuration that includes the operating system and the applications. This not only helps in maintaining a uniform standard across the enterprise; it also cuts the costs and time involved in a large-scale rollout of Windows 2000 Professional.

Remote Installation Service (RIS)   The RIS, part of Windows 2000 Server, allows client computers to install Windows 2000 Professional from a Windows 2000 Server with the service installed. The Remote Installation Services (RIS) facilitates installation of Windows 2000 Professional remotely on a large number of computers with similar or dissimilar hardware configurations. This not only reduces the installation time but also helps keep deployment costs low. Also, the Windows 2000 Remote Installation Services allow you a way to create an image of Windows 2000 Professional you can use to install Windows 2000 Professional on your network client systems. This image actually consists of the installation files from the Windows 2000 Professional CD-ROM.

Remote local printer   A print device connected directly to a print server but accessed by another print server or by workstations. The queue for the print device exists on the server, and the print server controls job priority, print order, and queue administration. Client computers submit print jobs to the server and can observe the queue to monitor the printing process on the server. Drivers for the print device are loaded onto the client computer from the print server.

Remote network printer   A network printer connected to a print server that is accessed by client workstations or other print servers. Like the remote local printer, the printer queue is controlled by the print server, meaning that the client computers submit their print jobs to the print server, rather than to the print device directly. This allows for server administration and monitoring of the printer queues. Drivers for the print device are loaded onto the client computers from the print server.

Renewal Time Value   The Renewal Time Value represents 50 percent of the lease period. If the lease period were eight days, then the Renewal Time Value (T1) would be four days. At T1, the DHCP client will attempt to renew its IP address by broadcasting a DHCPREQUEST message containing its current Internet Protocol (IP) address. If the Dynamic Host Control Protocol (DHCP) server that granted the IP address is available, it will renew the IP address for the period specified in the renewed lease. If the DHCP server is not available, the client will continue to use its lease, since it still has 50 percent of the lease period remaining.

Replay attack   This is when somebody captures the packets of a successful connection attempt and then later replays the same packets in an attempt to obtain an authenticated connection.

Request   After the client receives the DHCPOFFER message and accepts the Internet Protocol (IP) address, it sends a DHCPREQUEST message out to all Dynamic Host Control Protocol (DHCP) servers indicating that it has accepted an offer. The message contains the IP address of the DHCP server that made the accepted offer, and all other DHCP servers release the addresses they had offered back into their available address pool.

Reserved client   A reserved client is a Dynamic Host Control Protocol (DHCP) client that you configure to always receive the same Internet Protocol (IP) address. Creating reserved clients allows you to assign functionally static IP address to computers that require these, such as Windows Internet Name Service (WINS) and DNS servers. DHCP servers also require a static IP address. However, the DHCP server itself cannot be a DHCP client, so creating a client reservation for them would be a waste of IP addresses.

Resolver software   Resolver software on the Domain Name System (DNS) client formulates and issues query statements sent to the DNS server. Resolver software can be included in the WinSock application, or in the case of Windows 2000, be a component of the operating system. The Windows 2000 operating system has a system-wide caching resolver. Examples of WinSock programs that make use of resolver software include: Web browsers (such as Microsoft Internet Explorer), File Transfer Protocol (FTP) clients (such as the command-line FTP program found in Windows 2000), Telnet clients, and DNS servers.

Resource record   The resource record contains data about the resources contained in the domain. The resource record that you will use most is the A, or Host Address, record. This record contains the host name to Internet Protocol (IP) address mappings that most Domain Name System (DNS) clients will ask for when seeking to resolve a host name to an IP address.

Retry Interval   The Retry Interval defines the period of time the Secondary should wait until sending another pull request message. The Secondary will continue to retry the zone transfer until it is successful in contacting the Primary for its zone.

Reverse Address Resolution Protocol (RARP)   RARP does the same thing as the Address Resolution Protocol (ARP) in reverse; that is, it takes a physical address and resolves it to an IP address. The **arp –a** command can be used to view the current entries in the ARP cache.

Reverse lookup   The process of resolving a known Internet Protocol (IP) address to a host name is called a reverse lookup, in contrast to the forward lookup, in which a host name is resolved to an IP address. Reverse lookups query reverse lookup zones.

Reverse lookup query   A reverse lookup query resolves an Internet Protocol (IP) address to a Domain Name System (DNS) name, and can be used for a variety of reasons. The process is different, though, because it makes use of a special domain called in-addr.arpa. This domain is also hierarchical, but is based on IP addresses and not names. The subdomains are organized by the *reverse* order of the IP address.

For instance, the domain 16.254.169.in-addr.arpa contains the addresses in the 169.254.16.* range; the 120.129.in-addr.arpa domain contains the addresses for the 129.120.*.* range.

Reverse lookup zones   While forward lookup zones allow Domain Name System (DNS) clients to resolve a host name to an IP address, a reverse lookup zone allows the DNS client to do the opposite: resolve an IP address to a host name. Reverse lookup zones are especially helpful if your organization is using inventory or security software that depends on reverse lookups to identify the host names of the Internet Protocol (IP) addresses they discover.

RIPrep   *See* Remote Installation Preparation.

Rogue DHCP server   A rogue Dynamic Host Control Protocol (DHCP) server (a DHCP server that has not been approved by the IT department) is likely to contain invalid scopes and DHCP options. Rogue DHCP servers can assign inaccurate IP addressing information to DHCP clients, which may disrupt network communications for these hapless clients.

Rollback strategy   As with any upgrade, problems can sometimes require going back to the previous state. This possibility also applies to upgrading your domain to Windows 2000. You need to create a plan to roll back your network to its previous state if the upgrade to Windows 2000 fails. When upgrading the domain controllers, do not upgrade the Backup Domain Controller (BDC) that has the current directory database. Make sure the BDC is synchronized with the Primary Domain Controller (PDC), and then take it offline. Leave the BDC as is until the upgrade is successful. If you run into problems during the upgrade, you can bring the BDC back online, promote it to the PDC, and recover the Windows NT state. If this process is successful, you can upgrade the BDC to Windows 2000.

ROUTE command-line utility   ROUTE is used to display or make modifications to the local routing table.

Router   When the word "router" is used, typically people think of a physical box which is dedicated to just routing—Cisco, Bay Networks, Digital, and Cabletron

Systems, for example, are just a few of the best known vendors offering this kind of technology.

Router routing   Router routing occurs when a router receives a packet that is not destined for another computer so it must send the packet to either the destination computer (if directly attached) or another router.

Routing and Remote Access (RRAS)   Within Windows NT, a software routing and remote access capability combining packet filtering, Open Shortest Path First (OSPF) support, and so on.

Routing tables   Each router uses a list of known routes (either static routes or dynamic routes or a mixture of the two) that it amalgamates into one or more routing tables. When it receives a packet to forward, it consults its routing table to see which interface should be used to forward the packet. There may be more than one possible route, in which case the better path will also be evaluated to see which one should be used.

RRAS   *See* Routing and Remote Access.

Safe Mode   Safe Mode starts Windows 2000 using only some basic files and device drivers. These devices include monitor, keyboard, mouse, basic VGA video, CD-ROM, and mass storage devices. The system starts only those system services that are necessary to load the operating system. Networking is not started in this mode. The Windows background screen is black in this mode, and the screen resolution is 640 by 480 pixels with 16 colors.

Safe Mode with Command Prompt   This option starts the operating system in a safe mode using some basic files only. The Windows 2000 command prompt is shown instead of the usual Windows desktop.

Safe Mode with Networking   This mode is similar to the Safe Mode, but networking devices, drivers, and protocols are loaded. You may choose this mode when you are sure that the problem in the system is not due to any networking component.

SA *See* Security Association.

SAM *See* Security Accounts Manager.

Scavenging Scavenging is the process of removing stale entries from the zone. The default setting is not to allow scavenging from the Domain Name System (DNS) database. Scavenging can be set on a per-server or per-zone basis.

Scope A scope is a collection or pool of Internet Protocol (IP) addresses. A single scope includes all the IP addresses that you wish to make available to Dynamic Host Control Protocol (DHCP) clients on a single subnet. Only one scope can be created for each subnet. A single DHCP server can manage several scopes.

Scope options Scope options allow you to specify Dynamic Host Control Protocol (DHCP) options that apply to a single scope. A good example of when you want to set scope options is when you automatically want to configure the Internet Protocol (IP) address of the default gateway for the DHCP clients. Each subnet must have a different default gateway, since the default gateway must be local to each subnet. It wouldn't make much sense to assign the same default gateway to all the scopes. Therefore, you configure a scope option for the default gateway for each scope that has a different default gateway.

Scripted method This method for Windows 2000 Professional installation uses an answer file to specify various configuration parameters. This is used to eliminate user interaction during installation, thereby automating the installation process. Answers to most of the questions asked by the setup process are specified in the answer file. Besides this, the scripted method can be used for clean installations and upgrades.

SCSI *See* Small Computer System Interface.

Secondary Domain Name System (DNS) Server Secondary DNS servers provide fault tolerance and load balancing for DNS zones. A secondary server contains a read-only copy of the zone database that it receives from the primary server during a zone transfer. A secondary server will respond to a DNS request if the primary server fails to respond because of an error or a heavy load. Since secondary servers can resolve DNS queries, they are also considered authoritative within a domain, and can help with load balancing on the network. Secondary servers can be placed in remote locations on the network and configured to respond to DNS queries from local computers, potentially reducing query traffic across longer network distances. While there can be only one primary server in a zone, multiple secondary servers can be set up for redundancy and load balancing.

Secondary server   The server receiving the zone files can be called either a Slave server or a Secondary server. It is preferred to refer to the machine receiving the zone file as a secondary, because the term Slave DNS server has another meaning that refers to an inability to perform recursion for DNS clients.

Second-level domain name   The second-level domain name distinguishes your organization from all others on the Internet. Examples of second-level domains are microsoft.com, osborne.com, and syngress.com.

Secret key   Also called a shared secret, a digital code shared between two parties and used for both encrypting and decrypting data.

Secure callback   This is when the remote access server calls back the remote client after a successful authentication, and is used particularly when the connection charge should be the responsibility of the server rather than the client. Either the client can specify the number that should be called back (greatest flexibility so they can dial in from anywhere), or this feature can be restricted for security to call back only on a specific number (secure callback).

Security Accounts Manager (SAM)   The Security Accounts Manager (SAM) is the portion of the Windows NT Server registry that stores user account information and group membership. Attributes that are specific to Terminal Server can be added to user accounts. This adds a small amount of information to each user's entry in the domain's SAM.

Security Association (SA)   Security Associations (SAs) define Internet Protocol Security (IPSec) secured links. One of the tasks of IPSec is to establish a

Security Association between the two computers desiring to communicate with one another securely. This could include communications between remote nodes and the network, communications between two networks, and communications between two computers on a Local Area Network (LAN).

Security Groups   The Windows 2000 Security Groups allow you to assign the same security permissions to large numbers of users in one operation. This ensures consistent security permissions across all members of a group. Using Security Groups to assign permissions means the access control on resources remains fairly static and easy to control and audit. Users who need access are added or removed from the appropriate security groups as needed, and the access control lists change infrequently.

Security negotiation   Security negotiation ensures that the authentication and encryption methods used by the sending and receiving computers are the same. If they are not, reliable communication cannot take place. To provide for compatibility between the security systems being used, there must be protocols in place to negotiate the security methods. Internet Protocol Security (IPSec) uses ISAKMP and IKE to define the way in which security associations are negotiated.

Security Parameters Index   A Security Parameters Index (SPI) tracks each Security Association (SA). The SPI uniquely identifies each SA as separate and distinct from any other Internet Protocol Security (IPSec) connections current on a particular machine. The index itself is derived from the destination host's IP address and a randomly assigned number. When a computer communicates with another computer via IPSec, it checks its database for an applicable SA. It then applies the appropriate algorithms, protocols, and keys, and inserts the SPI into the IPSec header.

Security Templates   Windows 2000 comes with several predefined Security Templates. These templates address several security scenarios. Security Templates come in two basic categories: Default and Incremental. The Default or Basic templates are applied by the operating system when a clean install has been performed. They are not applied if an upgrade installation has been done. The incremental templates should be applied after the Basic Security Templates have been applied. There are four types of incremental templates: Compatible, Secure, High Secure, and Dedicated Domain Controller.

Segment   In discussions of Transmission Control Protocol/Internet Protocol (TCP/IP), segment often refers to the group of computers located on one side of a router, or sometimes a group of computers within the same collision domain. In TCP/IP terminology, "segment" can also be used to describe the chunk of data sent by TCP over the network (roughly equivalent to the usage of "packet" or "frame"). In discussions of the physical networking infrastructure, "segment" usually refers to a length of cable, or the portion of the network connected to a length of backbone between repeaters.

Sequenced Packet eXchange (SPX)   The communications protocol (from NetWare) used to control network message transport.

Serial Line Interface Protocol (SLIP)   The SLIP is an older Wide Area Network (WAN) link protocol that does not support encryption or compression, and requires a manually configured static Internet Protocol (IP) address. It can be used only on the Windows 2000 RAS client, and is used now primarily to connect to remote servers running the UNIX operating system.

Server   The word "server" can take on a variety of different meanings. A server can be a physical computer, such as "Check out that server over in the Accounting Department." A server can also represent a particular software package. For example, Microsoft Exchange 2000 is a mail and groupware server application. Often server applications are just referred to as "servers," as in "Check out what the problem is with the mail server." The term "server" is also used to refer to any computer that is currently sharing its resources on the network. In this context, all computers, whether Windows 3x or Windows 2000, can be servers on a network.

Server impersonation   This is when a bogus server appears to be a valid server so that it can capture credentials of a remote user trying to connect so it can use these to the valid server.

Server options   Server options apply to all scopes configured on a single DHCP server. Server options were known as global options on the Windows NT 4.0 DHCP Server.

Service identifiers   A computer running the TCP/IP NetBIOS interface actually has several NetBIOS names. Each name is used by a service to "advertise" that the service is running on that particular computer. It's like putting a sign on the door saying "these people live here." For example, if a Windows 2000 machine is running both the Server service and the Workstation (Microsoft Redirector) service, it will register two NetBIOS names, one for each of the services running. This is a way for the NetBIOS applications to let other machines know that they are running and available.

Service pack   A service pack typically contains bug fixes, security fixes, systems administration tools, drivers, and additional components. Microsoft recommends installing the latest service packs as they are released. In addition, as a new feature in Windows 2000, you do not have to reinstall components after installing a service pack, as you did with Windows NT. You can also see what service pack is currently installed on a computer by running the WINVER utility program. WINVER brings up the About Windows dialog box. It displays the version of Windows and the version of the service pack you are running.

Service record (SRV)   The SRV record provides information about available services on a particular host. This is similar to the "service identifier" (the hidden 16th character) in NetBIOS environments. If a particular host is looking for a server to authenticate against, it will check for a SRV record to find an authenticating host. SRV records are particularly important in Windows 2000 domains. Since the DNS server is now the primary domain locator for Windows 2000 clients, the appropriate SRV records must be contained on the DNS server to inform Windows 2000 clients of the location of a Windows 2000 domain controller that can authenticate a log on request.

Setup Manager   The Setup Manager is the best tool to use when you have no idea of the answer file syntax or when you do not want to get into the time-consuming task of creating or modifying the sample answer file. When you choose to use the Setup Manager for unattended installations, you need to do a lot of planning beforehand. It is understood that you will not be using Setup Manager for automating installations on one or two computers; that would be a waste of effort. Setup Manager is useful for mass deployments only.

SETUPACT.LOG   The Action log file contains details about the files that are copied during setup.

SETUPAPI.LOG   This log file contains details about the device driver files that were copied during setup. This log can be used to facilitate troubleshooting device installations. The file contains errors and warnings, along with a time stamp for each issue.

SETUPCL.EXE   The function of the SETUPCL.EXE file is to run the Mini-Setup Wizard and to regenerate the security IDs on the master and destination computers. The Mini-Setup Wizard starts on the master computer when it is booted for the first time after running SysPrep.

SETUPERR.LOG   The Error log file contains details about errors that occurred during setup.

SETUPLOG.TXT   This log file contains additional information about the device driver files that were copied during setup.

Shared folders   Sharing folders so that other users can access their contents across the network is easy in Windows 2000, as easy as right-clicking on the folder name in Windows Explorer, selecting the Sharing tab, and choosing Share This Folder. An entire drive and all the folders on that drive can be shared in the same way.

Shared folders permissions   As only folders, not files, can be shared, shared folder permissions are a small subset of standard NT File System (NTFS) permissions for a folder. However, securing access to a folder through share permissions can be more restrictive or more liberal than standard NTFS folder permissions. Shared folder permissions are applied in the same manner as NTFS permissions.

Shared printers   The process for sharing a printer attached to your local computer is similar to that for sharing a folder or drive. If the users who will access your printer will do so from machines that don't run the Windows 2000 operating system, you will need to install drivers for the other operating system(s).

Shared resource   A shared resource is a device, data, or program that is made available to network users. This can include folders, files, printers, and even Internet connections.

Shiva Password Authentication Protocol (SPAP)   The Shiva Password Authentication Protocol is a reversible encryption mechanism used by Shiva remote access servers. Although a remote access client might use SPAP to authenticate on a Windows 2000 Routing and Remote Access server, this protocol is more likely to be used by clients who need to connect to a Shiva remote access client. This protocol is more secure than Password Authentication Protocol (PAP), but less secure than the other protocols, and offers no protection against server impersonation. It is unlikely you would need it on a server running Windows 2000 Routing and Remote Access Service.

Silent Routing Information Protocol for Internet Protocol (Silent RIP for IP)   Silent RIP for IP is when an IP router (using the RIP routing protocol) dynamically updates its own routing table with information obtained from other RIP routers without sending out its own routing information. In this case, the routing "exchange" between the Silent RIP router and other routers is not complete because the information is one-way only—listening for routing information but not reciprocating. You can use Silent RIP on a workstation too, but this requires modifying the registry. On Windows 2000 RRAS router, it is configured as one of the RIP interface properties.

Simple Mail Transfer Protocol (SMTP)   The Simple Mail Transfer Protocol is used for sending e-mail on the Internet. SMTP is a simple ASCII protocol and is non-vendor specific.

Simple Network Management Protocol (SNMP)   The Simple Network Management Protocol provides a way to gather statistical information. An SNMP management system makes requests of an SNMP agent, and the information is stored in a Management Information Base (MIB).

Simple volume A simple volume is a volume created on a dynamic disk that is not fault tolerant, and includes space from only one physical disk. A simple volume is just that—it is a single volume that does not span more than one physical disk, and does not provide improved drive performance, extra capacity, or fault tolerance. One physical disk can contain a single, large simple volume, or several smaller ones. Each simple volume is assigned a separate drive letter. The number of simple volumes on a disk is limited only by the capacity of the disk and the number of available letters in the alphabet.

Single-Instance-Store (SIS) Volume When you have more than one image on the Remote Installation Service (RIS) server, each holding Windows 2000 Professional files, there will be duplicate copies of hundreds of files. This may consume a significant hard drive space on the RIS server. To overcome this problem, Microsoft introduced a new feature called the Single-Instance-Store, which helps in deleting all the duplicate files, thus saving on hard drive space.

SIS *See* Single-Instance-Store.

Site Server Internet Locator Server (ILS) Service This service supports Internet Protocol (IP) telephony applications. Publishes IP multicast conferences on a network, and can also publish user IP address mappings for H.323 IP telephony. Telephony applications, such as NetMeeting and Phone Dialer in Windows Accessories, use Site Server ILS Service to display user names and conferences with published addresses. Site Server ILS Service depends on Internet Information Services (IIS).

Slave server Slave servers are a special type of forwarder, which is configured not to attempt to resolve the host name on its own. The server receiving the zone files can be called either a Slave server or a Secondary server. It is preferred to refer to the machine receiving the zone file as a secondary, because the term Slave Domain Name System (DNS) server has another meaning that refers to an inability to perform recursion for DNS clients.

Slave server/caching-only forwarder   The slave server/caching-only forwarder combination is very helpful in protecting your intranet zone data from Internet intruders. We can use this combination to prevent users on the other side of a firewall from having access to information on our Internal Domain Name System (DNS) server.

SLIP   *See* Serial Line Interface Protocol.

Small Computer System Interface (SCSI)   A complete expansion bus interface that accepts such devices as a hard disk, CD-ROM, disk drivers, printers, and scanners.

Small Office/Home Office (SOHO)   A SOHO network typically has the following characteristics: a single segment network; peer-to-peer networking; a single protocol (such as TCP/IP); and a demand-dial or dedicated link connection to the Internet via an Internet Service Provider (ISP). A user on a SOHO networks frequently needs to use more than one computer, and also needs to be able to share resources from one computer to another, such as files, applications, and printers.

SMP   *See* Symmetric Multiprocessing.

SMS   *See* Systems Management Server.

SMTP   *See* Simple Mail Transfer Protocol

SNA   *See* Systems Network Architecture.

SNMP   *See* Simple Network Management Protocol

SOA   *See* Start of Authority.

SOHO   *See* Small Office/Home Office.

Spanned volume   A spanned volume is similar to a volume set in NT 4.0. It contains space from multiple disks (up to 32), and provides a way to combine small "chunks" of disk space into one unit, seen by the operating system as a single volume. It is not fault tolerant. When a dynamic volume includes the space on more than one physical hard drive, it is called a spanned volume. Spanned volumes can be used to increase drive capacity, or to make use of the leftover space on up to 32 existing disks. Like those in a basic storage volume set, the portions of a spanned volume are all linked together and share a single drive letter.

SPAP   *See* Shiva Password Authentication Protocol.

SPI   *See* Security Parameters Index.

SPX   *See* Sequenced Packet eXchange.

SQL   *See* Structured Query Language.

SRV   *See* Service record.

Stack   A data structure in which the first items inserted are the last ones removed, unlike control structure programs that use the Last In First Out (LIFO) structure.

Start of Authority (SOA)   The SOA identifies which Domain Name System (DNS) server is authoritative for the data within a domain. The first record in any zone file is the SOA.

Static Internet Protocol (IP) address   A static IP address allows users to use a domain name that can be translated into an IP address. The static IP address allows the server to always have the same IP address, so the domain name always translates to the correct IP address. If the address was assigned dynamically and occasionally changed, users might not be able to access the server across the Internet using the domain name.

Stripe set   The term "striping" refers to the interleaving of data across separate physical disks. Each file is broken into small blocks, and each block is evenly and alternately saved to the disks in the stripe set. In a two-disk stripe set, the first block of data is saved to the first disk, the second block is saved to the second disk, the third block is saved to the first disk, and so on. The two disks are treated as a single drive, and are given a single drive letter.

Stripe set with parity   A stripe set with parity requires at least three hard disks, and provides both increased storage capacity and fault tolerance. In a stripe set with parity, data is interleaved across three or more disks, and includes parity (error checking) information about the data. As long as only one disk in the set fails, the parity information can be used to reconstruct the lost data. If the parity information itself is lost, it can be reconstructed from the original data.

Striped volume   Like a stripe set in NT 4.0, a striped volume is the dynamic storage equivalent of a basic stripe set and combines free space from up to 32 physical disks into one volume by writing data across the disks in stripes. This increases performance but does not provide fault tolerance. A striped volume improves drive performance and increases drive capacity. Because each data block is written only once, striped volumes do not provide fault tolerance.

Striping   Striping is when the data are striped across the drives, and there is parity information along with the data. The parity information is based on a mathematical formula that comes up with the parity based on the data on the other drives.

Structured Query Language (SQL)   A concise IBM query language (only 30 commands) structured like English, widely used in database management applications for mainframes and minicomputers.

Stub areas   You can import external routes into an Open Shortest Path First (OSPF) AS with an AS Border Router, but to stop external routes from flooding into an area you can use what is called a stub area. A stub area applies the default route 0.0.0.0 to keep the topology database size small. In OSPF, you can assume that any destination that you can't reach through a designated route is reachable through the default route. To implement a stub area, one or more of the stub area's Area Border Routers must advertise the default route 0.0.0.0 to the stub area, and the route summary.

Subnetting Using several data paths to reduce traffic on a network and avoid problems if a single path should fail; usually configured as a dedicated Ethernet subnetwork between two systems based on two Network Interface Cards (NICs).

Supernetting Supernetting is a way of combining several small networks into a larger one. For example, a company may need a Class B network, but because those have all been assigned, it can't get one. However, Class C networks *are* available, so the company can be assigned multiple Class C networks with contiguous addresses. By "stealing" bits again, but in the opposite direction (sort of like taking from the poor and giving to the rich instead of vice versa), you can use some of the bits that originally represented the network ID to represent host IDs, reducing the number of networks but increasing the number of hosts available per network.

Superscope A superscope is a Windows 2000 Dynamic Host Control Protocol (DHCP) feature that lets you use more than one scope for a subnet. The superscope contains multiple "child" scopes, grouped together under one name and manageable as one entity. The situations in which superscopes should be used include these: when many DHCP clients are added to a network, so that it has more than were originally planned for; when the Internet Protocol (IP) addresses on a network must be renumbered; and when two (or more) DHCP servers are on the same subnet for fault tolerance purposes.

Symmetric algorithm A cryptographic algorithm that uses the same key to both encrypt and decrypt, also called a secret key algorithm.

Symmetric Multiprocessing (SMP) SMP is a system in which all processors are treated as equals, and any thread can be run on any available processor. Windows 2000 also supports processor affinity, in which a process or thread can specify which set of processors it should run on. Application Programming Interfaces (APIs) must be defined in the application.

Synthesis The process of design, formulation, integration, prediction, proposal, generalization, and showing relationships.

SYSPREP.INF   SYSPREP.INF is an answer file. When you want to automate the Mini-Setup Wizard by providing predetermined answers to all setup questions, you must use this file. This file needs to be placed in the %Systemroot%\Sysprep folder or on a floppy disk. When the Mini-Setup Wizard is run on the computer on which the image is being distributed, it takes answers from the SYSPREP.INF file without prompting the user for any input.

System Preparation (SysPrep)   SysPrep provides an excellent means of saving installation time and reducing installation costs. SysPrep is the best tool to copy the image of a computer to other computers that have identical hardware configurations. It is also helpful in standardizing the desktop environment throughout the organization. Since one SysPrep image cannot be used on computers with identical hardware and software applications, you can create multiple images when you have more than one standard. It is still the best option where the number of computers is in hundreds or thousands, and you wish to implement uniform policies in the organization.

System Monitor   The System Monitor is part of this Administrative Tools utility that allows you to collect and view data about current memory usage, disk, processor utilization, network activity, and other system activity. The System Monitor replaces the Performance Monitor used in Windows NT. System Monitor allows you to collect information about your hardware's performance as well as network utilization. System Monitor can be used to measure different aspects of a computer's performance. It can be used on your own computer or other computers on the network.

System policy   Group policies have mostly replace system policies, since group policies extend the functionality of system policies. A few situations still exist in which system policies are valuable. The system policy editor is used to provide user and computer configuration settings in the Windows NT registry database. The system policy editor is still used for the management of Windows 9x , Windows NT server and workstations, and stand-alone computers using Windows 2000.

Systems Management Server (SMS)   This Windows NT software analyzes and monitors network usage and various network functions.

Systems Network Architecture (SNA)   Systems Network Architecture (SNA) was developed by IBM in the mainframe computer era (1974, to be precise) as a way of getting its various products to communicate with each other for distributed processing. SNA is a line of products designed to make other products cooperate. In your career of designing network solutions, you should expect to run into SNA from time to time because many of the bigger companies (such as banks, healthcare institutions, and government offices) bought IBM equipment and will be reluctant to part with their investment. SNA is a proprietary protocol that runs over SDLC exclusively, although it may be transported within other protocols, such as X.25 and Token Ring. It is designed as a hierarchy and consists of a collection of machines called nodes.

Take Ownership Permission   This permission can be given to allow a user to take ownership of a file or folder object. Every file and folder on an NT File System (NTFS) drive has an owner, usually the account that created the object. However, there are times when ownership of a file needs to be changed, perhaps because of a change in team membership or a set of new responsibilities for a user.

Task-based model   This model is appropriate for companies in which administrative duties are functionally divided. This means that this model divides the management of Group Policy Objects (GPOs) by certain tasks. To apply this model, the administrators that handle security-related tasks will also be responsible for managing all policy objects that affect security. The second set of administrators that normally deploy the companies' business applications will be responsible for all the GPOs that affect installation and maintenance.

TCP/IP   *See* Transmission Control Protocol/Internet Protocol.

Telnet   Telnet is a Transmission Control Protocol/Internet Protocol (TCP/IP-based) service that allows users to log on to, run character-mode applications, and view files on a remote computer. Windows 2000 Server includes both Telnet server and Telnet client software.

Terminal Services   In application server mode, Terminal Services provides the ability to run client applications on the server, while "thin client" software acts as a terminal emulator on the client. Each user sees an individual session, displayed as a Windows 2000 desktop. The server manages each session, independent of any other client session. If you install Terminal Services as an application server, you must also install Terminal Services Licensing (not necessarily on the same computer). However, temporary licenses can be issued for clients that allow you to use Terminal servers for up to 90 days. In remote administration mode, you can use Terminal Services to log on remotely and manage Windows 2000 systems from virtually anywhere on your network (instead of being limited to working locally on a server). Remote administration mode allows for two concurrent connections from a given server and minimizes impact on server performance. Remote administration mode does not require you to install Terminal Services Licensing.

TFTP *See* Trivial File Transfer Protocol.

TKEY The TKEY resource record is used to transfer security tokens between the DNS client and server. It allows for the establishment of the shared secret key that will be used with the TSIG resource record.

Token Ring A Local Area Network (LAN) specification that was developed by IBM in the 1980s for PC-based networks and classified by the (Institute of Electrical and Electronics Engineers) IEEE as 802.5. It specifies a star topology physically and a ring topology logically. It runs at either 4 Mbps or 16 Mbps, but all nodes on the ring must run at the same speed.

Tombstoning Windows 2000 allows you to mark a record manually to eventually be deleted. This is called tombstoning. The tombstone state of the record replicates to other Windows Internet Name Service (WINS) servers, and this prevents any replicated copies of the deleted records from reappearing at the same server where they were originally deleted.

Top-level domain names Top-level domain names include .com, .net, .org, and .edu. Organizations that seek to have an Internet presence will obtain a domain name that is a member of one of the top-level domain names.

Trace log   The Windows 2000 DNS Server allows you to enable trace logging via the Graphical User Interface (GUI) interface if you require extremely detailed information about the Domain Name System (DNS) server's activities. The information gathered in the trace is saved to a text file on the local hard disk. A trace log can track all queries received and answered by the DNS server.

TRACERT command-line utility   TRACERT is used to trace the route a packet takes to a destination.

Transmission Control Protocol/Internet Protocol (TCP/IP)   A set of communications standards created by the U.S. Department of Defense (DoD) in the 1970s that has now become an accepted way to connect different types of computers in networks because the standards now support so many programs.

Transport Mode   When Internet Protocol Security (IPSec) is used to protect communications between two clients (for example, two computers on the same Local Area Network or LAN), the machines can utilize IPSec in what is known as Transport Mode. In this example, the endpoints of the secure communication are the source machine and the destination host.

Trees   Trees are groups of domains that share a contiguous namespace. This allows you to create a hierarchical grouping of domains that share a common contiguous namespace. This hierarchy allows global sharing of resources among domains in the tree. All the domains in a tree share information and resources with a single directory, and there is only one directory per tree. However, each domain manages its own subset of the directory that contains the user accounts for that domain. So, when a user logs into a domain, the user has global access to all resources that are part of the tree, providing the user has the proper permissions.

Trivial File Transfer Protocol (TFTP)   A simplified of the File Transfer Protocol (FTP), associated with the Transmission Control Protocol/Internet Protocol (TCP/IP) family, that does not provide password protection or a user directory.

Trust   The users in one tree do not have global access to resources in other trees, but trusts can be created that allow users to access resources in another tree. A trust allows all the trees to share resources and have common administrative functions. Such sharing capability allows the trees to operate independently of each other, with separate namespaces, yet still be able to communicate and share resources through trusts.

Trust relationship   A trust relationship is a connection between domains in which users who have accounts in and log on to one domain can then access resources in other domains, provided they have proper access permissions.

TSIG   The TSIG resource record is used to send and verify messages that have been signed with a hash algorithm.

Tunnel Mode   The second communication mode is a gateway-to-gateway solution. Internet Protocol Security (IPSec) protects information that travels through a transit network (such as the Internet). Packets are protected as they leave the exit gateway, and then decrypted or authenticated at the destination network's gateway. When gateways represent the endpoints of the secure communication, IPSec is operating in Tunnel Mode. A tunnel is created between the gateways, and client-to-client communications are encapsulated in the tunnel protocol headers.

Two-way initiated demand-dial connections   A two-way initiated demand-dial connection is where routers can both initiate a connection when needed, and also respond to the same router calling it over the same demand-dial interface. In other words, in a two-way initiated connection, both routers can be a calling router or an answering router on the same interface. Use two-way initiated connections when traffic from either router can create the demand-dial connection. This offers the greatest flexibility but also requires the greatest configuration, since not only do both routers need to be configured, but also they have to be configured similarly to ensure that their configurations match.

UDF   *See* Unique Database File.

UDP   *See* User Datagram Protocol.

Unattended method   The unattended method for Windows 2000 Server installation uses the answer file to specify various configuration parameters. This method eliminates user interaction during installation, thereby automating the installation process and reducing the chances of input errors. Answers to most of the questions asked by the setup process are specified in the answer file. In addition, the scripted method can be used for clean installations and upgrades.

UNATTEND.TXT file   The creation of customized UNATTEND.TXT answer files is the simplest form of providing answers to setup queries and unattended installation of Windows 2000. This can either be done using the Setup Manager or by editing the sample UNATTEND.TXT file using Notepad or the MS-DOS text editor. The UNATTEND.TXT file does not provide any means of creating an image of the computer.

UNATTEND.UDF   This file is the Uniqueness Database File, which provides customized settings for each computer using the automated installation.

UNC   *See* Universal Naming Convention.

UNICODE   UNICODE is a 16-bit character encoding standard, developed by the Unicode Consortium between 1988 and 1991, that uses two bytes to represent each character and enables almost all of the written languages of the world to be represented using a single character set.

Uninterruptible Power Supply (UPS)   A battery that can supply power to a computer system if the power fails. It charges while the computer is on and, if the power fails, provides power for a certain amount of time allowing the user to shut down the computer properly to preserve data.

Unique Database File (UDF)   When you use the WINNT32.EXE command with the /unattend option, you can also specify a Unique Database File (UDF), which has a .UDB extension. This file forces Setup to use certain values from the UDF file, thus overriding the values given in the answer file. This is particularly useful when you want to specify multiple users during the setup.

Universal Groups   Universal Groups are used in larger, multidomain organizations, in which there is a need to grant access to similar groups of accounts defined in multiple domains. It is better to use Global Groups as members of Universal Groups to reduce overall replication traffic from changes to Universal Group membership. Users can be added and removed from the corresponding Global Groups with their account domains, and a small number of Global Groups are the direct members of the Universal Group. Universal Groups are used only in multiple domain trees or forests. A Windows 2000 domain must be in native mode to use Universal Groups.

Universal Serial Bus (USB)   A low-speed hardware interface (supports MPEG video) with a maximum bandwidth up to 1.5MB per second.

Universal Naming Convention (UNC)   A UNC is an identification standard of servers and other network resources.

UPS   *See* Uninterruptible Power Supply.

USB   *See* Universal Serial Bus.

User account   The information that defines a particular user on a network, which includes the username, password, group memberships, and rights and permissions assigned to the user.

User classes   User classes allow Dynamic Host Control Protocol (DHCP) clients to identify their class membership to a DHCP server. The server can return to the client a specific set of options relevant to the class. The process is the same as how vendor class options are requested by the client and sent by the DHCP server.

User Datagram Protocol (UDP)   A Transmission Control Protocol/Internet Protocol (TCP/IP) normally bundled with an Internet Protocol (IP) layer software that describes how messages received reached application programs within the destination computer.

User Principle Name mapping   This is a special kind of one-to-one mapping only available through the Active Directory. Enterprise CA's insert an entry called a User Principle Name (UPN) into each of its certificates. UPN's are unique to each users account within a Windows 2000 Domain and they are of the format *user@domain* The UPN is used to locate the user account in Active Directory and that account is logged on.

Value bar   The value bar is positioned below the graph area. It displays data for the selected sample, the last sample value, the average of the counter samples, the maximum and minimum of the samples, and the duration of time the samples have been taken over.

Vendor class options   RFCs 2131 and 2132 define Dynamic Host Control Protocol (DHCP) vendor class options, which allow hardware and software vendors to add their own options to the DHCP server. These options are additions to the list of standard DHCP options included with the Windows 2000 DHCP Server.

Virtual Private Networking (VPN)   VPNs reduce service costs and long distance/usage fees, lighten infrastructure investments, and simplify Wide Area Network (WAN) operations over time. To determine just how cost-effective a VPN solution could be in connecting remote offices, use the VPN Calculator located on Cisco's Web site at www.cisco.com.

Volume set   The term "volume" indicates a single drive letter. One physical hard disk can contain several volumes, one for each primary partition or logical drive. However, the opposite is also true. You can create a single volume that spans more than one physical disk. This is a good option when you require a volume that exceeds the capacity of a single physical disk. You can also create a volume set when you want to make use of leftover space on several disks by piecing them together as one volume.

VPN   *See* Virtual Private Networking.

Windows 3x   Windows 3 changed everything. It was a 16-bit operating system with a user interface that resembled the look and feel of IBM's (at that time not yet released) OS/2, with 3D buttons and the ability to run multiple programs simultaneously, using a method called cooperative multitasking. Windows 3 also provided virtual memory, the ability to use hard disk space to "fool" the applications into behaving as if they had more RAM than was physically installed in the machine.

Windows 9x   In August of 1995, Microsoft released its long-awaited upgrade of Windows, Windows 95. For the first time, Windows could be installed on a machine that didn't already have MS-DOS installed. Many improvements were made: the new 32-bit functionality (although still retaining some 16-bit code for backward compatibility); preemptive multitasking (a more efficient way to run multiple programs in which the operating system controls use of the processor and the crash of one application does not bring down the others that are currently running); and support for filenames longer than the DOS-based eight-character limit.

Windows32 Driver Model (WDM)   The Win32 Driver Model (WDM) provides a standard for device drivers that will work across Windows platforms (specifically Windows 98 and 2000), so that you can use the same drivers with the consumer and business versions of the Windows operating system.

Windows 2000   Microsoft's latest incarnation of the corporate operating system was originally called NT 5, but the name was changed to Windows 2000 between the second and third beta versions—perhaps to underscore the fact that this is truly a *new* version of the operating system, not merely an upgrade to NT.

Windows 2000 Control Panel   The Control Panel in Windows 2000 functions similarly to the Control Panel in Windows 9x and NT, except that "under the hood" there are now two locations that information is stored, which is modified by the Control Panel applets. The Control Panel in previous operating systems was a graphical interface for editing Registry information.

Windows Backup   Windows Backup is a built-in backup and restore utility, which has many more features than the backup tool provided in Windows NT 4.0.

It supports all five types of backup: Normal, Copy, Differential, Incremental, and Daily. Windows Backup allows you to perform the backup operation manually or you may schedule it to run at a later time in unattended mode. Included with the operating system, it is a tool that is flexible and easy to use.

Windows Internet Name Service (WINS)   WINS provides name resolution for clients running Windows NT and earlier versions of Microsoft operating systems. With name resolution, users can access servers by name, instead of having to use Internet Protocol (IP) addresses that are difficult to recognize and remember. WINS is used to map NetBIOS computer names to IP addresses. This allows users to access other computers on the network by computer name. WINS servers should be assigned a static IP address, which allows clients to be able to find the WINS servers. Clients cannot find a WINS server by name because they need to know where the WINS server is in order to translate the name into an IP address.

Windows Internet Name Service (WINS) Name Registration   Each WINS client has one or more WINS servers identified in the network configuration on the computer, either through static assignment or through DHCP configuration. When the client boots and connects to the network, it registers its name and IP address with the WINS server by sending a registration request directly to the server. This is not a broadcast message, since the client has the address of the server. If the server is available and the name is not already registered, the server responds with a successful registration message, which contains the amount of time the name will be registered to the client, the Time To Live (TTL). Then the server stores the name and address combination in its local database.

Windows Internet Name Service (WINS) Name Release   When a WINS client shuts down properly, it will send a name release request to the WINS server. This releases the name from the WINS server's database so that another client can use the name if necessary. The release request contains the WINS name and address of the client. If the server cannot find the name, it sends a negative release response to the client. If the server finds the matching name and address in its database, it releases the name and marks the record as inactive. If the name is found but the address does not match, the server ignores the request.

Windows Internet Name Service (WINS) Name Renewal   As with Dynamic Host Control Protocol (DHCP), WINS name registrations are temporary and must be renewed to continue to be valid. The client will attempt to renew its registration when half (50 percent) of the Time To Live (TTL) has elapsed. If the WINS server does not respond, the client repeatedly attempts to renew its lease at ten-minute intervals for an hour. If the client still receives no response, it restarts the process with the secondary WINS server, if one is defined. The client will continue attempting to renew its lease in this manner until it receives a response from a server. At that time, the server sends a new TTL to the client and the process starts over.

Windows Internet Name Server (WINS) Proxy Agent   The WINS Proxy Agent has a single purpose: to resolve NetBIOS names for non-WINS clients. The non-WINS clients can be UNIX servers, or even Windows computers that are configured as b-node clients. Keep in mind that the WINS Proxy Agent resolves NetBIOS names; it does not register them. When a non-WINS client starts up, it may broadcast its name to the local segment, but the WINS Proxy Agent on that segment does not register the non-WINS client name in the WINS database. The WINS Proxy Agent solves the problem of NetBIOS name resolution for non-WINS clients. The other side of the coin is resolving the NetBIOS name of a non-WINS client. A non-WINS client does not register its name in the WINS database. If a WINS client tries to resolve the name of a non-WINS client, the attempt fails, because there is no entry in the WINS database for the non-WINS client. The solution to this problem is to add a *static entry* into the WINS database for the non-WINS client.

Windows Internet Name Service (WINS) Referral Zone   A WINS Referral Zone is usually a forward lookup zone that has no resource records in it. After creating the WINS Referral Zone, you disable WINS Referral for all other zones. After you have done this, any queries that are resolved via WINS are returned with the Fully Qualified Domain Name (FQDN) that contains the NetBIOS name returned from the WINS server with the WINS Referral Zone's domain name appended to it. In this way, it is easy to identify which queries have been resolved via WINS lookups.

Windows Internet Name Service (WINS) snap-in   With the snap-in, you can view the active WINS entries under the Active Registrations folder. In addition, you can supply static mappings for non-WINS clients on the network through the snap-in. To configure a static mapping, select the Active Registrations folder and the select New Static Mapping from the Action menu. Once a static mapping is entered into the WINS database, it cannot be edited. If you need to make changes to a static mapping, you must be delete and recreate the entry.

Windows NT   The NT kernel (the core or nucleus of the operating system, which provides basic services for all other parts of the operating system) is built on a completely different architecture from consumer Windows. In fact, NT was based on the 32-bit preemptive multitasking operating system that originated as a joint project of Microsoft and IBM before their parting of the ways, OS/2. NT provided the stability and security features that the "other Windows" lacked, albeit at a price, and not only a monetary one; NT was much pickier in terms of hardware support, did not run all of the programs that ran on Windows 9*x* (especially DOS programs that accessed the hardware directly), and required more resources, especially memory, to run properly.

WINNT.EXE program   The WINNT.EXE program is used for network installations that use an MS-DOS network client. The WINNT32.EXE program is used to customize the process for upgrading existing installations. The WINNT32.EXE program is used for installing Windows 2000 from a computer that is currently running Windows 95/98 or Windows NT.

WINS   *See* Windows Internet Name Service.

Workgroup   A workgroup is a logical grouping of resources on a network. It is generally used in peer-to-peer networks. This means that each computer is responsible for access to its resources. Each computer has its own account database and is administered separately. Security is not shared between computers, and administration is more difficult than in a centralized domain.

X25   X25 uses an international standard for sending data across public packet-switching networks. The Windows 2000 Routing and Remote Access server will only support direct connections to X25 networks by using an X25 smart card.

Zone delegation   Zone delegation provides a way for you to distribute responsibility for zone database management, and provides a measure of load balancing for Domain Name System (DNS) servers. When you create a delegation for a zone, you are "passing the buck" to another DNS server to answer DNS queries for a particular zone. Zones can be delegated to Secondary DNS Servers or Primaries.

Zone transfer   The zone transfer process can be considered a "pull" operation. This is because the Secondary Domain Name System (DNS) server initiates the zone transfer process. The Secondary DNS server will initiate a zone transfer when a Primary DNS server sends a "notify" message to the Secondary DNS server. informing it that there has been a change to the zone database, the Secondary DNS server boots up, or the Secondary DNS server's *Refresh Interval* has expired.

Zones of authority   The Domain Name System (DNS) name space is divided into zones, and each zone must have one name server that is the authority for the name mapping for the zone. Depending on the size of the name space, a zone may be subdivided into multiple zones, each with its own authority, or there may be a single authority for the entire zone. For instance, a small company with only 200–300 computers could have one DNS server handle the entire namespace.

Index

A

access control lists (ACLs), 519–525
    access control guidelines and, 531
    degree of granularity and, 520
    GPO Control and, 291–293
    object and attribute permissions
      and, 520
    permissions inheritance and, 521,
      525
    setting permissions and, 521–524
    special permissions and, 521
    standard permissions and, 520–521
accounts. *See also* user accounts
    creation of RIS accounts, 413
    manual creation of AD accounts,
      513–516
    scripting the creation of AD
      accounts, 516–519
accumulative counters, 536
ACLDIAG, AD tools, 547
ACLs. *See* access control lists (ACLs)
Active Directory (AD)
    background needed for, 33–39
      experienced NT administrators
        and, 38–39
      Microsoft networking concepts
        and, 33–34

      newbies and, 38
      terminology and, 34–37
      Windows 2000 concepts and, 34
    directory services and, 6
    exam topics and, 15–30
      backing up and restoring AD,
        21–22
      implementing OU structure, 21
      installing, configuring, and
        troubleshooting AD, 16–17
      integrating DNS with AD,
        22–24
      managing sites and subnets, 17
      using AD components, 29–30
      using AD security solutions, 30
      using domain controller roles,
        18–20
      using Group Policy, 24–27
      using RIS, 28–29
    features of, 3–4
    global services of, 8–13
      centralized management, 11
      control of user environment, 12
      DDNS integration, 9
      DHCP integration, 9

directory-enabled applications,
12

LDAP compatibility, 9

open interfaces and protocols, 10

security services integration,
12–13

support for industry standards, 9

TCP/IP support, 10

GPOs and

deleting GPOs, 313–314

locating GPOs, 285–286

role of directory services and, 5–8

self test, 42–44

self test, answers, 45–47

structure of, 13–15

logical structure, 14–15

physical structure, 13

two-minute drill, 40–42

what is covered in book, 31–32

Active Directory (AD), configuring.
See configuration, AD

Active Directory (AD), DNS and.
See Domain Name System (DNS),
AD and

Active Directory (AD), installing
components. *See* components, AD

Active Directory (AD), managing.
See management, AD

Active Directory (AD), troubleshooting.
See troubleshooting

Active Directory Installation Wizard

Database and Log Locations window
of, 59

default permissions for users and
groups and, 62

DNS and, 61–62

domain controller types and, 55

forests and, 56

installing DNS and, 229

NetBIOS domain name window
of, 58–59

Network Credentials window of, 57

New Domain Name window of,
57–58

password specification and, 63

SYSVOL folder and, 60

trees or child domains and, 56

Active Directory-integrated zones

creating, 231

switching to, 232–234

Active Directory Objects (ADOs)

auditing, 634–637

delegating control of, 527–530

using, 29–30

Active Directory Replication Monitor, 584–586

Active Directory Services Interface (ADSI)

application programming interfaces (APIs) of, 504

definition of, 35

function of, 178

interoperability and, 7

overview of, 10

scripting interfaces and, 517

Active Directory Sites and Services Console

creating bridgehead servers, 83–87

creating connection objects, 97–101

creating global catalog servers, 102–104

creating site link bridges, 88–95

creating site links, 79–83

creating sites, 72–75

creating subnet objects, 576

creating subnets, 76–78

moving server objects, 134

Active Directory Users and Computers Console

AD/DNS integrated zones and, 591–592

creating objects, 156–157

creating OUs, 152–156

published resources and, 504

RIS naming and placement schemes and, 419–421

verifying AD domain controller, 129

Add Printer Wizard, 503–504

administrative templates. *See* templates, administrative

ADOs. *See* Active Directory Objects (ADOs)

ADSI. *See* Active Directory Services Interface (ADSI)

aging, DNS management and, 242–244

alerts. *See* Performance Logs and Alerts

alias records. *See* canonical name (CNAME) records

answer files

associating with CD-based images, 414–418

definition of, 408

RIStandard.sif and, 407

application programming interfaces (APIs)

definition of, 35

published resources and, 504

applications

application logs and, 532

global services and, 12

ARPANET, 219

asynchronous replication, 80

attended installation, RIS clients, 454

attributes

access control and, 520

adding and modifying, 543–544

definition of, 3

schema and, 543

auditing. *See also* security

ADOs and, 634–637

best practices for, 639

configuring, 630

domain controllers and, 631–632

files, folders, and printers and,
    637–639

implementing, 629–630

planning, 650

security policies and, 634

stand-alone computers and, 633

authentication, 35

authoritative restore

performing, 21

restoring AD and, 195

authorization, RIS, 404–406

process of, 405–406

why authorize, 405

AXFR (full zone transfer), 259

B

backing up. *See also* Backup Wizard

exam topics and, 21–22

exercise for, 194

NTBACKUP and, 191–193

restoring from backup media, 204

backup domain controllers (BDCs)

AD replication and, 566

intersite replication and, 581–582

Windows 2000 and, 19

Backup Wizard, 182–191

Backup Label screen, 189

Completing the Backup screen,
    185, 191

exercise for backing up AD, 194

How to Back Up screen, 188

Manual Backup screen, 184

Media Options screen, 189

Type of Backup screen, 187

Welcome screen, 183

What to Back Up screen, 183

When to Back Up screen, 190

Where to Store the Backup screen,
    185

BDCs. *See* backup domain controllers
    (BDCs)

Berkeley Internet Name Domain
(BIND)
   overview of, 234–235
   as UNIX based DNS servers, 587
binding information, 508
BINL. *See* Boot Installation Negotiation
   Layer (BINL)
Block Policy Inheritance, 298, 362
boot disks, RIS clients, 399, 452–454
Boot Installation Negotiation Layer
   (BINL)
      RIS client installation and, 465,
      473–474
      troubleshooting RIS and, 429,
      470–471
boot ROM, 399
BootP messages, RIS, 429
bridgehead servers, 83–86
      creating, 84–86
      definition of, 83
      designating servers as, 87
      replication and, 579–580
browser interfaces, IE options, 375

canonical name (CNAME) records
   creating, 246
   resource records and, 24
categorization
   changing categories and, 366–367
   packages and, 367–368
   software deployment and, 368–369
CD-based images
   associating answer files with,
      414–418
   modifying, 408
   RIS image types and, 407
child domains
   AD installation and, 56
   definition of, 35, 180
child objects, 14
CIW. *See* Client Installation Wizard
   (CIW)
classes
   adding and modifying, 545
   schema and, 543
client installation. *See* Remote
   Installation Services (RIS), client
   installation
Client Installation Wizard (CIW)
   definition of, 35
   options of, 466–469
      Automatic Setup, 466–467

C

cache, DNS, 244

Custom Setup, 467

Maintenance and
Troubleshooting, 468–469

Restarting Previous Install,
467–468

OS recovery and, 456

restricting installation options,
447–448

RIS and, 399, 401, 466

Welcome screen, 472

CNAME records. *See* canonical name
(CNAME) records

compatibility, directory services and, 4

components, AD

attributes and, 543–544

classes and, 545

DNS and, 540–542

installation of

assigning bridgehead servers,
83–87

creating connection objects,
96–101

creating global catalog servers,
101–105

creating site link bridges, 88–95

creating site links, 79–83

creating sites, 71–75

creating subnets, 75–78

schemas and, 542–543

computers

AD stored objects and, 510

assigning packages to, 348

computer scripts and, 318

publishing resources to, 504

configuration

auditing and, 630

configuration data and, 7, 508

configuration naming context
and, 564

network configuration and, 374–383

Internet Explorer options,
375–377

other options, 377–383

RIS and

assigning permissions and,
422–425

CD-based images and, 408,
413–418

computer account creation
and, 413

default location and computer
naming and, 419–421

image types and, 407

pre-staging client computers
and, 426–428

RISetup and, 407–413

security logs and, 645–646

software deployment and

advanced options, 365

categorizing packages, 367–368

filtering packages, 362–363

miscellaneous options, 363–368

using transforms, 368–369

configuration, AD, 126–173

AD installation and, 126–131

verifying DNS server, 128–131

verifying domain controller,
126–128

operations master roles and, 138–149

definition of, 138–140

domainwide assignment of, 146

forceful transfer of (seizing),
147–148

how to transfer, 141–144

identifying assignment of,
144–146

when to transfer, 140–141

OU structure and, 150–159

creating objects, 156–158

creating structure, 152–154, 159

design overview and, 150–152

setting properties, 154–155

self test, 163–167

self test, answers, 169–173

server objects and, 131–137

creating in sites, 131–133

how to move, 134

removing from sites, 136–137

when to move, 133–134

two-minute drill, 161–162

conflict resolution, domain controllers
and, 570–571

connection objects, 96–101

creating, 97–101

definition of, 96–97

connections

dial-up connections, 383

IE options, 375

contacts, AD stored objects, 508

contiguous namespace, 14

Control Panel, DNS and, 226

costs. *See* total cost of ownership (TCO)

costs, site links and, 576

counters. *See* performance

D

data collation, 51–52

data stores, 3

database layer, AD architecture, 177

databases

location of, 59

setting up security database, 622–623

storage required by, 53

DCPROMO

default permissions and, 62

DNS and, 61–62

domain controller types and, 55

forests and, 56

NetBIOS domain name window
and, 58–59

Network Credentials window
and, 57

New Domain Name window
and, 57–58

password specification and, 63

SYSVOL folder and, 60

trees or child domains and, 56

using, 54

verifying AD installation and, 131

DDNS. *See* Dynamic Domain Name
System (DDNS)

debug logging options, DNS, 541–542

degree of granularity, 520

delegation of control, 525–531

definition of, 35, 525

Delegation of Control Wizard and
AD objects and, 527–530

assigning permissions with,
422–425, 526

configuration of, 531

Group Policy and, 26

guidelines for, 531

how to delegate, 526–531

deployment. *See* software deployment

DHCP. *See* Dynamic Host
Configuration Protocol (DHCP)

dial-up connections, 383

directories

definition of, 3, 35

optimizing replication traffic and, 13

directory services. *See also* Active
Directory (AD); global directory
services

AD and, 6

definition of, 3, 35

interoperability of, 7

logs for, 533

replication of, 7

terminology of, 34–37

Windows NT and, 5–6

Directory System Agent (DSA), 177
Discover program, 345
Distributed Security Services, 12–13
DNS. *See* Domain Name System (DNS)
DNS Console, MMC
    creating zones with, 229–232
    dynamic updates with, 238
    managing DNS Servers with
        aging and scavenging and,
            242–244
        cache and TTL and, 244
        menu and commands and,
            239–242
    overview of, 223
    switching to AD-integrated zones
        with, 233–234
    zone transfers and, 234–235
document invocation, 349
domain controllers
    AD installation and, 55
    auditing, 631–632
    exam topics and, 18–20
    managing
        event logs and, 532–533
        Performance Logs and Alerts
            and, 538–539

        Performance Monitor and,
            533–534
        System Monitor and, 534–538
    placement of, 581–582
    replication and
        conflict resolution and, 570–571
        high-watermark vector and,
            567–568
        making changes to AD and,
            569–570
        up-to-dateness vector and,
            568–569
        update sequence numbers
            and, 567
    stored objects and, 510
    verifying after AD installation,
        126–128
        from Active Directory Users and
            Computers, 129
        from My Network Places, 127
domain forests. *See* forests
Domain Name System (DNS)
    counters for, 251–255
    debug logging options of, 541–542
    DNS server logs and, 533, 540–541
    master servers, primary servers, and
        secondary servers and, 588

resource records of, 24
RIS server configuration and, 445
serial numbers and, 590
Start of Authority (SOA) records
and, 590
troubleshooting, 542
Windows 2000 basics and, 24
zones in, 588
Domain Name System (DNS), AD
and, 218–276
AD installation and, 53, 61–62
dynamic updates and, 237, 238
event logs and, 256
integrating with non-AD DNS,
234–237
BIND and, 234–235
Microsoft and non-Microsoft
DNS and, 236–237
interoperability and, 220–234
creating zones, 226–232
installing DNS, 222–226
switching to AD-integrated
zones, 232–234
management tasks and, 239–247
aging and scavenging and,
242–244
cache and TTL and, 244

creating records and, 245–246
managing DNS and, 245
viewing records and, 247
overview of, 219–220
Performance Console and, 248–255
DNS counters and, 251–255
monitoring and troubleshooting
with, 248
System Monitor and, 249–250
replication and, 258–260, 587–595
AD-integrated zones and, 260,
591–592
DNS data and, 258–260
non-AD integrated zones and,
589–591
troubleshooting, 593–595
self test, 264–269
self test, answers, 270–276
troubleshooting, 23–24, 256–258
two-minute drill, 262–263
verifying DNS server after AD
installation, 128–131
zone configuration and, 23
domain namespaces. *See* namespace
domain-naming master roles
definition of, 139
operations masters and, 20

seizing, 147–148

domain trees. *See* trees

domains

creating, 246

definition of, 35–36

domain data and, 7

function of, 180

logical structure of, 14

moving ADOs and, 496–500

moving OUs and, 500–501

second-level domains, 221

subdomains and hosts in, 220

top-level domains, 221

domainwide operations master roles. *See also* operations master roles

definition of, 139

identifying, 144

transferring, 146

DSA (Directory System Agent), 177

DSACLS, AD tools, 547

DSASTAT, AD tools, 547

Dynamic Domain Name System (DDNS)

dynamic updates with, 237–238

global services and, 9

Dynamic Host Configuration Protocol (DHCP)

AD global services and, 9

RIS server configuration and, 445

RIS troubleshooting and, 429, 470

dynamic updates

configuring zones for, 238

what are dynamic updates, 237

E

enterprise networks, scalability and, 2

ESE (Extensible Storage Engine), 177–178

event logs. *See also* Event Viewer

AD replication and, 583

archiving security logs, 644–646

clearing security logs, 646–647

DNS and, 256

domain controller performance and, 532–533

interpreting security events and, 647–650

RIS and, 476

types of events to monitor, 640–643

Event Viewer

DNS events and, 540–541

domain controller performance and, 532–533

interpreting security events with, 647–649

logging options of, 256

Security Log dialog box of, 642–646

    archiving logs, 644–646

    clearing logs, 646–647

    configuring settings, 643–644

    filtering events, 643–644

software deployment and, 371–373

tracking events with, 641

viewing events with, 649

Windows Installer service and, 372–374

Everyone group, 639

.EVT files, 644

exam topics, 15–30

    backing up and restoring AD, 21–22

    implementing OU structure, 21

    installing, configuring, and troubleshooting AD, 16–17

    integrating DNS with AD, 22–24

        DNS troubleshooting and, 23–24

        DNS zone configuration and, 23

    managing sites and subnets, 17

    using AD components, 29–30

    using AD security solutions, 30

using domain controller roles, 18–20

using Group Policy, 24–27

    Delegation of Control and, 26

    group policy inheritance and, 26–27

    group policy objects and, 25–26

    managing software with, 27

    managing user environment with, 27

using RIS, 28–29

Extensible Storage Engine (ESE), 177–178

F

fast zone transfer format, 234

FAT volumes, 626

File Replication service logs, 533

File Replication System, 138

files

    auditing, 637–639

    monitoring access to, 641

    setting security for, 627–628

    setting user rights for, 624, 626

filtering

    Event Viewer and, 643–644

Group Policy and, 301–309
    applying filters, 303–307
    filtering with security groups,
      308–309
    why filter, 302–303
    software deployment and, 362–363
first domain controller, 103
flexible single-master operations
  (FSMO), 19
folders
    auditing, 637–639
    Folder Redirection and, 340
    monitoring access to, 641
    publishing, 504, 505
    searching for shared folders, 511–512
    stored objects and, 510
forced removal, software deployment,
  360
forests
    AD features and, 4
    AD installation and, 56
    definition of, 14, 36
    function of, 181
forestwide operations master roles.
    See also operations master roles
    definition of, 139
    identifying and transferring,
      141–142

formats, log files, 644
forward lookup zones, DNS
    creating, 227–228
    definition of, 588
fresh installs, RIS clients, 455–456
FSMO (flexible single-master
  operations), 19
full replica, 565
full zone transfers (AXFR), 259

G

garbage collection, 570
global catalogs (GCs)
    AD features and, 3
    creating, 102–104
    definition of, 102
    domain controllers and, 18–19
    placing, 581–582
global directory services, 8–13. *See also*
  directory services
    centralized management with, 11
    control of user environment with, 12
    DDNS and, 9
    DHCP and, 9
    directory-enabled applications
      and, 12

LDAP and, 9
open interfaces and protocols and, 10
security services integration and,
12–13
support for industry standards in, 9
TCP/IP support and, 10
globally unique identifiers (GUIDs)
definition of, 36
domain controllers and, 567, 569,
570–571
prestaging and, 413, 426, 429
PXE devices and, 399
GPCs (Group Policy containers), 611
GPT (Group Policy templates), 611
Group Permissions, 362
Group Policy Console, 278–338
AD features and, 4
assigning script policies, 320–324
exercise for, 323–324
user vs. computer scripts,
321–322
controlling user environments, 27,
314–319
administrative templates and,
316–318
exercise for, 318–319
what can administrator control,
315–316

creating GPOs, 278–284, 614
deciding where to apply, 281
exercise for, 284
how to create, 281–283
what are GPOs, 279–280
definition of, 36, 611
delegating GPOs, 26, 288–295
exercise for, 295
how to delegate, 289–294
why delegate, 289
disabling Group Policy snap-in, 294
filtering GPOs, 301–309
applying filters, 303–307
exercise for, 288
filtering with security groups,
308–309
how and why to link, 286–287
location in Active Directory and,
285–286
why filter, 302–303
inheritance and, 26–27, 296–301
changing GPO inheritance,
299–300
exercise for, 300–301
managing inheritance, 298–299
what is inheritance, 296–297

RIS clients and, 447–451
security policies and, 309–314
    applying policies, 610–612
    changing policies, 310–313
    deleting policies, 313–314
    how to apply, 613
    when to use, 612–613
selecting Group Policy snap-in,
    281–283
self test, 328–332
self test, answers, 333–337
two-minute drill, 326–327
Group Policy containers (GPCs), 611
Group Policy editor
    changing security settings with,
    615–617
    creating security policies with, 613
Group Policy, network configuration,
374–383
    Internet Explorer options, 375–377
    other options, 377–383
    self test, 390–391
    self test, answers, 394
    two-minute drill, 386
Group Policy, software deployment
    configuring, 361–369
        advanced options, 365

categorizing packages, 367–368
filtering packages, 362–363
miscellaneous deployment
    options, 363–368
using transforms, 368–369
deploying, 27, 340–374
    applying to OUs, 348–355
    when and why to deploy
        software with GPOs, 346–347
    Windows Installer service and,
    341–346
maintaining, 356–361
    redeploying, 359–360
    removing, 360–361
    upgrades, 356–359
self test, 387–390
self test, answers, 392–393
troubleshooting, 369–374
    Event Viewer and, 371–373
    package fails to install, 369–370,
    371
    package install incomplete,
    370–371
two-minute drill, 385–386
Group Policy templates (GPTs), 611
groups
    AD stored objects and, 510

assigning RIS permissions to,
422–425
default permissions for, 62
publishing AD resources and, 504

H

HAL (Hardware Abstraction Layer), 457
hardware
AD installation and, 52–53
RIS clients and, 444–447, 475–476
Hardware Abstraction Layer (HAL), 457
Hardware Compatibility List (HCL),
181
hierarchy, domains and, 14
high-watermark vectors, 567–568
HINFO (host information) records, 246
HKEY_CURRENT_USER (HKCU),
316, 318
HKEY_LOCAL_MACHINE (HKLM),
316, 318
Host (A) records
creating, 246
resource records and, 24
host ID (host address), 227
host information (HINFO) records, 246
hosts, domains and, 220

I

IEEE (Institute of Electrical and
Electronics Engineers), 5
images
creating RIPrep images, 400
restricting OS image options,
449–450
RIS image types and, 407
imaging utilities, 455
inbound connections, 96
incremental zone transfers (IXFR),
259, 590
infrastructure master roles
definition of, 140
seizing, 148
inheritance, 296–301
Block Policy Inheritance option
and, 362
changing, 299–300
exercise using, 300–301
managing, 298–299
overview of, 26–27
permissions and, 521
what is inheritance, 296–297
.INI files, 346
installation
AD, 50–70

data collation and, 51–52

DCPROMO process for, 54–63

exercises for, 67–70

prerequisites for, 52–54

self test, 110

self test answers, 117

two-minute drill, 107

verifying install, 64–66

AD components, 71–124

assigning bridgehead servers, 83–87

creating connection objects, 96–101

creating global catalog servers, 101–105

creating site link bridges, 88–95

creating site links, 79–83

creating sites, 71–75

creating subnets, 75–78

self test, 111–115

self test answers, 117–122

two-minute drill, 107–109

RIS, 401–404

installation process, 402–404

prerequisites for, 401–402

Security Configuration and Analysis tool, 618

Institute of Electrical and Electronics Engineers (IEEE), 5

IntelliMirror

feature, benefits, and technologies of, 340

troubleshooting RIS and, 431

International Organization for Standardization (ISO), 5

Internet Explorer, options, 375–377

browser interface, 375

connections, 375

programs, 377

security, 376–377

URLs, 375–376

Internet Protocol (IP), site links in, 80, 82

interoperability

directory services and, 7

DNS/AD and, 220–234

creating zones, 226–232

installing DNS, 222–226

switching to AD-integrated zones, 232–234

Windows NT and, 235–237

intersite replication, 13

definition of, 36

exam topics and, 30
managing, 578–582
    BDCs and, 580–581
    domain controller and global
      catalog placement and,
      581–582
    password changes and, 581
    replication protocols and,
      579–580
Intersite Topology Generator, 579
intrasite replication, 13
    definition of, 36
    exam topics and, 30
    managing, 577–578
IP addresses, 227
IP (Internet Protocol), site links in,
    80, 82
IP Security (IPSec), 52
IPCONFIG, 257–258
ISO (International Organization for
    Standardization), 5
IXFR (incremental zone transfers),
    259, 590

J

Jscript, 517

K

Kerberos, 36
Knowledge Consistency Checker (KKC)
    AD replication and, 571–573
    creating Connection objects with,
      578
    site links and, 79

L

laptop computers, RIS troubleshooting,
    476
LDAP. *See* Lightweight Directory Access
    Protocol (LDAP)
LDP, AD tools, 547
leaves, 180
Lightweight Directory Access Protocol
    (LDAP)
    definition of, 36
    function of, 178

global services and, 9

standards and, 5

link costs, 92

links. *See* site links

load balancing, 141

local area networks (LANs), 563

Local Security Policy Settings dialog
  box, 632, 633

log file format, 644

logging

    DNS counters and, 251–255

    event logs and

        archiving security logs, 644–646

        clearing security logs, 646–647

        interpreting security events,
          647–650

        types of events to monitor,
          640–643

    Event Viewer and, 256

    types of logs and, 532–533

logical sites, 575

logoff

    auditing, 639

    scripts, 378, 381

logon

    auditing, 639, 641

    authentication traffic, 13

    scripts, 378–381

LOGON.BAT, 322, 323–324

lookup zones, 227

M

Mail Exchanger (MX) records

    creating, 246

    resource records and, 24

maintenance

    operations master roles and, 141

    RIS option for, 468–469

management, AD, 494–560

    accounts, 513–519

        manual creation of, 513–516

        scripting creation of, 516–519

    component performance, 539–548

        attributes and, 543–544

        classes and, 545

        DNS and, 540–542

        schemas and, 542–543

    delegation of control, 525–531

        guidelines for, 531

        how to delegate, 526–531

        why delegate, 525

    domain controller performance,
      532–539

event logs and, 532–533

Performance Logs and Alerts and, 538–539

Performance Monitor and, 533–534

System Monitor and, 534–538

global services, 11

locating objects, 508–513

searching AD, 510–513

searching for shared folders, 511–512

what is stored in AD, 508–510

moving objects, 495–503

across domains, 496–500

within domains, 496–498

how to move objects, 495–496

moving OUs across domains, 500–501

NETDOM utility and, 502

why move objects, 495

permissions, 519–525

degree of granularity and, 520

guidelines for, 531

inheritance and, 521, 525

object and attribute permissions and, 520

setting, 521–524

special permissions, 521

standard permissions, 520–521

publishing resources, 503–508

how to publish a resource, 503–504

publishing network services, 506–508, 509

publishing shared folders, 504, 505

publishing shared printers, 504–506, 507

publishing users, groups, and computers, 504

what are published resources, 503

self test, 552–556

self test, answers, 557–560

tools for, 545–548

two-minute drill, 550–551

Messaging API (MAPI), 178

Microsoft DNS (MS DNS), 235–237

Microsoft Management Console (MMC)

Active Directory Sites and Services Console. *See* Active Directory Sites and Services Console adding security snap-ins to, 618

centralized management with, 11–12

changing group policies with,
    310–313

DNS Console. *See* DNS Console

Group Policy Console. *See* Group
    Policy Console

Performance Console. *See*
    Performance Console

Security Configuration and Analysis
    Console. *See* Security
    Configuration and Analysis
    Console

Security Templates Console. *See*
    Security Templates Console

Microsoft Software Installation (.MSI)
    files. *See also* Windows Installer service
    creating .MSI package, 343–345
    .MST files and, 341, 368–369
    overview of, 341

migration, 7

monitoring. *See* System Monitor

MOVETREE utility
    moving AD objects with, 496, 499
    moving OUs with, 500–501

MS DNS (Microsoft DNS), 235–237

.MSI files. *See* Microsoft Software
    Installation (.MSI) files

.MST (.MSI tranform) files
    overview of, 341
    using, 368–369

multimaster replication
    definition of, 36
    operations master roles and, 19, 138
    overview of, 566–567

MX records. *See* Mail Exchanger (MX)
    records

My Network Places, 127–128

N

Name Server (NS) records, 245–246

namespace
    comparing AD and Windows NT
        namespaces, 4
    contiguous namespaces and, 14
    DNS and, 220–221

naming contexts, 564–565

naming conventions, RIS, 419–421

native mode, 36

native packages, 342

NetBIOS domain name window, 58–59

NETDOM utility, 496, 502

NETLOGON.DNS file, 65

network adapters

    RIS support and, 465

    RIS troubleshooting and, 475–476

network cards, 398

network configuration, 374–383

    Internet Explorer options, 375–377

        browser interface, 375

        connections, 375

        programs, 377

        security, 376–377

        URLs, 375–376

    other options, 377–383

        connections, network and

          dial-up, 383

        logon scripts, 378–381

        offline files, 383

        printers, 382

    self test, 390–391

    self test, answers, 394

    two-minute drill, 386

network connections, 383

Network Credentials window, 57

network errors, RIS, 470–472

network ID (network address), 227

network resources, 629

network services

publishing AD resources and,
    506–508, 509

    setting user rights and, 624

network topologies, 577

networking concepts, 33–34

New Domain Name window, 57–58

New Zone Wizard, 232, 589

NLTEST, AD tools, 547

No Override, inheritance, 298, 362

non-authoritative restore, 195

NS (Name Server) records, 245–246

NSLOOKUP, 256, 593

NTBACKUP, 191–193

NTDSUTIL, 204

NTFS

    permissions and, 413

    security and, 451

    volumes and, 626

O

objects

    access control and, 519–525

        AD administration and, 531

        degree of granularity and, 520

        object and attribute permissions
          and, 520

permissions inheritance and, 521, 525

setting permissions, 521–524

special permissions, 521

standard permissions, 520–521

AD components and, 176

creating, 156–158

definition of, 3, 36, 494

locating, 508–513

searching AD, 510–513

searching for shared folders, 511–512

what is stored in AD, 508–510

moving

across domains, 496–500

within domains, 496–498

how to move objects, 495–496

moving OUs across domains, 500–501

NETDOM utility and, 502

why move objects, 495

permissions and, 520

site objects and, 574

offline files, 383

open interfaces, 10

operating system (OS)

deploying, 454–455

restricting OS image options, 449–451

operations master roles, 138–149

definition of, 138–140

domain controllers and, 19–20

domainwide assignment of, 146

identifying, 144–146

replication and, 580–581

seizing roles, 147–148

transferring, 140–144

organizational units (OUs), 150–159

actions performed on, 151

AD stored objects and, 510

creating objects and, 156–158

creating OU structure, 152–154, 159

definition of, 37

deploying software to, 348–355

design overview, 150–152

exam topics and, 21

function of, 180

hierarchical models for, 151–152

moving between domains, 496–498

setting OU properties, 154–155

OS recovery, RIS, 456

OSChooser.exe, RIS, 401
overhead, auditing and, 637

P

packages. *See* software deployment
parameters, NTBACKUP, 192–193
parent domains, 180
parent objects
    definition of, 37
    domain hierarchies and, 14
partial replica, 565
partitions, RIPrep, 465
passwords
    AD installation and, 63
    intersite replication and, 581
PCI cards, RIS, 397
PDC emulators
    operations masters and, 20
    replication and, 580–581
    seizing, 148
PDCs. *See* primary domain controllers
  (PDCs)
performance
    balancing with security, 637
    Group Policy and, 323
    performance counters

exam topics and, 30
    types of, 536
Performance Console, 248–255
    DNS counters and, 251–255
    monitoring and troubleshooting
      with, 248
    System Monitor and, 249–250
Performance Logs and Alerts, 538–539
Performance Monitor
    compared with Performance
      Console, 248
    domain controller performance
      and, 533–534
    troubleshooting AD replication
      and, 583
permissions
    assigning RIS permissions, 422–425
    default permissions, 62
    degree of granularity and, 520
    Group Policy and, 292–293
    inheritance of, 521
    NTFS permissions and, 413
    object and attribute permissions
      and, 520
    setting, 521–524
    software filtering and, 362
    special permissions and, 521
    standard permissions and, 520–521

physical sites, 575
PING, 593
pointer (PTR) records
    creating, 246
    definition of, 24
preinstalled software, 456–457
prestaging, 458–461
    computer account creation and, 413
    RIS client installation and, 426–428,
        456–457
    troubleshooting RIS and, 429
primary domain controllers (PDCs).
    See also PDC emulators
    AD replication and, 566
    definition of, 139–140
    Windows 2000 and, 19
primary zones, 231
printers
    AD stored objects and, 510
    auditing, 637–639
    network configuration options
        and, 382
    print services and, 624
    publishing AD resources and,
        504–506
    publishing shared printers, 507
privileges
    delegation of, 641
    setting user rights and privileges, 624

programs, IE options and, 377
properties, OU properties, 154–155
PTR records. *See* pointer (PTR) records
public data, 7
publishing resources, 503–508
    definition of, 503
    how to publish a resource, 503–504
    publishing network services,
        506–508
    publishing shared folders, 504, 505
    publishing shared printers, 504–506,
        507
    publishing users, groups, and
        computers, 504
    what are published resources, 503
PXE-based boot ROM
    GUIDs and, 399, 426
    RIS and, 397–398, 452
    troubleshooting, 476

queries, 4

R

ratio counters, 536

RBFG.EXE. *See* Remote Boot Disk Generator (RBFG.EXE)

RDNs (relative distinguished names), 37

records. *See* resource records

recovery, system failure and, 203–205

registry, 316, 318

relative distinguished names (RDNs), 37

Relative ID (RID) master roles
  definition of, 139
  operations masters and, 20
  seizing, 148

Remote Boot Disk Generator (RBFG.EXE)
  creating boot floppies with, 400, 452–454
  installing, 398
  overview of, 397
  PCI adapters and, 446

Remote Installation Preparation (RIPrep)
  advantages and disadvantages of, 462
  Hardware Abstraction Layer (HAL) and, 457
  partitions and, 465
  preparation for using, 463
  RIPrep images and, 400, 407, 475

RIPrep wizard and, 28

RIS client installation and, 457–465

running, 463–465

Remote Installation Services (RIS), 396–441
  authorizing, 404–406
    process of, 405–406
    why authorize, 405
  configuring, 28, 407–428
    assigning permissions and, 422–425
    CD-based images and, 408, 413–418
    computer account creation and, 413
    default location and computer naming and, 419–421
    image types and, 407
    pre-staging and, 426–428
    RISetup and, 407–413
  definition of, 37
  installing, 28, 401–404
    prerequisites for, 401–402
    process of, 402–404
  overview of, 396–401
    how RIS works, 399
    PXE and, 397–398

RIS components and, 400–401
RIPrep wizard and, 28
security issues with, 28
self test, 435–438
self test, answers, 439–441
troubleshooting, 28, 429–431
    common errors and, 429
    RIS troubleshooter and, 430–431
two-minute drill, 433–434
Remote Installation Services (RIS), client
installation, 444–491
    installing image to client machine,
        452–469
        automatic setup and, 466–467
        CIW options and, 466
        custom setup and, 467
        fresh installs and, 455–456
        Maintenance and
            Troubleshooting option and,
            468–469
        OS recovery and, 456
        preinstall vs. prestage and,
            456–457
        restarting previous install and,
            467–468
        RIPrep and, 457–465
        RIS boot disk and, 452–454

preparation for, 444–451
    group policy settings and,
        447–451
    restricting installation options,
        447–448
    restricting OS image options,
        449–451
    supported hardware and,
        445–447
self test, 480–485
self test, answers, 487–490
tips for, 477
troubleshooting, 469–477
    BINL service and, 473–474
    hardware issues, 475–476
    network errors, 470–472
two-minute drill, 479–480
Remote Installation Services Setup.
    See RISetup
repackaging process, 342
REPADMIN, AD tools, 547
replicas, restoring from, 205
replication
    definition of, 37, 562
    directory service information and, 7
    File Replication

domain controller
  synchronization and, 138
  service logs for, 533
intersite replication, 13
  definition of, 36
  exam topics and, 30
  managing, 578–582
intrasite replication, 13
  definition of, 36
  exam topics and, 30
  managing, 577–578
overview of, 93
protocols for, 80, 82, 579–580
scheduling, 96
topology of, 96–97
replication, AD
  domain controllers and, 567–571
    conflict resolution and, 570–571
    high-watermark vector and,
      567–568
    making changes to AD and,
      569–570
    up-to-dateness vector and,
      568–569
    update sequence numbers
      and, 567
  exam topics and, 30

KCC and, 571–573
overview of, 4
self test, 599–601
self test, answers, 604–605
sites, subnets, and links and,
  574–577
troubleshooting, 582–587
  event logs and, 583
  monitoring replication and,
    583–586
two-minute drill, 597
what is AD replication, 563–567
  naming contexts and, 564–565
  single-master and multimaster
    replication and, 566
  store and forward model and,
    566–567
replication, DNS, 258–260, 587–595
  AD-integrated zones and, 260,
    591–592
  DNS data and, 258–260
  non-AD integrated zones and,
    589–591
  self test, 601–603
  self test, answers, 606–607
  troubleshooting, 593–595
  two-minute drill, 597–598
replication (REPL), 179

REPLMON, AD tools, 547
resource records
　creating, 245–247
　DNS and, 24
　viewing, 247
RESTORE DATABASE, 202
RESTORE DATABASE VERINC, 202
RESTORE SUBTREE, 202
RESTORE SUBTREE VERINC, 202
Restore Wizard
　Advanced Restore Options screen,
　　196, 201
　Completing the Restore Wizard
　　screen, 198, 201
　How to Restore screen, 200
　operating system selection screen,
　　196
　What to Restore screen, 198
　Where to Restore screen, 199
restoring, 193–203
　authoritative restore and, 195
　exam topics and, 21–22
　non-authoritative restore and, 195
　performing a restore, 196–203
　restoring from backup media, 204
　restoring via a replica, 205
reverse lookup queries, 228
reverse lookup zones, DNS

creating, 228
definition of, 588
RIDs. *See* Relative ID (RID) master
　roles
RIPrep. *See* Remote Installation
　Preparation (RIPrep)
RIS. *See* Remote Installation Services
　(RIS)
RISetup, 407–413
　preparing for setup and, 400
　RISetup Wizard and, 408–412
RIStandard.sif, answer files, 407
roles. *See* operations master roles
root domains, 180
RPC replication, 579

S

SAM (Security Accounts Manager), 178
scalability, 2
scavenging, 242–244
schema
　AD features and, 3
　definition of, 37
　overview of, 542–543
　schema data and, 7
schema master roles

definition of, 139

operations masters and, 20

seizing, 147

transferring, 142–144

schema naming context, 564

script policies, 320–324

assigning, 323–324

user vs. computer scripts, 321–322

scripts

account creation and, 513, 516–519

comparing user and computer, 318

execution order of, 381

logon, 378–381

startup/shutdown, 380

Windows Scripting Host (WSH) and

ASDI and, 517

Group Policy and, 27

SDCHECK, AD tools, 547

searches

searching AD, 510–513

searching for shared folders, 511–512

secondary zones, 231

security, 610–663

AD global services and, 12–13

AD subsystem for, 4

auditing and, 626–639

ADOs and, 634–637

audit policies on domain
controllers, 631–632

audit policies on stand-alone
computers, 633

best practices for, 639

configuring auditing, 630

files, folders, and printers and,
637–639

how to implement audit policies,
629–630

security policies and, 634

why audit, 629

event logs and

archiving security logs, 644–646

clearing security logs, 646–647

interpreting security events,
647–650

types of events to monitor,
640–643

exam topics and, 30

Group Policy and, 610–613

applying security policies with,
610–612

how and when to apply security
policies, 612–613

IE options and, 376–377

monitoring and analyzing events, 640–651

security issues and, 28

self test, 654–659

self test, answers, 660–663

two-minute drill, 652–653

Security Accounts Manager (SAM), 178

Security Configuration and Analysis Console, 613–626

installing, 618

Security Templates Console of, 619–621

setting policies for local file system, 626, 627–628

setting up security database with, 622–623

setting user rights and privileges with, 624–625

why perform security analysis, 621

security groups, 308–309

security ID (SID), 499

Security Log dialog box, Event Viewer, 642–643

archiving security logs, 644–646

clearing security logs, 646–647

configuring settings, 643–644

filtering events, 643–644

options of, 642–643

security logs, 532

archiving, 644–646

clearing, 646–647

configuring, 645–646

filtering events and, 643

locating events in, 642

settings for, 643–644

security policies, 610–613

auditing and, 634

how to apply, 613

when to use, 612–613

Security Services Provider Interface (SSPI), 10

Security Templates Console, 619–621

areas of application, 619–620

importing security templates with, 620–621

list of security templates, 621

self tests

component installation, 110–115

configuring AD, 163–167

directory services, 42–44

DNS/AD interoperability, 264–269

Group Policy, 328–332

managing AD, 552–556

network configuration, 390–391

replication, 599–603

RIS, 435–438

RIS client installation, 481–486

security, 654–659

software deployment, 387–390

troubleshooting, 208–212

self tests, answers

   component installation, 117–122

   configuring AD, 169–173

   directory services, 45–47

   DNS/AD interoperability, 270–276

   Group Policy, 333–337

   managing AD, 557–560

   network configuration, 394

   replication, 604–608

   RIS, 439–441

   RIS client installation, 487–491

   security, 660–663

   software deployment, 392–393

   troubleshooting, 213–215

server objects

   creating in sites, 131–133

   moving between sites, 131–137

   removing from sites, 136–137

service (SRV) records

   creating, 246

   resource records and, 24

setup, RIS clients

   automatic, 466–467

   custom, 467

SETUP.EXE, 342

shared system volume. *See* SYSVOL

  folder

shutdown scripts, 381

SID (security ID), 499

Simple Mail Transfer Protocol (SMTP)

   replication and, 579

   site links in, 80, 82

Single Instance Store (SIS), 400

single-master operations, 19

single-master replication, 138, 566

single-master update model, 233

SIS (Single Instance Store), 400

site link bridges

   creating, 90–92, 95

   definition of, 89

   network topologies and, 577

site links, 79–83

   costs of, 576

   creating, 80–83

   definition of, 79

   site creation and, 574–576

sites, 71–75

   approving/disapproving, 379

   creating, 72–75, 574–577

   definition of, 37, 71–72, 574

   exam topics and, 17

   installing AD and, 51–52

optimizing traffic and, 13

physical and logical, 575

server objects and

creating in sites, 131–133

moving between sites, 134

removing from sites, 136–137

SMTP. *See* Simple Mail Transfer Protocol (SMTP)

SOA records. *See* Start of Authority (SOA) records

software deployment, 340–374

configuring, 361–369

advanced options, 365

categorizing packages, 367–368

filtering packages, 362–363

miscellaneous options, 363–368

using transforms, 368–369

maintaining, 356–361

redeploying, 359–360

removing, 360–361

upgrading, 356–359

managing, 27

overview of

applying to OUs, 348–355

when and why to deploy, 346–347

Windows Installer service and, 341–346

self test, 387–390

self test, answers, 392–393

troubleshooting, 369–374

Event Viewer and, 371–373

package fails to install, 369–370, 371

package installation incomplete, 370–371

two-minute drill, 385–386

Software Installation and Maintenance technology, 340

redeploying software and, 359–360

using with Windows Installer service, 341

software, preinstalled, 456–457

special permissions, 521

SRV records. *See* service (SRV) records

SSPI (Security Services Provider Interface), 10

stand-alone computers, 633

standard primary zones, 231

standard secondary zones, 231

standards, 5, 9

Start of Authority (SOA) records

creating, 245

DNS and, 590

startup scripts, 381

statistics counters, 536

store and forward model, 566–567

subdomains, 220

subnets, 75–78

    creating, 76–78

    definition of, 37, 75–76

    exam topics and, 17

    sites and, 574

synchronous replication, 80

system failure, recovery from, 21, 203–205

system logs, 533

System Monitor

    domain controller performance and, 534–538

    Performance Console and, 249–250

    performance counters in, 30

system policies, 323

System Policy Editor, 278

system services, 624–625

systems state data, 21

SYSVOL folder, 60

T

TCO. *See* total cost of ownership (TCO)

TCP/IP, 10

telephony services, 624

Template Security Policy Setting dialog box, 632

templates, administrative, 314–319

    controlling user environment with, 318–319

    creating and importing, 316–318

    definition of, 315

    Group Policy and, 27

    what can administrators control, 315–316

TFTP (Trivial File Transfer Protocol), 471–472

Time To Live (TTL), 244

tombstoning, 569–570

total cost of ownership (TCO)

    Active Directory and, 494

    IntelliMirror and, 340

    RIS and, 397

TRACERT utility, 593

transform, 367–368. *See also* .MST (.MSI transform) files

transitive trusts

    definition of, 14

    installing AD and, 51

Transmission Control Protocol/Internet Protocol (TCP/IP), 10

trees
  AD features and, 4
  AD installation and, 56
  definition of, 14, 36
  DNS and, 220
  function of, 180
Trivial File Transfer Protocol (TFTP),
  471–472
troubleshooting, 176–215
  AD components and, 176–181
    architecture and, 177–178
    logical components and,
      179–181
    protocols and APIs and, 178–179
    restoring, 193–203
  AD replication and
    event logs and, 583
    monitoring replication and,
      583–586
  backing up AD components,
    181–193
    Backup Wizard and, 182–191
    NTBACKUP and, 191–193
  DNS and, 256–258, 542, 593–595
  recovery from system failure,
    203–205
  RIS and, 429–431

  common errors, 429
  RIS troubleshooter and,
    430–431
  RIS clients and, 469–477
    BINL service and, 473–474
    hardware issues and, 475–476
    network errors and, 470–472
  self test, 208–211
  self test, answers, 212–215
  software deployment and, 369–374
    Event Viewer and, 371–373
    package fails to install, 369–370,
      371
    package installation incomplete,
      370–371
  two-minute drill, 206–207
trusts
  AD logical structure and, 14
  comparing AD and NT, 4
  definition of, 37
  nature of, 14
TTL (Time To Live), 244
two-minute drill
  component installation, 107–109
  configuring AD, 161–162
  directory services, 40–42
  DNS/AD interoperability, 262–263

Group Policy, 326–327

managing AD, 550–551

network configuration, 386

replication, 597–598

RIS, 433–434

RIS client installation, 479–480

security, 652–653

software deployment, 385–386

troubleshooting, 206–207

U

unattended installation, 454–455

up-to-dateness vectors, 568–569

update sequence numbers (USNs), 567

upgrading software, 356–359

    deploying, 358–359

    mandatory upgrades, 356–357

    optional upgrades, 358

URLs, 375–376

user accounts

    assigning packages to, 349–350

    assigning RIS permissions to, 422–425

    creating, 514–516

default permissions for, 62

publishing AD resources and, 504

publishing software to, 350–355

stored objects and, 508

user rights and permissions and, 624, 641

user environment

    AD global services and, 12

    administrative templates and, 314–319

        creating and importing, 316–318

        using, 318–319

        what can administrators control, 315–316

    Group Policy and, 27

user groups, 510

User Permissions, 362

user principal names (UPNs), 37

user scripts, 318

USNs (update sequence numbers), 567

V

VBScript, 517
Veritas Software Console, 346

W

well connected sites, 71–72
wide area networks (WANs)
    directory replication and, 563
    directory traffic and, 582
Windows 2000
    concepts of, 34
    DNS and, 24
    DNS replication and, 588–592
        AD zones, 591–592
        non-AD zones, 589–591
    mixed mode and native mode in, 581
    PDCs and BDCs and, 19
    role of Group Policy in, 299
Windows Components Wizard,
    225–226, 404
Windows Installer service
    deploying software and, 341–346
    IntelliMirror and, 340
    using with Software Installation and
        Maintenance, 341

Windows NT
    comparing with AD, 4
    directory services and, 5–6
    DNS interoperability issues and,
        235–237
    intersite replication and, 580–581
    NTBACKUP, 191–193
    NTDSUTIL, 204
    NTFS and
        permissions and, 413
        security and, 451
        volumes and, 626
    SAM database in, 12, 581
Windows Scripting Host (WSH)
    ASDI and, 517
    Group Policy and, 27
WinINSTALL LE, 343–345

X

X.500, 5

Z

zone configuration, 23

zone transfer
  AXFR (full zone transfer), 259
  BIND and, 234–235
  definition of, 37
  DNS and, 588
  IXFR (incremental zone transfers),
    259
zones
  creating, 226–232

  definition of, 37, 588
  dividing namespaces into, 221
  dynamic updates and, 238
  primary and secondary zones and,
    594–595
  switching to AD-integrated zones,
    232–234

INTERNATIONAL CONTACT INFORMATION

AUSTRALIA
McGraw-Hill Book Company Australia Pty. Ltd.
TEL +61-2-9417-9899
FAX +61-2-9417-5687
http://www.mcgraw-hill.com.au
books-it_sydney@mcgraw-hill.com

CANADA
McGraw-Hill Ryerson Ltd.
TEL +905-430-5000
FAX +905-430-5020
http://www.mcgrawhill.ca

**GREECE, MIDDLE EAST,
NORTHERN AFRICA**
McGraw-Hill Hellas
TEL +30-1-656-0990-3-4
FAX +30-1-654-5525

MEXICO (Also serving Latin America)
McGraw-Hill Interamericana Editores S.A. de C.V.
TEL +525-117-1583
FAX +525-117-1589
http://www.mcgraw-hill.com.mx
fernando_castellanos@mcgraw-hill.com

SINGAPORE (Serving Asia)
McGraw-Hill Book Company
TEL +65-863-1580
FAX +65-862-3354
http://www.mcgraw-hill.com.sg
mghasia@mcgraw-hill.com

SOUTH AFRICA
McGraw-Hill South Africa
TEL +27-11-622-7512
FAX +27-11-622-9045
robyn_swanepoel@mcgraw-hill.com

**UNITED KINGDOM & EUROPE
(Excluding Southern Europe)**
McGraw-Hill Education Europe
TEL +44-1-628-502500
FAX +44-1-628-770224
http://www.mcgraw-hill.co.uk
computing_neurope@mcgraw-hill.com

ALL OTHER INQUIRIES Contact:
Osborne/McGraw-Hill
TEL +1-510-549-6600
FAX +1-510-883-7600
http://www.osborne.com
omg_international@mcgraw-hill.com

NOTES

NOTES

NOTES

NOTES

NOTES

NOTES

Custom Corporate Network Training

Train on Cutting Edge Technology   We can bring the best in skill-based training to your facility to create a real-world hands-on training experience. Global Knowledge has invested millions of dollars in network hardware and software to train our students on the same equipment they will work with on the job. Our relationships with vendors allow us to incorporate the latest equipment and platforms into your on-site labs.

Maximize Your Training Budget   Global Knowledge provides experienced instructors, comprehensive course materials, and all the networking equipment needed to deliver high quality training. You provide the students; we provide the knowledge.

Avoid Travel Expenses   On-site courses allow you to schedule technical training at your convenience, saving time, expense, and the opportunity cost of travel away from the workplace.

Discuss Confidential Topics   Private on-site training permits the open discussion of sensitive issues such as security, access, and network design. We can work with your existing network's proprietary files while demonstrating the latest technologies.

Customize Course Content   Global Knowledge can tailor your courses to include the technologies and the topics which have the greatest impact on your business. We can complement your internal training efforts or provide a total solution to your training needs.

Corporate Pass   The Corporate Pass Discount Program rewards our best network training customers with preferred pricing on public courses, discounts on multimedia training packages, and an array of career planning services.

Global Knowledge Training Lifecycle   Supporting the Dynamic and Specialized Training Requirements of Information Technology Professionals

- ■ Define Profile
- ■ Assess Skills
- ■ Design Training
- ■ Deliver Training
- ■ Test Knowledge
- ■ Update Profile
- ■ Use New Skills

College Credit Recommendation Program   The American Council on Education's CREDIT program recommends 53 Global Knowledge courses for college credit. Now our network training can help you earn your college degree while you learn the technical skills needed for your job. When you attend an ACE-certified Global Knowledge course and pass the associated exam, you earn college credit recommendations for that course. Global Knowledge can establish a transcript record for you with ACE, which you can use to gain credit at a college or as a written record of your professional training that you can attach to your resume.

Registration Information

COURSE FEE: The fee covers course tuition, refreshments, and all course materials. Any parking expenses that may be incurred are not included. Payment or government training form must be received six business days prior to the course date. We will also accept Visa/MasterCard and American Express. For non-U.S. credit card users, charges will be in U.S. funds and will be converted by your credit card company. Checks drawn on Canadian banks in Canadian funds are acceptable.

COURSE SCHEDULE: Registration is at 8:00 a.m. on the first day. The program begins at 8:30 a.m. and concludes at 4:30 p.m. each day.

CANCELLATION POLICY: Cancellation and full refund will be allowed if written cancellation is received in our office at least six business days prior to the course start date. Registrants who do not attend the course or do not cancel more than six business days in advance are responsible for the full registration fee; you may transfer to a later date provided the course fee has been paid in full. Substitutions may be made at any time. If Global Knowledge must cancel a course for any reason, liability is limited to the registration fee only.

GLOBAL KNOWLEDGE: Global Knowledge programs are developed and presented by industry professionals with "real-world" experience. Designed to help professionals meet today's interconnectivity and interoperability challenges, most of our programs feature hands-on labs that incorporate state-of-the-art communication components and equipment.

ON-SITE TEAM TRAINING: Bring Global Knowledge's powerful training programs to your company. At Global Knowledge, we will custom design courses to meet your specific network requirements. Call 1 (919) 461-8686 for more information.

YOUR GUARANTEE: Global Knowledge believes its courses offer the best possible training in this field. If during the first day you are not satisfied and wish to withdraw from the course, simply notify the instructor, return all course materials, and receive a 100% refund.

In the US:

CALL: 1 (888) 762-4442

FAX: 1 (919) 469-7070

VISIT OUR WEBSITE:

www.globalknowledge.com

MAIL CHECK AND THIS FORM TO:

Global Knowledge

Suite 200

114 Edinburgh South

P.O. Box 1187

Cary, NC 27512

In Canada:

CALL: 1 (800) 465-2226

FAX: 1 (613) 567-3899

VISIT OUR WEBSITE:

www.globalknowledge.com.ca

MAIL CHECK AND THIS FORM TO:

Global Knowledge

Suite 1601

393 University Ave.

Toronto, ON M5G 1E6

REGISTRATION INFORMATION:

Course title —————————————————————————————————

Course location ————————————————— Course date ——————————

Name/title ——————————————————————— Company ——————————

Name/title ——————————————————————— Company ——————————

Name/title ——————————————————————— Company ——————————

Address ————————————— Telephone —————— Fax ———————————

City ————————————— State/Province ————— Zip/Postal Code —————

Credit card ————————— Card # ——————————— Expiration date ——————

Signature ————————————————————————————————————

LICENSE AGREEMENT